Stephanie Alexander's KITCHEN GARDEN COMPANION

If you have ever dreamed of picking fresh salad leaves for the evening meal, gathering vine-ripened tomatoes or pulling up your own sweet carrots, this is the book for you. Follow in the footsteps of one of Australia's best-loved cooks and food writers as she reveals the secrets of rewarding kitchen gardening. Be encouraged by detailed gardening notes that explain how adults and children alike can plant, grow and harvest over 70 different vegetables, herbs and fruit, and try some of the 250 recipes that will transform your fresh produce into delicious meals. Whether you have a large plot in a suburban backyard or a few pots on a balcony, you will find everything you need to get started in this inspiring and eminently useful garden-to-table guide.

Stephanie Alexander ran the acclaimed Stephanie's Restaurant in Melbourne for twenty-one years and was a partner in the popular Richmond Hill Café & Larder for eight years. Stephanie was awarded an Order of Australia in 1994 for her contribution to hospitality. In 2000 she became involved in initiating and promoting a primary school kitchen garden program in the belief that the earlier children learn about food through example and positive experience, the better their food choices will be through life. She is now a director and board member of the not-for-profit Stephanie Alexander Kitchen Garden Foundation, which supports kitchen garden school programmes throughout Australia. She is the author of numerous food and recipes books, including *The Cook's Companion*, one of Australia's best loved and most popular cookbooks ever published.

Stephanie Alexander's
KITCHEN GARDEN COMPANION

PHOTOGRAPHY BY
SIMON GRIFFITHS
AND
MARK CHEW

Quadrille
PUBLISHING

CONTENTS

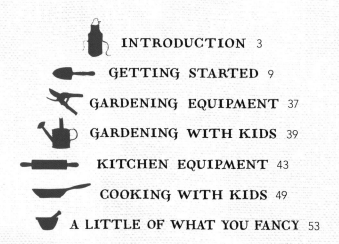
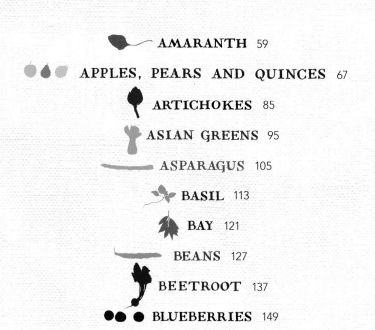

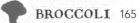

The initial inspiration for this book sprang from my work establishing kitchen gardens in Australian primary schools. I know that children who cultivate and harvest food themselves and are then shown how to turn these crops into delicious dishes are well on the way to enjoying fresh, healthy food for the rest of their lives.

Developing your own productive kitchen garden is very satisfying, and nothing tastes as special as home-grown produce. Inevitably, creating your first food garden will involve much trial and error, and probably frustration, as you begin to understand your garden. However, you and your family can be confident that the food you are eating is not only fresh and seasonal, it is also free of any harmful chemicals, it has not been transported long distances, and that by returning all your scraps back to the soil you are contributing to the long-term health of the land.

I was raised in a food-loving household where what we ate (much of it home-grown) was often discussed, always appreciated and was inspired by the flavours and practices of many cultures. I know what it did for me. I believe it is only by educating young children about good food and gently showing by example how to put healthy, well-balanced dishes on the table at home every day that we will influence their food choices for the future and contribute to a healthier diet for the next generation.

'Just do it' has been the catch-cry from the beginning, in 2001, of my work with children and kitchen gardens in primary schools. This work has been the catalyst for my growing interest in encouraging people at home as well as school children to become enthusiastic kitchen gardeners. Although few of us can expect to be self-sufficient, 'Just do it' resonates with those at home who are keen to start growing at least some of their own food.

The French term *potager* refers to a home kitchen garden that grows a mixture of annual and perennial fruit, vegetables and culinary herbs. It exists to supply a household with food.

The Collingwood College kitchen garden, Melbourne

This is what I mean by a kitchen garden. Modern-day organic gardeners tend to replace ordered rows (still seen in many kitchen gardens) with more informal plantings. This practice stems from the belief that underplanting, interplanting and companion planting not only adds interest to the garden but that this mix improves growing conditions by offering plants protection from hot sun or strong wind, discourages or confuses attacking insects while encouraging beneficial insects into the garden, and more truly reflects nature's diversity. In my own experience I have found that interplanting permits me to grow plants I had previously thought I had no room for. Rainbow chard, for example, grows happily among my rose bushes, and my broad beans climb against a wall in front of the espaliered apple tree (see page 689) at just the time when it is losing its leaves.

This book does not aim to be encyclopaedic or a complete reference book for gardeners. Rather, it is a guide to growing, harvesting, preparing and sharing the vegetables, fruits and herbs used most widely in home kitchens, along with a few of my favourite less well-known ingredients, such as amaranth and kohlrabi. There are many fruits and vegetables I have not included, sometimes because the necessary growing conditions are very specific, making them unsuitable for the majority of home gardens. Others I have excluded simply due to a lack of space. Learning about gardens and gardening is a lifetime journey. Just when I feel I have understood how to tackle a problem I meet another gardener who approaches the same problem in a different way. As with cooking, I am never comfortable claiming that there is only one way to do anything, so this book records my personal experiences of gardening at home and with the School Kitchen Garden Program in Australian schools.

New converts will want to start planting straight away. In the gardening notes, harvesting advice and recipes given for individual ingredients (see pages 59–683), I have aimed to keep enthusiasm high. At the same time I have included detailed and helpful cultivation notes for each of the plants covered, prepared by my colleague and Senior Project Officer at the Stephanie Alexander Kitchen Garden Foundation, Jacqui Lanarus, a successful and passionate food gardener and cook, as well as a mother of two keen young kitchen gardeners.

My underlying philosophy is that food gardens should be created and cared for without using damaging chemical sprays; that the soil should be fed with compost made simply by gathering food scraps (some of which will eventually come from ingredients you have grown and harvested yourself), fallen leaves, poultry, sheep or cow manure, torn-up paper, lawn trimmings and the like; that water should be used as efficiently and sparingly as possible; and that garden beds should be mulched to keep them adequately moist.

Just as a good cook needs to be sure that he or she has the necessary ingredients for a dish before starting to chop and whisk, to achieve success gardeners must consider basics such as their garden's soil types and needs, differences in climate, when to sow seeds and how to care for the growing plants. The gardening notes for each ingredient include information on the type of soil best suited to each plant, as well as when to plant and harvest them.

I have assumed that most home gardeners are not dealing with virgin soil, but that you will already have some plantings, which may include trees, shrubs and flowers, and possibly herbs. This book also offers advice on container planting as a practical option for food lovers who live in apartments or who have paved courtyards or balconies instead of a piece of land to work with.

Clockwise from top left: Radish (*Raphanus sativus*); Pumpkin (*Curcumis maxima*); Onion (*Allium cepa*); Runner bean (*Phaseolus coccineus*)

When deciding what to grow in your kitchen garden, make sure you choose crops that you love to eat!

Children can be part of this adventure. Gardening, cooking and eating engage all of a child's senses. Their sense of satisfaction and pride is guaranteed from the very first harvest. Wherever possible I have indicated special activities or points of interest to be shared with young gardeners and cooks (see the **Especially for kids** section included for each ingredient). With suitable tools children can help in both the garden and the kitchen, and will be eager to do so. The more involved they are, the more interested they will be in the harvest or the finished dish.

My dream is that every child will receive a broad and pleasurable food education as early as possible, at home and at school. By experiencing such magical moments in the garden and around the table, they will choose to include fresh, simply prepared seasonal food in their lives and will have the skills to do so forever.

When the time comes to gather and cook the fruit and vegetables from the garden, the recipes in this book are mostly simple. Almost all can be prepared in less than 45 minutes from start to finish (although there are a few that require stock or involve another lengthy preparation or some advance planning). I suggest gathering all equipment together before starting to cook. There is a list of the cooking equipment I use, including my **Basic toolbox**, on pages 44–47.

I hope that making these recipes will be a communal activity, with a parent or older sibling working alongside younger children. All recipes provide plenty of ways in which children can participate; however, adult supervision is needed whenever hot trays, boiling water or difficult slicing are involved. Inevitably, some recipes are more suitable for preparation by older children.

With sustainability and recycling in mind, I suggest keeping a small bucket with a lid near your kitchen bench top for collecting all appropriate kitchen scraps (such as vegetable and fruit peelings, seeds and any stems) that can be composted – this is second nature to me now and I empty these scraps into my compost bin outside each day. By returning composted kitchen scraps to your garden the link between your kitchen and garden is continued. For the same reason, I also save any water used for washing, blanching or cooking fruit or vegetables, and then use it to water a thirsty plant in my garden.

I hope by recounting my own kitchen garden experiences – particularly those gained over the last five years – I will encourage you to think of how you can start gardening. Remember, regardless of where you live and how much land you have around you, you can grow at least some of your own food. Just do it!

Holding a ripe tomato (top); Picking snow peas

GETTING STARTED

With my own ongoing kitchen garden successes (and failures) I have become more and more fascinated by the process, and entranced by the pleasure, of stepping out and picking just what I need for the next meal. This is always accompanied by a moment of meditative bliss, interrupted sometimes by the vicious seizing of a green caterpillar, which I dispose of ruthlessly! But I want to grow more; I want beans to climb up poles, and pumpkins and cucumbers to twine and twist. I want to dig my own potatoes. I want a more successful garlic crop. And that's just for starters.

I have decided to take a bold step and increase the amount of food I grow for my household of one (boosted by fairly frequent, hungry guests). Up until now I have been reasonably content with growing salad greens, globe artichokes and fancy silver beet (Swiss Chard) among the roses and bulbs in my sunny front garden, and in the not-so-sunny patch of garden at the rear of my house. The rosemary hedge, the bay tree in the pot and the spreading groundcover of various thymes and oregano are all healthy, and my flat-leaf parsley grows freely. Wherever possible I have planted a fruit tree: dwarf nectarines and peach, apple and several citrus plants.

The Evolution of My Own Kitchen Garden
During a major makeover of the house several years ago I outlawed the lawn – a waste of water – and opted instead for a largish area of paved terracotta, broken up by geometric plantings of four beautiful crabapple trees. Of course the paving gets the best sun of all and, as every vegetable gardener knows, all vegetables crave sunshine for at least six hours per day. For the last two planting seasons I have experimented with placing half-wine barrels and large pots on this paved area to benefit from the hours of sunshine it gets, and the results have been bumper warm-weather crops of eggplant, tomatoes, sweet peppers and chillies, and reasonable harvests of broccoli, broad beans and cabbage during the colder months.

A productive garden bed including, clockwise from top left: rhubarb; calendula; curly parsley; and a variety of red and green lettuces

Creating a Garden Bed If you are a new gardener, you need to get to know the soil in your garden: to recognise those areas that get the most sun and the places that are buffeted by wind, as well as the patches that tend to hold moisture and so on. This way, you can group the most demanding plants together and give them the extra care they need. Similarly, you can position less fussy plants in the driest or more difficult areas in the garden. Lastly, you can plant legumes, such as peas and all sorts of beans, to improve the soil for future crops (see **Green manure** on page 690).

Different plants respond best to different types of soil and methods of soil preparation, so check the sections on **Soil type** and **Soil preparation** in the gardening notes for each of the plants you wish to grow. However, if, for example, you just plant a tomato plant straight into the ground in the early summer, the plant will often grow anyway. It may not be the best possible tomato plant but it will still grow, so don't be too anxious – just do it. A spindly tomato plant may convince you to read up a bit next time.

Gardeners who decide that their soil is not suitable for vegetable growing (such as a heavy clay soil or a particularly light sandy soil or soil you are concerned may be contaminated) should consider constructing a raised no-dig garden, as I've done myself (see page 24).

Garden compost Garden compost is the ultimate soil improver. When garden compost is worked through it, soil becomes more porous, allowing air and water to reach growing roots more easily. Garden compost also releases important nutrients from the organic matter it contains as it decomposes.

An easy way to remember what goes into garden compost is to think of it as a mix of dry, brown materials (straw, dry leaves and torn paper) and fresh, green materials (lawn clippings, kitchen waste, such as that from preparing fruit, vegetables and herbs, cooked vegetable scraps and garden prunings). Don't compost diseased plants, plants that may have been sprayed with chemicals, or weeds with seeds that might survive the composting. Also avoid adding meat, bones, dairy products or oil, so as not to attract rodents. Never add cat or dog droppings. Traditionally citrus rinds and onion skins, garlic and other Alliaceae family members have been banned as it is said that the worms we hope to attract don't like them. I am not sure how this conclusion has been reached! I generally go along with this advice but don't fret if a bit of lemon peel or garlic gets mixed up with other scraps. The material added to the compost heap is broken down by bacteria in the soil, worms and various micro-organisms.

All compost heaps or bins should be sited on bare soil so that the compost can drain freely. You can buy expensive but very easy-to-use compost bins that aerate the mixture without any effort from the gardener or ones which are easily tumble-turned, or you can buy a very simple bin to collect materials that will need to be turned by hand. Simple bins can be made from timber, corrugated iron, off-cuts of trellis, bales of straw or posts and chicken wire. There are step-by-step instructions on how to make a simple compost bin at **www.greenfingers.com/articledisplay.asp?id=340.htm**

If you have enough space, you might decide to simply start a compost heap at the bottom of the garden, preferably with two or three compartments. It will need to be covered with something to keep out heavy rain. The composted materials are turned regularly and moved from one bay to the next to make room for fresh materials to be composted. If you wish to

Clockwise from top left: Ready-made compost bin; Rotating compost bin; Garden bed with rhubarb (top), cos lettuces (centre) and basil (bottom)

disguise the compost heap, grow nasturtiums or even a pumpkin vine near by.

A good compost heap should not be too wet, nor should it be too dry. Some gardeners become obsessed with compost – and swear by their own recipes. If you fall into this group, there is no end of information available. A good starting point is *Compost – the natural way to make food for your Garden* by Ken Thompson, published by DK Publishing. The charity Garden Organic has a video and advice on its website **www.gardenorganic.org.uk/ composting.**

Recipe for Compost 'Lasagne'

1 bucket vegetable scraps, fresh grass or weeds (avoid weeds with seeds)	ADD TO THIS *ONE* ITEM FROM THE NITROGEN LIST BELOW:	AND TWO ITEMS FROM THE CARBON LIST BELOW:
	1 bucket manure	1 bucket woody prunings
	2 cups pelleted manure (see page 693)	1 bucket shredded paper
	1 bucket lucerne	1 bucket straw
	1 cup fish, blood and bone	

To create a balance of carbon and nitrogen in your compost, add alternate layers between the three groups, not adding too much of the one component. After 3 weeks of layering during spring and summer (or 4–5 weeks in winter), turn the pile over and transfer to a second bay – the top becomes the bottom, so the bottom is now the top. After another 2–3 weeks, turn the pile over again and transfer to a third bay, then cover with a piece of old carpet (this is known as 'putting it in the oven'). Once the matter is broken down completely – this will take 2–6 months – it is ready to spread on the garden.

Composting in Apartments The Bokashi composting system is ideal for apartment living. Kitchen scraps are combined in a container with a special mix of sawdust, bran or grains infused with beneficial micro-organisms. The scraps speedily ferment in two or three weeks (rather than slowly rotting, as they do in the conventional compost system) and are then transferred directly to the garden or pots.

Worm Farms

Most kids just love worms and will need little encouragement to establish, look after and observe a worm farm. Worms have been converting organic scraps into usable humus forever! Almost half of all household material that ends up at the tip is organic waste. Get a worm farm going and these industrious creatures will quickly convert your food scraps into nutrient-rich worm castings, as well as liquid worm waste that, when diluted, is a powerful plant tonic (see **Worms and worm tea** on page 695). A worm can consume about half of its weight each day – in other words, 500 grams of worms will dispose of 250 grams of scraps each day – just don't feed them any citrus, onion or meat products. Ideally the scraps should be quite small (some worm farm owners have been known to blitz the scraps in a food processor before adding them, but my nieces and nephews, for example, put quite large scraps into their worm farm and the worms still thrive). Composting worms are surface dwellers (not the earthworms you find when digging that are equally as industrious workers) and can be bought by mail order from **www.wormsdirectuk.co.uk** or **www.wigglywigglers.co.uk.** They are sold by weight, which helps in the calculation of how much food they can consume in a day, and also how much space they need. For example, 500 grams of worms need a container that is 60 centimetres × 60 centimetres × 20 centimetres deep. A worm farm can be purchased, complete with worms, bedding and a drainage tap for the resulting liquid – a great present for a garden-loving household.

Once your worm farm is assembled in a cool, shaded corner of the garden, you will need to moisten the bedding. It must always be moist, but not noticeably wet. Children will be fascinated when they lift the lid to add new food scraps to see how quickly the worms retreat from the light. When worms mate they produce tiny cocoons, each of which incubates up to five baby worms. Conditions can get crowded as the growing numbers of worms compete for food. This is the time to transfer two-thirds of the converted scraps or humus (the nutrient-rich worm casings) to the garden and start the process again. A quick way of emptying the farm is to tip the contents onto a plastic sheet or small tarpaulin. The worms will burrow to the bottom of the pile and the humus can be lifted from the top for use in the garden. New bedding is added to the box and then moistened and the worms are returned to feed and breed again. In very hot weather it is important to keep the bedding moist and cover the farm with wet hessian.

Don't forget to check the liquid waste containers every so often. The draining liquid from the worm farm is diluted to a ratio of 1 cup worm juice to a full 9 litre-capacity watering can of water, which can then be sprayed or watered onto all plants.

DIY Worm Farm

A simple worm farm is easy to make. Basically you need a box (wooden, metal, plastic or otherwise hard-to-dispose-of polystyrene foam) with about four 3 centimetre-diameter holes punched or cut in the base for drainage. The box should be no more than 20 centimetres or so deep, but could be 60 centimetres square, allowing plenty of air to penetrate the worm farm. Line the bottom of the box with shadecloth to prevent worms escaping through the drainage holes (or cover the drainage holes with a piece of coarse mesh such as old flywire screen), then add a 1–2 centimetre layer of a reasonably fine pebble such as you would find in a fish tank or gravel and cover this with shadecloth again. The gravel will assist in providing good drainage. The box must be half-filled with suitable bedding, which could be finely shredded dampened newspaper or damp straw, plus a scattering of well-aged manure mixed with soil. Site the worm farm in a cool place, elevating it on bricks or something similar and placing small containers under the drainage holes to collect the precious liquid waste (see **Worms and worm tea** on page 695). Now add 500 grams of worms, then create a hole in the bedding and add some chopped-up food scraps. Cover the box with an old piece of carpet or a piece of plywood to keep out the light and leave the worms to feed and breed.

A worm farm... and a worm

Clockwise from top left: Making the most of an inner-city courtyard; Learning to be water-wise; Space to grow a plentiful harvest on a quarter-acre block

Container Planting Your local garden supply store will sell containers of many shapes and sizes. Terracotta looks beautiful but is very heavy and expensive if it is frost-resistant. It is fine for plants, such as trees, that have permanent homes, but most pots will need to be moved to ensure the plants receive enough sunlight, so portability is an important consideration. The advantage of plastic pots is that they are not porous and so retain more moisture in the soil than terracotta pots, and some are tinted a traditional terracotta colour so they look good as well as being easier to move.

The most useful-sized pot in a small garden is around 30–40 centimetres in diameter and holds around 15 litres of soil. The depth of the pot should be at least 40 centimetres to provide adequate room for the root system to develop. I grow either a single eggplant, sweet pepper or tomato plant in a pot of this size. It is not good for plants to have boggy roots so always sit a container on an old tile or a couple of pieces of a broken terracotta pot to lift it a few centimetres out of its drainage saucer. (You can buy small plastic pot feet at nurseries if you have nothing suitable to hand.)

Half-wine barrels look fantastic in the garden and have a large planting area (ideal for rambling vines such as zucchini or cucumbers), but once filled they are very heavy and difficult to move. Slip a few tiles or pieces of broken terracotta underneath the barrel before filling it with soil to improve drainage. Other container possibilities are hollow masonry blocks that can be stacked, or even 'found' objects such as old enamelled baths, laundry troughs or wheelbarrows. You may need to drill drainage holes in the bases to prevent the soil becoming waterlogged.

For an ambitious range of planters and raised bed systems, the following mail order suppliers are a good starting point: Harrod Horticultural, upmarket timber (**www.harrodhorticultural. com**), LinkaBord, recycled plastic (**www.linkabord.co.uk**) Recyle Works, budget timber (**www.recycleworks.co.uk**), coloured timber beds for schools (**GYOFood.com**) and metal beds Ever Edge (**www.everedge.co.uk**).

Just as a good cook needs to find an excellent butcher and fishmonger, gardeners should find the nearest nursery that supplies certified organic potting mixes, certified organic compost and certified organic manure. Check with your local nursery, gardening club or Organic Gardening catalogue (**www.organiccatalog.com**), or read the ads in a gardening magazine, or Google organic garden products and your nearest town. Buying these products in bulk is always considerably cheaper than purchasing them in smaller amounts, but bear in mind the difficulty of transporting large bags and bales, and make sure you have somewhere to store them.

Preparing a Container To prepare a pot or other small container for planting, mix about one-third of well-rotted organic manure or garden compost with the certified organic potting mix. In areas where low rainfall is an issue, mix some water gel, wetting crystals or Hydrostore (see page 691) with the potting mix. Plants in pots or containers can't send their roots deep into the earth to search for nutrients as they can if planted in the ground, which is why applying a **Liquid fertiliser** (see page 691) such as diluted seaweed emulsions is recommended every two to three weeks for plants in containers. Once an annual plant has completed its growing cycle, tip the original soil into your compost bin, then replace the contents of the pot as I've

Clockwise from top left: Globe artichoke; Bok choy seedlings; Lemon tree; Chilli plant. Following pages: Chervil (*Anthriscus cerefolium*)

described on page 16. (See also **Container planting** on page 688 and **Window boxes** on page 695.) Perennial potted plants should be replanted into a larger pot every two years.

What is a No-dig Garden?

No-dig gardens can be created almost anywhere. Although they are typically built straight onto bare earth or a lawn (one Kitchen Garden Program school has created several very successful no-dig garden beds on top of a disused tennis court). If they are constructed directly onto a patch of earth or piece of lawn it is important to start with an initial newspaper layer to suppress weed growth. There is no need to consider drainage as moisture will simply drain directly into the earth. This system is more versatile than my apple-crate garden (see page 24), as this is a special use of the method suitable for a paved area. If you have decided to make a no-dig garden, then you can disregard the **Soil preparation** section of the gardening notes for your chosen crop (see pages 59–683). The layering process used to create the no-dig garden provides all the organic material that your plants will need for their growing cycle. You will need to replenish the organic material in the no-dig garden every year.

Gardeners usually create edges for their gardens. The very simplest method (and a good idea if you have the space) is to outline the garden bed with bales of straw – they are great for sitting on with a cup of tea while contemplating your growing plants. After a year or so the straw will have started to decompose and can be added to the garden as mulch (see opposite), and the bales can be replaced. More elaborate edges can be constructed from untreated pine planks, timber railway sleepers from timber yards, galvanised iron, rocks, woven willow edging from a nursery, bricks, upturned flower pots, roofing tiles placed diagonally to make a sawtooth edge, just to name a few. Treated pine is not rcommended in gardens (especially ones where children are active) because it has been treated with copper, chrome and arsenic, all of which are poisonous.

Blueberries (*Vaccinium corymbosum*); Tomato seedlings growing in a no-dig bed (opposite)

Making a No-dig Garden

While any gardener already interested in the no-dig method has their own 'recipe' for creating a no-dig garden, here is the '*lasagne*' or six-layer method recommended to primary schools by the Stephanie Alexander Kitchen Garden Foundation, just to get you started. For a no-dig garden of approximately 1 metre × 1 metre, you will need:

one bale of pea straw
strong scissors to cut the twine on the bales
strong wheelbarrow
a bucket
newspapers
(if constructing the no-dig bed directly onto the earth or lawn)
one bale of lucerne
(easier to use than pulverised lucerne. If lucerne proves to be difficult to obtain you can always substitute spent hops or a locally obtained form of hay or straw instead.)

liquid seaweed fertiliser
large watering can
four 25-kilogram bags of organic well-rotted and pulverised manure
waterproof gardening gloves (see page 690)
a small tarpaulin (to collect flyaway lucerne or straw and especially useful if you are emptying your own compost bin for the compost layer)
four 25-litre bags of certified organic compost (see page 688)

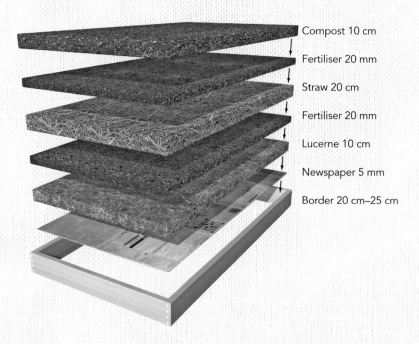

Compost 10 cm
Fertiliser 20 mm
Straw 20 cm
Fertiliser 20 mm
Lucerne 10 cm
Newspaper 5 mm
Border 20 cm–25 cm

Before You Start Break straw into a few manageable sections and put them into a wheelbarrow, then tip several buckets of water over and leave it to soak for at least two hours. The pea straw will swell considerably and be easier to handle; wetting also prevents tiny fragments that are easily inhaled from flying around, and provides moisture for the plant roots.

Layer One This layer is necessary if your garden is being built directly on the earth or on a grassed area such as a lawn. If you are using a fruit crate or other container with a base it is not necessary. Spread a 5 mm–1 centimetre-thick layer of newspapers (don't use glossy magazines) over an area equivalent to a square metre. The newspapers inhibit weed growth.

Layer Two Snip the twine off the bale of lucerne, if used. Peel off in sections that are approximately 10 centimetre-thick – they will separate easily and remind me of nothing so much as giant Weetbix biscuits! Pack lucerne sections over the newspaper tightly to form a dense, 10 centimetre-thick layer. Add 1 tablespoon of liquid seaweed fertiliser to about 4 litres of water in a watering can and pour evenly over the lucerne.

Layer Three Split open two bags of the manure. Tip the manure over the lucerne and, wearing gloves, spread it out into a 2–3 centimetre-thick layer.

Layer Four Peel off sections of the soaked straw that are approximately 20 centimetre-thick. Pack the sections tightly over the manure to form a dense 20 centimetre-thick layer. Add 1 tablespoon liquid seaweed fertiliser to about 4 litres water in a watering can of water (you could use the soaking water from the straw) and then pour evenly over the straw.

Layer Five Split open the two remaining bags of manure. Tip the manure over the straw and, wearing gloves, spread it out into a 2–3 centimetre-thick layer.

Layer Six Split open the bags of compost and, wearing gloves, spread it out into a 10 centimetre-thick layer. Water the compost well. Leave for a few days to settle and then your garden is ready for planting; any remaining straw can be used to mulch the plants as they grow. The garden level will settle over time, and needs to be topped up regularly by adding extra layers of lucerne, pea straw, manure and compost. The best time to do this is after harvesting one crop and before planting the next.

My Apple-crate Garden

In addition to the various pots I have in my courtyard, and the interplanting of vegetables among the flowers, I have decided to install square apple crate 'gardens' on my paved terrace. There are plenty of other options for large containers, so I encourage you to research via the Internet or visit your local garden supply business for advice, but aesthetically I liked the idea of using weathered wood. It should be noted that wood is not forever, whereas metal, in comparison, probably is, although unless treated it will rust. Essentially you are looking for a large box that must have a base, unlike other container garden shapes (such as those made from metal) which are intended to sit directly on the ground.

The first step I took was to chalk out my paved area to decide how many no-dig garden beds it could accommodate – the answer was three. To protect the base wood from rotting, I opted for a bottom liner inside each box made of pre-painted pressed steel (Colorbond), with a 10 centimetre upstanding lip. Several drainage holes were drilled through both the fitted tray and the wood at regular intervals. The lining of each box is a doubled piece of hessian and is to prevent the soil oozing out through the gaps between the wooden planks and spilling. In fact, I now believe this step is probably unnecessary as the layers compact very quickly.

Each of these boxes is just over a metre square. They have strong lockable castors attached so that if I really need to move them (say for my annual Christmas party when I need the paving), the boxed gardens can be rolled aside. They are **No-dig gardens** (see page 20), inspired by my sister's stories of how straightforward she has found this method (her no-dig garden was built directly on top of a lawn), and I have also been inspired by reading *Leaves of Life*, written by the pioneer of this movement, Esther Deans. I wanted flexibility and mobility, which also influenced my decision: if I had decided to fill the crates with soil the weight would have been several times greater than the no-dig gardens and it would have been virtually impossible to move them.

Still in planning mode, the first problem to be resolved was how to water these beds. Although the rainwater tanks were full, getting the water to my gardens without having exposed pipes that may trip someone (probably me) was tricky; underground piping was also out, as I had specified that pneumatic drills were not to be used. I was reassured this wouldn't be necessary after consulting with Adam Richards (also known as 'Mr Turf',) who subsequently installed the system that connects all rainwater to my water tanks. The water supply to the apple crates comes via spaghetti lines tapped into the drip irrigation system that waters each of my crabapple trees. These drip lines can be switched to access mains water during particular timed watering periods if the levels in the rainwater tanks are low. The connecting lines to the crabapple trees are quite long so I can still move the no-dig apple-crate garden beds around to ensure that they receive the maximum amount of sunlight possible.

Stephanie at work on her apple-crate garden

Drainage was also an important consideration: as I did not want any mess on the pavers, I needed some sort of drip tray to collect the liquid that drains from the bottom of the boxes. Initially I used 2 heavy-duty deep baking trays under each crate. Having two drip trays, side-by-side, means that each one is easy to remove. Even so, when they are full, they are still tricky to slide out without sloshing the liquid around, so keep an eye on the liquid level every couple of days and, of course, after heavy rain. The collected liquid is a very potent liquid fertiliser which should be diluted and distributed among all the plants in your garden. A more expensive option (but more efficient in the long-term, is to install a properly plumbed central drainage outlet in the crate when the pressed steel liner is being installed. I have since done this and the drainage hose is tucked out of sight at the foot of a nearby tree. The result is no more mess and a very vigorous crab apple tree.

Taking into account the quantities of materials needed for filling the boxes (see **Making a no-dig garden** on pages 22–23), and the labour I employed to deliver the boxes, fix the linings and castors and drill the holes, my apple-crate garden beds cost around £245 each. Without the fancy castors or the pressed steel inner lining, a no-dig garden of these dimensions should cost much less.

So What Have I Planted? I did the initial planting in my no-dig apple crates at the end of a pretty cold winter. Box Number One now has some brave lettuce seedlings, some seedlings of corn salad and perennial rocket and an edging of marigolds. Box Number Two has snowpea (mangetout) seedlings planted around tall cane pyramid supports, bok choy seedlings and some directly-planted seeds of breakfast radishes and golden beetroot that are yet to emerge. Box Number Three has direct plantings of climbing beans; I will be erecting a simple support structure for these. I hope there will also be space to include some romping cucumber vines.

After three weeks I noted that the salad leaves were growing very well, the first crop of radishes was nearly ready to pull, the golden beetroot had germinated, the climbing beans were just poking through, and I had just planted the seeds for my cucumbers.

Three months later I am harvesting small glossy Lebanese cucumbers for my lunchtime salad, along with flat yellow pole beans. I have just pulled the last of the initial planting of gloriously sunny golden beetroots, the leaves of which were also absolutely delicious. The climbing beans are reaching for the sky and the continuous supply of salad greens continues. Box Number One now has heritage tomatoes growing strongly.

Tomatoes growing in apple-crate beds

What to Plant? After all this preparation comes the exciting moment of planning what you will grow. Your selection will depend on the time of the year, whether you are planting seeds directly (such as peas and beans) or have 'hardened-off' seedlings to plant out. Hardening-off happens after the seeds have germinated and you have 'pricked out' the tiny plants into small pots and then grown them some more in sheltered conditions, perhaps under a plastic cover, a homemade shelter, a protected part of the garden or in a cold frame (see page 690). After the plants have grown to about 8 centimetres they are left uncovered in the open garden for parts of the day to toughen up before finally being transplanted into the garden. You may also want to consider the advice on **Companion planting** included in the gardening notes for each ingredient when deciding what to plant where.

Once you've planted and watered, it is important to place mulch around the base of your growing plants. This is done both to conserve water and suppress weeds. Straw and fine barks make fantastic mulch. New mulch can be layered over old mulch. Only mulch well-watered plants.

Deciding to Plant a Fruit Tree? Although some home gardeners can contemplate an orchard, space is an issue in most home gardens, and deciding to plant a fruit tree is a major decision as there may not be room for more than one or two. On my own standard-sized house block I have an espaliered apple tree (see page 689), four crabapple trees, a lemon, a quince, a passionfruit vine, a bergamot orange tree in a tub, a miniature peach tree, aromatic shrubs such as myrtle and lemon verbena, and I'm contemplating a blueberry bush instead of the very ordinary camellia that takes up a lot of space.

In selecting appropriate trees for your home garden, you will have to consider climate (the UK is not suitable for growing citrus fruits outside over winter, for example), aspect, and the amount of land available as well as other factors, such as which fruits you are likely to use most. While there are numerous fruit trees that can be included in a home kitchen garden, I have provided specific advice for growing, harvesting, preparing and sharing some of the most popular ones. See the chapters for **APPLES, PEARS AND QUINCES; LEMONS AND ORANGES; and STONE FRUIT.**

In very small areas Family trees (with several cultivars grown on the same tree) or miniature trees may be a solution. There are exciting developments in the world of miniature fruit trees – although the trees themselves are miniature, the fruit they bear is full-size. Most fruit trees are grafted onto rootstock that will determine the eventual size of the tree, so do take advice from a knowledgeable fruit tree specialist. Miniature trees are grafted onto miniature rootstock that reduces the tree size from half to two-thirds of normal. As there is an ever-growing variety of miniature fruit trees available, including not only apples, citrus and stone fruits but also avocadoes, figs, pomegranates and persimmon to name a few. I suggest talking to your local nursery for advice on which miniature fruit trees will suit your area.

Espaliered trees (see page 689) look fantastic and are practical if the garden has a wall for a boundary. Many of these trees can be pruned in such a way to keep them at a manageable height for harvesting.

Almost all fruit trees are deciduous and this means that the area underneath them will be

Clockwise from top left: Apples (*Malus domestica*); *Malus domestica* blossom; Figs (*Ficus carica*); Crabapple (*Malus domestica*) blossom

suitable for some planting in autumn and early spring, but will be in deep shade for most of the summer, which will have implications for planting. Ensure that the trees you select are self-pollinating ones, or else you may need to grow two. Most fruit trees will produce their first crop in their second or third year.

Autumn and winter are the best times of the year to buy and plant fruit trees. They then have the best chance of becoming well established before the heat of summer. The choice will be between a tree grown in a container or a bare-rooted plant. Bare-rooted plants are available only when the tree is dormant, and they tend to have thicker, stronger roots than a plant grown in a pot. You should prepare the planting hole in advance and then plant them as soon as you get them home from the nursery. You can plant a tree in a container any time but it will need plenty of water and constant surveillance to make sure it does not dry out.

Digging in plenty of well-rotted organic matter can help the soil retain moisture as can an annual mulch of rotted manure. An automatic irrigation system can be installed to keep the fruit watered in the growing season for the first couple of years. It is worth using one rigged up to a timer so the water is automatically turned off after a certain period.

It is worth mentioning that the netting sold to cover fruit trees to exclude predators is not shade-cloth. It is usually a very fine mesh that allows full sun to penetrate and ripen the fruit but it is fine enough to inhibit birds, squirrels and most insects from attacking the fruit. A tree is never netted until after the fruit has set as in most cases the netting is so fine that it will inhibit the entry of the bees that are needed for pollination. The netting of trees can be controversial as sometimes a bird is caught in the net and can't escape. Some orchardists leave one or two trees unnetted and hope the birds will accept this as their share of the crop.

Gardening and frost dates Most parts of the UK have a frost-free growing season, usually from May to October although much depends on the area you live, microclimate and the weather in any particular year. Most vegetables are annuals and will be sown or planted out at the start of the season and harvested at the end. Growing undercover, in a polytunnel, greenhouse or conservatory will help to extend the growing season and there are crop covers and cold frames to help extend the growing season as well.

Sowing temperatures There are the minimum temperature at which vegetables will germinate and all crops will germinate much more quickly as the soil temperature rises. The exception to this is lettuce, which germinates poorly at soil temperatures above 21°C. So there is little point sowing outdoors too early. Wait until the soil temperature is a minimum of 5°C, a soil thermometer is a useful tool. All the leafy cabbage family, including Asian greens, broad bean, lettuce, pea, radish and turnip will germinate at 5°C, followed by beetroot, carrot, leek, onions, parsnip and silver beet (Swiss chard) at 7°C. The minimum temperature for most beans, pole bean, cucumber, pumpkin, squash, corn and tomato is 13°C or higher.

Tender vegetables such as tomato, corn, eggplant and pepper that need high temperatures to bear fuit can be started earlier, providing a longer season. This is especially worthwhile in cold or northern areas or where the soil is cold and wet in spring. However, even in the warmer south, you can extend the growing season by up to three weeks by starting plants indoors before conditions are ideal outdoors.

Even small areas can yield a decent bounty and provide a lot of enjoyment

Starting off plants Tender plants are those that germinate and grow best when the temperature is a steady 21°C at the minimum. Because these are tender vegetables, you'll need to keep them warm. On a table by a well-lit windowsill in a heated room will be fine, but avoid direct sunlight or the seedlings may be scorched. To grow a range of veg a greenhouse is worthwhile; you will need to provide a heating mat to provide constant bottom heat—one with a thermostat so they do not overheat them on sunny days. All you need for hardy plants is somewhere with good light and frost-free or preferably higher than the minimum germination temperature. A porch is suitable, as is an old-fashioned cold frame. This is basically a square frame positioned over the soil with a window on top. Because these plants grow rapidly and can be planted outdoors after as few as four weeks, seed-starting trays are ideal. Sow a couple of seeds per cell and if more than one emerges, use nail scissors to clip all but the strongest later on.

Hardening off A simple technique for acclimatizing young plants to life outdoors after they have been raised under controlled conditions indoors is known as hardening off. The shock of moving tender seedlings straight from a warm sheltered place to cold soil will interrupt, or slow down their growth and can even kill them.

Tender or hardy? There are several vegetables that will be more successful if you start them off in pots. For the more tender types, it is important that you carefully harden them off before transplanting them outdoors. Tender fruiting crops include; cucumber, eggplant, melon, pepper, pumpkin or squash and tomato. These will need starting off early in order to fruit before the end of the growing season, the sowing time and temperature is critical. If you cannot provide the warmth that early in the year, buy young plants instead. Some crops such as Brussels sprouts, cabbage, cauliflower, celery, leek, lettuce, kale and onions are particularly hardy and do not need a greenhouse. If you live in an area prone to late frosts, don't be tempted to buy plants too early. Wait until they can go straight outdoors, otherwise you'll have to keep them protected from frost and watered regularly.

Caring for ready grown plants When you get your ready-grown plants, either from a garden centre or a mail order supplier, check the local weather forecast. A calm spell of mild weather is ideal for planting hardy plants; wait for an average temperature of at least 16°C before planting tender vegetables. If conditions are not ideal, keep the plants somewhere sheltered and well lit. Water regularly to keep the compost mix moist but not wet. If you can't plant outdoors for a few weeks, give the plants a little diluted plant food, and make sure you harden off the plants before planting outside. Finally, keep crop covers such as fleece handy in case of a sudden cold snap. They should keep new plantings warm even in a late frost.

Clockwise from top left: Basil (*Ocimum basilicum*); Nasturtium (*Tropaeolum majus*); Pumpkin (*Cucurbita maxima*); Tomato (*Lycopersicon lycopersicum*)

What to Consider Before Starting Your Kitchen Garden

Are you going to plant directly into the soil, container plant in a series of pots, or build a no-dig garden?

Choose your site carefully (the ideal site in the UK is south or west-facing, out of the shade, in an open but sheltered spot).

Decide what to plant and enjoy your garden and its produce!

Feed and prepare the soil according to the specific advice given for the plants you wish to grow in the alphabetical listing of plants (pages 59–683).

Establish a composting system (see page 10) and possibly a worm farm (see page 13).

Container plantings: large pots or half-wine barrels are great for citrus trees such as lemons, limes or oranges as well as a bay tree. Smaller pots are ideal for herbs, single plants of sweet peppers, eggplant, tomatoes, quick-growing salad plants and strawberries.

Install a water butt if possible.

Plant flowers for companion planting (see page 688) and to adorn your table at meal times.

Harvesting the crop can be a fun family activity

GARDENING EQUIPMENT

This is a list of equipment I have in my garden shed. I suggest, where possible, that you purchase good-quality tools that will last for a long time.

- bamboo canes
- broom
- buckets
- garden stakes to support plants
- gardening fork
- gardening gloves
- hose (although not used while water restrictions are in place, they are useful for designing

garden beds as they can be used to indicate a curved bed very well)
- pots (a range of sizes), including peat trays for seedlings
- propagating tray
- rake
- secateurs
- seed trays
- shady hat

- small tarpaulin
- soap
- soft gardening ties
- spades
- spray bottles
- trowel
- watering can
- weed fork
- wheelbarrow
- wooden spoon (for mixing sprays)

If you plan on undertaking any small building projects you will need:

- hammer
- mallet
- rope

- saw
- scissors
- wire

- wire mesh

An ornamental grape vine adds a splash of colour

GARDENING WITH KIDS

Hopefully your child will enjoy gardening so much that he or she will want to continue the activity. It has to be fun. If children are only asked to carry out orders or to do tasks as directed by adults working in their own garden, their enthusiasm will quickly disappear. Gardening time must make allowances for the short attention span of very young children and, of course, for their limited physical strength. Caring for the garden must be seen as a game, not a task or a chore. The aim is to share in discovering the magic of growth rather than impressive production. I have found that in order to capture children's interest and maintain their enthusiasm, they need to see the results of their involvement fairly quickly.

Throughout this book I have included ideas and ways to engage the interest, curiosity and energy of your children under the heading, **Especially for kids**. Mostly I have been thinking of children who are old enough to understand simple instructions that will ensure their safety in the garden, and to enjoy stories about plants or ideas about how to enjoy what they have grown. This probably means children who are at least four years old.

By the time children are seven or eight, they are able to understand concepts such as planting a few seeds now and a few more in several weeks to ensure there will be a continued crop to harvest. They understand that plants belong to 'families' (see pages 689–690) and that one should not plant members of the same family in the same spot year after year as this depletes the nutrients in the soil and can spread soil-borne diseases. Children can also understand seasonality and that not everything grows at the same time in the year. They will certainly have a lively interest in the life of the garden: the worms, snails, caterpillars and ladybirds. They will be able to appreciate which insects are their friends and which are enemies.

Planting spinach seeds

A Garden Bed of Their Own

To really capture your child's interest in the kitchen garden, I suggest setting aside a small section of it that is their own. This garden can be small (even just one sunny pot or several containers), or a space the size of the average backyard sandpit. But it must belong to the child. This is his or her garden – you are there to advise (perhaps on aspect), and to help construct the garden if necessary, but to do very little else. It is probably inevitable that very young children will pull up a seedling to see if it has grown into a carrot. Too bad. You might suggest that, if there is nothing at the end of the feathery leaves this time, they wait a bit longer before trying again. Maybe a calendar where they can colour the next six to eight weeks orange (to represent carrots) might make the wait a bit more interesting. Maybe they have also planted radish seeds at the same time as the carrots which will be ready much sooner. Radishes are an ideal first crop for a young gardener.

The size of the garden should never be so big that the child cannot reach the centre without overbalancing. A three-year-old can perhaps work with tiny child-sized tools, but from five years old onwards I think the child is best equipped with a hand trowel, a three-pronged tool commonly used to dislodge weeds that can be a used as a rake-substitute, and a small garden fork (the same size as the one you use). These are much stronger than the tools really intended for playing at gardening, and will do a much better job. Children will also need comfortable well-fitting gloves. Do not choose gloves that are so thick that it is impossible for them to flex their fingers or plant a seedling. Garden centres and even supermarkets offer a great range of easy-to-wear gloves.

Watering cans, however, must be child-sized and probably never filled more than halfway. Everyone in the world has to become water-wise in the face of a changing climate, and children should also understand that although their plants need regular watering and must not dry out, they will not survive if they are drowned or washed away.

It is a good idea to start a child's first garden in spring, when the ground will have warmed sufficiently to ensure successful germination of the first planted seeds. Maybe bush beans, certainly salad crops that can be harvested leaf by leaf, radishes as mentioned above, and snowpeas (mangetout) are all good choices. Don't forget to suggest planting some flowers as well. And not every crop needs to be started from seed. At the end of spring, a young child will enjoy a trip to the nursery to select a single tomato plant, or a single zucchini seedling or a small punnet of basil seedlings that might have to be shared with Mum or Dad for their garden.

Even though I have stressed that this is the child's garden there are times when an adult will need to offer advice. Perhaps it would be a good idea to construct a support for the growing tomato? Perhaps the weather is so hot that all the growing plants need to be carefully mulched, especially if the family is going on a holiday. Maybe the plants need to be fed (and this will be a popular activity), either mixing some liquid seaweed fertiliser with water (or making **Worm tea**, see page 695) and sprinkling it around, or digging in some compost. It will be an important bonus if caring for the garden is seen as a valued family activity. Nothing is more likely to reinforce the enthusiasm of the young gardener than seeing Mum or Dad or Grandpa out in their garden often. If the 'big' gardeners sometimes have failures, that can only be reassuring and probably satisfying to the beginners. And the big gardeners can set a good example by always cleaning their tools and storing them properly at the end of a gardening session and mentioning that you must always be mindful of others in the garden when walking with tools or wheelbarrows.

A 'show-and-tell' table in the garden featuring a never-ending display of interesting bits and pieces is a delightful and fascinating feature for young children. At different times it might display a fallen bird's nest, abandoned birds' egg shells, an insect cocoon, an intriguing seed pod, a fork-shaped carrot, flowers for drying, a sunflower seed-head or a damp saucer of sprouting seeds.

As well as being fun, the kitchen garden can be a place where your children are active learners in a very physical sense. Here they can connect with the natural world and all it has to offer, from straightforward sensory contact with earth, sunshine, rain and wind to developing an understanding of how to create healthy soil in order to nurture and harvest healthy plants. They have the opportunity to observe nature in action while helping to grow some of the food they eat in a sustainable manner.

Primary school-aged children can become competent kitchen gardeners

KITCHEN EQUIPMENT

I have first listed the cooking equipment that forms the basic toolbox of items I use everyday, such as knives, a chopping board and pots and pans; with these you will be able to prepare almost every recipe in this book. I have then listed other much-used items in my kitchen, such as utensils and baking equipment. The final list is of extra equipment that, while by no means being essential, I use when cooking some of the recipes in this book that require specific preparation, such as a hand-cranked pasta machine, candy thermometer and potato ricer.

As with gardening tools, buy the best-quality kitchen equipment that you can afford. It is not only exasperating but dangerous to cook with wobbly pans, blunt knives and rusted utensils. I am fascinated by kitchen bits and pieces and tend to choose bowls and platters that are beautiful as well as functional. Whenever I travel I inevitably collect a bit of kitchenalia to remind me of my time in Morocco, the remote north of Australia or rural France and so on. I also like to look at my treasures, so most of my shelves are open. As I move about my kitchen I can enjoy a glimpse of my copper couscous pot, extra-large English breakfast tea cups, the woven basket from Arnhem Land that I use to store my garlic, or some small copper saucepans I bought in France that are perfect for presenting individual serves of buttered green peas.

Basic Toolbox

apron
baking dishes (ceramic)
baking trays

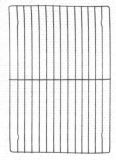

cake cooling rack

chopping board (plus
   kitchen wipes for
   resting board on)
colander (metal or
   enamelled)
egg lifter/slice (suitable
   for using with a non-
   stick frying pan)
electronic scales
food processor with
   slicing and grating
   attachments
3 (non-stick) frying pans:
   small (20cm/8in),
   medium (24cm/9½in)
   and large (30cm/12in)

gratin dishes (wide,
   shallow ceramic dishes
   in varying sizes with
   a large surface area so
   that whatever is grilled
   or baked in them gets
   crisp and well-browned)
kitchen scissors
knives:
   long, non-bendy
     serrated bread knife
   sharp cook's knife
     (18cm/7in blade,
     although some cooks
     may prefer a larger or
     smaller knife)
   sharp paring knife
     (12cm/5in blade,
     although some may
     prefer a smaller knife)
metric and imperial
   measuring spoons and
   measuring cups
3 mixing bowls (small,
   medium-sized and large)
paper towels
pepper mill
cling film
6 porcelain 100/3½ and
   150ml/5fl oz-capacity
   soufflé dishes (for
   baked custards and
   other desserts)

roasting pan
   (made from metal and
   used for roasting meat
   and vegetables)

rubber/nylon spatula (for
   transferring cake batter
   from bowls to cake
   tins or scraping down
   the bowl of a food
   processor)

salad bowl
salad servers
salad spinner
3 saucepans: small (1
   litre/1¾ pint), medium
   (2 litre/3½ pint) and
   large (4 litre/7 pint)
small washable bucket
   with lid (for compost
   scraps)
6–8 litre/10½–14 pint-
   capacity stockpot/
   pasta pot (plus steamer
   insert)
tea towels

tongs
vegetable peeler
wooden spatula
wooden spoons

Other Much-used Items in My Kitchen

baking paper

box grater
citrus juicer
electric kettle
electronic timer
fine-meshed sieve (for
     sifting flour and icing
     sugar and straining seeds
     from juice)
foil

jug
kitchen string

ladles

**large stainless-steel
     mixing spoon** (for folding
     in egg whites or mixing
     ingredients in a bowl)
loaf tin

muffin tin
oven gloves
ovenproof plate

pastry brush

pastry scraper (either
     a rigid plastic half-moon
     shape or a stainless-steel
     rectangle with a wooden
     handle – both used
     for chopping butter
     into flour when
     making pastry)
pastry weights
rolling pin

simmer mat (also called
     a heat diffuser, placed
     between a saucepan
     and the heat source to
     prevent food sticking
     to the bottom of the pan)
slotted spoon
small bowls (for organising
     prepared ingredients)
22cm/9in springform cake
     tin

22cm/9in square cake tin
20cm/8in and 24cm/9½in
     tart tin with removable
     base

tin opener
toaster
whisk

Extra Equipment

bamboo skewers and
toothpicks
bamboo steamer with lid
blender

4 litre/7 pint-capacity
bucket with lid (if you
plan to make any pickles)
candy thermometer (if you
plan to deep-fry)
cast-iron frying pan
with lid
Chinese clay pot
(24cm/9½in)

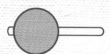

coarse-meshed
stainless-steel sieve
counter-top deep-fryer
disposable gloves
electric mixer (with dough
hook attachment if you
plan to make bread)
enamelled cast-iron or
other heavy-based
casserole with a tight-
fitting lid
fish pliers/tweezers
flexible filleting knife
(thin 22cm/9in blade)
flexible palette knife
food mill
friand tins

hand-cranked pasta
machine and pasta
cutters (if you plan to
make fresh pasta)
hand-held electric beaters
ice cream machine (if you
plan to make ice cream)
ice cream tray
jam funnel
long-handled brass
skimmer (for quickly
retrieving items that are
being deep-fried)
metal egg/hamburger
rings

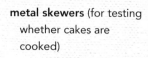

metal skewers (for testing
whether cakes are
cooked)

Microplane grater (for
finely grating citrus zest,
parmesan and other hard
cheeses, nutmeg and
ginger)

mortar and pestle
muslin

parisienne spoon (also
known as a melon baller)

plastic vegetable
slicer or mandoline
(for thinly slicing
vegetables) – there are
various designs, many
of which are made in
Japan although they are
increasingly being made
in Europe. All of these
are very sharp and **not**
suitable for use by
young children.

potato ricer (if you plan
   to make gnocchi or the
   Beetroot and Potato
   Pierogi on page 145, but
   otherwise a hand-held
   masher is fine – although
   in my opinion a ricer
   makes incomparable
   mashed potato)

18–20cm/7–8in pressed-
   steel crêpe pan (made
   from pressed steel, crêpe
   pans have a low lip or
   rim and don't need to be
   washed,
   just wiped and put
   away – they last forever
   if properly cared for.)

ridged cast-iron
   char-grill pan or
   barbecue with
   grill-plate

sauté pan with lid
   (a very useful pan with
   a relatively wide base
   and shallower sides than
   a saucepan but deeper
   than a frying pan,
   a well-fitting lid and an
   ovenproof handle – ideal
   for cooking small braises
   that start on the top of
   the stove but may need
   to be transferred to
   the oven.)

serving platters

spatter screen or lid that
   will cover your frying
   pan (to prevent oil
   spitting when pan-frying)

speed peeler (also called
   an asparagus peeler,
   this vegetable peeler
   has a blade that is set
   crossways. I not only use
   it for peeling asparagus
   but also for peeling
   quinces, green tomatoes
   and sweet peppers.)

wide shallow pasta bowls
   (bowls perfect for any
   main dish that has lots of
   juice. The French have
   a perfect name for this,
   assiette creuse, meaning
   hollow plate.)

wok sang (spade-like
   utensil with a long handle
   used for stir-frying)

wok with lid

COOKING WITH KIDS

I can still remember my first solo cooking efforts. I was about seven when I made toast and heated tinned tomato soup for myself. Hardly a stellar beginning. The next year I moved on to attempting to bake cakes whenever my mother was out shopping. They did not succeed and I now believe that I did not understand the difference between plain flour and self-raising flour. I had a heavy hand with the red colouring bottle too, and my flat-as-a-pancake cakes were a startling lolly-pink. Mum became pretty tired of returning home to a disaster zone in the kitchen and a few ground rules were established: if you cook, you clean up. I think at about this time she decided that my interest should be encouraged. By the time I was twelve I was capable of preparing and cooking a pretty straightforward family dinner. Typical of the time, it would probably have involved lamb chops or a chicken, vegetables from the garden and some sort of simple baked pudding. I was hooked and have never looked back. By fourteen I was allowed to plan and cook 'special occasion' dinners every now and then, and I was encouraged to bigger and better efforts by the enthusiasm and praise I received from my family.

Children love the idea of helping in the kitchen, just as I did when I was a child. They certainly love to eat. As soon as possible, engage your children and allow them to stand on a stool or a chair next to you at the kitchen bench. Four- to five-year-olds can mix ingredients with a wooden spoon or a whisk, so making sweet or savoury muffins might be a good first dish to try. They can also spoon fillings into savoury tarts (a bit might slop over the bench or floor), or spread soft fillings or dips onto toast or savoury biscuits if you are offering a snack to guests.

Anything to do with boiling water, lifting heavy pots of hot food, putting food into or taking it out of a hot oven, or slipping food into hot oil are all tasks that need to be done by an adult, although an experienced teenager could certainly tackle these tasks on their own.

Cooking freshly harvested produce

Homemade pasta (see page 474) was not on the radar when I was a teenager. Nowadays, though, it is a great way to start cooking real food with children. From the age of around seven they can assist with kneading the basic dough (not that different to playdough really) and will enjoy helping feed the pieces through the rollers of a hand-cranked pasta machine – seeing the strips fall so perfectly from the cutting rollers is a pretty thrilling sight.

Children over the age of seven or eight can also use good-quality knives, providing they are shown how to curl the fingers of the non-cutting hand over the food to be chopped and to slice, not force, the blade through the food. They will also love to wash and spin dry the salad – though you may have to curb their enthusiasm for the spinner if the leaves are delicate. Children can make dressings and consider the flavours. They can knead dough, shape breadsticks or rolls and roll pastry. They can pound spices with a mortar and pestle, grate cheese and citrus zest, shape meatballs and mix savoury fillings for pies or pasta with energy. With all of these skills under their belt, a child of eight or nine is able to make homemade pasta (see Fresh Pasta, page 474) with meatballs (see Very Basic Meatballs, page 649) and homemade tomato sauce (see Fast Basic Tomato Sauce, page 649) – with some adult help, of course.

By the time they are about ten, children who have been encouraged to feel comfortable in the kitchen and around all manner of ingredients will know how to follow a recipe. They will be able to weigh basic ingredients, separate eggs, and sauté, fry and grill – all with confidence and enthusiasm. They won't be frightened of hot water or hot ovens, but will approach both with sensible caution and will feel comfortable about asking for assistance.

Perhaps most importantly these children look forward to tasting what they have made and are open to trying unfamiliar flavours, as well as enthusiastically falling upon old favourites. My message is to let children help. A bit of a mess doesn't matter. Nothing succeeds like success. As the first batch of cheese muffins cool on a cake rack, and as the family fights for a taste, the young cook will swell with pride and be eager for the next session. Remember, children are just as capable of cooking delicious savoury food as sweet dishes.

Most of the recipes involve plenty of weighing, chopping, sifting and peeling. I have done this intentionally to provide opportunities for your family to enjoy cooking together.

Hopefully, as much as possible, the food you prepare will be picked from your own garden, supplemented by ingredients bought from a farmers' market or the freshest local source you can find. All eggs will be free-range, maybe from your own hens, and any chicken used will be free-range. Everyone can help, which will make it a lot of fun. And remember – if you cook, you clean up!

Preparing a salad for the family to share

A LITTLE OF WHAT YOU FANCY

All the recipes in this book showcase one or more vegetables and herbs or fruit harvested from your own garden. Most dishes can be served alongside some other dish or dishes. For example, the Broccoli with Crunchy Garlic Breadcrumbs on page 172 can be served with a roast chicken, a grilled piece of fish or a barbecued sausage. The Moong Dal with Potato and Green Vegetables on page 505 can be one of a series of spicy dishes, or it can be a simple lunch on its own. I have deliberately intended to move the focus of the meal away from protein with a bit of vegetable on the side to regarding the recipes as 'special' vegetable dishes that can be augmented with some protein if you wish. Vegetarian families will probably choose to serve two or three different dishes at each meal, as will those who do not wish to eat meat, fish or poultry at every meal. There are certainly dishes cooked with meat, poultry or fish, but they are in the minority. Using these recipes will expand your repertoire of vegetable dishes considerably. I have indicated throughout the book when I think a dish would go well with a grilled lamb rack, sausages or a roast chicken, but usually the meal could just as easily take a different turn by combining it with another vegetable dish and I have mentioned these options too.

I am never comfortable expounding nutritional advice. Talk of pyramids, food groups and numbers of servings makes me shudder. My food philosophy has always been to embrace the widest possible range of seasonal, locally produced fruit and vegetables and cheeses, to augment this with carefully selected free-range poultry and plenty of fish, and to seek out a good butcher who selects their meat with care and concern for how the animals are raised – oh and how I love eating eggs! I also make sure that I have a large bowl of green salad almost every day . . . but I still struggle to really enjoy yoghurt!

On the days that I choose not to prepare meat, poultry or fish I may cook with grains, pulses and legumes – especially in the colder months, when a substantial soup is almost my

A selection of salads, including Orange, Radish and Mint Salad (foreground, see page 366) and Sweet-and-sour Pumpkin with Mint (background, see page 516)

standard lunch. I will often have a simple evening meal of pasta with a vegetable sauce and a shower of the best parmesan.

I have included recipes that feature staples such as rice, chick peas, barley or lentils as they are wonderfully versatile ingredients that offer endless possibilities in the kitchen, especially during the winter months when the harvest from the garden is greatly reduced. The addition of small quantities of winter greens, herbs, spices and nuts all help to make these simple and sustaining dishes exciting.

For vegetarians, pulses and legumes are often the major source of protein in the diet and dishes based around these form the central dish of the meal. Such dishes are among the most traditional, widely known and most revered, and there are many different versions. In many cultures, different types of lentils are used as an inexpensive and sustaining form of protein – none more so than in India, although Middle Eastern cooks utilise them too. For those unacquainted with Indian cookery it can be bewildering to encounter the different varieties of lentil or dals used. Visit an Indian grocery store and be amazed. They vary in colour and flavour, and can be whole or split, and skinned or not to make purées, soups or more complicated combinations. The highly regarded small green lentils are imported from France and Italy.

There is no question that buying the best organic food to supplement what you grow in your kitchen garden is expensive. It may be tastier, it may be better for you and the planet, but it is difficult to do if you live on a modest budget. Even more reason to grow as much of your own food as you can, and to discover that you can make your own tomato sauce, chutney, relishes and curry pastes, and pickle your own lemons, olives and cucumbers for a fraction of what they cost in the shops. And remember, delicious meals do not need to include meat, fish or poultry every day.

Nettles in a jug

INGREDIENTS

AMARANTH

Amaranthaceae family
Annual

Soil type
Well-drained, light, sandy, fertile soil.

Soil preparation
Apply well-rotted manure 6 weeks prior to planting.

Climate
Suitable for all climates, but prefers warmer weather.

Position
Prefers full sun.

How to grow
Sow seed in small pots under cover in mid April, then plant out when 15cm high. Or sow seed direct into ground from May to mid June (min soil temperature 10°C). As the seeds are small, mix with coarse wet sand and then directly sow at a depth of 5mm. Thin once the seedlings have developed at least four new leaves – this should take around 2–3 weeks. Allow a space of 50–60cm between each plant. Poor germination rates are common. Amaranth can also be grown from cuttings.

Water requirements
Keep soil moist.

Successive planting
Every 2 weeks for maximum yield.

Harvest period
If grown for grain, 6–8 weeks from sowing to reach cropping stage, although the young leaves can be used much earlier.

Pests and organic control
Possible pests include caterpillars and cutworm. Plant calendula and other daisies to attract natural enemies, or use a pyrethrum spray (see page 700). Physically remove young caterpillars and their eggs.

Companion planting
Strawberries, eggplant and corn. Don't plant with beetroot.

Special information
Loosen the soil around the plant to prevent it becoming compacted.

Quantities to plant for a family of four
For grain, 8–12 plants, and 3–4 plants if only harvesting the young leaves.

Amaranth (*Amaranthus* sp.)

Growing and Harvesting 'What on earth is amaranth?', I hear many readers asking in amazement. Amaranth is a little-known plant in the Anglo-Saxon world but it is an important leafy vegetable for many African and Asian populations, and is well known to Greek and Chinese communities. It is native to Central America and very popular in Mexico. Amaranth has many names, including Joseph's coat; *callaloo* (Caribbean); *chaulai* (India); and *yin choy* (China). The name 'amaranth' is derived from the ancient Greek *amarantos* (unfading), because of an ancient belief that it lived forever.

A mature amaranth plant looks very striking with its magenta or gold tassels closely resembling in colour and texture the cord of a chenille dressing-gown. Some cultivars have leaves with brilliant splashes of pink or purple while those of others are a solid green. Amaranth is unusual in that, like buckwheat and quinoa, its grain (the seeds that are contained in those spectacular tassels) can be used as a cereal crop, and yet it is not a grass like 'true' cereals.

Smaller cultivars are grown principally for their leaves, and taller cultivars for grain. Taller amaranths will benefit from close planting so that the plants support each other. Some gardeners like to plant amaranth in regimented rows, but they look more handsome and add greater interest to the gardenscape if planted in informal clumps here and there among other plants. The plants bear both male and female flowers and self-pollinate. If allowed to flower and cast seed, amaranth can become a weed.

Tender leaves are best for cooking, so if you are not interested in collecting the grain, pick the green or green-splashed-with-purple tops when the plants are 15–30 centimetres high.

Container Planting Amaranth is ideal to plant along with other cut-and-come-again green things to provide quick pickings for dinner. You might like to sow the seeds with those of mild mustard, rocket, cress, mizuna or spinach and so on. Be prepared to cut the seedlings (with scissors, please!) as you need them – probably when they are around 10 centimetres high. Most of these young plants will oblige by re-shooting at least twice. At this smaller size, even greens that will develop quite a bite when older and larger can be added to a salad.

Preparing and Sharing Amaranth leaves are little known but quite delicious. I have started to see bunches of amaranth on sale at farmers' markets and they are a regular item in Asian food stores. They can be combined with many seasonings and flavours, reflecting their wide popularity across a range of different ethnic communities. The flavour of the leaf is earthy and spinachy, and not at all sharp or bitter. However, after brief cooking amaranth has more texture than lightly cooked spinach. It is also more tender than silver beet and the cooked leaves keep their structure and colour.

If very young leaves are picked they can be added to the salad bowl, but the salad will be more appealing if mixed with other less assertively flavoured salad leaves.

Remove the leaves from the strong main central stem so you have bouquets of leaves attached to smaller tender stems. Like silver beet and spinach, amaranth needs to be washed very well. Don't use leaves that are tough, yellow, wilted or slimy. The leaves can be briefly steamed or boiled and dressed with olive oil and lemon juice – for example, a Greek friend puts a little posy of these lightly cooked and dressed leaves alongside soft white cheese and olives to accompany an aperitif. The leaves can also be sautéed with garlic, shallots, chilli and sesame oil or stir-fried with garlic, garlic chives and spring onions, then drizzled with oyster sauce. Jamaican recipes combine salt pork with chopped amaranth or they shred the leaves and cook them like spinach, then serve them with poached eggs on top. I first encountered amaranth many years ago in a small Jamaican village. Callaloo soup (see page 65) is a popular country dish with plenty of shredded green leaves among the pieces of salt pork and chunks of potato, simmered in coconut milk and spiced with chilli.

I rather fancy adding steamed amaranth leaves to some cooked young stinging nettles and maybe another exotic green such as purslane or mountain spinach, or even common old silver beet leaves, to make a version of Janni Kyritsis's Wild Weed Pie (see page 64). Another idea is to add the leaves and tender stems to a vegetable stew that includes some pumpkin. The roughly chopped leaves can be added to a risotto or a dish of simmered dried beans much as you might add silver beet to wilt just before serving.

To collect the seeds to eat or plant later, rub the tassels over a plate to extract them. It is a good idea to wear thick disposable gloves when handling the tassels as they are quite rough and can stain your hands. The seeds are tiny and white, tan or black. They can also be ground and added to bread dough or other baked goods. Their flavour is mild and nutty.

Especially for Kids I am told that the method used to get at the grain in Mexico is to lie the dry tassels on a tarpaulin, then cover them with another sheet and *dance* on the top layer to knock the shiny seeds free. Smaller amounts can be rubbed off in a paper bag; use a small fan to blow away the chaff. Otherwise, shake the seeds and debris in a very coarse-meshed sieve; the seeds will fall through and the remaining chaff goes to the compost heap.

Amaranth seeds can be popped like popcorn – heat them in a dry frying pan over medium heat for 30 seconds; for maximum yield use a spatter screen or they will pop right out of the pan. This 'fairy popcorn' can be added to muffin batter as you might use poppy seeds, or stirred into a vegetable fritter batter – cauliflower or zucchini, for instance – or scattered over muesli.

Amaranth and Mint as a Flatbread Filling

SERVES 2 This is a very straightforward way to cook and season all manner of edible greens. However, blanching times will vary, depending on the variety of leaves being used, for example beetroot leaves would take longer than the brief dunking described here for amaranth. This filling also makes a great toasted sandwich filling, or you can wrap it in a warmed tortilla. You might have made some falafels (see opposite) or spicy meatballs such as the koftas on page 249 and you could tuck in a few of those too.

1 tablespoon amaranth seeds
  (optional)
1 teaspoon salt
1 tablespoon extra-virgin olive oil
1 large onion, halved lengthways
  and thinly sliced
1 fresh red chilli, halved lengthways,
  seeded and very thinly sliced

4 small handfuls loosely packed
  amaranth leaves and their tender
  stems, soaked in a bowl of water
4 sprigs mint, leaves picked and
  torn (about 16 leaves)
125g/4½oz coarsely grated firm
  mozzarella (see page 704)
2 flatbreads or Turkish bread rolls

EXTRA EQUIPMENT
spatter screen or
  lid that will cover
  the frying pan
  (optional)

If you have amaranth seeds, heat a non-stick frying pan over medium heat and 'pop' seeds, covering pan with a spatter screen or large lid. Once most of seeds have turned white, tip them into a small bowl and leave until needed.

Fill a large saucepan with water and bring to the boil over high heat, then add salt.

Meanwhile, heat olive oil in another frying pan over low heat. Drop in onion and fry slowly, stirring from time to time; the onion will soften, then become yellow and, after about 10 minutes, finally start to darken. Add chilli and reserved amaranth seeds, if using.

Transfer amaranth leaves to the pan of simmering water. Give a big stir with a wooden spoon and as soon as the water has returned to the boil, drain leaves in a colander. Rinse very briefly with cold water, wrap in a clean tea towel and squeeze hard, then drop blanched leaves into frying pan with onion. Stir together for about 1 minute, then stir in mint and grated mozzarella. Tip mixture into a bowl. Taste for salt and season if necessary.

Briefly warm flatbreads in same frying pan used to toast amaranth seeds. Cut each flatbread in half, open and scoop in half of the amaranth mixture.

Janni Kyritsis's Wild Weed Pie

SERVES 6 I have eaten this pie cooked by Australian chef Janni on several occasions. Every time the filling has been different. If 'wild' greens are not available, try 'tamed' ones such as silver beet. Here I have substituted (with Janni's permission) commercial filo pastry for the very tricky handmade version.

1 teaspoon salt

1kg/2lb mixed bitter greens (2 small handfuls loosely packed amaranth leaves combined with nettles, sorrel, silver beet and/or chicory to make up the balance), washed

150ml/5fl oz extra-virgin olive oil

2 red onions, finely chopped

1 free-range egg, lightly beaten

dried Greek oregano (*rigani*), to taste

500g/1lb fresh ricotta

sea salt and freshly ground black pepper

9 sheets filo pastry

250ml/9fl oz olive oil, for brushing

EXTRA EQUIPMENT

26cm/10in pizza tray

Bring water and salt to the boil in a large saucepan. Add amaranth leaves to pan, give a big stir with a wooden spoon and, as soon as the water has returned to the boil, scoop the leaves into a colander in the sink. Rinse very briefly with cold water, squeeze hard in a clean tea towel and drop blanched leaves into a mixing bowl.

Place other greens in a sauté pan or saucepan with the washing water still clinging to them, then cover and cook over medium heat until just wilted. Drain and squeeze out excess liquid. Coarsely chop, then add to bowl with amaranth. Heat olive oil in same pan and cook onion over low heat for 8–10 minutes or until soft. Remove from heat and combine with greens, then add egg and oregano. Gently fold in ricotta, season with salt and pepper, then cover and refrigerate.

Preheat oven to 200°C/Gas 6. Place 1 filo sheet on a chopping board, then using a 26cm/10in pizza tray as a guide, cut out a 26cm/10in round. Repeat with another 4 filo sheets. Cover rounds with some foil lined with a slightly damp tea towel and set aside. Line the pizza tray with a round of baking paper.

Brush 1 whole sheet of filo with oil and place widthways across the lined pizza tray. Brush another whole sheet of filo with oil and place lengthways across the pizza tray to form a cross with the first sheet. Brush a third whole sheet of filo with oil and place diagonally across the pizza tray, then brush another whole sheet of filo with oil and place it on the other diagonal.

Brush 2 of the filo rounds with oil and place it in the centre of the tray. Spread amaranth filling across the filo round, right up the edge of the tray. Fold up overhanging filo sheets, pleating it to cover and enclose the filling. Working one at a time, brush the remaining 3 filo rounds with oil, then place over the filling, allowing each one to crumple as it settles over the filling. Brush any exposed filo with more oil.

Bake for 20 minutes or until golden. Serve warm or at room temperature.

Callaloo

SERVES 6 Callaloo is the name of this traditional West Indian soup as well as the local name for the amaranth leaves, which are its key ingredient. There are many versions, but I was shown this spicy one when I visited Jamaica in the mid-1960s. If you prefer a less spicy soup, omit the sliced chilli.

EXTRA EQUIPMENT
blender or
food processor

40g/1½oz unsalted butter
2 tablespoons vegetable oil
500g/1lb smoked bacon, cut into
  1cm/½in dice
1 onion, coarsely chopped
2 cloves garlic, coarsely chopped
1 fresh red chilli, thinly sliced
6 small handfuls loosely packed
  amaranth leaves and tender stems,
  washed and dried

¼ small handful loosely packed
  flat-leaf parsley leaves, washed
  and dried
2 tablespoons celery leaves,
  washed and dried
1 litre/1¾ pints water
250ml/9fl oz coconut milk
sea salt and freshly ground
  black pepper

Heat butter and oil in a large saucepan over medium heat and sauté bacon until it starts to colour and is crisp around the edges. Scoop out bacon, drain on paper towel and set aside.

Add onion to pan and cook over medium heat for 5 minutes or until golden. Add garlic and chilli and cook for a further 2 minutes. Add amaranth, parsley and celery leaves to pan. Increase heat to medium–high and cook, stirring from time to time, for 7 minutes or until greens have wilted. Add water and bring to the boil. Cover and cook over medium heat for 10 minutes or until greens are soft.

Transfer soup to a blender (or food processor). Cover blender lid and flask with a dry tea towel; hot liquids can force up the lid of a blender, spraying hot liquid that can burn. Purée soup in batches in blender until perfectly smooth. Return soup to saucepan, add coconut milk and season with salt and pepper. Bring to a simmer over medium heat, then scatter in bacon bits and serve in warmed soup bowls.

APPLES, PEARS AND QUINCES

Rosaceae family (includes raspberries and strawberries) Deciduous tree

Soil type
Will tolerate most soils, providing they are deep and well-drained.

Soil preparation
Dig out a generous-sized hole, enrich the soil by mixing with well-rotted organic matter. Plant the tree the same depth it was in the original pot or ground.

Climate
There is an apple variety to suit all areas whereas pears and quince need warmer temperatures so in cold areas, in all cases seek local advice. Trained forms of pear can be grown against south-facing walls.

Position
Prefer full sun. Protect trees from strong wind.

How to grow
Plant bare root plants in the dormant season (October to March) and container-sold trees anytime but avoid prolonged dry spells. Trees may need staking for the first 2 years. Keep the ground beneath the tree clear of weeds and grass until the tree is established, mulch the ground each spring.

Water requirements
Needs regular watering during dry spells for the first 2 years. Dwarf forms might need extra watering.

When to fertilise
Feed in spring with an organic general-purpose fertiliser.

Pruning
Pruning varies greatly depending on the age and training of the tree when purchased. Free-standing trees just need damaged wood cut out in winter but trained forms also need pruning in summer. Developing fruit may need thinning.

Harvest period
Depends on the variety, the fruit matures at different times from late summer to autumn.

Pests and organic control
Control codling moth with traps or a biological control, winter moth by grease bands or pyrethrum. Aphids can be controlled by natural pesticides or by encouraging birds. Fungal diseases are bet prevented by careful choice of variety and keeping the tree growing well, Bordeaux mixture (see page 698) can be used as a last resort. Fireblight is a serious bacterial disease. There is no cure for it but mildly affected branches can be cut back to healthy wood otherwise dig up and burn the tree.

Special information
Most varieties will crop better if cross-pollinated by a compatible variety. Where it is not possible to plant more consider a Family tree (several varieties grafted onto one tree).

'Beurre Bosc' pear (*Pyrus communis*)

Growing and Harvesting Apples, pears and quince trees are usually sold on dwarfing rootstock which reduces the tree size. Apples and pears can be purchased with more than one variety grafted onto the same tree. This is a practical choice for a small family with room for just one tree in their garden, as the harvest period is extended.

Prepare the hole before taking delivery of the tree: it should be wide enough to spread the roots well. Soak the root ball for an hour in a bucket of water before planting or if in a container soak the plant while still in its container. Loosen the tree roots if at all twisted when removed from the pot. Slightly mound the soil in the centre of the hole and settle the tree over this mound, spreading the roots carefully, and shaking the tree very gently into the hole to settle it well. Backfill the hole with soil to cover the roots, pressing it firmly. Finish filling the hole, shaping the surface into a slight saucer shape to maximise water penetration. The graft (the bump on the lower trunk) must always be above the soil line. Trim branches so they are not wider than the spread of the roots.

Do not allow these trees to dry out, especially during their first two years. Quinces will tolerate dry conditions better than apples and pears.

Keep the area underneath young fruit trees clear of weeds and grass so the trees can establish. This usually takes two years. After this time the ground can be used. As apples, pears and quinces are deciduous, the area underneath them will be suitable for other plantings in autumn and early spring as it will still receive sunshine. Fast-growing leafy greens or shade tolerant herbs such as chervil can be grown underneath these trees during winter and spring. However, once the leaves have grown, this area will be in deep shade for most of the summer, so don't plant summer crops in this area.

Apples adapt well to shaping by an expert pruner – they can be espaliered (see page 689) along a wall, become a hedge or cover an arch. Pears may also need light summer pruning as they are more vigorous than apples. Quinces may need thinning as they can lose branches that are overloaded with fruit.

The very destructive codling moth heads the list of pests. One experienced gardener told me you need to be prepared to be quite active in its control, and if not, then it is best not to grow susceptible trees. It is important to understand the life cycle of the codling moth. They emerge in spring when fruit trees are in flower. The female lays eggs on the leaves and they hatch from June to July. The tiny caterpillars feed on the leaves before burrowing into the growing fruit and stay there munching for three to five weeks. They then leave the fruit (and their faeces), move to another place further down the tree (or on the ground) to spin a cocoon. Larvae remain in cocoons for months until the cycle repeats.

There are two main organic methods for dealing with codling moths that are the cause of maggots in apples and pears (not a problem with quince). The first, is to hang pheromone traps in the tree from mid-May to August. These attract and trap the males before they can mate with egg-laying females. This is only partly effective if there are other fruit trees in your area but by monitoring the appearance of males in the traps, other control methods can be applied in time. Gardeners can also purchase a biological control (a nematode Steinernema carpocapsae) to spray on a tree in the autumn (September to October). This small worm invades the caterpillars and gives them a bacterial disease. A wide range of natural and biological controls are available from www.harrodhorticultural.com.

Caterpillars of the winter moth can eat foliage which can weaken the tree. The damage is seen in late spring and early summer. Birds, such as tits, will eat the caterpillars but another option is to spray small trees with pyrethrum. The problem first starts when the female moth crawls up the tree trunk to lay its eggs. Putting a grease band around the tree trunk in autumn (late October) will block her path. Grease bands are available in garden centres or by mail order.

There are various types of aphids such as woolly aphids can attack apple and pear foliage, natural pesticides such as those based on pyrethrum or fatty acids are available but spraying is only practical on small trees. On larger trees, let the birds prevent the aphid populations from building up.

There are various fungal diseases such as powdery mildew, scab and canker that can appear in some years. Aim to choose resistant varieties and to grow them so they are healthy and little control should be needed. If an infection is severe then Bordeaux mixture can be used.

Fireblight is a serious bacterial disease that affects many member of the rose family. Blossoms and shoots wilt and die, as if burnt. White slime may appear from cankers on the stems. There is no cure but mildly affected branches can be cut back to healthy wood. Disinfect tools afterwards to prevent spread to other plants. The tree may have to be dug up and burned.

Apples, pears and quince trees all fruit in late summer through to autumn and winter. Early ripening varieties often have softer fruit than later varieties. Not all fruit varieties change colour when ripe. Mature apples and pears will separate easily from the tree; if you have to tug, the fruit is not ripe. Pears must be picked mature but hard. As they ripen quickly at room temperature and deteriorate equally fast, store some in the refrigerator so they don't ripen all at once.

Be sure to cut fruit cleanly from the tree (a long-handled cutting tool is ideal for this), rather than simply twisting it off. This prevents damage to the branches.

Container Planting Dwarf apples, pears and quinces are ideal specimens for large pots or tubs (at least 60 centimetres in diameter). More varieties are becoming available all the time. Depending on their growth, they may need to be re-potted every two to three years.

Preparing and Sharing Fresh fruit, eaten ripe from the tree, or mature fruit picked and ripened off the tree as is recommended for pears, will always be a treat. Some apple varieties are better for cooking than for eating, and vice versa. Pears are best picked before they are fully ripe and are then allowed to complete the process at room temperature or in a controlled atmosphere (for a commercial crop). If they are left on the tree after maturity to soften they will have lost texture and the centre of the fruit will be over-ripe. Depending on the fruit, it generally doesn't require much preparation beyond washing or peeling. Quinces cannot be eaten raw.

Plainly poached fruit, be it pears or quinces, rarely get many marks from young gourmets. Maybe they don't appreciate the nuances possible in a poaching syrup or maybe a white pear might be reminiscent of a tinned product. However, many delicious dessert options start with poached fruit – think always-popular crumbles (see page 76) and some fruit tarts (see page 82). Apples are rarely poached. Apple chunks or slices for crumbles, cakes or fillings are better cooked in butter than in water, or at least in butter with a spoonful or two of water. An exception might be apple sauce to go with roast pork. Cooked apple, either chunky or smooth, can also be the basis of a sponge pudding or one of my childhood favourites, apple snow (see page 74) or the classic apple Charlotte, where apple chunks are spooned into a cake tin lined with buttery crunchy bread slices, usually flavoured with cinnamon.

Apples, pears and quinces are frequently baked. The time taken will depend on the variety used; ripeness of the fruit; whether it is whole, halved, quartered or sliced; and whether it is a quince or a hard pear (both of which will always take a long time to bake); see the recipe for Oven-roasted Pears or Quinces on page 78.

Ripe pears can be halved, cored and sliced, then layered in a well-buttered shallow gratin dish – first dot with your favourite jam or fruit jelly (or even marmalade), then with coarsely crushed amaretti biscuits, then finally with butter. They should be tender in about 25 minutes in a 200°C/Gas 6 oven. Halved and cored hard pears or quinces could be arranged in a similar dish and the hollows filled with a piece of butter, a squeeze of lemon juice and a good spoonful of honey and then covered and bake for at least an hour. The quinces may need double this time to become tender.

Don't forget that both pears and apples are wonderful served just as they are with cheese, and both can appear in salads, such as the Apple and Bacon Salad with Quail Eggs and Hazelnuts on page 72.

Especially for Kids Take children to visit an orchard, either at blossom or at harvest time. The National Fruit Collection is one of the largest fruit collections in the world. Located at Brogdale Farm, near Faversham, Kent (www.brogdalecollection.co.uk) the collection includes 3,500 named apple, pear, plum and other fruit varieties. They offer family days, tours and an apple festival in October. Apple festivals, typically held in October, offer many child-friendly activities from tastings to games. See www.applesandorchards.org.uk for local events.

Apple (*Malus domestica*)

Apple and Bacon Salad with Quail Eggs and Hazelnuts

SERVES 4 AS A STARTER Quail eggs will definitely appeal to any children in the household. Their flavour is delicate; they fry in seconds and look so pretty on top of these individual salads. However, their shells are very tough and will not crack readily like hens' eggs. I find it easiest to saw the egg shell gently with a serrated knife until you break through the shell and then let the tiny egg slide into a small bowl. Each egg will need its own small bowl. This is the sort of starter I love as it has plenty of interest in terms of both flavour and texture but is not too filling, leaving you with an appetite for the next course. And almost everything is prepared in advance. Walnut halves could be used instead of hazelnuts, but be sure they are fresh and don't taste at all rancid.

50g/2oz hazelnuts or walnuts

8 quail eggs

2 crisp eating apples, cored, quartered and cut into thin pieces

juice of ½ lemon

salt

250g/9oz green beans, as small and tender as possible

100g/3½oz rindless streaky bacon or thin slices pancetta, cut into 1cm/½in-wide strips

4 small handfuls tender rocket leaves, washed and dried

4 small handfuls other tender salad leaves, washed and dried

DRESSING

60ml/2fl oz extra-virgin olive oil

1 tablespoon hazelnut or walnut oil

2 teaspoons red-wine vinegar

sea salt and freshly ground black pepper

EXTRA EQUIPMENT

4 tiny bowls for quail eggs (soy sauce bowls are ideal)

salad spinner

Preheat oven to 150°C/Gas 2. Put nuts on a baking tray and roast for 8 minutes or until golden. If using hazelnuts, rub hard in a dry tea towel to remove most of the skins, then pick nuts from debris and set aside until needed. Gently cut through end of each quail shell and slide each egg into its own small bowl. Place apple in a bowl and drizzle with lemon juice.

To make the dressing, whisk together all ingredients and taste for salt and pepper. Reserve until needed.

Bring a saucepan of lightly salted water to the boil and drop in green beans. Cook for 5 minutes or until bite-tender. Drain and transfer to bowl of dressing.

Sauté bacon or pancetta in a non-stick frying pan over low heat, stirring from time to time. When crisp, transfer to an ovenproof bowl and keep warm in the oven. Slide quail eggs into the frying pan and cook for 1 minute or until set. Transfer salad greens to a large bowl, scatter over crisped bacon or pancetta, apple and nuts, add green beans and dressing and mix. Taste for seasoning. Divide salad among 4 bowls. Slip 2 quail eggs on top of each salad and serve.

Apple Pancakes

MAKES 16 These light-as-air pancakes are perfection when drizzled with real maple syrup (beware of products labelled 'maple syrup flavour'). They need to be eaten as soon as possible as they will deflate if kept waiting. Use two large non-stick frying pans so you can make a large number all at once and have your hungry guests assembled, ready to eat them as soon as they are cooked.

2 crisp eating apples, unpeeled, quartered and cored
1 tablespoon caster sugar
juice of ½ lemon
100g/3½oz plain flour
a pinch salt

¼ teaspoon bicarbonate of soda
2 free-range eggs (at room temperature), separated
180ml/6fl oz buttermilk or milk
40g/1½oz butter, melted and cooled, plus extra for cooking

EXTRA EQUIPMENT
food processor with grating attachment or box grater
electric mixer
large metal spoon

Grate apples in a food processor with a grating attachment or using a box grater. Put apple into a bowl with sugar and lemon juice. Cover with plastic film.

Sift flour, salt and bicarbonate of soda into a mixing bowl. In another bowl, whisk egg yolks with buttermilk or milk and melted butter. Make a well in flour mixture and pour in egg mixture, then whisk to form a smooth batter. Stir in apple mixture.

Beat egg whites in an electric mixer to form snowy peaks, then fold into batter with a large metal spoon.

Brush a large non-stick frying pan (or 2 smaller ones) with a little extra butter. Drop small ladlefuls of batter into the pan/s. They will spread a little, to about 8cm/3in rounds. Wait until you see bubbles on the uncooked side (about 1 minute) before flipping pancakes over with a wide spatula and cooking for another 1–2 minutes. Serve at once.

Apple Snow

Peel and slice 5–6 eating apples, then gently cook over low heat in a little water, in a tightly-covered saucepan until very soft. Drain well in a colander. Firmly whisk 2 free-range egg whites, then beat in 55g/2oz caster sugar to make a soft meringue. Fold gently but thoroughly into the warm stewed apple. Pile into a large glass bowl or individual bowls and serve.

Apple and Cinnamon Cake

SERVES 8 This is a cake with an identity crisis as it could just as easily be described as a pudding. It remains damp and a bit crunchy after baking (as the apples are lightly cooked) and is delicious served warm with cream as a pudding or cut into slices to serve with coffee when it is quite cold. The texture is best on the day it is baked. It is very simple to make.

EXTRA EQUIPMENT
food processor with
slicing attachment
(optional)
20cm/8in springform
cake tin
electric mixer
large metal spoon

60g/2oz butter, plus extra for greasing
4 Granny Smith apples, peeled, quartered and cored
2 teaspoons white sugar
½ teaspoon ground cinnamon
25g/1oz fresh breadcrumbs
2 free-range eggs
150g/5oz caster sugar
150g/5oz plain flour

Preheat oven to 180°C/Gas 4.

Melt butter in a large non-stick frying pan.

Slice apples in a food processor fitted with a slicing attachment or slice them very thinly with a sharp knife. Tip apple into pan of melted butter and cook over medium–high heat, stirring and shaking, for 3 minutes. Tip apple into a large bowl and leave to cool.

Mix sugar and cinnamon and set aside until needed.

Thoroughly grease a 20cm/8in springform cake tin with extra butter. Tip in breadcrumbs, then turn and shake the tin until its base and side are well coated.

Beat eggs and caster sugar in an electric mixer until pale and thick. Sift flour over egg mixture and fold in lightly but thoroughly using a large metal spoon. Tip in apple and quickly fold in. It doesn't matter if the apple is not thoroughly mixed – speed is more essential so as not to deflate the batter.

Tip batter into the prepared tin. Smooth the top and scatter over cinnamon sugar mixture. Bake for 30 minutes or until the cake tests clean when tested with a fine skewer. Leave to cool in tin a little before serving warm, or cool completely in tin and then serve.

Individual Fruit Crumbles

SERVES 6 Individual fruit crumbles bake faster than one big family dessert. They are an excellent way to use up extra poached fruit and can be made with poached pears, quinces or a combination including cooked apple (see below) instead. If you choose to bake this in one large 1 litre/1¾ pint-capacity dish, expect it to take 30 minutes to cook.

600g/1lb 3½oz Poached Quince (see
    page 81) or pears
1½ tablespoons plain flour
butter, for greasing
double cream or ice cream, to serve

CRUMBLE MIXTURE
60g/2oz soft brown sugar
1 teaspoon baking powder
1 teaspoon ground cinnamon
75g/2½oz plain flour
2 tablespoons rolled oats
60g/2oz unsalted butter

EXTRA EQUIPMENT
6 × 150–180ml/
  5–6fl oz-capacity
  gratin dishes

Preheat oven to 200°C/Gas 6.

Put fruit into a mixing bowl. Sprinkle over flour and mix lightly. Lightly grease six 150–180ml/5–6fl oz-capacity gratin dishes with butter. Divide fruit among dishes, filling them nearly to the top.

To make the crumble, mix sugar, baking powder, cinnamon, flour and oats in a bowl. Rub in most of the butter so mixture is a bit crumbly and lumpy, then scatter it over fruit. Dot crumbles with tiny pieces of remaining butter.

Put dishes onto a baking tray and bake for 15 minutes or until crumble is golden and there are a few bubbles of juice around edges. These crumbles are very hot, so be careful. Serve with double cream or ice cream.

Cooked Apples for Crumble

If you want to make an apple crumble, peel, core and cut 4–6 apples into thickish slices and cook in a saucepan over medium heat with a good slice of butter and several tablespoons of water. Cover tightly and stir once or twice. The apples should be tender but not a mush. Some cooks might like to include 2 whole cloves or a cinnamon stick, or even 1–2 scented geranium or lemon verbena leaves.

Eve's Pudding

SERVES 6 This is a very old-fashioned family dessert that keeps on winning new fans. The soft sponge topping hides a thick layer of bubbling aromatic fruit. Sometimes I have added a sliced pear or even a few chunks of peach if I did not have enough apples. Strictly speaking, it is not Eve's pudding if the fruit used is not apple, but then I see no particular virtue in being strict (nor, I suppose, did Eve). The pudding can also be baked in six individual 200ml/7fl oz-capacity gratin dishes; just be sure you use plenty of fruit and not too much topping.

EXTRA EQUIPMENT
food processor with slicing attachment
1 × 1.5 litre/2¾ pint-capacity ovenproof gratin dish (mine is oval 18 × 26cm/ 7 × 10in) or
6 × 200ml/7fl oz-capacity gratin dishes

800g/1lb 12oz apples, peeled, quartered and cored
finely grated zest of 1 small lemon
80ml/3fl oz apple juice
55g/2oz caster sugar
butter, for greasing

SPONGE TOPPING
60g/2oz butter, softened
75g/2½oz caster sugar
2 free-range eggs
150g/5oz self-raising flour
60ml/2fl oz milk

Preheat oven to 180°C/Gas 4.

Slice apples thinly, either by hand or in a food processor using the slicing attachment. Transfer sliced apple to a bowl, scatter over lemon zest, apple juice and sugar. Mix through and cover with plastic film.

To make the sponge topping, cream softened butter and sugar in a food processor until pale and fluffy. Add 1 of the eggs, then 75g/2½oz flour and pulse to mix briefly. Repeat with second egg and remaining flour, pulsing to mix lightly. Add milk. Mix enough to just combine.

Grease base and sides of a 1.5 litre/2¾ pint-capacity ovenproof gratin dish (or six 200ml/7fl oz-capacity gratin dishes) with butter. Tip in apple. Drop spoonfuls of sponge topping over apple.

Bake for 30–35 minutes or until sponge is golden and apple is tender when tested with a fine skewer (individual puddings will cook in about 20 minutes).

Oven-roasted Pears or Quinces

SERVES 6 This way of cooking pears or quinces results in very intense flavour. Although it takes a long time, it requires no attention; once the fruit is tucked into an oven with a reliable thermostat you can safely spend two hours in the garden knowing that a delicious dessert is cooking itself. Bake either one fruit or the other, or combine the two. The quantities of butter and sugar are for one baking dish. If you are dividing the fruit between two dishes you will need to add a bit more butter and sugar. The pears will develop a pink tinge if cooked with the quinces and will be ready an hour or so before the quinces. Because quinces are so intense, I have estimated half a quince as one portion, whereas enthusiastic eaters will probably manage a whole pear. This oven-roasted fruit can be used instead of poached fruits to make an even more delicious Puff Pastry Pear Tarts (see page 82).

80g/3oz butter, chopped
6 pears or 3 quinces
150g/5oz caster sugar
juice of 2 lemons

6 lemon verbena leaves (or a vanilla bean, scented geranium leaf, citrus peel, cardamom pods, a cinnamon stick or a star anise)
honey-flavoured yoghurt or double cream, to serve

EXTRA EQUIPMENT
1.5 litre/2¾ pint-capacity baking dish
speed peeler (see page 47)
parisienne spoon (see page 46)

Preheat oven to 150°C/Gas 2. Melt the butter in a 1.5 litre/2¾ pint-capacity baking dish.

Peel pears, halve lengthways, remove cores with a twist of a parisienne spoon and roll in melted butter. Wash and peel quinces, halve lengthways and remove cores if you wish (they are quite edible after 3 hours' cooking). Roll in melted butter. Turn fruit so it is cut-side down in baking dish and scatter with sugar. Drizzle over lemon juice and add lemon verbena leaves or other flavouring. Cover tightly with a doubled sheet of foil and roast for 2 hours.

Turn fruit and baste with syrupy pan juices. The pears may be tender at this time and can be lifted onto a plate. Re-cover and bake quinces for another hour; they are ready when tender and highly glazed. Serve fruit with honey-flavoured yoghurt or double cream.

Poached Quince

SERVES 4–6 Poached fruit needs to be covered by the simmering liquid during cooking. Before starting to prepare any fruit, place it in the pan to check that it fits comfortably without being too crowded. You also don't want to choose a pan that is so wide that you will need to make huge quantities of syrup. Several varieties of fruit can be poached one after the other in the same syrup. The final syrup will gain in complexity and probably colour if this is done.

Quince cores and peel contain a lot of pectin. If you want to make quince jam, keep these to tie in a muslin bag and add to the pan when cooking. There is a wonderful recipe for quince jam in my earlier book *Cooking and Travelling in South-West France,* in which the quinces are neither peeled nor cored.

If you wish to poach pears instead, they first need to be washed and peeled. Either poach them whole or halved, in which case remove the core. A hard pear such as 'Beurre Bosc' can take up to an hour to cook, whereas ripe eating pears as little as 15 minutes.

Reduce the poaching syrup if it is to be used as a sauce for the cold fruit. You could also add the juice of a lemon to cut through any excessive sweetness, and serve the fruit lightly chilled. Carefully poached fruit is delicious served with cream, yoghurt or ice cream.

EXTRA EQUIPMENT
speed peeler
(see page 47)
parisienne spoon
(see page 46)
enamelled
cast-iron casserole
(optional)

4–6 quinces, washed

BASIC POACHING SYRUP
330g/11½oz white sugar
750ml/27fl oz hot water (up to ⅓ can be replaced with orange juice or wine)

a vanilla bean, lemon verbena or scented geranium leaf, citrus peel, cardamom pods, a cinnamon stick or a star anise

Wash quinces of furry down, then peel with the speed peeler. Cut in half, then core with a parisienne spoon and cut into wedges.

To make the poaching syrup, put sugar, hot water and your choice of flavouring into a heavy-based saucepan or enamel cast-iron casserole and heat over medium heat to dissolve sugar, stirring. Once all sugar has dissolved, simmer syrup for 3–4 minutes then carefully slip in fruit.

Cut a piece of baking paper to just fit inside pan and press it down onto surface of syrup; this will inhibit evaporation and also help keep fruit submerged (see Cartouche, page 703). You may need to weight the paper with a saucer to keep fruit under syrup. Poach for 1–3 hours or until just tender; test with a very fine skewer. The quince will turn from a creamy-yellow to copper-pink and finally to deep amber. (If you wish to cook in the oven, preheat to 150°C/Gas 2. Poach quince in a tightly covered pan to avoid any risk of the syrup evaporating during the cooking time.) Transfer quince to a tray to drain. Leave syrup to cool. Store any leftover fruit in the poaching syrup in the refrigerator for up to a few days.

Puff Pastry Pear Tarts

SERVES 6 Almond frangipane is a classic French preparation that can be made in moments. It provides a delicious base for raw or poached fruit and is spread over uncooked pastry to make simple tarts. It can be made in advance and stored in an airtight container in the refrigerator and softened at room temperature or in the microwave in less than a minute. This recipe uses ground almonds, but it can be made with ground hazelnuts or walnuts. A fun variation is to leave the poached fruit halves whole and to cut pastry shapes to echo the shape of the fruit being used, thus making individual pear (see opposite) or even peach or plum tarts. Each pastry shape must be chilled well before baking to prevent shrinking.

1 roll ready-made all-butter puff pastry, thawed overnight in the refrigerator or at room temperature for 1 hour, then rolled into a 25cm/10in-square sheet
1 free-range egg yolk
3–6 (depending on size) whole poached pears (see page 81), halved
2 tablespoons poaching syrup

double cream or ice cream, to serve

ALMOND FRANGIPANE
80g/3oz unsalted butter, softened
80g/3oz caster sugar
80g/3oz ground almonds
1 free-range egg

EXTRA EQUIPMENT
food processor

To make the almond frangipane, cream butter and sugar in a food processor until light and creamy. Add ground almonds and pulse briefly. Add egg and mix just until you have a smooth cream. Scrape into a bowl until needed.

Lift pastry sheet onto a baking paper-lined baking tray. Lightly mix egg yolk with a fork and brush it all over pastry with a pastry brush, ensuring that no egg drips over edges (this will impede rising). If making a rectangular tart, score a 1cm/½in border around edges and prick centre with a fork. Chill in the refrigerator for 20 minutes.

Spread chilled pastry with a 5mm/¼in layer of frangipane inside the scored border. (If using drained fruit halves for individual tarts, place a spoonful of frangipane on the pastry where the hollow of the fruit will cover it.)

Preheat oven to 210°C/Gas 6. Cut fruit into thick wedges, then lightly press into frangipane, arranging them in closely packed and slightly overlapping rows. (For individual tarts, place halves over spoonfuls of frangipane.) Brush fruit with a little reserved syrup. Chill in refrigerator for 15 minutes.

Bake for 10 minutes, then reduce heat to 170°C/Gas 3 and cook for another 25 minutes (15 minutes for individual tarts). Carefully paint fruit once again with reserved syrup. Bake for another 5 minutes; pastry should be the colour of toast so that it is really crisp and crunchy. Cool tart/s on a cake cooling rack before slicing with a serrated knife, if necessary, (use a sawing action rather than pressing through the pastry). Serve with double cream or ice cream.

ARTICHOKES

Asteraceae family (includes chicory, French tarragon, Jerusalem artichokes, lettuce and sunflowers)
Herbaceous perennial

Soil type
Well-drained sandy loam, enriched with organic matter.

Soil preparation
Dig in organic matter and manure 6 weeks prior. Grow in permanent beds, not as part of crop rotation.

Climate
Suitable for all climates.

Position
Like full sun or a sheltered site.

How to grow
Sow seed in February in a greenhouse, prick out strongest seedlings into pots in March. Or buy young plants, plant out in April to May. Suckers can be taken from mature plants and re-planted in a new site in spring. However you obtain your plants, set them out 1m apart in permanent beds rather than grow the plants as part of a crop rotation. Keep them well watered until established. The first summer after planting, snip off the flower buds as soon as they form but thereafter harvest flower buds in summer.

Water requirements
Keep soil moist and well drained to avoid crown rot. Water stress can cause buds to drop.

Successive planting
You should only need 2 or 3 plants, as they have a high yield.

When to fertilise
Mulch to control weeds, keeping it away from the main stem. Potash assists bud development.

Harvest period
10–15 weeks. After harvest, cut back the main stem to ground level, as new plants will have shot from the base. Leave to grow or, if space is a problem, separate and replant.

Pests and organic control
Aphid, specifically blackfly, is the main pest. They can multiply quickly, so wipe off with a damp cloth as soon as you see them or cut off any infested foliage. Leaves with pale yellow spots that then turn brown are a sign of lettuce downy mildew. Flower heads can shrivel and have a fluffy grey mould on them. Both these plant diseases can be prevented with good garden hygiene, that is picking or cutting off affected parts and disposing of them.

Companion planting
Parsley and pyrethrum distract natural enemies; nasturtiums will attract the aphids away from the plant.

Special information
After 4–5 years the plant will need to be dug up and divided.

Quantities to plant for a family of four
2–3 plants.

Purple artichoke cultivar (*Cynara scolymus*)

Growing and Harvesting   A mature globe artichoke plant takes up a lot of room in a garden but the space is justified as it is a truly spectacular plant with its flamboyant toss of elegant silver-grey leaves. If there is plenty of space in your garden, I would recommend growing even four plants, although a family will do well with two to three. A single artichoke plant may yield as many as twenty heads over the season. Even so, it is likely that just a few heads could be ready to eat on the same day, so rarely could you plan to serve your harvest of artichokes to a crowd! Make sure the plant has enough room to really spread in full, unfettered display. Its edible flower bud has a flavour unlike anything else (except perhaps, its close cousin, the cardoon). An artichoke plant will often not produce buds until its second year.

Artichokes can be green, green and violet, or purple. The plants look wonderful among flowering plants, so don't consign them to the bottom of the garden. A gardening friend tells me he grows a long row of artichokes in his extensive vegetable garden as a very effective windbreak. This year I have grown the cultivar 'Violetta'. The heads are deep purple and there is more heart (the best bit) than with the green varieties I have grown previously.

Sometimes recipes talk about 'baby' artichokes. Baby artichokes are not babies in the sense that they are not the progeny of the central head. They are more like siblings. The size of an artichoke depends on its position on the plant. The artichoke at the top of the plant can be enormous (it is sometimes confusingly called the 'mother'); those lower down are much smaller. Once the main head is cut the smaller ones will continue to grow, but will never be as large as the central head. It is an astonishing sight to see alongside a developed head a tiny dot of green or purple pressed close to the thick stem that swells in a few days to something that is now recognisable as an embryonic artichoke that just grows and grows.

Once the petals (bracts) begin to open, the artichoke is past its prime and is preparing to flower. A fresh raw artichoke squeaks when pressed.

One of the most welcome insects in an organic garden has to be any of the many species of ladybird. These delightful creatures are able to eat huge numbers of aphids – a common pest for artichokes – and their larvae eat even more than the adults do! Ladybirds seem to enjoy living and breeding among the leaves of artichoke plants. Leave them alone and they will help get rid of less desirable insects.

Container Planting   Artichokes are too large for planting in a small pot, although half a wine barrel would be a suitable container for a single plant. A single-person household would get all the drama and beauty of the plant this way and as the artichokes tend to develop one after the other rather than all at once, you could enjoy several artichoke feasts.

Preparing and Sharing   Artichoke preparation is comparatively complicated for a modest yield. Raw artichokes discolour almost instantly, so cooks need a halved lemon alongside to rub the exposed leaves or a bowl of water acidulated with lemon juice to drop the prepared hearts into to prevent them from browning. To prevent further discoloration, artichokes should be cooked in stainless-steel pans. Do remember to wash your hands most carefully after trimming them (or even wear disposable gloves), as the weird flavour they leave on your hands will transmit to whatever you touch next. And scrub the chopping board well too.

A newcomer to artichoke-eating may need to have this odd vegetable explained, as a sure way to turn them off artichokes is trying to eat an untrimmed specimen. The part we eat (after proper trimming) is in fact the flower bud. The stems can be eaten too, but only after the very tough and thick outer layer is peeled off. To prepare artichokes, see Trimmed and Cooked Artichoke Hearts on page 89.

Uncooked artichoke hearts are delicious when really young and fresh. Trim and halve, then remove any fibrous, hairy matter, known as the 'choke' with a sharp teaspoon and slice the heart thinly and serve with olive oil and either some shaved fennel, parmesan, or raw ham such as prosciutto, and salt and pepper to taste. Have a spoonful of olive oil in the salad bowl ready before you start slicing them and turn the slices in the oil instantly. The oil will delay the discoloration just as lemon does.

Trimmed artichokes will take 10–15 minutes to cook in simmering lightly salted water, depending on their size. They are cooked when a skewer slips through the thick base with little resistance. Cleaned young artichokes can also be fried in olive oil until crisp, then opened out like a flower – a very dramatic presentation and a specialty in Rome.

Cooked artichokes are also excellent tossed with hot potatoes, while the cooked artichoke hearts, scooped of their chokes, make edible containers for Aïoli (see page 314), the garlic mayonnaise used for dipping the leaves into. Children may enjoy helping to make aïoli, dribbling in the oil while mum or dad whisks. Artichokes like to be sautéed with oil too. They also work well when matched with capers, browned butter or crisp sage leaves.

Artichokes are especially appreciated in the Mediterranean countries of Italy, France, Spain and Greece. In France and Italy I have seen beautifully trimmed fresh artichoke hearts resting in bowls of acidulated water (see page 703) in the marketplace during their season. They would have been trimmed an hour beforehand and the expectation would be that they would be cooked and enjoyed soon after purchasing. Trimmed hearts can be sliced and sautéed to add to pasta sauces or risotto, or tossed with other luxury spring vegetables, such as asparagus, peas, young carrots and new season's garlic, to make a lovely garnish for a simple fish or meat dish. Or the hearts might be dipped in beaten egg and breadcrumbs, or breadcrumbs mixed with parmesan, and fried to enjoy as a starter or as part of a fritto misto selection (see page 560), perhaps with brains and thick strips of zucchini.

Especially for Kids Young gardeners will be intrigued to discover that this large vegetable is in fact the flower bud of a plant related to the common thistle and, if left unharvested, it will eventually burst into a spectacular purple flower that is very beautiful (and will attract bees to your garden) but totally inedible.

It is fun to show children how to scrape the cooked edible flesh from each petal against one's teeth and it can be an enjoyable family activity to share an artichoke feast. The pile of leaves at the end will be enormous! Cook the artichoke and drain it as described below and then divide up the 'petals' and the prized heart so everyone tastes both. Very young artichokes may not have any choke. An adult should remove the choke the first time as it is easy to gouge too deeply and damage the heart. Make sure children inspect the fibrous 'choke' so that they know exactly what to remove if they decide to have a go themselves.

Artichokes contain cynarin, a chemical that sweetens whatever you eat next. Ask children to drink water or orange juice after eating artichokes and report what they find.

Rustic Artichokes

SERVES 4 This dish represents artichoke-feasting at its most basic. If your artichoke plants are prolific you will certainly eat many prepared like this. The next recipe is more refined. I've given melted butter as a simple dipping sauce here, but try Hollandaise Sauce (see page 111) or a vinaigrette enriched with chopped herbs or tomatoes or both instead.

salt

4 globe artichokes

melted butter

EXTRA EQUIPMENT
disposable gloves

Bring a stainless-steel saucepan of salted water to the boil over high heat.

Meanwhile, wearing disposable gloves, snip away any pointed, prickly ends of exposed leaves using kitchen scissors. Snap or cut away the stalks so that each artichoke will sit more or less flat on a plate.

Drop artichokes into simmering water. Put a plate over them to weigh them down and keep them submerged. To check whether they are cooked, test artichokes by inserting a fine skewer into the thickest part after 10 minutes. The skewer should slip through without resistance; if not cook for another few minutes. Using tongs, first remove plate, then lift out each artichoke and invert it in a colander for a moment to drain. Be careful as boiling water can dribble onto your arm as you invert the artichoke.

Present each guest with their artichoke on a plate or shallow pasta bowl. Provide an extra plate for the leaf debris. Pull leaves away one by one and dip each into melted butter, then scrape the leaf against your teeth. The small amount of soft flesh at the base of each leaf will gradually increase as you move further into the centre of the artichoke. At the very centre is the prized heart, but before it can be enjoyed, you will almost certainly have to remove a tuft of fibrous matter known as the 'choke'. I know people who have unsuspectedly tried to eat this prickly straw-like stuff and rightly wondered what on earth all the fuss about artichokes was about. A sharp teaspoon does a very good job of scraping away the choke, leaving the pale-green hollowed heart to be enjoyed.

Trimmed and Cooked Artichoke Hearts

SERVES 4 This recipe requires more work than the preceding one, but the preparation is an indispensable step if you intend to add artichokes to either a braise, pasta dish or salad.

EXTRA EQUIPMENT
disposable gloves
slotted spoon

2 lemons
4 globe artichokes, stalks snapped
  off and reserved

1 litre/1¾ pints light chicken stock
  or water

Pull on a pair of disposable gloves. Have ready a bucket or basin of cold water with the juice of 1 lemon squeezed into it. Have another halved lemon at the ready.

Start pulling off dark outer leaves until you reach the point where leaves are uniformly pale (discarded leaves and trimmings go into the compost). Hold artichoke on its side on a workbench and use a serrated knife to very carefully cut off top half. Rub remaining artichoke with cut lemon. Use a paring knife to trim artichoke base and cut away nubs where discarded leaves were attached until you have a smooth cream-coloured surface. Don't cut too deeply as this is the best bit – the heart. Rub quickly with lemon.

Either dig into centre of artichoke with a sharp teaspoon to remove any prickly, pointy, pink-tinged leaves and underneath the choke (tuft of inedible fibrous matter), or halve the artichoke so that the prickly leaves and choke are exposed, then remove them. Rub with lemon and drop hollowed hearts into acidulated water. This all takes much longer to describe than to do. Repeat with remaining artichokes.

Cut a stalk into 6cm/2in lengths. Look at each cross-section and you will see a pale core surrounded by a circle of dark green. Strip away dark-green exterior, rub peeled stalk with lemon and drop into acidulated water. Repeat until all stalks are trimmed.

Immediately transfer prepared artichokes and stalks to a saucepan of either simmering light chicken stock or water and simmer for about 10 minutes until barely tender. Cool in liquid for a few minutes and then lift out with a slotted spoon to cool (once cooking liquid is cold it is a good idea to store trimmed hearts in it to prevent discolouration). They are now ready to use in a salad or to sauté. Alternatively, trimmed and par-cooked artichokes can be braised in olive oil with a bay leaf with a good-sized sprig of thyme added and then can be kept in the oil for a few days, refrigerated, until needed.

Spring Ragoût of Artichoke Hearts, Broad Beans, Peas and New-season Garlic

SERVES 4 AS A STARTER This exquisite first course is a labour of love as not only does it feature double-peeled broad beans, peeled baby turnips and artichokes trimmed to the heart, but also properly prepared shelled peas straight from the bushes. As such, the cook must be congratulated. This delicious dish could also be served alongside a grilled or sautéed chicken breast or an escalope of veal or with grilled wood-fired bread for sopping up the pan juices (see opposite). Thin slices of pancetta could be crisped in the butter with the artichokes.

8 cloves new-season garlic
1kg/2lb broad beans in pods, shelled
ice cubes
60g/2oz unsalted butter, chopped
4 Trimmed and Cooked Artichoke
   Hearts (see page 89), halved or
   quartered, depending on size
12 baby turnips, peeled

250ml/9fl oz light chicken stock
500g/1lb peas in pods, shelled
   (to yield 200g/7oz peas)
2 teaspoons coarsely chopped
   French tarragon
1 tablespoon finely chopped
   flat-leaf parsley
freshly ground black pepper

Put garlic in a saucepan and cover with water. Bring slowly to the boil over low–medium heat, then drain. Repeat this process and then slip skins off each clove and set aside in a bowl.

Refill saucepan with water and return to the boil over high heat. Drop broad beans into boiling water for 1 minute only. Immediately drain in a colander and tip into a bowl of iced cold water. Enlist help and double-peel broad beans. Reserve until needed.

Melt 30g/1oz of the butter in a sauté pan over medium heat. Once it starts to froth add artichoke pieces, turnips and peeled garlic and sauté until artichoke pieces become golden flecked with brown. Add chicken stock and peas, then cook, covered, for 5 minutes. Uncover, scatter over broad beans and herbs and shake gently to mix; there should be very little liquid remaining in the pan. If it still looks sloppy increase heat to high and continue to shake the pan. Add remaining butter to form a small amount of sauce. Taste for seasoning; there probably won't be any need to add salt. Grind over pepper and serve at once.

Salad of Raw Artichoke Heart with Celeriac, Fennel and Parmesan

SERVES 4 This lovely salad needs to be eaten as soon as it is prepared as both the raw artichokes and the celeriac discolour after a short time. Expect the preparation to take no more than fifteen minutes, then eat the salad immediately. The portions may look small but this is a very sustaining salad with plenty of crunch! A nice accompaniment is a piece of sourdough bread toasted or grilled and lightly swiped with garlic. For a more substantial salad you could spread the hot toast with fresh ricotta, then scatter with freshly chopped flat-leaf parsley and chives.

EXTRA EQUIPMENT
salad spinner
food processor with
   slicing attachment
   or plastic
   vegetable slicer
   (see page 46)

2 lemons
1 celeriac, peeled and halved
   (to yield 150g/5oz)
2 globe artichokes, trimmed
   (see page 87)
4 small handfuls rocket leaves
   or any mix of small salad leaves,
   washed and dried
1 bulb fennel, outer leaves trimmed
   and fronds reserved

ice cubes
60ml/2fl oz best-quality extra-
   virgin olive oil (or a lemon-
   infused extra-virgin olive oil)
1 tablespoon coarsely
   chopped flat-leaf parsley
sea salt and freshly ground
   black pepper
50g/2oz parmesan

Half-fill a stainless-steel bowl with water and add the juice of 1 of the lemons. Drop celeriac and trimmed artichokes into acidulated water (see page 703).

Place rocket leaves in a medium-sized stainless-steel bowl.

Thinly slice fennel in a food processor or carefully with a plastic vegetable slicer and drop into a bowl of iced cold water to keep crisp. Leave for 2 minutes. Pat dry with paper towel and add to rocket.

Meanwhile, without washing food processor, use shredding disc to cut dried celeriac into thin sticks (julienne), then add to bowl with rocket and fennel. Immediately drizzle over 2 tablespoons of the olive oil. Lift and toss with a fork to coat evenly. Dry artichoke hearts and slice thinly with a knife. Add to celeriac mixture and mix again until well coated with oil.

Finely grate zest of half of second lemon and then juice it. Add lemon zest and juice, parsley and reserved fennel fronds, then season with salt and pepper. Taste and adjust seasoning if required.

Pile salad onto 4 plates, shave over some parmesan and add a final drizzle of remaining oil. Eat at once.

ASIAN GREENS

Brassicaceae family (includes broccoli, cabbage, cauliflower, cresses, radish and turnips)
Annual

Soil type
Can grow in most fertile soils.

Soil preparation
As long as the soil is well drained and rich in organic matter, no additional preparation is required.

Climate
Suitable for all climates, but not all frost hardy.

Position
Prefer sun to partial shade.

How to plant
Sow March to May for a crop of loose leaves used for cut and come again salads but sowing early increases the risk of bolting (see page 687). They are also useful follow-on crop after broad beans or peas, sow direct into the soil in June or start off in small pots. Grow seeds in seed-raising mix, then transplant among other plants. Sow seeds at a depth of 1cm in seed-raising beds. Transplant the seedlings when they are 5–6 weeks old. Plants can be placed 30cm apart. Inter-plant among companion plants to confuse the pests.

Water requirements
Keep soil moist at all times.

Successive planting
Leave about 3 weeks between each planting, throughout the growing season.

When to fertilise
Apply liquid seaweed fertiliser (see page 691) fortnightly to encourage rapid growth.

Harvest period
6–10 weeks from sowing, pick the young outer leaves as required.

Pests and organic control
Aphids, cabbage white butterfly and caterpillars can be kept off crops by a fine mesh crop cover. Sprinkle crushed egg shells around the base of the young seedlings to deter slugs and snails. Hand-picking off the caterpillars is a great activity for kids. Annual crop rotation helps avoid any disease problems.

Companion planting
Peas, beans, celery, beetroot, onions and potatoes. Calendula and nasturtiums are a good distraction for aphids. Red and white clover and aromatic plants such as dill, peppermint, sage and chamomile are useful to distract cabbage white butterfly. Don't plant with strawberries or tomatoes.

Special information
Mulch keeps plants weed-free and conserves water and nutrients. Extreme heat and drought will cause plants to bolt (see page 687).

Quantities to plant for a family of four
Plant 6–8 seedlings every 3 weeks.

Bok choy (*Brassica rapa* Chinensis group)

Growing and Harvesting There are hundreds of Asian greens in existence in the Brassicaceae family alone. With many of these available to the kitchen gardener, it can be tricky deciding what seed to plant as often there are several names for the same vegetable, not to mention different spellings. For example, there are several different bok choys. All have more or less spoon-shaped leaves. They can have green or white stalks, and the stalks can either be longer or shorter. Each has its own name in Chinese. It may be labelled bok choy, buk choy, pak choy or pak choi.

A walk through one of our many Asian fresh-food markets with an Asian friend can help sort out the names and the uses for what seems like a bewildering array of stunningly fresh, deeply green vegetables. However, the most likely selection for a home garden might include several of the mild brassica family (bok choy, choy sum, gai lan and maybe Chinese cabbage and mizuna) and maybe some of the mustard green brassicas that range from mildly spicy to very hot.

Asian brassicas grow fast and cook fast – many can be picked just four to six weeks after planting out seedlings. The flowering shoots of brassicas can also be eaten when they are young and tender and some are grown primarily for these flowering shoots (choy sum and gai lan). When the leaves of bok choy are just 10 centimetres long the entire plant can be picked and is quite delicious. In China this is charmingly known as the 'chicken feather' stage.

To make it hard for leaf-chewing pests, fine nets stretched over a row of bamboo hoops are a great help to the organic gardener but a nuisance when it is time to harvest just two or three plants or a few leaves. You might decide to scatter the planting throughout the garden hoping that at least some of the marauding insects will be distracted by other plants.

Mizuna grows easily in most conditions and can be added to a mixed salad. Cut the plants regularly and it will continue to grow. The feathery leaves are fine in a salad bowl but it is best to remove the stems as they can catch in the throat and cause choking. Mizuna will grow happily in between corn plants or under climbing beans to save space.

When deciding what to plant, think about the culinary potential of each variety. Rarely, if ever, would an Asian cook consider using these brassicas raw.

This brings me to mustard greens. Again, there are many varieties. Usually the leaves become hotter when the plants are about to run to seed or if they have been starved of water. Smaller, younger leaves are less hot than mature larger ones.

Container Planting Asian greens can be successfully grown in a tub or pot. They can be grown alone or together with other greens intended for quick stir-fries such as silver beet (Swiss chard) or spinach. They should be treated as cut-and-come-again seedlings with individual leaves or shoots picked when very young and the plant left to continue growing and to shoot again. As with all container planting, beware of the soil drying out.

You might want to consider a small 'themed' garden pot. An Asian-inspired pot might include coriander, a selection of Asian greens, maybe a chilli bush and Vietnamese mint.

Preparing and Sharing While everything from the garden needs a good wash, you need to pay particular attention to bok choy clusters, as their bases collect dirt and can be quite gritty if not cleaned well. If the plants are to be split for cooking, check that you have removed all sand from between the tightly furled stems. Bok choy, choy sum and gai lan all need to be cooked, even if very briefly. Gai lan stems are usually peeled before cooking. They are then chopped into manageable pieces, dropped into boiling water that has a spoonful of peanut oil added, or tossed in a wok, and are then often finished with oyster sauce. Chinese cabbage only needs to be cooked briefly, although there are classic recipes where it is cooked for a long time, such as in the dish known as Lion's Head Meatballs.

Most leafy brassica varieties are mild-flavoured and more or less crisp and crunchy when lightly cooked (the exception to 'mildness' being mustard greens, which can taste quite pungent). They respond well to all of the traditional Chinese flavourings such as ginger, garlic, black beans, dried shrimps, soy sauce, sesame oil and chilli. They are also good quickly cooked and drizzled with small quantities of fruity extra-virgin olive oil. All Asian greens can be stir-fried or steamed. Timings will vary depending on the structure of the specific vegetable being cooked. Look carefully at the vegetables you have harvested, then consider the following: Are they soft and leafy? Are they chunky with lots of stalk? Are they solid, such as the wide range of barrel-shaped Chinese cabbages, which can also be braised?

To stir-fry Asian greens successfully you need to use a wok over the highest heat possible. Don't try and cook too large a batch or the result will be a wok full of watery, limp vegetables. They can also be braised, steamed or added to broths for a few minutes before serving.

My advice to home gardeners is to be wary of planting mustard greens unless you particularly like them. The assertive character of mustard greens can be softened by combining them with bacon and sautéed onion or soy sauce and a few drops of sesame oil. As vegetable guru Elizabeth Schneider asserts in her encyclopaedic tome *Vegetables: From Amaranth to Zucchini*, 'little as they are, mustard greens can pack a wallop, combining the pungency of horseradish, the bite of rocket and the bitterness of broccoli raab'. In Asia, mustard greens are primarily used to make pickles, although young leaves are also stir-fried.

I try to always have at least ten small bok choy planted so they are ready to eat at the same time, with another batch coming along behind them. This way, I can always step outside my kitchen and cut a few leaves, or if the plants are well grown, cut an entire plant or two. With a few side shoots from the pot of broccoli and a chard leaf or two, I have an interesting and delicious mix of greens to enjoy with a grilled sausage. I usually steam them, but then again I could wash and shake them, then drop them into a frying pan with a sliced clove of garlic and a spoonful of olive oil. By the time the water has disappeared I have glossy green leaves ready to eat. By adding an egg in the centre of these leaves and covering the pan I make one of my favourite breakfasts.

By mastering the simple preparations on the following pages you will be able to cook any leafy Asian vegetable you grow. The preparation is much longer than the cooking time. Successful cooking of Asian greens requires that everything is ready before the wok is heated. I also give recipes for two useful sauces that are both very versatile and suggest two other flavour combinations. Spring Onion and Ginger Sauce (see page 99) is a classic accompaniment to a plainly cooked chicken.

Especially for Kids My overall aim is to entice and delight children with new flavours and textures, not to challenge them unnecessarily. Offering greens that need to be cooked as ingredients in a raw salad is a very bad idea. My feeling is that most mustard greens present a significant challenge to the palate of a young child. If they are grown, they should be introduced carefully and their properties discussed, rather than including them without comment in a bowl of mixed salad. As is the case with other vegetables, be guided by your family's tastes when choosing which Asian greens to plant in your garden.

In some of the Kitchen Garden Program schools it has been great fun when parents who volunteer in the kitchen or garden share their knowledge of the world of Asian vegetables. An expert lesson in the technique of stir-frying has been a valuable class experience. If you are unfamiliar with how to stir-fry successfully, see opposite.

Penne with Mustard Leaves, Ricotta and Pine Nuts

SERVES 2–4 Although this recipe specifies mustard leaves, the dish can also be made with other leaves that have some structure, for example, the outer leaves of a lettuce, silver beet, kale or rapini (see **BROCCOLI**).

salt	30g/1oz pine nuts	EXTRA EQUIPMENT
4 small handfuls mustard leaves and	150g/5oz fresh ricotta	long-handled brass
stems, cut into 1cm/½in-thick slices	2 cloves garlic, chopped	skimmer or
ice cubes	sea salt and freshly ground	slotted spoon
250g/9oz penne	black pepper	
2 tablespoons extra-virgin olive oil	25g/1oz grated parmesan	

Bring a saucepan of lightly salted water to the boil. Plunge in prepared greens. Once water returns to the boil, scoop greens into a colander with a brass skimmer or slotted spoon, then cool rapidly in a bowl of iced water, drain and press out excess water. Set aside until needed. Bring pan of water back to the boil.

Preheat oven to 100°C/Gas ¼ and put ovenproof serving bowls in to warm.

Cook pasta in boiling water for 10–12 minutes or until al dente. Meanwhile, use a tiny amount of the oil to fry pine nuts in a medium-sized frying pan over medium heat. Once golden, tip them onto a paper towel-lined saucer for a moment. Transfer to a mixing bowl and add ricotta.

When pasta is about 3 minutes away from being ready, heat remaining oil in the frying pan, then sauté garlic for a few seconds. Add blanched greens and sauté for 1 minute or so. Drain cooked pasta, give it a good shake and tip onto greens. Mix lightly and tip greens mixture into mixing bowl with ricotta and pine nuts. Quickly mix together, season with salt and pepper and add parmesan. Divide among warm serving bowls and serve at once.

Steamed Asian Greens

SERVES 4–6

EXTRA EQUIPMENT

wok

bamboo steamer
  with lid

4–6 small handfuls trimmed Asian
  greens
Sesame and Red Rice Vinegar

Sauce (see page 100) or Spring
Onion and Ginger Sauce
(see below), to serve

Half-fill a wok with water. Place bamboo steamer plus lid over water and turn heat to high. Once water is boiling, lift steamer lid and scatter in greens, then cover with the lid. Soft leafy greens such as amaranth, spinach and watercress will take 1 minute. Chunky, stalky vegetables such as halved bok choy, choy sum or gai laan will take 4–5 minutes. Transfer greens to a serving dish, then spoon over your choice of sauce.

Spring Onion and Ginger Sauce for Asian Greens

SERVES 4–6

EXTRA EQUIPMENT

wok or
  small frying pan

2 tablespoons finely chopped
  spring onion
2 cloves garlic, finely chopped
1 tablespoon finely chopped ginger

2 tablespoons peanut oil
2 tablespoons light soy sauce
1 tablespoon mirin (see page 704)
1 teaspoon sesame oil

Mix spring onion, garlic and ginger in a small heatproof bowl. Heat oil to smoking point in a wok or small frying pan over high heat. (A Chinese friend tells me that he tests that the oil is really hot by standing the end of a bamboo chopstick in it. If the oil around the chopstick hisses instantly it is hot!) Pour very hot oil over spring onion mixture. Stir and add soy sauce, rice wine and sesame oil, then stir again. Serve with cooked Asian greens.

Stir-fried Asian Greens with Oyster Sauce

SERVES 4–6

EXTRA EQUIPMENT

wok with lid

2 tablespoons peanut oil
1 clove garlic, finely chopped
1 teaspoon finely chopped ginger
4–6 small handfuls trimmed Asian
  greens

60ml/2fl oz water
oyster sauce or Sesame and Red
  Rice Vinegar Sauce (see page 100)
  or Spring Onion and Ginger Sauce
  (see above), to serve

Heat a wok over high heat. Splash in oil, then add garlic and ginger. Stir for a few seconds. Add greens and stir for a few seconds until shiny. Add water. Cover, reduce heat and cook for 3–4 minutes. Test the thickest stem to ensure it is tender. Scoop onto a serving dish and drizzle with a little oyster sauce (oyster sauce is salty so don't use too much) or your choice of sauce.

Blanched and Stir-fried Asian Greens with Black Beans

SERVES 2 This is an ideal way to prepare greens that are strongly flavoured or a little 'bitey', such as those from the mustard family or kale leaves.

2 teaspoons salted black beans (see page 705), soaked in hot water for 10 minutes
2 cloves garlic, finely chopped

2 small handfuls trimmed Asian greens
2 tablespoons peanut oil

EXTRA EQUIPMENT
wok with lid
long-handled brass skimmer or slotted spoon

Mash drained black beans with chopped garlic, using the back of a spoon.

Half-fill a wok with water. Bring to the boil over high heat. Drop greens into water for just 30 seconds. Scoop out to a plate with a brass skimmer or slotted spoon. Carefully tip out water, then return wok to high heat; it will dry almost instantly.

Add oil to wok, then add black bean and garlic mixture and stir for a few seconds. Return blanched greens to wok, give a swirling stir, then cover with lid for 30 seconds before scooping greens onto a serving plate.

Sesame and Red Rice Vinegar Sauce for Asian Greens

2 tablespoons sesame seeds
1 tablespoon white sugar
1 tablespoon light soy sauce

2 tablespoons red rice vinegar (see page 705)
1 hot fresh red chilli (optional), seeded and finely chopped

SERVES 4–6
EXTRA EQUIPMENT
mortar and pestle

Pound sesame seeds with a mortar and pestle until well crushed. Transfer to a small bowl and stir in remaining ingredients. Serve with cooked Asian greens.

Stir-fried and Braised Chinese Cabbage with Chinese Mushrooms

SERVES 2 Any leftover mushroom soaking liquid can always be added to a braise or soup, or used in place of water whenever stir-frying.

2 dried Chinese mushrooms, soaked
 in warm water for 30 minutes
2 tablespoons peanut oil
1 clove garlic, chopped

2 small handfuls thickly sliced
 Chinese cabbage
Sesame and Red Rice Vinegar Sauce
 (see page 100), to serve

EXTRA EQUIPMENT
wok with lid
wok sang (see
 page 47)

Squeeze excess water out of dried mushrooms, then strain soaking liquid and reserve 60ml/2fl oz. Slice off and discard stems, then thinly slice caps.

Heat a wok over high heat until hot. Splash in oil, then add garlic and stir. Add Chinese cabbage, mushrooms and reserved soaking liquid, then stir to mix well. Cover, lower heat to medium and cook for 4 minutes; the liquid should have evaporated. Scoop into a serving dish and spoon over a little Sesame and Red Rice Vinegar Sauce, then serve.

Sweet-and-sour Finale for Stir-fried Asian Greens

Mix 2 tablespoons white sugar with 2 teaspoons cornflour, 2 tablespoons rice vinegar, 2 tablespoons light soy sauce and 1 teaspoon mirin (see page 704) to form a smooth paste. While stir-fried greens are still in the wok, tip in paste mixture, then stir quickly for 30 seconds and serve. This would be an excellent side dish with some sliced Chinese roast pork bought from a specialist Chinese roast meat shop.

ASPARAGUS

Liliaceae family
Perennial

Soil type
Beds should be at least 30cm deep in well-drained sandy loam.

Soil preparation
Enrich with organic matter a few weeks prior to planting crowns.

Climate
Suitable for all climates.

Position
Prefers full sun, but will tolerate partial shade.

How to grow
It is possible to raise asparagus from seed but it takes three years to get a crop. The quickest way is to buy crowns (dormant bases of one year old plants) in April. Dig holes 30cm deep × 30cm wide, 30cm apart with 1.5m between rows. Place a small mound of well-rotted cow manure in the centre of the hole and put the crown on top. Spread roots over manure. Cover with compost to a depth of 7.5cm. As fern grows, cover with soil until hole is filled.

Water requirements
Keep moist when spears are forming to avoid woody stalks.

When to fertilise
Apply a general organic fertilizer in spring.

Harvest period
Don't harvest in first year. When 2 years old, harvest 30–50 per cent of the spears to encourage good growth and allow crowns to build strength. Harvest 3-year-old crowns in late spring. This harvest can last 8–10 weeks. Remove spears when 15–20cm long with a sharp knife just below the soil. Cut foliage to ground level in autumn.

Pests and organic control
The only serious pest is the asparagus beetle. The adults are small yellow and black beetles with red heads, they and their grubs eat the ferny top growth. Pick off and destroy adults and grubs when seen. Where there are a lot of infested plants, spray with pyrethrum (page 700). Clear old stems away at the end of the year and burn them. Slugs may nibble the spear tips but this isn't a major problem for gardeners.

Companion planting
Comfrey and wormwood will distract snails, but don't plant too much or too close. Parsley is said to encourage asparagus to grow faster. Don't plant near onions or garlic.

Quantities to plant for a family of four
Production increases annually, so 7–15 plants would be a good start. This will require an area of 2m × 2m.

Asparagus (*Asparagus officinalis*)

Growing and Harvesting Asparagus means spring. I know that it appears in the shops beforehand and continues long after spring has flown, but for me asparagus belongs to spring. Here is a fragment from one of my 2004–2005 travel diaries. It is easy to see that I was visiting a French market in the spring!

Today I made my first visit to the excellent market at Boulevard Richard-Lenoir, near to the Place de la Bastille in Paris. (If my memory is correct, it was here that George Simenon's Inspector Maigret lived and probably Mme Maigret shopped at this very market for the leeks and potatoes for the inspector's favourite soup.) The star of the show was undoubtedly the asparagus. Stacked in green or cream and mauve bundles it was arranged into gorgeous groupings alongside exquisite salad greens, the leaves of the broad-leafed escarole, or the finer wisps of frisée parted to display the pale-gold and crunchy centres. And alongside was the other essential harbinger of spring – artichokes: small, medium and enormous, green and purple, round or pointed, at very handsome prices too as to be expected for the first of the season. On every stall a still-life fit to inspire Cézanne. Purple beetroot next to posies of lamb's lettuce, cut chunks of brilliant deep-orange pumpkin next to deeply crinkled olive-green cabbages, towers of blood oranges, bulging wooden crates of oysters, giant scallops gently breathing on beds of black shiny seaweed, and farm eggs laid out in feather-lined wicker baskets.

Asparagus is the young shoot of a plant that is related to the lily family. It can be white, green or purple. The spears develop from a network of underground 'crowns' that accumulate starch throughout the summer to enable the plant to live through winter, and then when the weather is favourable in spring, the shoots appear. A well-established asparagus bed will produce each spring for many years and should not be disturbed. Depending on the age of the crowns planted it may not produce anything at all for its first two years.

Asparagus requires a fair amount of space and initial deep cultivation of the beds. For much of the year an asparagus bed seems to be taking up a lot of room for little reward, until the spears poke through in spring. Harvesting has to be done carefully, spear by spear.

Once picking ceases the bed throws up distinctive feathery fern-like foliage that lasts until it is killed by cold weather, or is cut down and mulched into the soil. Any spear that is not cut will send out a shoot from each of the 'scales' near the tip that grow tall and feathery. Tiny flowers can appear in the summer followed by red berries that are poisonous. Thus growing asparagus is a challenging but dramatic project for an enthusiastic kitchen gardener.

White asparagus is the same plant grown with all light excluded, either by earthing up the plants with soil or, much more likely these days, by surrounding the growing plant with black plastic. Excluding light from asparagus as it grows means that white asparagus develops a thicker skin than the green.

Preference for white or green asparagus seems to depend on what one is familiar with. In the UK it is overwhelmingly the green asparagus that is cultivated and enjoyed as a springtime treat. On the continent white asparagus is considered the finest. There is a significant difference in flavour. Green and purple asparagus are much 'grassier' in flavour, while fat continental white asparagus spears are delicate and luscious.

Container Planting Asparagus is not suited to growing in a pot, although a large rectangular planter box could be considered. Remember the depth of soil required and that this container cannot be used for anything else.

Preparing and Sharing To snap off the woody ends at the base of asparagus, slightly bend an asparagus spear and it will snap off at just the right point. While home-grown green asparagus needs no further trimming, bought asparagus sometimes needs to be peeled with an asparagus peeler (also called a speed peeler, see page 47) as their outer layer can be quite fibrous and tough. In my experience, the thicker skin of white asparagus always needs peeling, although some growers dispute this.

It is generally recommended that spears of cooked asparagus be eaten with the fingers; this gives a clue as to how long to cook it. Too many minutes and the spears droop in a very ungainly manner. I suggest boiling or steaming asparagus for just a few minutes and draining well before serving. Asparagus spears are a most successful ingredient in a vegetable stir-fry. They are also lovely grilled – the spears are delicious when brushed with light soy sauce before grilling. And try it raw, thinly sliced as part of a green salad that breathes springtime, perhaps topped with a few shavings of parmesan.

Traditional accompaniments are butter and eggs (especially when poached or soft-boiled). Freshly gathered and lightly cooked spears rolled in melted butter or a few drops of lemon-infused extra-virgin olive oil are hard to beat. Later in the season, when you may have had your fill of such simplicity, make scrambled eggs or omelettes with cooked sliced asparagus added at the last minute, or make a Hollandaise Sauce (see page 111) for dipping or Asperges à la Flamande (see page 108) – young cooks will especially enjoy squashing the boiled eggs with butter and parsley. I also like lightly cooked asparagus, sliced and piled onto well-buttered, hard crunchy toast. I suppose one could add crisp bacon but I usually don't.

Especially for Kids Growing asparagus is a test of a child's patience. They will probably lose interest while the bed is dormant, but what could be more dramatic than reporting the sudden appearance of the first spears!

Help young gardeners to understand how to cut the spears without damaging the food storage factory that lies underneath the ground by showing them how to do it and explaining why this is important.

Asperges à la Flamande

SERVES 4 Children will love this way of eating asparagus. They should be encouraged to pick up the spears with their fingers.

1 teaspoon salt
4 free-range eggs, at room temperature
12 spears asparagus, woody ends
  snapped off
60g/2oz unsalted butter, softened

juice of 1 lemon
2 tablespoons chopped
  flat-leaf parsley
sea salt and freshly ground
  black pepper

EXTRA EQUIPMENT
slotted spoon

Preheat oven to 100°C/Gas ¼ and put 5 ovenproof plates inside to warm.

Bring 1 large and 1 small saucepan of water to simmering point over medium heat. Add salt to the large saucepan. Slip eggs still in their shells into the smaller saucepan and cook for 5 minutes exactly. Drop asparagus into large pan of salted simmering water.

After 5 minutes lift eggs from the water using a large slotted spoon and put into a bowl, then cover with cold water for 1 minute. Drain eggs and carefully peel. Lift out asparagus spears and drain for a moment on a dry tea towel, then divide among 4 of the warmed plates.

Roughly mash eggs with a fork on the last plate; the yolks should still be very moist. Work in softened butter, a little lemon juice and plenty of parsley. Season with salt and pepper. Scoop a quarter of this pretty green, yellow and white sauce beside each asparagus portion. Serve at once.

Baked Asparagus Custards

SERVES 6 AS A STARTER This is a fancy beginning for a special dinner and will impress your guests or family members. Yet it is really very straightforward to make and can be prepared right up until the moment before baking a few hours before dinner, then cooked just before serving. This custard can also be made with broad beans in place of the asparagus. If you wish to try this, use 200g/7oz of double-peeled broad beans (see page 157) and proceed as described below. Just be sure to save a few double-peeled beans to drop into the butter sauce.

butter, for greasing
1 teaspoon salt
12 spears asparagus, woody ends
   snapped off
1 clove garlic, finely chopped
300ml/½ pint pouring cream
2 teaspoons chopped
   French tarragon
4 free-range eggs
sea salt and freshly ground
   white pepper

BUTTER SAUCE
juice of 1 lemon
1 tablespoon water
75g/2½oz unsalted butter, chopped
   into 6 pieces
1 teaspoon chopped French
   tarragon
1 teaspoon snipped chives
sea salt and freshly ground
   white pepper

EXTRA EQUIPMENT
6 × 100ml/3½fl oz-
   capacity soufflé
   dishes
6 rounds baking
   paper, cut to
   fit bases of
   soufflé dishes
long-handled
   brass skimmer or
   slotted spoon
blender or
   food processor

Preheat oven to 160°C/Gas 3.

Thoroughly grease six 100ml/3½fl oz-capacity soufflé dishes with butter and line the base of each one with a round of baking paper.

Fill a large saucepan with water and bring to the boil, then add salt. Cut tips from asparagus and slice spears as thinly as possible. Drop tips and sliced spears into simmering water for 2 minutes, then lift out with a brass skimmer or slotted spoon. Set tips aside for later use and drop sliced spears into a bowl.

Put garlic and cream into a small saucepan and bring very slowly to simmering point over low heat, stirring once or twice.

Combine asparagus spears, hot garlic cream and chopped tarragon in a blender or food processor and process until smooth and apple-green. Expect this to take several minutes.

Lightly whisk eggs in a bowl. Add creamy asparagus mixture and whisk to mix, then pour mixture through a strainer into another bowl or a jug. Season with salt and pepper. Boil water in a kettle or electric jug.

Put prepared soufflé dishes into a deep roasting pan placed on an oven shelf. Pour custard mixture into buttered dishes. Pour boiling water from the kettle into roasting pan to come no more than halfway up sides of soufflé dishes, then slide oven shelf back into oven. Carefully close oven door and bake for about 20 minutes (check after 15) or until the custards feel just firm when you touch the centre with your fingertip.

Carefully remove roasting pan from oven and lift custards from their water bath, then leave them to stand for 5 minutes before turning out.

Meanwhile, to make the butter sauce, add lemon juice and water to a clean small saucepan. Bring to the boil over medium heat. Whisk in a piece of butter at a time, then, when the last piece of butter has nearly melted, drop in the reserved asparagus tips and chopped herbs. Season with salt and pepper.

Carefully remove custards from moulds and spoon a little sauce with asparagus tips onto each one.

Hollandaise Sauce

Melt 200g/7oz chopped unsalted butter gently over low heat and leave to cool a little. Put 60ml/2fl oz white-wine vinegar or verjuice (see page 706), a pinch of coarsely ground white pepper and 2 tablespoons water in a small saucepan and reduce over medium heat to 1 tablespoon liquid. Transfer to a small bowl that fits comfortably over a small heavy-based saucepan half-filled with hot water; the bowl must not touch the water. Add 3 free-range egg yolks to the bowl and whisk over medium heat until thick and foamy. Whisk in melted butter, a little at a time. When all the butter is incorporated you should have a bowl of thick, creamy sauce. Add lemon juice to taste.

BASIL

**Lamiaceae family
(includes mint, rosemary,
sage and thyme)
Annual**

Soil type
Well-drained, moist.

Soil preparation
Use premium quality organic
potting compost if growing in
a pot.

Climate
Is very sensitive to frost
and drought conditions.

Position
Prefers full sun. Prefers
a protected position.

How to grow
Basil is very tender and blackens
if subject to cold or frost, so it
is best to wait until April before
sowing in a greenhouse or on an
indoor windowsill. Sow 3-4 seeds
in a small pot, take care not
to overwater. When the plants

are 15cm high, pinch out the
tips to encourage more leaves.
Gradually harden off the plants
to the outdoors in late May to
June. Basil can be planted out in
beds, leave 20cm between each
plant, but it often does better
kept in pots in a warm sunny
spot.

Water requirements
Water regularly to maintain
healthy growth.

When to fertilise
To maintain healthy growth,
use a liquid seaweed fertiliser
(see page 691) every few weeks.

Harvest period
The leaves will be ready for
harvesting within 60 days.

Successive planting
If plants are trimmed and
kept picked, initial planting
will provide basil for the
entire season.

Pests and organic control
Seedlings are prone to slug and
snail attack. Using crushed egg
shells at the base of the young
seedlings will help deter these
pests. Raising the seedlings
inside until they are mature
is also a good idea as they are
very tender and dislike cold,
damp conditions.

Companion planting
Tomatoes and capsicum.
Don't plant near raspberries.

**Quantities to plant
for a family of four**
8 plants.

Sweet basil (*Ocimum basilicum*)

Growing and Harvesting There are many varieties of basil: small- and large-leaved, some with the aroma of liquorice, some of cloves, some of lemon. Why not grow holy basil (*Ocimum tenuiflorum*) with faint hints of mint, cloves and camphor, or another of the Asian basils, Thai basil (*Ocimum basilicum* var. *thyrsiflora*), which has rather sweet, peppery notes overlaying the familiar aniseed scent of all basils? Both are much used in South-East Asian cookery, and are often confused in recipe books. Other varieties can be grown for interest and comparative tasting, such as the purple-leaved opal basil (*Ocimum basilicum* var. *purpurascens*), cinnamon basil (*Ocimum basilicum* 'Cinnamon') or lemon basil (*Ocimum × citriodorum*).

Watch for snails when the seedlings are young and most vulnerable. Pinch out the flowering tops throughout the summer to keep the plants bushy rather than leggy. Once basil plants start going to seed the flavour of the remaining leaves diminishes, so don't delay the pesto-making until too late in the season. Basil should generally be used fresh as it loses most of its fragrance when long-cooked or dried.

When deciding how many plants to put in your garden, remember that one or two may die, or more likely be eaten, and thus disappear at the seedling stage.

Container Planting Basil is a perfect choice for growing in a pot. Situate it in full sun and remember that pots dry out faster than garden beds, so mulch around the plants once they are well established. You could combine the basil with other herbs: if you have a pot of Thai basil, why not fill the spaces with a chilli bush and some coriander plants?

Preparing and Sharing I cannot use the leaves from my basil bushes fast enough. When using basil in a salad, it is best to tear it with the fingers rather than to cut with a knife, as that hastens the darkening of the cut edges.

Every food lover knows that basil is the partner par excellence of ripe tomatoes. Tear plenty of basil and scatter it over a plate of sliced home-grown tomatoes, then season with a generous drizzle of fruity extra-virgin olive oil. With the addition of a ball of very fresh creamy mozzarella it becomes the simple Italian classic, *insalata caprese*, one of my very favourite summer lunches.

Basil leaves can be quickly deep-fried (make sure they are very dry) to scatter over other dishes. Sprigs of basil can also be dipped in the batter given for Sage Leaf Fritters on page 560. The resultant fritters are appealingly crunchy, although the flavour of the basil itself becomes a bit lost in the crunchiness of the coating. If the leaves are spread out on a lightly oiled baking tray and quickly crisped in the oven at 200°C/Gas 6, they can be lightly crushed and sprinkled over all sorts of things, from cheese on toast to any combination of grilled vegetables. When mixed with thinly sliced mint and the juices of slowly roasted tomatoes and more olive oil, the same crisped leaves make a lovely sauce for prawns. These crisped leaves should be used at once as their flavour and crispness will quickly disappear.

Basil is delicious with soft white cheeses such as buffalo mozzarella, but also a very fresh ricotta or goat's curd, or fromage frais made from either cow's or goat's milk. It also works well with char-grilled Mediterranean vegetables such as eggplant, peppers and zucchini.

Even when I manage to use a good handful of basil every day in the summer months it is likely that there will be plenty left over. Fortunately it is the essential ingredient in Pesto (see page 119). Make large quantities of this marvellous condiment. Jars of pesto covered with a film of extra-virgin olive oil will last until the following summer in the refrigerator, meaning that winter pasta dishes or vegetable soups can be garnished with a dollop (I don't see the point in freezing pesto as it keeps well when stored like this). I also like to shake just-cooked slender green beans in a small spoonful of pesto, or try a spoonful of pesto with still-warm boiled potatoes.

Basil leaves can be preserved by layering them in a jar with extra-virgin olive oil. Pick the leaves from the plant when they are completely dry. The bonus is the resulting basil-flavoured olive oil that is perfect for drizzling over a pizza or a bowl of pasta. Another traditional preserving method is to layer the leaves with coarse salt in a clean ice cream container or similar, packing well and finishing with salt. Cover and refrigerate, then simply remove a leaf when needed, rinse off the salt, pat dry and use within a month or for as long as the leaves are still fragrant.

Holy basil and Thai basil are used in many salads, soups, curries and noodle dishes in South-East Asian and particularly Thai cookery.

Especially for Kids Encourage young gardeners to bruise a basil leaf while in the garden and inhale deeply. The sense of smell is very important in awakening appetite. I was happy to hear during a classroom discussion about 'food memories' that Kitchen Garden Program students at Collingwood College in Melbourne told how the smell of basil instantly reminded them of the annual pesto-making project, when large quantities were made to sell at the school fair.

When next making pesto with young children, you could try a comparison between making the Pesto on page 119 by pounding the ingredients in a stone mortar, and whizzing in an electric blender or food processor, then ask them to note any difference in texture, colour or flavour, and which one they prefer.

A taste test of different basil varieties can also be interesting. Does the flavour change with the size, shape or colour of the leaves? Many gardeners believe planting a circle of basil around each tomato plant will enhance the flavour of the tomatoes. Do you think this works? Try it and see.

Basil and Tomato Pikelets

MAKES ABOUT 12   I make these pikelets quite large (about 8 centimetres/3 inches) so that two or three make a lovely breakfast. The clever idea of adding the sliced tomatoes and basil came from reading *Fresh from the Garden* by the Adey family. Smaller or even tiny pikelets topped with a soft cheese would be good served as a party savoury. They should be served hot or warm. As an alternative to topping the cooking pikelets with tomato slices, a variation is to use 5 millimetres/¼ inch-thick slices of raw salmon (cut to pikelet size) instead, then continue to cook as described below. Serve topped with a tiny dab of crème fraîche or sour cream and torn basil leaves.

50g/5oz plain flour
¼ teaspoon bicarbonate of soda
½ teaspoon salt
¼ small handful chopped basil
1 free-range egg
60ml/5½fl oz milk, plus extra if
    needed
1 teaspoon white-wine vinegar

20g/¾oz unsalted butter, melted
freshly ground black pepper
clarified butter (see page 704),
    for cooking
2 large tomatoes, thinly sliced
24 basil leaves
goat's curd, to serve
sea salt

Preheat oven to 100°C/Gas ¼ and put an ovenproof plate inside to warm.

Sift flour, bicarbonate of soda and salt into a large mixing bowl. Stir in basil. Whisk egg lightly with milk, vinegar and melted butter. Make a well in flour mixture and tip in egg mixture. Stir with a wooden spoon to make a batter with a smooth dropping consistency; you may need 1–2 tablespoons extra milk to achieve this, depending on the size of the egg. Add some pepper.

Lightly coat a non-stick frying pan with a film of clarified butter, then heat over medium heat. When hot, place large spoonfuls of batter in the pan (they should instantly form 7–8cm/3in rounds). Cook pikelets until bubbles start to appear on the uncooked side. Carefully place a slice of tomato and 2 basil leaves over the uncooked side and turn the pikelet. Cook for another 1 minute or so and then lift out carefully, transferring the pikelets tomato-side up to the warm plate, then keep warm in the oven until all are cooked. Each batch will need a film of clarified butter added to the hot pan.

Put a dollop of goat's curd on each pikelet, then sprinkle with a little salt and grind over some more pepper and serve.

Italian Party Cocktail Sticks

MAKES AS MANY AS YOU LIKE These savouries are fun for children to make for a party. Even the very youngest cooks will enjoy assembling them.

cherry tomatoes, halved widthways
sea salt and freshly ground
   black pepper
extra-virgin olive oil

smallest fresh mozzarella balls,
   drained
small basil leaves

EXTRA EQUIPMENT
bamboo skewers
  (the prettiest ones
  have a little knot
  at one end)

Put halved tomatoes into a bowl, toss with a little sea salt, a grinding of pepper and a good drizzle of olive oil. Leave at room temperature for at least 20 minutes.

To assemble, push half a cherry tomato onto a skewer with the rounded side facing the end of the skewer. Follow with a basil leaf, then a mozzarella ball, then a basil leaf, then another cherry tomato half. Continue until all ingredients are used. Place on a tray until needed and drizzle any oily juices from the tomato bowl over them.

Offer small paper napkins if these are served as hand-around snacks as they will be a bit juicy.

Basil Butter

MAKES 250G/9OZ I originally published this recipe in *The Cook's Companion*, but I've included it here as it is an excellent way of using surplus basil from your garden. A slice of this butter floated on a bowl of fresh tomato soup is delicious, or use it to butter your breakfast toast if cooked tomatoes are on the menu. I also enjoy it dabbed on top of grilled lamb chops.

250g/9oz unsalted butter, at room
  temperature
1 small handful basil leaves, torn into
  small pieces

sea salt and freshly ground
  black pepper

EXTRA EQUIPMENT
food processor

Blend all ingredients in a food processor until bright-green. Scrape butter onto a sheet of baking paper and form into a sausage shape. Roll up and wrap in a doubled piece of foil. Twist ends to form a tight roll. Refrigerate. The butter can also be frozen and will keep well for a month.

Pesto

MAKES 250ML/9FL OZ This classic condiment is very well known. I have included my recipe here for easy reference. Kitchen gardeners always have heaps of basil and will want to make at least one large jar of pesto each season.

EXTRA EQUIPMENT
blender or
  food processor
250ml/9fl oz-
  capacity screw-
  top jar

1 small handful firmly packed basil
  leaves
125ml/4½fl oz extra-virgin olive oil,
  plus extra to seal

40g/1½oz pine nuts
2 cloves garlic, crushed
sea salt
60g/2oz parmesan, grated

Put basil leaves, olive oil, pine nuts, garlic and salt in a blender or food processor and blend/process until smooth. Stop the machine once or twice and scrape down the sides with a spatula. When evenly blended, scrape the green paste into a bowl and stir in cheese.

Spoon pesto into a clean and dry 250ml/9fl oz-capacity screw-top jar. Press down with the back of a spoon to ensure there are no air pockets and seal with a film of olive oil. Store in the refrigerator.

Pesto Muffins

MAKES 12 These muffins could be served alongside a bowl of soup for a simple but satisfying lunch.

EXTRA EQUIPMENT
1 × 12-hole
  muffin tin

20g/¾oz unsalted butter, melted
225g/8oz self-raising flour
2 tablespoons finely chopped
  sun-dried tomatoes

1 free-range egg
180ml/6fl oz buttermilk
2 teaspoons Pesto (see above)
125ml/4½fl oz vegetable oil

Preheat oven to 180°C/Gas 4. Use melted butter to grease a 12-hole muffin tin well.

Sift flour into a large mixing bowl. Stir in sun-dried tomatoes. In another bowl, whisk egg, buttermilk, pesto and oil until just mixed. Make a well in flour mixture and tip in liquid, then mix lightly. Spoon batter into muffin holes, filling each just two-thirds full. Bake for 20–25 minutes or until browned on top and springy when touched.

Leave for a minute or so in the tin before turning out onto a cake cooling rack to cool further.

BAY

**Lauraceae family
Evergreen shrub/tree**

Soil type
Deep, well-drained fertile soil but will also tolerate poor soil.

Soil preparation
As long as soil is well drained and rich in organic matter, no further preparation is required.

Climate
Unless in a mild area, grow in a container as it is only moderately hardy.

Position
Prefers full sun, but will tolerate partial shade. If possible, protect from strong winds.

How to grow
You can grow a bay tree from cuttings, but I recommend you buy a small tree from a nursery.

Water requirements
Water containers regularly to maintain healthy growth.

When to fertilise
Give a good liquid fertiliser (see page 691) feed in spring and at the same time trim back the tree to give good shape and encourage more growth.

Harvest period
Harvest leaves as you need them.

Pests and organic control
Naturally pest and disease resistant but can be affected by scale insects and sooty mould. Treat with a fatty acid spray (see page 699) in cool weather.

Special information
Long-lived and slow-growing, it will become a large tree if not pruned regularly. It is suitable for hedging in mild areas.

**Quantities to plant
for a family of four**
1 tree.

Bay (*Laurus nobilis*)

Growing and Harvesting Every kitchen garden needs a bay tree. Bay is one of the most widely recognised herbs in cookery, where it is often used dried.

Fresh bay leaves are not poisonous. There is often confusion between *Laurus nobilis*, the slow-growing evergreen aromatic bay tree used every day by me and many enthusiastic cooks, and the cherry laurel, *Laurocerasus officinalis* (a member of the Rosaceae family), which should never be grown in a kitchen garden. Apparently the cherry laurel is safe in tiny quantities, but it should not be grown where young harvesters might make a mistake – especially as the fruit of the cherry laurel looks so much like a garden cherry.

I prefer to use a fresh leaf rather than a dried one, but when pruning is necessary, hang any trimmed branches and bag the leaves once they are dried to prevent them becoming dusty and greasy.

Container Planting Although it is not uncommon to see a bay tree 2.5–3 metres in height, a small trimmed bay tree of less than 1 metre in a medium-sized terracotta pot (45 centimetres diameter) is more typical. A container-grown bay can continue to thrive without any special attention, other than being kept moist and having an annual trim. If you plant your bay tree in a slightly larger pot, you could include with it other herbs such as thyme and oregano. They will tumble most attractively over the edges.

Preparing and Sharing A bay leaf is an essential component of a Bouquet Garni (see page 635), marinades and most vegetable pickles. Just about every long-simmered dish of meat and vegetables has a bay leaf thrown into the pot.

A fresh bay leaf can be simmered in a white sauce that is destined to be used in a gratin or to be transformed into a mornay sauce by the addition of grated cheese. I also like the flavour of fresh bay leaves in a tightly covered, well-buttered dish of 'Beurre Bosc' pears that will take at least one hour to cook in the oven at 180°C/Gas 4. And I suggest you include several fresh bay leaves if you are braising sweet peppers that have been peeled while still raw (see page 487).

Bay leaves are also good interspersed with grilled quail or pork and chunks of bacon and bread on skewers intended for the barbecue. A vegetarian alternative would be to intersperse bay leaves between rustic bread chunks and soft mozzarella, brushed with olive oil and then quickly grilled on all sides.

They are also lovely as a bed for a sizeable chunk of fish to be oven-roasted. Be generous with the bay leaves and olive oil and, when the fish is just cooked, pour over the bay-scented oily juices and season with sea salt and freshly ground black pepper before serving.

Especially for Kids Children may want to make a bay wreath to commemorate some special occasion or special achievement as was done for successful athletes and warriors in the days of Ancient Greece and Rome. They may be interested to know that in olden times it was thought that wearing a garland of bay on your head during a thunderstorm would ensure that you would not be struck by lightning.

Italian Lentils with Boiled Sausage

SERVES 4–6 The proper sausage to use with this lentil dish is a *cotechino*, a fat Italian pork sausage that is made with plenty of gelatinous bits of pork cheek and skin so it is very sticky and unctuous. It is simmered in water and then thickly sliced. I live in Melbourne where there are still Italian butchers who celebrate their culinary traditions, so it is relatively simple to obtain one of these beauties, but only in winter. If you can't find a *cotechino* you will need to buy the most flavoursome pork boiling sausage you can find (such as a Polish *kielbasa*, French *saucisson* or German *cervelat*), but it won't be the same! If you use thinner sausages they will not need a preliminary long simmer. Instead, simply add them to the lentils right from the beginning of the cooking. *Cotechino* is almost always accompanied by lentils, and sometimes potatoes as well. A bowl of mustard fruits is sometimes offered or just mustard or a homemade spicy hot tomato sauce. Leftover sausages and lentils can be combined the next day as a delicious salad, moistened with a sharp vinaigrette.

EXTRA EQUIPMENT
1 × 2.5 litre/4½ pint-capacity enamelled cast-iron or other heavy-based casserole

1 × 800g/1lb 12oz *cotechino* sausage (or equivalent weight of other large boiling sausage)
1 bouquet garni (see page 635)
2 tablespoons extra-virgin olive oil
1 onion, finely chopped
2 cloves garlic, finely chopped
75g/2½oz fat bacon, pancetta or lightly smoked belly bacon, finely diced

1 carrot, finely diced
400g/14oz brown or red whole lentils, washed and drained
500ml/18fl oz chicken stock
small handful chopped flat-leaf parsley

Fill a pasta pot or large heavy-based saucepan with cold water. Prick *cotechino* with a skewer in several places and put into saucepan with bouquet garni. Bring slowly to simmering point over medium heat, then reduce to low and simmer with the surface barely breaking a bubble for 1½ hours.

When *cotechino* has cooked for 1 hour, start preparing lentils. Heat olive oil in an enamelled cast-iron casserole over medium heat and sauté onion, garlic, bacon or pancetta and carrot for 8–10 minutes. When vegetables have softened and started to colour, tip in lentils. Add chicken stock and stir to mix, then cover and cook gently over low heat for 20 minutes. (If using thinner Polish-style boiling sausages such as *kielbasa*, add now.) Check from time to time, stir and, if necessary, dribble in a few extra spoonfuls of water. When lentils are tender but still with a little bit of texture, stir in parsley.

Tip lentils into a serving dish. Carefully lift sausage to a chopping board. Pierce skin, strip and discard it. Cut sausage into 1cm/½in-thick slices on the diagonal and place along centre of lentils or around edges of the dish to serve.

Lamb Skewers with Fresh Bay Leaves

SERVES 4 Children like to help assemble these skewers. The best family barbecues involve the whole family helping in some way. Although I've cooked the skewers on a metal grill over charcoal (see opposite), they are just as good when cooked in a char-grill pan or on the barbecue.

Enjoy these lamb skewers with a salad made from ingredients picked fresh from your kitchen garden.

1 red onion, unpeeled
2 tablespoons extra-virgin olive oil
2 tablespoons oregano leaves
8 fresh bay leaves, halved widthways
4 small lamb fillets, cut into
  3 pieces each

freshly ground black pepper
2 small lemons, halved widthways
4 flatbreads
juice of 1 lemon
sea salt

EXTRA EQUIPMENT
4 metal skewers
ridged cast-iron
  char-grill pan
  or barbecue
  grill-plate

Place onion in a saucepan and cover with cold water. Bring to the boil and simmer for 5 minutes. Drain onion in a colander, then rinse briefly with cold water and, as soon as you can handle it, peel and quarter it. Separate onion quarters into 3–4 'petals'.

Place olive oil, oregano, bay leaves, lamb and onion in a deep dish and grind over some pepper. Mix lamb and onion around so that they are coated with olive oil/herb mixture. Leave at room temperature for 1 hour.

To assemble the skewers, alternate onion, bay leaf halves and lamb pieces among 4 skewers, finishing with a lemon half.

Heat a char-grill pan or barbecue grill-plate until very hot. Grill skewers, turning once or twice and brushing them with any oil remaining in the marinating dish, until lamb is tender. They will be cooked in about 5–8 minutes, depending on how pink you like your lamb. The onion pieces should look charred on the edges.

Warm flatbreads on the barbecue grill-plate, if using, or in a non-stick frying pan over high heat. Place a lamb skewer in each flatbread, pull out the skewer, squeeze with some lemon juice, then add a sprinkle of sea salt and roll to eat.

BEANS

**Fabaceae family
(includes broad beans,
borlotti beans and peas)
Annual**

Soil type
Well-drained and rich in
organic matter.

Soil preparation
Add an organic blood-and-bone
mix just before planting.

Climate
Suitable for all climates, but prefer
warmer weather. Frost sensitive.

Position
Prefer full sun, but will tolerate
partial shade. Sheltered spot.

How to grow
Sow seed in small pots in a
heated greenhouse in April
to May, they need 10–12°C to
germinate. Grow on in warmth
(minimum 7°C). Towards the
end of May, gradually harden-
off plants to get them used to
outdoor conditions. Plant out in
June when there is no danger of
frost, in exposed areas protect
from cold winds. Climbing beans
need supports, wind young
plants around support until they
cling themselves. Dwarf beans
need minimal support and can
be grown under cloches.

Water requirements
Over-watering will destroy seeds
and seedlings. Water plants
when the first flowers start to
form.

Successive planting
Every fortnight during the growing
season for maximum yield.

When to fertilise
Apply organic liquid fertiliser
(see page 691) after 7–10 days of
the first flower appearing. Mulch
with compost or pea straw in hot
weather. Keep mulch 5 cm away
from the main stems in order
to prevent contact with micro-
organisms.

Harvest period
8–12 weeks from sowing, pick
beans when pods are young and
tender. Harvesting every 2–3 days
prolongs production.

Pests and organic control
Protect from snails by using
crushed egg shells around the
base of the plant. If you cut the
bottoms out of plastic yoghurt
containers or rinsed cardboard
milk cartons and put them over
the plants when they are small,
it will deter pests such as
cutworm. Toilet rolls also work.

Companion planting
Capsicum, cabbage, lettuce,
cucumber and potato. Don't
plant next to garlic or onion.

Special information
Some bean varieties grow up to
2m, so it is important to provide
windbreaks if your area is windy.
Spray flowers with cold/chilled
water to help the pods set.

Quantities to plant
for a family of four
6 seeds every 2 weeks.

Climbing beans (*Phaseolus vulgaris*)

Growing and Harvesting Green beans, French beans and string beans are just some of the common names applied to cultivars of the common bean (*Phaseolus vulgaris*). I adore green beans and find it difficult to think of them as 'common'. They are all annuals and legumes. As with all legumes, beans enrich the soil they are grown in by adding or replenishing nitrogen – a vital element for plant growth, especially leafy plants. At the end of their growing season, cut off the bean plants at ground level, then chop up the plants and dig them back into the soil or compost the spent stalks, then plant leafy vegetables such as lettuce, silver beet (Swiss chard) or cabbage in this spot. Sometimes legumes are grown specifically as a green manure to be dug back into the garden to improve the soil.

Some beans grow up to 2 metres high and are perfect specimens to train onto fences, an old garden gate, cane tepees or other supporting structures – which can include growing corn stalks, or even the stalks of tall sunflowers. Climbing beans are sometimes called 'pole' beans. In order to be stable, the stakes of tepees or other supports should be pushed at least 20 centimetres into the soil or container. Other cultivars grow into small or medium bushes needing various degrees of support.

Bean pods are most often green, but they can also be yellow, purple or green streaked with red. Some cultivars have tough strings down the side of the pod that need to be removed before eating, while others are stringless. Most are rounded but some are flat; others are long and skinny; some flat and wavy.

To keep the bushes productive, beans should be picked every few days. The biggest frustration I find is when the beans stay on the bushes too long and become tough, stringy and unpleasant to eat – when this happens, the bush will also stop producing any new beans.

If, like me, you plan to holiday away from home during the summer months, it is wise to also stagger your plantings. Successive planting ensures supplies throughout the summer, although if I will be away for some of that time I delay planting another crop until just before I leave. If possible, arrange for a family member, friend or neighbour who enjoys freshly picked beans to harvest your beans regularly while you're away. This is not always possible, so you may need to look at recipes for using up the overgrown beans that were allowed to get away (see Cooking Runaway Beans on page 131).

Scarlet runner beans (*Phaseolus coccineus*) are undeniably spectacular with their pretty scarlet flowers (which are edible, by the way, but once eaten there will be one less bean on the bush!) but are particularly prone to toughness when over-mature. Because they are a different species, they cannot be treated in same way as the French stringless bean or other slender bush beans. They are an excellent choice, however, to grow near a wire fence or you could even twine them up a small tree, which will offer the plant some shade on the hottest days.

Once you can see bulges through the pods of scarlet runners it is certain that the pods will be fibrous and tough. If you plan to eat the whole bean, you should harvest them before this stage. You can allow some of the crop to dry on the vine so that you can pod the last beans and use the inner beans either in cooking (as for any other dried bean, see **BROAD BEANS AND BORLOTTI BEANS**) or for planting the following year.

Runner beans need to be cross-pollinated by bees, so include some bee-attracting plants in the garden, such as lavender, myrtle or borage.

Container Planting A half-wine barrel or wide pot can be used to grow climbing or pole beans. Make sure you plant a support structure in the tub and then the beans on either side of each leg of the support, so they can grow up each strut. Select dwarf varieties of bush beans for smaller container planting, although they yield much less than a climbing bean. Bush beans will still benefit from some support, such as bamboo hoops in the pot.

Preparing and Sharing Many beans are eaten pod and all, such as green beans (also called *haricots verts* or French beans), but some beans are allowed to become fully mature before podding the beans inside, which are then either eaten fresh or they may be fully dried for storage. This is often done with scarlet runner beans (see **BROAD BEANS AND BORLOTTI BEANS**).

Young beans are a delight, especially the stringless varieties. They should be cooked until just bite-tender. The biggest mistake inexperienced cooks make when cooking beans (or other green things, for that matter) is to jam a large quantity into a small saucepan and put on the lid. Inevitably grey and flabby beans will result. Always cook them in a stainless-steel or other non-reactive saucepan with plenty of water. The chlorophyll in the beans can react with acids in the cooking water, turning the beans a greyish colour, so using plenty of water dilutes these acids. I recommend cooking them uncovered as this also allows these acids to disperse. Cooked this way, they make beautiful warm salads with just-cooked waxy potatoes or Roasted and Peeled Sweet Peppers (see page 488).

I dislike crunchy beans, which I have always described as 'squeaky beans'. Cooks differ about this, but the late Christopher Lloyd, author of *Gardener Cook*, was a man after my own heart: 'The fashion for undercooking beans and serving them virtually raw has spread like a virus into every restaurant and many homes. This is supposed to be chic, but ill serves the purpose of cooking, which is to bring out the flavour of whatever is being cooked.'

I also disapprove of transferring beans from boiling water to ice-cold water, supposedly to retain the bright-green colour. I find that it makes the beans taste of water rather than bean. Instead, try spreading the cooked, well drained beans quickly onto a warm shallow plate or bowl and then tossing them with butter or oil. Most of their colour will be retained. I prefer my beans to be served either hot (with butter and seasonings), or warm (with olive oil and seasonings). Chilled beans make me shudder to even think of them.

The flavour of scarlet runner bean flowers is quite 'beany' and although a few look stunning on a salad, I find eating one or two quite enough. I prefer to leave them on the plant so I can eat the beans that develop later. The pods of scarlet runners have a strange rasping quality that is not pleasant to eat unless well-cooked. I suggest shelling over-mature beans and putting the tough outer pods into the compost. Alternatively, over-mature bush or pole beans or scarlet runners can be strung, cut into sections and braised with onion, garlic, tomatoes and assertive herbs such as oregano or savory until tender. They are quite unsuited to being briefly boiled to serve with butter or oil as described earlier, and can cause great disappointment if served in this way.

Especially for Kids Children will really enjoy building supports for growing climbing beans. These can be made from bamboo canes tied together at the top to make a tepee shape. Alternatively, pruned branches from trees gathered into a rough bunch and again tied at the top make wonderfully eccentric bean supports. A friend has grown her climbing beans trailing over a pair of old iron gates. And in one of the Kitchen Garden Program schools the beans climb a marvellous sculpture made from bicycle wheels. Any of these options for supports look really interesting in the garden.

Spicy Green Beans with Cashews and Coconut

SERVES 4 This was a creation from my days at the Melbourne restaurant, Jamaica House, back in the late 1960s. Inspired by an Indian or Sri Lankan recipe, my version is a very loose adaptation. In those days I served it as a topping on a beef curry, which itself was a fairly loose interpretation of a curry that ought to have been made with goat.

EXTRA EQUIPMENT
food processor

2 tablespoons olive oil or
   vegetable oil
300g/10½oz green beans, trimmed
   and cut into 2cm/¾in lengths
80g/3oz raw cashews
125ml/4½fl oz coconut milk
125ml/4½fl oz water
sea salt and freshly ground
   black pepper

SPICE PASTE
1 teaspoon cumin seeds
45g/1½oz desiccated coconut
2 French shallots, peeled
1 fresh long green chilli, halved
   lengthways and seeded
2 cloves garlic, peeled
¼ teaspoon ground turmeric

To make the spice paste, dry-roast cumin seeds in a small frying pan over medium heat until fragrant and transfer to a food processor. Wipe pan clean with paper towel. Cook desiccated coconut in the frying pan over medium heat, stirring, until golden. Add to food processor along with shallots, chilli, garlic and turmeric and process to form a smooth paste. Scrape paste into a small bowl.

Heat oil in a large heavy-based frying pan over medium heat, then add spice paste and fry, stirring, for 2 minutes. Add beans and cashews. Give a big stir. Add coconut milk, water and a good pinch of salt. Stir to mix well, cover frying pan, then reduce heat to low and cook for 8 minutes, depending on how crunchy you like your beans. Season to taste with salt and pepper if needed.

Cooking Runaway Beans

The best way to cook overgrown beans is to sauté 2 sliced onions in olive oil with crushed garlic over medium heat for 3 minutes, then add 3cm/1½in sections of strung runner beans, herbs of choice, salt, pepper, and 250ml/9fl oz homemade Fast Basic Tomato Sauce (see page 649) or 1 × 400g/14oz tin diced tomatoes with their juice. Cover pan, reduce heat to low and cook for about 15 minutes until beans are tender and sauce is thick. Serve with garlic-swiped toast, or crack 2 free-range eggs into the mixture, cover the pan and cook for another few minutes for a quick, complete meal.

Green Beans with Lime-green Pepper and Sesame

SERVES 4 Indian cooks can draw from a huge repertoire of interesting ways to prepare vegetables. Such dishes often accompany a meat or fish-based curry. For non-meat eaters, serving a few dishes such as this with rice could make a well balanced meal.

2 tablespoons sesame seeds
¼ teaspoon chilli flakes
salt
300g/10½oz green beans, trimmed
   and cut into 4cm/1½in lengths
2 tablespoons olive oil or
   vegetable oil
1 teaspoon mustard seeds

4 cloves garlic, finely chopped
1 long lime-green pepper, halved,
   seeded and thinly sliced
1 × 1cm/½in long piece ginger,
   finely chopped
¼ small handful coriander leaves
   with stems, coarsely chopped
lemon juice, to taste

EXTRA EQUIPMENT
mortar and pestle
long-handled brass
   skimmer or slotted
   spoon

Preheat oven to 100°C/Gas ¼.

Place sesame seeds on a baking tray and toast in oven for 4–5 minutes or until golden. Pound sesame seeds and chilli flakes with a mortar and pestle to form a coarse powder.

Bring a large saucepan of lightly salted water to the boil over high heat. Cook beans, uncovered, for about 8 minutes or until barely cooked. Scoop from water to a colander with a brass skimmer or slotted spoon and (contrary to my usual advice) quickly run cold water over the beans to stop them cooking any further. Drain well and set aside.

Heat oil in a large heavy-based frying pan over medium heat. Add mustard seeds and stir with a wooden spoon. As soon as they start to pop (several seconds only) add garlic and pepper slices. Stir for 30 seconds or until fragrant, then add ginger, sesame/chilli powder, beans and coriander. Stir to mix well. Taste for salt and add lemon juice, then serve.

Green and Yellow Bean Salad

SERVES 4 This lovely salad evokes all those summer lunches I've enjoyed al fresco. It would probably be one of a number of dishes set out so that guests could help themselves, maybe to accompany either a barbecue, a roast chicken or a baked fish. With grilled garlic-swiped sourdough bread it would make a delicious lunch, probably with a few garden-ripened tomatoes and some torn basil served alongside in another bowl. I don't believe this salad needs any vinegar, as using it (or lemon juice) will both alter the colour of the beans and muddy the taste of the superb olive oil you have selected. If you prefer a sharper-tasting salad, cover a finely chopped French shallot with red-wine vinegar while the beans are cooking, then drain and scatter the diced shallot over the salad. When it comes to the olives used, I like to chop and change between the ever-increasing range of local olives becoming available. An extra touch might be to add some marinated goat's cheese to the finished salad, as shown here (see opposite).

salt
1 tablespoon extra-virgin olive oil
2 tablespoons of your favourite olives
2 teaspoons small salted capers,
   soaked in water for 5 minutes,
   drained and patted dry
2 tablespoons chopped flat-leaf
   parsley

2 teaspoons chopped chives
150g/5oz green beans, trimmed
150g/5oz yellow beans, trimmed
sea salt and freshly ground
   black pepper
marinated goat's cheese (optional),
   to serve

EXTRA EQUIPMENT
long-handled brass
   skimmer or slotted
   spoon

Bring a pasta pot or large heavy-based saucepan of lightly salted water to the boil. Meanwhile, put olive oil, olives, capers, parsley and chives into a mixing bowl.

Cook green and yellow beans separately in the saucepan of boiling water, uncovered, for about 8 minutes each, scooping each type into a colander with a brass skimmer or slotted spoon to drain; I don't run cold water over them as it leaves them tasting of water rather than of bean. Add drained beans to the mixing bowl. Mix very well, then taste and season with salt and pepper; careful – the capers will add some salt to the salad. Lift the salad onto a beautiful platter or shallow salad bowl and serve topped with marinated goat's cheese, if using.

BEETROOT

**Chenopodiaceae family
(includes silver beet/Swiss
chard and spinach)
Biennial grown as an annual**

Soil type
Well-drained. If the soil has
a high clay content, then
I recommend a no-dig garden
(see page 20).

Soil preparation
A few weeks prior to planting,
dig in well-rotted organic matter.

Climate
Suitable for all climates.

Position
Grow in full sun to partial shade.

How to grow
Sow seed in direct into the
ground in April, earlier sowings
can be made in March under
cloches. To store a main crop
of beetroot for the winter, sow
May–June. Sow at a depth of
1.5cm into a moist seedbed.
Keep the bed damp until the
seedlings emerge then thin them
out to 10cm between plants.
An alternative technique is
multi-seeding. Beetroot seeds
are actually clusters of 1–4 true
seeds. Two of these clusters
can be sown in modular trays
or small pots and then planted
out in a cluster of 6–8 seedlings.
There is no need to thin the
clusters.

Water requirements
Water the seedlings but then
aim to keep soil evenly moist,
spells of drought then heavy rain
checks the growth which can
lead to bolting or woody roots.

Successive planting
Leave about 3 weeks between
each sowing.

Harvest period
3–4 months after sowing, harvest
when the root is the desirable
size for the recipe you will be
using. Young beets and young
leaves are delicious.

Pests and organic control
Seldom any problems, except
the occasional leaf miner or leaf
spot. The best control is to pick
off the damaged leaves.

Companion planting
Onions, lettuce, cabbage, silver
beet (Swiss chard), kohlrabi,
cauliflower and peas.

Special information
In hot, dry conditions the root
may become stringy and tough.

Quantities to plant
for a family of four
6 seeds every 3 weeks.

Beetroot (*Beta vulgaris*)

Growing and Harvesting The colour of beetroot is gloriously opulent. It puts me in mind of Thai silk, velvet or even rubies. I love its unique satiny smoothness when cooked and its unusual sweet yet savoury flavour. All beetroot leaves are highly decorative, making it a very attractive plant in the garden. In a small garden beetroot plants can be inter-planted among flowers and other plants.

Do try to grow some of the heritage cultivars of beetroot as well as the regular ones. 'Burpee's Golden' (a glorious rich golden-yellow) and 'Chioggia' (with pinwheel stripes) are two personal favourites. By planting several types, you can greatly extend your harvest through the year.

Check development of the vegetable by gently probing the earth at the base of the plant to see how large the beetroot has grown. Beetroot can be harvested when golf-ball sized – I recommend harvesting each alternate beetroot so that those remaining continue to grow into a larger bulb. You may like to plant a small ring of beetroot in a cluster rather than in a long row. As the beetroot develop, they lean on each other for a bit of support and force the bulbs from the soil when they are ready for harvest.

You can take several leaves from a growing plant for a quick sauté without pulling the bulb. Just be sure to leave the central growing leaves intact and cut from the outside of the plant. When harvesting the leaves, use scissors so as not to dislodge the plant and cut them without too much stalk, as the stalk remains tough and mostly inedible.

Container Planting Small crops of beetroot can be grown in pots most successfully.

Preparing and Sharing Unlike other vegetables (such as peas and beans), the flavour of small and larger beetroots are equally good. The golden and striped beetroot cultivars don't bleed crimson juices all over chopping boards, hands and dishes as the ruby-red ones do. Disposable gloves are still a good idea in the kitchen when handling red beetroot. To prevent excessive bleeding of colour, don't cut the tap roots off before cooking your beetroot.

The appearance of the striped variety does become less dramatic when cooked, turning them an overall pink.

Beetroot bulbs can be served raw. Salads made with raw grated beetroot bleed less than salads made with cooked beetroot. Try coarsely grated or shredded raw carrot, beetroot and celeriac lightly tossed with a delicate dressing of cider vinegar and extra-virgin olive oil. Sour cream and chives go well with many beetroot dishes, both raw and cooked, and beetroot's very definite flavour is excellent combined with strongly flavoured green leaves such as rocket, lamb's lettuce (corn salad) or watercress. My friend, the Australian cook Maggie Beer, found the golden variety too bitter to enjoy raw. I planted some in my garden, and looked forward to testing this myself when they were ready to harvest. I can now say that my golden beetroot were excellent raw – a different palate or different soil, perhaps?

Whole small beetroot can be boiled for about 20 minutes to become tender. I wouldn't bother cutting larger beetroot into smaller pieces to boil as they will bleed excessively. For an even faster method, peel, coarsely grate (wear disposable gloves) and sauté beetroot in butter, stirring it for about 5 minutes over medium heat, then season with salt and pepper and serve. A teaspoonful of balsamic or good red-wine vinegar and cooked sliced potato can be added at the very end. All beetroot varieties can be cooked in this manner.

Beetroot seems to have greater intensity of flavour when it is baked, but it does take a while – even up to 90 minutes in a 180°C/Gas 4 oven for medium-sized whole beetroot; the time can be shortened by peeling and cutting the bulbs into small wedges or cubes and baking them sprinkled with olive oil in a baking dish, covered with foil, for about 45 minutes. So as not to waste energy, I often bake beetroot in one pan and cook the Roasted Vegetables with Rosemary on page 553 at the same time in another.

Cooked beetroot is at its most flamboyant when puréed. At a dinner on Hamilton Island in Queensland a few years ago, chef Darren Simpson prepared a delicious entrée of fat smoked eel with young leeks, a coarse red beetroot purée, sliced cooked golden beetroot and horseradish cream.

A popular French bistro lunch dish involves offering a parade of white china bowls in which various cooked or marinated vegetables are served, dressed with chopped herbs and olive oil and red-wine vinegar, together with a basket of crusty bread. Beetroot is always included. Other dishes might include Celeriac Rémoulade (see page 229), grated raw carrot, sliced cucumber and potato salad.

There are dozens of beetroot recipes in the Russian and Polish repertoires of which the soup borscht (see page 146) is probably the best-known. It is worth making for the excitement of the colour alone.

The leaves are also edible but require thorough washing before being eaten. They are not particularly appetising raw unless very tiny. However, they are fantastic when braised, steamed or sautéed. Once cooked they have a very mineral-y flavour that complements the sweetness of the bulbs, so they are great when served together. When baking beetroot whole or in chunks as described above, I like to interrupt the cooking halfway through by strewing several handfuls of well-washed wet beetroot leaves over the bulbs. Re-cover and continue cooking. The finished dish looks really interesting as the deep-green leaves with their purple markings mingle with the shiny bulbs.

Especially for Kids The sweetness of beetroot may come as a surprise to many children. They may also not know that one variety, sugar beet, is processed to create pure sugar.

Children are usually astounded at the brilliant crimson colour of a beetroot dip. If they have also made some labna from yoghurt (see page 637), the two things can be offered together, spread onto oven-crisped or grilled flatbread.

The very delicious recipe for Beetroot and Chocolate Muffins in my book *Kitchen Garden Cooking with Kids* has been a huge hit and will provide an extra talking point. To make them, see page 147.

Avocado, Grapefruit and Beetroot Salad with Toasted Walnuts

SERVES 4 The colours of this salad are so beautiful and the contrasting texture and flavour of the buttery avocado, sharp tang of the grapefruit, crispness of the green leaves and the sweetness of the beetroot are delightful. In winter, many farmers' markets offer marvellous freshly shelled new season's walnuts. If you are doubtful about the freshness of the walnuts you can buy (long-stored walnuts are quite disgusting) substitute toasted pine nuts or roasted almonds.

2 pink grapefruit or 3 blood oranges
12 golf-ball sized beetroot, washed,
  leaves trimmed (set big leaves aside
  for braising but wash and dry any
  small ones and add to salad)
olive oil, for cooking
50g/2oz walnut halves
1 large avocado
4 handfuls salad leaves, washed
  and dried

WALNUT OIL DRESSING
1 tablespoon extra-virgin
  olive oil
1 teaspoon walnut oil
½ teaspoon red-wine vinegar
1 tablespoon finely chopped
  chives (optional)
sea salt and freshly ground
  black pepper

EXTRA EQUIPMENT
salad spinner
disposable gloves

Using a small or large sharp knife carve skin from grapefruit or blood oranges. Holding a grapefruit in one hand over a large bowl to catch all the juices, slip knife down one side of a single segment and then down other side of the segment, cutting flesh away from membrane. Drop segment into the bowl. Continue until all segments are in the bowl, then work on the next grapefruit. Squeeze 'skeletons' so that the juice falls over the segments.

Preheat oven to 180°C/Gas 4. Put beetroot into a baking dish filled with water to a depth of 1cm/½in, then add a splash of olive oil and cover with foil. Bake for 45 minutes or until tender.

Toast walnuts in a frying pan over medium heat, tossing them for about 5 minutes, or place on a small tray in the oven and roast for about 5 minutes or until golden. Tip into a small bowl to cool.

To make the dressing, mix the ingredients in a separate bowl and set aside.

Uncover baking dish and, when beetroot are cool enough to handle, put on disposable gloves and slip off skins. Halve each beetroot and drop into bowl with the dressing.

Halve avocado and remove the stone. Using a large spoon, slip flesh out of the skin. Place each half cut-side down on a chopping board and cut into 1cm/½in-thick slices. Set out 4 salad plates. Toss salad leaves with beetroot, then place a quarter in the centre of each plate. Arrange avocado and grapefruit around beetroot. Taste remaining dressing, then add a little grapefruit juice and drizzle over salad. Scatter over walnuts and serve at once.

Baby Beetroot with Spinach, Crisp Ginger and a Curry-flavoured Dressing

SERVES 2 The curry-flavoured dressing is a surprise but combines well with the sweetness of beetroot. The crisp ginger sticks are stunning – try them scattered over other vegetables. These quantities can easily be multiplied to serve more.

EXTRA EQUIPMENT
salad spinner
mortar and pestle
disposable gloves

12 golf-ball sized beetroot, washed, leaves trimmed (wash and dry any small leaves and add to salad)

1 tablespoon extra-virgin olive oil

6 long thin slices ginger, peeled and cut into julienne

2 handfuls small spinach leaves or other salad leaves from the garden, washed and dried

1 Lebanese cucumber, peeled, quartered lengthways and cut into 8–10cm/3–4in-long pieces

CURRY-FLAVOURED DRESSING

1 clove garlic, crushed

½ teaspoon sea salt

2 teaspoons Tony Tan's Simple Curry Powder (see below)

2 teaspoons lemon juice

2 tablespoons extra-virgin olive oil

Preheat oven to 180°C/Gas 4. Put beetroot into a baking dish filled with water to a depth of 1cm/½in, then add 3 teaspoons of olive oil. Cover with foil. Bake for 45 minutes or until tender. Use remaining olive oil to fry ginger in a small frying pan over medium heat until golden and crisp. Drain on paper towel.

To make the dressing, pound garlic and salt with a mortar and pestle. Stir in curry powder and lemon juice. Scrape paste into a small bowl and whisk in olive oil.

Uncover baking dish and, when beetroot are cool enough to handle, put on disposable gloves and slip off skins. Halve beetroot, if necessary, and place in a mixing bowl. Add leaves and cucumber, then pour over dressing and toss well. Divide salad between 2 plates and scatter crisp ginger over each one, then serve.

Tony Tan's Simple Curry Powder

MAKES ABOUT 40G/1½OZ Tony is a fine cook. He stresses that the spices used must be very fresh. This recipe does not make a large quantity as one should not store curry powder for too long. Chopped fresh garlic and fresh ginger would be sautéed in the saucepan before adding the curry powder when making a curry. Grind a 5cm/2in cinnamon stick to a fine powder in a spice grinder or coffee grinder and tip into a mixing bowl. Dry-roast 1 tablespoon cumin seeds and 2 tablespoons coriander seeds separately in a small frying pan over medium heat until fragrant. Grind cumin, coriander, 3 cloves and at least 1 teaspoon chilli flakes to a fine powder and add to the cinnamon, then stir in 1 teaspoon ground turmeric. Store in an airtight jar and use within a month.

Beetroot and Potato Pierogi

MAKES AT LEAST 50 The Ukrainians call these delicious dumplings *vareniki*, the Poles *pierogi*. As I was given this recipe by a Polish friend, I've called my version *pierogi*. There are many different fillings, including sauerkraut, cheese or even sour cherry. This beetroot and potato version looks pretty sensational with its lipstick-pink filling showing through the thin dumpling dough. I like them best as a starter, rolled in light sour cream with plenty of chives, pepper and sea salt, while others prefer to roll them in melted butter. They could even be served alongside a rustic pork or veal stew. This is a good job to do when there are plenty of hands to help. The quantities I've given here make fifty dumplings as I find it is not worth making this in smaller amounts. However, the filled dumplings can be chilled, bagged, labelled and frozen and then dropped, still frozen, into a saucepan of simmering water to cook the next time you wish to serve them.

EXTRA EQUIPMENT
disposable gloves
electric mixer with
  a paddle beater
  attachment
potato ricer
food processor
6 cm scone cutter
slotted spoon

125ml/4½fl oz sour cream or 60g/2oz
  butter, melted
salt
2 tablespoons chopped chives
freshly ground black pepper

PIEROGI DOUGH
1 free-range egg
1 teaspoon salt
250ml/9fl oz water
60g/2oz butter, melted
525g/1lb 1oz plain flour, plus extra
  for rolling

BEETROOT AND
POTATO FILLING
200g/7oz beetroot, peeled
  and cut into 3cm/1½in
  cubes
125ml/4½fl oz water
salt
250g/9oz waxy potatoes,
  peeled and halved
60g/2oz butter, melted
sea salt and freshly ground
  black pepper

To make the dough, put egg, salt, water and melted butter in an electric mixer with a paddle beater. With the motor running, spoon in flour, beating on medium speed until you have a smooth and elastic dough. Transfer the dough to a floured chopping board or bench and knead for 1 minute or so, then put into a bowl and cover with a damp cloth for 1 hour.

Preheat oven to 180°C/Gas 4.

To make the filling, put beetroot into a baking dish with water, cover with foil and roast for 45 minutes or until tender. Meanwhile, cook potatoes in a saucepan of lightly salted boiling water until quite tender. Drain vegetables.

Push potato through a potato ricer into a mixing bowl. Process beetroot in a food processor until quite smooth. Combine beetroot with potato, transfer to a mixing bowl and work in melted butter using a wooden spoon. Taste for

>>>

seasoning and add salt and pepper if desired. Allow filling to cool completely.

Divide dough in half and cover one piece with a damp cloth. On a well-floured surface and using a well-floured rolling pin, roll out the other dough half until very thin. Cut into rounds using a 6cm/2½in scone cutter.

Place ½ teaspoon filling in the centre of each round, then fold dough over to enclose filling and pinch edges together. Transfer to a floured baking tray or chopping board (make sure that the *pierogi* don't touch as they will stick together) and continue until all rounds are filled.

Repeat rolling, cutting and filling process with the second piece of dough. Remember you can freeze any leftover *pierogi* you don't wish to cook yet.

Preheat oven to 100°C/Gas ¼. Place either sour cream or melted butter in 2 ovenproof serving dishes and transfer to oven to warm.

Bring a wide pan of lightly salted water to the boil over high heat. Drop in as many dumplings as will fit comfortably in a single layer. When they rise to the surface (about 6 minutes), scoop them out with a slotted spoon, then leave them to drain for a moment on a folded dry tea towel. Transfer to serving dishes and stir to coat with sour cream or butter.

When all dumplings are cooked, add chopped chives and season with salt and pepper, then serve.

Very Simple Cold Borscht

SERVES 4 Cook 4 medium–large beetroot in a saucepan of simmering water for 2 hours until tender, then rub off and discard skins; reserve cooking water. Cut beetroot into chunks and blend with enough of the reserved cooking water to make a thickish soup; don't aim for a super-smooth purée. Sauté 2 finely chopped white onions and 2 sticks finely chopped celery in 1 tablespoon olive oil over low heat for 10 minutes or until well softened, stirring occasionally. Drain well and add to soup with 1 tablespoon aged red-wine or sherry vinegar, 2 tablespoons chopped flat-leaf parsley and sea salt and freshly ground black pepper to taste. Whisk in 200ml/7fl oz sour cream. Serve chilled.

Buttered Beetroot

SERVES 4 This very simple dish, first published in *The Cook's Companion,* looks splendid and tastes excellent with any richly flavoured winter stew – cubed shoulder of lamb with raisins, or the classic rabbit with prunes are just two that come immediately to mind.

EXTRA EQUIPMENT
disposable gloves
food processor
with grating
attachment

300g/10½oz raw beetroot, peeled
40g/1½oz unsalted butter
1 tablespoon water

2 teaspoons red-wine vinegar or vino cotto (see page 706)
sea salt and freshly ground black pepper

Preheat oven to 100°C/Gas ¼ and put an ovenproof serving dish inside to warm.

Grate beetroot in a food processor fitted with a grating attachment. Put beetroot, butter, water and vinegar in a small saucepan and cook, covered, over low heat for 8 minutes, stirring once or twice. Uncover and check that the beetroot is just tender, but still a little crisp. Increase heat to high and boil off any extra liquid, stirring at the same time. Season with salt and pepper to taste. Turn into the warmed dish and serve.

Beetroot and Chocolate Muffins

MAKES 12 Preheat oven to 180°C/Gas 4. Grease a 12-hole muffin tin with melted butter. Grate 1 large peeled beetroot in a food processor with a grating disc attachment and set aside; you need 250g/9oz grated beetroot. Sift 175g/6oz plain flour, 1 teaspoon baking powder, and 2 tablespoons cocoa into a mixing bowl. Lightly whisk 2 free-range eggs with 60ml/2fl oz milk. Process 60g/2oz softened butter, 60ml/2fl oz vegetable oil, 55g/2oz caster sugar and 110g/3¾oz firmly packed soft brown sugar in a clean food processor until creamy. Gradually add egg/milk mixture, then transfer to a large mixing bowl. Sift in flour mixture, folding to mix, then stir in grated beetroot. Spoon mixture into greased muffin tin. Break 100g/3½oz dark chocolate into 12 squares and poke 1 square into the top of each muffin. Bake for 20–25 minutes or until well-risen and springy to touch. Cool in tin for a few minutes, then turn onto a cake cooling rack and leave to cool.

BLUEBERRIES

Ericaceae family
Deciduous shrub

Soil type
Well-drained, friable soil rich in organic matter. Blueberries require an acid soil.

Soil preparation
Add lots of organic matter and well-rotted chook manure 3 months prior to planting.

Climate
Fairly hardy but container-grown plants should have roots insulated in winter.

Position
Prefer sun, but will tolerate partial shade.

How to grow
Purchase container-grown plants in spring for best results. Don't plant too deeply; prepare a shallow hole and place the plant on a slight mound in the hole, then cover the roots with soil. Plant 1 m apart to avoid crowding. Mulch immediately to retain moisture once plant has been watered in.

Water requirements
Water well after planting. Keep soil moist, and don't allow to dry out. Use rainwater if possible.

When to fertilise
Don't over-fertilise. An annual application of well-rotted poultry manure should do the trick.

Harvest period
Allow blueberries to ripen on the bush, and harvest the largest and darkest berries as they ripen at different times. Harvest spread over late summer (July to September).

Pests and organic control
Blueberries are prone to few diseases and pests. Birds eating the fruit is a problem so be sure to cover plants with a bird net.

Special information
Although most blueberries are self-pollinating, growers recommend planting 2 bushes to ensure more fruit. Keep the soil moist and weed-free by applying an acidic mulch such as pine needles or pine bark. This also keeps fruit clean and helps avoid diseases. Don't overcrowd blueberries with other shrubs as good circulation is important for plant health. After 1 year prune weak or dead growth. Remove flowers for the first and second years, to allow the plant to establish.

Quantities to plant for a family of four
2–3 plants. Choose a couple of different cultivars such as an early and a late season, as this will give you a longer harvest period.

Blueberry (*Vaccinium corymbosum*)

Growing and Harvesting   Blueberries hail from the United States and only in the last five years have they been widely grown in the UK by gardeners. The first blueberry nursery was established in Dorset in 1949 and is still thriving today (www.dorset-blueberry.com).

Most varieties are deciduous and, although self-pollinating, tend to produce better fruit if more than one bush is planted. However, there are hybrid plants that don't need help with pollination. Ask the staff at your local nursery which variety is best for your area and whether you need to plant a second bush. A useful rule of thumb is that blueberries will grow wherever a camellia or an azalea thrives. Most will reach 1–1.8 metres high.

Blueberries are deservedly popular. They are delicious, full of antioxidants and the bush itself is highly ornamental, with pretty lily-of-the-valley-like flowers in spring followed by large clusters of blue-black fruits in the summer, and glorious autumn colouring. The bushes are ideal for the home garden. They have considerable advantages over many of the other berry species: they have no thorns; the bushes are self-supporting; non-invasive; they don't need spraying; they crop heavily; and the berries keep well for a week or two after harvesting.

A blueberry bush will not fruit for two to three years. The fruit is borne on suckers that shoot from the crown of the plant. Each sucker is exhausted after three seasons and needs to be cut away. Birds adore blueberries, so netting is essential. Ensure the nets cover the bushes right to the ground – drape them over poles to keep the netting off the actual bushes. The berries change from green to red and then to blue-black, and maximum sweetness develops about a week after this final colour change. Taste a berry to decide if it is time to start picking. Not every berry in a cluster will ripen at the same time, so the best idea is to pick every few days. Roll the berries off the cluster into a bowl rather than tugging at them, which will damage the plant.

Container Planting   Provided the potting mix is lime free (an ericaceous compost) and is kept moist, it is possible to grow a blueberry bush in a large tub. (Better still, grow two.)

Preparing and Sharing   Blueberries are just made for adding to muffins, cakes and tarts. The berries burst when they are cooked, releasing lovely blue-black juices. The fruit is also very popular scattered over breakfast cereals, as they offer a crisp bite and then a flood of juice. Because the berries ripen over a series of days, a small bowlful can stay in the refrigerator until the next batch is ripe; stored this way they will not lose their condition for at least a week. Blueberries have many close relatives that are foraged for in the countryside The European bilberry (*V. myrtillus*) or myrtille is found on moorlands. The berries are tiny and blue-black in colour.

Especially for Kids   Picking blueberries is an excellent way to discuss the difference between ripeness and under-ripeness. Children will very soon work out which berries to pick!

Blueberry Friands

MAKES 12 These cakes are best baked in small moulds, either traditional oval friand tins or small muffin tins. As they contain a lot of ground almonds they are richer than regular muffins and have quite a dense texture. The batter should be made at least one hour ahead of baking – even the day before. It is preferable to make the batter ahead of time rather than bake the cakes too early as the little cakes are at their best freshly baked and they take just 15 minutes to cook. They are absolutely delicious for afternoon tea. Try also making them with a mixture of blueberries and raspberries. Like many cooks, I often have frozen egg whites stored in my freezer and friands are one of the very best ways to use them up. Always date and label the egg whites and mark the container with the number of whites stored. (If in doubt, it is useful to know that an average-sized egg white is approximately 30ml/1fl oz.)

EXTRA EQUIPMENT
food processor
12 × friand tins

160g/5½oz unsalted butter, chopped, plus extra softened butter for greasing
160g/5½oz ground almonds
160g/5½oz caster sugar
a few drops pure vanilla extract
6 free-range egg whites
60g/2oz plain flour, plus 2 teaspoons extra for dusting
125g/4½oz blueberries

Melt butter in a small frying pan over medium heat until lightly golden. Strain carefully into a small bowl leaving all sediment behind. Cool.

Put ground almonds, sugar, vanilla and egg whites into a food processor. Whiz to mix, then add flour. Stop the machine and scrape down the sides. Don't over-mix. Add melted butter, then scrape batter into a bowl and leave, covered, for at least 1 hour or up to 24 hours.

Preheat oven to 220°C/Gas 7.

Thoroughly grease 12 friand tins with extra softened butter. Lightly dust tins with extra flour and shake to coat lightly. Turn upside-down and tap to remove excess.

Stir blueberries into batter. Scoop spoonfuls of batter into prepared tins, filling them no more than two-thirds full. Bake for about 15 minutes or until pale golden and firm when lightly pressed in the centre with your finger. The berry juices will have bubbled through the batter.

Cool friands in tins for a couple of minutes and then turn out on a cake cooling rack to cool. Serve as soon as possible.

Blueberry and Panettone Puddings

SERVES 4 This is an excellent way to use some of the extra panettone that often lands in households around Christmas time. Panettone is the super-light eggy vanilla-scented loaf beloved of Italians. If you don't have any, use a light egg-based bread or even croissants.

softened butter, for greasing
2 tablespoons caster sugar
4 free-range eggs
100g/3½oz crustless panettone
   or other light bread, cut into
   5mm/¼in cubes

200g/7oz blueberries
400ml/14fl oz milk
2 tablespoons raw sugar

EXTRA EQUIPMENT
4 × 250ml/9fl oz-
   capacity gratin
   dishes
slotted spoon
roasting pan

Preheat oven to 180°C/Gas 4. Grease four 250ml/9fl oz-capacity gratin dishes well with butter. Whisk together sugar and eggs. Stir panettone and blueberries into egg mixture. Bring milk to scalding point in a small saucepan over high heat, then tip over the panettone/berry mixture and stir. Stand for 5 minutes for panettone to swell. Using a slotted spoon, divide panettone/berry mixture among gratin dishes. Top with sugar and egg mixture. Boil water in a kettle.

    Position filled dishes in a roasting pan and rest on a pulled-out oven shelf. Pour boiling water from kettle into roasting pan to come halfway up sides of dishes and slide shelf back into oven. Bake for 20 minutes or until firm and lightly golden on top. Carefully remove roasting pan from oven and remove puddings. Scatter a little raw sugar on top of each pudding and serve.

Blueberry and Banana Smoothies

MAKES 4 Smoothies make a fast breakfast. Freezing some of the fruit makes the smoothie thicker as well as colder – just put on a tray in the freezer for 30 minutes before making the smoothies. As over-ripe bananas can be frozen at any time, they are a convenient resource to have to hand whenever a smoothie is planned.

300g/10½oz blueberries
2 bananas, chopped into
   bite-sized pieces
280g/10oz Greek-style yoghurt
   (see page 706)

375ml/13fl oz milk
1 tablespoon maple syrup or honey
½ teaspoon ground cinnamon,
   to serve

EXTRA EQUIPMENT
blender

Spread fruit on a baking tray and freeze for 20–30 minutes or until partially frozen. Blend fruit, yoghurt, milk and maple syrup in a blender until thick and smooth. Pour into 4 glasses. Dust cinnamon over the top of each drink.

BROAD BEANS AND BORLOTTI BEANS

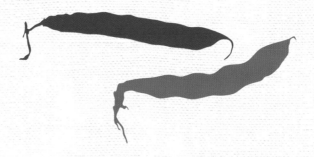

**Fabaceae family
(includes beans and peas)
Annual**

Soil type
Moist, fertile soil.

Soil preparation
Sandy soils will require a general organic fertiliser before sowing.

Climate
Suitable for all climates.

Position
Prefer full sun and an open but sheltered site.

How to grow
Sow in small pots under cover in February to March or sow a month later outside in the ground. Plants are hardy but need hardening off (see page 692) to cope with conditions early in the year. The traditional way to grow them is in rows 45cm apart with the plants 15–20cm apart, or grow in a double row just 20cm apart but with a wide path between double rows for easier picking. Growing in rows makes it easy to support them with a length of string but the plants can also be grown in blocks with plants 20–30cm apart and fitted in all around the garden. Borlotti beans have two types – dwarf or climbing – so check which you have before you start building a climbing structure.

Water requirements
Water in after saving or planting. Thereafter watering not usually required until the flowers form.

Successive planting
Leave about 3 weeks between each planting throughout the growing season.

When to fertilise
Broad and borlotti beans produce their own fertiliser in the form of nitrogen.

Harvest period
Pods should appear after 10 weeks. Pick young to ensure great flavour and quality. At the end of the harvest, chop plants and dig back into soil. Harvest borlotti beans young to eat fresh or leave on the vine to mature for drying.

Pests and organic control
Aphid, particularly blackfly, are a problem with early sowings. Pinch out the growing tips of the plants at the first sign of attack, or spray with pyrethrum or plant oil. Chocolate spot and rust are two fungal diseases that can infect foliage in damp, cold crowded conditions. Prevent problems by growing at the correct spacing to avoid overcrowding and removing and destroying affected foliage and plants (do not compost), there are few control options for gardeners.

Companion planting
Carrots, cauliflower, silver beet (Swiss chard), potatoes and peas. Calendula and nasturtiums are a good distraction for aphids.

**Quantities to plant
for a family of four**
5 plants every 3 weeks.

Broad bean (*Vicia faba*)

Growing and Harvesting Broad beans Broad beans are one of the very few vegetables that have defeated those who would make everything available all of the time. They are an early summer (June to July) treat. Broad beans are the most familiar of a group of beans sometimes collectively described as 'shelling beans' – you don't eat the pod but shell it for the bean within. These beans can also be dried for long-term storage. From the large group of shelling beans, which also includes lima beans, cannellini beans and black-eyed peas, home gardeners will probably only encounter broad beans and maybe borlotti beans or flageolet beans in nurseries and seed catalogues. The most common cultivar of broad bean has white flowers, but a heritage variety with crimson flowers is also now more widely available.

When supporting broad beans, be gentle as the stalks are fragile and if bent vigorously will snap – and there go the beans from that stalk! Use soft cloth as ties. Positioning broad beans in blocks randomly around the garden offers the hope that aphids will not find them among other plants. Plant with species known to attract aphid-loving insects, such as nasturtiums or globe artichokes. Once the broad bean plant is full of flowers, pinch out the growing tops to prevent further growth. The pinched off tops can be lightly steamed and enjoyed as a bonus crop.

For the sweetest and most tender broad beans, harvest the crop when the pods are 10–15 centimetres long. Even smaller pods can be sliced and steamed, pods and all. Pick the pods frequently to keep the plants productive.

As with all legumes, broad beans enrich the soil they are growing in by adding or replenishing nitrogen – a vital element for plant growth, especially in the case of leafy plants. At the end of the growing season, chop up the plants and dig them back into the soil or compost the spent stalks and follow the broad beans by planting other leafy vegetables, such as lettuce, silver beet (Swiss chard) or cabbage in the same spot.

Borlotti beans These are the same species as regular beans, but to a cook it makes sense to list them alongside broad beans as both are podding beans. They are one of a range of kidney-shaped beans and have attractive pink-and-white-splashed pods. They can be grown and harvested fresh but will take much longer to cook than broad beans.

Most are sold dried and are a great standby for winter cooking, so if the aim is to dry your own crop, don't harvest the plants until the leaves are dry and yellow and the beans themselves are completely without moisture. If the sun has not done the job, I recommend pulling up the whole plant and draping it over a rail or something similar in a warm and dry potting shed until there is no more moisture left in the bean. If the beans are stored with even a little moisture they will turn mouldy.

Container Planting 'Aquadulce', a dwarf cultivar of broad bean, grows no more than 1 metre tall. As long as the container selected is placed where the beans will be protected from wind damage and receive plenty of sunshine, broad beans can be a very successful container plant. The growing plants will benefit from some support. There is also a dwarf borlotti bean cultivar but the quantity you could harvest from a 30-centimetre pot would not justify growing this cultivar rather than something offering better yields for the home kitchen.

Preparing and Sharing **Broad Beans** Broad beans are mostly double-peeled to reveal their brilliant colour and superb texture. To do this, the beans are first podded from the shells, then immersed in boiling water for 30 seconds, then quickly run under a cold tap to cool. You nick the outer skin with a fingernail and flip out the green bean within. It is a very time-consuming task but the beans are virtually cooked by the time the skins are off. It is an ideal job to do with a friend or family member, or to share with a group. You chat and peel and before you know it, the beans are all ready.

Unpodded broad beans take up a lot of space and once podded, yield a lot less beans than you may think, so it is useful to remember that 1 kilogram/2 pounds of fresh beans in the pod will yield about 350 grams/12 ounces of beans when podded and approximately 225 grams/ 8 ounces after double-peeling. However, it is not necessary to double-peel broad beans to be used in puréed soups and dips. Nor is it necessary to peel them if the pods are picked when only 8–10 centimetres long.

While very young broad beans can be eaten raw, it is important to note that anyone taking antidepressants that contain monoamine inhibitors should *never* eat raw broad beans; one reference I've seen suggests that this combination can be fatal, so check with your doctor if you have any concerns. According to Harold McGee in his book *On Food and Cooking*, 'People of Mediterranean background may suffer from favism, a serious anaemic condition that results from eating undercooked broad beans or inhaling the plant's pollen. The condition appears to involve a genetically determined sensitivity to the broad bean toxin vicine, which causes damage to the red blood cells of susceptible individuals.'

One of the loveliest of all vegetable dishes is a combination of early spring vegetables (think baby turnips, carrots, peas, asparagus tips and broad beans), each cooked for just the right amount of time to be tender but not crunchy, then brought together with a knob of butter and some freshly chopped herbs, such as flat-leaf parsley, chervil or mint.

For another of my favourite vegetable stews I combine young leeks, artichoke hearts, French shallots and peas. The double-peeled broad beans would be added 2 minutes before serving, just long enough for them to heat through. An extravagant finish would be a tablespoonful of crème fraîche melted into the stew just before serving.

These delectable vegetable combinations are so special that they deserve to be offered as a course in their own right. You could maybe add a slice of grilled sourdough that has been lightly rubbed with cut garlic, then serve some grilled lamb cutlets or fish afterwards.

Broad beans are also lovely in salads (see my Salad of Broad Beans, Cherry Tomatoes, Feta and Olives on page 159). Broad beans also go well with cheeses (especially pecorino and ricotta salata, see page 705).

Borlotti Beans Freshly podded borlotti beans are best simmered gently in stock for 25–30 minutes. Otherwise you can simmer them for a few minutes and then drain and add to a vegetable soup for the last 20 minutes or so of the cooking time. The dramatic pink-and-white colouring disappears when the beans are cooked, transforming them into a deep brick-red. Unlike broad beans, they can't be eaten raw.

If you have dried your own borlotti beans (see opposite) or are using bought ones, they will need to be soaked for eight hours and will then take more than 90 minutes to cook. Gentle simmering in stock or water with onion, garlic and herbs such as sage, rosemary, thyme and bay leaves works best for soaked, dried borlotti beans. Sometimes a piece of cured pork is thrown into the pan for added flavour and richness. It might be a slice of smoked bacon, a piece of salted belly pork or an already-cooked ham hock. Salt is only ever added at the end of the cooking time as it can toughen the skin of the individual bean, and may not be needed if the beans have been cooked with a cured pork product. Like all dried beans, they are best if cooked in a wide-based saucepan so that there are not too many layers because this helps them to cook more evenly – if the pan is crowded some will become tender while others remain tough. Always stir the beans very gently to avoid breaking them up. Leave them to cool completely in their liquid before draining and proceeding with your next step, such as adding them to soups or casseroles or dressing them to make a sustaining warm salad. Borlotti beans can be used instead of chick peas in any of the chickpea salads on pages 175, 461 or 488.

Also, cooked and well-drained fresh borlotti beans, dressed with a little finely chopped French shallot or mild onion, plenty of chopped flat-leaf parsley and the very best extra-virgin olive oil, makes a stunning lunch dish to enjoy with the best-quality tinned tuna chunks.

During winter, when the harvest from the garden is dramatically reduced, it is acceptable to resort to good-quality tinned products that can make attractive salads or braises with the addition of herbs, onions and green leaves from your winter garden.

Especially for Kids   One of the Kitchen Garden Program students at Collingwood College in Melbourne was entranced by fresh broad beans. She wrote in her school diary, 'The inside of the broad bean pod is so soft to feel – each seed (sic) is in a soft little nest.'

Shelling dried bean pods can be difficult as the pods become hard and raspy. To make it a fun activity that even children will enjoy, select a clean and dry hessian bag, then cut a 10-centimetre hole in one corner of the bag and tie the hole shut with kitchen string. Put in the beans, pods and all, and then suspend the bag from a hook on the garden shed. Now beat the bag quite vigorously with a stick (as if cleaning a rug on the clothesline – does anyone ever do this these days?). Put a bowl or bucket under the bag and untie it. Most of the beans will have separated from the pods. Separate the beans from the pods and, before storing, put the dried beans into a container in the freezer for twenty-four hours to kill any weevil eggs they may be carrying.

Salad of Broad Beans, Cherry Tomatoes, Feta and Olives

SERVES 4 This is an example of the sort of salad I make frequently, depending on what is in season and to hand. It takes much longer to describe than to do and the quantities I've given are very approximate. Pick whatever is ready in the garden and create a *salade impromptue*.

EXTRA EQUIPMENT
salad spinner
long-handled brass
skimmer or
slotted spoon

100g/3½oz day-old Turkish bread, cut into 2cm/¾in-thick slices and cut or torn into bite-sized pieces
2 tablespoons extra-virgin olive oil
1 French shallot or ½ red onion, very thinly sliced
2 tablespoons red-wine vinegar
salt
1kg/2lb broad beans in pods, podded
12 cherry tomatoes, halved widthways
2 tablespoons of your favourite olives

1 small handful smallest spinach leaves or rocket leaves or a mixture, washed and dried
12 mint leaves, torn
2 tablespoons coarsely chopped flat-leaf parsley
freshly ground black pepper
juice of 1 lemon
100g/3½oz marinated feta-style goat's cheese

Preheat oven to 160°C/Gas 3.

Brush all sides of bread with some of the olive oil and place on a baking tray. Bake bread for 10 minutes or until golden and crisp.

Place shallot in a small bowl and cover with red-wine vinegar, then set aside until needed.

Bring a large saucepan of lightly salted water to the boil. Drop broad beans into the water for 1 minute. Scoop into a colander with a brass skimmer or slotted spoon, then run the cold tap briefly to stop them cooking (I rarely do this as it wastes precious water, but make an exception here). Drain well.

Place remaining olive oil in a large mixing bowl. Double-peel broad beans, dropping them into the bowl (the outer skins are for the compost). Add cherry tomatoes, olives, salad leaves, bread cubes, mint and parsley, then grind on some pepper. Drizzle over lemon juice and lift to mix with your hands. Taste for salt, allowing that the cheese is quite salty.

Arrange the salad in a shallow bowl or on a platter and, last of all, add cheese and well-drained shallot, then serve.

Stefano's Smashed Broad Beans

MAKES AS MUCH AS YOU CAN WITH THE BEANS YOU'VE PICKED This recipe and the one on page 162 for Antonio's Braised Broad Beans in their Pods are from two fine Italian cooks. They are both rather flamboyant characters and express themselves very forcefully. Stefano de Pieri once persuaded me into designing and helping prepare a dinner for 150 in his hometown of Mildura. The dinner was held in a giant marquee set up beside the Murray River in Victoria. The temperature was in the high thirties. As the guests assembled they were treated to a chug past by the local paddle-steamers, accompanied by much tooting. The first taste to be offered was of orange juice squeezed from fruit freshly picked just before the dinner – a mind-blowing experience for me. And then the next taste was offered by Stefano and his helpers, who smashed impressive quantities of freshly podded broad beans in a giant mortar. The roughly crushed beans were mixed with plenty of grated pecorino and local extra-virgin olive oil, which was piled onto grilled bread. A pepper mill was on hand, as was a bowl of the pink Murray River sea salt for guests to season to taste themselves.

sourdough bread	extra-virgin olive oil	**EXTRA EQUIPMENT**
garlic cloves, halved	pecorino, grated	ridged char-grill pan
double-peeled young broad beans	Murray River sea salt	or barbecue
(see page 157)	freshly ground black pepper	grill-plate
		large mortar
		and pestle

Grill the bread on both sides until crunchy in a hot char-grill pan or on a barbecue grill-plate, then rub lightly with a cut clove of garlic. Place slices somewhere warm.

Place the broad beans in the mortar and pound them to a very rough mash with the pestle. Slosh in some olive oil and transfer to a mixing bowl. Stir in some grated pecorino and season the mix with salt and pepper. Pile onto the grilled bread and enjoy without delay.

Antonio's Braised Broad Beans in their Pods

SERVES 4 Antonio Carluccio is a passionate cook and an enthusiastic eater; he tells us that this idea of eating what he describes as 'cradle-snatched' broad beans in their pods comes from Sardinia. It is quite delicious. This recipe is for all the home gardeners who have an embarrassment of broad beans in the springtime and are prepared to sacrifice a kilo or so of the very youngest pods, probably around 8–10 centimetres in length. I have slightly reduced Antonio's cooking times. Perhaps my beans were even smaller than he intended.

100ml/3½fl oz extra-virgin olive oil
100g/3½oz fatty pancetta or streaky
  bacon (from one of our specialist
  rare-breed pork farmers), cut into
  thin strips
2 onions, thinly sliced
1kg/2lb baby broad beans in pods

80ml/6fl oz water
20 mint leaves, chopped
100g/3½oz chorizo or fresh
  pork and chilli sausage, cut
  into small cubes
sea salt and freshly ground
  black pepper

Put olive oil into a heavy-based frying pan and fry pancetta together with the onion over medium heat. Let onion become soft, about 5 minutes, then add broad beans and water. Cook for 15 minutes and then add mint and sausage. Cook for a further 10 minutes, then season to taste with salt and pepper.

Pasta e Fagioli with Fresh Borlotti Beans

SERVES 12 To make this classic Italian pasta and bean-based soup, sauté 1 finely chopped onion in a large saucepan with a little olive oil over low heat until pale gold, then add 150g/5oz finely diced streaky bacon, 2 finely diced large carrots and 2 finely diced celery sticks, then cook for 3–5 minutes or until bacon crisps. Add 500ml/18fl oz Fast Basic Tomato Sauce (see page 649) and 250ml/9fl oz water and bring to the simmer. Add 550g/1lb 3oz podded fresh borlotti beans and 2 litres/3½ pints light veal or chicken stock and simmer for 45 minutes or until tender. Remove 250ml/9fl oz solids from pan and purée in a food processor, then return to the pan. Stir and season to taste with salt and pepper. Add 280g/10oz cooked pasta (I use macaroni) and serve with a drizzle of extra-virgin olive oil and grated parmesan.

Dried Borlotti Beans with Pork

SERVES 4 This recipe is one for baked bean lovers. Although it takes a while to cook, the beans require no attention once in the oven. It can be served with grilled duck legs or sausages, or it can be a comforting winter dish in its own right served with plenty of crusty bread. Extra stickiness can be achieved by stirring in a spoonful of maple syrup or treacle at the end of cooking. Chilli-lovers could add chilli to the pan; you could enclose the beans in a tortilla, roll it and fry it to create a taco, usually eaten with a fresh salsa and/or guacamole. The beans can be reheated and will become a little drier in the process.

To use tinned beans, you will need 450–500 grams/15–16 ounces drained and well rinsed beans. Stir the tomato paste into 250 millilitres/9 fluid ounces water, then add the tinned beans to the casserole when you add this mixture. Cooking times can vary depending on the age of the dried beans (hopefully the current season's), the thickness of the casserole, and whether it is metal or earthenware, its shape and depth, so the cooking times given are approximate. An extra hour or so might be necessary if the resulting beans are too liquid.

200g/7oz dried borlotti beans, soaked overnight in plenty of cold water	a generous bouquet garni (2 bay leaves, 4 sprigs thyme, 4 flat-leaf parsley stalks and 6 sage leaves), tied in a bundle with kitchen string
2 tablespoons extra-virgin olive oil	1 fresh red chilli (optional)
200g/7oz pork belly, skin removed and cut into 1cm/½in dice	2 tablespoons tomato paste
	2 tablespoons vino cotto (see page 706) or red-wine vinegar
3 large cloves garlic, sliced	sea salt and freshly ground black pepper

Put drained and rinsed beans into a medium-sized saucepan with enough cold water to cover them by about 5cm/2in. Bring to simmering point over low heat and simmer for 45 minutes. Drain beans in a colander placed over a large bowl. Reserve 250ml/9fl oz of cooking water. Set beans aside.

Preheat oven to 150°C/Gas 2. Heat olive oil in a heavy-based casserole over medium heat and sauté pork, stirring with a wooden spoon until it sizzles and looks golden and a bit crispy here and there. Stir in garlic, bouquet garni, chilli, if using, and beans. Mix gently.

Stir tomato paste into reserved cooking water and pour over beans; the mixture should look a bit sloppy at this stage, but certainly not dry. If you feel there is not enough liquid add an extra 125ml/4½fl oz water. Stir in vino cotto or vinegar, season with pepper, then cover tightly and bake for 1–1½ hours. Test whether the beans are cooked after 1 hour; they must be tender and the sauce should be slightly sticky, very aromatic and garlicky and not at all sloppy at this stage. Taste and adjust the seasoning, adding salt if necessary.

BROCCOLI

Brassicaceae family (includes cabbage, cauliflower, cresses, radish and turnips) Annual

Soil type
Prefers heavy soil well enriched with organic matter and a neutral or slightly alkaline soil (see pH, page 694).

Soil preparation
Apply lime if needed to raise the pH at least a month before digging in well-rotted manure a few weeks before planting into final positions.

Climate
Suits all climates.

Position
Prefers sun, does well undercover almost all year round.

How to grow
Sow in March in small pots undercover where temperature is at least 13°C and grow on in frost-free conditions. Harden-off (see page 692) and plant out in their final positions in April to May when 7–10cm tall, allow 30cm between plants.

Water requirements
Dislikes waterlogging, so raised beds are a good idea. Water during dry spells to keep soil moist. Never allow soil to dry out, as this causes it to become bitter and bolt (see page 687).

Successive planting
Sow every 8 weeks from April to July.

When to fertilise
Use a liquid fertiliser (see page 691) or worm tea (see page 695) every 2 weeks.

Harvest period
10–12 weeks from seedling and 16–20 weeks from seed. Remove primary head when it is tight. Harvesting the primary head encourages side shoots to grow.

Pests and organic control
Highly prone to pests and diseases. Aphids, cabbage white caterpillars and cabbage root fly can be prevented by using crop covers (see page 697) or controlled by picking off pests or by spraying with natural insecticides such as those based on garlic or pyrethrum or using a biological control. Downy mildew can sometimes be a problem, pick off and destroy affected foliage. Crop rotation will help prevent clubroot but once it is in the soil it will last for 20 years, so then your only option is to grow in containers.

Companion planting
Aromatic plants, including sage, dill, chamomile, beetroot, peppermint, rosemary, beans, celery, onions, potatoes and dwarf zinnias. Dill attracts wasps, which will control the cabbage butterfly, and zinnia attracts ladybirds to protect the plants. Don't plant with tomatoes or strawberries.

Quantities to plant for a family of four
6 plants every 2 weeks.

The one large central head of calabrese broccoli (*Brassica oleracea* var. *italica*)

Growing and Harvesting There are many varieties of broccoli. Calabrese (or green broccoli) is sometimes known as American broccoli or broccoli although it came from Italy originally. Calabrese develops a large central head and later has smaller side shoots; these tender shoots are delicious. If the plant is fed regularly they sometimes continue for a long time after the central flower head has been harvested.

The head of broccoli is actually made up of densely packed flower buds. Left unharvested, the central head will become less compact and the buds will loosen, then flower and turn yellow. This is a sign of age and broccoli heads should always be picked before this stage.

The cabbage white caterpillars are a constant pest. Fine net crop covers stretched over hoops is a good deterrent (to stop butterflies laying eggs) but a nuisance when you want to harvest the crop. Alternatively, inter-plant calabrese with strong-smelling herbs such as dill, sage and other companion plants (see page 165) that may discourage insect pests.

You could also try organic sprays (see pages 698–700). Note also that one of your daily tasks in the garden should be to check the underside of all brassica leaves for small green caterpillars. Pick these off and either destroy them or feed them to the chickens.

My own experience suggests that small seedlings are the most vulnerable to aphids and leaf-eaters of various kinds. If the plants are healthy and the soil is good, many plants will survive the attack and grow to maturity with just a few holey leaves to show for it. In my own garden this year I found that although the cabbage white butterfly did considerable damage to the leaves, they left the calabrese heads untouched.

Sprouting broccoli exists in several cultivars, and I especially like the delicious purple-sprouting one – this plant takes a long time to mature but the flavour is worth it. White-sprouting broccoli is another one, sometimes called Italian broccoli. These plants don't produce a central head but a profusion of smaller, looser heads. They are best cut when 10 centimetres long, together with their surrounding leaves. All parts are edible. The sprouting broccoli come into their own as winter veg.

Broccoli raab or rapini is an Italian favourite and seeds are available for growing it. The leaves are harvested with the developing flower buds and stems. This plant needs to grow quickly to avoid stringiness. It does have a slightly bitter flavour, prized by many but disliked by others. It may not appeal to children.

I once successfully grew something sold as 'miniature broccoli' from seedlings I bought at a farmers' market. Each very compact head was about 6 centimetres across and the stems were very tender.

Lastly, don't forget gai lan or Chinese broccoli (see **ASIAN GREENS**).

Container Planting All varieties of broccoli can be grown in a tub or large pot. No more than four plants could be accommodated in a container the size of a wine barrel, though. The yield will consist of one central head and some later side shoots. You will need to decide whether this is a good use of your container as opposed to planting several small cabbages or mini-cauliflowers, for example.

Preparing and Sharing Not everyone knows that calabrese stems are also edible. Once they are peeled, they are as tender as asparagus. In fact I have friends who only eat the stems, which I find hard to understand as well as very wasteful!

Broccoli is frequently badly cooked. Separate the florets with a knife. Peel the chunky stems and cut them into manageable pieces, then cook them briefly and uncovered in a large saucepan in plenty of simmering salted water. They should be very well drained and served bright-green with absolutely no trace of mushiness or that awful sulphurous smell associated with overcooked brassicas. Make sure the serving dish is warmed as broccoli loses its heat fast. With a knob of butter or a drizzle of extra-virgin olive oil your dish of broccoli is a treat and a revelation for many who have been subjected to mushy broccoli. Another option is to include the cooked and drained florets and stems in a mixed vegetable stir-fry.

I never transfer broccoli from boiling water to ice-cold water, which supposedly helps to retain the bright-green colour. I find that it makes it taste of water rather than broccoli. The key is to not overcook it in the first place.

Especially for Kids Young gardeners need to be shown how to cut the central head of each calabrese plant and then to watch for the development of the small side shoots. Make sure the cut is made on the diagonal to prevent the stem from collecting water and rotting.

I have had great success in converting several young broccoli-haters into broccoli-lovers by pulsing briefly cooked broccoli in a food processor and then tossing this coarsely chopped mixture with sautéed garlic and sautéed pine nuts through hot pasta. What these children disliked, they said, was the lumpiness of broccoli. Plus they hadn't realised it could be so brilliantly green, which told me that their previous experiences had featured overcooked broccoli. On the other hand, some other small gourmets I know love the lumps and bumps of broccoli shoots left whole and describe broccoli florets as 'little trees'.

Once converted, a variation of the 'broccoli plus pasta' theme is to use tiny florets of cooked broccoli in a carbonara-style dish (see page 171) by adding some sautéed ham or bacon and a couple of well-whisked eggs to the hot pasta, then finishing with grated parmesan.

Having converted the children in question to brilliantly green, tender broccoli it is a good opportunity to discuss why this is so different from the drab grey-green stuff they may have tasted before. The chlorophyll in the vegetable reacts with the acids in the cooking water, changing the broccoli to a dull green. Using lots of water dilutes these acids. Leaving the pan uncovered and quick cooking also allows the acids to disperse, resulting in perfect broccoli.

Broccoli and Orecchiette

SERVES 4 I tasted this specialty of Puglia several times during a delightful two-week stay in this lovely region of Italy. The pasta is shaped like little ears and I learnt to make it by hand. The first time I had ever heard of making pasta using ricotta was in this recipe. The Italian woman who shared the recipe came from Sicily and assured me this was how it was done in her hometown. It is a fun thing to do with a group of friends or all the family helping and you can dry the orechiette and store them if you don't wish to cook them right away. I have included the recipe and technique as shown to me here but the dried version is readily available in specialty Italian grocers; if you don't want to make the homemade version, use 250 grams/9 ounces dried orecchiette instead. As with much Italian regional cooking there are many variations of this recipe to be found.

salt
350g/12oz broccoli, head cut into small
  florets and stems peeled and cut into
  thin rounds
80ml/3fl oz extra-virgin olive oil
4 cloves garlic, finely chopped
6 anchovy fillets, chopped
1 fresh red chilli, seeded and chopped
20g/¾oz butter

2 tablespoons grated
  parmesan

HOMEMADE ORECCHIETTE
250g/9oz plain flour
1 teaspoon salt
100g/3½oz fresh ricotta
1 large free-range egg
2 teaspoons water

EXTRA EQUIPMENT
long-handled brass
  skimmer or slotted
  spoon

To make the homemade orecchiette, mix flour and salt. Tip onto a workbench and work in ricotta with your fingertips. Lightly whisk egg with water. Make a well in the middle of flour and tip in egg mixture. Drawing in the flour little by little with one hand, bring everything together to form a fairly stiff dough. Knead for 5 minutes. Wrap in plastic film and leave at room temperature for 15 minutes.

Return to dough and knead some more until it feels supple and very smooth. Break off a piece the size of a small egg. Roll it on a workbench to form a 1cm/½in diameter sausage-shape with your hands. Cut into 3mm-thick slices.

Hold each slice in the palm of your hand and press the ball of your thumb in the centre and give it a slight twist; this is only successful if you have very well-trimmed fingernails! Continue with remaining dough until all orecchiette are shaped.

Preheat oven to 100°C/Gas ¼. Put in large ovenproof serving bowl to warm.

Bring a large saucepan of salted water to the boil over high heat. Drop in trimmed broccoli. When water returns to the boil, cook for 2 minutes exactly and then scoop broccoli with a skimmer or slotted spoon into a colander resting over a large mixing bowl.

>>>

Bring pan of water back to the boil and drop in pasta. Homemade orecchiette will only take 5 minutes to cook, but dried orecchiette takes longer to cook than many other pasta shapes so expect it to be ready in 15 minutes.

When pasta has 3–4 minutes cooking time left, heat olive oil in a large heavy-based non-stick frying pan over medium heat. Sauté garlic for a few seconds until it smells fragrant and add anchovy fillets. Stir with a wooden spoon until anchovies have melted. Tip in chilli and the reserved broccoli. As soon as pasta is ready, drain it, give it a big shake and then tip it into the frying pan, together with butter and parmesan. Toss well and transfer to heated serving bowl. Serve at once.

Broccoli Carbonara

SERVES 4 The inclusion of broccoli is a 'ring-in' addition to a classic way with spaghetti. I actually prefer to use penne for this variation as it seems to complement the weight of the broccoli pieces.

EXTRA EQUIPMENT
long-handled brass
skimmer or
slotted spoon

salt
250g/9oz penne or pasta of choice
350g/12oz broccoli, head cut into
　　small florets and stems peeled and
　　cut into thin rounds
3 free-range egg yolks

2 tablespoons pouring cream
2 tablespoons grated parmesan
2 tablespoons extra-virgin olive oil
75g/2½oz streaky bacon, cut into
　　thin strips
sea salt and freshly ground pepper

Preheat oven to 100°C/Gas ¼ and put in an ovenproof serving bowl to warm.

Fill 2 large heavy-based saucepans with lightly salted water and bring to the boil over high heat. Drop penne into one and boil for about 12 minutes or until al dente.

Drop broccoli into second pan. When water returns to the boil, cook for 2 minutes exactly and then scoop broccoli with a brass skimmer or slotted spoon into a colander resting over a large mixing bowl.

Put egg yolks, cream and parmesan in a bowl. Lightly whisk and set aside.

When pasta has 3–4 minutes cooking time left, heat olive oil in a large heavy-based non-stick frying pan over medium heat and sauté bacon. When bacon starts to crisp, tip in broccoli and toss to heat through.

Drain pasta in a colander, reserving a spoonful of cooking water. Immediately add pasta to broccoli and bacon mixture. Toss to mix well. Add reserved pasta water to egg mixture. Remove frying pan from the heat, then tip in egg, cream and cheese mixture and shake to thicken. Immediately transfer everything into the heated serving dish and season to taste with salt and pepper. Serve at once.

Cooking Sprouting Broccoli

Tender sprouting broccoli is a very special and luxurious vegetable. Either steam it for a few minutes or cook it briefly in a saucepan of plenty of simmering lightly salted water, then drain it on a dry tea towel and transfer it to a heated plate and serve with Hollandaise Sauce (see page 111) as a delicious and stylish first course. You could vary the hollandaise sauce by making it with the strained juice of a blood orange instead of using lemon juice – this version is known in French as *Sauce Maltaise*.

Broccoli with Crunchy Garlic Breadcrumbs and Olives

SERVES 4 AS AN ACCOMPANIMENT This method of finishing and serving a dish with crisp breadcrumbs is delicious with broccoli and just as great with cauliflower – do choose a really substantial bread for making the breadcrumbs for the best result. It is a particularly good way of using the many slender side shoots that continue to appear once the main head of broccoli has been harvested. Or you may have planted sprouting broccoli, which produces many tender shoots rather than a large central head and you could use this instead. Both broccoli and cauliflower are full-flavoured and robust vegetables and can be used interchangeably in recipes such as this. I think a dish of either would be perfect with barbecued Italian-style pork sausages, especially ones with a little chilli or fennel seed in the mix, or a barbecued chunk of fresh tuna.

salt
50g/2oz coarse fresh breadcrumbs
1 fresh small red chilli, seeded
 and chopped
finely grated zest of 1 lemon
80ml/3fl oz extra-virgin olive oil,
 plus extra for drizzling
2 cloves garlic, bruised and
 flattened but not chopped

¼ small handful chopped flat-leaf
 parsley
350g/12oz broccoli or broccoli
 shoots, trimmed and head cut into
 small florets
20 black olives, pitted
sea salt and freshly ground
 black pepper

Preheat oven to 100°C/Gas ¼ and put an ovenproof serving dish inside it to warm.

Fill a large heavy-based saucepan with lightly salted water and put over medium heat.

Mix breadcrumbs, chilli and lemon zest. Heat olive oil in a large heavy-based frying pan, then add garlic and sauté for 1–2 minutes. Tip in breadcrumb mixture and stir to mix. Continue to stir for 8–10 minutes as crumbs start to toast and change colour; you are aiming for golden crumbs that feel almost sandy. When crumbs are nearly ready, remove and discard garlic cloves, then add parsley and stir to mix. Remove from heat.

Drop broccoli into boiling water and cook until just al dente; maybe 3 minutes after water returns to the boil – taste a piece to be sure. Drain broccoli in a colander and give it a big shake. Transfer to a mixing bowl and toss through the toasted breadcrumb mixture. Scatter over olives, then season with salt and pepper to taste. Transfer to warm serving dish and serve drizzled with a little more olive oil.

Chickpea Salad with Broccoli and Goat's Cheese

SERVES 4 I have included the recipes for my three favourite chickpea salads in this book and this is one of them. The other two are the Chickpea Salad with Preserved Lemon, Caramelised Onion, Chilli and Parsley on page 461 and Chickpea Salad with Roasted Sweet Red Peppers and a Spicy Dressing on page 488. Each of these salads is at its best if allowed to sit a little before you eat it, and even better served when the chick peas are still a little warm.

EXTRA EQUIPMENT
long-handled
  brass skimmer or
  slotted spoon

350g/12oz Cooked Dried Chick
  Peas (see page 203) or
1 × 440g/15oz tin chick peas,
  rinsed and drained
2 tablespoons extra-virgin olive oil
2 tablespoons flaked almonds
  (optional)
salt

1 head broccoli, cut into tiny
  florets and stalk peeled
  and cut into small pieces
finely grated zest and juice of
  1 lemon
2 tablespoons torn mint
80g/3oz marinated goat's cheese
sea salt and freshly ground
  black pepper

Put chick peas in a serving bowl.

If using the almonds, heat a small amount of the oil in a small frying pan over medium heat and fry almonds until golden. Tip onto a paper towel-lined plate to drain.

Bring a large saucepan of lightly salted water to the boil, then cook broccoli florets and stalks for 1 minute only. Quickly transfer to a colander with a brass skimmer or slotted spoon to drain, then add to chick peas. Add lemon zest and juice, mint, goat's cheese and olive oil to chick peas and season to taste with salt and pepper. Mix gently but well. Scatter with fried almonds, if using, and serve.

BRUSSELS SPROUTS

Brassicaceae family (includes broccoli, cabbage, cauliflower, cresses, radish and turnips)
Annual

Soil type
Prefers heavy soil well enriched with organic matter and a neutral or slightly alkaline soil (see pH, page 694).

Soil preparation
Apply lime if needed to raise pH at least a month before digging in well-rotted manure a few weeks before planting into final positions. To prepare a seed-bed, often in another part of the garden, dig over a small area of ground, then rake until level.

Climate
Frost tolerant.

Position
Prefer full sun in open but sheltered site.

How to grow
Sow March to mid-April for a winter crop, either sow in small pots and keep outdoors in a sheltered place or for more plants use a seed bed (see page 697). Sow 1cm deep in rows 15cm apart. Thin out seedlings to 8cm apart. Lift seedlings and plant out in their final positions when 10–15cm tall (May-June), allow 80–90cm between plants.

Water requirements
Water regularly during growth, but ease off prior to harvesting.

Successive planting
Leave about 3 weeks between each planting, throughout the growing season, or stick to one sowing for winter crops.

When to fertilise
Apply liquid fertiliser (see page 591) every 2 weeks to encourage rapid growth.

Harvest period
Harvest 3–5 months after planting, starting at bottom of plant, and harvest frequently.

Pests and organic control
Highly prone to pests and diseases. Aphids, cabbage white caterpillars and cabbage root fly can be controlled by picking off pests or by spraying with natural insecticides such as those based on garlic or pyrethrum or using a biological control. Downy mildew can sometimes be a problem, pick off and destroy affected foliage. Crop rotation will help prevent disease problem.

Companion planting
Aromatic plants, including sage, dill, chamomile, beetroot, peppermint, rosemary, beans, celery, onions, potatoes and dwarf zinnias. Dill attracts wasps that will control the cabbage butterfly and zinnias attract ladybirds. Don't plant with tomatoes or strawberries.

Special information
When sprouts begin to appear, remove any leaves from base of plant to give sprouts more room to develop.

Quantities to plant for a family of four
3 plants every 3 weeks.

Brussels sprouts (*Brassica oleracea* var. *gemmifera*)

Growing and Harvesting Brussels sprouts have a long growing period, taking several months to mature and take up a lot of room. However, they do provide welcome fresh greens over the winter period. The biggest sin is to let them grow too large.

There is a very pretty burgundy-red dwarf variety, Falstaff, available through the Thompson & Morgan seed catalogue (www.thompson-morgan.com).

Preparing and Sharing Brussels sprouts should never be overcooked but nor should they be left hard and undercooked. They need butter, olive oil, duck fat, bacon or a little warmed cream to mellow their flavour. Their relative unpopularity is probably because many people, especially children, have only experienced overcooked ones, and/or overmature sprouts.

Brussels sprouts can be quartered or sliced. Some cooks cut a deep cross in the underside of each sprout as an attempt to achieve more even cooking. The outside leaves can be separated and the hearts sliced; time-consuming but it achieves a brilliant result. They can be boiled; just use plenty of water and cook uncovered, or, alternatively, steam the sprouts.

Especially for Kids I hated Brussels sprouts as a child but the family rule was to 'try just a little bit'. I used to swallow one whole with a huge gulp of water. The fact that I enjoy them now should encourage other parents. Palates do change as long as one does not force the issue.

Steamed Brussels Sprouts with Butter Sauce

Make the butter sauce on page 110, then keep warm. Thickly slice Brussels sprouts, then place in a bamboo steamer over a wok of simmering water. Steam for 3 minutes; the sprouts should be bright-green and barely tender. Tip steamed sprouts into a warm serving dish, then spoon over butter sauce and serve scattered with chopped flat-leaf parsley. If you have harvested young carrots, steam them too and mix the two vegetables with butter sauce before serving.

Brussels Sprouts and Smoked Bacon

SERVES 4 Flabby Brussels sprouts are the single most important reason for their relative unpopularity, and not just with children. So keep the sprouts a bit crunchy, however they are going to be served (with the sole exception of the long, slow-cooked Brussels sprouts in duck fat which I have described in *The Cook's Companion*).

salt
1 tablespoon extra-virgin olive oil
2 cloves garlic, bruised and peeled
250g/9oz smoked bacon, rind removed and cut into 1cm/½in-thick slices
2 × 1cm/½in-thick slices sourdough, cut into 1cm/½in cubes

750g/1lb 10oz small Brussels sprouts
20g/¾oz butter
1 tablespoon red-wine vinegar
sea salt and freshly ground black pepper

Preheat oven to 100°C/Gas ¼ and put a plate and an ovenproof serving dish inside to keep warm.

Bring a large saucepan of lightly salted water to the boil.

Heat olive oil in a medium-sized non-stick frying pan over medium heat and add garlic and bacon. Stir occasionally with a wooden spoon for about 5 minutes or until bacon starts to crisp and is well coloured. Transfer bacon to warm plate in oven, leaving bruised garlic in the pan. Add bread to pan and fry for 5 minutes or until golden and crisp, shaking the pan and stirring so that croûtons colour evenly, then transfer to plate in oven with bacon.

Drop Brussels sprouts into pan of boiling water and cook for 3–5 minutes until just tender when inserted with a fine skewer. Drain Brussels sprouts, then quickly transfer them to the frying pan and add butter. Increase heat to medium–high and sprinkle sprouts with vinegar; take care as it will hiss and splutter. Return bacon and croûtons to pan, stirring and shaking to mix together. Discard garlic. Season with pepper and salt, if necessary, then tip into warmed serving dish and serve at once.

CABBAGE

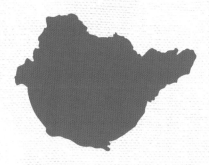

Brassicaceae family (includes broccoli, Brussels sprouts, cauliflower, cresses, radishes and turnips)
Biennial grown as an annual

Soil type
Prefers heavy soil well enriched with organic matter and a neutral or slightly alkaline soil (see pH, page 694).

Soil preparation
Apply lime if needed to raise the pH at least a month before digging in well-rotted manure a few weeks before planting into final positions. To prepare a seed-bed, dig over a small area of ground, then rake until level.

Climate
Suits all climates. Many types withstand frosts.

Position
Prefers full sun and open sites.

How to grow
There are different cabbages for every season, their sowing and planting times vary but all can be either sown in small pots and keep outdoors in a sheltered place or for more plants use a seed bed (see page 697). Planted out in their final positions, spacing is usually 30–45cm between plants. Summer and autumn cabbages are sown in March, planted out when 10–15cm tall (April-May). Winter cabbage are sown in May, planted out in June. Spring cabbage is sown in July, planted out in September-October.

Water requirements
Cabbages like a lot of water, so keep soil moist at all times.

Successive planting
Leave about 3 weeks between each planting throughout the growing season.

When to fertilise
Apply liquid fertiliser (see page 591) every 2 weeks to encourage rapid growth.

Harvest period
Summer and autumn cabbages are harvested June to November.

Pests and organic control
Aphids, cabbage white caterpillars and cabbage root fly can be prevented by using crop covers (see page 697) or controlled by picking off pests or by spraying with natural insecticides. Downy mildew can sometimes be a problem, pick off and destroy affected foliage. Crop rotation every year will help avoid disease problems.

Companion planting
Peas, beans, celery, beetroot, onions and potatoes. Calendula and nasturtiums are a good distraction for aphids. Red and white clover and aromatic plants such as dill, peppermint, sage and chamomile are useful to distract cabbage white butterfly. Don't plant with strawberries or tomatoes.

Special information
Mulch established plants to aid in water and nutrient retention.

Quantities to plant for a family of four
3 plants every 3 weeks.

Cabbage (*Brassica oleracea* var. *capitata*)

Growing and Harvesting Cabbage has to be one of the hardiest crops in the whole world. There are cabbage cultivars that will be at their best right through the springtime and into early summer. There are cabbages with dense round heads, ones that form cone-shaped heads and others that have loose, crinkly leaves (such as my favourite, Savoy). Then there are cabbages with purple leaves, or with blue-green leaves tinged with pink. There are large cabbages and small cabbages. All are very attractive plants, and their heads are framed by handsome leaves.

Kale is most often grown as a decorative plant, and is indeed extremely attractive with its shades of pink, grey and cream, often with prettily ruffled edges. Most mature plants are totally inedible, although there are edible kales: curly kale and the aristocrat of them all, Tuscan kale. Curly kale is well worth growing for winter/spring greens. Only the tiniest leaves of curly kale are suitable for inclusion in a salad mix. Even so, I am deeply dubious about its suitability for children learning to love their greens, as even when young curly kale can be aggressively flavoured and the leaves are never as tender as those of other more approachable brassicas. Tuscan black kale (*cavolo nero* in Italian) is a handsome plant. It suits growing in the coldest possible weather, so it is not surprising that it features in the Italian winter soup, minestrone. On a recent holiday in Italy the gathered Italian cooks assured me that it is the frost that makes the leaves tender and sweet and they were adamant that it was contrary to nature to grow or use *cavolo nero* outside of winter. This makes me feel guilty, for as I write this in late spring, I still have Tuscan kale plants in my garden and they are still delicious. Tuscan kale can grow as big as a rose bush and its plumes of leaves will re-sprout in the second year from the top of its long, thick stem. It is not suitable as a salad vegetable.

The cabbage white butterfly is a very persistent pest. Organic control measures are given on pages 697–700 but the best control method is to hunt down caterpillars that hide on the underside of the leaves during the day and destroy them.

After cutting the main head off spring cabbages, if the stump and outer leaves are left, young shoots will often emerge. These are one source of sensational spring greens. They are tender and may also appear on spent stalks of Brussels sprouts.

Container Planting One cabbage goes a long way in a small family and will yield enough for a few meals. Therefore, planting two or three cabbages in a tub, perhaps inter-planted with herbs or quick-growing salad varieties, is not a waste of time. Scatter some carrot and parsnip seeds in the pot and maybe beetroot seeds too. By the time the cabbages have all been harvested you should have some root vegetables growing well, possibly needing thinning. Or plant some dill seeds or sage in the same pot in the hope of confusing the cabbage white butterfly. One advantage of growing cabbage in a large container is that it will be easier to net to protect if those wretched butterflies are about!

Preparing and Sharing Raw cabbage makes great salads and coleslaw is the best-known. Make a mixed coleslaw of red, green and crinkly-leafed cabbage and dress with a mustardy vinaigrette, made with red-wine vinegar, extra-virgin olive oil, perhaps a little finely chopped garlic, sea salt, freshly ground black pepper and either Dijon or wholegrain mustard. To make a fancier version, add a little crumbled bacon or pancetta, fried capers or thinly sliced fennel, inner stalks of celery or celeriac. Cabbage leaves of all varieties make perfect wrappers for other ingredients, such as cooked rice mixed with minced pork, veal or beef (see the recipe for Braised Pork-stuffed Cabbage on page 192). To use them in this way, always blanch the leaves in boiling water for a minute and then carefully lift out with tongs and lay on a tea-towel-covered tray to dry before filling. The initial blanching makes the leaves limp and pliable so that they can be rolled or used to layer between fillings and baked as a savoury 'cake', to be cut into wedges and served.

A general piece of good advice is to either cook cabbage briefly or to cook it long and slowly in a casserole with other ingredients after a preliminary blanching in a saucepan of plenty of simmering lightly salted water for 3–5 minutes. The worst thing to do is to boil it confined in a too-small pan so that it becomes a watery mess with the lingering smell of rotten eggs.

Some of the most glorious classic dishes result from the mellow character of slow-cooked cabbage. There are many examples, such as the numerous one-pot stews or soups from France, the most well-known being the *garbure* from the south-west of France, which contains potatoes, turnips, sometimes a little salt pork or duck or goose confit but always cabbage, or lion's head meatballs from China, made by braising pork-based meatballs in stock with Chinese cabbage. A very specific cabbage preparation is Sauerkraut (see page 191), popular throughout the north of France, Germany and Central Europe. Cabbage is salted and stored for the coldest months and then re-cooked with potatoes and all manner of smoked pork products. A French version of this, *choucroute garni,* is a most substantial meal and always enjoyed with plenty of mustard.

A favourite use for leftover cooked cabbage is 'bubble-and-squeak', whereby chopped cabbage and chopped cooked potato are fried together until crusty and brown on the bottom. Those who love this specifically cook cabbage leaves and potatoes just so that they can make bubble-and-squeak! The Irish version is called Colcannon (see page 190).

In many cuisines, there is a long tradition of combining sweet and savoury flavours in the one dish. I have a recipe said to originate in Provence that combines cabbage with apples and sugar and we tried this in a Kitchen Garden Program class at Collingwood College in Melbourne. We lined loose-bottomed tartlet tins with crinkly cabbage leaves, then dotted the leaves with butter and filled them with plenty of thinly sliced apple finished with a sprinkle of white sugar. The 'tarts' baked in a 180°C/Gas 4 oven for nearly 45 minutes. The exposed edges of the cabbage became crisp and crunchy, while the leaves on the bottom absorbed some of the sugary apple juices and the top layer of apple became brown and delightfully caramelised. These desserts had to be eaten with a spoon and fork, though, and were generally voted as pretty good. If I were to do it again I might settle the apples on an Almond Frangipane Cream (see page 625) base to soak up some of the delicious apple juice, or even a thin slice of bread.

Curly kale is a very popular cabbage-family variety for winter or early spring. It is usually cooked for quite a long time until it becomes soft and cabbage-like in flavour. It is often chopped or puréed and combined with mashed potato to make the Dutch dish, *boerenkool stampot,* made into soups, or braised and added to meatballs. Curly kale does not shrink as much as many other cabbage-like greens when cooked. It can also be blanched for a few minutes, then drained and sautéed with olive oil, garlic and anchovies as a simple accompaniment for grilled or sautéed meat or fish.

To me, Savoy is the pick of the cabbage varieties for its glorious crinkled leaves, sweet flavour and many culinary uses, which include stuffing and wrapping as well as more conventional applications like braising and sautéing.

Tuscan kale (*cavolo nero*) is the traditional leafy green to use in an authentic minestrone. Remove the central rib as it will never soften. The trimmed leaves can be simmered in stock, wine or water, or braised with pork or added to sausage dishes. Tuscan kale is also excellent sautéed with potatoes, olive oil and garlic. When it is cooked, the leaves darken and become blue-black. It has a full flavour that is never bitter. Tuscan kale is not suitable for stir-frying. A few years ago I visited Tuscany to observe the new olive oil being pressed at various mills. We were fed magnificently at every stop. At Fattoria di Fubbiano in Lucca we were welcomed by Baron Gianpiero Andreas de Fubbiano and his wife, Lucia. A wonderful vegetable soup featuring Tuscan kale was offered, each portion served in a round loaf, and as I scraped around the bottom of the 'bowl' the soaked bread came away like a dumpling.

Red cabbage is also worth growing – just never cook it in an aluminium pan as it will make the cabbage go a dirty drab purple. It is usually cooked with an acid ingredient such as apples, vinegar or wine to counteract its tendency to discolour if exposed to slightly alkaline conditions like hard water.

Chinese cabbage (*wong bok*) is shredded for salads or cut into chunks for stir-frying, steaming or adding to long-cooked dishes (see the recipe for Stir-fried and Braised Chinese Cabbage with Chinese Mushrooms on page 102).

Especially for Kids Give young gardeners a magnifying glass and send them out to examine the cabbage plants. Make a game out of examining the under-leaves where caterpillars hide. They can then pick them off as a tasty lunch for your chickens; if there are no chickens the caterpillars will have to be squashed! Alternatively, collect a couple of caterpillars (if your children have never handled a caterpillar, they may find the experience challenging), and a leaf that already has tiny caterpillar eggs on it and put them in a large clean jar together with some cabbage (or nasturtium) leaves and observe as the eggs hatch into caterpillars and the caterpillars pupate and finally hatch as a new butterfly. The life cycle will take three to four weeks. However, the hatched butterflies will need to be disposed of. Handing kids a butterfly net is a great way to chase down and capture cabbage white butterflies.

With adult supervision, young cooks will enjoy pushing wedges of cabbage down a food processor chute and seeing it turn into fine shreds. Follow it with carrots to add colour and interest to the salad. A question for keen young cooks might be, 'Why do we add the dressing to a cabbage salad ahead of time when we never do this with a soft leafy green salad?' The answer is that the salt and acids (lemon juice, vinegar) in the dressing help to soften the leaves of the more resistant cabbage, whereas they will wilt softer leaves.

Children can help with blanching cabbage leaves but will need supervision as with any kitchen task involving boiling water. They need a special warning not to invert tongs that may have picked up some boiling water from the pan that could then trickle onto their arms or hands and scald.

Winter 'Tabbouleh' with Cabbage

SERVES 10–12 This useful variation on the much-loved classic preparation came about because of a Collingwood College Kitchen Garden workshop held in the middle of winter. Tomatoes and cucumber were nowhere to be seen, whereas cabbages and carrots were flourishing. If you happen to have celeriac in the garden one could be thickly peeled and grated to add along with the carrot. This recipe can easily be halved to serve five to six.

175g/6oz burghul (see page 703)
2 spring onions, trimmed and
   thinly sliced
1 clove garlic, finely chopped
2 carrots (about 300g/10½oz)
3 pale inner sticks celery
500g/1lb cabbage

¾ small handful chopped flat-leaf
   parsley
20 mint leaves, shredded
2 tablespoons extra-virgin olive oil
juice of 1 lemon
sea salt and freshly ground
   black pepper

EXTRA EQUIPMENT
food processor
   with grating disc
   attachment or
   box grater

Place burghul in a medium-sized mixing bowl and cover with hot water. Soak for 30 minutes, then drain in a strainer. Press out as much liquid as possible with the back of a spoon. Tip burghul onto a thick tea towel and fold it over to wrap and enclose it, like a sausage. Two people are now needed to each hold one end of the tea-towel sausage, and to twist in opposite directions to remove more liquid from the grain. Carefully unwrap tea towel so as not to lose any burghul.

Rinse and dry soaking bowl and carefully shake burghul into it. Add spring onion and garlic to burghul.

Using a food processor with a grating disc attachment or a box grater, shred carrot and add to mixing bowl. Slice celery as thinly as possible and put into mixing bowl. Roll up inner cabbage leaves and slice as thinly as possible, then add to mixing bowl, along with flat-leaf parsley and mint. There should be plenty of parsley.

Add olive oil to lemon juice to make a dressing, then add to bowl. Mix everything together very well and taste for salt and pepper, then season if desired and serve.

Buckwheat Pasta 'Maltagliati' with Cabbage, Sage and Potatoes

SERVES 6 Buckwheat pasta is easy to make and very different from pasta made from all-wheat flour. Owing to the lack of gluten in buckwheat flour, this pasta is very tender and inclined to tear. This doesn't matter as the 'maltagliati' of the title means 'badly cut' in Italian. It is worth taking the trouble to find Italian taleggio or fontina cheese as they add an authentic flavour to the dish.

EXTRA EQUIPMENT
food processor
hand-cranked pasta
    machine
pasta cutting wheel

fine semolina
100g/3½oz unsalted butter
4 cloves garlic, bruised
12 sage leaves
salt
300g/10½oz waxy potatoes, cut into
    bite-sized pieces
300g/10½oz cabbage, cut into bite-sized
    pieces
100g/3½oz taleggio or fontina, coarsely
    grated or chopped (it is difficult to grate
    these soft, squashy cheeses)

50g/2oz parmesan, grated
freshly ground black pepper

BUCKWHEAT PASTA
175g/6oz buckwheat flour
125g/4½oz plain flour
3 large free-range eggs
½ teaspoon salt

To make the buckwheat pasta, process all ingredients in a food processor until dough comes together in a ball. Remove and wrap in plastic film, then leave at room temperature for 20 minutes.

Spread a dry tea towel near a pasta machine and dust it with fine semolina. Cut pasta dough into 3–4 pieces. Set rollers on machine to the widest setting and pass dough through. Fold it in 3, turn it 90 degrees and roll it through again. Go to the next-thickest setting and pass dough through, repeating this process another 3–4 times. If pasta lengths are too long it is more likely to stick or tear. Keep rolling pasta this way until you reach the third-last notch only. Spread lengths on semolina-dusted cloth and leave to dry while you prepare the other ingredients.

Preheat oven to 100°C/Gas ¼. Put in an ovenproof serving dish to warm.

Heat butter, garlic and sage in a small non-stick frying pan over medium heat. When butter is golden brown, pour it through a fine strainer. Set aside strained butter and sage leaves, discarding garlic and other solids left in strainer.

Bring a large saucepan or pasta pot of lightly salted water to the boil over high heat and cook potato for 5 minutes. Add cabbage and cook for another 5 minutes.

Cut pasta sheets into rough diamond shapes with a sharp knife. Cook pasta in saucepan with cabbage and potato for 2–3 minutes or until al dente.

Drain saucepan contents in a colander in the sink and give them a good shake. Tip into heated serving dish and immediately pour over garlic-scented butter, scatter with cheeses and scatter over sage leaves. Toss, season and serve.

Colcannon

SERVES 4 It is really important to make this dish with lovely bright-green spring cabbage. Colcannon is a good recipe for using up cold boiled potatoes; however, freshly cooked potatoes go through a potato ricer much more easily. It helps to know what sized potato cake you are making, so I have given precise weights. Feel free to ignore them! In *Jane Grigson's Vegetable Book*, the late Jane Grigson states that colcannon was a favourite dish in Ireland for fast-day celebrations, and that 'at Hallowe'en, the eve of All Saints' day, a wedding ring would be pushed into the crusty mass; whoever found it would be married within the twelvemonth'. Colcannon is a superb accompaniment to good pork sausages. It will always be fairly soft and will break easily. If there is any left over the next day, cut wedges or pieces and put them on a baking paper-lined baking tray in a 180°C/Gas 4 oven for 10–15 minutes to warm and regain a crusty exterior.

salt
250g/9oz all-purpose potatoes,
   such as Desiree, cut into 1cm/½in-
   thick slices
250g/9oz spring cabbage, cut into
   1cm/½in-thick slices

sea salt and freshly ground
   black pepper
20g/¾oz butter
1½ tablespoons olive oil
½ large onion, finely chopped

EXTRA EQUIPMENT
potato ricer or
   food mill

Fill 2 large heavy-based saucepans with lightly salted water and bring to the boil over high heat. Drop potato into one and cook for 10 minutes or until very tender, then drain. Meanwhile, drop cabbage into the other and cook for 5 minutes, then drain.

Press potato through a potato ricer or food mill into a mixing bowl. Squeeze drained cabbage in a dry tea towel and then chop fairly finely. Mix with potato and season with salt and pepper to taste; it needs to be well seasoned.

Heat half of the butter and 3 teaspoons of the oil in a non-stick frying pan over low heat. Cook onion quite gently for 8–10 minutes or until it is golden. Press potato and cabbage on top of onion and cook for 10 minutes. Slip an egg lifter around edges and invert potato cake onto a flat plate. Return pan to the heat and add remaining butter and oil. Slide colcannon back into the pan and cook for another 10 minutes, then serve.

Cocktail Party Cabbage and Prosciutto Rolls

MAKES AS MANY AS YOU LIKE These unusual savouries are quick to make and very appealing. They could also be made with other leaves as wrappers instead – young silverbeet leaves, or even the outsides of cos lettuce are just two ideas.

EXTRA EQUIPMENT
wok
bamboo steamer
  with lid
bamboo toothpicks

**Savoy cabbage or other cabbage with bright-green leaves, core removed
soft spreadable goat's cheese (or blue cheese mixed with mascarpone to a spreadable consistency)**

thin slices of prosciutto (about 3 for each half-leaf), fat discarded

Turn cabbage upside-down and, with a small, sharp knife, cut base of leaves around core. Remove as many outside leaves as you can; each leaf will make around 8 of these cocktail savouries.

Half-fill a wok with water, place bamboo steamer in position, and when the water boils, steam each leaf for around 4 minutes. Transfer each leaf to a tea towel-lined baking tray, then leave to cool completely.

Spread a leaf on a chopping board. Using a sharp knife, shave the raised-up rib section away so that the leaf is fully pliable. Cut each leaf in half. You should now have 2 roughly rectangular pieces of cabbage. Turn 1 half-leaf so that its longest, straightest edge is nearest to you. Spread leaf with a thin layer of selected cheese. Cover cheese with trimmed prosciutto slices. Roll up tightly like a miniature Swiss roll. Trim each end and then cut the long sausage-shape you have made into 4 mini-rolls. They may need to be secured with a toothpick. Pack tightly together on a plate, cover with plastic film and chill until needed.

Sauerkraut

MAKES 1KG/2LB Sterilise an earthenware crock or heavy, wide-mouthed jar. Remove core from a cabbage weighing approximately 1kg/2lb. Pierce 2–3 large cabbage leaves with a knife and set aside. Finely shred remaining cabbage leaves and toss with 2 teaspoons caraway seeds, ½ teaspoon juniper berries and 2 bay leaves. Wearing disposable gloves, layer cabbage mixture and 1 tablespoon pure rock salt or sea salt into the crock, packing down each layer firmly. Finish with a layer of salt. Cover with reserved leaves and drape over a clean calico cloth. Place a close-fitting plate on top and weight it down. Store at a constant temperature of 15–20°C/60–68°F, inspecting every few days to skim off scum. Stir and replace cloth, plate and weight. Fermentation will take up to 3 weeks. When brine stops bubbling, transfer to sterilised jars and store for up to 3 months. Remove sauerkraut with clean tongs and ensure cabbage left in jar is still covered by brine. Rinse before cooking.

Braised Pork-stuffed Cabbage

SERVES 8 There are so many recipes for stuffed cabbage. Russians, Poles and Hungarians as well as the French all have their own versions. Sometimes a whole cabbage is stuffed, sometimes it is a layered terrine, sometimes individual leaves are stuffed and rolled and sometimes the cabbage is included in stuffing that is encased in pastry or noodle dough. I rather like eating these cold as well as hot. The pork mince should contain about twenty per cent fat. A little bacon could be added if the mince has no fat. Frozen or preserved homemade tomato sauce can be used instead of tinned tomatoes.

1 cabbage
salt
2 tablespoons extra-virgin olive oil
½ onion, finely chopped
3 cloves garlic, finely chopped
350g/12oz minced pork (with 20% fat)
1 teaspoon sweet paprika

1 tablespoon chopped thyme or oregano
sea salt and freshly ground black pepper
200g/7oz tinned diced tomatoes
125ml/4½fl oz well-flavoured veal or beef stock
25g/1oz grated parmesan

EXTRA EQUIPMENT
long-handled brass skimmer or slotted spoon
20cm × 26cm/8in × 10in baking dish

Turn cabbage upside-down and, with a small, sharp knife, cut the base of the leaves around the core. Remove as many outside leaves as you can. You will need at least 9 perfect leaves, although a few extra will be helpful. Bring a large heavy-based saucepan of lightly salted water to the boil over high heat. Simmer cabbage heart for 10 minutes, then scoop out with a brass skimmer or slotted spoon and transfer to a bowl of cold water to stop it cooking further. Drain, then squeeze hard in a dry tea towel and finely chop. You need 100g/3½oz for the filling. Return saucepan to medium heat.

Working in batches, cook cabbage leaves in pan of simmering water for 5 minutes. Carefully transfer to a tea towel-lined baking tray. When cool enough to handle, shave heavy central rib flat without cutting out completely – try to keep leaf intact but flat so it is pliable enough to wrap around filling. Set aside.

Preheat oven to 180°C/Gas 4.

Heat olive oil in a non-stick frying pan over low heat and sauté onion for 8–10 minutes or until very soft. Add garlic and stir for 1 minute, then tip into a mixing bowl. Add pork, chopped cabbage, paprika, thyme or oregano, salt and pepper. Mix very well with your hands. Take a small amount of filling and sauté in the frying pan until cooked to check for seasoning, then adjust if necessary.

Divide stuffing into 8 balls. Line a 20cm × 26cm/8in × 10in baking dish with the extra cabbage leaves. Wrap each ball in a leaf and tuck them into the dish, seam-side down. Spoon tomatoes and stock over and around parcels and scatter over parmesan. Cover with foil and bake for 45 minutes. Remove foil and bake for another 15 minutes to brown tops of cabbage parcels, then serve.

CARROTS

**Apiaceae family
(includes celery, chervil,
fennel, parsley and parsnip)
Biennial grown as an annual**

Soil type
Deep, loose, light soil. Root
development may be restricted
or uneven in compacted or
rocky soil.

Soil preparation
For poor quality soil, dig in
a small amount of organic
compost a month prior to
planting. If soil was fertilised for
the previous crop, no further
treatment is required.

Climate
Suitable for all climates.

Position
Prefers full sun, but will tolerate
partial shade.

How to grow
Directly sow seeds at a depth of
5 mm. Mixing seeds with washed
sand helps spread them when
sowing. Place a piece of wet
hessian over planting area until
seedlings emerge to keep them
moist but let light through. When
seedlings are 5cm high, thin out
to 2cm apart. Thin out again
when seedlings are 15cm high,
leaving 5cm between seedlings.

Water requirements
Once carrot seedlings are
growing they do not need
watering unless very dry.
Container-grown carrots
need watering so compost
is kept moist.

Successive planting
Leave 3–4 weeks between
plantings, throughout the
growing season. Avoid
successive crops in the
same plot.

Harvest period
2–4 months after planting.

Pests and organic control
Carrot root fly is the main
pest. Use a crop cover or a
resistant variety.

Companion planting
Lettuce, peas, leeks, chives,
onions, cucumbers, beans,
tomatoes, wormwood, sage
and rosemary will deter carrot
fly. Nasturtiums are a bait
plant for aphids.

Special information
Keep bed free of weeds by
mulching. Over-feeding will
cause the root to split. Harvest
a few young carrots. If they
are pale, this is a sign that the
soil is too acid. A dose of lime
sprinkled around the plants and
watered in will improve colour.

Quantities to plant
for a family of four
20 or more every 3–4 weeks.

Purple and orange carrot cultivars (*Daucus carota* var. *sativus*)

Growing and Harvesting Not all carrots are orange. This will surprise many gardeners. Why not investigate the heritage varieties available with red, yellow or purple skins, or the small golf-ball variety? At my local farmers' market the heirloom carrots are tied in multi-coloured bunches. They both look and taste wonderful. There are also stumpy cultivars, such as 'Chantenay Red Cored'.

Carrots prefer to be planted in soil that has previously grown a 'hungry' crop, such as tomatoes or cabbages. Too much nitrogen, manure, stones or other obstructions in the soil will result in forked carrots (although kids love these!).

As carrots (and parsnips) are slow to germinate, it is a good idea to mix their seed with that of a quick-growing crop such as radish or beetroot to mark the rows and protect the very fine foliage of the carrot seedlings from being accidentally crushed. Emerging seedlings resemble fine blades of grass.

As carrot seed is so fine it is easy to over-plant. Thin seedlings early as overcrowding can also lead to twisted carrots. Once the carrots have started to develop, you can always use subsequent tiny carrot thinnings in the kitchen or enjoy them as a gardener's treat. Pull them as soon as they have attained full colour. Having said that, it is good to know that carrots will keep better when left in the ground rather than pulled and put in the refrigerator. Only harvest what you need and allow the rest of the crop to grow larger. Mature carrots are still delicious, but they taste a bit different.

Container Planting Carrots can be sown in containers, provided the container is at least 20 centimetres deep. Cut-and-come-again salad greens could go into the container before you sprinkle in the carrot seed (mixed with radish and/or beetroot seed) to maximise the yield from a single container. Alternatively, plant leeks or chives in the same pot. The same applies to parsnips.

Preparing and Sharing Home-grown carrots tend to come in many shapes and sizes. However they come, I think carrots should be lightly peeled or at least scrubbed before eating. There is bitterness to the skin that can turn off young palates, if that is a concern in your household. Some will disagree, and of course munching on a just-pulled carrot in the garden is a pretty important moment for a first-time carrot grower, whatever the age! The depth of flavour in freshly pulled home-grown carrots compared with bagged carrots bought from a supermarket can be quite startling.

Carrots tend to be dismissed as a banal vegetable, so the challenge is to make them exciting. Their natural sweetness means that they caramelise when sliced and sautéed or roasted slowly. This has also made them a favourite ingredient for cakes such as the Italian Almond and Carrot Cake on page 204 and for fritters (see the Carrot Fritters on page 199).

Carrots are delicious raw – especially grated in salads with a good extra-virgin olive oil and lemon juice, or with spicy Asian flavours such as those found in Vietnamese or Indian salads, or accompanied with roasted cumin and coriander seeds to lend a Middle Eastern flavour – as well as cooked in every possible way. Small quantities of very fresh carrot tops may be included in salads or soups.

Cooked carrots combine very well with basil and a small amount of cream (one or two spoonfuls is plenty for two to three cups of cooked vegetable). They are also excellent rolled in melted butter with a liberal quantity of chopped French tarragon.

Especially for Kids Understanding the different needs of 'hungry' and 'not-so-hungry' crops is important for young gardeners and growing carrots is a very good way to introduce the concept. Over-feeding will cause the root to split. Some split or twisted carrots can be very woody. Taste one to see if it still tastes sweet. If not, it may need to be chopped and used as the base of a soup or some other dish, rather than having the star treatment.

As it is so easy to step on emerging wisps of carrot, I suggest that children make large colourful markers and plant them alongside the sown carrot seed to alert other gardeners. Planting in swirls or patterns is a great way to add interest in the garden. If the household is small, maybe encourage young gardeners to limit the amount of seed planted and to mark off a few weeks on the calendar before sowing another crop.

Inexpensive graters are available from Asian kitchenware shops that enable fine strings of carrot or Asian radish (daikon) to be pared by turning the handle. Children *love* to do this and the grated vegetables can be used in rice-paper rolls, dipping sauces and salads.

Carrot Pickle for Antipasto

SERVES 6 AS PART OF A MIXED ANTIPASTO I find that commercially prepared jars of Italian-style vegetable pickles are processed and stored in such sharply flavoured vinegar that they leave me gasping. This is a more gentle preparation. As long as the pickle is stored in a clean jar it will stay crisp for several months in the refrigerator (mine are still crisp after six months). Combine the vegetables with sliced salami, olives and some good bread and you have a palate-stimulating first course.

400g/14oz carrots, cut into thick
  julienne or thick slices on the
  diagonal
salt
1 stick celery, cut on the diagonal into
  5mm/¼in-thick slices, leaves reserved
8 slices fresh long red chilli

1 fresh bay leaf
1 teaspoon sea salt
12 black peppercorns
375ml/13fl oz verjuice (see page
  706) or white-wine vinegar for
  a sharper flavour
extra-virgin olive oil, to serve

EXTRA EQUIPMENT
1 × 750ml/27fl oz-
  capacity glass jar
  with lid, sterilised
  (see page 706)

Cook carrots in a saucepan of plenty of lightly salted simmering water for about 5 minutes or until barely tender. Drain in a colander and immediately transfer to a 750ml/27fl oz-capacity sterilised glass jar. Add celery, chilli, bay leaf, salt and peppercorns.

Pour over verjuice or vinegar, ensuring that the vegetables are covered, and tightly seal with the lid. Invert the jar a couple of times to mix the ingredients and leave upside-down until cool. Leave undisturbed for 24 hours. Once opened, the carrot pickle should be stored in the refrigerator.

When you wish to serve, remove the quantity you need with tongs or a fork, then drizzle with a few drops of olive oil.

Glazed Carrots

Put 200g/7oz peeled small even-sized carrots into a saucepan, cover with water and simmer for 6 minutes; they should still be firm. Drain. Melt 20g/¾oz unsalted butter in a heavy-based frying pan, then add carrots and roll in butter. Add 125ml/4½fl oz stock (or juices from a beef, lamb or chicken casserole if you are serving this alongside, diluted with water to yield 125ml/4½fl oz if necessary), then cover and cook over medium heat for 6 minutes or until tender. Remove lid, increase heat to medium–high, then shake the pan so juices evaporate and carrots develop a lovely shine. As liquid evaporates, remove pan from heat and scatter over 1 tablespoon chopped flat-leaf parsley (if serving with beef or lamb) or French tarragon (if serving with chicken). Maybe add a touch of freshly ground black pepper but the reduced stock will be salty enough. Serve at once.

Carrot Fritters

MAKES 8 These eggless fritters are quite delicious. It is difficult to make less batter than the quantity given below so maybe have some lightly cooked cauliflower or broccoli florets at the ready to use up the excess batter. To make dainty, bite-sized fritters cook teaspoons of the mixture, then serve with Red Pepper and Saffron Sauce for Almost Anything (see page 491) or dukkah, for dipping into.

EXTRA EQUIPMENT
wok
bamboo steamer
   with lid
mortar and pestle or
   spice grinder
food processor
candy thermometer
slotted spoon

1 teaspoon cumin seeds
1 teaspoon coriander seeds
200g/7oz carrots, cut into
   1cm/½in-thick slices
1 teaspoon finely chopped
   fresh ginger
¼ teaspoon salt
2 tablespoons chickpea flour

grapeseed oil or sunflower oil, for
   deep-frying
lemon wedge, for squeezing
fresh young coriander sprigs, to serve

BEER BATTER
100g/3½oz self-raising flour
200ml/7fl oz light beer

Fill a wok half-full of water. Place a bamboo steamer over the water and turn heat to high.

While waiting for water to boil, separately dry-roast cumin seeds and coriander seeds in a small frying pan over medium heat until they smell fragrant. Tip into mortar and grind to a powder with pestle or use a spice grinder.

Scatter carrot slices in a single layer in the bamboo steamer and cover with a lid. Steam for 10 minutes or until quite tender. Tip cooked carrot slices into a food processor. Add ground spices, ginger and salt and process to form a coarse purée. Stop processor, scrape down sides, then scatter over chickpea flour and process again. Scrape mixture onto a flat plate, then cover with plastic film and chill in the refrigerator.

Preheat oven to 100°C/Gas ¼ and put a paper towel-lined ovenproof plate inside to warm.

Carefully discard water in wok, wipe it dry, then add oil for deep-frying and heat over high heat until it registers 175°C/345°F on a candy thermometer.

To make the beer batter, place flour in a bowl, tip in beer and mix it quickly with a slotted spoon to form a loose batter. It doesn't matter if there are still a few lumpy bits.

Using a dessertspoon, scoop 1 portion of carrot mixture at a time and roll it quickly in batter, then carefully transfer to the hot oil. Turn each fritter once. Lift each fritter from the oil and allow any excess oil to drain back into the wok. Place cooked fritters on the warm plate and return to the oven until all are cooked. Repeat this process until the fritter mixture has been used.

Serve fritters with a lemon wedge to the side and topped with some coriander.

Carrot, Parsnip and Sausage One-pot Dinner

SERVES 4 I created this colourful dinner one evening after a morning visit to my local farmers' market. One stallholder had a spectacular display of heirloom carrots, as beautiful as bunches of flowers – yellow, purple, orange and white with perky green tops. They were irresistible, so I bought a bunch and a bunch of fresh young parsnips. At another stall I bought pure pork sausages from a young farmer who believes that unless one eats the produce of her rare-breed pigs, these breeds will disappear. Not everyone will have heirloom carrots growing in the garden. This dish will be successful when made with any fresh carrots and fresh parsnips.

2 large onions, halved and sliced
  into rings
60ml/2fl oz extra-virgin olive oil
8 carrots, peeled and halved
  lengthways if very thick

4 parsnips, peeled and halved
  lengthways if very thick
2 garlic cloves, unpeeled
2 bay leaves
8 pure pork sausages

EXTRA EQUIPMENT
large baking dish
  or casserole (it
  needs to hold
  vegetables and
  sausages in
  a single well-
  packed layer)

Put onion slices in a microwave-safe container with a lid. Add 1 tablespoon of the olive oil, stir, cover and microwave on high for 4 minutes. Carefully remove lid, then stir, cover and microwave for another 4 minutes or until onion slices are a deep-golden colour. Set aside. Otherwise, heat 2 tablespoons of the oil in a frying pan and cook onion, stirring frequently, over low heat for 20 minutes or until deep golden brown.

Preheat oven to 180°C/Gas 4.

Pour remaining olive oil into a baking dish, then add carrots, parsnips, garlic and bay leaves. Cover with foil and bake for 20 minutes. (This step could be done several hours in advance if that is more convenient.)

Unwrap and turn vegetables. Tuck pork sausages among vegetables, rolling them in oil. Scatter over onion. Replace foil and return to oven for another 20 minutes. Remove from oven and turn everything over. It should all be colouring beautifully at this stage and the vegetables should be tender.

Increase oven temperature to 200°C/Gas 6 and bake uncovered for another 10–15 minutes, then serve with a big green salad to the side.

Chicken with Chick Peas, Carrots and Couscous

SERVES 4 This is a very simple version of what can be a very complicated and splendid Moroccan specialty. This version is made in around 40 minutes from beginning to end and can be managed perfectly by an experienced young cook. The meal is best served with the couscous in one dish and the chicken, carrots, chick peas and broth in another deep serving dish. If it is all served in the same dish, the couscous will 'drink' up all the broth.

12 free-range chicken drumettes (the
   fleshy mini-drumstick part of the
   chicken wing) or 4 skinless chicken
   thighs, cut into 3 pieces each
sea salt
1 teaspoon cumin seeds
1 teaspoon coriander seeds
2 tablespoons extra-virgin olive oil
1 onion, sliced
2 cloves garlic, sliced
1 × 2cm/¾in-long slice ginger,
   chopped
1 pinch saffron stamens
½ teaspoon harissa (see page 704)
   or chilli paste

4 carrots, peeled and cut
   into chunks
500ml/18fl oz reserved chickpea
   stock (from cooking chick peas),
   chicken stock or water
350g/12oz Cooked Dried
   Chick Peas (see opposite) or
   1 × 440g/15oz tin chick peas,
   drained and rinsed
2 preserved lemon quarters, flesh
   discarded and rind wiped of
   excess liquid and thinly sliced
185g/6½oz couscous
¼ small handful chopped coriander

EXTRA EQUIPMENT
mortar and pestle
1 × 2 litre/3½pint-
   capacity
   enamelled cast-
   iron or other
   heavy-based
   casserole

Lightly season chicken pieces with salt.

Dry-roast cumin and coriander seeds separately in a small frying pan over medium heat until fragrant. Tip seeds into a mortar, then grind to a fine powder with pestle.

Heat oil in a 2 litre/3½ pint-capacity cast-iron casserole over low–medium heat and sauté onion, garlic, ginger, saffron, harissa and ground spices, stirring for 8–10 minutes or until onion has softened. Add chicken pieces and stir to mix. Add carrot and liquid or stock, then cover and bring to simmering point over medium heat. Reduce heat to low and cook for 20 minutes. Add chick peas and preserved lemon and cook for a further 15–20 minutes or until chicken is completely tender. Taste broth for salt and season if desired.

Reconstitute the couscous according to directions on the packet, then transfer to a serving bowl and fluff with a fork.

Ladle chicken, vegetables and broth into a deep serving dish, then scatter with chopped coriander and serve with couscous.

Cooking Dried Chick Peas

The flavour of a chickpea-based dish is better when you start with dried chick peas. They will need to be soaked in cold water overnight, then will take 45–90 minutes to cook in a saucepan of simmering water, depending on their freshness. As a guide, 220g/7½oz dried chick peas triples in volume after soaking; the final yield will depend on how fresh they are and how long they've been soaked. They will continue to swell in the cooking process. Another advantage of starting from scratch is being able to add a big bouquet of herbs or a sautéed *soffritto* of onion, carrot and celery to the cooking pot to give the chick peas extra flavour. Don't add salt until they are cooked as this can cause them to toughen. When time is pressing, tins of chick peas can be used instead. Always drain them well, and rinse them in fresh water.

Carrot Flan

Many years ago the Sydney-based chef Damien Pignolet delighted me with a carrot flan served as a side dish. Since then, I have cooked this recipe in small buttered moulds and served it as a first course with a fresh tomato sauce. The mixture could also be baked in a blind-baked pastry case and served as a tart. Quantities are always approximate as it can be made with two or three carrots or twenty. The purée is then measured and the other ingredients calculated accordingly. First, peel and slice carrots thinly, then sweat them in a baking dish in butter in a 180°C/Gas 4 oven with plenty of your favourite herb (over the years I have used flat-leaf parsley, chervil, thyme or French tarragon, sometimes just one, sometimes in combination). When carrots are quite soft (maybe after 15–30 minutes, depending on how many carrots and the size of baking dish used), process carrots and herbs in a food processor to an almost-smooth purée. For every 250ml/9fl oz purée, mix in 250ml/9fl oz pouring cream, 3 whole free-range eggs and 1 additional yolk. Season very well with sea salt and freshly ground black pepper and bake in buttered 150ml/5fl oz-capacity moulds for about 20 minutes in a baking dish half-filled with hot water. If baked as a tart (or in a buttered ring tin) it may take an additional 10–15 minutes to cook.

Italian Almond and Carrot Cake

SERVES 10 This recipe is closely based on a recipe for carrot cake in *Jane Grigson's Vegetable Book*. The mixture wants to stick to the tin so a piece of baking paper at the base of the pan is an essential precaution. It can also be baked in ten greased and baking paper-lined holes of a 12-hole muffin tin. In this case, fill each hole two-thirds full with batter, then scatter a few pine nuts over each one. Little cakes will take about 20 minutes to cook until firm and golden on top.

20g/¾oz butter, for greasing
120g/4oz raw almonds
125g/4½oz (1 or 2 depending on
   their size) carrots, peeled
2 tablespoons self-raising flour

finely grated zest of ½ lemon
2 free-range eggs, separated
125g/4½oz caster sugar
2 tablespoons pine nuts

EXTRA EQUIPMENT
22cm ×10cm/
   9in × 4in loaf tin
food processor
   with grating
   attachment
slotted spoon
electric mixer

Preheat oven to 180°C/Gas 4.

Melt butter in a small frying pan over low heat or in a microwave on high heat for 20 seconds. Using a pastry brush, grease a 22cm × 10cm/9in × 4in loaf tin well with melted butter, then line with baking paper and grease again.

Process almonds in a food processor to form a fairly fine powder. Scrape into a mixing bowl. Without washing processor, attach grating disc and grate carrots. Add carrot to mixing bowl, then add flour and lemon zest. Mix well, using your fingers to make sure there are no lumps of unmixed carrot.

Beat egg yolks and sugar in an electric mixer until thick and pale. Stir in carrot mixture using a slotted spoon. Scrape mixture into a large mixing bowl.

Wash and dry electric beaters and bowl very well. Whisk egg whites until stiff peaks form. Fold into carrot batter gently but thoroughly. Spoon batter into prepared loaf tin. Scatter pine nuts over the batter. Bake cake for around 40 minutes or until a skewer inserted in the centre tests clean.

Leave cake to cool in tin for a few minutes before running a knife around and turn out carefully onto a cake cooling rack to cool completely.

CAULIFLOWER

Brassicaceae family (includes broccoli, Brussels sprouts, cabbage, cresses, radishes and turnips)
Biennial grown as an annual

Soil type
Prefers heavy soil well enriched with organic matter and a neutral or slightly alkaline soil (see pH, page 694).

Soil preparation
Apply lime if needed to raise the pH at least a month before digging in well-rotted manure a few weeks before planting into final positions. To prepare a seed-bed, often in another part of the garden, dig over a small area of ground, then rake until level.

Climate
Suitable for all climates.

Position
Prefers full sun and even temperatures.

How to grow
Sow seed in modular tray at a depth of 1cm, spaced 5cm apart. Seedlings will appear in 6 weeks and will be ready for transplanting at 10–12 weeks. Plants should be positioned 40cm apart.

Water requirements
Keep soil moist at all times. Avoid watering directly over the head.

Successive planting
Leave about 3–4 weeks between each planting, throughout the growing season.

When to fertilise
Cauliflowers are very fertiliser-hungry. Four weeks after sowing, water with a comfrey tea or liquid seaweed fertiliser (see pages 688 and 691). A good dose of lime when transplanting seedlings helps to promote healthy growth.

Harvest period
After 4–5 months, or when the head is 20cm wide. Always pick when the head is firm and a lovely white.

Pests and organic control
Highly prone to pests and diseases. Aphids, cabbage white caterpillars and cabbage root fly can be prevented by using crop covers (see page 697) or controlled by picking off pests or by spraying with natural insecticides such as those based on garlic or pyrethrum or using a biological control. Downy mildew can sometimes be a problem, pick off and destroy affected foliage. Crop rotation will help prevent clubroot but once it is in the soil it will last for 20 years, so then your only option is to grow in containers.

Companion planting
Beetroot, silver beet (Swiss chard), celery, dill, nasturtiums, garlic, peas and potatoes. Don't plant with climbing beans, tomatoes or strawberries.

Quantities to plant for a family of four
8 plants every 4 weeks.

Cauliflower (*Brassica oleracea* var. *botryoides*)

Growing and Harvesting The head of a cauliflower may be white, cream, yellow, green or purple, depending on the cultivar. The cultivar 'Snowball' can be grown as a baby cauliflower by planting closer than normal and, if planted 30 centimetres apart, will mature in seventy to ninety days with heads 10 centimetres across. If the seedlings are planted even further apart and given extra time they will develop larger heads. Cauliflower is a good plant to demonstrate the effect of 'blanching' (see page 687), whereby the largest leaves are pulled across the developing flower head and pegged loosely.

A young cauliflower is milky white (assuming the gardener is growing a 'white' cultivar). The head should be picked when the curd (white part) is perfect, is tightly nestled among the inner leaves and is blemish-free. In organic gardens, however, there will often be holes in leaves where caterpillars have had a good munch, so aiming for completely blemish-free cauliflower is unrealistic. The head gradually becomes creamy, then yellows and dulls as it becomes over-mature. The curd starts to separate from the leaves as it ages, by which time it is past its best.

The cabbage white butterfly is a very persistent pest and attacks all brassicas. Effective organic controls are available (see pages 697–700), but the most effective method is to carefully inspect the leaves every two days, pick off any hatched caterpillars and brush off any eggs. Caterpillars must be destroyed or fed to the chickens.

Container Planting The smaller cultivars of cauliflower are suitable for growing in a large pot or planter box. Beetroot and dill would be good companion plants.

Preparing and Sharing Freshly picked cauliflower can be broken into small pieces and used raw or very lightly blanched (note the cooking as opposed to gardening meaning of 'blanched' here) as a scoop for dips. Older examples will taste unpleasantly bitter when raw. Garden-picked cauliflower can often harbour small insects. Before using or cooking, soak the separated florets for a few minutes in plenty of lightly salted water to flush out any remaining tiny creatures.

Over-cooking and plain bad cooking is responsible for the terrible smell that many associate with cauliflower. The smell is often the result of cramming too much cauliflower into a small pan with cold water and jamming on the lid. Instead, I suggest either steaming the florets in a bamboo steamer over a wok (see page 210), or plunging the florets into a saucepan filled with plenty of lightly salted boiling water – much as you would cook pasta – and test a piece after five minutes. As with pasta, cauliflower should still be 'al dente', that is, have a little resistance when you bite it. It will continue to cook as it sits in the serving dish or any accompanying sauce. Drain it very well before saucing and always heat the serving dish. Use a non-aluminium pan to avoid the cauliflower taking on a yellowish tinge. The challenge is how to make cauliflower exciting and using Browned Breadcrumbs (see page 210) is one of the best ways of doing this. They add crunch and colour and can be combined with many other ingredients to vary the flavour.

Boiled or steamed cauliflower is delicious when presented as Cauliflower and Blue Cheese (see page 212). Raw or steamed cauliflower is delicious when sautéed until tender with such ingredients as pine nuts, garlic, breadcrumbs, chilli, anchovies and olives, or in the Asian spectrum, with mustard seeds, garlic, ginger and turmeric (see the Spiced Cauliflower

Masala recipe on page 215). Cauliflower works well in risottos and fritters or baked with a spicy tomato sauce. It also makes a lovely purée, extended with a very small amount of cream. Such a purée is absolutely delicious when served with seared scallops.

Green and purple cauliflowers are somewhat reminiscent of broccoli in flavour. They are both very attractive plants and look lovely when cooked to just-tender and served together in a wide bowl so the colours can be admired, glistening with a little melted butter or extra-virgin olive oil on the top.

Especially for Kids When blanching your cauliflower to make it white, children will be intrigued to be asked to peg the largest leaves across the cauliflower's head. This would be a good moment to call attention to the two different meanings of the term 'blanching' (see page 687 and page 703).

Caring for your cauliflower provides a good opportunity to talk about the importance of regularly feeding all brassicas as they are 'hungry crops'. Children will be fascinated and maybe initially a little disgusted when asked to assist in the making of compost 'tea' or 'moo poo tea' made with manure (see **Liquid fertiliser**, page 691) to fertilise your garden.

To get rid of caterpillars, hand over a magnifying glass that will make spotting any butterfly eggs a bit easier (see instructions for doing this with **CABBAGE** on page 185). Buy a butterfly net to use as an effective way of catching then destroying at least some of the cabbage white butterflies.

Four Ways with Lightly Steamed Cauliflower and Browned Breadcrumbs

SERVES 4 AS AN ACCOMPANIMENT The method I've given here for browned breadcrumbs yields more than the amount used with steamed cauliflower, so if you don't wish to use them immediately, then pack them in containers, label and freeze for up to a month. All of the following ideas can also be used with all varieties of broccoli (refer to the recipes in **BROCCOLI** for other ideas that can be used interchangeably for cauliflower). Many recipes require the crumbs to be mixed with other flavourings (see opposite for some ideas; each recipe requires one quantity of Steamed Cauliflower and one quantity of Browned Breadcrumbs). Prepare the other ingredients first of all so that the crumbs just need to be added to the pan for a final toss before serving.

choice of Additional Flavourings
　(see opposite)

STEAMED CAULIFLOWER
400g/14oz cauliflower florets

BROWNED BREADCRUMBS
1 loaf day-old good-quality bread
　(could be either white or multigrain)
60ml/2fl oz extra-virgin olive oil or
　clarified butter (see page 704)
1 clove garlic, crushed

EXTRA EQUIPMENT
food processor
wok
bamboo steamer
　with lid

To make the browned breadcrumbs, slice the crusts away from the loaf of bread, then discard and cut the remaining bread into thick slices. Spread slices on a baking tray and leave overnight.

The next day, preheat oven to 100°C/Gas ¼.

Put bread into oven for 20 minutes, turning once after 10 minutes. When bread feels crisp, remove and leave it to cool completely. Break each slice into a few pieces and process in batches in a food processor, then transfer each batch to a bowl. Be warned, it will make a terrible noise and you should not go too far away as food processors have been known to rock themselves to the edge of benches when processing breadcrumbs.

Heat olive oil or clarified butter in a heavy-based non-stick frying pan with garlic over medium heat. Tip in 50g/2oz breadcrumbs (the rest can be frozen to use later) and stir with a wooden spoon. At first the crumbs will just look a bit damp and clumpy, but as you stir them they will start to become crisp and golden. Expect this process to take at least 5 minutes. When crumbs are golden, tip into a bowl and leave to cool until needed.

Fill a wok half-full of water. Place a bamboo steamer over water and turn heat to high. Once water is boiling, scatter cauliflower florets inside steamer, cover with lid and steam for 5 minutes or until tender.

Tip cauliflower florets into a large mixing bowl and serve with browned breadcrumbs mixed with your choice of flavouring (see opposite).

Additional Flavourings:

1. Anchovy and Parsley

2 tablespoons extra-virgin olive oil
6 anchovy fillets, chopped
2 cloves garlic, chopped

2 tablespoons chopped
  flat-leaf parsley
freshly ground black pepper

Heat olive oil in a frying pan over medium heat and sauté anchovies and garlic until anchovies have melted. Stir in steamed cauliflower, crumbs and parsley and season to taste with pepper. Tip into a hot serving dish.

2. Egg and Parsley

60g/2oz butter, melted
¼ small handful chopped flat-leaf
  parsley

2 hard-boiled eggs, peeled
sea salt and freshly ground black
  pepper

Tip steamed cauliflower into a frying pan of hot melted butter and stir over medium heat. Sprinkle over the parsley and crumbs. Crush the eggs with a fork and scatter them over the cauliflowers. Season and tip into a hot serving dish.

3. Red Pepper and Paprika

60ml/2fl oz extra-virgin olive oil
2 tablespoons sweet paprika
1 fresh long red chilli, seeded
  and finely sliced

1 Roasted and Peeled Sweet Pepper
  (see page 488), diced
sea salt

Heat olive oil in a frying pan over medium heat, then sauté paprika, chilli and red pepper until the red pepper is well softened. Tip in cauliflower. Toss to mix well, then season with salt. Add crumbs and tip into a hot serving dish.

4. Capers and Parmesan

60g/2oz butter
2 teaspoons salted capers, rinsed and
  drained
finely grated zest and juice of 1 lemon

25g/1oz grated parmesan
sea salt and freshly ground
  black pepper

Melt butter in a frying pan over medium heat until just starting to foam. Add capers, lemon juice and zest. Toss in cauliflower, parmesan and crumbs. Toss to mix well. Season with salt and pepper and tip into a hot serving dish.

Cauliflower and Blue Cheese

SERVES 4 AS A SIDE DISH OR 2 AS A LUNCH DISH This is best served straight from the oven while it is still puffy. If you cannot find a soft blue cheese, you might like to try a garlic and herb cheese such as Boursin or a soft goat's milk cheese instead.

200g/7oz trimmed cauliflower
   florets
40g/1½oz unsalted butter
½ small onion, finely chopped

2 free-range eggs
80ml/3fl oz milk
50g/2oz soft blue cheese
2 tablespoons plain flour

EXTRA EQUIPMENT
wok
bamboo steamer
   with lid
18cm × 14cm/
   7in × 5½in
   gratin dish
blender or food
   processor

Preheat oven to 180°C/Gas 4.

Half-fill a wok with water. Place a bamboo steamer over water and turn heat to high. Once water is boiling, scatter cauliflower florets inside steamer, cover with lid and steam for 5 minutes or until tender. Tip cauliflower florets into a large mixing bowl.

Melt butter in a small frying pan over low heat. Use a little melted butter to thoroughly grease an 18cm × 14cm/7in × 5½ in gratin dish. Increase heat to medium and sauté onion in remaining butter for 3–4 minutes until golden. Tip onion into another mixing bowl.

Put eggs, milk, cheese and flour in a blender or food processor and blend to form a smooth batter. Tip into bowl with onion and stir to mix. Add cauliflower and tip everything into the gratin dish; make sure florets are evenly placed in the gratin dish. Transfer to the oven and bake for 30 minutes or until puffed and golden brown, then serve.

Spiced Cauliflower Masala

SERVES 4 AS A SIDE DISH This colourful dish can be served as part of an Indian-inspired meal with other side dishes, or it could just as well be part of the accompaniments to a Western-style barbecue. It is based on a recipe given in the excellent book *Singapore Food* by Wendy Hutton. The cauliflower is quite spicy, and while some young palates can surprise their elders with their enjoyment of spicy food, the chilli could easily be omitted or reduced. The last time I made this dish, I cut 200 grams/7 ounces of chunky white fish (use blue-eye trevalla or hapuku) into bite-sized pieces and added them to the pan at the same time as the tomato and it made a satisfying lunch for four (see opposite), but this is optional.

60ml/2fl oz peanut oil
½ teaspoon mustard seeds
2 tablespoons finely chopped ginger
2 cloves garlic, finely chopped
½ teaspoon cumin seeds
½ teaspoon ground turmeric
1 onion, halved and thinly sliced

400g/14oz trimmed cauliflower
   florets
220g/8oz tinned chopped tomatoes
1 fresh long green chilli, seeded
   and sliced
½ teaspoon salt
a handful of coriander sprigs,
   to serve

Heat oil in a large non-stick frying pan over medium heat. Add mustard seeds and wait a few seconds until they start to pop. Add ginger, garlic, cumin, turmeric and onion and stir for 8 minutes or until the onion is well softened. Add cauliflower and turn until every piece is well coated with spice mixture, then add tomato, chilli and salt. Stir to mix, then cover. Cook for 8–10 minutes, stirring once or twice until cauliflower is just tender. Serve scattered with coriander sprigs.

Spinach Pasta with Cauliflower, Rocket, Vino Cotto Butter and Fried Almonds

SERVES 4 AS A STARTER AND 2 AS A MAIN Vino cotto or *vincotto* is an Italian syrupy condiment that adds a subtle sour-sweetness to many dishes. An excellent vino cotto is made by my friend Maggie Beer, a well-known Australian cook, and I use it often. I think it is much more exciting, and certainly better value, than the thin industrial so-called 'balsamic vinegars' that are widely available. My supermarket sells a very pretty mixed green and white pasta labelled *Foglie d'ulivo*. Its slightly rough texture and shape is intended to mimic that of olive leaves. If you can find it, it is a good choice in this recipe (see opposite). This dish looks particularly appetising when made with half broccoli and half cauliflower.

20g/¾oz unsalted butter
30g/1oz flaked almonds
300g/10½oz dried or fresh
   spinach pasta
salt
300g/10½oz trimmed cauliflower
   florets
sea salt and freshly ground
   black pepper
2 big handfuls rocket leaves, washed
   and dried

VINO COTTO BUTTER
2 cloves garlic, very
   finely chopped
75g/2½oz unsalted butter,
   softened
1 tablespoon vino cotto
   (see page 706)
½ teaspoon sea salt

EXTRA EQUIPMENT
food processor
wok
bamboo steamer
   with lid

Make the vino cotto butter first of all. Pulse all ingredients in a food processor until well combined. Scrape into a large bowl and set aside.

Melt butter in a small frying pan over medium heat. Sauté flaked almonds until golden and quickly tip them onto a plate lined with lots of paper towels.

Preheat oven to 100°C/Gas ¼. Put in an ovenproof serving dish to warm.

Cook pasta in a large saucepan or pasta pot of boiling lightly salted water until al dente. Cauliflower takes just 5 minutes to steam so plan accordingly, depending on whether the pasta is dried or fresh. Dried pasta will take at least 10 minutes to cook (read what it says on the packet), while fresh pasta will only take moments, and, in this case, the cauliflower should be cooked first of all.

Half-fill a wok with water. Place a bamboo steamer over water and turn heat to high. Once water is boiling, scatter cauliflower florets inside steamer, cover with lid and steam for 5 minutes or until tender. Tip cauliflower florets into large mixing bowl with vino cotto butter.

Drain pasta, and add to bowl with cauliflower and vino cotto butter. Toss gently to thoroughly coat cauliflower and pasta in vino cotto butter. Season to taste with salt and pepper. Mix in rocket and transfer to warm serving dish. Scatter over fried almonds and serve at once.

CELERY AND CELERIAC

**Apiaceae family
(includes carrots, chervil,
fennel, parsley and parsnip)
Biennial grown as an annual**

Soil type
Rich, fertile well-drained soil
enriched with organic matter.

Soil preparation
Prepare the soil with well-rotted
organic compost a few weeks
before planting.

Climate
Prefers damp, cool climates.

Position
An open position in full sun.

How to grow
Sow seeds in March-April in a
heated greenhouse at 18°C.
Sow in modular seed trays at a
depth of 3cm and 2cm apart.
Keep well watered through the
2–3 week germination period.
Harden off plants and plant out
after last frosts. Transplant into
a permanent position, spaced
25cm apart, when the seedlings
are 10–12cm tall.

Water requirements
Frequent watering from seed to
maturity. A lack of water leads
to tasteless and stringy celery.

Successive planting
Leave about 4 weeks between
each planting, throughout the
growing season.

When to fertilise
As celery should be grown fast,
a fortnightly application of liquid
fertiliser (see page 691) will be
required for a good crop.

Harvest period
Celery: 4 months after planting
the whole plant will be ready.
Crop the outside stalks as you
need them. Celeriac: harvest
when the root is 8–10 cm wide.
This can take 6 months or more.

Pests and organic control
Snails, slugs and celery fly can be
a problem. Use crushed egg shells
around base of young plants to
deter snails and slugs. Pyrethrum
spray will help with insects.
If a fungal disease known as leaf
spot affects your celery, check
your seed as it is seed borne.

Companion planting
Brassicas, leeks, chives,
tomatoes and dwarf beans;
nasturtiums and calendula
as bait plants for aphids. Don't
plant with carrots and parsnips.

Special information
Keep the soil moist and free
from weeds by mulching.
Keeping the soil moist will
stop it bolting.

Quantities to plant
for a family of four
Plant 3–4 seedlings every
4 weeks in the growing season.

Celery (*Apium graveolens* var. *dulce*)

Growing and Harvesting Celery Celery is a shallow-rooted plant and needs well-mulched soil. I recommend planting self-blanching celery in blocks rather than long rows so that the densely packed growing plants will be better protected from wind. The close planting will also achieve some degree of self-blanching (see page 687). I have seen celery growing very successfully in a row, however it was planted against a west-facing wall. In another garden I visited celery plants were successfully growing here and there among other vegetables. Self-blanching varieties such as 'Victoria' are less work than traditional trench celery.

When the stalks are ready to harvest it is not necessary to cut the entire head. Individual stalks can be cut just below ground level. This is such a sensible way to use the crop. How often have you bought a bunch, used a few stalks and a week or so later found the rest of the bunch looking sad and limp at the bottom of the fridge, suitable only for the stockpot?

Celeriac Celeriac has the same growing requirements as celery but it will take longer to be ready to harvest. As the plant grows, remove any side shoots that appear. When ready to harvest, you will see the base pushing through the soil with a tuft of small, dark-green and unmistakeably celery-like leaves attached. The stems are not used as they are very bitter.

This warty-looking vegetable will almost certainly be unknown to most young gardeners, and they will find it fascinating because it looks so unappealing. Like common celery, celeriac has developed over time from a smaller wild plant, but in this case the base of the stem has become as large as a softball and grows mostly underground.

Container Planting Celery Celery could be grown in a pot provided the pot is placed out of the wind. Because celery is greedy for water, ensure that the pot does not dry out. You will have to wait four months before harvesting and, as with all slow-growing vegetables, you may have to be content with a single harvest as there may not be space for successive planting.

Celeriac Celeriac could be grown in a container. As it will be nearly six months before it is ready, fill the spaces in the tub or pot with fast-growing salad greens, radishes and maybe some rainbow chard. Many crops planted in containers will yield one harvest only, as there will not be space for successive planting.

Preparing and Sharing Celery Crispness and crunchiness without any bitterness is what is expected from celery. If garden-grown celery has not been blanched it is absolutely fine to include small quantities in the stockpot or soup pot, or add it to a bouquet garni (see page 635) or a stuffing. In Asian cookery, the thinner stalks of celery that have not been blanched are preferred for adding to cooked dishes. Try a few of the coarser stalks sliced and stir-fried with other vegetables and fresh ginger – they are too aggressively flavoured to be enjoyed raw as a salad vegetable.

When handling a full head of celery remember that the base of the bunch – the white, solid part that has been naturally blanched under the ground – is extremely delicious and tastes just like celeriac. Discard just the thinnest slice from the base that might be dirty into the compost bucket and then slice or dice the solid base to add to a salad.

Raw celery is a great addition to the salad bowl. The hollowed side of the stalk just asks to be stuffed with some savoury mixture, often based on a creamy cheese – I like using cream cheese seasoned with a small amount of finely chopped garlic, some snipped chives and chopped toasted walnuts.

The pale inner leaves of blanched celery are absolutely delicious when dipped in tempura batter and fried. Mix them with a selection of other vegetables also dipped in tempura batter, or serve celery fritters alongside fried fish coated in the Eggwhite Batter on page 678.

Celery can also be braised or it can be the major player in a soup. I was recently served a delicious smooth-as-silk chilled celery soup topped with a floating island of airy salmon mousse.

Celeriac Celeriac tastes like celery but has a totally different texture. It has none of the crunchy character of celery stalks and the flesh is quite dense. Celeriac must be peeled thickly to remove all the knobbles and crevices where dirt collects. It is a vegetable that discolours quickly when prepared, so drop chunks into a bowl of water acidulated with the juice of a lemon without delay. Everyone seems to love the classic French preparation, Celeriac Rémoulade (see page 229), where the grated flesh is tossed through a mustard mayonnaise.

Chunks or slices of celeriac can be added to braises (see Lamb Shanks Braised with Celeriac on page 227) or roasted with other root vegetables (try adding it to the Roasted Vegetables with Rosemary on page 553). Thin slices of celeriac make great chips.

Especially for Kids **Celery** If blanching young celery plants with cardboard or milk cartons, children will need to keep an eye out for slugs and snails that may enjoy this shelter too. Again, caring for your celery could be the starting point for a discussion about the two meanings of 'blanching', (see pages 687 and 703).

In the kitchen, older children will enjoy cutting celery sticks into short lengths, slitting each end of the piece and watching them curl in a bowl of cold water. Or involve them in making the Celery and Blue Cheese Party Sticks on page 222 to hand around the next time you are entertaining. Some young gourmets I know like their celery stalks spread with a little crunchy peanut butter!

Celery and Blue Cheese Party Sticks

MAKE AS MANY AS YOU LIKE This is another hand-around savoury like the Italian Party Cocktail Sticks on page 118 that can be made by young cooks with minimal assistance. They will feel pretty proud handing these around.

pale inner celery sticks	**your choice of blue cheese, rind removed**	
iced water	**mascarpone or softened butter**	

EXTRA EQUIPMENT
piping bag with star
    nozzle (optional)

Cut inner sticks of celery into pieces about 8cm/3in long. Using a paring knife, cut slits in the last 2cm/¾in of each piece, about 3mm/¹⁄₁₀in apart. Place in a bowl of iced water for about 1 hour or until the slitted ends start to curl.

Put blue cheese in a small bowl and mash with a fork. Work in as much butter or mascarpone as you need to make a spreadable paste (not too soft if the party sticks are going to be at room temperature for more than a few minutes). Lift out celery and pat dry with paper towel. Using a teaspoon or a piping-bag with a star nozzle, fill the celery pieces with blue cheese mixture. If using a piping bag, the easiest way is to drop the bag into a jug and fold its top over the rim like a cuff. Spoon in blue cheese mixture, unfold the top and twist the bag to force all the mixture to the bottom end of the piping-bag. Place filled sticks on a tray, then cover and refrigerate until needed.

Deep-fried Crunchy Celery Leaves

MAKES AS MANY AS YOU HAVE These crunchy leaves are addictive. Prepare just as you want to eat them. They are the best garnish for simply grilled or fried fish, and a wonderful addition to a plate of vegetable fritters (see page 560).

grapeseed or sunflower oil, for	**BATTER**
deep-frying	**60g/2oz plain flour**
celery leaves from pale inner sticks	**1 teaspoon bicarbonate of soda**
sea salt	**½ cup iced water**

EXTRA EQUIPMENT
wok or heavy-based
    saucepan
candy thermometer
long-handled
    brass skimmer

Preheat oven to 100°C/Gas ¼ and put a plate lined with several layers of paper towel inside to warm. Heat oil for deep-frying in a wok over high heat until it registers 175°C/345°F on a candy thermometer or try the chopstick test (see page 602). To make the batter, quickly mix batter ingredients. Dip in a celery leaf, allowing excess batter to drip back into the bowl. Gently lay leaf in hot oil. Continue adding batter-coated leaves until surface of oil cannot fit any more. Turn leaves once; they will be crisp and golden. Remove leaves, allowing excess oil to drain back into wok. Transfer leaves to lined plate. Scatter with salt to serve.

Stir-fried Celery with Chinese Sausage

SERVES 4 AS PART OF A MULTI-DISH MEAL Dried Chinese sausage is known as *lap cheung*, and it is sold in Asian grocery stores. It is a great product to have on hand in the refrigerator if you have Asian vegetables growing in your garden as it keeps for several months. It must always be steamed before use to make it soft. Be careful as the sausage is very slippery after steaming and it can therefore be dangerous to cut.

1 dried Chinese sausage (*lap cheung*)
1 tablespoon light soy sauce
1 tablespoon mirin (see page 704)
1 teaspoon rice vinegar
2 tablespoons peanut oil
1 clove garlic, chopped

1 teaspoon chopped ginger
2–3 sticks celery, cut on the diagonal into 5cm/2in-long pieces
2 tablespoons water
1 teaspoon white sugar

EXTRA EQUIPMENT
wok
bamboo steamer with lid
wok sang (see page 47)

Half-fill a wok with water. Place a bamboo steamer over water and turn heat to high. Once water is boiling, drop sausage inside steamer, cover with the lid and steam for 15 minutes or until tender. Remove sausage, pat dry with paper towel and, using a serrated knife, carefully cut it into thin slices on the diagonal.

Mix soy sauce, rice wine and vinegar.

Discard steaming water and dry wok over high heat. Add peanut oil and swish up sides of wok with a wok sang. Add sausage and stir-fry for 30 seconds. Add garlic and ginger and stir-fry for another 30 seconds. Add celery and stir-fry for 30 seconds, then add water and cook for another 2 minutes, lifting and tossing all the time. Cover with lid, reduce heat to medium and cook for another 1 minute. Lift the lid, then return heat to high, stir in soy mixture and scatter over sugar. Stir-fry for another 30 seconds and serve at once.

Lamb Shanks Braised with Celeriac

SERVES 4 This splendidly hearty autumn dish is easy to prepare and, once it's in the oven, cooks itself without any further attention required. Lamb shanks were once considered to be very ordinary. Now that they are sold carefully trimmed by the butcher (described as 'French-trimmed' or 'frenched'), with the shank bones sawn off so that the meat shrinks back along the bone as it cooks, they are regarded as a rather fancy food.

Preserved lemons are a speciality of the Middle East and the unique tang of their softened rind is unlike anything else. Made by covering lemons with salt, preserved lemons are readily available in specialty food stores but they are very simple to make at home (see page 371). I like to serve this dish with a pile of wilted fresh leafy greens (see opposite) such as chard, silver beet or Tuscan kale (*cavolo nero*). If there is extra room in the casserole pot, add chunks of carrot or whole small potatoes. Alternatively, you could serve it with Barley with Parmesan (see page 228).

EXTRA EQUIPMENT
mortar and pestle
cast-iron casserole
  with tight-fitting
  lid (or 24cm/
  9½ in Chinese
  claypot)

80ml/3fl oz extra-virgin olive oil
4 lamb shanks, French-trimmed
1 onion, sliced
3 cloves garlic, sliced
10 sprigs thyme, tied together with
  kitchen string
1 quarter preserved lemon, flesh
  discarded, rind rinsed and sliced
  (or 3 wide strips of lemon zest)
1 celeriac (about 300g/10½oz after
  peeling)
500ml/18fl oz meat-based stock
sea salt and freshly ground
  black pepper

1 teaspoon grated lemon zest
2 tablespoons chopped
  flat-leaf parsley
1 tablespoon chopped coriander

SPICE MIX
1 teaspoon cumin seeds
1 teaspoon coriander seeds
1 teaspoon paprika
sea salt and freshly ground
  black pepper
1 tablespoon plain flour

To make the spice mix, separately dry-roast cumin and coriander seeds in a small frying pan over medium heat until fragrant. Grind to a fine powder in a mortar with the pestle. Tip into a bowl and mix in paprika, salt, pepper and flour. Spread mixture on a plate and roll shanks in it. Reserve extra flour mixture.

Preheat oven to 180°C/Gas 4.

Heat 2 tablespoons of oil in a cast-iron casserole or heavy-based frying pan over high heat and seal shanks very well until browned on all sides. Set aside. Discard oil in pan and wipe it out. Add remaining oil and fry onion and garlic over medium heat for 8–10 minutes or until well softened. Return shanks to pan, or if using a 24cm/9½in Chinese claypot, transfer contents of frying pan now. Add thyme and preserved lemon or lemon zest. Scatter over reserved flour mix.

>>>

Peel celeriac and cut into big chunks. Tuck chunks around shanks, then pour over stock; it should come a little over halfway up sides of meat. Cut a round of baking paper and press it down over the meat. Cover with the lid and place in the oven. Cook for 1 hour 45 minutes or until meat is very tender. Taste the sauce and adjust seasoning with salt and pepper if necessary. If sauce is too thin, ladle it into a wide frying pan and reduce by rapid boiling over high heat, then pour back over shanks.

Mix lemon zest, parsley and coriander and scatter over the shanks and celeriac, then serve.

Barley with Parmesan

SERVES 4 I met Skye Gyngell, the Australian chef at the highly regarded Petersham Nurseries just outside London, when she was a guest at the 2008 Melbourne Food and Wine Festival. We quickly sensed a similar approach to culinary matters – minimum of fuss and a maximum of flavour. Skye cooked a succulent slow-roasted shoulder of lamb flavoured with anchovies, fennel seeds and sage. It was accompanied by a dish of the ancient wheat variety farro. It is very difficult for a home cook to locate farro but I adjusted the quantities and cooked this dish in the way Skye instructed using pearl barley instead – it was very delicious, and very easy. Put 100g/3½oz barley in a small saucepan, then cover generously with cold water and add a large pinch of sea salt. Bring to the boil over high heat, then skim the surface. Reduce heat to low and cook for 25 minutes. Taste barley to see if it needs an additional 5 minutes to become tender. Watch at this point to make sure it is in no danger of boiling dry; add a little extra hot water if necessary. Preheat oven to 100°C/Gas ¼ and put an ovenproof serving bowl inside to warm. Drain cooked barley, give it a good shake and tip into the warmed bowl. Stir in 30g/1oz unsalted butter, 2 tablespoons red-wine vinegar, 1½ tablespoons extra-virgin olive oil and 40g/1½oz shaved parmesan, then season with salt and pepper to taste. Stir gently to mix, taste and adjust seasoning, then drizzle with another 1½ tablespoons olive oil and serve.

Celeriac Rémoulade

SERVES 2–4 I've included this recipe in many of my cookbooks, including *The Cook's Companion*, but it has been such a runaway success story in every Kitchen Garden workshop I have given that I feel it has to be repeated here. Time and time again I've encountered teachers and even gardeners who had never even seen this funny warty vegetable before, and time and time again they were enchanted with this classic French bistro dish. Celeriac rémoulade can be served as one of a selection of cold vegetable starters, such as the Avocado, Grapefruit and Golden Beetroot Salad with Toasted Walnuts on page 140 or the Green and Yellow Bean Salad on page 134. The mayonnaise can be made in a food processor but with this small a quantity there is a danger that the egg yolks will not emulsify with the oil and the mixture may curdle, so it is easier to do it by hand. Ask someone to help – it's so much easier to have one person whisking while the other slowly adds the oil.

EXTRA EQUIPMENT
food processor with grating/shredding disc attachment

juice of 1 lemon
1 celeriac (about 300g/10½oz after peeling)
sea salt and freshly ground black pepper
1 tablespoon chopped flat-leaf parsley

MAYONNAISE
2 free-range egg yolks
1 tablespoon Dijon mustard, plus extra if desired
1 pinch sea salt
180ml/6fl oz extra-virgin olive oil or 125ml/4½fl oz extra-virgin olive oil and 60ml/2fl oz grapeseed or other neutral-flavoured oil
1 teaspoon white or red-wine vinegar (optional)

Set aside 1 tablespoon of the lemon juice and put the rest into a mixing bowl half-filled with cold water. Drop in squeezed lemon halves. Peel celeriac and cut into large chunks that will fit down the feeder tube of your food processor. Put the chunks into the acidulated water (see page 703).

To make the mayonnaise, place egg yolks in a round-bottomed bowl resting on a damp tea towel or a non-stick mat. Add mustard, salt and reserved lemon juice. Whisk well for about 30 seconds. Start adding oil, a few drops at a time, whisking all the while. If you have a helper, one person can drip in the oil and the other whisk, changing over halfway if your arm gets tired. When two-thirds of the oil is incorporated, taste the mayonnaise. If it needs to be a bit sharper, either whisk in vinegar or extra mustard. Whisk in remaining oil.

Dry celeriac chunks and shred them in the food processor. Transfer shredded celeriac without delay to mayonnaise and mix very well. Taste for salt, pepper and 'mustard-ness', adding more of these if desired. Stir in parsley and serve.

CHERVIL

**Apiaceae family
(includes carrots, celery,
fennel, parsley and parsnips)
Biennial**

Soil type
Moist, well drained and rich in
organic matter.

Climate
Suitable for all.

Position
Prefers partial shade.

How to grow
Sow March onwards directly
where you want it to grow,
planting seeds in a small
depression and covering with
5 mm of seed-raising mix.
Germination should take
10 days. When the seedlings
are 3cm tall, they should be
thinned to 25cm apart, leaving
the strongest.

Water requirements
Frequent watering is required to
keep soil moist.

Successive planting
Leave about 4 weeks between
each planting, throughout the
growing season.

When to fertilise
To promote foliage growth,
fertilise with liquid fertiliser
(see page 691) or worm
tea (see page 695) once
every 4 weeks.

Harvest period
Harvest 6–8 weeks after planting.
Harvest frequently to prevent it
from running to seed.

Pests and organic control
Use crushed egg shells around
the bases of the young plants to
deter snails and slugs. Pyrethrum
spray (see page 700) will help
with aphids.

Companion planting
Planting with lettuce helps deter
aphids, snails and slugs.

Special information
Keep the soil moist and free
from weeds by mulching.
Use taller companion plants
to provide shade during
the hotter months.

**Quantities to plant
for a family of four**
2–4 plants.

Chervil (*Anthriscus cerefolium*)

Growing and harvesting Chervil has a faint aniseed flavour and is very highly regarded in French cooking. Chervil does not like excessive heat, so plant it in the shadiest part of your herb garden, or sow it between rows of taller plants to give it shade. If the leaves turn pink the plant is too hot and the flavour will almost completely disappear. Chervil starts off as a compact rosette of leaves close to the ground but develops to a height of around 25 centimetres. Use scissors to snip stems of chervil from the outside of the plant.

Container Planting Chervil, like most herbs, is ideal to grow in a pot. If you move the pot out of the hottest midday sun and keep it moist, the plant should flourish. It will happily coexist in the same pot with tarragon, chives and flat-leaf parsley, these being so often used in combination.

Preparing and Sharing After picking, each little leaf has to be nipped from the stem. The stems go into the compost bin. The tiny triangular leaves can be pulled apart into their sections. Chervil is prettier used in this way than chopped to an anonymous green dust.

Chervil is at its best matched with delicate foods such as eggs, fish or soft, fresh cheeses or with freshly harvested produce such as asparagus, peas or tomatoes. Use it generously to appreciate its aniseed-accented flavour.

It is a delicate herb that ought to be used on its own or else in the classic combination of flat-leaf parsley, chives and tarragon that makes the *fines herbes* mixture frequently used in French cookery. It is also part of another classic combination, Sauce Ravigote (see page 235) and Beurre Ravigote (see page 235), where finely chopped flat-leaf parsley, chives, tarragon and chervil are combined with either oil and vinegar or butter. A slice of Beurre Ravigote is delicious melted over quickly cooked fillets of a delicate fish such as King George whiting.

The flavour of chervil is destroyed by heat so it is always added at the end of cooking or as a final garnish. It does not dry successfully.

Especially for Kids Young gardeners need to be shown how to snip individual stalks from the outside of the plant, preferably using scissors. If the stalk is pulled it is likely that the entire plant will be uprooted. The new shoots grow from the centre of the plant.

Sauce Ravigote

MAKES ABOUT 250ML/9FL OZ This sauce is one of a largish family of cold herb-based sauces that are used in the French and Italian repertoires to spoon over plainly cooked (for example, poached or steamed) meats, poultry or fish. A poached nut of veal could have this sauce spooned over the slices instead of the more usual (and richer) tuna mayonnaise used to make the classic Italian dish, *vitello tonnato*.

There are many variations on a theme – some sauces include chopped hard-boiled eggs and some don't; others include finely chopped French shallots and others don't; and some methods involve blanching the herbs in boiling water. However it is made, ravigote always includes chervil. I have decided to follow (more or less) the version offered by Elizabeth David in her book *French Provincial Cooking*. Her quantities are rather vague but it hardly matters as long as the flavour combination is essentially the same as the following. This recipe could just as well have been located under **TARRAGON** or even **PARSLEY**.

a handful picked flat-leaf
　parsley leaves
a small handful tarragon leaves
a small handful young
　watercress leaves
a small handful chervil leaves
10 chive stems
3 anchovy fillets
2 teaspoons salted capers, soaked
　in hot water and drained
2 cornichons (tiny, crunchy cucumbers
　pickled in vinegar)
80ml/3fl oz extra-virgin olive oil
2 teaspoons tarragon vinegar
1 teaspoon lemon juice
sea salt and freshly ground black pepper

Chop the herbs with the anchovies, capers and cornichons very finely; don't be tempted to process ingredients in a food processor as the herbs will be bruised and not cut correctly. Transfer to a bowl, then stir in olive oil, vinegar and lemon juice and taste for salt (probably not needed) and pepper and season as required. This sauce should be quite thick.

Beurre Ravigote

To make a delicious compound butter, finely chop the exact same ingredients as for Sauce Ravigote (see above) finely. Instead of using olive oil, work them into 120g/4oz softened unsalted butter (this can be done in a food processor). Add 2 teaspoons tarragon vinegar and 1 teaspoon lemon juice and taste for salt (probably not needed) and pepper. Spoon mixture onto a piece of baking paper and shape into a log, then roll in a double thickness of foil. Chill in the refrigerator until firm, then label, date and freeze for up to 1 month if not using immediately. Try a slice melted over a grilled lamb chop.

CHIVES AND GARLIC CHIVES

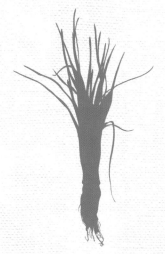

Alliaceae family (includes garlic, leeks and onions)

Herbaceous perennial

Soil type
Moist, well drained and rich in organic matter.

Soil preparation
Dig in organic matter or well-rotted manure a few weeks prior to planting.

Climate
Suitable for all climates.

Position
Prefer full sun, but will tolerate partial shade.

How to grow
In March-April, directly sow seeds at a depth of 1cm, in clumps of 5–10 seeds per hole. When seedlings are 12cm tall, thin to 10cm apart with 15cm between rows. Or buy a potted plant and divide it.

Water requirements
Water well during hot months.

When to fertilise
To ensure vigorous growth, fertilise with liquid fertiliser (see page 691) or worm tea (see page 695) every few months.

Harvest period
Chives and garlic chives are ready to harvest when they are 15 cm tall – this will take around 3 months. Cut to the ground, leaving 5 cm stem to continue growing. Regular harvesting will promote more growth. Chives die down in winter, which is a good time to divide the clumps and replant. Do this every 2 to 3 years.

Pests and organic control
Use crushed egg shells around the bases of the young plants to deter snails and slugs.

Companion planting
Chives deter aphids on lettuce and roses and will help prevent black spot on roses. Chives are a good companion to carrots. Grow under apple trees to prevent apple scab. Don't plant near peas or beans.

Special information
Keep soil moist and free from weeds by mulching.

Quantities to plant for a family of four
6–8 plants.

Chives (*Allium schoenoprasum*)

Growing and Harvesting **Chives** Chives come in two sizes. There are very fine chives and another type that grows taller and has thicker leaves. Both become straggly or die back completely in winter and both have exactly the same cultivation needs. Cutting off the flowers as they appear will keep the leaves growing. However, the flowers are very pretty and young gardeners may want to cut one or two of these lilac-pink pompoms to strew over a salad. Be aware that the flowers have the same onion flavour as the leaves and are pretty strong, so don't scatter too many petals!

New growth will return quickly in the springtime if the clumps are not disturbed or accidentally dug up during winter. Sink a plant marker in the soil next to the chive clump and label it so that you remember not to disturb this spot when digging over the garden. However, if you wish to replant, then it is a good idea to divide the clumps in winter while they are dormant and replant them about 20 centimetres apart.

Garlic chives Garlic chives are quite different from regular chives. They grow more vigorously and grow much taller. The leaves are strap-like rather than hollow and the tight-green pointed buds open to flowers that are white and prettily star-shaped. Garlic chives are very heavy feeders and the leaves die back in winter. Lift and divide the clumps every three years.

Container Planting Chives and garlic chives, like most herbs, are ideal to grow in a pot. Keep the soil moist and the plant should flourish. Combine with other sun-loving herbs in the same pot.

Preparing and Sharing **Chives** Before chopping chives, inspect them closely. Sometimes the harvester will inadvertently include stems that are yellow or slimy. Children may need to be alerted to this so they are more discriminating next time they pick them. It is often easier to snip chives directly onto the food to be garnished using kitchen scissors rather than chopping on a board with a knife. Chives are part of the classic French herb combination of flat-leaf parsley, chives, chervil and tarragon that makes *fines herbes*. Used either alone or in the *fines herbes* combination, they add a delightful and discreet onion note to dishes featuring smoked fish, beetroot, fresh cheeses and scrambled eggs. Another classic herb combination has finely chopped chives, chervil and tarragon mixed with butter to make the flavoured compound butter, Beurre Ravigote (see page 235). Chives are also often used as a finishing garnish on soups, especially tomato-based ones or those incorporating seafood. Like their *fines herbes* companion chervil, chives should be added at the end of cooking as heat destroys their flavour.

Garlic chives Chives and garlic chives are certainly not interchangeable. Garlic chives are very 'garlicky' and need only the very briefest cooking. Some cooks insist they are better steamed than stir-fried. Chinese cookery authorities are just as definite in their preference for stir-frying. Chinese cooks also prefer garlic chives before the bud has opened as this guarantees that they are young and tender. Sometimes garlic chives are blanched in the garden (see page 687), so that their flavour is milder. Blanched garlic chives are easily recognised in Chinese markets as they are yellow rather than green.

Especially for Kids Children need to be shown how to harvest chives. Cut what is needed with scissors, leaving about 8 centimetres of stem behind, which will continue to grow.

Cultural differences in attitudes towards how best to prepare garlic chives can be discussed when cooking with garlic chives, offering a good moment to initiate a discussion about there rarely being only one way that is the right way (and that appreciating cultural differences is fascinating and often illuminating).

Garlic chives

Chive Omelette

SERVES 1 Chives and fresh free-range eggs are a great combination. A thin moist omelette with a generous quantity of chives takes maybe five minutes to make, including chopping the chives and cracking the eggs. You can also make the omelette super-thin, flip it onto a clean cloth and, when it is cool, roll it lightly, cut it into thin strips and drop them into a clear broth, or add them to fried rice.

2 free-range eggs	1 tablespoon finely
1 tablespoon water	chopped chives
sea salt and freshly ground black pepper	30g/1oz unsalted butter

Break eggs into a bowl and add water, a pinch of salt and some pepper. Whisk lightly. Stir in two-thirds of the chopped chives.

Heat a small non-stick frying pan over medium heat. Add 20g/¾oz of the butter. As soon as it is foaming, tip in egg mixture and immediately tilt the pan so that the egg runs all over the bottom where it will start to set at once. Using a wooden spatula, drag cooked edges to the middle and again tilt the pan so that the uncooked mixture flows to the edges. The uncooked surface should still look moist and shiny. The omelette is cooked.

Give the pan a sharp shove away from you to start the furthest edge flipping up the sides and rolling over and the near side of omelette to fold over. Slide omelette onto a heated serving plate (the omelette will taste just as good if you serve it unfolded on your plate!). Skim surface with remaining butter and scatter over remaining chives, then serve.

Blini with Chives

MAKES 12–15 These tender little yeast pancakes are the perfect accompaniment to smoked salmon, trout or eel. Sift 60g/2oz plain flour, 50 g/1¾oz buckwheat flour and a pinch of salt into a bowl. Stir in 2 teaspoons dry yeast. Separate yolk and white of 1 free-range egg into separate bowls, then lightly whisk yolk. Warm 150ml/5fl oz milk to just warm and add to egg yolk. Whisk in 60ml/2fl oz sour cream. Make a well in dry ingredients and pour in egg yolk mixture, then stir to form a smooth batter, cover, then leave for 1 hour or until well risen and bubbly. Whisk egg white to snowy peaks and fold into batter. Leave batter for another 30 minutes. Heat clarified butter (see page 704) in a non-stick frying pan. Working in batches, add as many ladlefuls of batter as fit in the pan, using about 1 tablespoon batter for each blini. Leave blini to set. When bubbles appear on the uncooked side generously sprinkle with chopped chives and turn over. Cook other sides, dribbling in a little extra melted clarified butter if necessary. Transfer blini to a warmed plate and continue until all are cooked.

Prawn, Pork and Garlic Chive Wonton Soup

SERVES 4 The best wrappers to use for these wontons are round and known as gow gee wrappers. They are sold in Asian grocery stores and the refrigerator section of larger supermarkets and are considerably smaller in diameter than gyoza wrappers. If you can't find them you will need to cut down gyoza or square wonton wrappers so that the dumplings look dainty in the soup bowl. Wrappers freeze and thaw perfectly. Each packet usually holds around fifty. It is smart to divide the packet and freeze what you don't intend to use in this recipe. Remember to label and date the containers.

EXTRA EQUIPMENT
wok
food processor
long-handled brass
  skimmer or slotted
  spoon

1 teaspoon peanut oil
1 small handful garlic chives, cut
  into 5mm/¼in lengths
20 gow gee wrappers (available
  in Asian food stores)
1.25 litres/2 pints well-flavoured
  chicken stock
1 teaspoon red rice vinegar (see
  page 705) or black vinegar

WONTON FILLING
100g/3½oz prawn meat, roughly
  chopped
125g/4½oz minced pork
1 teaspoon grated ginger
½ teaspoon white sugar
½ teaspoon sesame oil
½ teaspoon light soy sauce
2 teaspoons oyster sauce
¼ teaspoon salt

Heat a wok over high heat and splash in peanut oil. Stir-fry garlic chives for about 30 seconds or until a vivid green. Turn onto a paper towel-lined plate and leave to cool.

To make the wonton filling, put all ingredients into a food processor. Add two-thirds of the stir-fried garlic chives, then process to form a smooth paste. Scrape into a bowl and chill in the refrigerator for at least 30 minutes.

Set out a bowl with a small amount of cold water and a pastry brush. Place 1 heaped teaspoonful of filling mixture in a wrapper and brush edges with cold water to slightly dampen them. Fold edges over to make a half-moon shape and pinch to seal. Continue with filling and wrappers until all wontons are made.

Bring a saucepan of water to simmering point over high heat. Place chicken stock in another saucepan and bring to a simmer over high heat, then reduce heat to low and keep warm. Drop wontons into simmering water and cook for 6 minutes. Lift out using a slotted spoon and drain. Drop cooked wontons into barely simmering chicken stock for 2 minutes.

Divide vinegar among 4 soup bowls. Scoop wontons into bowls and ladle over broth. Scatter with reserved garlic chives and serve.

Shanghai Noodles with Sliced Beef and Garlic Chives

SERVES 2 This delicious dish can easily be doubled but you will need to use a very large wok unless you cook it in batches.

150g/5oz rump steak, topside or
   porterhouse, thinly sliced against the grain
250g/9oz thick fresh Shanghai wheat noodles
1½ tablespoons peanut oil
1 tablespoon oyster sauce
2 teaspoons dark soy sauce
1 teaspoon white sugar
1 lime-green pepper or 1 sweet red pepper,
   seeded and sliced into 5mm/¼in-wide strips
60g/2oz garlic chives, cut into 5mm/¼in
   lengths

MARINADE

1 clove garlic, finely
   chopped
2 teaspoons oyster sauce
2 teaspoons light
   soy sauce
1 teaspoon white sugar
2 teaspoons cornflour
a few drops sesame oil

EXTRA EQUIPMENT
wok
wok sang (see
   page 47)

To make the marinade, mix all ingredients in a bowl. Add beef, then cover with plastic film and refrigerate for 30 minutes or longer.

Bring a saucepan of water to the boil over high heat. Drop in noodles, then stir briefly to ensure they are not clumping together. Simmer for 3 minutes and drain in a colander in the sink, then run under cold water. Shake to drain, then add a few drops of the peanut oil and mix through. Set aside until needed.

Mix together oyster sauce, dark soy sauce and sugar and set aside.

Heat a wok over high heat, then splash in remaining oil. Stir-fry sliced pepper for 1 minute. Add beef and marinade and stir-fry for 1 minute. Add noodles and garlic chives and stir-fry for about 2 minutes or until noodles are a glossy brown and everything is very hot. Tip in oyster sauce mixture and stir to mix. Serve at once.

CORIANDER

Apiaceae family (includes carrots, celery, chervil, fennel, parsley and parsnips)

Annual

Soil type
Moist, fertile, well-drained soil.

Soil preparation
As long as the soil is well drained and enriched in organic matter, no additional preparation is required.

Climate
Suitable for all climates.

Position
Prefers full sun or partial shade.

How to grow
Sow direct into the ground in April-May. Thin out seedlings to 20cm apart. Coriander can also be sown in autumn on window sills.

Water requirements
Keep soil moist.

Successive planting
Leave about 2 weeks between each planting.

When to fertilise
Use a liquid fertiliser (see page 691) or worm tea (see page 695) every 2–3 weeks.

Harvest period
Leaves can be cut and used after 6 weeks. If you require the roots for cooking, you can pull the plant out of the ground if it is more than 15cm tall. The seeds can also be collected and dried.

Companion planting
Coriander is reputed to repel aphids, so it can be used as a companion for plants with aphid issues, although it should not be planted near roses or fennel. Plant with potatoes, spinach and radishes.

Special information
Keep soil moist and free from weeds by mulching. Coriander will bolt to seed very quickly in hot weather (see page 687).

Quantities to plant for a family of four
2 plants every 2 weeks, throughout the growing season.

Coriander (*Coriandrum sativum*)

Growing and Harvesting Coriander loves sunshine yet prefers to be protected from extreme heat and can bolt (see page 687) in very hot weather. You can start cutting the leaves about six weeks after sowing, once the plants are around 15 centimetres tall, or you can harvest an entire plant at this stage if you need the roots for cooking as well as the leaves. Allow some plants to continue to grow and flower. Coriander has very pretty pale-pink flowers.

If you wish to collect the seeds, cut the whole plant as soon as the green 'fruits' start to change colour to a pale brown or they will quickly drop from the plant. Dry the plant completely on a tray or newspaper away from wind or flying dust. Separate the seeds from the dried seed head by shaking it in a paper bag, then dry the seeds thoroughly and spread out on a tray before storing for use in the kitchen or the garden.

Only use plants that are green without any traces of yellow. You can harvest leaves and stems as you need them, only pulling the roots if you require them for a specific recipe.

Container Planting Like most herbs, coriander is ideal for growing in a pot. You may wish to combine it with another herb or herbs, especially those suited to Asian food, such as mint, Vietnamese mint or garlic chives.

Preparing and Sharing In the cuisines of many countries coriander seeds are as highly prized as the leaves. They combine well with many different spices and aromatics and, perhaps surprisingly, taste totally unlike the flavour of the leaves or roots. Coriander seeds are reminiscent of the smell of slightly scorched orange peel. They are used in breads and cakes, in spice mixtures such as rubs or marinades and in vegetable braises, such as vegetables cooked in the style known in French as *à la grecque*. Add a few roasted crushed seeds to a lamb or pork casserole. They can also lend a mysterious note to marmalade.

If using the seeds, always roast them in a small, dry frying pan over medium heat until fragrant before grinding (this is called dry-roasting), and only prepare what you are going to use in the next day or so. Dry-roasted ground coriander combines magnificently with dry-roasted ground cumin seeds and I use this combination almost as often as I use freshly ground pepper. I usually use up to four parts coriander seed to one part cumin seed. Some cooks will prefer more cumin.

Coriander roots and stems hold lots of dirt so each plant must be washed very well before using. Never wash the leaves until you are just ready to use them. They will lose aroma and also become very dank and start to deteriorate as soon as they are wet.

Coriander leaves are an essential garnish in so many South-East Asian dishes, either chopped or picked as sprigs. In Indian cooking they are used in cooling yoghurt-based sauces called raitas to accompany curries. The roots are pounded with garlic and black peppercorns to give Thai food its distinctive flavour. In most of these cultures the leaves and stems are used fresh, as a final garnish to a dish. Coriander leaves lose their aromatic oils when they are heated, so they are generally not cooked. Recipes from the United States will refer to coriander as cilantro.

I have given both weight and bunch estimates in the following recipes just in case you don't have a lush patch of coriander in your garden.

Especially for Kids Children will be intrigued to notice how different the aroma of the leaves is from the aroma of the roasted, ground seeds. An interesting comparison would be with the leaves and seeds of fennel.

Using a mortar and pestle is one of the favourite tasks for young cooks. Buy the largest one you can find as small mortars will have spices bouncing all over the bench. The mortars made of volcanic rock found in Asian food shops are good value and come in many sizes. Children may need to be shown how to crush the seeds gently first before grinding them to a powder with other ingredients. Similarly, when making a paste of coriander roots with black peppercorns (or any other spice paste) the action will involve a combination of thumping the pestle down into the mortar, and then using it to grind ingredients against the sides.

Coriander is prized by so many cultures and used in such widely diverse ways that it is an excellent plant to illustrate culinary diversity. When your coriander is growing prolifically, it might be fun to make and taste dishes using coriander that originate in the Middle East, South-East Asia (the Coriander and Coconut Sambal on page 250), India (the Kofta Curry with Coriander Sauce on page 249), Portugal, South America and Mexico (the Tomato and Coriander Salsa on page 251) over the course of a few days or weeks, and talk about the differences.

The leaves are sometimes said to smell like squashed ants. What do you think?

Kofta Curry with Coriander Sauce

SERVES 4 Every Indian and Middle Eastern food writer is enthusiastic about the deliciously spiced meatballs known as kofta. It does make you wonder why our own hamburger tradition is so unadventurous! The sauce for this simple curry uses masses of coriander and you can use the stems as well as the leaves. The kofta can also be fried and served without the sauce, simply slipped into flatbreads with some fresh yoghurt and a flat-leaf parsley and green leaf salad.

EXTRA EQUIPMENT
food processor
mortar and pestle
electric mixer with
    paddle beater
    attachment
simmer mat

Simple Flatbread (see page 294, or use purchased) or steamed rice, to serve

KOFTA
20g/¾oz coriander leaves and stems (about ½ bunch), well washed
1 onion, roughly chopped
1 × 1.5cm/½in long piece ginger, peeled and roughly chopped
3 cloves garlic, roughly chopped
2 teaspoons cumin seeds
2 teaspoons coriander seeds
500g/1lb minced lamb
1 teaspoon sea salt
1 teaspoon chilli powder
1 free-range egg

CORIANDER SAUCE
1 fresh long green chilli, seeded and sliced
50g/2oz coriander leaves and stems, well washed and dried
1 × 2cm/¾in-long piece ginger, peeled and roughly chopped
4 cloves garlic, roughly chopped
60ml/2fl oz extra-virgin olive oil
8 green cardamom pods, lightly bruised with back of a knife
2 tablespoons Tony Tan's Simple Curry Powder (see page 143)
1 large onion, finely chopped
1 × 400g/14oz tin chopped tomatoes
60ml/2fl oz water
sea salt
140g/5oz Greek-style yoghurt (see page 706)

To make the kofta, put coriander leaves and stems, onion, ginger and garlic in a food processor and whiz to form a smooth paste. Separately dry-roast cumin seeds and coriander seeds in a small frying pan over medium heat until they smell fragrant. Grind the spices with a mortar and pestle to form a fine powder. Put minced lamb, coriander/onion mixture, roasted spices, salt, chilli powder and egg into an electric mixer fitted with a paddle beater attachment. Beat the mixture on medium–high speed for 5 minutes until it looks very smooth and pasty. With wet hands, shape mixture into 4cm/1½in-diameter balls; you should have 16–20 kofta. Cover with plastic film and refrigerate.

To make the coriander sauce, put chilli, coriander leaves and stems, ginger and garlic into a food processor and whiz to form a smooth paste. Heat oil in a large heavy-based non-stick frying pan or sauté pan over medium heat and sauté cardamom pods for 30 seconds. Add curry powder and cook for another 30 seconds. Add onion, stir well and cook for 4–5 minutes or until well softened.

>>>

Add chilli/coriander paste and cook for 2 minutes, then add tomato, water and a good pinch of salt. Stir well and cook over low heat for 10 minutes or until well thickened. You can set the sauce aside at this stage if you want to prepare it in advance, then reheat it gently before proceeding with the recipe.

Stir yoghurt into sauce, a spoonful at a time. You may need to add a little water to the sauce at this point, if it seems a little thick. Slip in kofta. Cover pan and simmer over low heat for 30 minutes, using a simmer mat so the sauce doesn't stick. Give the pan a gentle shake every 10 minutes but don't stir as yoghurt may split. Serve with Green Chutney (see below), your choice of vegetable accompaniment and some simple flatbread (see page 294) or steamed rice.

Green Chutney

MAKES ABOUT 180ML/6FL OZ Make this chutney as close to eating it as possible as the vibrant green dulls after a few hours. It can be made as hot as you like. I like it spooned onto almost any vegetable, even steamed new potatoes.

		EXTRA EQUIPMENT
1 fresh long green chilli (or more if you like), seeded and sliced	20g/¾oz coriander leaves and stems (about ½ bunch), well washed, dried and roughly chopped	food processor coarse-meshed stainless-steel sieve
15 large sprigs mint, leaves picked	1 tomato, chopped juice of ½ lemon sea salt	

Put chilli, mint leaves, coriander leaves and stems, tomato and lemon juice into a food processor, then process to form a coarse green paste. Scrape the paste into a coarse-meshed sieve resting over a bowl and let excess liquid drain for 15 minutes. Taste for salt and season if necessary. Transfer drained chutney to a small serving bowl and serve.

Coriander and Coconut Sambal

MAKES 125ML/4½ FL OZ This pungent Malaysian side dish (sambal) uses shrimp paste or *blachan*. Made from salted fermented tiny shrimps, it smells astonishing, but when combined with hot, sweet and sour elements it becomes a tantalising sambal that is perfect with grilled seafood. Palm sugar is becoming increasingly available in supermarkets; otherwise it can be found in Asian food stores. The base will keep for weeks in the refrigerator without the coconut, lime and coriander. Once you have stirred in the fresh ingredients, use within two days. Add additional chillies if you want extra punch!

>>>

EXTRA EQUIPMENT
food processor

1 fresh long green chilli, seeded and sliced
1 large French shallot (or 2 smaller), roughly chopped
1½ tablespoons shrimp paste (see page 706)
2 cloves garlic, roughly chopped
1 × 2cm/¾in-long piece ginger, peeled and roughly chopped

1 tablespoon grated palm sugar or soft brown sugar
2 tablespoons peanut oil
2 tablespoons desiccated coconut
juice of ½ lime
40g/1½oz coriander leaves and stems (about 1 bunch), well washed, dried and finely chopped

Put chilli, shallot, shrimp paste, garlic, ginger and sugar into a food processor and process to form a fine paste. Transfer to a small bowl and stir in peanut oil. Heat a medium-sized non-stick frying pan over medium heat and tip in paste. Stir continuously for 2 minutes; it will darken as the sugar caramelises.

Scrape paste into a bowl, then stir in coconut, lime juice and coriander. Taste to check there is a balance of sweet, salty, hot and sour.

Tomato and Coriander Salsa

MAKES 500ML/18FL OZ This fresh-tasting salsa is great spooned over eggs, grilled meats or fish, or used as a topping on flatbread. Simple combinations like this are a staple of the Mexican diet. This salsa is at its best when made from home-ripened tomatoes and home-grown coriander.

½ red onion, finely diced
2 tablespoons red-wine vinegar
2 fresh hot red chillies, finely chopped
2 cloves garlic, finely chopped

4 large ripe tomatoes, halved widthways, gently squeezed to remove seeds and finely diced
30g/1oz coriander leaves and stems, well washed and dried (about ⅓ bunch)

Put onion into a small bowl, cover with vinegar and leave for 30 minutes. Drain onion, pressing hard with the back of a spoon to extract as much vinegar as possible. Discard vinegar. Wash and dry bowl and tip onion back in. Stir in chilli, garlic, tomato and coriander and serve.

CORN

Poaceae family

Annual

Soil type
Well drained deep soil rich in organic matter.

Soil preparation
Plant in a bed after a nitrogen-fixing crop such as broad beans or peas, or dig in well-rotted manure a few weeks prior to planting.

Climate
Prefers a warm, sheltered site and a climate with a long growing seasons.

Position
Prefers full sun with protection from wind.

How to grow
Sow seed in April in small but deep pots in warmth (needs a minimum 15°C to germinate). Grow on in heated greenhouse, gradually harden-off (see page 692) and plant after there is no danger of frost (mid May

to June). In areas with a long growing season, seed can be sown direct from late May to June onwards. Space plants 30–35cm apart with 60cm between rows, grow in blocks rather than long rows to assist wind pollination.

Water requirements
Water plants in to keep soil moist, but take care after pollination not to wet the tassels. No need to water until flowering begins.

When to fertilise
Use a liquid fertiliser (see page 691) or worm tea (see page 695) when planting and then fertilise every 4 weeks.

Harvest period
12–14 weeks after planting.

Pests and organic control
Mice nibble the seeds, particularly when the seeds are sown direct into the soil. Starting off in pots helps. Frit fly maggots

can damage the plants, again raising in pots and growing under a crop cover until June can help.

Companion planting
Cabbages, lettuce, pumpkin and potatoes. Avoid growing near tomatoes. Can be used as a climbing frame for beans and peas. Squash can be grown at the base of corn as live mulch.

Special information
If plants are too close together poor pollination will result. Protect from wind. Earth up seedlings to encourage root growth. Keep the soil moist and free from weeds by mulching. One planting only – a block is made up of 18 plants.

Quantities to plant for a family of four
18 or more plants.

Corn (*Zea mays*)

Growing and Harvesting Corn is fast-growing, taking only twelve to fourteen weeks to reach maturity. It provides a useful windbreak for other plants during the hot summer and can also be used as a climbing frame for beans or peas. Pollination is all-important. Corn pollen is transferred by the wind from the male flower (the tassel) onto the the female flower (the silk).

Be clear whether you are planting a hybrid cultivar or a traditional non-hybrid. Refer to seed catalogue, if you are unsure. In traditional non-hybrids, the sugar in the young corn turns to starch within hours of being picked, so speedy preparation is essential! For maximum flavour, don't pick the crop one day and eat it the next. Hybrid cultivars, on the other hand, have had their sugar levels increased and the transfer to starch is delayed, making the speed of picking and eating not as critical. Most hybrids are either sugar-enhanced or super sweet. The latter are so sweet the cobs can be eaten raw.

Corn is a 'hungry' crop and is particularly good planted in a bed previously occupied by peas or broad beans. Try planting pumpkins and squash or quick-growing salad greens at the base of the growing corn to utilise the space between the rows.

Harvest corn when the silks have turned brown and the ear feels full – usually about three weeks after the silks appear. Children will enjoy checking the corn's progress: pull back a husk a little and press a thumbnail into a kernel. It should squirt a milky liquid. Clear liquid will indicate that the corn needs more time.

Container Planting Corn is not suitable for planting in a pot or tub.

Preparing and Sharing My grandpa grew magnificent corn and my siblings and I all sang the ridiculous line from the musical *Oklahoma* about how the corn was 'as high as an elephant's eye'. We ate fresh corn for breakfast, lunch and sometimes for dinner too. I chomped down each row with obsessive precision and always started back at the beginning of the next row, like shooting home the carriage of a typewriter ('What is a typewriter?' I am sure will be asked). The others preferred the bigger bite technique, taking in several rows at once. We all spread the corn with lots of butter. Mum also devised delicious corn fritters when she wanted a change. Made with an egg (probably a duck egg), a spoonful of plain flour, lots of sliced-off cooked kernels and a little milk if needed, they were delicious with smoked bacon or with a homemade tomato sauce (see page 649).

Everyone loves corn on the cob. One of the best ways of cooking it is on the barbecue, perhaps right in the garden. You pull back the husk, remove all the silk, dampen the husk and rewrap it around the ear of corn and then grill the corn cob on the hot barbecue. A Mexican alternative to grilled corn brushed with butter, salt and pepper is to brush the hot corn cob with cream and sprinkle it with chilli powder or sometimes grated cheese just before eating. If you are not barbecuing the cob, then strip off its husk and silk immediately prior to cooking, leaving the stems on for easy eating. When I boil corn cobs I don't salt the water first as I find this toughens the kernels.

As well as the well-loved corn on the cob, use your fresh corn to make dishes using scraped corn kernels such as Annie Smithers' Superb Corn Fritters on page 258 or Kylie Kwong's Sweetcorn Soup on page 257. Rake raw corn kernels with a fork to split the skins before slicing the kernels from the cob (see page 256). If children are helping it would be a good idea for an adult to be standing by to assist with this task.

It is also intriguing to understand the differences between the cornmeal (finely ground) used to make baked goods and bread, and polenta (coarser in texture), available in both white and yellow varieties which are used to make the porridgy Northern Italian staple of the same name. Cooked polenta can either be soft, like porridge, or firm, to be grilled. Cornflour is used as a thickening agent.

If you are lucky enough to harvest a bumper crop, I suggest freezing the cobs in dated freezer bags, husks, silk and all.

Especially for Kids Corn is a magical crop for children to experience. It is interesting for children to make the connection between the corn they eat on the cob and the coarse grain, polenta, and to realise that there are different families of corn that are each best for different uses. It could be a good time for older children to make their first batch of soft polenta. They will love to have a go at making a simple version of tamales using polenta and reserved husks as a wrapping. To do this, they could mound spoonfuls of cooled soft polenta in dampened corn husks and steam them to make a simple version of a tamale. If you have already made a batch they can experience both soft 'wet' polenta and grilled, cooled firm polenta.

It is possible to spend a lifetime investigating the history of corn and its importance to the diet and trade of those in the Americas and how its use spread to the rest of the world. Older children may be intrigued to know that maize (as corn is more correctly known) is one of the most important cereal crops in the world. A good discussion could be had about some of the surprising products derived from corn, such as cardboard cartons, soap and toothpaste.

Do all dried corn kernels pop? This is a good time to point out that you can't dry your own corn kernels for popcorn as it is made from a different variety whose kernels have hard outer skins.

Kylie Kwong's Sweetcorn Soup

SERVES 4 I was so pleased to find this recipe in Sydney chef Kylie Kwong's cookbook *Simple Chinese Cooking* as, like Kylie, I was dismayed to find that every other Chinese recipe that I consulted made versions of this soup using canned creamed corn. Corn is a favourite of mine and a very successful crop in the kitchen garden. The whole family will enjoy this delicious way of using fresh corn. Kylie says in the introduction to her recipe, 'The addition of eggs in the final stages of cooking creates a ribboning effect that subtly thickens the soup, and the combination of crunchy corn kernels and fluffy gelatinous eggs works perfectly.'

4 cobs corn, husks and
 silk removed
2 tablespoons vegetable oil
1 small white onion, finely diced
2 tablespoons ginger julienne
1 clove garlic, finely diced
1 teaspoon sea salt

125ml/4½fl oz shao hsing wine
 (see page 706) or dry sherry
1.75 litres/3 pints homemade
 chicken stock
1½ teaspoons light soy sauce
2 free-range eggs, lightly beaten
1 tablespoon thinly sliced
 spring onion

Remove kernels from corn cobs by first raking the corn kernels with a fork to split the skins, then cutting the kernels from the cobs with a sharp knife (see opposite). You should have about 3 cups of corn kernels.

Heat oil in a medium-sized heavy-based saucepan over medium heat and sauté onion, ginger, garlic and salt for 1 minute. Add wine or sherry and simmer for another minute or until liquid has reduced by half. Stir in corn and stock and bring to the boil. Reduce heat to low and simmer gently for 30 minutes. During the cooking time you may need to skim the surface of the soup occasionally to remove any impurities.

Stir in soy sauce. Slowly pour beaten egg into soup in a thin stream, stirring constantly with a fork. Remove soup from the heat as soon as you see the egg forming fine 'ribbons'.

Serve soup in bowls and garnish with spring onion.

Preparing corn for Kylie Kwong's Sweetcorn Soup

Annie Smithers' Superb Corn Fritters

MAKES ABOUT 15 FRITTERS One of the best reasons to visit Kyneton in Victoria is to eat at Annie Smithers' Bistrot. Annie worked with me for several years and we have an annual date to harvest my crabapple crop to make a fresh batch of her excellent crabapple jelly. Recently I happened to be in Kyneton and I had these stunning crisp-edged corn fritters with local bacon and green zebra tomatoes. What a treat. Annie believes the secret is cooking them in clarified butter rather than oil and I think she is correct. The batter must stand for at least one hour or up to two. I have also discovered that 250 grams/9 ounces peeled frozen broad beans or soy beans can be used instead of corn.

100g/3½oz butter
3 cobs corn, husks
   and silk removed
240g/8½oz plain flour
3 teaspoons baking powder
a pinch salt
1 free-range egg

430ml/15fl oz milk
1 tablespoon chopped
   flat-leaf parsley
1 teaspoon chopped chives
30g/1oz butter, melted
bacon and maple syrup (optional),
   to serve

EXTRA EQUIPMENT
small ladle (about
   50ml/2fl oz-
   capacity)

To clarify butter, melt butter in a small saucepan over low heat and cook for 5 minutes or until milk solids fall to the bottom of the pan like light-golden specks and butter resembles deep golden oil. Remove from heat at once. Spoon or tip through a very fine strainer, leaving brown specks in pan. Any extra clarified butter can be covered and stored in the refrigerator for several weeks.

Fill a large heavy-based saucepan or pasta pot with water and bring to the boil over high heat. Drop corn cobs into simmering water and cook for 8 minutes, then test if corn is tender by lifting out a cob and piercing a kernel with a skewer. If tender, remove cobs to a colander resting in the sink. Leave to cool a little. When cool enough to handle, stand each cob on its end, then remove kernels by running a sharp knife down sides of each one. You should have about 250g/9oz corn.

Sift flour, baking powder and salt into a large mixing bowl, then make a well. Whisk egg with milk and pour into dry ingredients. Whisk well until you have a smooth batter, then add herbs, corn and melted butter. Allow batter to stand for 1 hour at room temperature, covered with a tea towel.

Heat a film of clarified butter in a non-stick frying pan over medium heat, then use a small ladle to ladle in a few portions of batter. Leave to cook until underside is golden. Flip over and cook through. Continue until all batter is used, adding clarified butter as needed. Serve corn fritters immediately, with bacon and maple syrup, if desired.

CRESSES

Brassicaceae family (includes broccoli, cabbage, cauliflower, radishes and turnips)

Biennial

Soil type
Moist soil, rich in organic matter.

Soil preparation
Not required.

Climate
Suitable for all climates.

Position
Prefers partial shade.

When to plant
All climates: all year round.

How to grow
Seeds can be grown indoors or outdoors. To sow indoors at any time, place seeds onto a moist layer of seed-raising mix. Cover with a sheet of moist paper until seedlings emerge. Keep moist.

To sow outdoors (March–July), sprinkle seed onto seed-raising mix or fine soil and keep moist. Harvest seedlings as needed or thin out and grow into larger plants.

Water requirements
Water frequently to keep soil moist. Don't allow to dry out over summer or it will bolt (see page 687) and the leaves will become bitter.

Successive planting
Leave about 4 weeks between each planting, throughout the growing season.

When to fertilise
To ensure vigorous growth, use a liquid fertiliser (see page 691) or worm tea (see page 695) once every 4 weeks.

Harvest period
Harvest leaves before flowering. Cut with scissors when about 5–10 cm high.

Pests and organic control
Use crushed egg shells around the base of the young plants to deter snails and slugs.

Companion planting
Use companion plants such as corn or sunflowers for shade during the hotter months.

Special information
Keep the soil moist and free from weeds by mulching.

Quantities to plant for a family of four
2 plants every 4 weeks, throughout the growing season.

Watercress (*Nasturtium officinale*)

Growing and Harvesting Cress is the common name for more than a dozen sharp, pungent, small-leafed plants related to the mustards. The group includes watercress (which is closely related to the nasturtium, and it is easy to smell the relationship), upland cress and miniature cress shoots. Many cresses grow fast and without difficulty. The difficulty lies in getting them to the table at the right moment for maximum enjoyment.

All cresses are more or less sharp and very pungent. As one would for rocket, both watercress and upland cress should be picked while still young enough to be palatable without any hint of yellow or 'old radish' smell. If you overlook these considerations, you will ensure their rejection at the table.

Watercress requires moist soil at all times – it grows well in water and can be picked right through the winter once well established. The flavour diminishes once the plant flowers. Make sure children understand the danger of picking watercress from an unknown waterway. (Liver fluke, a parasite of cattle and sheep, can also infect humans and may contaminate streams if stock drink from the water.)

Container Planting Watercress can be grown in a container if you don't have a patch of very moist soil to use just for it. Keep the pots very well watered, or else place them in a container of water. In some school kitchen gardens I've seen old baths converted into containers for aquatic plants. This is a perfect place to grow watercress. Plant it in a porous pot that can be submerged up to its rim in the water.

Preparing and Sharing Only the tender stems and soft green leaves are edible. Stems that are almost hollow and thick are sure to be tough and stringy and should be consigned to your compost bin. Some people believe that watercress should always be cooked, others that it can be part of a salad of raw ingredients – a timely reminder of the adage that 'one man's meat is another man's poison'. 'Watercress stir-fried with beef but *never* in a salad,' says one Chinese cook I know. In contrast, watercress is often included in salads in South-East Asia, and little handfuls of peppery watercress served with salmon or a beefsteak are delightful. I personally enjoy adding the youngest sprigs to a mixed leaf salad for just a hint of peppery bite. Wholemeal bread sandwiches of mustard shoots and cress are superb with freshly shucked oysters. Cress shoots can be snipped over fish or egg dishes or over young cheeses just before serving. Watercress soup is delicious – try making the Watercress, Sorrel and Potato Soup on page 265.

Especially for Kids Even though most organic gardeners will prefer to grow watercress from seed, children will be fascinated to see the shoots that appear on the stems of purchased or picked watercress held in a water-filled glass jug after just a few days. These shooting stems can be successfully planted in the garden. Similarly, it is exciting for very young gardeners to grow mustard and cress seedlings together in a punnet on a windowsill. See also my comments about **Window boxes** on page 695. The mustard seedlings will appear a few days before the cress seedlings.

If children have grown mustard and cress the seedlings can be cut as needed (using sharp scissors) to make a spicy sandwich filling. The spiciness can be balanced by adding a soft mild cream cheese or sliced avocado.

Mustard Cress Butter

MAKES 120G/4OZ This butter is so wonderful to have on hand when making the quintessential afternoon tea treat of cucumber sandwiches. The bread used would ideally be wholemeal, the butter should be generously applied, the cucumber should be cut wafer-thin and there should be plenty of it. Very tiny mustard cress sandwiches would be superb served alongside freshly shucked oysters too.

EXTRA EQUIPMENT
food processor
(optional)

60g/2oz unsalted butter, softened
a few drops lemon juice

¼ small handful snipped mustard
cress, coarsely chopped
sea salt and freshly ground pepper

Either combine all ingredients in a food processor or work them all together in a bowl using a fork. Scrape butter into a piece of baking paper and form into a roll. Wrap roll in a doubled piece of foil and store in the refrigerator for a day or so or for up to 3 months in the freezer. Bring butter to room temperature before attempting to spread it on bread.

Chilled Stir-fried Watercress

SERVES 4 AS AN ACCOMPANIMENT Pick over a large bunch of watercress, reserving just the young stems with tender leaves. Wash, dry in a salad spinner, then pick off the leaves and cut the young stems into 5mm/¼in lengths. Mix leaves and chopped stems, then scatter over a little sea salt and leave in a colander for 30 minutes. Drain and squeeze in a tea towel to remove excess liquid. Heat a wok over high heat, then splash in a little vegetable oil. Stir-fry watercress for 30 seconds, scoop into a dish, add a few drops of sesame oil and then chill. Serve as an accompaniment to the Beancurd Salad on page 606.

Watercress, Sorrel and Potato Soup

SERVES 4 This recipe calls for more watercress than sorrel, but if you happen to have more sorrel than watercress on hand, just reverse the proportions given in the recipe below and the results will be fine. To remove the sorrel leaves from the stems, bend each sorrel leaf in half and pull the stem up and along the leaf (a bit like pulling up a zip). The stem end and the central stem will come away, leaving you with two pieces of leaf. If you like, you can float a slice of the Mustard Cress Butter on page 263 on top of the soup, or use the same quantity of watercress to make the butter and use this instead (see opposite).

EXTRA EQUIPMENT
blender, food
processor or
food mill
coarse-meshed
stainless-steel
sieve

30g/1oz unsalted butter (or even
    better, use the Mustard Cress
    Butter on page 263)
2 spring onions, trimmed and sliced
2 cloves garlic, finely chopped
450g/15oz waxy potatoes, cut into
    2cm/¾in cubes
1 bay leaf
1 litre/1¾ pints water

65g/2¼oz picked watercress leaves
    and tender stems, well
    washed and dried
60g/2oz sorrel leaves, well washed,
    dried and stems removed
sea salt and freshly ground pepper
Mustard Cress Butter (see
    page 263, optional), to serve

Melt butter in a large saucepan over medium heat and sauté spring onion and garlic for 2 minutes. Add potato and bay leaf and turn so that potato sweats in the butter. Stir with a wooden spoon. Add water, bring to the simmer over medium heat then cover and cook gently over low heat for 15 minutes or until potato is tender. Drop in watercress and sorrel, increase heat to medium and simmer for 2 minutes. Remove bay leaf.

Using a ladle or a measuring cup, carefully transfer batches of soup to a blender, food processor or food mill and purée soup; if using a blender don't over-fill and hold lid down with a tea towel-wrapped hand to ensure that steam does not force lid off during first few seconds of blending. For a lovely baby purée-smooth soup, pour each batch through a coarse-meshed stainless-steel sieve into a clean, large saucepan or mixing bowl if not using immediately (otherwise transfer directly to saucepan or mixing bowl). When all is smooth, taste for salt and pepper and season as required. Reheat gently to serve. Top each serve with a slice of mustard cress butter if desired.

CUCUMBERS

Cucurbitaceae family (includes melon, pumpkin and zucchini)

Annual

Soil type
Well drained and rich in organic matter.

Soil preparation
Dig in organic matter or well-rotted manure a few weeks prior to planting.

Climate
Suitable for all climates if you have a greenhouse.

Position
Prefer full sun and sheltered from wind.

How to grow
Sow seed in small pots in April indoors or in a heated greenhouse, they need 25°C to germinate. Grow on and then harden-off (see page 692) well before planting out after there is no danger of frost (mid May-June). As you only need a couple of plants, you can just buy potted plants from a garden centre. To grow outside a warm, sunny, sheltered spot is needed but they can also be grown in a greenhouse or polytunnel. Provide supports and tie in young growth.

Water requirements
Water frequently during the growing period. Under-watering may make vines drop fruit.

Successive planting
Plants are very productive so continued sowing is not necessary.

When to fertilise
To ensure vigorous growth, use a liquid fertiliser (see page 291) or worm tea (see page 295) once every 4 weeks.

Harvest period
8 weeks after planting (or when the small hairs of the fruit can be brushed off easily). Frequent harvesting increases production.

Pests and organic control
Powdery mildew tends to take its toll at the end of the season, keep plants watered and fed and keep good air circulation around plants to keep it at bay. Root rots and red spider mite can be a problem. Careful watering, avoiding the stem and damping down greenhouse paths to keep the air humid can help avoid problems.

Companion planting
Beetroot, carrots and peas. Dill will distract insect predators and nasturtiums are a good bait plant.

Special information
Keep the soil moist and free from weeds by mulching. Cucumber is ideal for planting in mounds or raised beds. Don't plant where you have grown any member of the Cucurbitaceae family the previous year.

Quantities to plant for a family of four
3 plants every 6 weeks.

Cucumber (*Cucumis sativus*)

Growing and Harvesting Cucumbers love hot weather and are fast growers. There are many different cultivars of cucumber, some varieties are recommended for growing outdoors and others for indoors. You can also grow the outdoors ones inside in a greenhouse, in border soil or in a polytunnel, but greenhouse ones need the extra warm under cover.

Most cucumbers are usually allowed to trail, but to save space you can train them over a trellis or similar supporting structure, such as the simple frame often sold to support tomatoes. This has several advantages: it provides height in a garden, it ensures good air circulation for the vines, and it lifts much of the crop away from ground-dwelling pests. Cucumbers are pollinated by bees but can be hand-pollinated. Early in the morning, hand-pollinate the female flowers (the smaller flower with a round swelling behind it) by transferring pollen from the male flower (the one on the long stalk) using a paint brush, or break off the male flower, bend back its petals and press it against a female flower.

Cucumbers should be picked while they have plenty of crunch, before they become flabby, watery or the seeds are over-developed. Pick often to keep your bushes or vines productive. Once the vines have started to produce, check them every two days as, like zucchini, cucumbers grow fast and can be hidden under leaves.

In terms of types, I prefer the long telegraph or small Lebanese, although the round apple type has its devotees.

Container Planting Two cucumber plants would grow happily in a half-wine barrel container with a supporting frame, as mentioned above. Choose a compact cultivar that will not grow more than about a metre wide. As with all container plants, keep the soil well watered.

Preparing and Sharing Cucumbers are a popular salad ingredient. They are often to be found in combination with tomatoes, soft cheeses, smoked fish, olives and salad leaves of all colours and shapes, and with Asian ingredients such as fish sauce, chillies and garlic. I particularly like recipes, such as Kylie's Hot and Sour Cucumber Salad on page 272, that add chillies, garlic and ginger to serve as a side dish or a refreshing appetiser.

Taste a slice to decide if the skin is tough and, if so, peel it before adding it to your salad. Garden-picked cucumbers will probably not need to have their seeds removed unless they 'got away' and have grown too big. Many Asian cooks use cucumbers to make brilliant fresh pickles and salads, and cucumber is frequently combined with yoghurt as a cooling dish in many cuisines such as those of India, Turkey and Greece – Tzatziki (see page 272) is a classic example of such a dish. Cucumber is also refreshing served as a chilled soup in summer (perhaps with a blue borage flower floating on it as a delicate and pretty garnish, if you happen to also grow them). And, of course, where would afternoon tea parties be without cucumber sandwiches?

All varieties can be pickled but there are cultivars especially developed for pickling that remain small in size and have small seeds. If you would like to give pickling a go, try the recipe for my sister Diana's Bread and Butter Pickled Cucumbers on page 271.

Cucumbers can also be cooked, but you do need to beware the slimy texture! (The texture most disliked by children in the fruit and vegetable department is slippery or slimy.) Some of the best cooked cucumber dishes have them salted, rinsed and dried before proceeding. They can then be sautéed gently in butter or simmered in a small amount of stock and served with a delicate fillet of veal or fish.

Dill is good with all cucumbers, as are mint and coriander.

Especially for Kids Children can become very competent at creating frames and trellises for growing cucumbers and other trailing plants. Often these structures are made from bamboo canes or lightweight tree branches and look most attractive. Remember to attach the growing plant with soft ties – strips of cloth work well.

It may be a good idea to pick all the very small cucumbers and have a cucumber pickling day so that everyone gets to enjoy the crop rather than to return from summer holidays to find vines heavy with unappealing over-ripe specimens.

Diana's Bread and Butter Pickled Cucumbers

MAKES ABOUT 2 × 400ML/14FL OZ JARS My sister Diana has always had great success with growing cucumbers. Her version of this well-known pickle is delightful. Not only is it great served with cold cuts, it also makes a wonderful addition to a good-quality cheddar sandwich. Once a jar is opened, store it in the refrigerator. I am still using a jar I made six months ago and opened four months ago.

EXTRA EQUIPMENT
food processor with
slicing attachment
or plastic
vegetable slicer
(see page 46)
2 × 400ml/14fl oz
jars, sterilised (see
page 706)

500g/1lb freshly picked young
   cucumbers, unpeeled (the
   crunchier the better)
1 onion (about 200g/7oz), very
   thinly sliced
1½ tablespoons kitchen salt
60ml/2fl oz hot water

PICKLING LIQUID
250ml/9fl oz white vinegar
220g/8oz white sugar
2 teaspoons mustard seeds
1 teaspoon chopped dill
¼ teaspoon ground turmeric
¼ teaspoon chilli flakes

Slice cucumbers very thinly in a food processor using the slicing attachment or with a plastic vegetable slicer (this is more accurate, but more dangerous than a food processor). Mix cucumber and onion in a mixing bowl. Dissolve salt in hot water in a stainless-steel saucepan over medium heat, stirring with a wooden spoon until completely dissolved, then pour this mixture over cucumber mixture. Mix through and leave for 3 hours. Rinse saucepan.

Tip cucumber and onion into a colander resting over a plate or bowl. Press with the back of a large spoon to extract as much liquid as possible.

To make the pickling liquid, mix all ingredients in the rinsed-out saucepan. Bring to the simmer over medium heat, stirring until sugar has dissolved. Tip cucumber and onion into pickling liquid and simmer for 2–3 minutes, stirring once or twice. Remove from heat and leave to cool in the saucepan, then spoon or ladle into sterilised jars, ensuring the cucumber mixture is covered with pickling liquid. Seal, label and date the pickle.

Kylie's Hot and Sour Cucumber Salad

SERVES 4 AS PART OF A MULTI-DISH MEAL The cuisines of most cultures seem to value the refreshing quality of cucumber. Although there are many other cucumber-based salad ideas, this Chinese way by Sydney chef Kylie Kwong, published in her book *My China*, is rapidly becoming a favourite.

2 Lebanese cucumbers (about
    400g/14oz), peeled, halved
    lengthways and cut into 5mm/
    ¼in-thick slices
1 fresh long green chilli, thinly sliced
½ fresh long red chilli, thinly sliced
1 spring onion, trimmed and
    thinly sliced

DRESSING
2 cloves garlic, finely chopped
2 teaspoons soft brown sugar
2 tablespoons brown-rice vinegar
2 tablespoons light soy sauce
1 teaspoon sesame oil
1 × 2cm/¾in-long piece ginger,
    peeled and finely chopped

Place cucumber, chillies and spring onion in a bowl. To make the dressing, mix all the ingredients together and pour over the cucumber. Stir and toss to mix, then serve.

Tzatziki

MAKES 250ML/9FL OZ The combination of yoghurt and cucumber occurs in many countries, but this way is typically Greek. Tzatziki can be served as one choice on a platter of dips with warmed flatbread, or offered as a sambal with a curry, in which case it would be called raita, or served alongside barbecued meats.

1 Lebanese cucumber (about
    200g/7oz)
1 clove garlic, finely chopped
30 mint leaves, chopped
juice of 1 lemon

300g/10½fl oz Greek-style yoghurt
    (see page 706)
½ teaspoon sea salt
freshly ground black pepper

EXTRA EQUIPMENT
box grater with large
    grating holes
1 piece muslin
    (30cm × 30cm/
    12in × 12in)

Peel strips of rind from cucumber, leaving it green-and-white striped. Halve lengthways and scoop seeds into compost bucket using a sharp teaspoon. Grate cucumber coarsely (I find that the grating disc on my food processor extracts far too much liquid that has to be drained away, so I prefer to grate cucumber by hand). Mix all ingredients together in a mixing bowl. Season if necessary.

Dampen a clean piece of muslin or Chux cloth. Wring it out, settle it inside a sieve resting over a mixing bowl and scoop in tzatziki. Leave to drain for 2 hours. Serve straightaway or refrigerate, covered with plastic film, until needed.

Preparing Kylie's Hot and Sour Cucumber Salad

DILL

**Apiaceae family
(includes carrots, celery,
chervil, coriander, fennel,
parsley and parsnips)**
Annual

Soil type
Well drained and rich in
organic matter.

Soil preparation
As long as the soil is well-drained
and rich in organic matter, no
additional preparation
is required.

Climate
Prefers warm, sunny sites.

Position
Prefers full sun.

How to grow
Directly sow seeds at a depth
of 5mm, with 20cm between
plants. Planting among
vegetables and fruit trees will
attract beneficial insects. Don't
raise in seed trays or pots, as
they won't transplant well.

Water requirements
Keep soil moist. Dry soil will
cause the plant to bolt (see
page 687).

Successive planting
Leave about 2 weeks between
each planting, throughout the
growing season. Dill plants
allowed to flower will
self-seed readily.

When to fertilise
To ensure vigorous growth, use
a liquid fertiliser (see page 691)
or worm tea (see page 695)
once every 4 weeks.

Harvest period
After 4 weeks from planting,
pick dill as required.

Pests and organic control
In wet or shady areas, fungal
diseases can be a problem,
so be sure to allow space for
ventilation.

Companion planting
Plant near broccoli for better
growth; dill will attract bees,
so plant among plants that
require bee pollination,
such as pumpkin, zucchini
and cucumber.

Special information
Keep the soil moist and free
from weeds by mulching.

**Quantities to plant
for a family of four**
3 plants.

Dill (*Anethum graveolens*)

Growing and Harvesting Dill resembles fennel both in look and taste, having an aniseed flavour with an overtone of caraway. The two plants can be identified by colour and height. Dill leaves are bluish green, while fennel leaves are yellowish green. Dill never grows more than a metre tall (and often less), whereas fennel can grow much taller than this.

Dill plants flower after six weeks and set seed quickly. To save seeds for the following year, see below.

Container Planting As with most herbs, dill is ideally suited for growing in a container. Perhaps combine it with other herbs, such as French tarragon or one of the thymes.

Preparing and Sharing The snipped foliage combines well with hot or cold boiled potatoes, cucumber salads, egg dishes and, most commonly, with smoked fish. Dill seeds are used in cooking as often as the foliage. The taste of the seeds is much more powerful than that of the foliage and they are used to flavour assertive-tasting vegetables such as beetroot, turnips and cabbage, or in the making of Sauerkraut (see page 191) and to make dill pickled cucumbers.

Despite the similarities in flavour between dill and fennel, each has a distinctive character and their use in recipes is not interchangeable. While I would happily combine dill with chives and flat-leaf parsley, I would never include it in the Mediterranean combo of rosemary and fennel. Dill foliage is essential for making the delicious cured salmon dish, gravlax. I would only put chopped dill in a potato salad that was to accompany smoked salmon, eel or herrings, not one to go with warm roast beef (and would include sour cream in the salad to accompany fish, but probably make a warm vinaigrette for the potato salad to accompany the roast beef). I have read that dill is used in North Vietnam, where it is generally not eaten raw but added to cooked dishes such as fish soups, combined with turmeric for coating grilled fish or added to fish cake mixtures. In Scandinavia, large quantities of dill are included in the simmering water used to cook freshwater crayfish.

Especially for Kids Collecting seeds from many different plants is an important activity in the garden. It requires concentration, a still day and a steady hand. Saved seeds must be fully dried before being stored in paper envelopes and carefully dated and labelled. Here the collected dill seeds have a double use – not just to provide continuity of the crop but to flavour food as well.

Children (especially those with younger siblings) might be interested to know that dill water made by infusing dill seeds in water was traditionally regarded as the best cure for colicky babies, nowadays more likely to be described as a baby being 'unsettled'. It is still recommended as a simple cure for indigestion in adults as well as children and babies. For adults and children, infuse 30 grams/1 ounce bruised dill seeds in two cups of hot water for several hours, then strain and sweeten with honey. Try a teaspoonful for children, more for an adult.

Salmon Patties with Dill

MAKES 8 LARGE OR 24 BITE-SIZED PATTIES Gravlax, raw salmon cured with dill, is quite delicious and is very well known; however, it does take several days to achieve. Here fresh salmon is combined with dill and used instead to make light-textured patties that are lovely served with waxy potatoes tossed while hot with dill-flavoured sour cream. For a party, tiny patties can be served on toothpicks with either dill-flavoured sour cream for dipping or topped with a dollop of mayonnaise (see page 229 if you want to make your own) and a sprig of dill, as I've done here (see opposite).

EXTRA EQUIPMENT
flexible narrow-bladed filleting knife, (optional)
fish pliers/tweezers for pin-boning (optional)
food processor

1 × 300g/10½oz salmon fillet, skin removed and pin-boned (you can ask your fishmonger to do this)
2 tablespoons thickened cream
30g/1oz fresh breadcrumbs (from about 1 thick slice bread)
30g/1oz marinated goat's cheese

1 free-range egg yolk
¼ small handful chopped dill
½ teaspoon sea salt
freshly ground black pepper
2 tablespoons plain flour
20g/¾oz butter
2 tablespoons olive oil

If salmon has not had its skin removed and been pin-boned, place it on a chopping board and insert the narrow blade of a filleting knife at the tail end or thinnest section of the fillet. Work it between the skin and flesh just enough so that you can hold the skin taut on the bench with one hand, while using the knife with the other hand to work in a slightly zig-zag action and separate the skin from the flesh. Pin-bones can be removed with strong fish pliers. Cut salmon into bite-sized pieces.

Pour cream over breadcrumbs and leave for 5 minutes.

Process salmon, cream-soaked crumbs and goat's cheese in a food processor; do this quickly as you want it all combined but not reduced to a paste. Scrape mixture into a mixing bowl and mix in egg yolk and dill, then season with salt and pepper to taste. (Fry a tiny ball of the mixture to check the salt and pepper if you can't bring yourself to taste it raw.) Cover mixture with plastic film and chill in refrigerator for 30 minutes. Dampen your hands and divide mixture into 8 large or 24 bite-sized patties. Roll each one in flour.

Heat butter and oil in a large non-stick frying pan over medium heat and fry patties for 2–3 minutes per side or until golden brown. Don't cook too long as salmon cooks very fast and is much nicer if still moist. Serve at once.

EGGPLANT

**Solanaceae family
(includes peppers,
potatoes and tomatoes)**

Perennial grown as an annual

Soil type
Moist but well-drained and
fertile.

Soil preparation
Eggplants are usually grown in
containers filled with a potting
compost or in the border soil of
a greenhouse or polytunnel.

Climate
Suitable for warm, mild areas as
a patio container crop, or grow
undercover in other areas.

Position
Requires sun, warmth and a
sheltered site.

How to grow
Sow seeds in March in small
pots, either indoors or in
a propagator in a heated
greenhouse. A germination
temperature of 20°C needed. As
seedlings develop grow on at a
minimum of 14°C. An alternative

to providing such heat to raise
seeds undercover is to buy small
potted plants from a garden
centre. Pot on into larger pots or
growing bags. Pinch out growing
tips and provide support (split
canes). In mild areas, harden off
(see page 692) and put outside
once all danger of frost has
passed (June), you may need
to return pots to greenhouse
towards end of season if the first
frosts are likely to come before
all the fruit has been harvested.

Water requirements
Container grown plants will need
daily attention to keep compost
moist but do not over water.

Successive planting
As the UK only just has a long
enough growing season to get
the fruit, just one sowing or
planting is done.

When to fertilise
When the first flowers start to
form, feed regularly with liquid
fertiliser (see page 691) or worm
tea (see page 695).

Harvest period
4–5 months from sowing/
planting.

Pests and organic control
Red spider mite, whitefly and
aphids can all attack plants
undercover. Use a biological
control (see page 698). Fruits
can suffer from grey mould and
blossom end rot, there is little
you can do to control these but
to prevent by removing infected
fruits and foliage and by regular
by careful watering.

Companion planting
Beans, basil and peas.
Amaranth is a good 'trap'
plant for pests.

Special information
Keep the compost moist and
free from weeds by mulching.
Stake to support the weight of
the fruit. Don't grow where any
Solanaceae family member was
grown the previous year.

**Quantities to plant
for a family of four**
4–5 plants.

Eggplant (*Solanum melongena*)

Growing and Harvesting Eggplant bushes crop very heavily and can be bowed down with the weight of the crop.

Don't pick the fruit if you don't intend to use them by the next day as they keep much better on the bush. Eggplant doesn't like being too cold and shouldn't be stored in the refrigerator. On the other hand, don't leave ripe fruit too long on the bush. Eggplants ready for harvest should be firm, feel heavy and the skin should be very glossy. Cut the fruit from the bush rather than pull it. If the skin is dull and wrinkled, the eggplant is past its prime (although it can still be used for baking and purées). If the bush produces a bumper crop, and your family can't face eating any more eggplant, it could be time to make eggplant pickles (see page 284).

I really recommend growing some of the beautiful heritage cultivars as well as the better-known purple fruit. There are a great number of eggplant cultivars: purple, pink, lilac, white, green, striped and orange. Some are large and some are very small. Some crop earlier and others later. One with lilac-and-white striped fruit is 'Violetti di Firenze'. The seeds in eggplants become more pronounced in larger cultivars as the fruit matures. However, some of the very small eggplant types preferred in South-East Asian dishes are very seedy and, as far as I am concerned, are an acquired taste.

Container Planting The slender variety known as Lebanese eggplant is excellent for growing in a pot. Include some support for the growing plant and feed it well. Arrange for a friend to water your eggplant if you will be away over summer, as this is their prime growing season.

Preparing and Sharing Cooks are often instructed to salt eggplant before cooking to extract any bitter juices. Salting eggplant definitely makes it absorb less oil when fried but if the eggplants are freshly grown and picked when young there shouldn't be any bitterness that needs to be extracted. If you wish to salt eggplant, rinse it very well and gently squeeze dry in a tea towel before cooking to ensure you have gotten rid of all of the salt and moisture.

Some eggplant dishes have the slimy texture detested by many children (and adults), so bear this in mind when selecting recipes to cook. Dips and fritters such as the Eggplant and Pork Patties on page 288 are likely to be more popular with children than braised chunks or whole baked eggplant. Having said that, a well-made eggplant parmigiana, with its bubbling cheesy topping, will be a hit with the whole family. To make, layer fried eggplant slices in a deep dish, spread with Fast Basic Tomato Sauce (see page 649), then top with grated parmesan and bake in the oven at 180°C/Gas 4 until golden.

Many recipes start by instructing the cook to sauté sliced eggplant. I find it best to cut eggplant lengthways into quite thin slices. I then brush each slice with olive oil on both sides and cook them in a non-stick frying pan over medium heat. This method dramatically reduces the quantity of olive oil needed. Badly cooked (that is, under-cooked) fried eggplant is truly disgusting, with a squeaky leathery texture guaranteed to make the unfortunate recipient an eggplant-hater for a long time.

Try fritters made by boiling a whole medium-sized eggplant for 10 minutes (or roasting it over a flame), squeezing it, splitting it and scooping out the flesh. Mix the chopped flesh with parsley, breadcrumbs and ricotta, then bind with an egg and shallow-fry in a non-stick frying pan over medium heat. Or make meatballs with plenty of cooked eggplant flesh (prepared as above), some fresh breadcrumbs and a small amount of minced veal, pork or beef and an egg to bind. These delicate meatballs are great simmered in a fresh tomato sauce such as the Fast Basic Tomato Sauce on page 649 or even with a tin of diced tomatoes, juice and all. Either of these recipes could be made with a char-grilled eggplant rather than a boiled one.

Because eggplant can differ quite dramatically in size, I have given the weight as well as number of eggplants required in the following recipes.

Especially for Kids Children can be shown how to cook whole eggplants on a barbecue grill-plate or char-grill pan over maximum heat; just remind them to prick the skins with a skewer here and there to avoid an explosion. I expect a medium to large eggplant to take around 15 minutes to become soft enough to purée. The eggplant needs to be turned several times to char the skin evenly. Children will be amazed at how quickly the skin collapses and the flesh becomes soft. It will also be very hot, so wait a while before splitting the eggplant open. Invite them to smell the smoky aroma that results from this way of cooking eggplant. The flesh of this eggplant, once scraped from its skin and chopped with flat-leaf parsley and garlic and seasoned with salt, pepper and lemon juice, makes a simple and popular dip that will be a hit served with warmed pita breads. With the addition of tahini, the paste made from ground sesame seeds, this dip becomes Baba Ghanoush (see page 285).

Children may be interested to know just how widespread the appreciation of eggplant is. Perhaps introduce them to names for eggplant in other languages. One Kitchen Garden Program school hung a poster in the classroom with some of the different names – *aubergine* (French), *badjan* (Arabic), *berinjela* (Spanish and Portuguese) and *melanzane* (Italian). Keen young cooks might like to research a new way of cooking it from each of these cultures.

Eggplant with Spicy Dressing and Toasted Coconut

SERVES 2 AS AN ACCOMPANIMENT OR 4 AS PART OF A MULTI-DISH MEAL This dish has been a great hit in my family. I like to eat it after it has cooled a little.

1 eggplant (about
  400g/14oz)
1 tablespoon desiccated
  coconut
2 tablespoons peanut oil
4 cloves garlic, finely
  chopped

SPICY DRESSING
2 teaspoons soft brown sugar
1 tablespoon brown-rice vinegar
1 tablespoon lemon juice
2 teaspoons fish sauce
1 fresh small red chilli, seeded and
  thinly sliced

EXTRA EQUIPMENT
barbecue grill-plate
wok
wok sang
  (see page 47)

Heat a barbecue grill-plate or until hot and roast eggplant, turning it 2–3 times to roast evenly; it will take about 15 minutes for skin to char and eggplant to feel soft. Remove with tongs. Cool a little. Peel away charred skin. Halve lengthways and put into a colander set over a baking tray to catch draining juices.

Meanwhile, toast coconut in a small frying pan over medium heat, stirring with a wooden spoon for 3–4 minutes or until golden brown. Tip into a small bowl and set aside until needed. Put drained eggplant in a clean tea towel and gently squeeze. Cut flesh into 5cm × 2cm/2in x ¾in pieces.

To make the dressing, mix all ingredients in a bowl and set aside.

Heat a wok over high heat. When very hot, quickly add peanut oil and swirl it up the sides of wok with a wok sang, then add garlic and stir. After a few seconds, tip in eggplant and stir-fry for 2 minutes or until it catches sides of the wok and has lovely bronze bits at the edges. Tip in dressing, stir-fry for another 1 minute, then scatter with toasted coconut and serve.

Maggie's Eggplant Salad

Legendary Australian cook Maggie Beer and I each have our own way of doing things but when I am a guest in her kitchen I follow instructions! This dish was cooked by me, following her instructions, for a breakfast feast for eighty guests the morning after an important wedding. Peel eggplant, then cut lengthways into 1cm/½in-thick slices, then into 1cm/½in-long strips. Fry in batches in a frying pan over medium heat using extra-virgin olive oil and a couple of crushed garlic cloves until well-coloured and tender, dribbling in olive oil as required. Drain on a paper towel-lined baking tray. When all eggplant is cooked, increase heat to high and return all eggplant to the pan. Add a generous slosh of verjuice and allow it to reduce rapidly. Season with sea salt and freshly ground black pepper and toss with chopped flat-leaf parsley.

Baba Ghanoush

MAKES 375ML/13FL OZ No one can claim an original way of preparing this very popular dip. It is found throughout the Middle East, India and the eastern Mediterranean, and has become a much-loved party dip. This is how I make it, resulting in a dip with texture. If you want a smooth cream it can be processed for about thirty seconds in a food processor. The Baba Ghanoush could be sprinkled with chopped flat-leaf parsley or dusted with paprika or sumac, and is frequently given a final drizzle of a fruity extra-virgin olive oil before serving.

EXTRA EQUIPMENT
barbecue grill-plate
food processor
(optional)
mortar and pestle

3 eggplants (about 1kg/2lb)
1 teaspoon cumin seeds
125ml/4½fl oz Greek-style yoghurt
 (see page 706)
sea salt
125ml/4½fl oz tahini

2 cloves garlic, finely chopped
juice of 3 lemons, to taste
freshly ground black pepper
warmed Simple Flatbread
 (see page 294 or use purchased),
 to serve

Heat a barbecue grill-plate until hot. Roast eggplants, turning them 2–3 times so they roast evenly; they will take about 15 minutes for skin to char and eggplants to feel quite soft. Remove with tongs. (This can also be done over a gas flame.) Cool a little. Peel away charred skin. Halve eggplants lengthways and put into a colander resting over a baking tray to catch draining juices. After 10 minutes, put drained eggplant into a clean cloth and gently squeeze. Chop flesh quite finely and put into a large mixing bowl (or blend in a food processor for a smoother result).

Dry-roast cumin seeds in a small frying pan over medium heat until fragrant. Tip into a mortar and grind to a powder with a pestle. Tip ground cumin into the mixing bowl with chopped eggplant.

Whisk yoghurt with a pinch of salt until it is smooth and creamy, then add yoghurt, tahini, garlic and half of the lemon juice to eggplant. Mix together and taste. Add more lemon juice if needed and season with salt and pepper.

Serve in a plate or shallow bowl so that your guests can easily dip their warmed flatbread into it.

Antonio's Eggplant and Pesto Medallions

SERVES 4 AS A STARTER This recipe is firmly based on the work of a fine cook, Antonio Carluccio. It comes from his book *Antonio Carluccio's Vegetables*. I have changed the cheeses used but otherwise the recipe is his. The format has been altered for consistency and to accommodate younger cooks. (Because of the way this dish is assembled I have contradicted my own advice on page 282 where I stated that I always slice my eggplants lengthways and very thinly if they are to be fried.)

1 vine-ripened tomato, cut into 5mm/¼in-thick slices and finely diced
80ml/3fl oz olive oil
1 eggplant (about 400g/14oz), cut into 8 × 1.5cm/½in-thick slices
2 tablespoons Pesto (see page 119)

16 small bocconcini, halved or 1 large fresh ball mozzarella, diced
2 tablespoons grated parmesan (optional)
sea salt and freshly ground black pepper
8 small basil leaves or sprigs

Preheat oven to 220°C/Gas 7.

Put diced tomato on a paper towel-lined plate while frying eggplant.

Heat 2 tablespoons of the oil in a large frying pan over medium heat and add eggplant slices. Cook for 5 minutes; don't despair if all the oil seems to have disappeared, all will be well. Turn slices. Now trickle in remaining oil if you think it is needed. After cooking for a further 5 minutes, lift out eggplant slices to a plate covered with a double thickness of paper towel. Tear off 2 more paper towels, then lie over fried eggplant slices and gently press to blot away any excess oil.

Transfer eggplant to a baking paper-lined baking tray. Divide pesto among eggplant slices and spread with a knife or the back of a spoon. Spoon some of the diced tomato onto each slice (any extra will be great in a salad or in some other dish).

Arrange a piece of bocconcini or mozzarella on top of the tomato. Sprinkle with parmesan if liked, then season each medallion with salt and pepper.

Bake in the oven for 10 minutes. Transfer medallions to a paper towel-lined plate to blot excess oil. Garnish each medallion with a basil leaf and serve.

Eggplant and Pork Patties

MAKES 10 These patties make a lovely lunch. They are also a great way of combining vegetables with a small amount of meat and have been very successful with young people who tend to be suspicious of eggplant in particular.

1 eggplant (about 400g/14oz)
200g/7oz spinach leaves, well
   washed and tough stems removed
200g/7oz minced pork, veal or beef
1 clove garlic, finely chopped
100g/3½oz fresh ricotta, crumbled
30g/1oz soft breadcrumbs
   (from about 1 thick slice bread)
25g/1oz grated parmesan

½ teaspoon salt
freshly ground black pepper
1 free-range egg
25g/1oz fine fresh breadcrumbs
60ml/2fl oz olive oil, for pan-frying
250ml/9fl oz Fast Basic Tomato
   Sauce (see page 649) or tinned
   chopped tomatoes (optional)

EXTRA EQUIPMENT
barbecue grill-plate
wok
bamboo steamer
  with lid

Heat a barbecue grill-plate until hot. Roast eggplant, turning it 2–3 times so it roasts evenly; it will take about 15 minutes for skin to char and eggplant to feel quite soft. Remove with tongs. (This can also be done over a gas flame.) Cool a little. Peel away charred skin. Halve eggplant lengthways and put into a colander resting over a baking tray to catch draining juices.

After 10 minutes, wrap eggplant with a clean tea towel and gently squeeze. Chop flesh quite finely and put into a large mixing bowl. Rinse colander and place it over the tray.

Half-fill a wok with water. Place a bamboo steamer with its lid over water and turn heat to high. Once water is boiling, put spinach in steamer, cover and steam for about 3 minutes. Tip leaves into colander, then press with the back of a spoon to extract as much liquid as possible. When spinach is cool enough to handle, squeeze it in a dry tea towel, then chop quite finely and add to eggplant.

Add minced pork, garlic, ricotta, breadcrumbs, parmesan, salt, pepper and egg to eggplant/spinach mixture and mix very well; I think this is best done with clean hands. Fry a tiny ball of the mixture to check the salt and pepper if you can't bring yourself to taste it raw. Cover mixture with plastic film and chill in the refrigerator for at least 30 minutes.

Dampen your hands, then divide the mixture into 10 balls. Slightly flatten them. Roll each patty in fine breadcrumbs. Heat 2 tablespoons of the olive oil in a large non-stick frying pan over medium heat and gently fry patties for 5 minutes on each side; they will brown very quickly because of the parmesan so watch them. Once patties are a rich brown you may prefer to finish cooking them in a frying pan with some fresh tomato sauce or even 250g/9oz tinned chopped tomatoes. If not, continue cooking over medium heat until cooked through, then serve. Repeat with remaining patties, adding oil as required.

EGGS

Growing and Raising Raising chickens in or near the kitchen garden is a sure-fire method of engaging the interest of children. They love visiting the birds, bringing them tiny treats of snails or caterpillars, refreshing their water bowls, removing uneaten food and, best of all, carefully collecting the eggs.

Gardeners who appreciate fresh seasonal food will also enjoy freshly laid eggs from hens that are happy, well fed and healthy. The gentle clucking made by contented hens is a very soothing and reassuring sound to have in the garden.

Chickens start to lay as soon as they are sexually mature – at around four months old (you don't need a rooster to ensure egg production). At this stage they are known as 'pullets' and the first eggs will be smaller than those laid once the birds are fully mature. Chickens lay fewer eggs in the winter. Different breeds average very different numbers of eggs per year. Anything over a hundred eggs per year would be considered a good result. Some breeds average more than 200. Most hens lay well for about four years.

Chickens appreciate fresh green plants as much as we do, so you will need to provide a secure, fenced area for them with as much free-ranging space as possible, away from the beds of growing vegetables. Enclose the chicken house to protect the birds from dogs, cats and foxes, and to protect growing plants from the chickens! As a further protection, I recommend shutting the birds in at night. Foxes and cats can climb wire enclosures, so construct the enclosure with wire walls that are slack rather than taut. The wire should also extend under the ground, as foxes can dig their way into an enclosure. A gruesome discovery of mauled birds will cause heartbreak and deep distress to children and adults alike.

Chickens love to scratch, and the ground beneath their run can become bare very quickly. Scatter fresh straw into the run and regularly rake it out and replace it. The used straw is an excellent addition to the compost heap.

Ingenious moveable chicken runs, often marketed as 'chicken tractors', may be ideal for the smaller home garden. The whole run, coop and scratching space is fenced and can be rolled to a different part of the garden once the birds have worked over (and manured) one area. The chicken manure-enriched space could then become a garden bed.

It pays to research what is involved first and how you will fit them into your garden. As well as books and websites you can also attend courses where you can learn to handle the birds (for example, www.cotswoldchickens.com). There are now many housing options, from traditional timber coops and hen houses (www.thechickensite.co.uk) to modern plastic ones such as the Omlet, which would suit urban dwellers or those with small gardens (www.omlet.co.uk). Omlet provide a 'ready-to-go' solution – you buy the birds, house and feed online and they will deliver, and someone will come and show you how to set everything up. As keeping chickens is now trendy, you need to be on your guard when buying them. There are many options, from going to a breeder or dealer direct (The Poultry Club of Great Britain can be contacted on 02820 741056 for further information) or buying ex-battery hens (www.bhwt.org.uk).

The best feed for chickens is a mixture of grain, grass and fresh greens such as the outside leaves of cabbage, lettuce or other scraps from the kitchen, including bread crusts or cooked vegetables. They must have some shell grit or roasted crushed eggshells so that they can produce eggs with strong shells. If you buy food, ensure that it is labelled 'certified organic', as pellets can include undesirable additives.

For healthy and happy chickens you need to supply a fresh and varied diet, fresh water and a clean, dry environment. If you are a new or prospective chicken owner, refer to specialist websites for more information.

Preparing and Sharing There is not much preparation involved with eggs. They are one of nature's perfect packages.

Most hens lay an egg a day so unless you have a large number of hens there will be no problem using eggs when they are absolutely fresh. A freshly laid egg, soft-boiled or poached, is about as near to perfection as is possible. Eggs that will not be eaten in the next 2–3 days should be stored in the refrigerator, as they do lose quality at room temperature after this.

Where hens have access to a large space to roam sometimes you may come across an egg and be unsure how long it has been there. As I've mentioned in *The Cook's Companion*, a fresh egg placed in a bowl of water will generally lie at the bottom while a stale egg will float blunt-end up. Discard any egg that floats, just to be safe.

Especially for Kids Eggs cook so quickly that they are an ideal way of getting children involved in the kitchen as the results can be almost instantaneous. A soft-boiled egg served with toast 'soldiers' for dipping is usually a childhood favourite. Scrambled eggs or a simple omelette are also sure to succeed the first time round. Hard-boiled eggs are great in salads (they are especially delicious if they are not *too* hard-boiled. I time my freshly laid eggs to cook for 6 minutes if for a warm salad, and maybe 8 minutes if to take on a picnic).

For baking or more advanced egg cookery it is often necessary to separate eggs. In my book *Kitchen Garden Cooking with Kids* I recommend showing 8–12-year-olds how to separate the yolk and the white by cracking the egg into clean hands held over a bowl and slightly opening the fingers so that the white slips into the bowl. Most children found this method easier than the usual adult method of giving the egg a sharp crack on the edge of a basin and then tipping the white into a bowl, holding back the yolk in one half of the shell. Experiment with your young cook to see which method works best for them. This would be a good moment to remind young cooks that the most successful way to remove a bit of egg shell from a mixing bowl is to use a cracked egg shell as a scoop.

It might be illuminating to have a taste test of a freshly laid egg against an egg from a battery-reared chicken bought from the supermarket.

When deciding whether or not to keep chickens it is important to consider who will care for them if you go away. Arrangements will need to be made for them to stay with a willing family member, friend or neighbour, or there must be a reliable roster of volunteers who will come to check on the birds, clean the run, remove uneaten food and ensure fresh food is provided, change the water and, of course, collect the eggs.

Baghdad Eggs on Simple Flatbread

SERVES 1 (MAKES 4 FLATBREADS) This combination of flavours is very typical of many dishes from the Middle East. I created this breakfast special during the years I owned the all-day café Richmond Hill Café & Larder in the Melbourne suburb of Richmond. It is still a popular seller, I believe. Freshly baked flatbreads are the perfect base for these eggs. The flatbread is also excellent alongside soup or a curry such as the Kofta Curry with Coriander Sauce on page 249. Extra flatbread can be frozen. If you have two small non-stick pans the ingredients for cooking the eggs can easily be doubled.

½ teaspoon cumin seeds
20g/¾oz butter
1 clove garlic, thinly sliced
1 tablespoon lemon juice
2 free-range eggs
sea salt and freshly ground black pepper
8 mint leaves, thinly sliced

SIMPLE FLATBREAD
125g/4½oz plain flour, plus extra
    for dusting
¼ teaspoon salt
2 teaspoons extra-virgin olive oil
80ml/3fl oz tepid water

EXTRA EQUIPMENT
food processor
rolling pin
mortar and pestle

To make the flatbreads, put flour and salt in a food processor. With the motor running, trickle in oil and enough tepid water to make a dough (add gradually as you may not need it all), processing for 1–2 minutes until mixture forms a ball. Turn dough onto a workbench lightly dusted with flour and knead until it feels smooth and silky. Place in a bowl and cover with a clean tea towel. Leave at room temperature for at least 30 minutes.

Preheat oven to 100°C/Gas ¼ and put a baking tray inside to warm.

Divide dough into 4 pieces each about the size of a small egg, then use a rolling pin to roll into flat rounds on a floured workbench.

Heat a heavy-based cast-iron frying pan over high heat until very hot; there is no need for any oil. Slap a dough round into it. Cook for 2–3 minutes and then turn to cook the other side. The cooked flatbread will have little burnt blisters on it. Keep warm on the baking tray in the oven while cooking remaining flatbreads and eggs.

Dry-roast cumin seeds in a small frying pan over medium heat until fragrant, then tip into a mortar and grind with a pestle to a powder. Tip into a small bowl until needed.

Melt butter over medium heat in a small non-stick frying pan. When butter starts to foam, drop in garlic and cook for 30 seconds until it just starts to change colour. Add lemon juice and eggs and fry gently until set. Sprinkle over cumin. Serve on warm flatbread or toast, seasoned with salt and pepper and sprinkled generously with thinly sliced mint.

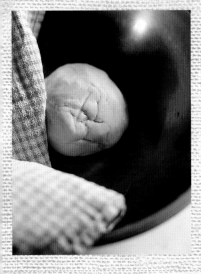

Egg and Tomato Breakfast 'Muffins'

MAKES 6 This recipe is based on the one given in *Mollie Katzen's Sunlight Café* by Mollie Katzen, a treasure-house of simple, practical ideas for breakfasts. These 'muffins' are akin to crust-less quiches and would be the perfect treat to whip up for a Mother's Day breakfast, or any time really. The recipe format has been changed for consistency and to accommodate younger cooks.

30g/1oz butter, melted
12g/⅓oz fresh fine breadcrumbs
4 free-range eggs
125g/4½oz fresh ricotta
¼ teaspoon salt

freshly ground black pepper
3 spring onions, trimmed and
   thinly sliced
1 tomato, cut into 5mm/¼in dice
1 tablespoon grated parmesan

EXTRA EQUIPMENT
1 × 6-hole muffin tin
food processor
flexible palette knife

Preheat oven to 180°C/Gas 4.

Brush sides and bases of a 6-hole muffin tin generously with melted butter. Divide breadcrumbs between the holes and tip and shake to coat them well. Turn tin upside-down and tap over the sink to remove excess crumbs.

Put eggs and ricotta in a food processor and briefly blend to form a smooth batter. Scrape into a mixing bowl. Add salt and pepper. Stir in spring onion and diced tomato.

Spoon mixture into prepared holes. Bake for 10 minutes. Open the oven and half-pull out the oven shelf. Scatter tops of muffins with parmesan, then close oven and bake for a further 10 minutes. Leave muffins to cool in their tins for at least 3 minutes before carefully easing them from the sides of the muffin holes with a palette knife. Carefully invert muffins on a cake cooling rack or a warm plate. They will deflate slightly.

These muffins are good served hot, warm or cold. Extra muffins can be stored in an airtight container in the refrigerator for a day and can be reheated in a 100°C/Gas ¼ oven.

Egg Custard

MAKES 750ML/27FL OZ Bring 250ml/9fl oz milk, 250ml/9fl oz pouring cream and a split vanilla bean to simmering point in a heavy-based saucepan. In a bowl, whisk 5 free-range egg yolks and 110g/3¾oz caster sugar until light and foamy, then whisk in warm milk and cream. Return mixture to rinsed-out pan and cook over medium heat for about 10 minutes, stirring constantly with a wooden spoon until mixture thickens and coats back of spoon. Strain immediately into a cold bowl, then scrape in vanilla seeds. Serve warm or cold. If using as a base for ice cream, use 375ml/13fl oz milk and 125ml/4½fl oz cream.

Greek Easter Eggs

MAKES 6–8 It is great fun to dye eggs for Greek Easter. Greek delicatessens sell the dye in paper envelopes with instructions included. The crimson eggs are pushed inside a traditional plaited Easter bread called *tsoureki*, and Greek families play the game whereby two people hold one red egg with the pointed end uppermost and crack eggs together. The person whose egg remains intact is said to have good luck. A family member will say '*Christos Anesti*' (Christ has risen), to which the reply is '*Alithos Anesti*' (Truly he has risen). The egg represents the renewal of life, and the colour red is said to symbolise the blood of Christ.

It is even more interesting to dye the eggs using onion skins. Don't expect them to be the intense crimson shade of the commercial dye. It doesn't seem to matter whether the onion skins are yellow, brown or red – the eggs end up a very handsome burnished copper colour. A Greek acquaintance volunteers the additional information that the colour improves if the eggs used are white rather than brown, and that there are other things that might be added to the onion skins to further 'redden' the finished product. Although I have not tried any of these, her suggestions were to try 'sumac, saffron, turmeric, dried hibiscus flowers, rosehip, dandelion root, beets or ripe blackberries'.

As onion skins are undesirable in the compost heap (they don't appeal to the wonderful worms that help break down the material) this is a fun thing to do with some of the skins you will generate when cooking in your kitchen. Save skins by storing them in a container in the freezer for up to one month.

EXTRA EQUIPMENT
stainless-steel
  strainer
stainless-steel
  mixing bowl
slotted spoon
stainless-steel cake
  cooling rack

300g/10½oz onion skins (5 firmly
  packed cups or the skins of about
  12 large onions)
2 tablespoons white vinegar

1.25 litres/2 pints cold water
6–8 free-range eggs,
  at room temperature
1 teaspoon olive oil

Put onion skins in a large stainless-steel saucepan with vinegar and cold water. Bring slowly to the boil over medium heat, then reduce heat to low and simmer with the lid on for 30 minutes. Strain contents into a mixing bowl, discarding the skins. Cool to room temperature.

Put eggs very carefully in a smaller stainless-steel saucepan; they should just fit in a single layer without too much extra space. Pour over cooled dye mixture which should cover the eggs completely. Bring slowly to the boil over medium heat, then reduce heat to low and simmer, covered, for 12 minutes. Gently remove pan from heat and leave eggs to steep another 5 minutes. Lift eggs out of dye with a slotted spoon and leave to cool completely on a stainless-steel cake cooling rack resting over a plate or tray to catch drips.

When completely cold and dry put a little olive oil on a paper towel and rub all over eggs to make them shine. Use more paper towel to lightly polish eggs.

FENNEL

**Apiaceae family
(includes carrots, celery,
chervil, coriander, dill,
parsley and parsnip)
Perennial**

Soil type
Prefers moist, well-drained soil
enriched with organic matter.

Soil preparation
Not required.

Climate
Suitable for warmer, milder
areas.

Position
Prefers full sun and warmth.

How to grow
To grow the bulbous Florence
fennel there is no point sowing
too early as the plant might bolt
(see page 687). Sow seed in May
or June in small pots, harden
off (see page 692) and plant out

after there is no more danger
of frost and weather is warm
(usually June to July). Space
plants 25–30cm apart. Harvest
late August to September.

Water requirements
Don't over-water, but do keep
soil moist.

Successive planting
Usually just one sowing.

When to fertilise
To ensure vigorous growth, use
a liquid fertiliser (see page 691)
or worm tea (see page 695).

Harvest period
3–4 months from planting.
Cut the swollen bulb just above
ground level when it is around
5–10cm in diameter. Harvest
the leaves as required.

Pests and organic control
No specific pests, although
slugs and snails can be
a problem for seedlings.
Using crushed egg shells
around the base should
deter them.

Companion planting
Fennel is good for repelling
the codling moth away from
susceptible fruit trees. Grow
fennel away from other plants,
as some organic gardeners
believe that many plants
don't like to be near it.

Special information
Keep the soil moist and free
from weeds by mulching.
Blanch the bulb by earthing
up the soil around the base.

**Quantities to plant
for a family of four**
1–3 plants.

Florence fennel (*Foeniculum vulgare* var. *azoricum*)

Growing and Harvesting   Fennels include common and bronze leaf fennel and the bulbous vegetable known as Florence fennel, which is enjoyed for its crisp, swollen leaf stems that overlap into one dense mass, usually referred to as a 'bulb'. All varieties of fennel have an aniseed flavour.

The best of the Florence fennel is the rounded 'female' part of the plant, at their best during spring and autumn. The flatter 'male' part of the plant tends to be stringier and lack sweetness. No one has been able to tell me how to grow fennel that is just 'female'. It might just be chance! Like sexing chickens, it is hard to know which sort one has until they approach maturity.

Bronze fennel is a much more manageable leafy fennel and a good choice for learning how to collect seeds from seed heads. Its flowers will attract beneficial insects to the garden. Don't plant fennel near dill as the two plants will hybridise, producing seedlings that are neither one thing nor the other. Don't let leafy fennel set seed on an allotment as it can self seed.

Container Planting   As all fennels are said to repel the codling moth, try planting a few seeds at the base of any susceptible fruit trees in the garden. As there are so many dwarf fruiting trees available these days intended for balconies or courtyards, this may well mean planting the fennel seeds in the same pot.

I planted four Florence fennel seeds in a pot with a miniature peach tree, and can report that my little tree produced a good crop of non-infested fruit in the recent drought-struck summer, so the fennel may have helped.

Preparing and Sharing   It is a mistake to combine fennel leaves, either the feathery tops of bulb fennel or common fennel, with delicate herbs, as they are overwhelmed by its assertive aniseed flavour. Flat-leaf parsley and rosemary are the only two herbs that can go head to head with fennel. I don't believe that fennel leaves should ever be included in a bundle with herbs such as tarragon, chervil or chives. However, common fennel is a necessary and welcome ingredient in a fish stock or fish soup and in other strongly flavoured Mediterranean dishes. For instance, I remember being served a rock lobster grilled with a generous quantity of fennel stalks and leaves in a tiny restaurant at Villefranche on the French Riviera many years ago. It was sensational and its accompanying mayonnaise was flavoured quite discretely with pastis, the local aniseed-accented aperitif. Fennel is an essential part of the Sicilian dish pasta with sardines and fennel (*pasta con le sarde),* where the leafy fennel greens are chopped and cooked with the pasta (my version of this is on page 304).

Entire heads of fennel, picked after the flowers have set seed, are an excellent flavouring to use when curing olives (see Cracked Green Olives on page 440). The seeds from dried heads of leafy fennel can be added in tiny quantities to bread doughs like the Fennel Seed Grissini on page 307. Fennel seed is also used in some Italian salamis and fresh sausages. One seed head of fennel from bronze or bulb fennel allowed to go to seed, will yield a good spoonful of seeds.

If you rub the flowers of common fennel you can collect the golden pollen. This can be scattered over fish or included in bread dough. It is more subtle than the seeds, yet unmistakeably 'fennel' in character.

The aniseed flavour of the fennel bulb is both enjoyed by many and disliked by many (especially children, in my experience). It is more noticeable when the bulb is eaten raw; the flavour mellows after braising. The bulbs generally need to have their tough, stringy outer layers removed and bases trimmed before you use them whole, halved, quartered, sliced, shaved or diced.

Raw fennel slices will become crisper if soaked in ice-cold water for 15 minutes before drying well on a clean tea towel or paper towel and adding to a salad. Slivers of raw fennel prepared like this are delicious in salads and combine well with citrus fruit, stone fruit, parmesan or pecorino and olives. Last weekend I chopped a small quantity of wild fennel leaves and tossed them with a salad of raw shaved fennel bulb, then added extra-virgin olive oil and generous flakes of parmesan. It was a good combination with poached salmon and boiled waxy potatoes. At Sydney chef Sean Moran's restaurant, Sean's Panaroma, I was recently served a most delicious dish of steamed clams with a generous quantity of chopped fennel and lime butter sauce spooned over them.

Another idea is to toss paper-thin slices of fennel with similarly paper-thin slices of inner celery and slices of mozzarella to make an attractive and simple salad dressed with extra-virgin olive oil and a squeeze of lemon.

Fennel bulbs can be braised (see the Master Recipe for Braised Fennel on page 302), grilled, sautéed, stir-fried or baked. Chunks or wedges will caramelise beautifully if the par-cooked pieces are roasted alongside a chicken or a leg of lamb. It is best to par-cook fennel in salted water before proceeding to bake, grill or braise, otherwise it will take a long time to cook. Fennel combines very well with all cheeses and is great as a tart filling or on a pizza.

Especially for Kids With adequate supervision teenagers can use a plastic vegetable slicer (see page 46) to shave fennel and other firm vegetables. These gadgets are very efficient and extremely sharp so I must emphasise the need to take great care when using them. Younger children would be better off using the slicing attachment of a food processor, with adult supervision.

Young children may also be intrigued to hear that fennel pieces were apparently once used as bandages for dog bites, snake bites, toothaches and ear aches.

Master Recipe for Braised Fennel

SERVES 4 AS A SIDE DISH Bulb fennel is at its best during spring and autumn. I find that the thinner, flatter, greener bulbs available during the heat of summer (and sold as 'baby' fennel) have none of the fleshy texture or the sweetness of the crisp fat bulbs available in cooler weather. The dominant flavour of aniseed is mellowed in this recipe and I have indicated some ways it can be varied (see opposite). It is a delicious side dish to serve with a whole grilled or oven-baked fish or a roasted chicken. I have recommended cutting the fennel into relatively small, bite-sized pieces; however, if you prefer, you can just quarter the fennel bulbs or cut thick slices, each still attached to the root end. In either case you should then blanch the fennel in lightly salted water for 10 minutes and drain it really well before proceeding with the recipe. If you are using large chunks or slices you will probably need to increase the amount of tomato used, or add a glass of white wine with the tomato and increase the cooking time.

1 large bulb fennel, trimmed, plus 2 tablespoons coarsely chopped fennel fronds
2 tablespoons extra-virgin olive oil
½ onion, finely diced
1 × 5cm/2in sprig rosemary, leaves picked and roughly chopped
2 cloves garlic, sliced
sea salt and freshly ground black pepper
3 large ripe tomatoes, chopped or 1 × 400g/14oz tin chopped tomatoes

Inspect fennel and, if necessary, discard damaged outside layer. Cut away root end. Halve bulb lengthways from top to bottom. Place one half cut-side down on a chopping board and cut into 4–6 sections. Cut across the sections into 1cm/½in-thick slices.

Heat oil in a heavy-based frying pan with a lid over medium heat and sauté onion and rosemary for 2–3 minutes until onion starts to soften. Add garlic and cook for 30 seconds, then add chopped fennel, salt and pepper. Cook, stirring for 2 minutes, then add tomato. Cover pan, reduce heat to low and cook for 10 minutes. Test tenderness of fennel; if it is not completely tender, then cook for a further few minutes.

Finish in one of the following three ways (see opposite), or invent your own dish.

Variations on Master Recipe for Braised Fennel

1. Braised Fennel Bruschetta

4 slices sourdough bread	1 quantity Braised Fennel (see opposite)
1 clove garlic, halved	100g/3½oz fresh mozzarella (see page 704)

SERVES 4 Toast or grill the bread. Rub lightly with garlic. Divide braised fennel among the toasted bread and top with slices of mozzarella. Grill under a hot griller for 3–4 minutes or until cheese is bubbling. Serve at once.

2. Braised Fennel Gratin

extra-virgin olive oil, for cooking	30g/1oz fine fresh breadcrumbs
1 quantity Braised Fennel (see opposite)	2 tablespoons grated parmesan
	grated zest of 1 small lemon

SERVES 4 Select a shallow 18cm/7in gratin dish. Brush with olive oil and pile braised fennel into the dish. Mix remaining ingredients together and scatter over braised fennel. Drizzle with more olive oil.

If fennel is cold, then finish the dish in a preheated 200°C/Gas 6 oven for about 15 minutes or until crumbs are golden and crunchy. If the braise has just been cooked and the gratin assembled at once, finish under a hot griller for about 5 minutes until the crust is golden.

3. Braised Fennel with Preserved Olives

50g/2oz dried preserved black olives	2 tablespoons chopped flat-leaf parsley
1 quantity Braised Fennel (see opposite)	

SERVES 4 Stir olives into braised fennel. Serve at room temperature, scattered with parsley.

Pasta with Sardines and Fennel

SERVES 4 This is a Sicilian treat – sardines and fennel in one recipe! These powerful flavours are combined with smooth pasta, sweet currants and irresistible pine nuts. The same combination occurs in the recipe for Warm Sauté of Zucchini, Pine Nuts and Currants on page 676. Sometimes this dish appears with spaghetti, sometimes with a hollow pasta such as rigatoni or bucatini, and I have also seen it layered between pasta sheets and baked as for a lasagne – an idea that is definitely worth trying.

50g/2oz currants
125ml/4½fl oz dry white wine
    or water
½ teaspoon saffron stamens
2 tablespoons warm water
100ml/3½fl oz extra-virgin
    olive oil
1 clove garlic, bruised
60g/2oz fresh breadcrumbs
salt

2 fennel layers, cut in half
500g/1lb dried pasta
1 onion, finely chopped
1 small handful very finely chopped
    fennel fronds (including some of the
    inner layers of fennel bulb)
1 teaspoon chilli flakes
80g/3oz pine nuts
12 fresh sardines, filleted
sea salt and freshly ground black pepper

Preheat oven to 100°C/Gas ¼ and put in 4 ovenproof pasta bowls to warm.

Soak currants in wine or water in a small bowl for 30 minutes. Soak saffron in warm water in another small bowl until needed.

Heat 2 tablespoons of the olive oil and bruised garlic in a large non-stick frying pan over medium heat, then stir in breadcrumbs. Continue stirring until crumbs are golden and feel a bit sandy. Tip breadcrumbs into a bowl and set aside; discard garlic. Wipe out pan with paper towel.

Fill a large saucepan or pasta pot with lightly salted water and add fennel (to flavour the cooking water), then bring to the boil over high heat. Drop in pasta and cook until al dente. (Be guided by the instructions on the packet but check several minutes earlier than indicated.)

Meanwhile, heat remaining olive oil in a heavy-based frying pan over medium heat and sauté onion and ½ small handful of the fennel fronds for 6–8 minutes or until well softened. Add currants and any liquid, chilli flakes, saffron and its soaking water and pine nuts and stir to mix. Add sardines, increase heat to high and stir with a wooden spoon for 1–2 minutes. Remove pan from heat.

Drain cooked pasta in a colander and shake well, discarding fennel pieces. Return it immediately to the hot pan. Tip in sardine/fennel sauce and shake and stir to mix; don't worry if the sardines have broken up, as this is how it should be. Add salt and pepper if necessary. If the pasta looks at all dry, add an extra drizzle of olive oil. Scatter with remaining fennel fronds. Divide pasta and sardine mixture among warm pasta bowls, sprinkle with breadcrumbs, then serve.

Fennel Fritters

SERVES 4 AS AN APPETISER There are many ways of preparing fennel fritters: cut into strips, slices or wedges; dipped in batter or in egg and breadcrumbs and shallow-fried in olive oil or deep-fried in lots of clean vegetable oil. In all cases I advise you to remove any possibly stringy outer layers, and that you blanch (see page 703) the fennel before proceeding with the recipe. Alternative coatings for these fritters include a very crunchy beer batter (see Carrot Fritters on page 199), another light beer-based batter (see Sage Leaf Fritters on page 560), and a very fine lacy batter such as the one on page 222 for Deep-fried Crunchy Celery Leaves.

2 bulbs fennel, trimmed and cut into strips, thin slices or wedges, plus 2 tablespoons chopped fennel fronds
salt
2 tablespoons plain flour

2 free-range eggs
2 tablespoons grated parmesan
sea salt and freshly ground black pepper
olive oil or vegetable oil, for shallow-frying
lemon wedges, to serve

EXTRA EQUIPMENT
long-handled brass skimmer or slotted spoon

Blanch fennel in a saucepan of lightly salted simmering water for 10 minutes over medium heat. Drain in a colander, then pat dry with paper towel.

Preheat oven to 100°C/Gas ¼ and put a paper towel-lined ovenproof plate inside to warm.

Set out a plate and put the flour on it. Whisk eggs, parmesan, chopped fennel fronds, salt and pepper in a bowl.

Pour oil into a wok or medium-sized heavy-based frying pan to a depth of 1.5cm/½in in the centre, then heat over high heat. It is hot enough when a drop of egg mixture added to the pan sizzles instantly to golden brown.

Quickly dip a piece of fennel into flour and tap to remove excess, then swish it through egg mixture and gently lay in hot oil. Continue to coat a few more pieces – there should be enough space for them to bob about a bit. Don't crowd the pan. Cook fritters for 3 minutes or until undersides are golden, then turn to cook other sides. Lift out with a skimmer or slotted spoon and transfer to the paper towel-lined plate in the warm oven. Continue with remaining fennel pieces, flour, and egg mixture until all fritters are cooked. Serve at once with lemon wedges to the side.

Fennel Seed Grissini

MAKES 20 This is a wonderful way of using any fennel seeds you have saved from plants in the garden. A few fennel seeds go a long way – too many give a not altogether pleasant tongue-numbing experience! Or substitute half a teaspoon of fennel pollen, shaken from fennel flower heads, for the seeds (see page 301).

EXTRA EQUIPMENT
mortar and pestle
electric mixer with
dough hook
attachment
pastry scraper

200g/7oz unbleached plain flour
50g/2oz semolina
½ teaspoon salt
2 teaspoons instant dried yeast
1 teaspoon olive oil, plus extra
  for greasing
160ml/5½fl oz warm water

FENNEL FLAVOURING
80ml/3fl oz extra-virgin olive oil
1 clove garlic, crushed
1 teaspoon fennel seeds, lightly
  crushed with a mortar and pestle
sea salt

Combine flour, semolina, salt and yeast in the bowl of an electric mixer. Add oil to warm water and, with motor running, add mixture to bowl and work to form a smooth dough. Transfer the dough to a lightly oiled mixing bowl and cover with a damp tea towel. Leave for about 1 hour or until doubled in size. Knock dough back gently, then cover with a tea towel and allow to double again (about 30 minutes).

Preheat oven to 200°C/Gas 6. Using a pastry scraper, divide dough into 20 pieces, each about 3cm/1½in in diameter. On a workbench, roll each piece into a thin sausage-shape about 20cm/8in long, using both hands. Spread out your fingers as the piece of dough stretches (young cooks will enjoy doing this!).

To make fennel flavouring, pour olive oil into a baking tray with a rim. Swish garlic in oil, then scatter in fennel seeds and salt. Drag dough pieces through oil mixture and transfer to another baking tray, spacing them well apart. Use a pastry brush to brush remaining fennel flavouring onto the dough. Bake for 10 minutes and then turn. Bake for another 5 minutes or until crisp. Cool on a cake cooling rack. Store in an airtight container.

Fennel and Fish 'Pie'

Slice cooked potatoes, toss with chopped flat-leaf parsley, chopped chilli and olive oil, then season well with sea salt and freshly ground black pepper. Spread in a shallow baking dish. Scatter with chopped fennel leaves and a few fennel seeds. Top with thin slices of fish (use flattish fillets such as John Dory). Season with salt and pepper, then scatter with fennel leaves and smear with a thinnish layer of homemade tomato sauce (see page 649). Top with fresh breadcrumbs mixed with grated lemon zest and chopped fennel fronds, then drizzle with olive oil and bake at 180°C/Gas 4 for 20 minutes or until crumbs are golden.

GARLIC

Alliaceae family (includes French shallots, leeks, onions and spring onions) Perennial that can be grown as an annual

Soil type
Moist, well-drained soil, enriched with organic matter. Don't plant in freshly manured or acidic soil.

Soil preparation
Dig in organic compost or well-rotted manure a few months prior to planting.

Climate
Suitable for all climates.

Position
Prefers full sun.

How to grow
Plant cloves in February to March or in the autumn. Sow garlic cloves directly into the ground, pointy end up, 3cm deep. Plant 15cm apart in rows 30cm apart or in a 2m × 2m block. Also plant around the bases of fruit trees, and inter-plant the blocks with beneficial flowering plants.

Water requirements
Keep soil moist, but don't over-water. Be sparing with water as bulb matures.

When to fertilise
Use a liquid fertiliser (see page 691) or worm tea (see page 695) once every 4 weeks.

Harvest period
6–8 months after planting.

Pests and organic control
Leek rust can be a problem. Destroy affected plants and do not put on compost heap. Practise crop rotation to avoid diseases such as white rot.

Companion planting
Good for tomatoes, roses and fruit. The secretions of sulphur from garlic are said to improve the scent of roses. Garlic repels aphids and borer. Don't plant with peas and beans.

Special information
Frost tolerant, once established garlic needs little attention.

Quantities to plant for a family of four
Depending on space, a 2m × 2m block will provide 50 heads of garlic.

Purple garlic cultivar (*Allium sativum*)

Growing and Harvesting You can plant garlic from the supermarket, but there is a risk of introducing plant diseases so it is best to start with certified disease-free bulbs from a garden centre or mail order supplier.

There are two main varieties of garlic: hard-neck and soft-neck. Most kitchen gardeners grow the soft-neck variety, as its soft stems make it suitable for plaiting. Softneck garlic types produce several layers of small cloves and store well for winter use. Hardneck or rocambole types produce a false flower shoot which hardens over the summer. Around this shoot a single layer of bulbs form. Hardneck types grow well in ares with cold winters. The bulbs tend to have stronger flavour than the softnecks but they do not store well. The flower shoot, also known as a scape, can be cut while it is still green and used in cooking.

An easy way to be aware of the garlic growing cycle is to remember the autumn equinox and the winter and summer solstices. The rule is to plant garlic before the shortest day, and harvest it around the longest day. In practice this means planting in late autumn or early winter; in a school garden, harvesting the garlic will be one of the last tasks before the summer holidays.

Keep an eye on newly planted cloves of garlic, as sometimes they are taken by birds. Garlic is ready for harvest when the plant tops have started to turn from yellow to brown. You can then lift the garlic bulbs and dry them before plaiting them or tying them in bunches. Once the garlic is properly dry – it will take at least two weeks – you can store it for months in a cool, dry spot. Imperfectly dried cloves will rot.

Some garlic growers plant early varieties that are harvested when the tops are still mostly green but streaked with yellow. In this case the bulbs will be rounded, with the individual cloves barely visible and completely covered by their papery veil. When the crop is picked a month or so later the bulbs will have broken through their damp covering, and the individual cloves will be clearly visible and starting to separate.

As each garlic plant sends up a relatively slender stalk, there is always space between the growing plants – you could use this space for another crop. Lettuces and Asian greens make good companions. Garlic requires little attention whilst it is growing, although watering in dry spells when the leaves are actively growing will increase the size of the bulbs. The most important thing is to keep the ground weed-free.

Garlic is reputed to have significant protective properties against all manner of complaints, ranging from the common cold to cancer. It is also frequently used as a companion plant to reduce aphid infestation in nearby plants (including roses).

Container Planting Garlic can be grown in a pot or planter box, but since you need to grow a lot for use throughout the year there are more productive crops you could grow if you only have a small space – garlic will take up the ground for at least six months. Small-scale gardeners would be better off buying several plaits of locally grown garlic at a farmers' market in the summer and finding a dry spot to hang and store it for winter use. I do this, as I don't have enough space for more than half-a-dozen plants in my own garden.

Preparing and Sharing Garlic is an indispensable ingredient in kitchens throughout almost the entire world – the Anglo-Saxons were the hardest to convince. Happily, this is changing in our multicultural society. Hardly a day passes in my kitchen without me reaching for the garlic basket.

Although most store-bought garlic is dried before selling (see opposite), newly harvested garlic can be used as soon as it is picked. It is a very special treat usually reserved for home gardeners. The cloves are crisp in texture (almost juicy) and the flavour is fresh and pungent. Wrap these freshly harvested heads in a piece of oiled foil and roast for 45–60 minutes in a 180°C/Gas 4 oven until quite soft, then squeeze this perfumed spread onto bread. Exquisite!

Even before harvesting the garlic, a few of the green tops can be cut and used as flavouring, snipped straight into sauces, omelettes, soups, casseroles or stir-fries. Green garlic is very pungent and is best cooked rather than added raw to a salad.

When garlic is cut the cell walls are damaged, releasing the distinctive odour. The more it is cut, the stronger the smell, so sliced garlic is milder than finely chopped and whole cloves are mildest of all. Heat destroys its strong odour and pungent flavour, so dishes that involve cooking garlic result in milder flavours than those where it is used raw (in a salad dressing or rubbed on grilled or toasted bread, for example).

A few of my favourite preparations starring garlic include: Aïoli (France, see page 314); al-i-oli (Spain); skordalia (Greece); Pesto (Italy, see page 119); and gremolata (also from Italy, see page 327), a mix of chopped flat-leaf parsley, grated lemon zest and finely chopped garlic that is magical scattered over cooked veal (most famously, osso bucco) and many vegetable dishes. Garlic is also a key ingredient in my Parsley Butter (see page 457). Roughly chopped potatoes sautéed in a frying pan in olive oil with rosemary and bruised cloves of garlic is a favourite side dish in many Italian cafes.

I had a marvellous 'garlic experience' at the end of a recent holiday in France in the lovely southern town of Uzès. I recorded it in my travel diary:

With two days to go I went to the Garlic Fair, held this year on 24 June. I marvelled at the mountains of white and violet garlic for sale. Too late in the holiday to justify buying a plait. I was persuaded, however, to try a confit clove of new garlic for breakfast and it was mild and crunchy and quite delicious. I was assured by the robustly healthy vendor that this treat was marvellous for my heart. Fresh garlic was 3–5 euros per kilo, the white from the local countryside, the violet from nearby Lautrec. Locals were buying it by the case, or by the *manouille*, where about twenty heads were gathered into two plaits and the plaits were joined to form a handle. This was also called a 'basket of Provence'.

Another great snack is to take a freshly harvested tomato, halve it and then use it to rub a piece of grilled bread that you have already rubbed with cut garlic. Rub it quite hard until you are left with nothing but the skin of the tomato in your hand. This is a very popular treat from the Catalan region in Spain. One day in Barcelona I watched a family of six at a restaurant for lunch, all rubbing their own small round split loaf vigorously with garlic and tomato, from grandpa down to the youngest child.

I've given three different ways of making garlic-scented bread or croûtons on pages 312 and 313. Bread slices or cubes can also be fried in butter, which is delicious but which I don't recommend indulging in too often.

Especially for Kids Children love grilling bread and then brushing it with olive oil and rubbing it with garlic – three or four gentle swipes will be enough. The grilling can be done on a barbecue, perhaps right in the garden, or use a ridged cast-iron char-grill pan over medium heat. Once children have mastered this technique, a good activity is to think of different toppings for the bruschetta they have made.

Children also love bringing their small fists down sharply onto the flat side of a knife blade that is steadily pinning a garlic clove on a chopping board. An adult hand should be holding the knife steady on the clove of garlic. The smashed garlic still has to have the papery skin lifted away before the clove can be chopped. Another favourite activity is roasting whole heads of garlic in loose, oiled foil parcels, or with a little water in a gratin dish tightly covered with foil in a 180°C/Gas 4 oven for 45–60 minutes.

Garlic plaits are fun for children to make. They will then need to hang their plaits in a place that is cool, dry and frost-free. Kitchens are usually too warm and humid, so try a cupboard under the stairs.

Garlic-rubbed Bruschetta

SERVES 4 This grilled bread is used as the base for bruschetta. Once prepared, the grilled bread is ready for any savoury topping, including tomato and basil, prosciutto and rocket leaves, spinach or kale leaves blanched and sautéed in a little olive oil or butter, or a million other ideas.

1 loaf day-old sourdough bread,
cut into 8 × 1.5cm/½in-thick slices

1 clove garlic
extra-virgin olive oil, for drizzling

EXTRA EQUIPMENT
ridged char-grill
  pan or barbecue
  grill-plate

Heat a ridged char-grill pan or light the barbecue. Adjust heat to medium. Place bread slices on the char-grill pan or barbecue grill-plate and grill slowly. After a few minutes, turn bread over and grill the other side; the distinguishing marks of grill bars are part of the charm. The bread should be quite firm on the outside but still a bit soft in the middle.

Transfer grilled bread to a chopping board. Cut garlic clove in half and gently rub cut surface over the bread, then drizzle bread with a little olive oil.

Garlic Croûtes

MAKES 12–16 PIECES This garlicky bread is best used to serve alongside a soup or to spread with a softish pâté, dip or very fresh ricotta.

1 baguette-style breadstick
extra-virgin olive oil, for brushing

1 clove garlic

Preheat oven to 200°C/Gas 6.

Cut 12 or 16 slices from the baguette on the diagonal. If the croûtes are to be served just as they are, for example with a soup, cut the slices 5mm/¼in-thick. If they are to be offered with a dip they can be a little thicker.

Pour a little oil into a small bowl and lightly brush each side of the slices, then transfer them to a baking tray/s. Bake for about 10 minutes until edges of slices are deep-gold and centres look faintly golden.

Transfer bread slices to a tray to cool. Cut garlic clove in half and gently rub cut surface over bread. Once completely cool, the croûtes can be stored for a day or so in an airtight container.

Garlic Croûtons

SERVES 6–8 These croûtons are used to drop into soups or to toss with a salad. You could also add a tablespoon of stripped rosemary leaves to the bowl of garlicky oil at the beginning if you like.

1 loaf day-old sourdough bread
60ml/2fl oz extra-virgin olive oil

2 cloves garlic, crushed

Preheat oven to 180°C/Gas 4.

Cut bread into eight 2cm/¾in-thick slices, remove crusts and cut or tear into 2cm/¾in cubes. Pour olive oil into a bowl and drop in crushed garlic. Add bread cubes and toss well to mix and moisten.

Spread bread cubes on a baking tray in a single layer, leaving crushed garlic in the bowl. Bake bread cubes for about 15 minutes until golden brown and crusty on the outside but still a bit soft in the middle. You will need to shake the tray around a bit halfway through to ensure croûtons are baking evenly.

Tip croûtons back into bowl and toss with crushed garlic cloves (the oil will all have been soaked up by the bread). Leave to cool in the bowl before adding to a salad or offering with a wintry soup. Use immediately or store for a few days in an airtight container (in which case it would be a good idea to 'refresh' croûtons by tossing in a dry frying pan to warm them before using).

Roasted Garlic

Roasting whole heads of garlic is a fun thing to do, either in a foil parcel (see below) or directly in an ovenproof dish, perhaps with a bay leaf (see opposite). The flavour of roasted garlic is sweet and mellow, quite different from that of raw garlic in a dressing or chopped or sliced and fried. The soft pulp can be squeezed onto toast, into a soup, added to mashed potato or enjoyed alongside a grilled lamb chop. For the sake of energy efficiency, plan to roast something else in the oven at the same time (a rack or leg of lamb, for example, or a baked pudding or cake that will take about the same time). Once the roasted garlic pulp has been removed from the skins, the skins can be dropped into some simmering chicken stock to make a lovely garlic-scented broth. Add a pinch of saffron and a small handful of risoni pasta for a delicious first course, garnished with chopped flat-leaf parsley and grated parmesan.

1 or more heads garlic   **extra-virgin olive oil**

Preheat oven to 180°C/Gas 4.

Weigh garlic. The weight will determine how long garlic will take to cook.

Carefully cut a slice right across the top of the garlic head. You will see a cross-section of each garlic clove, each wrapped in its skin. Take a 24cm/9½in-square sheet of foil and drizzle a little olive oil in the middle. Roll each garlic head in oil, then gather edges of foil together and scrunch into a loose parcel. Place parcels on an oven shelf and cook for 40–60 minutes, depending on the weight of the garlic. A small head (40–50g/1½–2oz) will take 30–40 minutes to roast. A larger head (80–100g/3–3½oz) will take 45–60 minutes to roast. Carefully remove parcel to a chopping board. Unwrap and test with a skewer; it should slip through garlic head without any resistance. If it still feels firm, reseal foil parcel and bake for a further 15 minutes. When ready, either serve whole head alongside roasted or grilled meat or vegetables or divide it into sections and share cloves between diners. Alternatively, press each clove with the back of a teaspoon so that garlic pulp squirts out, then use as a wonderful flavouring in soups, sauces or dips.

Aïoli

MAKES 375ML/13FL OZ Pound 6 cloves garlic and a pinch of salt with a mortar and pestle to form a pulp. Transfer to a large bowl and work in 2 free-range egg yolks with the pestle. Very gradually add 375ml/13fl oz olive oil, drop by drop at first. It will become very thick. When almost all oil is added, add juice of ¼ lemon and taste for salt. If it curdles, put an extra egg yolk into a clean bowl and work in curdled mixture a little at a time – it should fix it.

GRAPES AND VINE LEAVES

Vitaceae family
Deciduous woody vine

Soil type
Grow in most soils, although prefer well-drained soil.

Soil preparation
Not required.

Climate
Many varieties are available to suit most climates, except high humidity areas.

Position
Sunny position.

How to grow
A grapevine can be grown for its edible fruit outdoors in a mild, sunny area or it can be planted under glass in a greenhouse or conservatory. Pick a suitable 'indoor' or 'outdoor' one for your location and make sure you have a strong support to hold the vine. To grow outdoors,

plant in spring, spacing 1.5m apart. Apply a general organic fertiliser and a small amount of sulphate of potash each spring. Keep vines watered in dry spells, especially when they are fruiting. Traditionally, a greenhouse vine was planted outside, then the stem trained through a hole in the greenhouse. If you have no border soil under glass, then grow the vine in a large tub of loam-based compost. There are several training and pruning methods. Consult a local expert or a pruning book. Pruning is generally undertaken in January.

Water requirements
Allow the soil to dry out between each watering.

Harvest period
New vines will take 2–3 years to develop fruit. Grapes are ready from August-October. Allow fruit to ripen on the vine.

Pests and organic control
Grapes are susceptible to many fungal diseases, such as powdery mildew, black spot and botrytis. Improved air circulation and removing old lower foliage can help prevent these; also keep the vine well mulched.

Companion planting
Hyssop is said to stimulate the growth of grapes, while geraniums attract pests away from the vine.

Quantities to plant for a family of four
1–2 vines should provide enough grapes for the table. Choose an early harvester such as Early Muscat and a mid to late harvester such as Sultana to ensure an extended harvest.

Grape (*Vitis vinifera*)

Growing and Harvesting If you decide to grow grapes, be careful when choosing a grapevine that you select a fruiting rather than an ornamental one. A grapevine provides shade from the summer sun and glorious colour in autumn, and can provide wrappers for the cook in late spring when the leaves are young and supple (but inspect them carefully for caterpillars first). Grapevines are fast growers and can grow several metres in a season. They must have a strong support to climb on, such as a trellis or pergola.

Take advice regarding which variety to grow to suit your region. Different varieties require different growing conditions. Some vines want to droop while others want to shoot upwards, for example. Each variety will require different support and may need to be pruned differently. Some are much faster growers than others. If you intend to dry the fruit, you should grow seedless and smaller varieties, which will dry better. However, as I explain below, they don't have to be seedless to achieve a good result.

Grapevines are not without their problems. Uncared-for plants get very messy and tangled, and not only does this prevent the sun from penetrating efficiently to ripen the fruit, but the tangle offers an invitation to insects and diseases. Bunches of ripe grapes (or at least some of them) may need to be bagged to protect them from birds. If only the birds would understand that some bunches are for them and leave the rest alone!

I once spent a few days at a retreat in South Australia in late autumn and marvelled at an overhanging Muscat grapevine with its many bunches of grapes shrivelling to muscatel raisins, hardly touched by birds. The weather was magnificent: clear skies and temperatures in the mid-twenties. The owners were certain that it was the noise of clinking cutlery and conversation that kept the birds away. Rarely could you expect bunches of grapes to dry on the vine like that without swarms of birds eating most of them! These bunches tasted magnificent, warm from the sun, and with a delightful plumpness merging into chewiness.

Recently I also saw a most luxuriant fruiting grapevine growing on a frame built over and around an impressive compost heap. No doubt the vine benefited from having its roots in the compost, but it is also a beautiful way of screening the compost area during the summer months when the family spends more time in the garden. And I smiled when I saw a strongly growing grapevine curling around a pre-loved brass bedhead in a school kitchen garden.

When grapevines are pruned, the prunings can be bundled and dried and will give a marvellous aroma to a barbecue. Another idea is for schools is to sell these bundles at a kitchen garden stall at the school fair.

Preparing and Sharing There are many varieties of grapes that can be grown at home – red, black or green; large, small or very small – with flavours ranging from rich and highly aromatic to rather insipid. Skins can be thick or thin. A home-grown bunch of grapes is a treat and is a perfect accompaniment to the cheeseboard or offered as a simple dessert. Grapes don't ripen further off the vine so be sure to pick and wash ripe bunches directly before eating; they don't store well.

I have never peeled a grape in my life, although I do occasionally remove the seeds before adding grapes to a dish as the bitterness of crushed grape seeds can be unpleasant. If you haven't grown seedless grapes, simply halve them then flick out the seeds with the point of a small sharp knife.

The tendrils from grapevines can be included in any spring salad, which is a fun thing to do and will intrigue young cooks.

Late spring or early summer is the best time to pick the first leaves to appear on the grapevine to use as wrappers. Whether they are large or small indicates variety, and that some have grown a bit faster than the others. Choose tender leaves that are hidden from the sun so you won't need to blanch them (see page 703) to make them pliable before using. They can be oiled and wrapped around small fish (think sardines or red mullet), small birds (quail or chunks of boneless, skinless chicken thighs), savoury minced patties (lamb or beef) or firm, mature mozzarella or cheeses with more of a bite such as fontina or haloumi. Young vine leaves look beautiful as a lining for a cheese platter to catch all the crumbs or oozings.

Choose the largest leaves to make dolmades (savoury rice rolled in fresh or pickled vine leaves) as they need their ends to be tucked in to make a neat roll, and must cook gently for some time for the leaves to be tender. Line the pan with several layers of vine leaves before tucking in the rolls. This will prevent the dolmades sticking to the base of the pan. They take at least 30 minutes to cook.

Later in the season the leaves will toughen and be fully grown – they will need to be dunked briefly in boiling water before being used as wrappers for barbecued food as described above. These large leaves can also be used to line an oiled gratin dish: drizzle them with extra-virgin olive oil and pack the dish with flat mushrooms and some sliced garlic, then cover with more oiled leaves and bake in a 180°C/Gas 4 oven for about 45 minutes. As the leaves crisp, the mushrooms exude a rich, dark juice. Another item to contribute to a school fair might be jars of homemade Pickled Vine Leaves (see page 320).

Many Greek and Italian households make small quantities of wine for family consumption from backyard vines.

Especially for Kids Dried fruit is such a popular snack for young children, so why not dry some of your own grapes? The connection between fresh grapes and dried currants, sultanas and raisins may be obvious to you but can come as a surprise to your children. I have already described how grapes can be dried while still on the vine (see opposite) if you are able to discourage birds. If dried on the vine there is no need to worry about an overnight shower of rain as the sun will soon dry the fruit the next day. This is not the case if the bunches have already been picked.

Sun-drying picked bunches of grapes will only be successful in regions with high summer and autumn temperatures and low humidity. Even so, the grapes will need to be brought in at night to protect them from condensation. It can take up to fifteen days to dry a bunch of grapes. One unexpected rainfall will ruin the lot. Once well dried, they can be stored in an airtight container. Greek friends store their dried grapes in bags with home-dried bay leaves. I am unsure whether this is for flavour or whether the bay is there to protect the grapes from insects. My herb books suggest that as bay leaves dry they give off an acid gas that is protective against some insects, especially weevils.

An interesting project for older children could be to involve them in constructing a simple drying rack. You will need a stainless-steel (or plastic mesh) screen supported on bricks or cement blocks to raise the screen and the fruit well above the ground. (Don't use aluminium or galvanised mesh or copper. These metals can oxidise and leave harmful residues on the grapes, rendering them inedible.) Site the drying rack on concrete or asphalt, well away from cars or foot traffic and over a sheet of aluminium. The sun's reflection on the metal increases the temperature and hastens the drying. The drying grapes will need to be covered with a layer of muslin to keep away birds or insects. Put the drying rack somewhere where an inquisitive family dog cannot get to it. Apparently vets now advise not to give dogs grapes or sultanas (or any grape products) as they can cause renal failure in dogs, especially greedy ones! Peg the muslin securely to the underneath screen. And remember to take the grapes inside every night. An easier but less interesting way to dry grapes is to purchase a home dehydrator and follow the manufacturer's instructions.

Pickled Vine Leaves

MAKES 40 The leaves of your grapevine can be used for cooking regardless of whether the vine is an ornamental or a fruiting vine. Freshly picked leaves are really only suitable for stuffing or grilling when they are very young. For the rest of the year it is handy to have a few jars of pickled leaves set aside. Small fish such as sardines or red mullet are traditionally rolled in vine leaves before being grilled on the barbecue, or try wrapping them around a chunk of a firm cheese such as haloumi. And pickled vine leaves are needed to make dolmades unless the available fresh leaves are very tender.

40 vine leaves, cut from the vines without any stems	150g/5oz kitchen salt 2 litres/3½ pints water

EXTRA EQUIPMENT
1 × 1 litre/1¾ pint-capacity pickling jar with wide mouth, sterilised (see page 706) kitchen string

Tip boiling water into a large mixing bowl. Put vine leaves on a clean tea towel on a baking tray or workbench near the mixing bowl. Dip vine leaves, a few at a time, into the water. Push them under water using clean tongs for about 20 seconds. Remove leaves and spread on tea towel. Cover with a second tea towel and continue until all leaves have been dipped and spread out to dry. Discard this water.

Meanwhile, dissolve salt in 2 litres/3½ pints fresh water in a saucepan, bringing it to simmering point over high heat.

Make a stack of 8–10 leaves, fold them over on themselves and tie each bundle with kitchen string. When all bundles are tied, drop them into boiling brine. Count to 10 and then lift bundles from brine and transfer to a sterilised jar with string intact; they can be packed in quite firmly. Ladle boiling brine over bundles in jar to cover them completely. Cover and cool. Pickled vine leaves can be used after 1 week or stored for several months. To use, remove a bundle of leaves with tongs. Store the opened jar in the refrigerator.

Patrizia's Grape Fritters

MAKES 10 These delicious treats were cooked for me by my friend Patrizia Simone who, along with her husband George and son Anthony, operates the delightful Simone's Restaurant in the town of Bright in north-eastern Victoria. I spent two fascinating weeks with the family in Perugia in 2007. Patrizia has a seemingly never-ending repertoire of marvellous traditional Italian dishes and this is just one of them. We ate these lovely fritters as part of a very indulgent breakfast, but they would be just as welcome as dessert.

EXTRA EQUIPMENT
sifter or coarse-
 meshed sieve
sugar dredger or
 small sieve

200g/7oz self-raising flour
2 tablespoons caster sugar, plus
 1 tablespoon extra for dusting
¼ teaspoon salt
1 free-range egg

250ml/9fl oz milk
500g/1lb black grapes, preferably
 seedless, stems removed
grapeseed oil or vegetable oil,
 for frying

Preheat oven to 100°C/Gas ¼ and put a paper towel-lined ovenproof plate inside to keep warm.

Sift flour, sugar and salt into a mixing bowl. Lightly whisk egg with milk. Make a well in flour and stir in egg/milk mixture, then whisk to form a smooth, thickish batter. Leave to stand for 30 minutes.

Cut some of the grapes in half with kitchen scissors. Drop whole and halved grapes into the batter.

Pour grapeseed or vegetable oil into a medium-sized non-stick frying pan to a depth of 1cm/½in and heat over medium heat until hot. Test the heat by dropping in a small blob of batter. It should sizzle as it hits the oil and start to brown at once. Drop in heaped tablespoonfuls of batter and fry for 1 minute, then turn with an egg lifter. Press down lightly on each fritter with the egg lifter. Fry until golden brown on both sides. Remove to the warmed paper towel-lined plate. Continue with remaining batter until all fritters are cooked.

Dust with extra caster sugar and serve.

Chicken with Grapes

SERVES 4 Add a small handful of halved, seeded grapes to the pan when roasting a jointed chicken 20 minutes before it is ready, along with a generous slosh of verjuice. Turn each piece of chicken to coat with the juice. Both chicken and grapes will caramelise slightly.

Grape, Ginger and Yoghurt Brûlée

SERVES 4 This delicious and incredibly simple dessert relies on using the right-shaped dishes (shallow) and an efficient overhead griller. I love the tang of the ginger; however, younger palates may prefer it made with cinnamon instead – oh, and the yoghurt used must be thick!

350g/12oz seedless grapes,
  stems removed
200g/7oz Greek-style yoghurt
  (see page 706)

45g/1½oz soft brown sugar
1 teaspoon ground ginger
  or cinnamon

EXTRA EQUIPMENT
4 × 125ml/4½fl oz-
  capacity shallow
  oval gratin dishes

Pack one-quarter of the grapes really tightly in a single layer into four 125ml/4½fl oz-capacity gratin dishes; they will nearly fill the dishes. Spoon yoghurt over, then smooth and press it around grapes with the back of a teaspoon. You are aiming for a smooth surface, just glimpsing the dark shapes beneath. Chill filled dishes in the refrigerator for 1 hour (or even overnight).

Preheat overhead griller to maximum.

Mix brown sugar and ginger or cinnamon, ensuring there are no small lumps in sugar. Sprinkle and smooth an even layer of sugar mixture over yoghurt, using the back of a teaspoon, until no yoghurt is visible.

Place gratin dishes on a baking tray and slide under griller, then watch carefully. In less than 1 minute the sugar will caramelise and start to bubble. Remove baking tray and allow gratins to settle; don't try to eat this dessert until sugar has stopped bubbling, as it will be very hot!

Melita's Greek Grape Pudding (*Moustalevria*)

SERVES 6–8 This delicious and very simple Greek sweet may look like chocolate but is richly raisin in character. Every traditional Greek cook has their own version, but this is my friend Melita's. Bring 4 litres/7 pints grape juice (obtained by pressing freshly picked grapes in an electric juicer, or by using a food processor and forcing the purée through a coarse strainer) to the boil and reduce by half, skimming off any foam that rises to the surface. Leave to cool and let any sediment settle. Ladle the juice into a clean saucepan, leaving the sediment behind. Compost sediment. Stir in 200g/7oz semolina and 150g/5oz coarsely chopped roasted almonds, then cook, stirring continuously, until well thickened. Pour into a shallow, lightly oiled dish and sprinkle with sesame seeds and/or ground cinnamon. *Moustalevria* is nicest served cold.

HERBS

See also **BASIL, CHERVIL, CHIVES AND GARLIC CHIVES, CORIANDER, DILL, MINT, OREGANO, PARSLEY, ROSEMARY, SAGE, SORREL, TARRAGON and THYME.**

Growing and Harvesting Herbs are essential for good cooking. Most are easy to grow and they mature relatively quickly, so are likely to be among your first harvest. Every garden, no matter how small, can find space for the essentials: parsley, rosemary and thyme. And don't forget oregano, chervil, chives, basil, dill, mint, tarragon and coriander – all perfectly happy in pots, beds or on windowsills. Herbs are tolerant of most soils, although they will grow best of all in a garden bed or pot that has plenty of organic matter included. Before you pick any from the garden, you should reflect on how the herbs are to be used. A bunch of mixed herbs, picked without thought and chopped together, can confuse a dish so that your family never fully appreciates the special individual flavour of each herb from the garden.

Aromas, as well as what our eyes perceive, are the first signals for taste. They can tell us much about freshness, maturity and the special characteristics of each plant. The aroma of fresh culinary herbs begins to fade as soon as they are picked, so pick them just before they're required, if possible. Reject discoloured or wilted herbs, as these will not taste good. In most parts of the UK, herbs will not continue to grow throughout the winter outside. The shrub (such as sage and rosemary) and perennial (such as chives and mint) types might be hardy and survive, but there will be a lack of fresh new foliage and, even if the plant is evergreen, the leaves are often damaged by the weather. Don't despair – a few fresh herbs over winter are possible, either by potting up plants and moving them under cover, or protecting them in situ with a cloche, or raising from seed in pots indoors.

Clockwise from bottom: Sage (*Salvia officinalis*); Dill (*Anethum graveolens*); Flat-leaf parsley (*Petroselinum crispum* var. *neopolitanicum*); Mint (*Mentha* ×*spicata*).

If you want to dry some of a bumper crop to use during the winter, the flavour is best when the plants are just coming into flower. This is also when they are in full production and there is more likely to be a surplus. I recommend cutting them early in the morning then hanging them in bunches upside-down in an airy, shady place. Tarragon is an exception; although it does flower, the blooms are inconspicuous and the herb cannot be propagated by seed. Its lovely fragrance is best preserved in vinegar or in a frozen roll of tarragon butter (see page 629).

Some herbs are not at all dainty. Borage, the 'herb of gladness', with its irresistible sky-blue flowers, self-seeds readily and quickly invades every corner. Angelica, a handsome plant, can grow as high as 2 metres and lives for three years. It is known for its hollow stems and large pale-green leaves. It will grow in broken shade as well as full sun. The stems can be candied and the leaves reduce acidity, so are sometimes combined in small quantities with rhubarb in pies, fools or crumbles.

Comfrey is another sprawling herb; in fact unsafe to eat, it is grown in organic gardens for its leaves, which are used to make a good fertiliser (see **Green manure**, page 690). Comfrey is also valued as a compost accelerator. Comfrey is known as 'knit-bone' by herbalists because of its ability to heal damaged skin tissues. This is just one of the miraculous claims made for comfrey.

Container Planting Most herbs are ideal for planting in containers, either on their own if they are invasive, such as mint, or in combination with others. It can be interesting to plant herbs together in the groupings you frequently use in the kitchen: Asian herbs in one pot, for example, and aromatic woody herbs such as thyme, rosemary and oregano in another.

If the pots become overgrown, you should divide and re-pot the plants. I like potting up some of my divided herbs and giving them as gifts to friends moving into a new home. You can purchase special herb pots with several openings at different heights. These do look lovely. You don't plant the herbs directly into the small jutting-out openings, however, as there is insufficient potting mix there for their spreading roots. Rather, you plant the seedlings at different heights in the pot as you fill it with potting mix. You then gently tease and train the growing plants to peep out of their own hole. You add more mix to the pot up to the level of the next hole, then plant the next herb and so on. Another interesting idea is to fill octagonal terracotta drainage pipes with potting mix and stand them in a sunny corner of your garden, then use them to grow a single compact plant such as thyme.

Preparing and Sharing As soon as picked herbs touch water they start to deteriorate. It is better to store them in the refrigerator in a dry plastic bag lined with a sheet of paper towel, rather than standing them in a jug of water.

When herbs that have been hung to dry are absolutely dry, the leaves should immediately be stripped from their stalks and stored in clean, dry, dark glass containers. These dried herbs should be used for one winter only and then any leftovers discarded. Dried herbs are stronger than fresh, so when cooking use about one-third of what you might use if fresh.

Very thin omelettes made with a good quantity of a single herb are an excellent way of showcasing the special flavour of, say, basil, oregano or thyme. They can make quick roll-ups if simply spread with a fresh cheese such as ricotta or fresh goat's cheese.

Some herb combinations are very well known, such as:

- *bouquet garni:* bay leaf, flat-leaf parsley stalks, thyme (orange zest)
- *fines herbes:* flat-leaf parsley, chives, chervil, tarragon
- *gremolata:* flat-leaf parsley, lemon (or orange) zest, garlic
- *herbes de Provence:* rosemary, thyme, lavender, oregano
- *persillade:* flat-leaf parsley and garlic.

Especially for Kids Gathering tiny posies of herbs for the table, including their leaves and flowers, is a favourite activity and it is the best way to become familiar with different plants. You can investigate if the herb flowers have more or less fragrance than the leaves.

Encourage young gardeners to notice how beautiful these dainty plants are. Suggest that they run their hands over different plants to note the varieties in texture, and crush a few leaves to smell. If you grow a number of herbs, your children can play a game of finding four herbs that smell very different from one another, learning the name and studying the leaf shape of each one – this is a popular activity for the students of the school Kitchen Garden Program. Another activity could be to find herbs that smell similar to one another such as chervil and fennel leaves, lemon thyme and thyme, or flat-leaf parsley and chervil. Do these herbs belong to different family groups?

Moving into the kitchen, it is fun to introduce children to the pleasure of pounding herbs (and aromatics such as seeds, spices, chillies and garlic) with a large stone mortar and pestle.

An interest in using herbs for both culinary and medicinal applications is ancient indeed and this tradition can be drawn on to engage children with the herbs they grow in the garden. They will be interested in hearing some of the myths and stories that surround the names, origins and uses of herbs and aromatic plants that have been recorded and passed down through the centuries.

Orris root is one fascinating example, as it is the most common fixative used in perfume-making. It is the rhizome of a certain variety of iris, highly valued since the days of ancient Egypt. The iris is represented on the coat of arms of the city of Florence, where the cultivation of orris root has been important since the thirteenth century. The iris rhizomes are harvested after the flowers have died and are then peeled and dried. Sliced and powdered, they become orris root, which has a faint violet scent, but its more important attribute is of enhancing the scent of other ingredients and 'fixing' the scents for a longer time. Orris root powder is also an important ingredient in potpourri (see Lemon Potpourri on page 381 and Rose Potpourri on page 565).

When I spent some time in Tuscany ten years ago I met an elderly woman, Flora, whose family had grown irises for generations for the perfume trade. She told me that porcupines eat the valuable rhizomes before they are harvested so are regarded as absolute pests. Flora was especially proud of one of her specialties, roasted porcupine, although the creature is in fact protected!

Saffron and Herb Pancake Roll-ups

MAKES 6 I have used a combination of basil and chives in these pancakes, but they are good with many other herb combinations. Coriander and mint would work well, as would flat-leaf parsley, chives and chervil or dill, chives and flat-leaf parsley. Think about what you are intending to spread on the pancakes when deciding on the herb combination. I spread these pancakes with soft goat's cheese, but other possibilities might be hummus or taramasalata (which would work well with coriander and mint); smoked salmon (which would suit a combination that includes dill); or grated raw carrot (which would suit any of the suggested combinations).

Try spreading the pancakes with fresh ricotta seasoned with sea salt and freshly ground black pepper or roll the pancakes with a purée of cooked leeks, then place them in a buttered gratin dish and warm in the oven, dotted with more butter and parmesan. On another occasion, the pancakes can be rolled around just-cooked asparagus spears. Yet another thought is to allow the pancakes to cool completely, then spread them with the selected filling and stack them on top of each other. The stack can then be cut into wedges.

The pancakes can be successfully reheated if placed on a plate, covered with foil and transferred to a preheated 150°C/Gas 2 oven for about 15 minutes.

a pinch of saffron stamens	40g/1½oz unsalted butter, melted and slightly cooled	**EXTRA EQUIPMENT**
1 tablespoon hot water		1 × 18–20cm/7–8in
75g/2½oz plain flour	6 basil leaves, chopped or torn into tiny pieces	pressed-steel
¼ teaspoon salt		crêpe pan (see
1 free-range egg	1 teaspoon chopped chives	page 47)
180ml/6fl oz milk	soft goat's cheese or your choice of filling, to serve	

Soak saffron in a small bowl in the very hot water.

Sift flour and salt into a bowl. Lightly whisk egg and milk together. Make a well in flour and tip in egg/milk mixture, then use a whisk to bring the mixture together, whisking to form a smooth batter.

Add 2 tablespoons of the melted butter to the saffron mixture. Pour saffron mixture into batter and stir in with a wooden spoon; don't use a whisk as the saffron strands will catch in its wires. Stir in herbs and stand for 20 minutes at room temperature.

Spread out a clean tea towel near the stove. Heat a crêpe pan and brush its base with a little of the remaining melted butter. Using a ladle, tip in 2 tablespoons pancake batter and immediately swirl to cover base of pan. Cook for 30–40 seconds to set and then flip with an egg lifter (I find it easier to do this with my fingers, but I have had years of practice of dabbling my fingers in hot pans).

Slide cooked pancake onto the tea towel. Continue until all batter is used, re-brushing base of pan with extra melted butter if needed; as there is butter in the batter you may not need any more. Spread with goat's cheese or your desired filling, then roll up and eat immediately.

Salsa Verde

MAKES 125ML/4½FL OZ This is a wonderfully versatile sauce. I love spreading it on grilled eggplant or grilled zucchini. It is sensational eaten with a simple poached chicken breast or a grilled lamb chop. Try it with grilled asparagus or a barbecued or grilled fillet of fish or use it as a sauce for raw vegetables. There are many versions in both Italian and French cookbooks. The most common variations are to add a slice of day-old bread soaked in water, oil or vinegar and crumbled, or to include finely chopped or minced hard-boiled eggs, although I have done neither. Sometimes the finished sauce is quite loose, and sometimes it is made quite thick – there is no absolute right or wrong way.

1 spring onion, trimmed and
  very finely sliced
¼ small handful chopped flat-leaf
  parsley
1 tablespoon chopped rocket leaves
  (long ends removed)
1 teaspoon chopped French tarragon
1 teaspoon chopped lemon thyme

1 teaspoon chopped chervil
3 cornichons (see page 704), sliced
1 tablespoon salted capers,
  soaked in hot water and rinsed
60ml/2fl oz extra-virgin olive oil
sea salt and freshly ground pepper
finely grated zest and juice
  of ½ lemon

As each ingredient is chopped or sliced, transfer it to the same small bowl. Stir in oil and adjust seasoning with salt and pepper. Don't add lemon juice until you are ready to use the sauce, as it will dull its beautiful green colour. On the other hand, any leftovers will still taste great so don't throw them away, just store them closely covered with plastic film in the refrigerator.

JERUSALEM ARTICHOKES

Asteraceae family (includes globe artichokes and lettuce) Perennial; may be planted as an annual

Soil type
Not fussy about soil type so a good crop for the edge of a vegetable plot.

Soil preparation
None required apart from to clear the weeds before planting and fork in a general organic fertiliser at planting time.

Climate
Suitable for all areas but in windy sites be prepared to stake plants.

Position
Sun or partial shade.

How to grow
Use potted plant or tubers from the previous year's crop (these can also be purchased). Plant in February to March direct into the ground. Plant 10–15cm deep, 45cm apart, if you want to use them as a windbreak plant in two or three rows 1m apart.

Water requirements
None required.

When to fertilise
These plants do not need feeding.

Harvest period
7–8 months from planting. Top growth will die back in late autumn, cut back and then lift tubers as required. Clear ground of tubers by early spring.

Pests and organic control
Use crushed egg shells around the base of the young plants to deter snails and slugs.

Companion planting
Wormwood to deter snails.

Special information
Mound soil around the base of the plants as they mature to increase yield.

Quantities to plant for a family of four
4–6 plants.

Jerusalem artichoke (*Helianthus tuberosus*)

Growing and Harvesting Home gardeners are often delighted to share this crop, as once established it can become prolific. Plants can grow to a height of 2 metres and cast a lot of shade, so situate them where the shade will not cause problems to a neighbouring crop. Perhaps utilise the shade and plant a delicate herb such as chervil underneath, where it can grow in the filtered light. Although the plants have most attractive yellow flowers (showing the family connection with sunflowers) that can be added to herb posies, for best quality tubers, nip out the flower heads at budding stage and cut all flower stems close to the ground before harvesting the tubers.

The tubers are ready for harvest after the flowers and stems have died off. As there are usually plenty to choose from, reject any that are not firm or that have spongy patches. Tubers not harvested will produce even more plants the following year. However, it is better practice to harvest the crop completely and plant new tubers each season. As Jerusalem artichokes don't store well, harvest and use them as soon as possible.

When growing Jerusalem artichokes as a perennial crop, keep them out of a crop rotation system. Instead, plant them on some spare ground where little else will grow.

Container Planting It is perfectly possible to grow Jerusalem artichokes in a pot, but remember that you must wait 4–5 months before there will be any return. Thus only the most passionate Jerusalem artichoke eaters are likely to grow these tubers this way.

Preparing and Sharing Although raw Jerusalem artichokes are not universally enjoyed, they can be peeled, sliced thinly and dressed with a vinaigrette, especially one made with a small quantity of hazelnut or walnut oil, such as is used in the Apple and Bacon Salad with Quail Eggs and Hazelnuts on page 72. In fact, sliced raw Jerusalem artichokes could be added to that salad in place of some of the apple. The late Alan Davidson, editor of *The Oxford Companion to Food,* likened the flavour of young raw Jerusalem artichokes to that of Brazil nuts.

Their most annoying characteristic (apart from their well-deserved reputation for causing intestinal gas) is their many bumps and protuberances, which are usually found in large quantities. I believe Jerusalem artichokes need to be peeled as otherwise they seem to retain a faint taste of soil, so I just slice these bumpy bits away, dropping them in the compost bucket, and am prepared to find a few plants growing in the compost heap later on.

Jerusalem artichokes discolour once they are peeled, so have a bowl of water acidulated with lemon juice nearby and drop the pieces in as they are prepared.

Both the delicate flavour and creamy colour of Jerusalem artichokes are shown to advantage in a puréed soup. They are also delicious roasted with rosemary and maybe a clove or two of bruised garlic, either on their own or combined with chunks of carrot, parsnip and potato.

Especially for Kids You may need to clarify the confusion between Jerusalem artichokes and globe artichokes. Despite their name, Jerusalem artichokes have nothing to do with the city of Jerusalem, and while they look nothing like globe artichokes, both are in fact part of the Asteraceae family, which also includes sunflowers.

Jerusalem Artichoke Pakhoras

SERVES 4 These fritters are so delicious that I cannot imagine a child rejecting any vegetable presented in this way. The batter is light, crisp and tender and the spicing is delicate. Chickpea flour is often labelled gram flour or besan flour, especially in Indian shops. Pakhoras can be served simply sprinkled with sea salt or with a spicy dip such as the Tomato and Coriander Salsa on page 251. Chickpea flour is prone to weevils so I keep mine in the freezer in a sturdy sealed and labelled plastic container – I did once have a nasty surprise when I used chickpea flour instead of ground almonds in a cake. From then on I have been assiduous about labelling containers! Here I've used Jerusalem artichokes, but on another occasion I might make mixed vegetable pakhoras. Cauliflower, sweet peppers, whole chillies, sweet potato, eggplant or whole green beans can all be dipped in the batter and fried in the same way. Use your commonsense about timing. A chunk of raw potato will take longer (about 8 minutes) than a piece of eggplant (3 minutes) and a whole chilli will be ready in even less time. As with all fried food, these fritters are most delicious as soon as they are fried.

EXTRA EQUIPMENT
mortar and pestle
wok or counter-top
  deep-fryer
candy thermometer
long-handled
  brass skimmer
  or slotted spoon

150g/5oz chickpea flour
1 teaspoon salt
½ teaspoon bicarbonate of soda
½ teaspoon ground turmeric
½ teaspoon cumin seeds

½ teaspoon coriander seeds
½ teaspoon chilli flakes
250ml/9fl oz cold water
400g/14oz Jerusalem artichokes
375ml/13fl oz vegetable oi

Sift chickpea flour, salt, bicarbonate of soda and turmeric into a bowl.

Dry-roast cumin and coriander seeds separately in a small frying pan over medium heat until fragrant. Tip seeds into a mortar, then add chilli flakes and grind all to a fine powder with the pestle. Stir ground spices into flour mixture. Make a well in the centre and slowly stir in cold water to form a smooth batter. Leave for 15 minutes.

Cut knobby bits off Jerusalem artichokes, then peel and cut into 1cm/½in pieces. Drop into batter.

Preheat oven to 100°C/Gas ¼ and put a paper towel-lined ovenproof plate or baking tray inside to keep warm.

Heat oil in a wok or deep-fryer until it registers 180°C/355°F on a candy thermometer. Using your fingers, lift several pieces of Jerusalem artichoke out of batter, allowing excess batter to drip back into bowl. Gently slide artichoke into oil; *do not* drop pieces into the oil as it will splash and burn you. Don't crowd wok or deep-fryer; each piece should be able to bubble happily without sticking to the next. Fry for about 5 minutes. Separate pieces and turn over using a brass skimmer or slotted spoon. Lift a piece out and test for tenderness by inserting with a skewer. Lift pakhoras onto the paper towel-lined plate. Continue until all pakhoras are cooked. Serve at once.

Jerusalem Artichokes Provençale

SERVES 4 This style of vegetable dish instantly makes me think of an outdoor lunch. It is best cooked and presented in the same dish. It would make an excellent accompaniment to a whole baked fish (see opposite).

a pinch saffron stamens
1 tablespoon hot water
500g/1lb Jerusalem artichokes, peeled
2 tablespoons extra-virgin olive oil
25g/1oz fresh breadcrumbs
2 cloves garlic, finely chopped
1 × 400g/14oz tin diced tomatoes

a handful pitted black olives
sea salt and freshly ground black pepper
2 tablespoons chopped flat-leaf parsley, plus extra to serve
1 teaspoon lemon-infused extra-virgin olive oil (optional) or an extra drizzle of extra-virgin

EXTRA EQUIPMENT
wok
bamboo steamer with lid (or saucepan with steamer insert and lid)
1 × 1½ litre/ 2¾ pint-capacity gratin dish

Preheat oven to 180°C/Gas 4. Soak saffron in hot water.

Half-fill a wok with water. Place a bamboo steamer over water and turn the heat to high. As soon as water boils, scatter Jerusalem artichokes in a single layer in steamer and cover with lid. Steam for 5 minutes, then test with a skewer; they should still feel a little firm in the centre. Transfer artichokes to a bowl and leave to cool. Cut into bite-sized chunks, then put in a mixing bowl and drizzle with 1 teaspoon of the olive oil. Shake to coat each piece.

Heat half of the remaining oil in a non-stick frying pan over medium heat. Add breadcrumbs, then stir often until golden and sandy. Set crumbs aside. Wipe out pan with paper towel. Heat remaining oil in pan over medium heat, then briefly sauté garlic. Add tomato and saffron mixture. Bring to the boil and cook over high heat, stirring for 8–10 minutes or until tomato is well reduced. Drop in artichokes and olives. Stir to mix and season with salt and pepper. Tip mixture into a 1.5 litre/2¾ pint-capacity gratin dish, then scatter over mixed parsley and breadcrumbs.

Bake for 15 minutes or until bubbling around the edges. Drizzle with lemon-infused oil or olive oil and scatter with extra chopped flat-leaf parsley. Serve hot or warm.

Jerusalem Artichoke Chips

Choose and wash the longest tubers, then dry well and slice thinly with a plastic vegetable slicer (see page 46) or push them through the chute of a food processor with the slicing blade attached. Fry chips in hot clean oil. Chips are delicious scattered over fish, or added to a bowl of leafy greens, or served as a nibble.

KIWIFRUIT

Actinidiaceae family
Deciduous wood vine

Soil type
Moist but well-drained, fertile soil. Prefers acid soil.

Soil preparation
Dig in well-rotted manure and compost a few weeks before planting.

Climate
Most areas but to grow outside most types crop better in milder, warmer areas. In cold areas, *A. arguta* 'Issai' is worth a try outdoors against a warm wall. The alternative is to grow under glass in a large greenhouse or conservatory.

Position
Prefers sun, warmth and a sheltered position.

How to grow
Plant a bare-rooted plant in the dormant season in mild areas or a container-grown plant in spring in colder areas. Take care not to pile soil or mulch up against the plant stem. You will only need one plant of the newer self-fertile types such as 'Jenny' or *A. arguta* 'Issai' but if you are growing traditional varieties you will need one male variety for up to 8 female varieties. Where space is limited a male and female can be planted in the same planting hole and trained together. Kiwi fruit plants are vigorous vines that will need training against a strong support. Take expert advice on training and pruning of young plants for the first 3 years.

Water requirements
Keep soil moist during the growing season.

When to fertilise
Feed each spring (April) with an organic fertiliser for fruiting plants. Mulch with pine bark chips or other acidic mulch each spring.

Harvest period
Vines will produce fruit after 3–4 years, although *A. arguta* 'Issai' can set fruit within 1–2 years. Harvest fruit in September to October provided the weather is dry.

Pests and organic control
No major problems.

Companion planting
Marigolds, lavender and calendula.

Special information
Once trained vines are trained into a framework, in summer prune out excess new growth, tie in the rest, in winter prune old wood to form fruiting spurs.

**Quantities to plant
for a family of four**
1 self-fertile plant, or 1 male and 1–2 females.

Kiwifruit (*Actinidia deliciosa*)

Growing and Harvesting The beautiful emerald-green flesh of the kiwifruit is sweet and highly perfumed. In the home garden kiwifruit vines will weave sinuously over a trellis or an arbour in a remarkably short time, providing shade in summer and, because the vines are deciduous, allowing light in during winter. They do need protection from strong winds. Once well established, the vines are very long-lived and vigorous (growing up to 10 metres in height!), so their supporting structure should be sturdy. A well-established pair of vines can produce up to a hundred fruit in a season.

Kiwifruit is native to China, where there are many varieties (not all edible), but it was New Zealand that developed it into a crop of international importance and popularity, hence its common name. It is now grown worldwide. In recent years, self-fertile varieties, such as 'Jenny' or *A. arguta* 'Issai', that can be grown outdoors in the UK, have made it possible to grow this fruit without taking up valuable space. The latter is smooth-skinned and produces lots of smaller fruits. Where a variety is either male or female, you will need one of each. However, the male plant can be up to 6 metres away from the females and one male can service up to eight female plants. The female cultivar 'Hayward' is the best-known type, and the male cultivar 'Tomuri' is usually sold as the pollinator.

Bees do not pollinate kiwifruit efficiently as the flowers don't produce nectar, although they are very sweetly scented. I recommend planting bee-attracting plants such as marigolds and lavenders nearby, and being prepared to hand-pollinate the flowers. Children can help do this. Female flowers have a small swelling at the base of the petals. Early in the morning, hand-pollinate the female flowers by transferring pollen from the male flower using a paint brush, or break off the male flower, bend back its petals and press it against a female flower. Yet another plant in the garden that may initiate a discussion about sex!

Kiwifruit vines have most attractive heart-shaped leaves but will not bear fruit for the first few years. However, the fruit is worth waiting for and doubly welcome in that the harvest is in autumn, after all the other soft fruits have finished bearing. Don't pick during or within five days of rain – dry, sunny weather concentrates sugars in the fruit and wet weather does the opposite. Kiwifruit will keep for several weeks in the refrigerator after picking, but they can also remain on the vine until you are ready.

Container Planting Kiwifruit are unsuitable for growing in containers.

Preparing and Sharing A ripe kiwifruit should feel heavy when cradled in the hand; it should be neither rock-hard nor very soft, but give just slightly when gently pressed, like an avocado. The easiest way to enjoy the fruit is to cut it in half widthways and scoop out the flesh with a teaspoon. Otherwise, use a vegetable peeler to strip away the brownish, hairy peel then slice the fruit or cut it into wedges as you might do with a lemon. Kiwifruit is good sliced onto the top of a pavlova, perhaps combined with a sliced banana. It combines well with passionfruit and/or strawberries, in fruit salads, for instance. It also makes a pretty sorbet (see page 340). A drop of lemon juice heightens its flavour. Kiwifruit is not good cooked.

Especially for Kids Try halving the fruit lengthways, scooping out the flesh and freezing the shells (freeze them in an empty egg carton). Make a very simple sorbet (see Kiwifruit Sorbet on page 340) and spoon the sorbet back into the frozen shells for a spectacular dessert.

In school kitchen gardens, growing kiwifruit leads to a discussion about the word 'dioecious', which means a species that has separate male and female plants.

Kiwifruit and Banana Brûlée

SERVES 4 I make no apologies for repeating the idea for this lovely dessert, also included on page 322. This simple dish relies on using the right-shaped dishes (shallow) and an efficient overhead griller. I love the tang of the ginger, however younger palates may prefer cinnamon instead. And be sure to use thick Greek-style yoghurt. Bananas and passionfruit are included here, although it could be made with kiwifruit alone.

EXTRA EQUIPMENT
4 × 125ml/4½fl oz-capacity shallow oval gratin dishes

3–4 kiwifruit, peeled and cut into small pieces
1 small Lady Finger banana, halved lengthways and thickly sliced
pulp of 1 passionfruit
2 teaspoons honey

210g/7½oz Greek-style yoghurt (see page 706)
45g/1½oz soft brown sugar
1 teaspoon ground ginger or cinnamon

Place kiwifruit, banana and passionfruit pulp in a small bowl. Drizzle honey over fruit and mix lightly. Pack fruit mixture really tightly in a single layer into four 125ml/4½fl oz-capacity gratin dishes. It should nearly fill each dish. Spoon yoghurt over, then smooth and press it around fruit with the back of a teaspoon. You are aiming for a smooth surface, just glimpsing fruit beneath. Chill filled dishes in the refrigerator for 1 hour or even overnight.

Preheat overhead griller to maximum. Mix brown sugar and ginger, ensuring there are no small lumps in sugar. Sprinkle and smooth an even layer of sugar over yoghurt, using the back of a teaspoon, until no yoghurt is visible.

Place gratin dishes on a baking tray and slide under hot griller, then watch carefully. In less than 1 minute the sugar will caramelise and start to bubble. Remove baking tray and allow gratins to settle; don't try to eat this dessert until sugar has stopped bubbling as it will be very hot!

Kiwifruit and Passionfruit Compôte

SERVES 4 Compôte is a rather posh French word that usually means 'stewed fruit', but it can also be used to describe fruit that is very lightly cooked and allowed to macerate in its own juice. Made in minutes, this dessert is best served cold, perhaps spooned around some perfect garden-picked strawberries, or for a super-fancy dessert, alongside the Kiwifruit Sorbet on page 340.

6 kiwifruit, peeled and cut into 6 wedges, then cut into 1cm/½in-thick slices

pulp of 3 passionfruit
1½ tablespoons caster sugar
juice of 1 orange, strained

Place kiwifruit in a bowl. Scoop passionfruit pulp into a stainless-steel or other non-reactive saucepan or small frying pan. Add sugar and cook over medium heat for 2–3 minutes, stirring until sugar has dissolved. Pour resulting syrup over kiwifruit. Stir gently to mix, then leave to cool.

Add just enough of the orange juice to loosen compôte a little and brighten its colour. Chill in the refrigerator before serving.

Kiwifruit Sorbet

SERVES 12 To make this sort of sorbet you really do need an ice cream machine, but given the popularity of ice cream and frozen desserts, and the relative simplicity of making fruit-based sorbets, it could be a good investment. The first step of peeling and puréeing the fruit can be done in advance and the purée measured, labelled and frozen in an airtight container. This same recipe and technique could be used with apricots, plums or tamarillos – all fruits that can ripen in embarrassingly large numbers all at once.

500g/1lb kiwifruit (about 5–6 large), halved lengthways	**SYRUP**
	250g/9oz caster sugar
juice of 1 orange, strained (optional)	200ml/7fl oz hot water
	juice of 1 lemon, strained

EXTRA EQUIPMENT
food processor
coarse-meshed
   sieve (optional)
empty egg carton
   (optional)
ice cream machine

To make the syrup, dissolve sugar in hot water in a saucepan over medium heat, stirring with a metal spoon until sugar crystals have disappeared. Increase heat to high and bring syrup to the boil. Boil for 30 seconds. Remove from heat and pour into a measuring jug to cool. Add lemon juice to cooled syrup. With a sharp teaspoon, dig out as much kiwifruit flesh as you can, just leaving the thin brown shells. Pack shells into an empty egg carton or put on a small tray and freeze for at least 30 minutes.

Purée kiwifruit flesh in a food processor. If you wish to extract seeds, press purée through a coarse-meshed sieve. Measure flesh; you need 500ml/18fl oz. If you don't have this amount, add enough orange juice to make up the balance.

Combine purée with cold syrup and churn in an ice cream machine according to manufacturer's instructions. When firm, scoop purée into rigid kiwifruit shells, either piled up and rough, or levelled off, or smoothed to a rounded dome-shape. Cover with plastic film and return to freezer until needed. If you have not saved and frozen kiwifruit shells (or have leftovers), scoop finished sorbet into an airtight container, then seal, label and freeze.

Allow sorbet to soften a little at room temperature before serving.

KOHLRABI

Brassicaceae family (includes broccoli, cabbage, cauliflower, cresses, radishes and turnips) Annual

Soil type
Moist, well-drained soil, fertile and enriched with organic matter. Does best on slightly alkaline soil.

Soil preparation
Dig in organic matter or well-rotted manure a few weeks prior to planting.

Climate
Suitable for all climates.

Position
Prefers full sun or partial shade.

How to grow
In April–June, directly sow seeds at a depth of 1cm in clumps of 2 or 3, 10cm apart. Thin out to 15cm apart.

Water requirements
Frequent watering is required for rapid growth.

Successive planting
Leave about 2–3 weeks between each planting, throughout the growing season.

When to fertilise
Use a liquid fertiliser (see page 691) or worm tea (see page 695) once every 4 weeks, and water in immediately.

Harvest period
After 12–14 weeks, when the stem should be 5–10cm in diameter.

Pests and organic control
As it is a member of the cabbage family, in theory it can suffer from the same problems (see page 181). In practice, it grows fast and has thick leaves so usually escapes. Woody texture and split stems can occur if plants suffer a check to growth (usually irregular watering). Crop rotation every year will help avoid soil disease problems such as clubroot.

Companion planting
Cucumber, spring onions and silver beet (Swiss chard). Avoid potatoes, tomatoes and climbing beans.

Special information
Keep the soil moist and free from weeds by mulching. Kohlrabi is best grown quickly to ensure tender stems. Don't mound the soil around the swelling stem.

Quantities to plant for a family of four
2 every 3 weeks throughout the growing season.

'Purple Vienna' kohlrabi (*Brassica oleracea* var. *gongylodes*)

Growing and Harvesting Kohlrabi is a fascinating-looking vegetable; 'a bit like an alien', was the assessment of one young gardener. The edible part of the plant is the above-surface bulb it forms; it is actually a swollen stem from which grow thinner stems (that are not usually used) with deep-green leaves. The leaves can be eaten, although this is only recommended when the bulb is very small. The edible bulb can be purple, cream or pale green. I am advised by a kohlrabi grower that the green variety grows much faster than the purple one. Another gardening friend advises that the green variety is sweeter, while the violet one is hardier. I am yet to grow my own kohlrabi.

To enjoy kohlrabi at its best it needs to grow fast so fertilise with a liquid fertiliser (see page 691) or worm tea (see page 695) every 4 weeks. It is best picked at about the size of a small apple. It can be as small as a golf ball or as large as a grapefruit, and if starved of water or nutrients, the bulb can be very woody. If the plants are directly sown, thinnings can be used in a quick stir-fry.

Container Planting As kohlrabi is a very compact plant, it can be grown in a pot or tub with other plants such as silver beet (Swiss chard), spring onions or cut-and-come-again leafy salad greens.

Preparing and Sharing Kohlrabi is such a versatile vegetable, it deserves to be more widely known. It is always peeled and any fibrous layer under the skin should also be peeled away (as for turnips). The leaves of young bulbs are edible, but the tough stems are only good for the compost bucket.

Kohlrabi tastes like peeled broccoli stalks with a touch of turnip-like sweetness. Young kohlrabi can be peeled and sliced, then eaten raw as part of a plate of crudités served with a cream cheese or blue cheese dip (see Celery and Blue Cheese Party Sticks on page 222) or Salsa Verde (see page 329). It can also be grated and added to: a mixed slaw-style salad (see Winter 'Tabbouleh' with Cabbage on page 186); a filling for rice-paper rolls; or a rémoulade sauce as for celeriac (see page 229).

The bulb can be boiled, steamed, stir-fried, sautéed or braised. Like turnip, kohlrabi flesh soaks up cooking juices and other flavours, making it ideal to put into a casserole or to cook with a slow-roasted chicken or duck. Without a dominant flavour of its own, it will blossom in character when cooked with herbs, spices and other aromatics.

Especially for Kids The first time a young gardener sees a kohlrabi they are amazed at its appearance. At school, teachers might ask students to write a description or invent a story starring this curious-looking vegetable.

As the cabbage white butterfly is such a destructive pest, children may like to hunt for them with a butterfly net – but the butterflies will need to be disposed of, not released.

Kohlrabi Glazed with Vino Cotto

SERVES 2–4 Glazed vegetables are a classic French preparation. The same method is used for cooking small turnips or chunks of turnips (see page 662); small onions or French shallots; chunks of carrot or even whole garlic cloves. The time it takes for the braise to be complete varies depending on the vegetable. Often two or three glazed vegetables are combined to make a very pretty and delicious accompaniment to a slow-braised shoulder of lamb or a braised duck. This way of cooking vegetables can be made richer by replacing the water with chicken stock. Chopped herbs can be added at the last minute when the last few shakes of the pan are happening.

EXTRA EQUIPMENT
sauté pan or
saucepan (large
enough for
vegetables to
fit closely in
a single layer)

300g/10½oz kohlrabi (2–4), peeled,
  halved lengthways and cut into
  3–4 wedges
½ teaspoon salt
1 teaspoon white sugar

40g/1½oz butter
375ml/13fl oz water
1 teaspoon vino cotto (see page
  706) or balsamic vinegar

Preheat oven to 100°C/Gas ¼ and put in an ovenproof serving dish to warm.

Drop kohlrabi wedges into a sauté pan or saucepan and ensure that they will all fit snugly in a single layer without too much extra space.

Tear off a piece of baking paper and fold it in 4. Cut into a quarter-moon shape and open it out. You should have a circular piece of paper (called a **Cartouche**, see page 703) that fits reasonably neatly over the kohlrabi. Set aside.

Add salt, sugar, butter and water to kohlrabi; water should barely cover it. Cover with cartouche and cook over medium heat for 15 minutes, then test for tenderness by inserting a fine skewer. A few spoonfuls of water can be added if kohlrabi is not tender when almost all liquid has evaporated. If it is quite tender and there is still quite a bit of liquid present, remove cartouche, increase heat to high and keep a close watch to ensure kohlrabi doesn't catch on base of pan, then simmer until liquid has reduced.

Once there is only a little water remaining in the pan, dribble in vino cotto or balsamic vinegar and start shaking the pan every 30 seconds or so to prevent kohlrabi sticking. It should develop a lovely golden glow and a slight shine. As last drops of liquid evaporate, give a final shake and tip kohlrabi into warmed serving dish or around the meat or poultry dish it is to accompany. Serve at once.

Kohlrabi and Chickpea Soup

SERVES 4 This spicy soup is very fast to prepare and is a great way to use a relatively small harvest of kohlrabi. If you are using tinned chick peas, drain and rinse the chick peas with cold water. Use the remaining chick peas to make a salad such as the Chickpea Salad with Roasted Sweet Peppers and Spicy Dressing on page 488 or another dish like my recipe for Chicken with Chick Peas, Carrots and Couscous on page 202 the next day.

1 teaspoon cumin seeds
1 teaspoon coriander seeds
½ teaspoon chilli flakes
½ teaspoon ground turmeric
2 tablespoons extra-virgin olive oil
200g/7oz kohlrabi (2 smallish ones), peeled and cut into 1cm/½in cubes
200g/7oz cooked chick peas (or 200g/7oz tinned chick peas, drained)

200g/7oz ripe tomatoes, cut into 1cm/½in cubes (2 medium-sized, depending on variety)
1 tablespoon tomato paste
750ml/27fl oz water
1 teaspoon salt
⅓ small handful thinly sliced coriander (or fine sprigs) or chopped flat-leaf parsley

EXTRA EQUIPMENT
mortar and pestle

Dry-roast cumin and coriander seeds separately in a small frying pan over medium heat until fragrant. Tip seeds into a mortar, then add chilli flakes and grind to a fine powder with the pestle. Stir in turmeric.

Heat olive oil in a medium-sized saucepan over medium heat and fry spice mixture for 1 minute. Tip in kohlrabi and sauté, stirring, for 1 minute or so. Add all remaining ingredients (except coriander or parsley) and bring to simmering point. Simmer for 10–15 minutes or until kohlrabi is tender. Taste and add salt if necessary.

Ladle into bowls and scatter generously with coriander or parsley, then serve.

Kohlrabi with Salsa Verde

Steam small peeled kohlrabi for 3–5 minutes. Cut into 5mm/¼in-thick slices, then brush with olive oil and sear in a hot dry frying pan over high heat for 30 seconds or so on each side. Spread a little Salsa Verde (see page 329) on each slice and serve as one of several vegetable-based antipasti.

Kohlrabi, Carrot and Cucumber Salad with Mint and Peanuts

SERVES 4 The proportions of one vegetable to another really don't matter much in this salad as it can be varied according to your harvest. Whatever the final mix, this dish is fresh and a little spicy. Peanuts are of course optional. This Asian-style salad makes a light first course or it can be one of several side dishes offered alongside a platter of soy-braised chicken or a roast duck bought from an Asian takeaway shop specialising in cooked poultry.

1 large carrot (about 150g/5oz), coarsely grated
1 cucumber (about 200g/7oz), coarsely grated
300g/10½oz kohlrabi (2–4), coarsely grated
1 fresh small red chilli, halved, seeded and thinly sliced

2 teaspoons salt
1 teaspoon caster sugar
1 tablespoon rice vinegar
juice of ½ lime (optional)
1 tablespoon thinly sliced mint
2 tablespoons thinly sliced coriander
2 tablespoons coarsely chopped dry-roasted peanuts (optional)

EXTRA EQUIPMENT
food processor with grating attachment
heavy glass tumbler or a large pestle

Place vegetables and chilli in a mixing bowl and scatter with salt. Fork through and leave for 20 minutes.

Tip vegetables into a strainer placed over a mixing bowl. Press with the bottom of a tumbler or a pestle from a large mortar to extract as much liquid as possible. Discard liquid from bowl and wipe bowl clean.

Tip vegetables and chilli back into bowl, then add sugar and vinegar. Taste for balance and add more chilli, sugar or a squeeze of lime juice if necessary. Stir in mint, coriander and peanuts, if using, and serve at once.

Kohlrabi Crisps

Peel small kohlrabi, removing any fibrous layer. Slice very thinly with a plastic vegetable slicer (see page 46) or the slicing blade attachment in a food processor. Heat vegetable oil for deep-frying in a wok or counter-top deep-fryer to 180°C/Gas 4, then deep-fry kohlrabi slices until pale-gold. Drain very well on paper towel, then season with sea salt and freshly ground black pepper. Serve as a nibble or alongside a main course dish. A bowl of vegetable crisps made from kohlrabi, celeriac, beetroot, parsnips and Jerusalem artichokes is a surefire way of attracting attention to these lesser-known vegetables.

Kashmiri-style Slow-cooked Kohlrabi Leaves with Mustard Oil

SERVES 4 AS PART OF A MULTI-DISH MEAL I first read of this delicious way of cooking textured green leaves in Madhur Jaffrey's cookbook *A Taste of India*. Further research into Kashmiri specialties identified the dish as *haak*, many versions of which include the use of a number of spices, which I have done. This dish works well with freshly gathered kohlrabi leaves but is more commonly made with other greens such as silverbeet leaves, young beetroot leaves and young turnip tops (or even a combination). The final result is very soft and mellow; totally different from crunchy stir-fried greens. A non-traditional use for the finished dish would be as a topping for bruschetta (see page 312) in which case you could make it with Tuscan kale. The finished dish can also be served as a bed for a piece of fish; just arrange the two in a shallow ovenproof gratin dish. If you sprinkle the fish with a little olive oil and cover with a piece of foil before you bake it, you'll have a complete dinner in around 15 minutes. Mustard oil gives this dish its distinctive flavour. It is available in all Indian food stores and in many Chinese grocery stores also.

EXTRA EQUIPMENT
salad spinner
wok
wok sang
(see page 47)

60ml/2fl oz mustard oil
1 teaspoon cumin seeds
2 cloves
250g/9oz small kohlrabi (or other) leaves, washed, well dried and coarsely chopped

2 dried long red chillies, split lengthways and seeded
2 cloves garlic, thinly sliced
375ml/13fl oz water
½ teaspoon salt
2 teaspoons ghee (see page 704)

Heat a wok over high heat and pour in mustard oil. Allow it to come to smoking point, then as soon as it has just started to smoke quickly add cumin seeds and cloves and tip in kohlrabi leaves, chilli and garlic. Turn quickly for a few seconds and then pour in water and scatter over salt.

Cook kohlrabi leaves over high heat for about 15 minutes, stirring with a wok sang from time to time; they are ready when all water has evaporated. Tip ghee onto greens in wok. Mix through quickly and scoop greens into a serving bowl. Retrieve chilli, then chop into small pieces and stir it back into greens. Taste for salt and season if desired. Serve hot or warm.

LAVENDER

Lamiaceae family
Perennial

Soil type
Well-drained soil, can tolerate dry soil in summer but not waterlogged conditions in winter. Dislikes lots of organic matter.

Soil preparation
As long as the soil is well-drained, no additional preparation is required. The drainage of heavy clay soils can be improved by forking in horticultural grit and mixing in with the soil.

Climate
English lavender (Lavandula angustifolia) is hardy in most areas if its roots are not sodden overwinter.

Position
Prefers sun and an open position.

How to grow
Buy a young potted plant and plant in spring or summer (April-July). Plants can be propagated from cuttings taken in June to July and grown on in pots (keep them frost-free overwinter) to plant out the following spring. Plant 20–45cm apart depending on the variety. Lavender is very versatile, it can be grown as line of edging against a path or a single plant can be grown in a container of free-draining potting mix.

Water requirements
Water in young plants until they are growing away, thereafter plants are fairly drought-tolerant so no watering is required unless the plant is in a container.

When to fertilise
These plants do not usually need feeding unless they are growing in containers, a light sprinkling of an organic fertiliser for flowering plants will suffice.

Harvest period
Pick the flowers at their peak (usually June to July) if you want to dry or preserve them. Otherwise pick flowers and stems at anytime.

Pests and organic control
Lavender has few pests but look out for rosemary beetle, a small metallic green and purple beetle. Pick off and destroy any you find. Leaf spotting may occur if plants are overcrowded or growing in damp or wet conditions, remove affected leaves.

Companion planting
Lavender attracts many beneficial insects such as bees. It is often grown alongside garden pinks or at the edge of rose beds.

Special information
Lavender plants often become woody after a few years, they can simply be replaced but pruning from a young age can keep them looking good. Clip the flower heads off once they are faded but do not cut into the old brown wood. In spring, young plants can be cut back to the emerging young growth.

Quantities to plant for a family of four
1 plant.

English lavender (*Lavandula angustifolia*)

Growing and Harvesting There are more than thirty different species of lavender but most of us recognise just a few. English lavender flowers only in summer and grows as a bush with very showy flowers. The world's finest oil of lavender comes from English lavender, and is used for all manner of things from toilet waters to soaps to room fresheners. The scent is strongest when the stems are picked just as the flowers open. French lavender (*L. stoechas*) has flowers topped with eye-catching bracts. It is less hardy than English lavender and will only survive outdoors in mild areas. The flowers are less scented but the leaves have a camphor note so the English lavender is preferred for culinary use.

All lavenders are perennial. Bees love lavender and for that reason alone it is welcome in a kitchen garden.

Container Planting A pot of English lavender is a delightful feature in a small courtyard garden. A 60-centimetre pot will do well for a single plant. Fertilise once a year and don't over-water. Here's another word of warning: if very small children play in the courtyard, remember that your lavender bush will be a magnet for bees. It is not a good idea to place it right where a toddler might grasp the flowers.

Preparing and Sharing Lavender can be used in very small quantities to flavour lamb, rabbit or chicken dishes, usually as part of a bouquet garni (see page 635) as is done in Provence. Alternatively, a few flower heads can be infused in a sugar syrup that is then used to poach stone fruits. Some cooks add small quantities of dried lavender to biscuits, cakes and other baked goods.

To pick lavender for drying, the stems should be cut just where they meet the leaves on a still, dry day. Hang the bundles upside down in a dry place. When the flowers are quite dry they should be stripped from the stalks and stored in clean, airtight containers until needed. Like dried herbs, the dried flowers should not be stored beyond a season.

Especially for Kids Encourage children to brush against these plants, to crush a leaf here and there, to smell the fragrance, or to pick a dainty flower sprig to add to a posy for the kitchen table. Anything that increases the pleasure they experience of being in the garden and engages their senses is to be encouraged. (Despite my earlier comments about bees and young children, parents should not frighten children off lavender altogether, but it is sensible to be nearby if crushing and snipping lavender is happening.) It would be fun to help young children make lavender bags or sleep pillows as gifts for friends or for a school fair.

Lavender Sugar

Pulse a dried head of lavender with caster sugar in a food processor and then sift the sugar before using it. Lavender sugar can be sprinkled over freshly iced cup cakes, or used to make lavender meringues. The lavender flavour is quite powerful and can be an acquired taste.

Lavandula's Lavender Scones

MAKES 8–10 This lovely recipe comes from the proprietor of Lavandula, a delightful lavender farm at Shepherd's Flat near Daylesford in the state of Victoria (see below).

In France, a discreet touch of lavender is mixed with other herbs to flavour rabbit and lamb dishes, and sometimes baked goods too. The important point is that a small quantity of lavender imparts a lot of aroma, so it's a good idea to use discretion and a light hand.

EXTRA EQUIPMENT
pastry scraper

375g/13oz self-raising flour,
    plus extra for dusting
40g/1½oz pure icing sugar
½ teaspoon dried lavender flowers

125ml/4½fl oz thickened cream
160ml/5½fl oz milk
jam and double cream, to serve

Preheat oven to 240°C/Gas 9.

Sift flour and icing sugar into a mixing bowl and then add lavender. Cut cream in with a pastry scraper or broad spatula. Mix in milk quickly.

Sift a little flour over a chopping board and over a baking tray. Turn dough onto floured board. Pat into a rectangle and cut with decisive cuts into approximately even-sized 6cm/2½in squares. Separate and place dough squares onto floured baking tray. Bake for 5 minutes or until browned on top. Reduce oven temperature to 180°C/Gas 4 and bake for a further 10 minutes.

Line a large mixing bowl with a dry tea towel and place cooked scones inside. Fold ends of towel over scones to stop them becoming too hard. Split and serve with the best jam and thick double cream.

LEEKS

**Alliaceae family
(includes French shallots,
garlic and onion)
Biennial grown as
an annual**

Soil type
Well-drained, moist, fertile,
loamy soil.

Soil preparation
Dig in organic compost or
well-rotted manure a few
weeks prior to planting.

Climate
Suitable for all climates.

Position
Prefer full sun or partial shade.

How to grow
In March-April, sow in modular
trays at a depth of 5mm. When
seedlings are 20cm high,
transplant into its permanent
position. Prepare a 10cm-wide
× 15cm-deep hole for each
seedling, 15–20cm apart. Water
seedlings in; the soil will fall from

the sides and begin to cover
the roots; make sure all roots
are well covered. Cut the top
two-thirds of growth off each
seedling to help encourage root
development and reduce water
loss. Plant in blocks among
companion plants.

Water requirements
Water regularly in dry spells to
encourage strong growth. It is
important to keep soil moist.

Successive planting
Leave about 4 weeks between
each planting, throughout the
growing season.

When to fertilise
Use a liquid fertiliser (see page
691) or worm tea (see page 695)
every 2 weeks.

Harvest period
7–8 months when the stems
are 1.5–2.5 cm thick. Leeks will
continue to grow and are still
delicious when very large after
10 months' growth.

Pests and organic control
Seldom affected by pests but
crop rotation is important as
leeks are prone to leek rust.
Remove and destroy badly
affected plants (do not compost).
Look out for rust-resistant
varieties.

Companion planting
Onions, carrots, celery and
celeriac. Don't grow with corn,
cabbages, beans or potatoes.

Special information
Don't plant where other family
members grew the previous year.

**Quantities to plant
for a family of four**
8 plants every 4 weeks during
the growing season.

Leek (*Allium ampeloprasum* var. *porrum*)

Growing and Harvesting Leeks are a great winter and spring vegetable. While onion-like, they are much sweeter and they slow-cook to a mellow softness. They have the added advantage of looking very handsome in the garden and they need very little attention. The soil can be 'hilled up' to achieve the maximum white section at their base. This is called blanching.

Leeks can be picked when about the thickness of an adult's thumb. It is a good idea to harvest every alternate leek if you have planted the leeks quite close together. Once the very skinny ones have been harvested, those remaining will continue to grow fatter. Both skinny and fatter leeks are delicious. They can be left in the ground for many months, although I recommend harvesting them young if you intend to use the leeks whole in gratins, or cook them with other spring vegetables in a pot-au-feu, or serve them as a cooked salad vegetable. Fully grown leeks are excellent for turning into soups or for pie or tart fillings as long as the centre has not become woody. In fact, the sweetness increases in older leeks. Leeks are not suitable for eating raw.

Leeks will eventually bolt (see page 687) and produce a long stem topped with a very attractive ball of flowers that, if left in place, will eventually shower seeds over the garden bed. Alternatively, allow this seed ball to dry and collect it for next year's seed. Pull the leek out of the ground before the seeds start to fall and hang it upside-down in a dry, well-ventilated space over a sheet of white paper. Bag and label the collected seeds.

Container Planting As leeks are very compact plants, it is possible to plant them in a container together with other non-spreading plants such as spring onions, carrots and celeriac. Conventional gardening wisdom says you should not plant leeks or any other member of the onion family in the same container the following season. However, I have done just that due to lack of another suitable space and, after feeding the soil with well-rotted manure, the crop was just as successful in the second year. I will not grow them in the same container for a third year, though. For more information see **Crop rotation** on page 688.

Preparing and Sharing As the leeks may have been 'earthed up' with soil to achieve the maximum white section at their base, it follows that there will be quite a bit of dirt between the layers. Therefore, it is important to learn how to get leeks really clean before you cook them. This is easier if the white parts of the leeks are first cut into rounds and swished in a bowl of water (which can then be used to water a thirsty plant).

However, if whole leeks are required it is best to cut off most of the dark-green top section (a little leek top will be fine in the compost) and then trim the bases and make a slit down the white part of the leeks (see opposite). If the leeks are large, turn them and slit again so that the cuts make a cross; take care not to cut all the way through. Soak the whole leek in water for 15 minutes or so until there are no signs of dark patches underneath the top layer of leaves, then continue with the recipe.

Small slender whole leeks (sometimes called pencil leeks) can be steamed, then brushed with olive oil and grilled on a barbecue grill-plate. Accompany them with a bowl of the Red Pepper and Saffron Sauce for Almost Anything on page 491 for dipping into.

Leeks of any size are wonderful slowly cooked in butter in a covered pan to make what the French call a *fondue* (from the verb *fondre*, to melt), and can then be spooned under simply cooked fish, delicate poultry or meat dishes, or used to make tart fillings. Leeks can be sliced and sautéed; when combined with potatoes they make the classic leek and potato soup (served chilled, this soup is known as vichyssoise). Combined with other vegetables they can be baked in foil or as a gratin, either with or without a cheesy sauce.

Leeks must be thoroughly cooked until really soft. They are inedible if cooked al dente and can cause an unsuspecting diner to choke. I have encountered a few leek terrines in my time that were quite dangerous. Because of their long shape it is appealing to line a terrine dish with cooked leeks and maybe layers of fish or other ingredients and bind the whole with a savoury jelly. Not only are such terrines devilishly difficult to cut neatly, they are impossible to eat if the leeks are insufficiently cooked.

Thin shreds of leek are delectable if deep-fried. Try frying a mix of shredded carrot and leek and scattering these crunchy morsels over fish or scallops baked in the half-shell.

Especially for Kids Leeks may be quite unfamiliar to many children as they are not as widely appreciated as they deserve to be. Perhaps discuss the different members of the Alliaceae family and how they vary in strength of flavour. Does cutting leeks make your eyes water the way they do when you cut onions?

Leek, Ham and Goat's Cheese Gratin

SERVES 4 This gratin is easy to make and can be assembled several hours (or even the day) before it is needed. It is an ideal dish to have ready for lunch after a busy morning, or a true comfort dish perfect for a light evening meal, with some salad and some fruit to finish. All that is required is a moderate (180°C/Gas 4) oven and about 25 minutes for the gratin to be thoroughly hot and appealingly crusty.

butter, for greasing
6 medium-sized leeks (about
    600g/1lb 5oz), dark-green tops
    and bases trimmed
salt
150g/5oz ham, shredded

210g/7½oz plain yoghurt
2 free-range eggs
100g/3½oz marinated goat's cheese
50g/2oz parmesan, grated
freshly ground black pepper
25g/1oz fresh coarse breadcrumbs

EXTRA EQUIPMENT
1 × 1.5 litre/
    2¾ pint-capacity
    gratin dish (about
    26cm × 20cm/
    10in × 8in)
sauté pan
slotted spoon
heavy glass tumbler
    or pestle

Preheat oven to 180°C/Gas 4. Grease a 26cm × 20cm/10in × 8in gratin dish with butter.

Slice leeks into 1cm/½in-thick rounds and put them into a bowl of cold water for a few minutes, swishing with your fingers to release any sand or dirt.

Bring a sauté pan of lightly salted water to the boil. Drop leek into simmering water and cook for 8 minutes or until tender. Using a slotted spoon, transfer leek to a colander set over a mixing bowl. Press with the back of a slotted spoon, then press again with the base of a heavy glass tumbler or a pestle to extract as much water as possible. Tip drained leek into a bowl and add ham, then mix.

In another bowl, lightly whisk together yoghurt, eggs, goat's cheese and 25g/1oz of the parmesan. Taste for seasoning, remembering that both cheese and ham are salty. Grind in some pepper.

Mix cheese mixture with leek/ham mixture and tip into buttered gratin dish. Mix breadcrumbs with remaining parmesan and scatter over the top. Bake for 25 minutes or until golden and bubbling, then serve.

Leek Tart

SERVES 6 A great leek tart has a crisp crust, lots of leeks and not too much cream filling. Cook plenty of washed, sliced and well drained leeks (see above) in butter slowly in a covered frying pan over low heat for 20 minutes or until really soft. Blind-bake a 20cm × 4cm/8in × 1½in-deep tart shell (see page 510) for 20 minutes at 200°C/Gas 6. Lightly whisk 3 free-range eggs with 160ml/5½fl oz cream, stir in leek and season well with sea salt and freshly ground black pepper. Spread into prepared pastry shell, dot with butter and bake at 180°C/Gas 4 until filling sets. Lovely served with a tomato salad.

Leek Fritters

MAKES 12 These tender little fritters will be a huge hit. Serve them alongside sausages or grilled tomatoes for brunch, or as an accompaniment to a simple main course.

2 medium-sized leeks (about
  200g/7oz), white parts only
1 tablespoon extra-virgin olive oil
½ teaspoon salt
80ml/3fl oz water
2 free-range eggs (at room
  temperature), separated
1 tablespoon chopped flat-leaf parsley
1 tablespoon chopped basil,
  dill or mint

100g/3½oz soft cheese, crumbled
  (such as feta or plain or
  garlic-flavoured cream cheese)
1 tablespoon plain flour
sea salt and freshly ground
  black pepper
olive oil, for pan-frying

Quarter leeks by cutting along them in half lengthways, then turning them and cutting again. Cut widthways into 5mm/¼in-thick pieces. Float chopped leek in a bowl of cold water, swishing with your fingers to help release any sand or dirt. Scoop leek out onto a clean, dry tea towel and pat really dry.

Heat olive oil in a small saucepan. Tip in drained and dried leek, salt and water. Cook covered over low heat for 5–8 minutes or until leek is well softened and water has been absorbed. Tip into a bowl and leave to cool.

Lightly whisk egg yolks with herbs. Stir egg/herb mixture and cheese into leek mixture; it doesn't matter if cheese stays in smallish pieces. Sift over flour and mix through. Season to taste with salt and pepper.

Using a whisk or electric mixer, whisk egg whites to form soft peaks and fold into leek mixture with a large metal spoon.

Heat a non-stick frying pan over medium heat and brush it with a small amount of olive oil. Fry tablespoonfuls of leek mixture gently for 2 minutes on each side. Don't overcook as leek fritters are most delicious if still moist in the middle. Serve at once.

Baby Leeks with Fried Eggs and Parmesan

SERVES 4 This makes a very elegant first course or a brunch dish. It is only worth doing this with young leeks pulled from the garden when they are no more than 2 centimetres/¾ inch thick. If they are even smaller, allow three or four leeks per person rather than two. The ratio is one egg per serve, regardless of how many leeks you use. Choose rectangular gratin dishes that will allow the leeks to lie snugly side by side without too much extra space. The cooked leeks can be cut in half widthways if you want to use shallow round gratin dishes.

8 baby leeks (or more, depending on size), dark-green tops and bases trimmed
100g/3½oz unsalted butter
salt
4 free-range eggs
juice of 2 lemons, strained

2 teaspoons snipped chives
1 tablespoon chopped flat-leaf parsley
sea salt and freshly ground black pepper
1 tablespoon extra-virgin olive oil
50g/2oz shaved parmesan

EXTRA EQUIPMENT
4 individual gratin dishes (long enough to accommodate leeks)
sauté pan, large enough to hold the leeks in a single layer
Microplane grater that makes thin shavings (or vegetable peeler)

Slit leeks halfway down white parts, then turn and slit again. Soak leeks in a bowl of cold water for a few minutes, swishing with your fingers to help release any sand or dirt.

Preheat oven to 100°C/Gas ¼. Choose 4 small gratin dishes (preferably rectangular). Put 20g/¾oz of the butter in each gratin dish and put in oven to warm.

Bring a sauté pan of lightly salted water to the boil and lower in leeks. Simmer for 10 minutes over medium heat or until the point of a sharp knife penetrates leeks easily; cook an extra few minutes if there is any resistance as half-cooked leeks are horrible.

Spread a dry tea towel on a baking tray, then transfer leeks to the tray. Fold tea towel over leeks and weight with something heavy (a few tins of tomatoes lying on their sides would be ideal). Leave for 2 minutes to remove excess water. Slice leeks in half widthways if you are using round gratin dishes. Transfer leek to warm dishes and then roll in melted butter in gratin dishes. Return gratin dishes to oven.

Melt remaining butter in a medium-sized non-stick frying pan over medium heat. When butter just starts to foam, add eggs, then spoon bubbling butter over yolks. When egg whites are a bit crispy at the edges and just set, tip in lemon juice and herbs and increase heat to high for a few seconds so butter mixture bubbles. Remove gratin dishes from oven. Slip 1 egg on top of leeks in each dish, then season with salt and pepper.

Add olive oil to pan, swishing to mix, then spoon pan juices over leeks and scatter shaved parmesan over each egg. Serve at once.

LEMONS AND ORANGES

Rutaceae family
Evergreen tree

Soil type
Well-drained, fertile and preferably lime-free.

Soil preparaton
Citrus are grown in containers so a loam-based potting mix with added grit is usually used if citrus potting mix is not available.

Climate
All are frost tender to some degree.

Position
Prefers sunny, sheltered position with plenty of light.

How to grow
Buy a young potted grafted plant and plant in summer (June-July). Keep outside until September then bring into a heated greenhouse or conservatory, with a minimum winter temperature of 7°C. Pay particular attention to watering and feeding.

Water requirements
Require regular watering but prefer a soaking then allowed to dry out a bit rather than 'little and often'.

When to fertilise
Heavy feeding is required, a high nitrogen feed with trace elements during the growing season and a general purpose feed overwinter. Specialist citrus feeds for summer and winter are available.

Pruning
Minimal pruning, just tidy up or cut back unwanted growth in spring. Thin out fruitlets so only one per cluster develops. Remove any shoots below the graft line.

Harvest period
Can take 7–12 months for the fruit to ripen, many will hang on the tree until ready to use.

Pests and organic control
Most of the pest problems arise when the plant is under glass. Scale insects (with the associated black sooty mould) can disfigure the leaves and make them sticky, wash with soft soapy water. Red spider mite can be controlled with biological control, to prevent problems maintain the humidity with regular misting.

Companion planting
Not applicable.

Quantities to plant
for a family of four
2 or more plants.

Lemon (*Citrus limon*)

Growing and Harvesting There are few things more beautiful than a fully laden citrus plant grown well, often the plant is carrying both scented flowers and slow-ripening fruit at the same time, nestling in amongst glossy evergreen leaves. It is a challenge to grow citrus well in the UK, they are frost-tender plants and need a winter minimum temperature of 7°C or higher, yet good light levels. This necessitates plants being grown in containers so they can be moved to large heated greenhouse or conservatory, when necessary. Typically, the potted plants are placed on a patio or outdoor summer quarters in early June then bought inside well before the first frosts (mid-end September). The alternative is to grow them all year round under glass but then it is often too hot and dry for them over the summer period unless the structure is well-ventilated and the humidity raised. Put them outside where possible as this helps to ripen the wood, be aware that some carry sharp spines.

Container Planting Despite their lack of hardiness, citrus plants are long-term investments so care needs to be taken with the type of potting compost and feed. You may be able to get specialist potting mixes and feeds from a citrus nursery or garden centre, otherwise use a loam-based compost such as a John Innes No2 or No3 with extra horticultural grit mixed in for added drainage. An alternative, where pot weight is an issue, is to use a lime-free (ericaceous compost, usually peat-based) with perlite mixed. To maximise fruiting, it is best to keep the roots restricted in the same size pot, or to move up in pot sizes slowly until you reach a container diameter of 60 centimetres. Containers, such as terracotta or concrete, that keep the roots cool in summer are preferred of plastic and metal. The potting mix will need to be refreshed every couple of years or so, simply scrape the top few centimetres off the top and replace with fresh. Late spring, just before growth commences is the best time for potting on or topping up with fresh mix.

Make sure the graft (the swollen bump on the stem where the rootstock was joined to the top growth) is above the soil line.

Water plants thoroughly, then let the potting mix start to dry out before watering again. The plants dislike lime so in hard water areas, save rain water for them. Special citrus feeds are available and worth using, follow instructions as the feeding is often different in the growing season when they need high nitrogen and trace elements to that overwinter when they have a weaker general purpose feed.

Be sure to cut fruit cleanly from your plants (a pair of secateurs is ideal for this) rather than simply twisting it off, as this prevents damage to the stems. The plants are slow-growing so there is not much need for pruning, plants can be shaped in spring, cutting back long shoots. However, plants can be cut hard back if required and will respond well, although do cut back beyond the graft!

Citrus covers a wide range of fruits from lemons, oranges, limes – even grapefruits and kumquats. They vary in size and hardiness, so do a bit of research to find one that will suit the facilities you can provide (citrus specialist www.readsnursery.co.uk can advise and supply by mail order). It is well worth buying a pot-grown grafted plant rather than a seed-raised one, it will cost more initially but will fruit much sooner and the fruit will be more consistent. Two compact, easy-to-grow citrus are Meyer's lemon and lime 'Tahiti', both have relatively good cold-tolerance.

Other small ones include kaffir lime, whose aromatic leaves are used in Thai cooking, kumquat (not really a citrus but fruits can be used for drinks and decoration). One of the few citrus that is suitable as a houseplant is calamondin, it can cope with hot, dry spells and be grown in a small pot on a windowsill and fruits used in marmalade.

Orange trees tend to be slower growing but ultimately larger the lemon or lime bushes, again there are many available but 'Valencia' is one to look out for as the fruits are sweet and seedless.

Preparing and Sharing A bumper crop is unlikely unless you are lucky enough to have an orangery so enjoy the individual fruits as they are ready. One particular benefit is that they, unlike most lemons on sale, are unwaxed so you can use the zest in recipes or use cut slices for drinks. Marmalade-making, cordial-making, preserving lemons in salt, pickling and spicing oranges or lemons, preparing chutney, candying peel, freezing juice and enjoying puddings, cakes and tarts made with fresh juice are just some of the ways these marvellous fruits can be used. Salads made with assorted sliced citrus – perhaps blood orange, tangelo and navel orange – can be combined with savoury ingredients such as radishes or fennel and served as a starter, and are also a most refreshing and beautiful way to end a meal. In Morocco, orange slices are arranged on a shallow plate and then served with sliced dates scattered over them and a very faint sprinkling of ground cinnamon.

Especially for Kids The smell of chutney or marmalade cooking inevitably draws family members into the kitchen to sniff appreciatively. Children enjoy stirring a big pan of ingredients such as Greg Malouf's Lemon and Date Chutney on page 368 or Tom Jaine's Lemon Pickle on page 369. Special care should be taken when bottling jam, chutney or syrup as sugar burns are particularly painful.

Older children can be challenged to see how long a spiral they can make by peeling an orange. Spirals of orange peel can be hung up to dry and will add a lovely flavour to a bouquet garni (see page 635).

A good discussion could result from sitting down with children to consider all the many nuances of 'lemon-ness', which include lemon and lime-scented geraniums; lemongrass; lemon-scented verbena; lemon thyme; kaffir lime leaves; lemony sorrel; and lemon leaves, not to mention lemons themselves. All are prized for the sharp, cleansing quality that they offer the palate, often used to counteract the sweetness, richness or heat of other ingredients served over the course of a meal.

If several different citrus fruits are available (say an orange, a blood orange, a mandarin, and a pink grapefruit), it would be fun for your child and their friends to do a citrus tasting. They could smell the fruit, note the differences in the texture of the skin, cut the fruit, sip and taste the juices and comment on their similarities and differences.

Orange, Radish and Mint Salad

SERVES 4 AS PART OF A MIXED SALAD BUFFET One of the delights of the nightly bazaar in the main square of Marrakech is the brightly painted caravans selling the freshest citrus juices. Many of the caravan stalls are decorated with branches of orange trees, some with blossoms still attached. The addition of orange flower water is typical of such salads served in Morocco.

12 radishes
1 teaspoon sea salt
4 oranges
8 stems mint
1 tablespoon extra-virgin olive oil

juice of 1 lemon
½ teaspoon orange flower water
(see page 705)
¼ teaspoon chilli powder (optional)

EXTRA EQUIPMENT
food processor
with grating
attachment or
a box grater

Shred radishes in a food processor fitted with a grating attachment or use a box grater. Sprinkle with salt and leave for 15 minutes.

Using a small or large knife (whichever feels most comfortable), carve skin from oranges. Holding one of the oranges in one hand over a bowl to catch all the juices, slip knife down one side of a single segment and then down other side of segment, cutting flesh away from membrane. Drop segment into the bowl. Continue until all segments are in the bowl, then work on the next orange and so on. Squeeze orange 'skeletons' so that the juice falls over the segments.

Gently squeeze radish in a clean tea towel to remove excess juices. Arrange orange segments attractively on a wide serving platter. Scatter with radish. Tear leaves from mint stems and dot all over salad. Mix olive oil with a little of the orange juice and some lemon juice. Taste for balance and adjust with more orange juice, lemon juice or oil if necessary. Drizzle salad with dressing, then sprinkle with orange flower water and chilli powder, if using, and serve.

Orange Crème Caramels

SERVES 4 I just had to slip in a recipe for everyone's favourite dessert. Make a dark caramel with 220g/8oz white sugar dissolved in 125ml/4½fl oz hot water in a saucepan over medium heat (see page 376). Carefully divide caramel among four 150ml/5fl oz-capacity soufflé dishes, turning to coat sides and bases. Put a long strip of thinly peeled orange zest into a saucepan with 375ml/27fl oz milk and bring very slowly to scalding point over low heat. Lightly whisk together 2 free-range eggs, 2 egg yolks and 2 tablespoons caster sugar, then strain the orange-scented milk into bowl. Mix gently and then fill soufflé dishes. Put filled soufflé dishes into a baking dish that is filled halfway with boiling water, then bake at 160°C/Gas 3 for 25–30 minutes or until just set. Check after 20 minutes. Leave to cool, then chill soufflé dishes in the refrigerator for up to 12 hours before turning out.

Greg Malouf's Lemon and Date Chutney

MAKES 2 CUPS This delicious chutney, from Greg and Lucy Malouf's cookbook *Arabesque* is beautifully spiced and has some of the salty tang one associates with long-preserved lemons. The dates add a richness and gorgeous texture. The original recipe has been changed for consistency and to accommodate younger cooks.

10 lemons

2 tablespoons cooking salt

12 cardamom pods (to yield
   1 tablespoon seeds)

1 teaspoon coriander seeds

4 cloves garlic, finely chopped

100ml/3½fl oz cider vinegar

1 tablespoon freshly grated ginger

½ teaspoon chilli flakes

225g/8oz soft brown sugar

200g/7oz fresh dates, pitted and chopped
   into small pieces

EXTRA EQUIPMENT

food processor

mortar and pestle

simmer mat

2 × 250ml/9fl oz-
   capacity sterilised
   jars (see page
   706)

large metal spoon
   or jam funnel

Juice 4 of the lemons and set aside. Strip zest from remaining lemons, taking just the coloured part. Put zest into a food processor and chop finely, then scrape into a mixing bowl. Using a small or large knife (whichever feels most comfortable), carve white pith from lemons and discard. Cut flesh into tiny dice, flicking away seeds, and add flesh to bowl with zest. Stir in salt and leave for at least 6 hours or overnight.

Using a pestle, bruise cardamom pods and extract seeds. Put them into the mortar. Add coriander seeds and grind with the pestle to form a powder.

Put chopped lemon and zest, reserved lemon juice, spices, garlic, vinegar, ginger and chilli into a heavy-based saucepan and bring slowly to the boil over medium heat. Simmer for 5 minutes. Add sugar and dates. Stir well and bring to simmering point. Place saucepan on a simmer mat over low heat and stir frequently. The chutney will take at least 35 minutes, and maybe up to 50 minutes, to become very thick.

Spoon into two 250ml/9fl oz-capacity hot sterilised jars, then seal, label and date. Leave for at least 1 month before eating. The chutney in my house is still wonderful 6 months after making it. Like most preserves it is best to store an opened jar in the refrigerator.

Using Lemon Leaves

Although not edible, washed and dried lemon leaves can be used as a base for a whole fresh mozzarella ball to be grilled on the barbecue. The leaves impart their aroma as the cheese softens.

Tom Jaine's Lemon Pickle

MAKES 1 LITRE This is from Tom Jaine's charming book *Cooking in the Country*, the country referred to being Devon in the south-west of England. I have used this recipe often and find it foolproof, although I prefer to leave the spices rolling around in the mixture rather than being held in a muslin bag. I guess it depends on how you feel about crunching on a crushed coriander seed or a bruised cardamom pod. I love serving this pickle with a roast chicken. I have to admit that the last time I made this I used some of it on the very same day with my dinner of roast chicken, and it was still warm and quite delicious.

EXTRA EQUIPMENT
mortar and pestle
  or electric spice
  grinder
simmer mat
  (optional)
4 × 250ml/9fl oz-
  capacity sterilised
  jars (see page
  706)

8 lemons, juiced and zest cut
  into 3mm-thick slices
2 large onions, sliced
2 fresh long green chillies, halved,
  seeded and sliced
50g/2oz ginger, finely chopped
4 cloves garlic, finely chopped
25g/1oz cooking salt

600ml/1 pint white-wine vinegar
675g/1lb 7½oz caster or white
  sugar

SPICE MIXTURE
1 tablespoon allspice berries
2 teaspoons cardamom pods
2 teaspoons coriander seeds

Put sliced lemon zest and juice into a bowl, then add onion, chilli, ginger, garlic, salt and vinegar to bowl.

To make the spice mixture, put spices into a large mortar or a spice grinder and pound them coarsely with a pestle or give a quick pulse in the grinder; you don't want a powder. Add spices to lemon mixture and give it all a good stir, cover with plastic film and leave for 6 hours or overnight.

The next day, tip the lemon/spice mixture into a large heavy-based saucepan. Bring to the boil and simmer over low heat for about 1½ hours or until lemon zest is very tender; once the sugar is added they will stop softening. Add sugar, stir until dissolved and boil briskly for 20 minutes over medium heat. Stir frequently or use a simmer mat to prevent sticking.

Spoon into four 250ml/9fl oz-capacity sterilised jars, then seal, label and date. Leave for 1 month before eating. The lemon pickle in my house is still wonderful 6 months after making it. Like most preserves it is best to store an opened jar in the refrigerator.

Preserved Lemons

MAKES 40 QUARTERS Preserved lemons last for years without refrigeration. Traditional methods can mean waiting up to two months before the lemons are ready to use. These days I put the quartered lemons into the freezer for about four hours before proceeding. The softened skins mature in a much shorter time; check after four weeks.

EXTRA EQUIPMENT
1 litre/1¾ pint-
 capacity sterilised
 jar (see page 706)

250g/9oz coarse kitchen salt
10 thick-skinned lemons, scrubbed
 and quartered, plus extra lemon
 juice (optional)

1 fresh bay leaf, torn
2–3 cloves
1 cinnamon stick, broken into pieces

Scatter a spoonful of salt into a 1 litre/1¾ pint-capacity sterilised jar. Tip lemons into a wide plastic bucket with remaining salt and mix well. Massage salt into fruit vigorously, then pack into jar, curved-side up, inserting pieces of bay leaf, cloves and splinters of cinnamon stick at intervals. Press down hard on fruit to release as much juice as possible. Spoon salt mixture left in bucket over lemons. Cover with extra lemon juice, if required. (If a wedge of lemon is not covered in lemon juice, it sometimes develops white mould. It doesn't look great but it is harmless.) With a clean cloth dipped in boiling water, wipe neck of jar free of salt, and seal tightly. Let the lemons mature for 1 month in a cool spot (not the refrigerator) before using. The skins should feel really soft; if not, leave for another 1–2 weeks and check again.

Chilled Lemon Cream

SERVES 8 This very simple dessert was originally published in the cookbook *Stephanie Alexander and Maggie Beer's Tuscan Cookbook*. Use quite small containers; when in Tuscany we used small espresso cups and topped each one with raspberries. The biscuits are sprinkled with sweet wine, although orange juice could be substituted if making this for young children (but the quantities of wine are small and it is for special occasions!). Or you could divide the mix and make some with wine-soaked biscuits, and some with orange juice-soaked ones instead.

EXTRA EQUIPMENT
electric mixer
large metal spoon
8 × 100ml/3½fl oz-
 capacity cups

4 sponge finger (savoiardi) biscuits,
 broken into very small pieces
125ml/4½fl oz sweet wine, sherry or
 marsala (or orange juice)
finely grated zest and juice of 2 lemons

2 free-range eggs (at room
 temperature), separated
50g/2oz caster sugar
250ml/9fl oz thickened cream
raspberries (optional), to serve

>>>

Put biscuits into a mixing bowl (or two bowls if you are using wine for some and orange juice for others) and sprinkle with the wine (or orange juice) and lemon juice.

Using an electric mixer, beat egg yolks with sugar until pale and thick, then fold in lemon zest. In another bowl, beat egg whites until stiff peaks form, then fold carefully into yolk mixture using a large metal spoon.

Whip cream to firm peaks. Fold cream and soaked biscuits into egg mixture, then spoon into eight 100ml/3½fl oz-capacity cups. Cover each one with plastic film and freeze for no longer than 1 hour; it is not meant to be too hard.

Decorate tops of lemon creams with raspberries if you like, then serve.

Orange or Mandarin Jellies

SERVES 6 It may be old-fashioned, but a proper jelly is a lovely finish to a rich meal. I think these jellies look best of all set in pretty glasses so that you can pour a thin layer of cream over the top of each serve. Alternatively, set the jellies in fancy moulds and turn them out onto cold plates. They could have a few pieces of Caramel Oranges (see page 376) served with them. If the jellies are for a children's party, leave out the alcohol and make up the volume with additional strained citrus juice. The jelly could also be made with pink grapefruit or blood orange juice instead.

finely grated zest of
  1 orange or mandarin
100g/3½oz caster sugar
3 × 2g/.07oz gold-strength
  gelatine leaves (see
  page 704)

100ml/3½fl oz hot water
300ml/½ pint strained fresh orange juice
  or mandarin juice
strained juice of 1 lemon
2 tablespoons fortified wine (such as muscat,
  port, Punt e Mes or red vermouth)

EXTRA EQUIPMENT
Microplane or other
  fine grater
food processor
fine-meshed sieve
6 × 150ml/5fl oz-
  capacity moulds
  or glasses

Put grated zest and sugar in a food processor and process until sugar is a bright orange.

Soak gelatine leaves in a bowl of cold water for a few minutes until they feel quite soft.

Put sugar mixture and the hot water into a heavy-based saucepan and bring to simmering point over medium heat. Stir to ensure sugar has completely dissolved. Strain sugar syrup through a fine-meshed sieve into a clean bowl. Squeeze gelatine leaves and drop into hot syrup. Stir to mix, then leave to cool for 5 minutes.

Strain warm syrup into combined citrus juice, then add fortified wine. Stir to mix and ladle into six 150ml/5fl oz-capacity cold moulds or glasses already set out on a tray. Refrigerate until set.

Sally's Orange, Lemon and Coconut Cake

SERVES 8–10 This is a winner of a cake as it takes just minutes to mix. I have made a few tiny adjustments to the recipe as given to me by Sally from one of my favourite dress shops, where the service includes cake and coffee! If you want a less chewy cake, use desiccated coconut instead of shredded. Or, if you prefer more crunch, instead of using 100 grams/3½ ounces ground almonds, use 50 grams/2 ounces each of ground almonds and chopped slivered almonds. The cake can be cut into portions, then wrapped individually and frozen.

EXTRA EQUIPMENT
22cm/9in springform
cake tin
large metal spoon

butter, for greasing
90g/3oz shredded coconut
75g/2½oz plain flour
100g/3½oz ground almonds
220g/8oz caster sugar
grated zest of 1 orange
grated zest of 1 lemon
4 free-range eggs

125g/4½oz butter, melted and
  cooled
125ml/4½fl oz strained lemon juice
125ml/4½fl oz strained orange juice
250ml/9fl oz milk
icing sugar and double cream
  (optional), to serve

Preheat oven to 180°C/Gas 4.

Grease a 22cm/9in springform cake tin. Cut baking paper to line bottom of tin, then grease the paper. Place tin on a baking tray.

Combine coconut, flour, almonds, sugar and citrus zests in a large bowl. With a whisk or your hands, briefly mix zests in evenly. Lightly whisk eggs in a large bowl. Add cooled melted butter, citrus juices and milk and mix.

Make a well in dry ingredients and tip in egg mixture. Mix with a large metal spoon until you have a smooth and rather runny batter.

Tip batter into tin and bake for 1 hour or until golden brown on top and a skewer inserted in the middle of the cake comes out clean. Remove cake from oven, then cool in tin on a cake cooling rack for a few minutes. Run a butter knife around edge of cake to ensure it has not stuck. After 5 minutes, release spring on tin and remove outer ring. Cool completely before attempting to lift cake from the base.

Dust top with icing sugar, if desired. This cake is best of all when served with double cream.

Orange Chiffon Cupcakes

MAKES 12 Chiffon cakes are as light as air. The batter can't sit around so the cupcake cases should be placed inside muffin tins, the oven at the right temperature and a large spoon ready to scoop the batter into the paper cases as soon as the batter is made. To bake this as a large cake, choose a deep 20 centimetre/8 inch tube tin, don't grease it, and expect it to take 30 minutes to cook at 180°C/Gas 4. Large chiffon cakes made in a tube tin are inverted over a jam jar or jug to cool when they are removed from the oven to retain their just-baked airy texture.

125g/4½oz plain flour
110g/3¾oz caster sugar
½ teaspoon salt
1 teaspoon baking powder
1 teaspoon finely grated
    orange zest
60ml/2fl oz vegetable oil
60ml/2fl oz strained orange juice
30ml/1fl oz water
3 free-range egg yolks
unsprayed orange blossoms
    (optional), to serve

MERINGUE
4 free-range egg whites (at room
    temperature)
60g/2oz caster sugar
⅛ teaspoon cream of tartar

CREAM CHEESE AND ORANGE ICING
90g/3oz cream cheese
85g/3oz caster sugar
1 teaspoon finely grated orange zest
2 teaspoons orange juice

EXTRA EQUIPMENT
Microplane or other
    fine grater
12 large paper
    cupcake cases
1 × 12-hole muffin
    tin
electric mixer with
    paddle and whisk
    attachments
large metal spoon
food processor

Preheat oven to 190°C/Gas 5. Line a 12-hole muffin tin with paper cases.

Sift flour, sugar, salt and baking powder into bowl of an electric mixer fitted with a paddle. Mix zest with oil in a small bowl. Mix orange juice with water in another small bowl. With motor running, mix on low speed and gradually add oil/zest mixture, then egg yolks and finally orange juice/water mixture to flour mixture. Stop the machine once or twice to scrape sides and bottom of the bowl with a spatula. Continue beating until batter is just smooth, then scrape into a large bowl. Wash mixing bowl, rinse with cold water and dry.

To make the meringue, beat egg whites with the electric mixer using the whisk attachment until soft peaks form. Add sugar and cream of tartar in a steady stream until you have a soft but glossy meringue. Fold meringue mixture into batter speedily but thoroughly with a large metal spoon. Spoon cake batter into paper cupcake cases. Bake for 18–20 minutes. Transfer trays to a cake cooling rack, then after 1 minute, lift cakes in paper cases out of holes and leave them on the cake cooling rack to cool completely.

Meanwhile, to make the cream cheese and orange icing, process cream cheese, sugar and zest in a food processor until smooth and golden. Thin to required consistency with orange juice. Drop a generous blob of icing onto each cooled cupcake and smooth it with the back of a teaspoon, then top with orange blossoms, if using.

Caramel Oranges

SERVES 4 It is difficult to think of a better flavour match than that between this dark caramel and sharp yet sweet orange. Eat the oranges within two hours of pouring the syrup over them for maximum deliciousness. Otherwise, the oozing juice from the oranges will dilute the caramel and the dish will taste a bit watery. The Caramel Oranges can also be spooned into a buttered pudding mould and topped with a plain sponge pudding mixture (see Eve's Pudding on page 77) or used to fill a folded crêpe. If the folded crêpe is quickly sautéed in a little butter and flamed with brandy, you will make the classic dish Crêpes Suzette. And Caramel Oranges served alongside silky Orange Crème Caramels (see page 366) has to be an all-time favourite. If you prefer to carve skin and pith from oranges and then slice them widthways into simple rounds, you will need to use the juice of an extra orange for the caramel sauce.

6 oranges

110g/3¾oz caster sugar

60ml/2fl oz hot water

Using a small or large knife (whichever feels most comfortable), carve skin from oranges. Holding one of the oranges in one hand over a bowl to catch all the juices, slip knife down one side of a single segment and then down other side of segment, cutting flesh away from membrane. Drop segment into the bowl. Continue until all segments are in the bowl, then work on the next orange and so on. Squeeze orange 'skeletons' and collect this juice in a measuring cup or a small bowl. Place it near the stove.

Dissolve sugar in hot water in a heavy-based saucepan over medium heat. Have the orange juice close by. Stir mixture with a metal spoon until the sugar has dissolved. Increase heat to high (don't stir), and boil until bubbles on surface of syrup get larger. The syrup will first become golden and will quickly darken. When caramel is a deep amber, carefully pour reserved orange juice into it. It will hiss and splutter and rise up the pan. Reduce heat to low and stir until caramel and juice have combined to form a smooth sauce.

Leave orange caramel sauce to cool completely before drizzling it over the orange segments. Delicious!

Loretta's Shrewsbury Easter Biscuits

MAKES 40 Pastry chef Loretta Sartori and her team of young helpers produce delicious biscuits at the Jesuit Social Services building in Abbotsford, Melbourne. These young teenagers are all in need of support – financial, physical and emotional. After a few shifts in such a friendly and sweet-smelling environment they achieve real competence and skills that will be of value as they deal with the outside world. Some older recipes don't include currants while some include caraway seeds. In her book *The Observer Guide to British Cookery*, Jane Grigson states that Shrewsbury biscuits are at least three centuries old. She tells the reader that in a collection of myths, ghost stories and legends first published in 1837 as *The Ingoldsby Legends,* a Shrewsbury biscuit was thrown at a dog that had bitten off some unfortunate person's fingers and toes.

EXTRA EQUIPMENT
Microplane/grater or other fine grater
electric mixer with paddle attachment
large metal spoon

100g/3½oz currants
finely grated zest and juice of 1 orange
370g/13oz plain flour
¾ teaspoon baking powder
¾ teaspoon ground cinnamon
200g/7oz unsalted butter, softened

100g/3½oz caster sugar
50g/2oz soft brown sugar
1 free-range egg
1 free-range egg white
white sugar, for rolling dough in

Put currants in a bowl, then pour boiling water over them and leave for 5 minutes. Drain and return to bowl. Pour orange juice over currants and refrigerate them for 1 hour or even overnight. Drain currants, discarding orange juice.

Sift flour, baking powder and cinnamon together and set aside. Using an electric mixer with a paddle attachment, beat together butter, sugars and orange zest until light and pale, scraping down the bowl at least once with a spatula. With the motor running on low speed, add whole egg and mix to combine. Add flour mixture and beat on low speed only until just combined. Add drained currants and mix briefly so as not to tear the fruit.

Cover 2 baking trays with a sheet of baking paper each. Divide dough between the trays. Using paper as a guide, roll dough into a log, smoothing and squeezing with your hands. Twist paper at ends of each log to firm each roll. Chill dough rolls in the refrigerator until quite firm (even overnight).

Preheat oven to 170°C/Gas 3.

Lightly whisk egg white with a fork. Scatter a baking tray with sugar. Unroll biscuit dough logs and, using a pastry brush, brush all over with egg white and then roll in sugar. Re-line the baking trays with baking paper. Slice dough logs into 7mm/⅓in-thick slices and put onto baking paper-lined trays, then bake for 15 minutes or until golden brown.

Transfer trays to cake cooling racks and leave until biscuits are quite cold, then store in an airtight container for up to 1 week.

LEMON VERBENA

Verbenaceae family
Deciduous shrub

Soil type
Moist well-drained soil or a free-draining potting mix.

Soil preparation
Fork in grit if planting out directly into the soil.

Climate
Frost tender so only grow out all year in very mild areas, otherwise grow as a summer container plant.

Position
Prefers full sun.

How to grow
Buy a young potted plant in late spring to early summer (May-June). In most areas, re-pot into a larger pot and put out on a sunny patio once there is no more risk of frost. In mild areas, it can be planted out into ground and it may survive the frosts if heavily mulched in autumn. Summer cuttings are often taken as an insurance against winter losses. Take 5–10cm long cuttings, remove the leaves from the bottom part of the stem and insert into small pots of cutting mix. Put a propagator lid (or plastic bag) over them. Keep moist until rooted, keep some on the windowsill.

Water requirements
Water pot plants sparingly.

When to fertilise
Use a liquid fertiliser (see page 691) or worm tea (see page 695) ever 6-8 weeks during the growing season.

Harvest period
Pinch out the young leaves as and when required, this will promote a bushy habit. If you wish to harvest dry verbena for winter use, harvest leaves just as the plant is coming into flower.

Pests and organic control
Red spider mite and whitefly can be a problem if potted plants are kept under glass, moving the plants outside over the summer can prevent problems or increasing the humidity around plants by spraying with water will help prevent red spider mite. the plant is coming into flower.

Quantities to plant
for a family of four
1 plant

Lemon verbena (*Aloysia triphylla*)

Growing and Harvesting Lemon verbena is a deciduous herb that grows to a height of 90 centimetres x 60 centimetres wide in the UK. Move the pot under cover in winter. In winter the plant looks dead, and inexperienced gardeners may fear that they have lost it. But come the spring it shoots forth its long, slender, pale green leaves with their distinctive raspiness, soon followed by sprays of exquisite tiny pale mauve flowers on spikes at the end of each leaf cluster. The flowers will continue for many months. Cut the shrub back hard in autumn and do any extra pruning or shaping in the spring, just as it comes into leaf.

Lemon verbena is one of the most beautiful herbs to pick for putting in a vase or for drying, and it will also attract beneficial insects to your garden. To dry the leaves at the end of autumn, cut some of the branches from the shrub before it is pruned, and either hang them in a draught-free place until fully dried before storing the leaves, or strip the leaves from the branches, then lay the leaves on newspapers in a draught-free place until completely dry. Bag or put the dried leaves into very clean and dry jars and give to friends to make tea.

Container Planting Lemon verbena can be grown in a pot that is at least 45–50 centimetres in diameter and a similar depth – just ensure there is a rich potting mix. Fertilise every six to eight weeks and 'refresh' the pot with extra organic matter at the same time.

Preparing and Sharing The leaves are strongly lemon-scented and it takes just one or two to flavour poaching syrups, custards and fish dishes or to make a herbal tea. A baking tray of peaches or apricots dotted with butter and roasted in a 200°C/Gas 6 oven for 15 minutes can be given a special touch by adding a few lemon verbena leaves halfway through the baking time, while a few leaves can be added to any jam for a subtle citrus note. The citrus-scented flavour of lemon verbena pairs well with fruit such as pineapple or kiwifruit, either eaten fresh or infused in the syrup used to make a simple sorbet (see the Kiwifruit Sorbet on page 340).

Lemon verbena tea is known as an *infusion de verveine* in France and is regarded as one of the finest herb teas. The tea is equally refreshing and delicious if made with either dried or fresh leaves. Quite large bunches can be cut without damaging the plant and dried to store for herbal teas or for making potpourri (see opposite). The dried leaves retain their potency and therefore flavour for years.

Especially for Kids A fun activity for the garden involves comparing and scoring the degree of 'lemonness' between lemon verbena leaves, lemon leaves, lemon-scented geranium and lemon thyme.

Drying lemon verbena leaves is a great job for kids (see above) – another idea for the school fair perhaps? Children may also like to help pulverise some dried lemon verbena leaves with caster sugar in a food processor. This scented sugar can be used to make biscuits (maybe omit the lemon thyme in the Buttery Lemon Thyme and Vanilla Boomerangs on page 638 and substitute this sugar for the sugar in the recipe), or added to the stuffing for Baked Peaches Stuffed with Amaretti Biscuits on page 614.

Lemon Potpourri

Orris root powder can be purchased from good pharmacies. This recipe comes from Gilian Painter and Elaine Power's book *The Herb Garden Displayed*.

2 small handfuls lemon balm
  leaves
1 small handful lemon verbena
  leaves
zest of 1 Lisbon lemon, peeled
  thinly and finely chopped

½ small handful dried yellow petals
  from marigolds and other aromatic
  flowers
1 tablespoon orris root powder
9 drops of lemon verbena essential oil

Combine all ingredients, then store in an airtight glass jar or use to fill sachets.

Dried lemon verbena leaves

LETTUCE AND OTHER SALAD GREENS

Asteraceae family (includes globe artichokes and Jerusalem artichokes)
Annual

Soil type
Adaptable to most soils, but prefers moist, well-drained soil, enriched with organic matter.

Soil preparation
Green manures such as legumes, barley or mustard grown prior to planting are beneficial.

Climate
Suitable for all climates. High temperatures causes lettuce to bolt.

Position
Prefer full sun in cool weather and partial shade in hot weather.

How to grow
Directly sowing is preferable, but seedlings can be raised in modular trays and planted out. Sow a few seeds in a depression and cover with 1cm of seed-raising mix. Thin out to a single seedling when 8cm tall. Keep the soil moist and free from weeds by mulching. Avoid sowing in hot weather.

Water requirements
Keep soil moist but avoid over-watering, as it will cause fungal disease. Allowing the soil to become too dry reduces head size and makes lettuce bitter.

Successive planting
Leave 1–2 weeks between each planting, throughout the growing season.

When to fertilise
Use a liquid fertiliser (see page 691) or worm tea (see page 695) every 4 weeks.

Harvest period
8–10 weeks to mature. Cut the whole plant or harvest the outer leaves as required.

Pests and organic control
Use crushed egg shells around base of young plants to deter snails and slugs. Prevent diseases such as rot and downy mildew by using good watering techniques, including avoiding wetting the foliage. Crop rotation is important.

Companion planting
Cucumber, carrots, radishes, beetroot and strawberries. Plant among herbs and flowers, as they will deter pests. Marigolds are thought to be beneficial.

Special information
Lettuces can be grown with the cabbage family. They like the same soil conditions and they grow quickly, so they can fill space left by the slower-growing cabbage family.

Quantities to plant for a family of four
10 seedlings every 2 weeks throughout the growing season.

'Cos Verdi' lettuce (*Lactuca sativa*)

Growing and Harvesting   There seems to be an infinite range of salad greens available for the home gardener to try planting. Sometimes a very similar lettuce is known by different names – I have heard one cultivar called both 'Oak Leaf' and 'Sutton's Salad Bowl', for example. Do refer to seed catalogues and try something different – perhaps a 'Freckles', a 'Royal Oak Leaf' or another of the cut-and-come-again cultivars. You can pick leaves from the outside of these lettuces and the plant will continue to grow. Always ensure that you have chosen lettuces that suit the climate and the season.

Many of these plants are beautiful to behold – patterns of red, brown, gold and green can be achieved and will look stunning in your garden. You don't have to plant everything in a straight row. Why not try a triangle or a circle, maybe edged with young leeks or miniature French marigolds?

Salad greens grow quickly and both under-planting and inter-planting among other crops or flowers are recommended to maximise use of space in a small garden. In my own garden, I have tucked soft-leaved lettuces among my roses. Salad greens will appreciate the shade provided by tall corn plants, climbing beans or a cucumber vine in hot weather.

If you have planted out seedlings and there is a sudden heat wave, protect the infant seedlings by covering them during the hottest part of the day with a large leaf (such as a vine leaf or a zucchini leaf) weighted down with a handful of soil, or a shoe box. The leaves or shoe box can be removed in the cool of the evening. More permanent shade protection can be made with a piece of 30 per cent shadecloth either draped over hoops or tacked onto a light frame that can be moved from place to place. This diffuses sunlight and restricts water loss.

Given that parents are hoping to delight children with texture, flavour and novelty, don't plant lettuce varieties that are bitter, too peppery or have a preponderance of tough leaves before you get to the tender heart. In most cases this means the softer, loose-leaved varieties are preferable, and they are faster to grow too. Corn salad (also known as mâche or lamb's lettuce, another example of one plant with different names) is a great variety to add to the mix in cooler weather. The much-maligned 'Iceberg' is an excellent lettuce to grow, providing it is picked while the heart is still a bit loose and before it becomes as hard as a rock. And cos is another favourite. It is delightfully crunchy and best known as the classic leaf to use for a Caesar salad. Cos lettuce is also known as romaine. Although the round Chioggia radicchio is a bitter variety, it is not unduly so, and it not only has plenty of crunch but is also a spectacular crimson colour, streaked with cream.

A word about endive. Here I am referring to the curly-edged salad varieties, sometimes called frisée, frilly lettuce or broad-leaved escarole. (The name confusion stems from the fact that endive sometimes refers to what is usually grown and marketed as 'witloof'.) When offered for sale in a French market, the vendor always spreads these lettuces wide open to display their pale hearts, knowing that the dark-green outside leaves will be going to the chickens or the rabbits. The wastage is about two-thirds, so I doubt that endive can justify the space it takes up in a small kitchen garden. In France such lettuces are often bound with twine or similar to keep the hearts pale as they grow.

Never try to use leaves from a lettuce that shows any sign of bolting (see page 687), though. They will also have started to produce compounds that are intensely bitter. These plants can be kept for seed-saving purposes or composted.

Lettuce seed germinates at low temperature so it is worth considering sowing some at the start and end of the growing season as fresh salad leaves are particularly welcome overwinter. It is worth selecting a variety that does well in cold conditions either because it is resistant to downy mildew, a disease of cold damp weather, or because the variety is hardy. A cos variety such as 'Winter Density' usually does well. You can sow outside in August and cover with cloches once it gets colder. If you have a greenhouse, winter lettuce makes a good follow on crop once the tomatoes are cleared away. The greenhouse needs to be frost free, so it in needs insulating with bubblewrap and some background heat. Growth will be slower, so sowing once a month rather than every fortnight will suffice. Careful watering so the leaves are not wetted and good ventilation on warm days will help keep lettuce healthy.

Harvesting greens appropriately is an important part of learning in the garden, and young gardeners will need guidance. For cut-and-come-again varieties, pick from the outside of the plant, leaving the centre leaves to continue to grow. If lettuces have been separated so that they grow larger, pick whole plants when they are still young and tender.

Container Planting Salad greens are ideal container plants. Some salad seedlings are sold as mixes and these are intended to be planted close together. Often called *mesclun* (an old Provençal word meaning 'mixture'), these red, brown, green and speckled loose leaves make a delightful salad. As they are always picked very young there is never any bitterness, even if some frilly-leaved varieties and chicories have been included in the mix.

The method of close planting can be used with any loose-leaved salad green. Allow them to grow all together and cut them leaf by leaf with scissors, or separate them and grow as individual salads underneath a taller plant that will offer some sun protection. Pull thinnings of young plants as required and allow the remainder to continue to grow where they are, or to provide more young plants for successive sowings.

It is also possible to grow several individual lettuces to maturity in a spacious pot. Harvest either leaf by leaf or whole. Keep soil moist at all times.

Preparing and Sharing Don't forget to wash salad leaves well, then give them a gentle spin in a salad spinner. Wrapping them in a clean dry tea towel will ensure they are really dry in readiness for their dressing. Everyone in the family should be encouraged to mix and toss their salads with clean hands. This is the best way to learn to judge how much dressing a salad needs. The simplest method of all is to mix the dressing directly in the salad bowl. Use far less oil and lemon juice or vinegar than you think you need. The dressing only needs to coat every leaf lightly. There should never be any liquid left at the bottom of the bowl.

For easy reference I have included recipes for my preferred vinaigrette (see page 389), a Blue Cheese Dressing (see page 390), and the delicious Parmesan Dressing that is so good with Caesar-style salads (see page 390).

Inevitably some lettuces will grow faster than anticipated. Coarser lettuces that have not gone to seed can still be used in the kitchen as wrappers or in soups, braised or added to a frittata or risotto. If some bitter leaves or very spicy leaves have crept into the vegetable garden, they are best used by slicing or shredding them and combining with a much greater quantity of milder greens and perhaps crumbling some soft goat's cheese or cubes of

Gruyère-style cheese into the salad bowl. Another way would be to combine shredded large lettuce leaves (cos, for example) with cooked pulses such as butter beans or chick peas, then include some Caramelised Onion (see page 461) to add sweetness.

Especially for Kids One of the aims of the Stephanie Alexander Kitchen Garden Program is that every meal the students prepare and share includes a leafy salad. Other ingredients will appear in these salads but there should always be leaves! In fact, being part of the group each week that is invited to prepare the 'Salad of the Imagination' in Melbourne is a highly prized activity. This is the moment for petals of edible flowers or collected seeds from pumpkins or sunflowers to appear as garnish for some very colourful salads. The overwhelming importance of this part of the school kitchen gardens means that careful consideration is given to the varieties planted as discussed above and to establishing a continuous supply of leafy greens. Some seedlings should go into the ground just before the long summer holiday, providing there are volunteers to water them or an irrigation system, so that there will be salad leaves ready to use in the new school year.

Once a wonderful basket of salad leaves has arrived in the kitchen, children can firstly be shown how to handle these special leaves, including how to inspect, wash and gently dry them. Using a salad spinner is a favourite activity. It may be necessary to curb over-energetic use of this useful gadget or you may end up with bruised leaves. Salads made with an individual variety of very young leaves are extremely delicate and all washing and drying must be very gentle. Pat them dry with a clean tea towel rather than whirling them violently in a salad spinner.

Another popular task is creating a salad dressing. Offer children different oils, vinegars, citrus fruits and herbs. They may lean towards adding sweet ingredients such as honey that may not appeal to all adult palates. This can be discussed at the table perhaps, while you are all enjoying the salad.

Clockwise from top left: radicchio; green oak lettuce; baby cos

Stephanie's Everyday Salad Vinaigrette

SERVES 4 I always make my vinaigrette directly in the salad bowl as it saves fiddling around with small bowls. I cross the salad servers over the dressing, then pile the washed and dried leaves on top and transfer the whole bowl to the refrigerator until it is time to serve the salad. When it is brought to the table the salad servers are pulled away so that the leaves sink down in the bowl and are tossed gently but thoroughly. Simple! After a few goes you will not need the measuring spoons, but will be comfortable estimating the quantities of vinegar and olive oil. Every cook has a few obsessions. Mine is a dislike of balsamic vinegar in a classic green salad. I find the sweetness quite inappropriate. I can accept rubbing the salad bowl with a cut clove of garlic, but I would always prefer to add the garlic in the form of the Garlic Croûtons on page 313.

EXTRA EQUIPMENT
salad spinner

a pinch sea salt
1 teaspoon red-wine or
   sherry vinegar
freshly ground black pepper

1 tablespoon best-quality
   extra-virgin olive oil
4–6 handfuls washed and
   dried salad leaves

Sprinkle salt into a salad bowl, crumbling it as you do so, and add vinegar. Stir with one of the salad servers to dissolve salt. Grind on pepper and add olive oil. Taste for balance of salt and acid. Put salad servers in the bowl, crossed over to form a barrier.

Add salad leaves and refrigerate until needed. Remove salad servers and toss, then serve at once.

Extra Bits for Salads

This is a list of some of the garnishes that can be added to leafy salads. I am sure that there are many more that I have not thought of. And of course, young cooks will often want to combine different vegetables with their green leaves; the recipe for the popular Middle Eastern salad Fattoush on page 406 is a good example of a combination salad.

- avocado chunks
- bacon fried with a trace of oil until crisp, drained on paper towel and crumbled
- Caramelised Onion (see page 461)
- crumbled blue cheese
- cubes of Gruyère-style cheese
- flaked almonds fried in butter until golden and drained on paper towel
- fried quail eggs (see page 72)
- Garlic Croûtons (see page 313)
- marinated goat's cheese
- toasted pumpkin or sunflower seeds

Blue Cheese Dressing

SERVES 6 Blue cheese is wonderful with salad greens. Here it is included in the salad dressing but on another occasion you could use the Everyday Salad Vinaigrette on page 389 and crumble chunks of a creamy blue cheese into the bottom of the salad bowl with the dressing. The chunks soften in the dressing and breakdown as the salad is tossed. Another idea for using a firmer blue cheese, such as Roquefort, is to grate the cheese coarsely over the salad after it has been tossed. This is best done after you have portioned the salad to ensure that everyone has a fair share of this delicious cheese.

2 French shallots,
  roughly chopped
1 clove garlic, roughly chopped
200g/7oz blue cheese, crumbled
250ml/9fl oz sour cream
1 tablespoon red-wine vinegar

sea salt and freshly
  ground black pepper
lemon juice (optional), to taste
6 wedges iceberg lettuce or
  cos lettuce hearts, washed and dried,
  to serve

EXTRA EQUIPMENT
salad spinner
food processor

Process shallots, garlic, cheese, sour cream and vinegar in a food processor until smooth. Scrape into a bowl and season to taste with salt and pepper. Sharpen with a little lemon juice if you wish. Drizzle over salad greens and serve at once.

Parmesan Dressing

SERVES 6 This is the classic dressing for a Caesar salad. The best Caesar salads are made with crunchy cos leaves. Traditional accompaniments are anchovies, softly cooked eggs, Garlic Croûtons (see page 313) and crisp bacon. Caesar salad is best presented on a long or wide platter rather than a deep bowl so that everyone at the table gets a fair share of the crunchy offerings without having to hunt for them. If this dressing is stored in an airtight container it will keep well for several days in the refrigerator.

2 free-range eggs, at room
  temperature
1 clove garlic, roughly chopped
2 anchovy fillets, roughly chopped
50g/2oz parmesan, grated

1 tablespoon Dijon mustard
juice of 1 lemon
125ml/4½fl oz extra-virgin olive oil
sea salt and freshly ground
  black pepper

EXTRA EQUIPMENT
slotted spoon
food processor

Bring a small saucepan of water to the boil. Add eggs and simmer over low heat for 4 minutes. Remove with a slotted spoon and run under cold water. Crack eggs and scoop contents into a bowl. Check you have not added any fragments of shell – if you have, then the best way of removing them is by using the halved egg shell as a scoop. Tip eggs into a food processor. Add garlic, anchovies, parmesan, mustard and lemon juice and process until quite smooth. With motor running, slowly dribble in olive oil until dressing has consistency of a runny mayonnaise. Scrape dressing into a bowl and season to taste. Either drizzle the arranged salad with dressing or serve it in a jug alongside the salad.

Salade Niçoise

SERVES 4 This well-known combination is one of my all-time standbys. Individual salads are a good idea when catering for a big party – that way you are assured that everyone gets a bit of everything. Try not to cook the eggs and potatoes too far ahead as they are so lovely when served barely warm.

EXTRA EQUIPMENT
salad spinner

2 × 200g/7oz tuna steaks
80ml/3fl oz extra-virgin olive oil
2 medium-sized waxy potatoes such
  as nicola, desiree or kipfler
salt
1 tablespoon coarsely chopped
  flat-leaf parsley
sea salt and freshly ground
  black pepper

2 ripe tomatoes, sliced or halved
8 black olives
1 tablespoon torn basil
4 free-range eggs
2 handfuls small green beans
4 handfuls whole crunchy lettuce
  leaves such as cos or hearts of
  iceberg, washed and dried
4 anchovy fillets

Heat a char-grill pan or barbecue grill-plate until hot, then brush tuna with a little of the olive oil and grill briefly for 1–2 minutes on both sides. Set aside on a plate.

Cook potatoes in a saucepan of simmering salted water for 20 minutes or until tender, then drain, cut into bite-sized pieces and toss with a little of the olive oil and the parsley and season with salt and pepper. Set aside.

While potatoes are cooking, put tomato, olives and basil in a bowl, then drizzle over a little of the olive oil. Season with pepper.

Boil eggs for 6 minutes (you want the yolks to still be a little moist), then drain and tap shells. When just cool enough to handle, peel carefully.

Cook beans in a saucepan of salted boiling water for 4 minutes or until barely tender, then drain, tip onto a plate and drizzle with a little olive oil.

Divide salad leaves among 4 plates. Fill with warm potatoes, beans and tomato/olive mixture. Break tuna into bite-sized pieces and divide among lettuce leaves. Cut eggs lengthways and divide among lettuce leaves, draping anchovy fillets over eggs. Season with a very little salt and plenty of pepper. Drizzle remaining olive oil over salads and serve at once.

MELONS

**Cucurbitaceae family
(includes cucumbers,
pumpkin and zucchini)
Annual**

Soil type
Well-drained, light soil.

Soil preparation
Dig in plenty of organic matter.

Climate
Frost tender so only suitable
as an outdoor crop in warm,
mild areas. In other areas grow
under glass.

Position
Prefers full sun and shelter.

How to grow
In April-May, sow seed in small
pots in warmth of a heated
greenhouse or windowsill, a
temperature of 21°C is needed
for germination and 16°C for
seedling growth. If this cannot
be supplied, buy young potted
plants in late spring. Pot on the
strongest seedlings and grow
on, putting in a small cane to
support growth. Harden off

plants (see page 692) very
gradually. Plant out once there
is no more danger of frost
(usually end May-June) leave
1m between plants, or less
room if training up supports. Be
prepared to use a crop cover
such as fleece or polythene
overnight when temperatures
drop but open up during the day
for pollinating insects.

Water requirements
Water sparingly when first
planted to avoid rotting of the
stem, as the plant grows away
watering can increase.

When to fertilise
Use a liquid fertiliser (see page
691) or worm tea (see page 695)
every two weeks.

Harvest period
About 4 months from planting.

Pests and organic control
Neck rot caused by cold,
wet conditions or infection is
common, to avoid it practice
crop rotation and plant into a
mound to improve drainage.
Powdery mildew can be a
problem, pick off infected leaves.

Companion planting
Marigolds.

Special information
Fruit that falls off the vine during
early development indicates
poor pollination. Undercover it
is harder for the bees and other
insects to find the flowers so be
prepared to hand pollinate (see
page 690). A layer of straw or
black sheet mulch on the ground
under the developing fruit will
prevent soil disease and keep
fruit clean. Trained vines usually
need fruit supported with nets.

**Quantities to plant
for a family of four**
2–4 plants.

Cantaloupe (*Cucumis melo*)

Growing and Harvesting Outdoor melons are a marginal crop in the UK, anyone who succeeds in producing fragrant, sun-ripened fruit will feel a real sense of achievement. Some years the growing season is long enough to produce useable fruit, other years crops are disappointing. Growing undercover, a large greenhouse, polytunnel or coldframe, improves your chances greatly. Select an early variety that does well in the UK, 'Sweetheart' is a well-known older variety for under glass but look out for new varieties such as 'Alvaro' and 'Magenta' for growing outdoors and a wider range of heritage varieties (see **www.realseeds.co.uk**) are appearing too. Another new development that could help UK gardeners grow melons with more success is the appearance of grafted melons plants (see **www.suttons.co.uk**), these claim to crop earlier and are more robust. The growing season in the UK is not long enough for watermelons but there is a heritage variety 'Blacktail Mountain' (see **www.realseeds.co.uk**) that is said to be very early and a new variety 'Sugar Baby' so worth trying in a polytunnel or greenhouse .

Melon vines grow vigorously and need some support, in a greenhouse or polytunnel, canes or string tied to the roof offer support, tie the stems in with soft ties. An alternative, for melons grown in a coldframe, is to use some plastic netting on supports so they can scramble just above ground.

For maximum quality, gardeners should restrict the number of fruit allowed to set on each vine to two or three, and pinch out the growing tips of the vine to stop its growth when it has set that number of fruit. As mentioned in other entries for the Cucurbitaceae family (see **CUCUMBER**, **PUMPKIN** and **ZUCCHINI**), it may be necessary to hand-pollinate melons as sometimes bees don't do the job satisfactorily, particularly if the plants are growing under glass. Melon flowers are smaller than pumpkin flowers, making the task more difficult for both bees and humans.

Early in the morning, hand-pollinate the female flowers (the smaller flower with a round swelling behind it) by transferring pollen from the male flower (the one on the long stalk) using a paint brush, or break off the male flower, bend back its petals and press it against a female flower. Choose a female flower that is only partly opened for best results. The Cucurbitaceae family provides a dramatic way to introduce concepts of fertilisation and reproduction to children!

Cantaloupes are ready to harvest when there is a slight change of colour (this applies to most varieties) and when cracks appear in the stem where it joins the fruit. Many melons have a lovely fragrance when they are ripe, and the fruit will separate easily from its stem. Watermelons are ripe when knocking on them produces a hollow sound and when the tendrils nearest the fruit become brown and shrivelled.

Container Planting Nowadays you can select a melon that can be grown in a container. There are heritage cultivars with vines that grow to just 1 metre and produce small, sweet fruit.

Preparing and Sharing I have eaten the exquisite Charentais melons on many occasions in France. They are a small fruit, often the size of a large grapefruit, with a smooth pale jade-green skin with darker markings. The flesh is deeply orange in colour, highly perfumed and as one spoons it, the sweet juice runs copiously. One food writer recommends scooping out the seeds and replacing them with a glass of perfumed wine, such as a Frontignac or a late-harvested Semillon. I think a Charentais melon is best enjoyed at the end of a meal – unlike cantaloupe, it is not the perfect partner for ham.

Far better known is the melon most of us refer to as cantaloupe. Everyone seems to enjoy eating a ripe cantaloupe. Note how its flavour is heightened with a few drops of lemon juice.

Watermelon is a favourite summer thirst-quencher. Many commercial cultivars have had the traditional black seeds bred out, which seems to take some of the fun out of eating it.

Especially for Kids Children will enjoy making delicious cool drinks or granitas with puréed watermelon or cantaloupe (see Watermelon Granita on page 398). Puréeing watermelon with a few strawberries and a little lemon juice seems to deepen and heighten its flavour. Or at the beginning of a meal, introduce children to the Italian summer starter of ripe melon partnered with the thinnest slices of prosciutto as a change from serving melon with ice cream.

I read on the Internet that the record for watermelon-seed spitting is 68 feet, set in 1989! I think a competition of watermelon-seed spitting (outside, of course) would be a fun and different birthday party activity for small children.

Every child loves using a melon baller (see page 46). A salad of pink, green and apricot-coloured melon balls, squeezed with a little lemon juice, then turned with chopped mint or lemon verbena, is a lovely and delicious summer dessert.

Cantaloupe Gelo di Melone with Scented Leaves

SERVES 4 This exquisite dessert, of Sicilian origin, is basically fruit juice thickened with cornflour, but this description can't convey its delicacy and divine colour. I have made two different versions, this one using cantaloupe and lemon verbena leaves and a watermelon version with rose-geranium (see opposite). In Sicily one might find nuggets of pistachio or roasted almonds suspended in the dessert, which would probably have been perfumed with rosewater or jasmine. Because of the meaty character of cantaloupe flesh, the juice will never be as liquid as that of watermelon, so the finished *gelo* will probably be a little thicker than the watermelon one. If you prefer a looser *gelo*, stir in the strained juice of an orange before starting to cook the cantaloupe. Serve the *gelo* in small glass bowls or glasses to show off the beautiful colours. The desserts are best served well chilled.

1 small (600–700g/1lb 5oz–1lb 9oz) cantaloupe, halved, seeded, and cut into chunks (you need 500g/1lb flesh)
strained juice of 1 orange or water (optional)

1½ tablespoons cornflour
80ml/3fl oz water
75g/2½oz caster sugar
2 teaspoons lemon juice, strained
8 lemon verbena leaves

EXTRA EQUIPMENT
electric juicer
4 × 125ml/4½fl oz-capacity glass dishes

Juice cantaloupe chunks in an electric juicer; you should have 375ml/13fl oz juice – if not, make up the volume with strained orange juice or extra water.

In a medium-sized bowl, mix together cornflour, water, sugar, lemon juice and enough cantaloupe juice to form a very smooth paste without any lumps. Pour in remaining cantaloupe juice. Transfer mixture to a small saucepan with verbena leaves.

Have four 125ml/4½fl oz-capacity glass dishes alongside the stove. Cook cantaloupe mixture over medium heat, stirring continuously until it comes to the boil and has thickened. Remove lemon verbena leaves and immediately divide mixture among dishes. Leave to cool for a few minutes, then cover with plastic film and chill in the refrigerator before serving.

Watermelon Gelo

SERVES 4 As watermelons are usually quite large, what is leftover from making this recipe could be used to make the Watermelon Granita on page 398.

EXTRA EQUIPMENT
electric juicer
4 × 125ml/4½fl oz-
   capacity glass
   dishes

500g/1lb watermelon flesh, cut into chunks and seeded
2 tablespoons cornflour
2 tablespoons water

75g/2½oz caster sugar
2 teaspoons lemon juice, strained
2 rose-scented geranium leaves

Juice watermelon chunks in an electric juicer. You should have 375ml/13fl oz juice – if not, make up the volume with extra water.

In a medium-sized bowl, mix together cornflour, water, sugar, lemon juice and enough watermelon juice to form a very smooth paste without any lumps. Pour in remaining watermelon juice. Transfer watermelon mixture to a small saucepan with rose-scented geranium leaves.

Place four 125ml/4½fl oz-capacity glass dishes by the stove. Cook watermelon mixture over medium heat, stirring continuously until it comes to the boil and has thickened. Remove rose-scented geranium leaves and immediately divide watermelon mixture among dishes. Leave to cool for a few minutes, then cover with plastic film and chill in the refrigerator before serving.

Tony Tan's Watermelon with Prawns and Coconut

Dissolve 150g/5oz palm sugar in 100ml/3½fl oz hot water in a small saucepan over low heat, stirring. Add 1 well-washed coriander plant (leaves, stems and root) and simmer together until quite syrupy. While syrup is reducing, fry 70g/2½oz desiccated coconut in a dry non-stick frying pan over medium heat, stirring, until it is a rich golden brown. Remove coriander from cooled syrup, stir in desiccated coconut, some finely chopped chilli and fish sauce to taste. Cut chunky rectangles of watermelon, spoon over the coconut syrup and top each rectangle with either chopped stir-fried prawns or freshly picked crabmeat.

Watermelon Granita

SERVES 4 This refreshing iced dessert is absolutely child's play to make. Because watermelon contains so much water and is naturally very sweet, it is not necessary to make the sugar syrup that is needed for most other granitas. However, it will become very icy after several hours in the freezer so it is ideal to make, freeze and serve on the same day. If there is leftover granita that has become ice-block hard, leave it out of the freezer for an hour, and then work it with a fork. The texture will be almost as good as it was when freshly made.

If you are not making this for children, you might like to add a little white rum, vodka or clear fruit brandy to this recipe.

500g/1lb watermelon flesh, cut into
   chunks and seeded
6 strawberries, hulled

1 tablespoon pure icing sugar,
   or to taste
2 teaspoons lemon juice, strained

EXTRA EQUIPMENT
electric juicer or
   food processor
shallow metal ice
   cream tray

Purée watermelon chunks and strawberries in an electric juicer or food processor. You should have 375ml/13fl oz juice. Press icing sugar through a sieve into watermelon juice, then add lemon juice. Taste for sweetness and acidity and add extra icing sugar or lemon juice if required.

Pour watermelon mixture into a shallow metal tray and put into the freezer. After 45 minutes, remove the tray and use a metal spoon to scrape frozen edges into the centre. Repeat this scraping 30 minutes later. Your granita may be ready or it may need a further 30 minutes and a final scrape. It should be uniformly icy and still a bit slushy.

When it is ready, either pile straight away into chilled glasses and serve or transfer it to an airtight container, cover and serve within a few hours.

MINT

**Lamiaceae family
(includes lavender, rosemary,
sage and thyme)
Herbaceous perennial**

Soil type
Moist, well-drained soil.

Soil preparation
As long as the soil is well drained
and rich in organic matter,
no additional preparation
is required.

Climate
Suitable for all climates.

Position
Grows well in either full sun
or partial shade.

How to grow
For cuttings, take a woody
cutting about 5–10cm long
and place just over half the
length in good soil. Once the
roots have taken you can plant
in a permanent position in the
garden. For propagation by
division, dig up a plant and
divide it into several pieces.
Be sure each piece has a stem
and root system, and replant
the pieces.

Water requirements
Keep soil moist.

When to fertilise
Fertilise a couple of times a
year with a liquid fertiliser (see
page 691) or worm tea (see
page 695).

Harvest period
Can be harvested at any
time. Regular harvesting will
encourage production. The
plant will die down or become
straggly in winter; prune to the
ground at this point; the plant
will reappear in spring.

Pests and organic control
Powdery mildew can strike at the
end of the season. Cut down the
plant and feed and water it wll.
Mint rust is a serious disease.
Destroy the whole plant (do not
compost).

Companion planting
As mint repels pests,
it is beneficial planted near
broccoli and cabbage.

Special information
Keep the soil moist and free
from weeds by mulching.
Cut back after flowering.
Can be invasive.

**Quantities to plant
for a family of four**
1 healthy mint plant will be
more than enough.

Winter mint (*Mentha ×spicata*)

Growing and Harvesting Brushing past a pot of mint, especially after rain, releases a whoosh of a refreshing and uplifting aroma like that of no other herb. There are many varieties. The most common for culinary purposes are spearmint (*Mentha spicata*), with narrow leaves; or winter mint, with rounder, slightly pebbled leaves (*Mentha cordifolia*). Peppermints (*Mentha ×piperita*) are preferred for infusing to make peppermint tea, a fun thing to do in the garden as a refreshing break from digging. Apple mint (*Mentha suaveolens*) has a slightly furry texture but is prized for its delicate flavour.

Most mints are space invaders and need to be contained. A mint plant kept in a pot but settled into a suitable hole in the garden is a good idea. Sunk in its pot it is less likely to dry out, and is still contained. Make sure that the host pot has adequate drainage holes before digging it in, though. If you decide to inter-plant mint with vegetables and flowers, given its invasive nature you should still plant it in the garden bed in its own pot. Spearmint, in particular, is thought to repel insects such as cabbage white butterfly.

Container Planting A half-wine barrel is a perfect container for mint. A cheaper alternative is a cut-down plastic rubbish bin with a drainage hole cut in the bottom. The new shoots should be picked first to encourage side growth and the container should not be allowed to dry out. Mint plants form a dense mat of roots, so it is not a good idea to combine another herb in the pot or tub; it will have a hard time competing.

Mint plants need to be re-potted after about two years and I recommend refreshing the pot or barrel with plenty of compost at the same time. Take root cuttings in summer, pot up and bring indoors. Put on a windowsill for fresh leaves in winter.

Preparing and Sharing In traditional cookery mint is used with fresh peas and new potatoes or to make a mint sauce to go with roast lamb. It is also often scattered over fresh fruits such as melon or strawberries or added to summer fruit punches or cocktails. Mint is a much-loved herb in many other cuisines, such as those of South-East Asia and the Middle East, where the popular salad tabbouleh relies on large quantities of mint and flat-leaf parsley, not to mention the astonishing quantities of mint tea that are drunk in Arab countries. Mint tea can be made with either fresh or dried leaves.

In Indian and other Sub-continental cooking, mint is often mixed with coriander and basil, or chopped into yoghurt to make a fresh chutney to serve with curries. Mint is delightful torn or chopped into seafood salads made with prawns or calamari. It is chopped into salsas in Mexico and kneaded into fresh cheese in Greece.

Especially for Kids Make a jug of mint tea by infusing lots of freshly picked and chopped or bruised leaves with boiling water. After the leaves have steeped for five minutes, remove them and sweeten the drink with a small quantity of honey.

Another speedy and refreshing drink is made by puréeing watermelon or pineapple chunks in a blender, then adding a little finely chopped mint. Or make a refreshing yoghurt-based Mint and Cucumber Lassi (see page 407), a popular Indian cooler, and serve it the next time you have something spicy for dinner to see if it helps counteract the heat.

A good activity is to compare the taste, texture and colours of freshly made tabbouleh with a store-bought mix. Working out the comparative cost could also be interesting.

Spiced Chicken and Rice with Mint

SERVES 4 This is based on the classic Indian dish biryani, where spiced rice is mixed with chicken or lamb in a rich sauce and steamed. Although I have described how to present this dish in the traditional manner, I have simplified it to make it family-friendly and suggested serving the two components separately. To serve it more traditionally, you may want to fry some almonds to scatter over the chicken and rice and decorate the dish with extra sprigs of mint. Yoghurt is inclined to split when it is overheated, especially when it is added to dishes such as this one which contain acidic ingredients like tomatoes. To minimise the chance of the yoghurt splitting I recommend not adding the yoghurt mixture to the dish until it is ready to serve. This is an exciting dish for young cooks and is a simple introduction to the magical world of spices.

EXTRA EQUIPMENT
simmer mat
  (see page 45)
mortar and pestle
1 × 2 litre/3½
  pint-capacity
  enamelled cast-
  iron or other
  heavy-based
  casserole with a
  tight-fitting lid

SPICED RICE
1 tablespoon vegetable oil
½ onion, finely chopped
2 cardamom pods, bruised
2 cloves
1 × 2cm/¾in-long piece cinnamon
  stick
10 saffron stamens, soaked in
  1 tablespoon water for 5 minutes
¼ teaspoon ground ginger
salt
250g/9oz basmati rice, washed
  and drained
500ml/18fl oz water
40g/1½oz sultanas

CHICKEN STEW
½ teaspoon cumin seeds
½ teaspoon coriander seeds
½ teaspoon chilli flakes

½ teaspoon ground turmeric
½ teaspoon salt
2 tablespoons vegetable oil
1 onion, finely chopped
2 cloves garlic, finely chopped
1 × 2cm/¾in-long piece ginger,
  finely chopped
3 medium-sized tomatoes, peeled,
  seeded and chopped (see page
  645) or 250g/9oz tinned chopped
  tomatoes with juice
20 mint leaves, torn
500g/1lb skinless free-range chicken
  breasts, cut into bite-sized pieces
1 teaspoon cornflour
1 tablespoon water
140g/5oz Greek-style yoghurt
  (see page 706)
30g/1oz flaked almonds (optional)
butter, for frying (optional)

>>>

To make the spiced rice, heat vegetable oil in a medium-sized saucepan over low heat and sauté onion for 8–10 minutes or until soft and golden, stirring from time to time. Add spices and salt, stir together and then add rice. Give a good stir to coat rice grains and add water. Bring to the boil over medium heat, then reduce heat to lowest possible (use a simmer mat if necessary). Cover saucepan tightly and cook undisturbed for 20 minutes. Lift lid, scatter in sultanas, replace lid and leave rice off heat but still tightly covered until you wish to serve.

To make the chicken stew, dry-roast cumin and coriander seeds separately in a small frying pan over medium heat until fragrant. Tip seeds into a mortar, then grind to a fine powder with the pestle. Tip them into a bowl, then add chilli flakes, turmeric and salt.

Heat oil in a 2 litre/3½ pint-capacity enamelled cast-iron casserole dish over medium heat. Sauté onion, garlic and ginger for 8–10 minutes or until well softened and golden, stirring from time to time. Add spice mix and cook for 1–2 minutes. Add tomato and mint (reserve a few leaves to scatter over before serving, if desired). Stir to mix and then add chicken. Place casserole on a simmer mat over low heat, then cook gently for 20 minutes or until chicken is very tender.

Mix cornflour and water to form a paste. Heat yoghurt in a small frying pan over low heat until barely warm. Remove from heat and stir in cornflour paste. Add 1 ladleful of the sauce from the chicken stew to yoghurt, then stir very gently. Remove chicken stew from heat, then gently stir in yoghurt/cornflour mixture.

Traditionally the chicken stew is stirred through the spiced rice and the whole lot is steamed in a covered steamer until hot and served mounded on a platter. If you wish, fry 2–3 tablespoons flaked almonds in a little butter and scatter them over the mound. Otherwise, you can serve it family-style with the rice in one dish and the chicken stew, scattered with mint, in another (see opposite).

Fattoush

SERVES 2 This popular salad is included in every collection of Middle Eastern recipes I've ever seen. Constants seem to be toasted pita bread, tomatoes, cucumbers, parsley and mint; beyond that the versions vary. Some contain lettuce leaves, some include red onions or spring onions; others suggest flavouring the salad with sumac, a dark red spice ground from a berry that adds tartness to Middle Eastern dishes just as tamarind adds a similar quality to South-East Asian and Indian dishes. Melbourne chef Greg Malouf massages spices into raw onion rings in his version, while Claudia Roden suggests adding a final sprinkling of pomegranate seeds.

I had no pita bread the day I wanted to test this recipe so, although it may be sacrilege, I cut very thin slices of sourdough, brushed them with olive oil and fried them in a dry frying pan in the same manner as described here. There is no question that pita bread gives a more authentic result, but when you are looking for ways to cook with what you've just harvested from the garden, sometimes you need to improvise.

6 cos or other salad leaves, cut or
  torn into large pieces
1 ripe firm tomato (an oxheart
  variety is the very best for this),
  cut into bite-sized pieces
1 Lebanese cucumber, peeled and
  cut into bite-sized pieces
20 mint leaves, chopped
½ small handful flat-leaf parsley,
  chopped

½ pita bread
2 tablespoons extra-virgin olive oil,
  plus extra, for brushing
1 clove garlic, halved
juice of 1 lemon
a pinch sea salt
freshly ground black pepper
2 spring onions, trimmed and
  thinly sliced

Place lettuce leaves, tomato and cucumber in a bowl. Mix in herbs.

Open out pita bread and brush lightly on both sides with olive oil. Place bread in a dry non-stick frying pan over medium heat and toast, turning after 3 minutes so that both sides have coloured and it feels crisp. Remove bread to a chopping board and very lightly rub cut garlic over it. Set garlic aside to add to dressing. Leave bread to cool and then cut or tear into bite-sized pieces.

To make the dressing, finely chop reserved garlic and mix with lemon juice, salt, pepper and remaining olive oil in a small bowl. Set aside.

When ready to serve, add spring onion and crisped bread to salad and pour over dressing. Mix well and serve at once.

Mint and Cucumber Lassi

SERVES 1 This is a very refreshing drink and should be served icy cold. Lassis are frequently made with yoghurt thinned to the required consistency with iced water; however, here I have used commercial buttermilk. Although I've said to remove the seeds from the cucumber, with very small home-grown cucumbers the seeds are insignificant and can be left in place. It makes a great accompaniment to a spicy curry.

EXTRA EQUIPMENT
blender or food
processor

1 crisp Lebanese cucumber, peeled,
  halved lengthways, seeded
  and roughly chopped
250ml/9fl oz buttermilk
a pinch salt

1 spring onion, trimmed and
  roughly chopped
10 mint leaves, roughly chopped
sprig mint, to serve

Place all ingredients (except mint sprig) in a blender or food processor and whiz until smooth. The lassi will be a very delicate pale-green with a few darker green flecks. Pour into a chilled glass and garnish with a mint sprig, then serve.

Mint and Apple Jelly

MAKES 2 × 250ML/9FL OZ-CAPACITY JARS This lovely jelly is adapted from the recipe given to Australian cook Maggie Beer by her friend Kathy Howard for a wild crabapple and sage jelly, first published in Maggie's book, *Maggie's Harvest*. I used apples bought at my local farmers' market and added a handful of my unripe crabapples because they were available. Roughly chop 1kg/2lb firm whole unpeeled apples in a food processor. Put apple and 1½ small handfuls mint leaves into a heavy-based saucepan and barely cover with cold water, then bring to boil over medium heat. Reduce heat to low, then cover and simmer for 45 minutes or until apples are completely soft. Put a colander inside a large bowl, then line it with damp muslin, leaving plenty of overhang. Tip apple/mint mixture into colander and leave overnight at room temperature. The next day, compost solids and measure liquid (I had 750ml/27fl oz). Transfer liquid to a wide saucepan or preserving pan, then add 180ml/6fl oz white-wine vinegar and 600g/1lb 5oz sugar (for each 250ml/9fl oz liquid add 60ml/2fl oz vinegar and 200g/7oz sugar). Heat over medium heat, stirring until sugar dissolves. Increase heat to high and boil without stirring for about 12–15 minutes. Skim froth that rises to the surface. When setting point is reached (about 105°C/220°F on a candy thermometer, or test by spooning a little onto a cold saucer and then seeing if your finger leaves a clear trail when dragged through), remove from heat immediately and stir in 2 teaspoons finely chopped mint. Ladle into sterilised jars and seal. Unopened jars will keep for at least 6 months. Once opened, keep the jar in the refrigerator.

Mint and Tamarind Chutney

MAKES 180ML/6FL OZ Tamarind is a fascinating ingredient. The tree produces long pods that are used extensively in Indian and South-East Asian cookery. Inside the pods are seeds covered in a dense and sticky pulp whose flavour is sweet yet sour. Tamarind pulp is available in Asian and Indian food stores. It is possible to buy already seeded tamarind but I have given instructions for separating the pulp from the seeds as I find that I often buy a block of what I believe is pure tamarind pulp and get it home to find it still has all the seeds embedded in it. Recipes often refer to tamarind water and that is what one ends up with after following the process described below. It is a confusing term as frequently the tamarind water is quite thick, as it is in this recipe.

This delicious chutney can be served as a side dish with a curry or as a condiment with pakhoras such as the Jerusalem Artichoke Pakhoras on page 333. It would be well received as an accompaniment to tiny seasoned meatballs or the Salmon Patties with Dill on page 279.

EXTRA EQUIPMENT
coarse-meshed stainless-steel sieve
pestle (or other device for forcing tamarind through sieve)
food processor

150g/5oz tamarind pulp (see page 706)
180ml/6fl oz boiling water
2 tablespoons chopped coriander
¼ small handful chopped mint

55g/2oz dark brown sugar
1 tablespoon chopped ginger
½ teaspoon sea salt
¼ teaspoon chilli flakes
juice of ½ lemon

To make tamarind 'water' or paste, put tamarind into a mixing bowl and pour over the boiling water. Allow to cool until just warm. Work the rather murky mixture with your fingers to start separating pulp from embedded seeds. Place a strong sieve over a second mixing bowl and tip in tamarind mixture. Push and press mixture with a pestle or other device to force as much pure pulp through as you can. Scrape paste several times from bottom of sieve into bowl. At the end of this process you will have about 150ml/5fl oz smooth rather thick tamarind water (any excess can be frozen for another use) and a tangle of strings and seeds in the sieve or strainer to be discarded in the compost bucket.

Put all ingredients in a food processor and process to form a smooth paste. Taste for salt and sharpness; you can add extra salt or lemon juice if desired. Scrape into a container, then cover and refrigerate. This chutney will keep for at least 1 month stored in an airtight container in the refrigerator.

Making tamarind water

Lamb, Mint and Lentil Patties (*Shami Kebab*)

MAKES 8 These patties make great picnic food, folded into Indian flatbread or pita bread. Start preparing them the day before you intend to eat them. Serve with yoghurt and your favourite pickle; I sometimes offer Tom Jaine's Lemon Pickle on page 369 (see opposite). At the risk of scandalising Indian readers, I have to admit to baking the mixture in a shallow oiled gratin dish for 20 minutes at 180°C/Gas 4 to add to a party table with other shared dishes. The idea is to scoop a portion onto a plate or a piece of warmed flatbread. The 'surprise' is offered as a condiment to sprinkle on a portion when it is served in this way.

50g/2oz red lentils or yellow split peas, rinsed
250ml/9fl oz water
450g/15½oz finely minced lamb
10 cloves
1 teaspoon black peppercorns
½ teaspoon ground cinnamon
6 cardamom pods, bruised and seeds
   removed
3 bay leaves
1½ teaspoons salt
1 × 2cm/¾in-long piece ginger, peeled and
   finely chopped

1 large free-range egg
vegetable oil, for cooking
sprigs mint, to serve

'SURPRISE'
2 tablespoons very finely
   chopped onion
1 tablespoon very finely
   chopped mint
1 teaspoon very finely
   chopped fresh small
   green chilli

EXTRA EQUIPMENT
food processor

Put lentils or split peas, water, lamb, cloves, peppercorns, cinnamon, cardamom seeds, bay and salt in a heavy-based non-stick saucepan and bring to the boil. Cover, reduce heat to medium and simmer for 20 minutes or until lentils or split peas are cooked. Remove lid and increase heat to medium–high, then cook, stirring constantly, until meat is very dry; there should be no hint of liquid. Turn off heat and allow meat to cool. Discard bay leaves. Grind lamb mixture in a food processor until you have a fine paste; no whole spices should be visible (this will take quite a few minutes). Add ginger and egg and whiz again to mix. Taste and add more salt if necessary. Put lamb mixture into a bowl, then cover and refrigerate for several hours.

To make the 'surprise', mix together all ingredients. Divide lamb mixture into 8 portions, then use wet hands to form smooth balls. Take 1 ball at a time and press a deep indentation in it with your thumb. Stuff one-eighth of the 'surprise' mixture into the indentation, then squeeze the meat mixture to completely cover the 'surprise'. Flatten into a patty and chill. Repeat with remaining lamb and 'surprise' mixtures.

Pour 5mm/¼in vegetable oil into a large, heavy-based non-stick frying pan and heat over medium heat. Fry patties in batches for 3–4 minutes on each side or until slightly crisp and golden. Drain on paper towel. Garnish with mint.

MUSHROOMS

Agaricaceae family

Soil type
Rich, moist compost containing well-rotted manure.

Climate
Suitable for all climates in a controlled environment indoors.

Position
Prefers a dark aspect, but will tolerate some light.

How to grow
Usually grown indoors over winter. If you choose to use a mushroom farm kit (see page 414), follow the enclosed instructions. If not, there will be 3 stages to growing mushrooms:
1 Preparation: you will need to have a container to grow the mushrooms in (such as a cut-down rubbish bin or broccoli box).
2 Spawning (planting): spawn can be purchased from mushroom growers. Plant 1cm pieces of spawn 2cm deep and 25cm apart, into prepared compost. Water lightly.
3 Casing: after a couple of days, the compost will need to be covered with a layer of topsoil. Just water and watch them grow.

Water requirements
Water 2–3 times a week; keep compost moist but not wet.

Harvest period
Mushrooms can be harvested after 4 weeks. The crop appears in flushes. Cut stalks at the soil level. Regular picking will encourage further flushes.

Pests and organic control
Mushroom flies are attracted to wet compost. Use a fine net crop cover.

Special information
Mushrooms require a constant temperature of 18–23°C.

Quantities to plant for a family of four
1 mushroom farm will be enough to satisfy curiosity but perhaps not appetite.

Cultivated or button mushroom (*Agaricus bisporus*)

Growing and Harvesting Technically mushrooms are not a garden crop but the visible fruiting body of a fungus. Whether they are a plant or fruiting body, for adults and children alike they are a most fascinating form of life.

While making a television series, I was travelling in north-eastern Tasmania, and the crew was searching for a 'beauty shot'. We came across a hillside strewn with field mushrooms, each as big as a small dinner plate. We picked about twenty and then wondered how to enjoy them, given that we were staying in very basic motel units. The solution was to send the cheekiest member of the team to the kitchen of the local pub and ask the chef to cook them for us. He was happy to oblige. So dinner was grilled scotch fillet and the chef delivered a big bowl of our mushrooms simply cooked with butter, a touch of salt and some freshly ground pepper. They were magnificent and we all mused about the mushrooming expeditions of our childhood and agreed that you rarely see mushrooms like this any more.

What saddens me is that when we do see regular field mushrooms in paddocks or roadsides, fewer people are prepared to pick and eat them. I am the first to urge caution with unknown fungi, but it seems disappointing that the highly valued field mushroom of my youth is now treated with such suspicion. Mushroom enthusiasts are familiar with many different varieties, but as far as most young children are concerned, they are more likely to experience cultivated mushrooms. An outing with a knowledgeable adult may expand a child's mushroom repertoire, but again, caution and expertise are needed.

Another option is to grow your own using a mushroom farm kit, available from good nurseries. These come as a bag or box, complete with compost and spawn, which will grow to become mushrooms. Follow the enclosed instructions. Temperature control may mean that mushroom farms have to be located indoors, as most gardens will be too cold and the farms must be kept away from direct sunlight. A garage or non-draughty shed will be suitable. A commercial mushroom kit will usually produce mushrooms over a period of at least eight weeks. They can be harvested in all stages of button, cup and fully opened mushrooms, known as 'flats' – a useful and very visual way to explore the idea with children that things can be useful at different stages of their life cycle. (Sometimes flat mushrooms are sold or described on restaurant menus as 'portobellos'.) A button mushroom will never mature into a flat cap once it is picked. A wider range of mushrooms can be grown on logs and stumps (see **www.gourmetmushrooms.co.uk** for advanced techniques).

Once the mushrooms cease, their compost can be added to the garden compost pile. The growing mushrooms will have used up most of the nutrients in the mushroom compost, however, so don't rely on it on its own but mix it with aged animal manure or your own compost before spreading it on the garden.

Container Planting For those not buying a kit, mushrooms can be grown in a cut-down rubbish bin or broccoli box (see page 413).

Preparing and Sharing Mushrooms should not be washed before preparing them. Any dirt or growing medium can be brushed away with a soft cloth or you can even buy a mushroom brush in cookery equipment stores if you are a mushroom-lover. Mushrooms should never be stored in plastic bags or covered with plastic film as they need air circulating around them to prevent them deteriorating quickly. Vendors always provide paper bags for mushrooms. Cultivated mushrooms never need peeling.

Mushrooms are very versatile and cook in just a few minutes. Whole mushrooms can be grilled, sautéed or stuffed. I know it is said that life is too short to stuff a mushroom, but I am not so sure! A quick mixture of garlic, chopped mushroom stems, chopped flat-leaf parsley, grated parmesan, butter and breadcrumbs spooned into the hollows and baked in a 180°C/Gas 4 oven means that in 20 minutes you have a delectable first course.

I find that if I cook flat cultivated mushrooms with a nut of butter and a little water in a covered shallow pan over medium heat, they develop flavours and juices that make you hesitate and wonder if perhaps they are real field mushrooms. Try it! Never crowd mushrooms in a frying pan as they will stew rather than sauté.

To make a quick topping for a steak or toast, sauté 250 grams/9 ounces sliced flat mushrooms in a frying pan in melted butter with a little chopped garlic. When softened, add a heaped tablespoonful of Greek-style yoghurt, chopped flat-leaf parsley and snipped chives, then season to taste with sea salt and freshly ground black pepper.

Chopped mushrooms can be sautéed, deep-fried as fritters or added to stir-fries. Mushrooms pair beautifully with garlic, flat-leaf parsley, thyme and olive oil or butter. The youngest buttons are delicious sliced and served raw in salads, with or without other ingredients (see the Raw Mushroom, Rocket and Bread Salad on page 420).

Especially for Kids Mushroom 'farms' are thrilling for children to observe. The first time they see the tiny white dots growing into mushrooms, it seems like pure magic.

Mastering the art of making a Mushroom Omelette (see page 416) can be one of the first dishes in a young cook's repertoire. It takes ten minutes from start to finish and could well be a lifeline dish for the rest of their life. It is one of my absolute standbys.

Some schools may be able to organise excursions to look for field and wild mushrooms with an expert, so it is well worth asking. Wild mushrooms must be expertly identified and no one should ever experiment with eating an unknown mushroom.

Mushroom Omelette

SERVES 1 A moist omelette with a generous quantity of mushrooms takes maybe ten minutes to make, and that includes chopping the mushrooms and cracking the eggs. Keep a pan just for making omelettes and crêpes. It will only ever need to be wiped with a piece of paper towel and will reward you by never sticking.

60g/2oz unsalted butter
6–8 small button mushrooms, sliced
2 free-range eggs
1 tablespoon water

sea salt and freshly ground
   black pepper
1 tablespoon finely snipped chives

EXTRA EQUIPMENT
1 × 18–20cm/7–8in
   pressed-steel
   crêpe pan
   (see page 47) or
   small non-stick
   frying pan

Heat 30g/1oz of the butter in a small crêpe or frying pan over medium heat and drop in mushrooms. Stir and keep moving for 4–5 minutes. Tip into a bowl and keep warm.

Break eggs into another bowl and add water, a pinch of salt and some pepper. Whisk lightly. Stir in most of the chives.

Heat pan over medium heat. Add 20g/¾oz of the remaining butter. As soon as it is foaming, tip in egg mixture and immediately tilt pan so that egg runs all over the bottom where it will start to set at once. Using a wooden spatula, drag cooked edges to the middle and again tilt the pan so that uncooked mixture flows to the edges. Tip mushrooms across centre of omelette. The uncooked surface should still look moist and shiny. The omelette is cooked.

Give the pan a sharp shove away from you to start the furthest edge flipping up the sides and rolling over. Encourage the near side of the omelette to fold and slide the omelette onto a heated serving plate. Skim omelette surface with the last of the butter and scatter over remaining chives. The omelette will taste just as good if you serve it unfolded onto your plate!

Mushroom Custard for a Tart

Cook mushrooms as instructed in the above Mushroom Omelette recipe, then add to a custard made by whisking together 600ml/1 pint pouring cream (or 300ml/½ pint each pouring cream and milk), 3 whole free-range eggs and 2 free-range egg yolks. Pour mixture into a blind-baked 22–24cm/9–9½in tart shell (see page 510) and bake at 170°C/Gas 3 for about 20 minutes or until set. Leave tart to cool a little before slicing and serving warm.

Sautéed Mushrooms

SERVES 2 This is a basic recipe. It can either be the topping for Bruschetta (see page 312), served as breakfast mushrooms on toast, a slightly fancier filling for an omelette than the one on page 416, a filling for delicate crêpes, the basis of a mushroom tart, or transformed into a party entrée by spooning the mushrooms onto freshly baked rectangles of puff pastry (see opposite). The combination of mushrooms, butter, garlic and parsley is hard to beat. While delicious with just one size and type of mushroom, this recipe becomes more interesting if you include a few sliced oyster mushrooms, and combine a mixture of flats and buttons. In the autumn you may find a few pine forest mushrooms to add to the mixture. Just be certain that any mushrooms gathered in the wild have been identified authoritatively. The hot toast or baked warm pastry case should be absolutely ready before you start to cook the mushrooms as they are at their best immediately after they are cooked. If they are to become a tart filling, the custard (see page 416) should already be mixed and the pastry shell be blind-baked until golden.

40g/1½oz butter
2 tablespoons extra-virgin olive oil
250g/9oz mushrooms, sliced or
    quartered, depending on size
    (leave whole if tiny
    button mushrooms)

1 clove garlic, finely chopped
1 tablespoon chopped
    flat-leaf parsley
60ml/2fl oz pouring cream (optional)
sea salt and freshly ground
    black pepper

Heat butter and olive oil in a large non-stick frying pan over medium heat and, when it foams, tip in mushrooms. Cook mushrooms for 5 minutes, stirring constantly with a wooden spoon. Cover and cook for 1–2 minutes, then increase heat to medium–high, uncover and add garlic. Stir for 30 seconds, then add parsley and cream, if using; the cream will form a small amount of sauce. Remove from heat, season with salt and pepper and serve at once.

Puff Pastry Shells for Sautéed Mushrooms

Cut rectangles from ready-made and rolled out all-butter puff pastry making decisive cuts with a very sharp knife (uneven cuts will cause the pastry to rise unevenly). One 27cm/10½in-square sheet can be cut into 6 pieces. Invert pastry rectangles onto a baking tray and chill for 20 minutes. Brush with a whisked free-range egg yolk. (A pastry chef passed on the hint of turning cut puff pastry shapes upside-down before baking as it seems to assist the pastry to rise evenly.) Bake for 10 minutes at 200°C/Gas 6, then reduce temperature to 170°C/Gas 3 and bake for another 15 minutes. Split each pastry rectangle in half, then spoon on sautéed mushrooms and top with other half (see opposite).

Raw Mushroom, Rocket and Bread Salad

SERVES 4 This is a favourite salad of mine. Raw mushrooms have an unusual nutty flavour that combines wonderfully with rocket and the slightly salty cheese, ricotta salata (see page 705). This pressed and salted style of ricotta is not easy to find. You should head to a delicatessen that is patronised by Italians. If it is not obtainable, you can substitute pecorino or even parmesan; although parmesan is a bit aristocratic (and much more expensive) for what is really a pretty rustic salad.

2 slices sourdough bread, crusts removed (about 100g/3½oz)
150ml/5fl oz extra-virgin olive oil
1 clove garlic, halved
300g/10½oz button mushrooms, bases trimmed and caps thinly sliced

100g/3½oz shaved ricotta salata (see page 705) or pecorino
sea salt and freshly ground black pepper
1 tablespoon lemon juice
4 handfuls rocket leaves, washed and dried

EXTRA EQUIPMENT
speed peeler (see page 47)
salad spinner

Brush bread slices with 1 tablespoon of the olive oil and toast in a dry large non-stick frying pan over medium heat, turning after 3 minutes, until both sides have taken colour and look crisp. Transfer bread to a plate, then rub lightly with cut garlic. When cool enough to handle, cut into 1cm/½in cubes and drop into a salad bowl. Add mushrooms, cheese, salt and pepper to the bowl, then drizzle over lemon juice and remaining olive oil.

Turn salad over and over with a large spoon and then leave for about 10 minutes to allow flavours to mellow and mushrooms to soften. Taste a mushroom slice for salt and pepper and adjust seasoning if desired.

At the last minute toss rocket leaves through salad and serve. An extra drizzle of olive oil may be a good idea.

Stuffed Flat Mushrooms

MAKES 12 In this recipe the mushroom stems are used in the stuffing for the mushrooms themselves. The same stuffing can be used to fill halved and hollowed baby squash or even zucchini that are a bit bigger than you would ideally like; in which case you may like to include a few whole mushrooms to make the stuffing go further. Quantities are not really that important as the stuffing often varies according to what is on hand. Sometimes I have added shredded ham.

12 flat mushrooms (about
  6–8cm/2½–3in diameter), stems
  removed and reserved
80ml/3fl oz extra-virgin olive oil
sea salt and freshly ground
  black pepper
20g/¾oz butter
1 small onion, finely chopped

2 cloves garlic, finely chopped
½ teaspoon freshly grated nutmeg
25g/1oz fresh breadcrumbs
25g/1oz grated parmesan
35g/1¼oz Gruyère-style cheese or
  mozzarella, grated
⅓ small handful chopped flat-leaf
  parsley

Place mushroom caps on a baking paper-lined baking tray and brush each one with some of the olive oil. Season with salt and pepper. Finely chop mushroom stems.

Preheat oven to 180°C/Gas 4.

Heat 3 tablespoons of the olive oil and the butter in a large non-stick frying pan over medium heat and sauté onion for 5 minutes or until it has started to soften. Add chopped mushroom stems, garlic and nutmeg to the pan and cook for a further 3 minutes, then scrape into a mixing bowl. Stir in breadcrumbs, cheeses and parsley and season with salt and pepper to taste.

Press some stuffing mixture onto each mushroom cap, smoothing it right to the edge. Drizzle with last of the olive oil.

Bake mushrooms for 10 minutes or until bubbling and golden brown. Serve straight away; warn your family or guests that the mushrooms will be very hot.

Grilled Mushrooms with Lemon

Drizzle fully opened large mushroom caps with extra-virgin olive oil. Add 2–3 very thin slices of garlic to each mushroom and season well with sea salt and freshly ground black pepper. Grill under a hot griller for 5 minutes. Sprinkle each mushroom with a few drops of lemon juice and serve at once.

Mushroom Soup with Porcini

SERVES 6 This is a rustic autumnal soup, woodsy in colour and flavour. Dried porcini mushrooms are sold in small envelopes in larger supermarkets and specialty food stores. They have a unique fragrance that is much prized. They need preliminary soaking as described below. Fresh horseradish is available during the autumn and winter months and looks a bit like a very rustic parsnip. Peel it and grate either with the grating attachment of a food processor or a Microplane-style grater. If you can do this near an extraction fan you won't cry so hard, as the fumes from fresh horseradish are very powerful and even cause strong men to cry (and everyone else too!). A reasonable compromise if fresh horseradish is not available is to use commercially prepared horseradish, squeezed of excess vinegar and folded through some whipped cream.

EXTRA EQUIPMENT
Microplane or other fine grater
food processor
coarse-meshed sieve
pestle

250ml/9fl oz boiling water
15g/½oz dried porcini mushrooms
500g/1lb mushrooms
40g/1½oz butter
1 onion, sliced
2 cloves garlic, chopped
2 teaspoons thyme leaves
1 tablespoon chopped flat-leaf parsley
1 thick slice sourdough bread, cut into 2cm/¾in cubes

1 litre/1¾ pints chicken stock, vegetable stock or water
2 tablespoons tomato paste
sea salt and freshly ground black pepper

HORSERADISH CREAM
125ml/4½fl oz pouring cream
30g/1oz freshly grated horseradish
juice of ½ lemon
sea salt

Pour boiling water over porcini and soak for 15 minutes. Lift porcini from liquid and chop roughly, then set aside. Strain soaking liquid through a fine-meshed sieve and reserve. Coarsely chop fresh mushrooms in a food processor.

Melt butter in a large saucepan over medium heat, then cook onion for 5 minutes or until it starts to soften. Add garlic, thyme, parsley and chopped porcini and sauté for 1 minute, then tip in strained porcini juice. Bring to the boil. Add chopped mushrooms, bread, stock or water and tomato paste. Stir and bring to simmering point. Taste and add salt and pepper. Reduce heat to low and simmer for 10 minutes.

Meanwhile, to make the horseradish cream, whip cream with a whisk or hand-held electric beaters to form soft peaks. Dampen horseradish with lemon juice and fold through whipped cream. Season with salt.

Blend soup in a food processor and press it through a coarse-meshed sieve resting over a deep bowl. Press on soup with a pestle to force as much through the mesh as possible. Adjust seasoning. If the soup is too thick, add a little hot water. Serve in wide soup bowls and swirl or dollop horseradish cream into each bowl.

Barley and Mushroom Risotto

SERVES 4–6 The cooking method is the same as for a classic risotto, but even though the barley has been 'pearled' (see page 705) it still takes longer to cook than rice. Barley will always retain a slight chewiness in the grain and it has a delightfully nutty flavour.

EXTRA EQUIPMENT
fine-meshed sieve

250ml/9fl oz hot water
15g/½oz dried porcini mushrooms
500ml/18fl oz chicken stock
40g/1½oz butter
1 tablespoon extra-virgin olive oil
½ onion, finely chopped
2 cloves garlic, finely chopped
220g/8oz pearl barley (see page 705)

60ml/2fl oz vino cotto (see page 706) or red-wine vinegar
100g/3½oz button mushrooms, trimmed and sliced
sea salt and freshly ground black pepper
¼ small handful chopped flat-leaf parsley

Pour boiling water over porcini and soak for 10 minutes. Lift porcini onto a chopping board and strain liquid through a fine-meshed sieve into a small saucepan. Add stock to saucepan and heat over low heat until hot. Roughly chop porcini.

Melt 20g/¾oz of the butter with the oil in another small saucepan or wide-based pan over high heat, then cook onion and garlic for 1 minute, stirring. Add chopped porcini and barley and stir well for 1 minute or until each grain is shiny with oil and butter. Add vino cotto or vinegar and let it sizzle and evaporate.

Reduce heat to medium, then start adding hot stock one ladleful at a time. Stir after each addition. A barley risotto will take 30 minutes to cook so be patient. After half of the stock has been added (after perhaps 15 minutes), add sliced mushrooms. Leave them to soften for 1–2 minutes before stirring them through barley. Continue adding remaining stock a ladleful at a time, until all stock is used and the barley is tender. Season with salt and pepper, then stir in parsley and remaining butter. Turn off heat and leave, covered, for 3 minutes or so before serving.

MYRTLE

Myrtaceae family
Evergreen shrub

Soil type
Rich moist soil, but will tolerate dry conditions.

Soil preparation
Enrich with organic matter.

Climate
Suitable for all climates, but prefers moist, warm areas.

Position
Full sun to partial shade.

How to grow
Buy as a small shrub from a nursery or grow from a cutting. To plant from cuttings, take a 5–10 cm-long cutting, remove leaves from the bottom half of the stem and place just over one-third of the length in good soil. Once the roots have taken you can plant the cutting in a permanent position. Use woody cuttings in autumn and soft cuttings in summer.

Water requirements
Water moderately to keep soil moist.

When to fertilise
Use a liquid fertiliser (see page 691) or worm tea (see page 695) every 6 months.

Harvest period
Allow berries to ripen fully before harvesting; leaves can be harvested all year.

Pests and organic control
There aren't usually any problems. However, aphids can attack. Watering the leaves can deter these pests, as can a soap or pyrethrum spray (see page 700).

Quantities to plant for a family of four
1 plant.

Myrtle (*Myrtus communis*)

Growing and Harvesting This attractive shrub deserves to be better known. It is native to the Mediterranean, evergreen, very drought-resistant and grows to about 3 metres. The foliage is dark-green, dense and shiny; it is covered with small creamy flowers in late spring through to summer, followed by very attractive small elongated berries in the autumn. The berries are dark-blue, with a bloom like a damson plum, and are highly aromatic when crushed, as are the leaves.

Myrtle can be hedged to create an aromatic border between sections of the garden, or you can do as I have and plant a single specimen. I have grown it in various positions and even moved it when it was practically fully grown. After a period of melancholy it picked up and is now fully recovered and flourishing. I find I can take substantial sprigs from the shrub without there being any ill effects.

Quite apart from its value as a powerful flavouring plant, myrtle earns its place in the garden by providing height, by acting as a windbreak (by virtue of its evergreen foliage), and by attracting bees.

Container Planting Myrtle can be grown in a large tub. Select a pot or other container that is at least 50 centimetres in diameter and a similar depth. Ensure that the soil contains plenty of organic matter. Fertilise once a year and 'refresh' the pot with extra organic matter or well-rotted manure at the same time. After several years the plant may need to be moved to a larger container. A container this size will be very heavy, so its permanent position must ensure it receives full sun.

Preparing and Sharing Myrtle was used in ancient times to season wild boar or small birds, and it does complement pork, quail, squab pigeon or venison particularly well. The best way to appreciate its flavour is to either roast some pork on a bed of myrtle sprigs and lightly crush the berries into the roasting juices, or to tie sprigs to an opened-out (butterflied) quail, a piece of pork or venison and grill it on a barbecue or over hot coals.

Especially for Kids In summer when the myrtle bush is covered in its pretty, fuzzy, cream flowers, sprigs can be cut to add to herb posies for the table – just be cautious that you are not disturbing a bee. And crushing one of the ripe berries in autumn can be part of a 'sniff-and-tell' plant identifying game for children in the garden.

Barbecued Quail with Myrtle

SERVES 4 Quail has a delicate flavour that is complemented by those of many other ingredients and it cooks very quickly. It is at its best when grilled over hot coals. If this is not an option, a ridged char-grill pan or a conventional barbecue grill-plate will have to do. One quail per person is the usual portion. You could easily double this recipe. It is mandatory to lick your fingers! It can get a bit messy, so offering damp cotton towels might be a good idea at the end of eating this.

EXTRA EQUIPMENT
hinged metal grill so the birds can be held flat and turned easily (if using a charcoal fire)
basting brush

4 quail
80ml/3fl oz extra-virgin olive oil
2 tablespoons vino cotto (see page 706)

8 × 10cm/4in-long myrtle sprigs (with or without berries)
freshly ground black pepper
sea salt

Using kitchen scissors, cut up the back of each quail either side of the backbone right through to the neck opening. Pull backbone out and drop it into a bowl. Open out each bird and remove the heart and liver (if present) and add to the bowl. Rinse bird quickly under cold water and then pat really dry with paper towel. Turn each quail skin side-up and press firmly on the breastbone to flatten it with your hand. Repeat with all the quail. (This is called 'spatchcocking' or 'butterflying' and is also often done with a small chicken weighing around 400–500g/14–16oz, frequently sold as a 'poussin'.)

Mix oil and vino cotto in a baking dish. Roughly squash any berries on myrtle sprigs into the mixture. Grind in a good amount of black pepper and drop in myrtle sprigs. Add quail and turn over and over for 1 minute or so, then leave to rest in marinade, flesh side-down, for up to 1 hour (any longer and you will have to refrigerate them).

If using a charcoal fire, ensure coals are white-hot. Otherwise, heat a char-grill pan or barbecue grill-plate until hot. Lift quails from marinade, letting any extra marinade drip back into the baking dish; hopefully the myrtle sprigs will be sticking to the birds at this stage.

If using a hinged metal grill, arrange the quail evenly on one side and close the hinge firmly. Cook quail flesh-side facing heat for about 6 minutes. Turn carefully and crisp skin-side for about 2 minutes. Turn back to the other side if you are concerned that they are not sufficiently cooked for your taste. (Quail is especially delicious if cooked so that the breast meat is still faintly pink.) The myrtle sprigs should be nicely charred.

Transfer quail to a warm platter and leave to rest, skin-side down, for 5 minutes before serving. Quickly heat remaining marinade to boiling point in a small saucepan and spoon over resting quail. Sprinkle with salt before eating.

NETTLES

Growing and Harvesting Nettles are commonly thought of as weeds and the instinct has been to get rid of them. Even though few gardeners would choose to plant these, I have included them here as nettles, both the tall-growing variety and the smaller plant, both have important and useful properties.

Nettles are rich in nitrogen and iron and provide nutrients to the soil for nearby crops. They can be used to make a liquid fertiliser (see page 691). Be pleased if you find nettles appearing near your potatoes, horseradish or tomatoes. It is a host plant for many creatures and attracts beneficial insects to the garden, including ladybirds, who feast on the insects living among its prickles. Nettles like to have cool feet but seem to be indifferent to whether they grow in full sunshine or in shade.

Before setting out to pick nettles, select a thick pair of gardening gloves. The slightest touch of a nettle is enough to cause anguish. Various remedies suggested to ease the sting include rubbing the area with a handful of dry soil, common dock leaves, a handful of mint or sorrel leaves. Hopefully one or other of these plants is growing conveniently nearby! Avoid water, however, as it can reactivate the sting.

Only attempt to gather and cook the youngest nettles, preferably the new shoots that appear in the garden in springtime. The smaller plants will always be more tender than the larger. Over-grown patches of long-ignored nettles will taste rank and tough, no matter how they are treated. Don't use damaged or slimy leaves. Remember that the nettle leaves will collapse dramatically when cooked, so gather plenty. Nettles deteriorate very quickly, so pick and use them on the same day. Strip the leaves from the stalks – still wearing those gloves! – and consign the stalks to the compost or to the chickens, who will enjoy them.

Nettle (*Urtica dioica*)

Preparing and Sharing When handling stinging nettles it is important to wear thick rubber gloves at all times. Cut the leaves and fine stems away from the thick central stalk with scissors. They need to be washed well, then blanched for 2 minutes in a saucepan of plenty of lightly salted boiling water. Swish them around using tongs or a wooden spoon and then drain very well before proceeding. They can then be chopped and sautéed in butter or oil if they are to be part of a pasta sauce or risotto, or they can be added, chopped or not, at the last minute to a vegetable soup that is then puréed, or to a crêpe batter such as the Nettle and Buckwheat Crêpes on page 434. Prepared nettles can be frozen and reconstituted for the filling of Janni Kyritsis's Wild Weed Pie (see page 64) or as needed.

Good partners for nettles include leeks and sorrel, such as in a soup; potatoes and eggs for a frittata; or onions, butter and maybe mint if adding to a risotto.

In times past, nettles were thought of as a springtime tonic, to be consumed regularly to regenerate the body after the rigours of winter. (Old herbalist books charmingly advise to 'pick nettles before the swallows arrive'.) I own a marvellous little book called *Les Secrets de l'Ortie* (*Nettle Secrets*) by Bernard Bertrand, which not only lists in exhaustive detail his knowledge of nettle lore and their historical use, but describes how to use them in the garden, medicinally and in the kitchen. It also lists societies of nettle-lovers (all in France!). One of the most fascinating pages in this book details how nettles were used to make cloth in ancient Egypt and Europe for hundreds of years. The stalks were gathered, dried, soaked, bruised, shredded into fibres, combed and spun. Nettles are a natural insecticide and fungicide, and this cloth was used as the wrapping for Egyptian mummies. More recently, this book claims, nettle fibres were included in the fabric used to make packs and caps for German soldiers during World War I and at the same time the American Army used the strong cloth to store gunpowder. The best muslin for cheese-making apparently included fibre from the nettle family in its manufacture. Extraordinary!

Few of us will have the opportunity to eat many nettles, which is probably a good thing, as excessive intake is considered bad for the kidneys.

Especially for Kids It is intriguing for children to discover that a 'weed' that can deliver such a nasty sting can be tamed by cooking. Harvesting stinging nettles to cook can lead to a good discussion about what constitutes a 'weed'. Janni Kyritsis's recipe for Wild Weed Pie on page 64 could lead to a discussion of how people in many different cultures gather wild plants to eat as part of their everyday diet.

It is interesting to find out how plants have been and are still grown to become fibre. Australian Aborigines collected rush-like sedges. Some sedges produce tubers or seeds that were edible, while the rush-like leaves of others were soaked, dried and then used to weave mats and baskets.

For an interesting website devoted to nettles, go to **www.nettles.org.uk** to read facts about nettles and wildlife, and uses. There is a 'Be nice to nettles' week held in May most years.

Nettle, Fennel and Potato Soup with Saffron

SERVES 4 This soup is not very far from the classic leek and potato soup. On this occasion I've substituted the leeks with nettle leaves, to reinforce the fact that young nettles are not to be regarded only as a nuisance. Alternatively you could use sorrel leaves or young beetroot leaves, or a combination of these.

EXTRA EQUIPMENT
blender or
  food processor
coarse-meshed
  sieve
pestle (or other
  device for pushing
  solids through
  a sieve)

salt
150g/5oz young nettle leaves
60ml/2fl oz extra-virgin olive oil
1 onion, finely chopped
1 bulb fennel, cut into 2cm/¾in
  pieces (reserve some leaves and
  chop, for garnish)
2 cloves garlic, chopped
1 bay leaf

a pinch saffron stamens
600g/1lb 5oz potatoes (about 4),
  cut into 2cm/¾in chunks
sea salt and freshly ground
  black pepper
2 free-range egg yolks
2 handfuls Garlic Croûtons (see
  page 313), to serve

Half-fill a large saucepan or pasta pot with lightly salted water and bring to the boil. Using tongs, drop nettle leaves into pan and swish for 1 minute. Drain nettles in a colander, then press hard on them (they will have lost their sting). Chop roughly. Dry the pan.

Heat olive oil in the pan over low–medium heat, add onion, fennel and garlic and cook for 5–8 minutes or until onion is well softened. Add nettle leaves, bay leaf, saffron and potato. Stir to mix and then barely cover with cold water.

Bring to the boil over high heat, then reduce heat to low and simmer for 20 minutes or until potato is quite tender. Purée potato/nettle mixture in a blender (or food processor). Cover blender lid and the flask with a dry tea towel; hot liquids can force up the lid of a blender, spraying hot liquid that can burn. Carefully blend until smooth.

Tip each batch into a large coarse-meshed sieve placed over a large mixing bowl and force through into the bowl with a pestle or another device. When all soup has been puréed, rinse and dry pan again.

If serving immediately, return soup to pan and reheat to simmering point. Taste and add salt and pepper. Whisk egg yolks in a small bowl with a ladleful of the hot soup. Remove soup from heat and tip in egg yolk mixture. Stir for 1 minute until the soup thickens slightly. The soup mustn't boil again after the egg yolks have been added, so don't complete this final step until you are ready to serve.

Ladle into wide soup bowls, scatter over chopped fennel leaves and offer a bowl of garlic croûtons separately.

Nettle and Buckwheat Crêpes

MAKES 6 Buckwheat blini (small yeast pancakes, see page 240) are the classic accompaniment to smoked fish. They are usually about 5mm/¼in thick. Here I suggest that these thin buckwheat crêpes, with their flecks of dark-green nettles, are equally as good as traditional blini when spread with sour cream or crème fraîche and smoked salmon (or, as is done in Brittany, with thin slices of cooked ham and thin shavings of Gruyère). Alternatively, the crêpes can be cooled completely, then spread with your choice of filling, stacked one on top of the other and the stack then cut into wedges. The crêpes can be successfully reheated if placed on a plate, covered with foil and transferred to a 150°C/Gas 2 oven for about 15 minutes. A very fancy option is to put the cooked crêpes on a cake cooling rack in a 200°C/Gas 6 oven for a few minutes until the edges are well crisped. When they are removed from the oven a small handful of soft salad leaves is placed in the centre, then draped with a slice of smoked salmon and sprinkled with finely chopped herbs such as dill or flat-leaf parsley (see opposite). A final dollop of sour cream could be offered as well.

salt	¼ teaspoon salt	**EXTRA EQUIPMENT**
½ small handful loosely packed	1 large free-range egg	1 × 18–20cm/7–8in
young nettle leaves	250ml/9fl oz milk	pressed-steel
50g/2oz plain flour	60g/2oz butter, melted and cooled	crêpe pan (see
2 tablespoons buckwheat flour		page 47)

Half-fill a large saucepan with lightly salted water and bring to the boil. Using tongs, drop in nettle leaves and swish for 1 minute. Drain nettles in a colander, pressing hard on them (they will have lost their sting). Chop roughly.

Sift flours and salt into a bowl. Lightly whisk together egg, milk and 40g/1½oz of the cooled butter. Make a well in flour and tip in milk mixture. Using a whisk, bring mixture together, whisking to form a smooth batter. Stir in chopped nettle with a wooden spoon (if you use a whisk the chopped nettle will catch in the wires of the whisk). Leave to stand for 20 minutes.

Spread a clean tea towel near the stove. Heat a crêpe pan over medium heat and brush its base with a little of the remaining butter. Using a ladle, tip in 2 tablespoons of crêpe batter and immediately swirl it to cover base of pan; buckwheat flour takes a little longer to cook than plain flour so leave crêpe for nearly 1 minute before flipping it over. Flip with an egg lifter (I find it easier to turn them with my fingers, but then I have had years of practice of dabbling my fingers in hot pans). Cook second side for 30 seconds, then slide the cooked crêpe onto the tea towel.

Continue until all batter has been used, brushing base of pan with extra butter if needed. As there is butter in the batter you may not need any more. Spread or top with your desired filling, roll up and eat immediately.

OLIVES

Oleaceae family
Evergreen tree

Soil type
Well-drained soil or potting mix.

Soil preparation
As long as soil is well drained and rich in organic matter, no additional preparation is required.

Climate
Only hardy down to minus 10°C so in cold areas grow in containers and bring underglass in winter. Only likely to produce fruit in mild regions or cities and warm summers in the UK.

Position
Prefers full sun.

How to grow
Olives are now popular plants in UK, although they are mostly grown as an ornamental container plants. The sizes of potted plant sold vary greatly from small 30cm high ones sold alongside other herbs to 3m mature specimen trees imported from Italy as instant 'features' and various sizes and prices in between. Plant in ground only in mild areas or city gardens where winters are cool, soil needs to be well-drained and the site warm. For how to grow in containers, see overleaf.

Water requirements
The plant is tolerant of dry soil conditions but container-grown plants will need watering. Extra watering is needed during flowering and fruit setting.

When to fertilise
During the growing season keep the compost moist and feed with a liquid fertiliser every month.

Harvest period
Harvest fruit in late autumn or winter, plants may not fruit every year.

Pests and organic control
Few pests but long spell of cold can cause leaf drop, dieback and splits in bark, plants recover but a harvest may be lost.

Special informaton
When it is in flower give the tree a good shake to spread the pollen around.

Quantities to plant
for a family of four
1-2 trees.

Olive (*Olea europea*)

Growing and Harvesting The olive tree symbolises peace. It is a most beautiful tree, long-lived and rich in association, and requires very little attention. It can be grown as a single specimen or several trees can be planted close together

I once read a lovely story in the memoir of Pietro Demaio, an Italian-Australian, called *Preserving the Italian Way*, describing how he had planned to harvest the olives from five trees planted outside his suburban office. The night before the planned harvest, someone stripped the fruit from the trees. Once the fruit was nearly ready to pick the following year, determined not to let it happen again, he sprayed the tree with a harmless bright-blue food dye and attached a notice that read: 'Don't eat – sprayed with poison.' It worked and he was able to harvest the crop and wash away the dye!

It is a challenge to get the trees fruiting in the UK but it is possible in mild areas and in a hot summer. To flower and fruit, the trees need eight weeks of cold (below 10 degrees C but too long below 7 degrees C and fruiting will be reduced) and a fluctuation between day and night time temperatures, so outdoor plants are more likely to fruit than those kept indoors. Fruit is produced at the tips of the previous year's growth, so avoid drastic pruning however it is worth thinning the crop (reduce the fruit numbers to three or four per 30 centimetre of branch within three weeks of flowering) to prevent premature fruit drop.

Container Planting Olive trees make beautiful specimen trees in large tubs. Choose a tub at least 60 centimetres in diameter so that the tree does not need to be transferred to a larger pot. Plant herbs around the tree; maybe one of the prostrate rosemary varieties that will tumble over the edge, and one or two varieties of thyme or oregano. A potting mix such as loam-based John Innes No 3 with added horticultural grit for improved drainage is recommended. Olive trees in containers make attractive additions to a sunny patio in summer and cab then be moved into a cold conservatory, porch or greenhouse over winter. Where the container is too big to move, the rootball should at least be insulated by wrapping several layers of bubblewrap around the container. While olive trees are drought-tolerant, container-grown specimens need regular watering and feeding to produce fruit. During the growing season keep the compost moist and feed with a balanced liquid fertiliser every month. In winter, you can reduce watering, but don't let the compost from dry out completely.

Preparing and Sharing Travellers to France, Spain, Italy, Greece or North Africa are likely to have seen markets with piles of differently sized, coloured and flavoured olives, all ready to eat. It can be such fun choosing and trying a different olive each day of your holiday.

Olives are inedible straight from the tree, no matter how ripe they are. They must be treated with water or brine to remove the glucosides that make the fruit impossibly bitter. Olives can be pickled at all stages of ripeness, and the flavour and texture of the finished product will vary accordingly. The fruit starts off green, then moves through rose, purple-pink, deep-purple, chestnut, reddish-black and finally violet-black. There are variations in this spectrum, depending on variety. The safest way to pickle olives when children are helping is to stick to methods based on water and salt, rather than using caustic soda-based solutions that can burn. Most pickling methods are based on traditional home recipes and involve weeks of soaking and rinsing the fruit. Black, that is ripe, olives can also be dry-salted to produce the richly wrinkled black olives that I love but which are very oily and probably not very appealing to many children.

Whatever method you use to preserve olives there are certain basic rules you need to follow. Always use fresh, unbruised fruit. Make sure all utensils are scrupulously clean and that you use glass, ceramic, stainless-steel or unchipped enamel bowls. When bottling, ensure the brine covers all the olives and wipe the rim of the jar to ensure that the seal is tight. Once pickled, they don't need to be stored in the refrigerator, but if you choose to do so, take them out a while before serving as they taste much better at room temperature.

Once the bitterness has been removed from green olives all sorts of flavours can be added (see page 440). Pickled olives are very good when gently braised in extra-virgin olive oil and scooped into the pan juices of a braised rabbit a few minutes before serving, or served with seared fillets of a rockfish such as flathead or red mullet.

If you are dry-salting black olives, the finished dried olives can be stored in airtight containers or zip-lock bags and frozen for later use. Thaw them at room temperature and then flavour as you like, perhaps adding preserved lemon, chilli, garlic or fennel. Fresh ingredients won't last forever so add these to a batch you plan to consume within a few days. Once thawed, the olives can be marinated in extra-virgin olive oil with a little red or white-wine vinegar.

If a recipe calls for chopped olives I find the easiest way to remove the stones is to press the flat blade of a chef's knife onto each olive to split them, making the pit easy to remove. *Never* buy sliced 'black' olives such as those found on inferior pizzas. This is actually an unripe green olive, soaked in a bath of lye (a caustic solution) and then pumped with oxygen, which turns it an unlikely solid black and gives it a soapy flavour.

Pastes and spreads are simple to make using green or black pickled olives. Tapenade is a famous one (see page 444), as is *anchoïade*, another French combination which includes anchovies. These pastes are great spread on bruschetta before topping with grilled vegetables, chopped tomato or anchovy fillets.

Especially for Kids Although no one at home is going to press their olives for oil, it is an important part of the story for young helpers to understand that the extra-virgin olive oil we cook with and use in our salad dressings is in fact the juice of this extraordinary fruit. I have found that children are fascinated by the entire pickling process – from changing the water each day and making the brine, to bottling the olives and the final tasting.

Children studying the history of the olive will be studying the history of a large part of the world, including that of Egypt, and Ancient Greece and Rome. There are many biblical references to olives and they are mentioned in the Koran. Homer lauds the olive in the stories of Odysseus. There are centuries-old murals, frescoes and mosaics depicting olive harvests from ancient times. There are countless myths involving the olive tree. Today olive oil is an international commodity, with Spain being the largest producer in the world.

Cracked Green Olives

MAKES 5 KILOGRAMS/11 POUNDS There are dozens of ways to cure olives and everyone who does it has their favourite. I have included other recipes for home-cured olives in my book *The Cook's Companion*, but this recipe for green olives, repeated here for easy reference, is one of my favourites, not least because it has intrigued many children – the fact that they've helped crack the olives at the very beginning leads to increased interest in the process. In French markets olives preserved by this method are invariably sold in a container immersed in their brine. It has always reminded me of buying a goldfish! If the finished olives are left out of the brine, they will still taste all right but they will darken in a few hours and look pretty unloved. Although the recipe here is for a good-sized batch, it is worth processing even quite a small amount. Adjust the quantities if your tree has a smaller yield.

5kg/11lb fresh green olives
1kg/2lb kitchen salt
5 fresh bay leaves
finely grated zest of 2 bright oranges

2 fennel seed heads
  (see page 300)
2 tablespoons coriander seeds

EXTRA EQUIPMENT
wooden mallet
clean bucket with lid
very large heavy-
  based stock pot
sterilised containers
  (see page 706),
  such as glazed
  earthenware or
  pottery or
  2 litre/3½ pint-
  capacity glass
  preserving jars

Tap each olive firmly with a wooden mallet to split its flesh without cracking the pit. Put olives into a clean bucket, ensuring that no leaves or bruised fruit are included. Cover olives generously with water, then leave in a cool place with the lid on the bucket to soak for 9 days.

Each day, tip olives into a colander in batches, transferring each batch into a clean basin until all are drained. (Tip soaking water into the garden. It is fine to pour around trees or developing root crops but not onto salad greens that will be eaten in the next few days.) Return olives to bucket and cover with fresh water. Taste an olive after 9 days and if it is still bitter, soak olives for another 2–3 days, continuing to change the water each day.

Once olives no longer taste bitter, prepare the brine. Place 10 litres/17½ pints water and remaining ingredients in a very large heavy-based stockpot and bring to the boil over high heat. Cool brine mixture completely.

Once brine is cold, drain olives a final time, then pack into sterilised containers and pour cold brine over them to immerse them completely. Leave for a further 6–8 days before eating. These olives are best eaten within 2 months.

Very Speedy Chicken with Cherry Tomatoes and Olives

SERVES 4 This simple summery dish is cooked in minutes – twenty to be exact. The same recipe can be made with a whole jointed chicken, but then it will take more like forty minutes to cook. Its charm lies in the last-minute addition of cherry tomatoes and olives, meaning that both of these ingredients taste fresh and not stewed. I like to serve it with fresh fettuccine.

EXTRA EQUIPMENT
sauté pan or flameproof casserole dish with a lid (just big enough to hold chicken in one layer)

2–3 free-range chicken breast fillets (500–600g/1–1lb 5oz), skin removed, cut into 4–5cm/1½–2in pieces
sea salt
¼ small handful oregano, roughly chopped
60ml/2fl oz extra-virgin olive oil
2 cloves garlic, sliced, plus 1 clove garlic, very finely chopped, to serve
1 fresh small red chilli, seeded and thinly sliced

125ml/4½fl oz verjuice (see page 706) or dry white wine
16 pitted black olives (home-cured of any size are great. If purchasing, go for Kalamata or the tiny Ligurian-style olives)
16 cherry tomatoes
sea salt
2 teaspoons chopped flat-leaf parsley

Place chicken pieces on a baking tray. Season with salt, sprinkle with oregano and drizzle with a little of the olive oil.

Heat remaining olive oil in a sauté pan or flameproof casserole dish over medium heat. Add the 2 cloves sliced garlic and chilli and stir for 30 seconds. Add chicken pieces and spread in a single layer, then cook for 3–4 minutes, turning with a wooden spoon, to seal on both sides. Add verjuice or wine and season with salt, then let it bubble quite fiercely for 1 minute. Reduce heat to low and cover with a lid. Cook for 10 minutes, then lift lid and test chicken is cooked through by inserting a fine metal skewer; it should slip in easily. Tip in olives and tomatoes. Replace lid and cook for another 4–5 minutes or just until the tomato skins start to burst.

Shake the pan to allow juices to mingle, remove from heat and leave chicken to rest for 2–3 minutes before serving. Combine remaining finely chopped garlic and parsley. If serving in its cooking dish, scatter over garlic/parsley mixture. Alternatively, divide chicken and juices between individual shallow pasta bowls and scatter each one with a little garlic/parsley mixture.

Olive and Cheese Loaf

MAKES 1 LOAF This loaf can be served warm straight from the oven alongside a vegetable soup or toasted (best when it is a day old).

250g/9oz self-raising flour

100g/3½oz firm mozzarella (see page 704) or Gruyère-style cheese, coarsely grated

100g/3½oz sliced ham, chopped

50g/2oz black olives, pitted and halved

a pinch salt

½ teaspoon freshly ground black pepper

3 free-range eggs

100ml/3½fl oz olive oil

1 tablespoon extra-virgin olive oil

EXTRA EQUIPMENT

22cm × 12cm/
9in × 5in
loaf tin

large metal spoon

Preheat oven to 200°C/Gas 6. Grease a 22cm × 12cm/9in × 5in loaf tin with olive oil and line with baking paper.

Combine flour, cheese, ham, olives, salt and pepper in a mixing bowl. In another bowl, whisk eggs and olive oil. Make a well in flour mixture, then tip in egg mixture. Mix quickly but thoroughly to form a thick batter. Spoon into tin and smooth top with a large metal spoon. Drizzle with extra-virgin olive oil.

Bake loaf for 30 minutes or until a skewer inserted in the middle comes out clean. Turn out onto a cake cooling rack.

Tapenade

Remove the pits from a good handful of black or green olives and weigh the flesh, then transfer it to a food processor. Add half the weight each of capers, tinned tuna and anchovy fillets (so for 200g/7oz pitted olives use 100g/3½oz capers, 100g/3½oz tinned tuna and 100g/3½oz anchovies). Process all the ingredients in the food processor to form a rough paste, adding Dijon mustard to taste. Gradually add enough extra-virgin olive oil in a thin steady stream to form a thick paste; the finished tapenade should be quite thick. Season with freshly ground black pepper. Many cooks advise adding a few drops of brandy to tapenade.

OREGANO

**Lamiaceae family
(includes basil, lavender, mint,
rosemary, sage and thyme)
Perennial**

Soil type
Moist, well-drained soil, enriched
with organic matter.

Soil preparation
As long as soil is well drained
and rich in organic matter,
no additional preparation
is required.

Climate
Suitable for all climates except
frost tender ones.

Position
Prefers full sun.

How to grow
Buy small potted plants. Plant
in spring or, if frost-tender, early
summer. There are three ways
to grow oregano: from seed,
from cuttings and by division.

Raise seeds in modular trays
in April at a depth of 1cm. For
cuttings, take stem cuttings
5–10cm long and insert into pots
of gritty cutting mix. Once the
roots have taken you can plant
it in a permanent position in the
garden. For division, dig up a
plant and divide it into several
pieces. Be sure each piece has
a stem and root system and
replant the pieces. All herbs are
great planted among vegetables
as they attract beneficial insects.

Water requirements
Don't over-water; once a week
should be enough.

When to fertilise
Use a liquid fertiliser (see page
691) or worm tea (see page 695)
every 2–3 months.

Harvest period
Harvest the leaves as required.
If you wish to dry oregano for

winter use, harvest just as the
plant is coming into flower.

Pests and organic control
Aphids can be a problem, but
can be controlled with a garlic or
pyrethrum spray (see page 700).

Companion planting
Cucumber, zucchini, pumpkin,
cabbage and beans.

Special informaton
Keep the soil free from weeds
during early development by
mulching. Give a good prune
after flowering if you are not
harvesting often.

**Quantities to plant
for a family of four**
1 plant.

Oregano (*Origanum* sp.)

Growing and Harvesting Much confusion exists as to what oregano is, what marjoram is, and which variety of either one has in the garden. It is a botanist's challenge to separate the different plants. One authority says that 'oregano' is the name given to a flavour obtained from only some of the *Origanum* genus. This flavour and aroma varies, not only between the different species but depending on where the plant is grown and how much sun and rain it receives. Oregano or wild marjoram (*Origanum vulgare*) is hardy and grown as a perennial, the species is a native of the Mediterranean where it has a very pungent flavour. In the cooler conditions of the UK the flavour is less pronounced, there are several named garden worthy forms including a golden-leaved form. Pot marjoram (*O. onites*) is a similar hardy perennial type, winter marjoram (*O. x applii*) is a small half-hardy one, very good in a container. Sweet marjoram (*Origanum marjorana*) is the most fragrant of all the origanums and is the most elusive to find. It is also frost tender. It can be propagated by cuttings or root division. It is often known as knot marjoram, referring to the whorl of leaves that opens to a tiny white flower. Its flavour is delicate and it is best added to dishes at the end of cooking – try it with egg dishes or cooked tomatoes.

Oregano is thought to repel the cabbage white butterfly from vegetables planted nearby. My advice is not to rely on this and to regularly pick off those munching caterpillars and chase down and dispose of any butterflies.

Container Planting Oregano is ideal for growing in containers. See also **HERBS**.

Preparing and Sharing Many Italians, Greeks and Mexicans prefer to dry this herb and then use it in this more intense form rather than fresh – oregano is one herb where the flavour and aroma increases when dried. They also like to dry the herb when it is just coming into flower as this is when its flavour is at its peak. When I use a stalk of dried oregano, I rub it over the food to be grilled or marinated so that the leaves and flower heads separate from the stems and stalks. I dislike finding tiny twigs in my salad, although I can cope if they are charred a bit on a barbecue. Only use dried herbs harvested in the last growing season.

Oregano (or pot marjoram, as it should probably be known), goes very well with tomatoes and zucchini, and is popular scattered over pizzas, grilled lamb and chicken, or used to season a Greek salad. Strip fresh leaves from the stalks, then add them whole or chopped to your dish a few moments before serving; I find its flavour is best when it is not cooked but just warmed through. Try mixing fresh oregano with finely chopped garlic, breadcrumbs and chopped tomato and using this as a topping for baked mussels on the half-shell.

I once read in an American cookbook that it is a good idea to pick several long sprigs of oregano and to tie them in loosely around a bamboo skewer, interspersed with tomatoes and any meat you fancy to cook on the barbecue. While this sounds a lovely idea it's not so easy to do (see Fresh Mozzarella, Bread and Oregano Skewers with Anchovy Sauce on page 450).

Especially for Kids You could make a 'pizza garden' by planting oregano around the edge of a tomato bush. The two plants are perfect together as companion plants and because it is likely that you will pick both at the same time, as oregano is used so often with tomatoes.

Turkish Bread 'Pizza'

MAKES 2 These scrumptious snacks can be made from start to finish in 15 minutes. If the ingredients are on hand they can easily be assembled by older children without assistance (just keep an eye on the initial slicing of the chunk of bread). If you don't have oregano, basil is an excellent substitute.

1 × 14cm/5½in square piece
  of Turkish bread, cut in half
  horizontally
2 tablespoons extra-virgin olive oil
1 clove garlic, halved
80ml/3fl oz Fast Basic Tomato Sauce
  (page 649) or any homemade

tomato-based relish
4 anchovy fillets, torn
8 black olives, halved and pitted
2 tablespoons chopped oregano
50g/2oz coarsely grated firm
  mozzarella (see page 704)
freshly ground black pepper

Preheat oven to 200°C/Gas 6.

Put the 2 bread slices on a baking paper-lined baking tray, crust-sides down. Brush with 1 tablespoon of the olive oil. Bake for 5 minutes. Remove from oven and lightly rub each slice with cut clove of garlic. Spoon on tomato sauce and smear it right to the edges with the back of a spoon. Dot with torn anchovy fillets and olives and scatter over oregano. Divide grated cheese and spread it right to the edges. Grind over some black pepper and drizzle with remaining olive oil.

Bake for 10 minutes. Remember that the cheese will be very hot so wait a minute or so before taking your first bite.

Oregano Onions

Pound or process ½ small handful oregano leaves with a good pinch each of sea salt and freshly ground black pepper and a good slosh of extra-virgin olive oil with a mortar and pestle or in a food processor to form a coarse paste. Halve large peeled onions widthways and microwave them for 4 minutes on the highest setting. Top halved onions with oregano paste, then grill under a hot griller until well coloured and a bit scorched at the edges. Great served with roasted or barbecued meats, or chopped and used as a pizza topping or instead of leeks to make an onion and oregano tart (see page 358).

Fresh Mozzarella, Bread and Oregano Skewers with Anchovy Sauce

SERVES 4 These can be made very small for hand-around snacks or a little larger to be served on a bed of inner cos leaves or baby spinach, either raw or just wilted, as a simple starter. The lengths of oregano can be tied onto the skewers or inserted into pieces of cheese, making it less likely to lose the herbs in the first few seconds under the griller.

4 thick slices day-old bread (from a sourdough or other substantial loaf), crusts removed
extra-virgin olive oil, for brushing
8 × 10cm/4in-long oregano sprigs, plus extra oregano, chopped
4 balls fresh mozzarella (see page 704), cut into 4–6 pieces depending on size
60g/2oz unsalted butter, melted
4 handfuls inner cos or baby spinach leaves (optional)

ANCHOVY SAUCE
100ml/3½fl oz pouring cream
1 clove garlic, chopped
a tiny pinch salt
20g/¾oz unsalted butter
4 anchovy fillets, chopped
1 teaspoon chopped flat-leaf parsley
1 tablespoon chopped oregano

EXTRA EQUIPMENT
mortar and pestle
8 bamboo or metal skewers (if making hand-around snacks use 12 small metal cocktail skewers)

To make the anchovy sauce, boil cream in a small saucepan over medium heat, stirring for about 2 minutes until it has thickened and is a little reduced. Set saucepan aside. Pound garlic and salt with a mortar and pestle to make a paste and transfer to a small non-stick frying pan. Add butter and anchovy. Stir together over low heat until anchovy has dissolved. Stir in cream, parsley and oregano and set sauce aside until needed.

Line a griller tray with foil, then preheat griller. Lightly brush bread with olive oil and toast in a dry non-stick frying pan over medium heat until it starts to colour, then tear or cut each slice into very rough 2cm/¾in pieces. Tie 2 oregano sprigs onto each skewer (or tear sprigs into smaller pieces and push into each piece of cheese). Slip pieces of bread and cheese onto skewers, starting and finishing with bread. Balance skewers across a baking tray or heatproof platter so that bread doesn't touch the bottom. Brush all sides with melted butter and scatter over chopped oregano.

Place skewers on griller tray and grill for 2 minutes per side or until cheese just starts to soften and edges of oiled bread are just starting to toast.

Serve as hand-around snacks still on skewers, drizzled with a little anchovy sauce. If serving as a starter you might want to place skewers on top of some salad or baby spinach leaves on each plate and drizzle with sauce.

PARSLEY

Apiaceae family (includes carrots, celery, coriander, dill, fennel and parsnip)
Biennial, but does less well in its second year

Soil type
Moist, well-drained soil enriched with organic matter.

Soil preparation
As long as soil is well drained and rich in organic matter, no additional preparation is required.

Climate
Suitable for all climates.

Position
Prefers full sun, but will tolerate partial shade.

How to grow
Directly sow or raise seeds in small pots . Plant seeds at a depth of 5mm in clumps of 2 or 3, with 30cm between clumps for direct-sowing. Parsley is slow to germinate. Sow from March-July outside, or all year round if growing on kitchen windowsill.

Water requirements
Keep soil moist. If the soil dries out, the plant will bolt (see page 687).

Successive planting
Leave about 4 weeks between each planting.

When to fertilise
Use a liquid fertiliser (see page 691) or worm tea (see page 695) every 2–3 months.

Harvest period
Harvest the outside stalks as needed 2–9 months after planting.

Pests and organic control
Place crushed egg shells around the base of the young plants to deter snails and slugs. Pick off caterpillars by hand.

Companion planting
Roses, tomatoes and asparagus.

Special information
Keep the soil moist and free from weeds by mulching. Cutting back the flower stalk will increase production of leaves.

Quantities to plant for a family of four
3–4 plants.

Flat-leaf parsley (*Petroselinum crispum* var. *neapolitanum*)

Growing and Harvesting There are both curly parsley (*Petroselinum crispum*) and flat-leaf parsley (*P. hortense filicinum*), and there is also parsley root (or Hamburg parsley). Everyone is familiar with parsley, but I bought my first Hamburg parsley (*P. crispum* var. *tuberosum*) very recently and found it to be quite delicious.

For everyday cooking, my preference is for flat-leaf parsley, which has a more pronounced flavour and can be torn into small pieces for salads, whereas curly parsley is best chopped or fried. Be aware that because of its 'curliness' it is possible for it to catch in the throat, especially if it is not in its first flush of youth! Flat-leaf parsley is sometimes also called Italian parsley or continental parsley. If you have plenty of space, why not grow both, since parsley is used so often? Grow several plants of whichever variety you prefer.

Parsley has a reputation for being very slow to germinate. If you are growing parsley for the first time, expect germination to take fourteen days. Parsley is hardy but, to keep the leaves clean and top quality over winter, use a cloche over winter or move pots into cold greenhouse or indoors. Never pick parsley that has gone to seed for the table as the leaves will taste bitter, although I think such stems look most attractive in a flower arrangement.

Bunches of deep-green curly parsley look especially wonderful among other plants and in large garden spaces can be a good choice as a border plant, perhaps alternating with some of the fast-growing but less aromatic oregano/marjorams (see **OREGANO**). The late Christopher Lloyd grew curly parsley 'Bravour' at his Great Dixter garden, in amongst French marigolds and red lobelia. Its deep-green colour sets off bright displays of summer annuals and it looks fresh into the autumn.

Parsley must be picked young; the leaves should feel delicate and soft, not rough like sandpaper. Lightly bruised with the fingers, it should have a wonderful fragrance. Pick it stem-by-stem, from around the outside of the plant. Children will need to be shown how to pick parsley so as not to damage the plant.

Container Planting Like all herbs, parsley is a perfect plant to grow in a pot. In fact, it is probably *the* most essential herb for a beginner to grow. See also **HERBS**.

Preparing and Sharing Can you ever grow enough parsley? When freshly chopped its marvellous zing and sprightly note is welcome in so many dishes – buttered potatoes, scrambled eggs, vegetable cream soups, combined in a gremolata (see page 327) with finely chopped lemon or orange zest and garlic and sprinkled over veal, especially osso buco – the list is endless.

If your parsley is dusty or muddy, wash it before chopping, then pat really dry with paper towels or a clean tea towel and chop away. There is no need to chop parsley so small that it looks like green dust. Chopped parsley loses its fragrance after about 30 minutes, so chop the leaves just before using. Stored chopped parsley is horrible. After picking the leaves from the stems, you can add the stems to a stock, or tie them with a bay leaf and a good-sized sprig of thyme to make a bouquet garni for any casserole or braise.

Curly parsley makes the best deep-fried parsley. Dry sprigs carefully and deep-fry for less than a minute in hot but not smoking clean oil (around 180°C/Gas 4). Drain very well. Deep-fried parsley complements all sorts of seafood, from lightly floured and fried whitebait and calamari to baked mussels on the half-shell and battered fillets for fish and chips.

If you have parsley root or Hamburg parsley growing, this long tapered vegetable is very versatile. The feathery tops can be used exactly as you would use flat-leaf parsley, but have the bonus of a root you can use as well. Looking almost exactly like a smooth parsnip or perhaps horseradish, parsley root has a mild flavour, with a hint of celeriac and even carrot. It can be grated into salads as you would use carrot, or long peelings can be quickly deep-fried in a little oil and served as a snack or a garnish for a grilled piece of fish or sautéed scallops – anything really where the flavour of parsley and a bit of crunch would be welcome. It can also be grated or shredded and added to a tabbouleh or mixed with a little mayonnaise as if making a Celeriac Rémoulade (see page 229). It adds an intriguing 'otherness' to mashed potato. Use two parts potato to one part peeled parsley root and cook and mash in the usual manner. It can also be added to a *soffritto* (usually a chopped mix of onion, carrot, and celery) and used as the base for vegetable and bean soups or meat stews.

Especially for Kids Once a parsley plant has flowered and gone to seed, children can help to shake some of the seed heads over the ground and hopefully they will germinate where they fall. Collect the rest of the seeds and use for seed-saving or to give as a gift to a friend. Store the seeds in a dry, labelled and dated envelope.

Compare the flavour and especially the aroma of freshly chopped parsley with a bowl that has been stored and covered in the refrigerator for a day.

What does this proverb mean? 'Parsley seed goes to the devil and back seven times before it comes up, and the devil likes it so much he always keeps some.'

Parsley and Parmesan 'Bread Balls'

MAKES 10 I tasted these unusual fritters in Puglia and was delighted to find a recipe in Nancy Harmon Jenkins' book *Flavors of Puglia*. I have slightly altered her version and included a quantity of grated stretchy mozzarella. Those I enjoyed in Tricase Porto oozed strings of mozzarella with each forkful. They are a fine example of what Italians mean by *cucina povera* – where very inexpensive and readily available ingredients are combined in a creative manner to make something tasty and sustaining.

150g/5oz day-old bread, either multi-grain or sourdough, crusts removed, cut or torn into rough pieces
125ml/4½fl oz milk
1 free-range egg
40g/1½oz parmesan, grated
1 tablespoon coarsely grated firm mozzarella (see page 704)

⅓ small handful chopped flat-leaf parsley
1 clove garlic
sea salt and freshly ground black pepper
250ml/9fl oz Fast Basic Tomato Sauce (see page 649)
60ml/2fl oz extra-virgin olive oil

EXTRA EQUIPMENT
food processor

Put bread into a mixing bowl and pour over milk, then leave for 5 minutes. Squeeze bread and drop into a food processor, discarding excess milk. Pulse briefly to form a mass of wet crumbs. Transfer to wiped-out bowl.

In another bowl, mix together egg, grated cheeses, parsley and garlic, then add to soaked crumbs. Add some salt and pepper to wet bread mixture and use your hands to squeeze and mix well. Taste and adjust seasoning with salt and pepper, if desired.

Wet your hands and form the mixture into 2cm/¾in balls, then place on a plate. Line another plate with paper towel and have it nearby. Warm tomato sauce in a small saucepan over medium heat.

Heat olive oil in a large non-stick frying pan over medium heat. Slide in fritters and flatten slightly with a spatula, then shallow-fry until golden on both sides. Transfer fritters to paper towel-lined plate. Serve fritters with tomato sauce spooned over and around them.

Parsley Butter

MAKES 160G/5½OZ This classic combination, sometimes referred to as garlic butter, is well known. It is also called maître d'hotel butter (I often wonder why). Garlic bread is usually made by cutting slits along the length of a breadstick, inserting a thin slice of this butter in each slit, then wrapping the breadstick in foil and baking it in a 200°C/Gas 6 oven for 15 minutes or so. The butter melts into the bread and the crust becomes hot and crisp. A slice of this butter is also a speedy and excellent garnish for a grilled lamb chop, a fillet steak or a baked potato. It will make a delicious sauce if gently shaken into just-cooked green peas or baby carrots, drained of all but one spoonful of their cooking water. Another idea is to work a little under the skin of chicken breasts or drumsticks before roasting. Other herbs can be added as well as parsley – tarragon is particularly successful. It goes without saying that the parsley (or other herb) must be absolutely fresh. The instructions here are to form the parsley butter into a roll and to store any not used in the freezer. Make sure it is well wrapped and use it within a few weeks or it risks tasting 'fridgey'.

EXTRA EQUIPMENT
food processor

100g/3½oz softened unsalted butter, chopped
1 clove garlic, finely chopped

sea salt and freshly ground black pepper
a few drops lemon juice
¼ small handful chopped flat-leaf parsley

Process all ingredients together in a food processor until thoroughly combined. Scrape butter mixture onto a sheet of baking paper. Fold paper over and form into a sausage-shape. Twist ends of paper to enclose and firm up the shape, then wrap in a doubled sheet of foil and place in the refrigerator to harden. Slice as needed. Label, date and freeze what is not needed within 2 days. A slice can be fairly readily cut from the frozen roll if you use a knife dipped in boiling water.

Stracciatella

SERVES 4 To make this Italian egg-drop soup, whisk 4 free-range eggs, then season with sea salt and freshly ground black pepper and stir in 2–3 tablespoons chopped flat-leaf parsley. Bring 1 litre/1¾ pints well-seasoned and full-flavoured chicken or beef stock to the simmer. Remove from heat and slowly pour in egg mixture, stirring gently as you pour; the egg will set in the hot broth. Serve at once in warm bowls.

Parsley and Hazelnut Picada with Scallops

SERVES 6 Spanish recipes sometimes add a finely chopped mixture of bread-crumbs, nuts, parsley and garlic (called a *picada*) right at the end of cooking to a chicken or rabbit braise, to thicken the juices as well as add a fresh and enticing aroma. French cooks use *persillade,* a mix of raw garlic and flat-leaf parsley, to do the same thing. Northern Italian cooks might scatter gremolata – a mix of parsley, garlic and grated lemon zest – onto a dish of osso buco, just before serving. Parsley and garlic are common to all of these great-tasting garnishes. I find that this Spanish combination has many uses. It is stunning sprinkled over scallops (as I've done here) or mussels baked on the half-shell, or over baby clams. Also try it on grilled or steamed zucchini, or poached or steamed chicken and fish. *Picada* should be used the day it is made, preferably as soon as it is made – the orange zest and parsley won't survive storage.

12 scallops in the half-shell,
   roe removed
extra-virgin olive oil, for brushing
squeeze of lemon juice
lemon wedges (optional), to serve

PICADA
20 hazelnuts
¼ small handful chopped flat-leaf
   parsley

1 clove garlic, finely chopped
finely grated zest of
   1 orange
30g/1oz fresh breadcrumbs
2 tablespoons extra-virgin
   olive oil
sea salt and freshly ground
   black pepper

EXTRA EQUIPMENT
mortar and pestle
   (optional)

Preheat oven to 160°C/Gas 3.

To make the *picada,* place hazelnuts on a baking paper-lined baking tray and toast for 10 minutes. Tip hot nuts onto a dry tea towel, then fold over and rub towel vigorously. Open towel and pick out skinned nuts (don't worry if a few have not shed all of their skin). Chop coarsely with a knife or pound with a mortar and pestle and put into a bowl. Add parsley, garlic and orange zest to bowl.

Place a plate lined with a doubled piece of paper towel near the stove. Heat olive oil in a small non-stick frying pan over medium heat. Tip in bread crumbs and stir constantly until crumbs are golden and feel sandy. Immediately tip onto lined plate, spreading them with a wooden spoon. Shake crumbs into parsley mixture. Add salt and pepper and mix very well. Use as soon as possible.

Increase oven temperature to 200°C/Gas 6. Wipe scallops and shells to remove any grit. Trim and discard any black intestinal thread. Brush scallops with olive oil, then place on a baking tray and roast for 4–5 minutes or until they feel springy. Remove from oven, then squeeze a little lemon juice over each scallop. Spoon a little of the *picada* over each scallop, then serve at once, with lemon wedges to the side, if using.

Chickpea Salad with Preserved Lemon, Caramelised Onion, Chilli and Parsley

SERVES 4 I have included the recipe for Caramelised Onion here as, although few families will have the space to devote to growing storage onions in their vegetable patch, all cooks buy onions. Caramelised Onion lasts for months in the refrigerator. And it is such a useful standby – to top a steak, garnish a pizza, stir into a stew, or, as I've done here, to add a deep rustic note to this simple chick pea and parsley salad.

350g/12oz Cooked Dried Chick Peas (see page 203) or 1 × 440g/15oz tin chick peas, rinsed and drained
2 preserved lemon quarters (see page 371), flesh scraped off and discarded, rind wiped and finely diced
2 tablespoons chopped flat-leaf parsley

½ teaspoon chilli paste such as harissa (see page 704)
sea salt (optional)

CARAMELISED ONION
125ml/4½fl oz extra-virgin olive oil
4 large onions, halved and thinly sliced

To make the caramelised onion, heat olive oil in a large non-stick frying pan over medium heat. Tip in onion and cook over medium heat, stirring every few minutes until it softens, becomes golden, starts to darken and eventually is a deep golden brown. This may take up to 20 minutes. Scrape onion and all the oil into a bowl and set aside. Extra caramelised onion with its oil can be stored in a screw-top jar in the refrigerator for several days. (Alternatively, you can try this speedy microwave method. Drizzle sliced onion with olive oil and cook on high for a few minutes in a covered dish, remove, uncover, stir, and repeat in three or so 3–4 minute bursts until onion is deep-gold.)

Put cooked chick peas into a serving bowl. Add preserved lemon, parsley, chilli paste and as much of the caramelised onion as you wish. Mix well and taste for salt; you will probably not need to add any as the preserved lemon is salty. Similarly you probably will not need to add extra olive oil as the onion is oily. Serve at once.

PARSNIPS

Apiaceae family (includes carrots, celery, chervil, dill, fennel and parsley)
Biennial grown as an annual

Soil type
Friable, well-drained and deep soil, preferably slightly on the acid side.

Soil preparation
Dig over the soil to loosen compacted soil and fork in a general fertiliser. Parsnips should follow a previous crop that has been well-manured rather than have the manure added prior to sowing.

Climate
Suitable for all climates.

Position
Prefers sun. Tolerates partial shade.

How to plant
Sow seed in March to April direct into the ground as parsnip does not transplant well from pots, the timing should depend on the weather as germination is tricky in cold, wet soils. Sow at 1cm deep in rows 30cm apart. Sow at thinly as possible, the seed takes several weeks to germinate so mark the rows carefully. Keep the ground moist and weed free.

Water requirements
Once the plants are growing no regular watering is needed unless it is very dry.

Successive planting
Further sowings can be made in summer for baby parsnips but successive sowing is not required for maincrop parsnips.

When to fertilise
Not usually required.

Harvest period
7–9 months after sowing although baby parsnips can be harvested earlier if required. Once the tops have died down, use a garden fork to lift the roots out of the ground. Harvest just what you need, the roots will keep underground. However, in very cold areas cover the row with straw to insulate the ground and roots. Where ground is very wet it is better to lift the whole crop or it can rot in the ground.

Pests and organic control
There are few pest problems but canker can be a serious disease so look for resistant varieties such as 'Avonresister'. Forked roots are due to fresh manure or organic matter not being properly broken down or to poor soil preparation.

Companion planting
Lettuce, peas, chives and shallots, and nasturtiums are a bait for aphids.

Special information
Always use freshly purchased seed each year for parsnip as its seed life is short.

Quantities to plant for a family of four
12 plants every 4 weeks.

Parsnip (*Pastinaca sativa*)

Growing and Harvesting Parsnips are a delicious vegetable and they develop their best flavour if left in the ground over winter and harvested progressively and as you need to use them, right into spring. They are cultivated in the same manner and have the same soil needs as carrots (see **CARROTS**), although they are even slower to germinate.

Container Planting Parsnips can be sown in containers, provided the container is at least 20 centimetres deep. Cut-and-come-again salad greens could be planted in the container before you sprinkle in the parsnip seeds to maximise the yield from a single container. Alternatively, plant leeks or chives in the same pot.

Preparing and Sharing The most common preparations for parsnips are to bake or mash them or use them in soups. All the family will adore deep-fried parsnip chips, made by thinly shaving the peeled root with a vegetable peeler. One parsnip yields a lot of paper-thin chips. A very delicious and irresistible snack is a bowl of mixed fried wafer-thin slices of parsnip, carrot, beetroot and celeriac.

Small parsnip chunks can be oiled and roasted in a 200°C/Gas 6 oven, with or without similarly sized chunks of carrot, potato or sweet potato or a combination of all four. Thick slices or wedges can be oiled and grilled on a hot char-grill plate; keep an eye on them and turn frequently. Not to mention that parsnip purée made with some good homemade stock instead of water is lovely served alongside almost any meat dish (see opposite).

Especially for Kids An interesting exercise might be to have a taste test comparing your own kitchen garden-grown parsnips with shop-bought ones. Is there a taste difference? Which tastes sweeter? Are there any other comments?

Slow-braised Beef with Parsnip Purée

SERVES 4–6 The sweetness of parsnips is a perfect partner for slowly braised beef. Here I have used my favourite braising cut, a single piece of oyster blade. The meat will always benefit from a rest and you also need some of the finished rich juices to make the purée.

The beef could even be cooked the day before, and some of the juice removed to make the purée. The next day, skim off any fat that has risen to the surface, make the purée and gently reheat the beef in its juices. It will only get better. If you have also made the purée in advance, reheat it in a steamer or microwave. A scattering of gremolata (see page 327) would add a lovely final touch.

>>>

EXTRA EQUIPMENT

enamelled cast-iron
    casserole or other
    heavy-based
    casserole
food processor or
    blender

1 × 1.5kg/3lb beef oyster blade
2 teaspoons brandy (optional)
freshly ground black pepper
1 × 200g/7oz piece pork skin, with
    some fat still attached
    (ask your butcher for this)
1 bouquet garni (see page 635)
1 tablespoon olive oil
1 onion, sliced
1 carrot, sliced
3 cloves garlic, peeled
250ml/9fl oz dry red wine
1 litre/1¾ pints well-flavoured veal
    stock or chicken stock

PARSNIP PURÉE
250ml/9fl oz beef cooking juices
40g/1½oz butter
6 parsnips, thinly sliced
1 Hamburg parsley root
    (see pages 454–455, optional) or
    celeriac, peeled and thinly sliced
1 bay leaf
sea salt and freshly ground
    black pepper

Pat beef with brandy, if using, and season with pepper. Place pork skin, fat-side down, in base of an enamelled cast-iron casserole, then top with bouquet garni and place beef on top. Cover with the lid and leave in the refrigerator for a few hours or even overnight.

When ready to cook, preheat oven to 150°C/Gas 2.

Heat olive oil in a frying pan over medium heat, then add onion and carrot and cook for 6–8 minutes or until softened. Add to casserole with garlic, wine and stock. Press a piece of baking paper right down over beef, then cover with the lid and cook in the oven for 2 hours. Turn beef over and cook for another hour. Remove from oven, then check it is tender by inserting a skewer; if it does not slide easily through the meat then cook for another hour. If tender, set aside while making the purée. Put an ovenproof plate inside oven to warm.

To make the purée, remove 250ml/9fl oz beef cooking juices with a ladle and set aside. Heat butter in a heavy-based saucepan over medium heat, then add parsnip and Hamburg parsley and stir for 3 minutes until well coated in butter. Add bay leaf and reserved cooking juices, then cover with a tight-fitting lid and cook over medium heat for 20 minutes or until vegetables are completely tender. Remove bay leaf. Working in batches, purée cooked vegetables in a food processor or blender, adding some of the cooking juices to each batch. The aim should be a smooth, somewhat flowing purée, not a stiff mixture. Return excess juices to casserole. Season purée with salt and pepper and set aside.

Transfer beef to the warm plate, then strain juices and reduce them over high heat in a frying pan until well concentrated. Thickly slice beef and spoon over reduced juices, then serve with parsnip purée.

Parsnips Bravas

SERVES 4 This recipe is my own invention. I have enjoyed *patatas bravas* at various tapas bars in Spain, where I loved the combination of fried potatoes with a very spicy sauce, and thought why stop at potatoes? This parsnip dish would be a perfect side dish at a barbecue. The Spanish would also serve a bowl of garlic mayonnaise-like sauce, although if it is made without eggs it is authentic *all-i-oli*, but I use homemade Aïoli (see page 314). As parsnips are at their best during the cooler months, the spicy sauce will need to be made with tinned or preserved tomatoes.

400g/14oz parsnips, cut on the
   diagonal into bite-sized pieces
80ml/3fl oz extra-virgin olive oil
sea salt
Aïoli (see page 314), to serve

SPICY TOMATO SAUCE
60ml/2fl oz extra-virgin olive oil
2 onions, finely chopped

4 cloves garlic, sliced
1 fresh red chilli, seeded
   and sliced
1 × 400g/14oz tin diced tomatoes
1 good pinch white sugar
1 good pinch Spanish smoky
   paprika (see page 706)
1 good pinch saffron stamens

Preheat oven to 200°C/Gas 6.

Roll parsnip pieces in olive oil and put into a baking dish. Roast for 45 minutes or until perfectly tender and golden brown.

Meanwhile, to make the spicy tomato sauce, heat olive oil in a wide heavy-based frying pan. Add onion and garlic and cook over medium heat, stirring for 6–8 minutes or until well softened and starting to colour. Add remaining sauce ingredients and continue to cook for 10 minutes or until sauce is well reduced, stirring from time to time. Taste for seasoning and adjust if desired. The sauce should be thick and quite spicy. Toss parsnip chunks in sauce and sprinkle with sea salt. Serve with a bowl of aïoli.

Parsnip Hash Browns

MAKES 4 Mix 2 coarsely grated parsnips with 2 finely chopped spring onions, then bind with 1 free-range egg white beaten to form very soft peaks. Season to taste with sea salt and freshly ground black pepper, then fry tablespoonfuls of mixture in a non-stick frying pan in melted butter and a splash of olive oil. Even better, mix grated sweet potato with the grated parsnips. Great served alongside a simply cooked piece of fish.

PEAS (PODDING, SNOWPEAS AND SUGAR SNAP PEAS)

**Fabaceae family
(includes beans)
Annual**

Soil type
Prefer moist, well-drained soil, enriched with organic matter.

Soil preparation
Dig in organic matter a few weeks prior to planting.

Climate
Suitable for all climates.

Position
Prefer full sun or partial shade in a sheltered position.

How to grow
In March-April, directly sow seeds at a depth of 3–5cm in moist soil, 10cm apart, at the base of a climbing structure. If sowing dwarf varieties, plant in blocks rather than rows.

Water requirements
To avoid seed rot, don't water seeds until they have germinated, then water regularly.

Successive planting
Leave about 3 weeks between each planting, throughout the growing season.

When to fertilise
If you did not fertilise before planting, use a liquid fertiliser (see page 691) or worm tea (see page 695) once every 4 weeks.

Harvest period
Pick at your desired eating size, usually 10–14 weeks from sowing. At the end of the harvest, chop and dig the plant into the soil.

Pests and organic control
Mice or other rodents eat the pea seeds. Starting off in pots might help. Peamoth grubs are an unpleasant find in podding peas. Sow early or late to avoid them or try snowpeas (mangetout) instead. To avoid the risk of diseases, don't grow peas in a bed that was previously used for a bean crop or broad beans.

Companion planting
Corn, beans, tomatoes, radish, carrots, turnips, cucumbers, eggplant and spinach. Don't plant with garlic, onions or chives.

Special information
Keep the soil moist and free from weeds by mulching. Peas don't germinate well in cold, wet soil. Sow under cloches (see page 687) or start off in small pots in a greenhouse or cold frame.

**Quantities to plant
for a family of four**
10 plants every 3 weeks.

Pea (*Pisum sativum*)

Growing and Harvesting Regular green peas are often known as 'podding peas' or 'shelling peas' to distinguish them from snowpeas (mangetout) and sugar snap peas. Podding peas should be picked when they are bright green and waxy to the touch. They should look full but not have bulges, which indicates that the peas are past their best. Only pick as many peas as you can use in the following hour or so, as the rich sugars in peas convert to starch a few hours after picking, so they lose much of their sweetness. Pick sugar snap varieties when the pods are rounded and smooth without any bulges. Pick snowpeas when the pods are quite flat, with just a hint of the developing peas within. Better still, pick them when the white flower petal residue is still clinging to the pea – this indicates a really young snowpea.

Be clear as to whether you are planting dwarf, semi-dwarf or tall peas. Dwarf peas grow to less than 1 metre; semi-dwarf varieties to around 1 metre, and tall varieties can grow to 2 metres. All peas need support as they grow. This can start off as a collection of twigs inserted into the ground and loosely circled with a doubled length of string – sow a pea plant at the base of each twig – or you can buy simple stakes or bamboo canes. As the plants grow, the twigs will need to be backed up by proper stakes or wigwam supports. Blocks of dwarf and semi-dwarf peas may benefit from a circle of mesh placed around them, with each individual plant supported by a central stake. If left unsupported, pea plants risk falling over and their tendrils become hopelessly tangled, offering an attractive home for snails and other chewing pests. Young pea plants also need shielding from strong wind, so it is a good idea to plant the peas among taller plants that will offer protection, globe artichokes for example.

Sow hardy varieties, such as 'Feltham First' and 'Meteor', in autumn to enjoy fresh peas in the springtime. A second crop could be sown in October–November – spare borders in a greenhouse or a polytunnel could be used. Pick peas every few days to keep the bushes producing. Compost any pods that are yellowish, bulging, have split or look dry. You could save a few of the dried peas still hanging on the vine to plant next year.

Asian gardeners sometimes grow peas very close together just to harvest pea shoots (the top pairs of leaves at the tip of the stem), which stir-fry in moments to a brilliant green.

As with all legumes, peas enrich the soil they grow in by adding or replenishing nitrogen – a vital element for plant growth, especially for leafy plants. At the end of the growing season, chop up the plants and dig them back into the soil or compost the spent stalks and follow the peas with leafy vegetables, such as lettuce, silver beet (Swiss chard) or cabbage.

Container Planting Dwarf varieties can be grown in containers provided they are supported, as described above, and are not exposed to blasting winds. My choice would be sugar snap or snowpeas, as their yields are far greater, given that the pods are edible. You would need to grow a lot of podding peas to get more than the few meals that could be grown in most containers.

Preparing and Sharing Podding peas can be nibbled raw, and are delicious and sweet if they are young and juicy. I think it would be a shame if the entire crop disappeared this way, though. Peas are so good when cooked, but many children who dislike cooked peas will happily snack on them raw. Snowpeas are edible raw but again, in my opinion, are not as delicious raw as cooked. Brief cooking develops their sweetness, colour and flavour. The shells of podding peas are inedible, although some cooks use them to add flavour and colour to soups; for an example, see Risi e Bisi on page 480. As a general guide, 500 grams/1 pound of whole podding pea shells will yield about 200 grams/7 ounces shelled peas, which is just enough to serve two. Check the pods for small green grubs and discard any hard peas.

The very first podding peas of the season are the sweetest of all and such a treat that little needs to be done to them. If only a small quantity of podding peas have made their way into my kitchen, I blanch them in a saucepan of lightly salted boiling water for several minutes, drain, and then make a quick sauce by simmering them for a minute or two with a little pouring cream and some torn basil leaves to spoon over homemade fettuccine. Another idea is to combine the blanched peas with just-cooked young carrots before adding cream and some chopped flat-leaf parsley instead of basil. This spring stew is lovely with simply cooked fish. Either way, an entire meal can be created in less than fifteen minutes.

A beautiful spring salad might combine double-peeled broad beans and podding peas, both lightly cooked, then combined with very fresh firm ricotta and young salad leaves, drizzled with a lemon-infused extra-virgin olive oil. Young tendrils and shoots from the vines are also good in salads mixed with other choice salad leaves.

Later in the season, when the runaway podding peas have become a bit over-mature and mealy, consider making a kitchen garden soup (see page 473 for a guideline), which by its very nature will probably vary every time you make it. The idea is to use what is fresh and available from the garden, including the shelled pea pods.

The pods of sugar snaps and snowpeas are entirely edible. I endeavour to pick my crop when they are young, small and therefore more tender. Approximately 500 grams/1 pound should be sufficient to serve four to six. Both varieties require careful stringing before eating. To do this, snap off the stem ends, then pull the string downward on one side. Use a small, sharp knife to cut the string from the other side, then pull it downward to remove.

Sugar snap peas need fast cooking (2–4 minutes) to bring out their brilliant flavour and colour. Both sugar snaps and snowpeas are at their best in stir-fried dishes mixed with Asian flavours. They go wonderfully well together and look stunning when combined with bright-pink king prawns – the addition of a little finely chopped ginger is a must.

Especially for Kids Children will enjoy making supports for the peas and can help to secure the young plants to the supports using soft ties. I save torn pillow slips (or even a torn bed sheet) for tearing into narrow strips for the garden. The cotton is soft and tears and ties easily. One pillow slip has kept me going for a couple of years. Children can also be trusted to maintain a close eye on the young plants for any leaf-chewing insects.

A good taste test is to offer freshly gathered and cooked podding peas versus frozen peas – at the very least, children will notice the difference in flavour (be prepared for some to prefer the frozen flavour because that is what they are used to). However, if children have grown and harvested the peas themselves, most will prefer the fruit of their own labour. A more elaborate taste test would also include a sample of purchased shelled peas. I have never yet tasted pre-shelled peas that were as sweet as garden-picked specimens.

Encourage young gardeners to also try raw pea shoots (the top pairs of leaves at the tip of the stem) or white pea blossoms – but not too many or there will be no more peas!

Spicy Potato and Green Pea Samosas

MAKES 12 These famous Indian snacks are delicious, but undeniably fiddly to make. They are good to prepare as a group activity, as three or four cooks can all have a go at rolling, folding and filling their own samosas. I find myself to be all thumbs when folding the pastry (just as I am when trying to make dainty dim sum) but younger cooks are often more nimble! If you can't face making the traditional pastry, a cheat's version uses square spring-roll wrappers instead. Each wrapper is cut in half on the diagonal to make two samosas, then dampened, folded and sealed as described below. A wonderful accompaniment is the Mint and Tamarind Chutney on page 409.

vegetable oil, for deep-frying

PASTRY
10g/3¾oz plain flour, plus extra
   for dusting
½ teaspoon salt
2 teaspoons vegetable oil
25ml/4½fl oz warm water

PEA AND POTATO FILLING
300g/10½oz (2 medium-sized)
   potatoes, peeled
½ teaspoon cumin seeds

½ teaspoon coriander seeds
1 fresh small red chilli, seeded
   and finely chopped
375g/13oz peas in pod (to yield
   150g/5oz shelled peas)
1 × 1cm/½in-long piece ginger,
   finely chopped
½ teaspoon salt
1 tablespoon lemon juice
2 tablespoons vegetable oil
1 small onion, finely chopped
2 tablespoons water
2 tablespoons finely chopped mint

EXTRA EQUIPMENT
food processor
mortar and pestle
sauté pan
wok
slotted spoon or
   long-handled
   brass skimmer

To make the pastry, put flour and salt into a food processor. Add oil to warm water. With motor running, add oil/water mixture and process to form a ball of soft dough (if necessary, add an extra 1–2 teaspoons water). Knead briefly, then put into a bowl, cover with plastic film and refrigerate for at least 20 minutes. The dough can be made a few hours in advance if that is more convenient.

To make the pea and potato filling, boil potatoes in a saucepan of lightly salted water for 20 minutes or until just tender. Drain, cool for a few minutes and then chop into 5mm/¼in cubes. Place in a bowl.

Meanwhile, dry-roast cumin and coriander seeds separately in a small frying pan over medium heat until fragrant. Tip seeds into a mortar, then grind to a fine powder with the pestle.

Place cumin/coriander mixture, chilli, shelled peas, ginger, salt and lemon juice in a bowl.

Heat vegetable oil in a sauté pan over medium heat and fry onion for 5 minutes or until golden. Add spiced pea mixture and stir to mix well. Add water, then cover and cook over low heat for 7 minutes or until peas are cooked,   **>>>**

stirring once or twice. Add potato cubes to pan and mix together. Cover pan and cook for a further 5 minutes. Scrape mixture into a bowl, stir in mint and leave to cool completely.

To assemble samosas, divide dough into 6 balls. Keep the rest covered with plastic film while you work with 1 ball (or give 1 ball of dough to each samosa-maker and all work together). Each ball will make 2 samosas.

Line a baking tray with plastic film. Put a small bowl of cold water near the workbench. Dust bench with extra flour. Using a rolling pin, roll 1 ball to form a 15cm/6in round. Cut in half.

Dampen cut edge of a dough semi-circle with a finger dipped in water and pick it up. Form a cone or pouch by lifting and folding one wet edge to the centre and bring the other edge to overlap, forming a seam. Press to seal. Fill this pouch with 2 heaped teaspoons of filling mixture and then dampen exposed edge and fold it over to seal filling. Transfer to baking paper-lined baking tray. Don't worry if your samosa does not look wonderful; practice makes perfect. Repeat with remaining dough and filling. When all samosas are filled and sealed, refrigerate until needed.

Preheat oven to 100°C/Gas ¼ and put a paper towel-lined baking tray inside to keep warm.

Heat vegetable oil in a wok over medium heat. Slide in as many samosas as will fit comfortably in a single layer. Fry until golden brown on one side. Carefully turn over in the oil with a slotted spoon or brass skimmer and fry the second side until golden. Lift samosas onto paper towel-lined tray and keep warm in oven. Continue until all samosas are cooked.

Spring Kitchen Garden Soup

Start with some butter, a chopped onion, some sliced garlic if you like, maybe some torn outer lettuce leaves, and a chopped potato or two in a saucepan over medium heat – cook just until onion has softened. Moisten with stock or water and add a handful of pea pods, then simmer. When the potato is quite tender, blend the soup in a blender for several minutes to a pretty shade of apple-green. Strain through a coarse-meshed sieve to remove any pea pod strings, reheat and drop in a handful or two of podded peas. Simmer just until peas are tender (maybe 5 minutes). Season with salt and pepper. A spoonful of crème fraîche is delicious stirred into each bowl just before serving.

Pappardelle with Peas, Lettuce and Prosciutto

SERVES 4 Every child loves making pasta and it is such a simple and useful skill to have that I think the whole family should become comfortable with whipping up a small amount of pasta without any fuss. The instructions may at first look long and off-putting, but with two or three people working together this amount of pasta can be made from scratch in less than 15 minutes (excluding the one-hour resting time). While I like to hand-cut pappardelle, you could just run the dough through the pasta machine cutters if you prefer. This delicate and gentle sauce is perfect with tender homemade pasta.

40g/1½oz unsalted butter
2 tablespoons extra-virgin olive oil
6 slices prosciutto, cut widthways
   into 1cm/½in-wide strips
12 cos lettuce leaves, hard stalks
   cut away, leaves cut widthways
   into 3cm/1½in-wide strips
2 cloves garlic, thinly sliced
salt
500g/1lb peas in pod (to yield
   200g/7oz shelled peas)
250ml/9fl oz pouring cream

2 tablespoons chopped
   flat-leaf parsley
sea salt and freshly ground
   black pepper
grated parmesan, to serve

FRESH PASTA
300g/10½oz plain flour, plus extra
   for dusting
3 free-range eggs, lightly beaten
1 free-range egg yolk (optional)

EXTRA EQUIPMENT
food processor
hand-cranked pasta
   machine

To make the pasta, put flour into a food processor. With motor running, add eggs. Process for a few minutes until dough clings together and feels springy (it should not feel sticky); if mixture is too dry, add an extra egg yolk. Tip dough onto a workbench, knead it for a few minutes, then wrap in plastic film and rest for 1 hour at room temperature.

Clear a large space on your workbench and have a bowl of plain flour nearby. All surfaces must be dry. If serving pasta immediately, bring a large saucepan or pasta pot of lightly salted water to the boil. Divide dough in half. Press each piece into a rectangle about 8cm/3in wide. Pass this piece of dough through pasta machine rollers set to its thickest setting. If dough comes through ragged at the edges, fold it in 3, then turn it 90 degrees and roll it through twice more. Change to next-thickest setting and pass the dough through 3–4 times. Continue in this manner until dough has passed through thinnest setting desired. If dough gets too long to handle comfortably, cut it into 2–3 pieces and roll each piece separately. Either cut pasta sheets into 10–15mm/½–¾in-wide pappardelle, or run them over cutting rollers. Lay cut pasta on flour-dusted bench or a clean tea towel and roll and cut remaining dough. Use as soon as possible, or hang over a length of dowelling (or a broom handle) or the back of a chair to dry. It will take 10 minutes or so for pasta to dry in a well-ventilated room.

>>>

Heat butter and olive oil in a large non-stick frying pan or sauté pan over low heat and gently sauté prosciutto until the fat starts to run. Add lettuce and garlic, then cover pan and cook gently over low heat for 5 minutes or until lettuce is limp.

Cook pappardelle in pan of lightly salted boiling water. It will take just a couple of minutes to be correctly al dente. Drain pasta, then return it to hot empty pasta pot while you finish the sauce.

Add peas and cream to prosciutto/lettuce mixture, cover and cook for 5 minutes or until peas are tender. Uncover pan and increase heat to medium, then cook for 2–3 minutes or until cream starts to thicken and deepen in colour. Toss in pasta and parsley, then season with salt and pepper to taste. Toss to mix well and tip into a warmed serving dish and serve. Offer grated parmesan.

French-style Peas with Crisp Sage

SERVES 4 This is a slight variation on the classic recipe for *petits pois à la Française*. The peas combine with the other ingredients in a sort of sauce and are great served with a delicate fish or meat dish, such as quickly grilled fillets of sole brushed with butter and scattered with herbs (see opposite), or sautéed escalopes of veal. The fish or meat will not need any other sauce.

EXTRA EQUIPMENT
sauté pan

80g/3oz butter, plus 1 teaspoon
   extra (or use Parsley Butter on
   page 457)
12 sage leaves
10 lettuce leaves (inner cos,
   or iceberg or other lettuce with
   a crunchy texture), hard stalk
   cut away, leaves rolled up and
   thinly sliced into fine ribbons

4 spring onions, trimmed and
   very thinly sliced
500g/1lb peas in pod (to yield
   200g/7oz shelled peas)
¼ teaspoon salt
80ml/3fl oz water
1 tablespoon chopped
   flat-leaf parsley

Heat 40g/1½oz of the butter and sage leaves in a large sauté pan over medium heat until leaves are crisp and butter is nut-brown. Quickly scoop out sage leaves and place on a paper towel-lined plate.

Heat remaining butter in sauté pan over medium heat and drop in lettuce, spring onion, peas, salt and water. Cover tightly and cook for about 10 minutes. Peas should be bright green and unwrinkled and lettuce should be quite limp. Taste a pea to see if they need further cooking. When tender, add parsley, extra butter and crisp sage leaves. Shake very gently to melt butter. Serve at once.

French-style Peas with Crisp Sage

Spicy Stir-fried Snowpeas or Sugar Snap Peas with Deep-fried Eggs

SERVES 4 The spice paste used in this recipe is speedy to make and it can be stored in a jar in the refrigerator, ready to bring a touch of magic to many simple vegetable dishes, or try it mixed into a pan of sautéed prawns. It can be safely stored, covered, in the refrigerator for at least one month. I have also used it as an unconventional spread on hot corn fritters (see page 258)!

4 free-range eggs
vegetable oil, for deep-frying
6 spring onions, trimmed and
    cut into 4cm/1½in lengths
300g/10½oz snowpeas or sugar
    snap peas, strings removed

SPICE PASTE
½ onion, roughly chopped
¼ small handful roughly chopped
    coriander, including stems

3 × 1cm/½in-long pieces ginger,
    peeled and roughly chopped
3 cloves garlic, roughly chopped
2 fresh small red chillies, halved
    and seeded
250g/9oz ripe, firm tomatoes,
    seeded and diced
2 tablespoons vegetable oil
2 tablespoons dark brown sugar
1 tablespoon fish sauce
2 teaspoons lemon juice

EXTRA EQUIPMENT
food processor
wok
long-handled brass
    skimmer or slotted
    spoon
wok sang (see page
    47) or large metal
    spoon

To make the spice paste, put onion, coriander, ginger, garlic and chilli in a food processor and pulse to form a paste. Add tomato and process again. Heat oil in a medium-sized frying pan over medium heat and cook the paste, stirring frequently for 5 minutes or until it has dried out considerably. Stir in sugar and fish sauce and cook for another 2–3 minutes until mixture resembles a thick paste. Stir in lemon juice and taste for balance of sweet, sour, salty and hot; adjust with more sugar, fish sauce or lemon juice, if desired. Cool and then store in an airtight container in the refrigerator for up to 1 month. Makes about 200g/7oz.

Boil eggs in a small saucepan of simmering water for 6 minutes. Lift from water, cool in a bowl of cold water, then dry and carefully peel.

Heat enough vegetable oil in a wok to a depth of 4cm/1½in in the centre. Carefully slide eggs into hot oil and fry, turning once until they are golden brown on all sides. Lift from oil with a brass skimmer or slotted spoon and put on a plate nearby. Cut each egg in half lengthways. Carefully tip most of the oil into a bowl, leaving just 1 tablespoon in the wok.

Heat wok over high heat, then quickly stir-fry spring onion for 30 seconds, then toss in snowpeas or sugar snap peas. Keep vegetables moving for 1 minute, then add 2 tablespoons of spice paste and the eggs. Stir to mix thoroughly and then serve at once.

Risi e Bisi

SERVES 4 This dish is a specialty of Italy's Veneto region and is a must-taste dish in Venice. *Bisi* is the local word for peas. Italian cookbook author Marcella Hazan insists this is not a risotto but a soup and that it must be eaten with a spoon. Her recipe uses best-quality homemade chicken broth. Another recipe from one of Venice's finest restaurants, Da Fiore, makes a broth using the pea pods. I like this idea. Of course one could always infuse the chicken stock with pea pods instead. This would be a good time to draw a young cook's attention to the special type of rice used to make this dish as well as risotti.

750g/1lb 10½oz peas in pod (to yield 300g/10½oz peas), pods reserved
1.5 litres/2¾ pints water or stock (or 850ml/30fl oz chicken stock)
1 tablespoon extra-virgin olive oil
70g/2½oz butter
½ onion, finely chopped
30g/1oz pancetta or bacon, finely chopped

200g/7oz Arborio or Carnaroli rice (see page 703)
sea salt and freshly ground black pepper
2 tablespoons chopped flat-leaf parsley
25g/1oz grated parmesan

EXTRA EQUIPMENT
enamelled cast-iron or other heavy-based casserole with lid

If you are making pea-pod infused stock, put pea pods in a large heavy-based saucepan or pasta pot with 1.5 litres/2¾ pints water or stock. Bring to simmering point and cook over medium heat for 45 minutes. Strain and measure; you should have 850ml/30fl oz of pea pod-infused stock. Set aside. Otherwise, heat 850ml/30fl oz chicken stock in a heavy-based saucepan.

Heat oil and 50g/2oz of the butter in a heavy-based casserole over medium heat. Sauté onion and pancetta, stirring for 6–8 minutes or until onion is soft and golden. Add peas and just a little of the stock and simmer for 5 minutes. Add rice and salt and stir well to coat with buttery onion/pea mixture. Add one-third of the remaining stock at a time, waiting for each lot to be absorbed before adding the next (as if making a risotto), stirring constantly. This should take about 15 minutes. Taste rice after last addition; it should still be a little al dente and the consistency quite sloppy. If rice is still too hard, add a little extra water and continue to cook for a few more minutes. Taste for salt and pepper and adjust seasoning if desired.

Stir in parsley, grated parmesan and remaining butter and serve.

PEPPERS AND CHILLIES

**Solanaceae family
(includes eggplant,
potatoes and tomatoes)
Perennials grown as annuals**

Soil type
Well drained soil rich in organic
matter or a potting mix.

Soil preparation
Dig in organic matter a few
weeks prior to planting.

Climate
Frost tender.

Position
Prefers full sun, but will tolerate
partial shade.

How to grow
In February to March, sow
seeds in small pots in a heated
propagator at 20°C in a heated
greenhouse or on a windowsill.
Grow on at 16°C and then
gradually get them used to lower
temperatures. An alternative
to seed raising is to purchase
pot-grown young plants in late
spring. Pot on into 2-litre then
5-litre pots of potting mix, either

keep them in a greenhouse or
gradually harden-off the plants
and put out on a sunny sheltered
patio well after the last frosts
(early June). It is also possible
to plant them out into soil beds
either in a greenhouse or outside
under a crop cover, allow 45cm
between each plant.

Water requirements
Keep soil moist.

Successive planting
Growing season not long
enough for successive plantings.

When to fertilise
After flowering and fruit-setting,
use a liquid fertiliser (see page
691) or worm tea (see page 695).

Harvest period
3–4 months from planting.
Regular harvesting improves
production.

Pests and organic control
Plants grown undercover may
be attacked by aphids, whitefly
or red spider mite. Check
plants regularly as in the early

stages, simply picking off and
destroying affected foliage may
be sufficient. Biological controls
are worth considering under
glass for aphids, whitefly or red
spider mite. Outside, use a soft
soap spray. Blossom end rot,
where the end of the fruit turns
black, is not a disease but a
physiological condition bought
on by erratic watering leading to
poor calcium uptake.

Companion planting
Coriander, okra, basil, thyme,
peppermint and marigolds.

Special information
Protect from wind; staking
helps. If seed-saving maintain a
distance between sweet peppers
and chillies as they can cross-
pollinate. Chillies need hot
weather more than peppers.

**Quantities to plant
for a family of four**
2 plants every 6 weeks.

Capsicum (*Capsicum annum*)

Growing and Harvesting All peppers and chillies originated in Central and Southern America. They are the most widely used seasoning in the world and were 'discovered' in the Caribbean by Christopher Columbus.

Peppers There are many different cultivars. The best known are the sweet peppers (also known as bell peppers or capsicums), which come in a rainbow of colours: red, cream, orange, yellow, black, white, purple and green. Children (and some adults) may not realise that all coloured peppers start life green. A green pepper is unripe, but perfectly edible.

Green peppers change colour in late summer. Temperatures between 18–25°C cause the colour change, not exposure to sunlight. Peppers can be harvested when the colour change is about 75 per cent complete. They will continue to ripen and change colour in the next day or so at room temperature. You may choose to grow the longer and narrower varieties of sweet pepper, which have a waxy skin. Their colour changes from lime-green to yellow to orange or red. Sometimes these long peppers are described as 'fryers'.

As all peppers have compact bushes they are a perfect plant to dot here and there in the garden. Home-grown peppers feel as tight and firm as a drum when picked. They snap cleanly from the bush and are very shiny. Only pick as many as you will use immediately. Once picked, the shine and the tautness will start to diminish within a few hours.

A few years ago in Barcelona I made the acquaintance of the most delectable green pepper, known there as *pimientos de Padrón*. I was lunching at the port with my daughter and noticed a platter of something brilliantly green being served to almost every Spanish group. I asked the waiter for clarification. Within minutes we too had a platter of fried *pimientos de Padrón*. The waiter said that eating them is always a bit of a game – some will be more *piccante* (spicy) than others and you can never tell which ones will give you a surprise. These small (6–8 centimetres long), fat, mildly hot peppers were sensational! They still had the bitterness of a green pepper but also a rich ripeness that counteracted the bitterness. The skins were blistered from their brief bath in good, hot olive oil and a sprinkling of salt was the only addition. Seed of 'Padrón' is available in the UK (**www.nickys-nursery.co.uk**).

Chillies Chillies can be long or short, thick or thin, orange, purple, yellow, green or red, with heat levels ranging from 1–10 on the Scoville scale. The available range increases every season, it seems, including many that are often mentioned in Mexican and American cookery books, such as poblano, jalapeño and habañero. Some of these varieties are extremely hot. Habañero is claimed to be one of the hottest chillies available. Jalapeño is most commonly used raw and green. Mexican varieties are often roasted to increase their flavour and to remove their rather tough skins, or they may be dried or smoked and dried. Freshly harvested chillies should not be refrigerated unless first wrapped in several layers of paper towel; stored this way they will remain in good, supple condition for a week. Below 7°C they will start to deteriorate rapidly and the temperature of the average domestic refrigerator is around 4°C. Otherwise store at room temperature in a basket where they will dry naturally after a couple of weeks. To dry, string red and green chillies using a needle and waxed cotton and hang in a dry, protected place.

Container Planting All peppers and chillies make excellent container plants, although peppers need support if they produce a heavy crop of fruit. As with eggplant, the plant may continue to produce well into the autumn before it is killed by frost. Bring potted plants back into a greenhouse at the end of season to get the last fruits. As with eggplant, if you are planning a summer holiday ensure these pots are kept watered by a friend, as this is the main growing season for all peppers.

Preparing and Sharing Peppers The riper red, orange and yellow peppers are the sweetest and the most digestible of all. Simply roasted and peeled (see page 488), then cut into strips, they are lovely as they are, dressed with a drizzle of extra-virgin olive oil and a few drops of vinegar. With the addition of the best anchovy fillets, the salad becomes a bit fancier.

Freshly harvested peppers can be sliced and eaten just as they are in salads, but many people (particularly children) find all raw peppers bitter and indigestible (especially green ones). If you can, wait until the colour change from green to red, yellow or orange has happened before harvesting them. Apart from the increased sweetness, the magical colour change is very exciting for young gardeners to observe.

If you can't wait and want to harvest and use a green pepper, then either peel it raw with a speed peeler (see page 47) or roast as described on page 488. Alternatively, you could shallow-fry it in extra-virgin olive oil. Peppers that are peeled raw with a speed peeler and then slowly braised with a little good quality extra-virgin olive oil, fresh bay leaves and peeled garlic cloves have a totally different texture and a significantly different flavour from roasted ones. The oil deepens in colour and the peppers almost melt into it. This has to be one of my all-time favourite vegetable dishes and I serve it often with a piece of crisp-skin salmon. The fish needs no other sauce.

Chillies Green chillies can be added to salads or used to make pickles. Fully ripe red chillies can be used in condiments and general cooking. Chillies need to be handled with care. It is best to use disposable gloves when slicing and seeding chillies, and even then you still need to wash your hands after dropping the gloves in the rubbish bin. Don't just rinse your hands but use a nailbrush and soap and scrub under your fingernails. Whenever I prepare a seeded chilli, I first slice it lengthways and then take it to the compost bucket that sits beside my kitchen sink and then, with the point of a small knife, I scrape the seeds directly into the bucket so as to be sure that there are no stray seeds on my work surface.

When I have an abundance of chillies in my garden, I add them to all manner of dishes, including curries (see Kofta Curry with Coriander Sauce on page 249), pasta sauces (see Spicy and Speedy Cherry Tomato Sauce for Pasta on page 651), stews, stir-fries (see Spicy Stir-fried Snowpeas or Sugar Snaps with Deep-fried Eggs on pages 478) and vegetable dishes (see Spiced Cauliflower Masala on page 215), but I also make a Chilli-Infused Oil (see next page), which I sometimes drizzle over hot boiled potatoes or the Tiny New Potatoes in a Paper Bag (see page 497); pasta dishes; and almost always over barbecued seafood and grilled fish.

Especially for Kids I have never met a child who is not amazed the first time they are asked to roast a pepper until it is completely black (see page 488) – they can't believe they have not ruined it! Children can learn how to roast sweet peppers over a flame either by holding them with tongs or sitting the peppers directly on a gas burner or barbecue grill-plate, then turning; or on a heavy cast-iron char-grill plate; or under a hot griller. If using the open gas flame you may need to balance the peppers on a small cake cooling rack settled over the burner to facilitate even scorching (it won't be much good for cakes after this but you will want to roast peppers often). Watch peppers carefully and turn to roast all sides. When blackened all over, the peppers must be enclosed in a paper or plastic bag or loosely wrapped in a cloth to steam so the skins will lift off easily. Try to achieve this without washing the peppers as some of their flavourful juices will go down the sink.

An interesting and telling flavour comparison could be to taste the differences between a garden-grown, sun-ripened red pepper and a commercial red pepper, often grown under hydroponic conditions.

Chillies can be dried for long-term storage – stringing chillies together and hanging the strings to dry is a fun activity for kids. The strings must be stored indoors well away from any chance of rain. These strings are known as *ristra*s in Spanish, and in Spain, New Mexico and Mexico houses are hung with dozens of these colourful strings.

Chilli-infused Oil

MAKES ABOUT 250ML/9FL OZ Heat 250ml/9fl oz extra-virgin olive oil in a heavy-based saucepan or wok over high heat until very hot but not smoking, then add 60g/2oz freshly chopped long red chillies (including the seeds). Remove from the heat and leave to cool completely. Strain the cold oil into a sterilised bottle (see page 706) and refrigerate for up to 2 months. You can buy an inexpensive stainless-steel oil pourer in kitchenware shops that fits firmly into a standard bottle and allows for a controlled amount of chilli oil to be poured. A few words of warning – don't prepare more than the amount I've specified in one batch. My brother did, and the hot oil and chillies overflowed from the pan.

Peeling and Preparing Raw Peppers

This alternative method is fiddlier than the more common roasting or grilling one described on page 488, but it does result in raw peeled peppers. This is an advantage if the cook wants to make a slow-cooked dish combining peppers with other ingredients; for example, a ratatouille. If you start with already roasted and skinned peppers they will collapse into the sauce, contributing flavour certainly, but no texture. If you use raw unpeeled peppers your finished dish will have little scraps of pepper skin in the sauce. The peeled peppers can either be stuffed; slow-cooked with extra-virgin olive oil, whole peeled garlic cloves and fresh bay leaves; or used in a braise.

EXTRA EQUIPMENT
speed peeler
(see page 47)

sweet peppers (as many as you need)

Practice makes perfect with this technique. Peel peppers with zigzag strokes of the peeler, aiming for a loose-wristed action. Because peppers have lots of bumps you will probably have to leave some crevices and grooves unpeeled. Another way of doing it is to first cut each pepper into pieces following its natural grooves. This makes for easier peeling but you will end up with small pieces of pepper, which may not always be what you want. (Put peelings in compost bucket.) Cut tops from each pepper and scoop seeds into compost bucket, then proceed with your recipe.

Habañero chillies

Roasted and Peeled Sweet Peppers

Most recipes using sweet peppers recommend removing the skins, which can be bitter (especially green peppers) or indigestible (all colours). The most common way of doing this follows. The prepared peppers are then ready to be sliced or diced and used in many different ways, either sautéed, mixed with other ingredients, or served just as they are as a salad or as part of an antipasti platter.

sweet peppers (as many as you need)

Heat a griller or barbecue grill-plate to maximum. Place whole sweet peppers on griller tray or grill-plate, then grill, turning frequently using tongs, until skin on all sides has plenty of black scorched patches. Using tongs, place blackened sweet peppers in a plastic or brown paper bag, then seal and leave to cool completely.

Carefully peel away skins and place in compost bucket. Slice off tops and scoop seeds into compost bucket. Use in the following recipes or with the antipasto suggestions on page 491.

EXTRA EQUIPMENT
griller or barbecue
  grill-plate

Chickpea Salad with Roasted Sweet Red Peppers and a Spicy Dressing

SERVES 4 This salad features the gorgeous mellow flavours of Roasted and Peeled Sweet Peppers (see above).

350g/12oz Cooked Dried Chick Peas
  (see page 203) or 1 × 440g/15oz
  tin chick peas, drained and rinsed
2 Roasted and Peeled Sweet
  Peppers (1 red and 1 orange
  or yellow, see above)
sea salt
2 handfuls coriander sprigs

SPICY DRESSING
1 teaspoon cumin seeds
1 teaspoon coriander seeds
1 clove garlic, finely chopped
1 teaspoon chilli paste such as
  harissa (see page 704), or to taste
juice of ½ lemon
2 tablespoons extra-virgin olive oil

EXTRA EQUIPMENT
mortar and pestle

To make the spicy dressing, dry-roast cumin and coriander seeds separately in a small frying pan over medium heat until fragrant. Tip seeds into a mortar, then grind to a fine powder with the pestle. Mix with remaining dressing ingredients.

Put chick peas into a serving bowl. Cut roasted and peeled peppers into strips and mix them with chick peas. Pour over dressing and mix well, then taste and season with salt if desired. Scatter salad with coriander and serve.

Roasted and Peeled Sweet Peppers with Olive and Cheese Loaf (see page 444) and Rocket

Stuffed Red Pepper 'Boats'

MAKES 4 BOATS These stuffed pepper halves are easy to assemble and look colourful and inviting as part of an antipasti platter. They are best served warm or at room temperature.

extra-virgin olive oil, for cooking	**STUFFING**	**EXTRA EQUIPMENT**
2 Roasted and Peeled Sweet Peppers (see page 488), halved widthways and seeded	2 tablespoons currants	20cm × 24cm/
	1 tablespoon verjuice (see page 706) or red-wine vinegar	8in × 9½in gratin dish
	2 tablespoons extra-virgin olive oil	
	2 tablespoons pine nuts	
80ml/3fl oz Fast Basic Tomato Sauce (see page 649), tomato sauce or relish (or use 1 tablespoon tomato paste diluted with 2 tablespoons hot water)	25g/1oz fresh breadcrumbs	
	2 teaspoons salted capers, rinsed and drained	
	12 black or green olives, pitted and chopped	
	2 tablespoons chopped flat-leaf parsley	
	30g/1oz soft goat's cheese, crumbled	

To make the stuffing, put currants into a small bowl with verjuice or red-wine vinegar and leave for at least 15 minutes to plump; they will absorb all or most of the liquid. Heat 1 tablespoon of the oil in a small frying pan over low heat and fry pine nuts, stirring constantly with a wooden spoon. When golden, quickly tip pine nuts into a sieve resting over a bowl. Transfer pine nuts to a paper towel-lined plate to drain and return reserved oil in bowl to frying pan. Add another tablespoon of oil to the pan and fry breadcrumbs over medium heat, stirring until they are golden and feel sandy. Tip crumbs into another bowl and add remaining stuffing ingredients and mix well.

Preheat oven to 180°C/Gas 4.

Brush a 20cm × 24cm/8in × 9½in gratin dish with a little olive oil. Divide stuffing among the 4 pepper halves and put them in the oiled gratin dish; they should fit very snugly. Spoon tomato sauce over and around to just moisten the boats; on no account should they be swimming in sauce. Drizzle with a few drops of olive oil.

Bake 'boats' for 20–30 minutes or until stuffing is bubbling. Serve warm or at room temperature.

Red Pepper and Saffron Sauce for Almost Anything

MAKES 375ML/13FL OZ This wonderful sauce enhances so many other ingredients. It is based on my own recipe for rouille, the fiery French paste that is stirred into a fish soup. This sauce is magnificent with plainly cooked fish or with baked scallops or prawns. It is an excellent dipping sauce for vegetable fritters and a great accompaniment to roasted Jerusalem artichokes, potatoes and onions – as I have said, almost anything really.

EXTRA EQUIPMENT
blender or food processor

1 Roasted and Peeled Sweet Pepper (see page 488), cut into strips
1 potato, cut into chunks
2 cloves garlic, chopped

1 fresh small red chilli, seeded
½ teaspoon saffron stamens
500ml/18fl oz water
1 teaspoon salt
2 tablespoons extra-virgin olive oil

Put all ingredients except olive oil in a small saucepan, then cover and simmer over low heat for about 20 minutes or until potato is completely tender.

Remove and reserve about 125ml/4½fl oz liquid from the pan to prevent sauce from being too runny. Place capsicum/potato mixture in a blender (or food processor). Cover blender lid and flask with a dry tea towel; hot liquids can force up the lid of a blender, spraying hot liquid that can burn. Carefully blend until you have a smooth, brilliantly coloured sauce. Taste for salt and adjust seasoning if desired. Return reserved liquid to the sauce if it is too thick, remembering that the sauce will thicken further as it cools. (Don't throw away any leftover reserved liquid – it can be added to a soup, stew or curry.) Continue to blend, adding the olive oil. Pour sauce into a container, then seal, store in the refrigerator and use within 5 days.

Antipasto Suggestions for Roasted and Peeled Sweet Peppers

Strips of roasted peppers (see page 488) can be combined with any of the following:

- capers
- Caramelised Onion (see page 461)
- chopped flat-leaf parsley
- eggs to make a frittata
- extra-virgin olive oil
- fresh goat's cheese
- grilled bread to make bruschetta

- pitted olives
- red-wine vinegar
- rocket or other young salad greens
- sautéed eggplant
- toasted pine nuts
- toppings for a pizza
- torn basil and ripe tomatoes

POTATOES

Solanaceae family (includes chillies, eggplant, peppers and tomatoes)
Perennial grown as an annual

Soil type
Moist, well-worked soil enriched with organic matter. Don't grow in soil that has been used for members of the Solanaceae family in the last 3 years.

Soil preparation
Dig in organic matter or well-rotted manure a few weeks prior to planting.

Climate
Suitable for all climates.

Position
Prefer full sun or partial shade. Dislike extreme heat and frosts.

How to grow
Buy certified seed potatoes in January-February, lay the tuber out in trays with the end with the most eyes uppermost. Place in a cool, dry light place such as a windowsill until sprouts form, this process called 'chitting' gives the tubers a head start when the ground is cold. Early and second early varieties are planted in March-April, maincrops towards end of April. Plant tubers 13–20cm deep, 30–40cm apart in rows 60–75cm apart depending on vigour of the variety and how long it will be in the ground.

Water requirements
Potatoes growing in the ground do not need regular watering except when it is dry when the tubers are swelling. Container grown potatoes need the compost to be evenly moist so some watering is required.

Successive planting
Leave a few weeks between planting early, second early and maincrop varieties.

Harvest period
New potatoes can be harvested 12–16 weeks after planting. Maincrop potatoes are left in the ground until the plant has died down; this will take an extra 3–4 weeks.

Pests and organic control
Aphids need controlling as they spread potato viruses, use a suitable organic spray. Blight is an increasing and most serious problem in wet years, destroying plants and rotting tubers. There is no control for it, only a few varieties are resistant to the new strains but Bordeaux mixture (see page XXX) can help prevent it if applied at the right time.

Companion planting
Peas, celery, savory, marigolds and corn. Nasturtiums distract aphids. Planting a broad bean crop before potatoes may reduce some fungal diseases; growing horseradish among potatoes is also said to help. Don't plant near cherry trees, apricots, rosemary or tomatoes.

Special information
1 seed potato should yield 10.

Quantities to plant for a family of four
6–8 seed potatoes every 4 weeks from March-April.

Potato (*Solanum tuberosum*)

Growing and Harvesting There are hundreds of potato varieties and cultivars in existence but far fewer are available for home gardeners. Although all potatoes originated in South and Central America, many of the so-called 'new' varieties have been well known for a long time. This is especially so of the yellow-fleshed, waxy varieties, some of which are described as 'fingerling' potatoes.

It is a very welcome development that potatoes are now more often than not identified by name. Be aware that some names seem to change in different countries and it can be very confusing to follow the recommendations in an American, New Zealand or Australian recipe. Better to concentrate on whether a waxy or floury potato is specified (see opposite).

Many waxy cultivars are narrow like chubby fingers, such as 'Anya' or 'Pink Fir Apple'. But some, such as 'Rocket' are roundish, and one of my favourites, the all-purpose 'Nicola', is oval.

Popular cultivars of floury potatoes include 'Home Guard', 'Maris Piper', Rooster' and 'King Edward'. And there are cultivars that seem to be somewhere in between, which means they are firm when cooked but can be mashed. 'Desiree' is the best example.

The flesh of potatoes can be white, cream, yellow, pink or blue. Not every potato has a brown skin. The blue-skinned, purple-fleshed cultivar 'Purple Congo' is pretty spectacular.

It is important to understand the difference between 'new' potatoes and 'maincrop' potatoes – so often wrongly described in fruit shops and supermarkets, where anything small is inclined to be described as 'new'. New potatoes are harvested before the plant tops die down. They are not necessarily small, but they all have paper-thin skins that rub off readily. They should be cooked straightaway after lifting, as they deteriorate fast without thick skins to protect them. Shield them from light if you have to wait for a day or so before cooking them. All varieties of potato can be harvested at this stage, and even the flouriest will be firm and waxy when newly harvested.

Main crop potatoes are those that are harvested when fully grown, after the tops have died down; they may be left in the ground for an extra two weeks to develop thicker skins. They can be either floury, waxy or all-purpose varieties and are not all large, but large ones are best for baking in their skins.

There are many growing methods advocated for potatoes, all aimed at protecting the growing tubers from light. Home gardeners with limited space will be interested in the following method. Prepare the soil and place three or four seed potatoes on top; create a cylinder of chicken wire (about 60 centimetres diameter) to enclose the planted space, holding it together with four stakes. Cover the potatoes with straw and manure. As the potato plants grow, add more straw so that only the top two leaves are visible. Continue to do this until the leaves die down. This method is a variation of a 'no-dig' garden. Other gardeners plant their seed potatoes 20 centimetres deep into well-prepared soil and only commence the mulching and earthing up of the plants once the tops start to sprawl.

When harvesting, always dig from well outside the plant, as you don't want to put the garden fork straight through one of your precious potatoes. Allow newly dug potatoes to dry for a few hours, away from the sun, before storing them in a basket or box in the dark, preferably covered with a hessian sack.

Container Planting It is possible to grow three or four potato plants in a 60 centimetre pot or container if the soil is fertile and at least 40 centimetres deep. Plant radishes, spring onions and salad greens along with the potatoes – these will be ready long before the potatoes. You can now buy patio potato planters, these are flexible bags with drainage holes and a carrying handle. Typically around 10–15 litre capacity, these will produce a meal-sized crop from one seed tuber.

Preparing and Sharing The most important distinction to make when cooking with potatoes is whether a potato is considered waxy or floury, as this will influence what you use it for.

Floury potatoes have a high starch and low water content. They bake and mash well and are fine for chips, but disintegrate when boiled to serve whole. They are the varieties to choose when making the popular dish gnocchi. Floury potatoes are also good baked whole in their jackets for at least an hour in a 180°C/Gas 4 oven, then split and spread with butter, sour cream or hummus. Don't forget about potato cakes – either using grated raw potato or cold mashed potato, or a mixture of both (see Crusty Potato and Tarragon Cakes on page 498). Fried home-grown potato cakes and crisp bacon are so good together. Then let's not forget oven-baked potato wedges. Toss 3–4 centimetre-long unpeeled potato wedges in a bowl with olive oil and a little salt, spread out on a baking tray and bake in a 180°C/Gas 4 oven for about 40 minutes, or until tender and golden brown.

In contrast, waxy potatoes have a low starch and high water content. They remain whole when boiled, but don't mash well at all. I also wouldn't use them to make chips. They are the potatoes to use in salads or serve buttered to accompany simply cooked fish or grilled meat. For many food lovers, waxy potatoes are the aristocrats of the potato family. Waxy potatoes make the very best potato salads. I like to boil the potatoes in their skins, then drain and peel them while they are still warm (they can burn you, so try cradling each one in a clean tea towel). Slice into chunks and add the very best extra-virgin olive oil, chopped herbs such as French tarragon, dill, mint or flat-leaf parsley (depending on what is to be served alongside) and season with sea salt and freshly ground black pepper as quickly as possible, then allow the salad to soak up all those flavours. This sort of potato salad should be served still faintly warm or at room temperature – never chilled.

All-purpose potatoes such as 'Desiree' and 'Nicola' seem to do everything well. They are good boiled or mashed, and hold together well for salads; both make lovely gnocchi. The odd-looking 'Purple Congo' potato has a most unusual flavour when cooked – similar to a chestnut or a very dry sweet potato. It makes a very dry, stiff mash.

I tend not to peel potatoes before cooking, as I enjoy eating the skins, and the potato is less likely to break up. Try par-boiling either waxy, floury or all-rounder potatoes and then roasting them in a pan around a chicken with garlic cloves and rosemary sprigs. Alternatively, you could slice par-boiled waxy potatoes into a saffron-scented fish soup or a dish of braised tripe and tomatoes; or sauté them with Spanish chorizo and perhaps some Roasted and Peeled Sweet Peppers (see page 488) to serve as a light lunch.

If you have not already done so, make the acquaintance of a potato ricer. This wonderful gadget is the best way to mash potatoes, whether for gnocchi, potato cakes or just for everyday smooth mash. It is also great fun to use. If you are in the kitchen with young cooks, they will fight to be the one to use the ricer!

Look to Indian recipes for some delicious and different ways with potato: try serving the filling for the Potato, Ginger and Coriander Semolina Dosas on page 503 as an accompaniment to a curry-based meal.

Potatoes exposed to light can develop green patches that are toxic. If there is just a small bit of green, cut it away. If extensive, discard the potato or alternatively replant it in the garden. Potatoes don't like cold and below 10°C/50°F the starch can turn to sugar; the potato will taste very peculiar and most unpleasant. For this reason never store potatoes in the refrigerator. A sprouting potato is one that is past its prime. That said, there have been desperate times when the only potato I have in the kitchen has a sprout. I just knock it off and proceed to cook it, but it will never be an outstanding potato.

Especially for Kids   I have found that digging for potatoes is one of the most magical moments for young gardeners. The first time they see a cluster of potatoes dangling from a clump of stems, leaves and roots is a moment of instant understanding.

A bountiful potato harvest offers an ideal opportunity to talk about how some foods are just made for each other. Examples include potatoes and:

- butter
- extra-virgin olive oil and chives
- garlic
- garlic mayonnaise (see Aïoli on page 314)
- mushrooms
- onions and parsley

What are some other 'perfect matches' for potatoes?

An interesting practical activity could be to look at and cook with different varieties of potato. Not every potato can be mashed! This can also help you work out which potato varieties you prefer and help you decide which type to plant next time.

In school kitchen garden classrooms the potato harvest has led to a fascinating discussion about all the vegetables brought back from the New World after Columbus's voyages.

Tiny New Potatoes in a Paper Bag

SERVES 4 This is such a fun way to cook very special tiny home-grown potatoes. The parcels could also be made from foil or baking paper, but I think paper bags are more fun to serve. Parcels made from baking paper need their edges to be very carefully folded and pressed to stop them opening up during baking in the oven. A few button mushrooms added to each parcel is a delicious variation; adding three to four per bag would do. Once these potatoes are served they are very hot, so do warn your family or guests to wait a few minutes before biting into one. They could be accompanied by a shower of freshly chopped flat-leaf parsley or bowls of a savoury sauce such as the Green Chutney on page 250, Yoghurt with Spinach on page 590, Mint and Tamarind Chutney on page 409 or Red Pepper and Saffron Sauce for Almost Anything on page 491.

EXTRA EQUIPMENT
4 new small paper bags

24–28 tiny new potatoes (no bigger than 3–6cm/1½–2½ in), washed and dried well with paper towels
sea salt and freshly ground black pepper

2 tablespoons extra-virgin olive oil
40g/1½oz butter
4 cloves garlic, crushed

Preheat oven to 200°C/Gas 6.

Put well-dried potatoes into a mixing bowl, then season with salt and pepper and turn in olive oil. Divide potatoes, butter and garlic between bags. Close bags firmly and put on a baking tray.

Bake in the oven for 35 minutes; turn bags over after about 15 minutes. Take a bag from the oven and carefully open it, watching out for a gush of steam, then test whether potatoes are tender by inserting a fine skewer or the point of a sharp knife into one. If it is still resistant, cook potatoes for a further 5 minutes. Otherwise, remove bags (which will be beautifully puffed up) and serve on large plates. Each person tears open their own bag and enjoys the potatoes.

Crusty Potato and Tarragon Cakes

SERVES 4 This mix is best baked in individual egg rings on an oiled baking tray lined with baking paper. The tops become deliciously crusty, yet the cakes remain tender in the middle. The tarragon contributes a touch of spring. At other times of the year flat-leaf parsley, dill or chives might be picked to use instead.

1 tablespoon extra-virgin olive oil
1 onion, finely chopped
2 large floury potatoes (see page 495), peeled
80ml/3fl oz pouring cream
1 tablespoon chopped French tarragon

1 large or 2 small free-range eggs (at room temperature), separated
sea salt and freshly ground black pepper
20g/¾oz butter, chopped

EXTRA EQUIPMENT
food processor with coarse grating attachment or box grater
pestle or other heavy device for pressing potato gratings
4 metal egg or hamburger rings

Preheat oven to 200°C/Gas 6.

Heat 2 teaspoons of the olive oil in a small frying pan over medium heat and sauté onion, stirring from time to time, for 8–10 minutes or until it is deep-gold. Set aside to cool.

Grate potatoes in a food processor using a coarse grating attachment, or use a box grater. Press grated potato firmly with a pestle and tip it into a clean dry tea towel. Roll up and twist tea towel ends in opposite directions to extract as much liquid as possible. Tip squeezed potato into a dry bowl and immediately mix in onion, cream, tarragon, egg yolk/s, salt and pepper.

Whisk egg white/s to form firm peaks and fold into potato mixture. Using a pastry brush, brush baking tray and inside 4 metal egg rings with remaining olive oil. Line the tray with baking paper. Place rings on the tray. Divide potato mixture among oiled rings, pressing it down firmly. Dot potato mixture with butter and bake for 35 minutes.

Remove rings with tongs and return potato cakes on tray to the oven for a further 5–10 minutes to crisp the sides of each one. Serve at once.

Potato Galettes with Baked Goat's Cheese

SERVES 4 This dish is for goat's cheese lovers and would be a very special first course for a fancy dinner, or then again, maybe a light lunch or brunch dish. If you don't want to serve grilled goat's cheese on top of the galettes, why not add a spoonful of cherry tomatoes quickly sautéed with basil leaves instead? The anchovy dressing is optional, but is excellent with either choice.

400g/14oz floury potatoes, peeled
1 free-range egg,
  plus 1 free-range egg yolk
125ml/4½fl oz pouring cream
sea salt and freshly ground
  black pepper
4–5 tablespoons plain flour
100g/3½oz butter, clarified
  (see page 704)
8 × 1cm/½in-thick slices of a round
  goat's cheese log

rocket or small salad leaves, washed
  and dried (optional), to serve

ANCHOVY DRESSING
2 anchovy fillets, chopped
1 clove garlic, very finely chopped
40g/1½oz unsalted butter
juice of ½ lemon
2 teaspoons chopped
  flat-leaf parsley

EXTRA EQUIPMENT
salad spinner
potato ricer
food processor
  with grating
  attachment or
  box grater
griller

Preheat oven to 100°C/Gas ¼ and put a paper towel-lined ovenproof plate inside to keep warm.

Cook 1 of the potatoes in a saucepan of lightly salted simmering water for 20 minutes or until quite tender. Press through a potato ricer into a mixing bowl. Add whole egg, egg yolk and cream, mix, then season with salt and pepper.

Grate remaining potato in a food processor with a coarse grating attachment, or use a box grater. Tip potato into a clean, dry tea towel. Roll up and twist tea towel ends in opposite directions to extract as much liquid as possible. Tip squeezed potato into a dry bowl and immediately add potato/egg mixture and enough flour to bind the mixture so it will hold its shape when fried.

Heat clarified butter in a non-stick frying pan over medium heat and drop spoonfuls of the potato mixture into the pan; you should have enough for 8 galettes. Fry undersides until golden, then turn and fry other sides. Transfer galettes to paper towel-lined plate and keep warm in the oven until you are ready to serve.

Heat a griller to maximum. Top each galette with a slice of goat's cheese and grill until cheese starts to bubble and develop a golden crust. Quickly remove cheese-topped galettes to serving plates. (I like to settle the galettes on a bed of rocket or a mixture of garden-picked small salad leaves.)

To make the anchovy dressing, heat anchovy and garlic in a small frying pan over high heat for 30 seconds, swirl in butter and, as it foams, add lemon juice and parsley. Spoon a little over each cheese-covered galette, then serve.

Potato Tortilla

SERVES 4–6 I have been making thickish potato omelettes for most of my cooking life but recently I've been checking the recipes of various Spanish cooks and I wonder whether I should claim to be making a 'tortilla', an omelette or an Italian-style frittata. Whatever it is called, it tastes good and is best not served straight from the pan, but not refrigerated either. The omelette can be cut into wedges or squares, and then served with salad or with a drink as an appetiser or as part of a cold buffet. When I holidayed in San Sebastian a few years ago a potato tortilla was served as part of the daily breakfast buffet. Although not done in Spain, I have frequently added chopped herbs, cooked spinach and even grated parmesan to the mixture.

EXTRA EQUIPMENT
1 × 20–22cm/8–9in heavy-based cast-iron frying pan with a lid

125ml/4½oz olive oil
1 large onion, halved and thinly sliced
3 large (about 600g/1lb 5oz) waxy potatoes such as nicolas or desirees, peeled, halved and cut into 5mm/¼in-thick slices

6 large free-range eggs
sea salt and freshly ground black pepper

Heat 60ml/2fl oz of the olive oil in a cast-iron frying pan over medium heat and fry onion slices gently, stirring often to prevent sticking or burning, until onion becomes deep yellow, about 8–10 minutes. Tip onion into a sieve placed over a bowl. Transfer drained onion to a mixing bowl and return strained oil to the pan. Add another 2 tablespoons of oil to the pan and slide in potato. Cover and cook over low heat for about 15 minutes, lifting the lid and moving potato around every 5 minutes with a wooden spoon. Check potato slices are tender and then tip them and their oil into the sieve again. Once potato has drained, add it to bowl with onion and set strained oil aside.

In a separate bowl, lightly whisk eggs to mix. Combine eggs, onion and potato and season well with salt and pepper.

Return pan to the heat and add strained oil to the pan; if necessary, add an extra tablespoon of oil to pan. Heat over high heat until quite hot. Carefully tip in egg/potato mixture; it should hiss and splutter very satisfactorily as it hits the hot oil. Immediately turn heat down to medium. Cook for 5 minutes or until you can see underside is becoming golden brown when lifted to inspect with a flexible egg lifter. The Spanish way is to turn the tortilla onto a plate, reheat the oil and then slip it back to cook the other side. (I suggest you slide the pan into a 200°C/Gas 6 oven or under a preheated griller to cook the top of the tortilla.) If you wish to have a go at the authentic Spanish method, use 2 dry tea towels to invert the tortilla onto a plate over a bench in case of a mishap; don't be surprised if a bit of liquid runs out. Carefully return tortilla to pan to cook the other side. Serve tortilla warm or at room temperature.

Potato, Ginger and Coriander Semolina Dosas

MAKES 8–10 I have long been fascinated by Indian breads and pancakes and have made several types. Dosas are traditionally cooked on a tawa – a flat griddle very similar to the hotplates used to make buckwheat pancakes in Brittany. The batter is pushed around the hot stone with a clever gadget to make the pancake thin with crispy edges. The semolina dosa recipe given here is a popular breakfast pancake in southern India. The batter is fast to prepare and the dosas simple to cook, once you have mastered the trick of spreading the batter effectively.

If you don't have time to make the dosas, the filling given here can be used to fill samosas (see page 472) or as a curry side dish. Alternatively, other savoury mixtures, such as the samosa filling on page 472 or a creative mix of leftover cooked vegetables, heated through with some chopped fresh chilli or a spicy sauce, can be used to fill these dosas.

EXTRA EQUIPMENT
mortar and pestle
food processor
plastic pastry
scraper

**POTATO, GINGER AND
  CORIANDER FILLING**
650g/1lb 7oz potatoes (about 4),
  quartered
salt
60ml/2fl oz vegetable oil
1 teaspoon black mustard seeds
2 onions, diced
1 fresh small green chilli, seeded
  and chopped
2 × 1cm/½in-long pieces ginger,
  finely chopped
½ teaspoon ground turmeric
2 tablespoons chopped coriander
160ml/5½fl oz water

SEMOLINA DOSAS
1 teaspoon cumin seeds
160g/5½oz fine semolina
90g/3oz rice flour
1 fresh long green chilli, seeded
  and roughly chopped
1 × 2cm/¾in-long piece ginger,
  grated
½ teaspoon bicarbonate of soda
1 teaspoon salt
600ml/1 pint buttermilk
80ml/3fl oz vegetable oil

For the filling, cook potato in a pan of lightly salted simmering water for 15–20 minutes or until tender. Drain, leave to cool and cut into 1cm/½in dice. Set aside. Heat oil in a large non-stick frying pan over medium heat. Add mustard seeds; they will pop after a few seconds. Stir in onion and cook for about 5 minutes, stirring from time to time, until translucent but not browned. Stir in chilli, ginger, turmeric and coriander and cook for 1 minute. Add potato and stir. Transfer to a large, heavy-based saucepan and add the water and salt to taste. Cook over medium heat, stirring often, for 10 minutes or until water has evaporated and mixture thickened. Transfer to a bowl and set aside. Warm just before serving.

To make the semolina dosas, dry-roast cumin seeds in a small frying pan over medium heat until fragrant. Tip into a mortar and grind to a fine powder

>>

with a pestle. Wipe out pan with paper towel. Process ground cumin, semolina, rice flour, chilli, ginger, bicarbonate of soda and salt in a food processor until chilli is very finely chopped through dry ingredients. With motor running, add buttermilk; stop machine halfway through processing and scrape down sides with a spatula. Transfer batter to a jug.

As semolina swells if left to stand, it is best to proceed with cooking the dosas at once (if you do need to delay, you may need to add 1–2 tablespoons water to thin the batter). It should be the consistency of yoghurt, not porridge.

Preheat oven to 100°C/Gas ¼ and put in an ovenproof plate to keep warm.

Heat a large non-stick frying pan over high heat. Reduce heat to medium and wipe pan with a smear of the vegetable oil. Fill a ladle with batter and tip into centre of pan. Immediately use a pastry scraper to smooth batter to a thin 20cm/8in round. Dribble oil around and over edges of pancake and cover pan with 24cm/9½in lid. After about 40 seconds, remove lid and use a flexible spatula to gently flip dosa to cook on other side, uncovered, for another 30–40 seconds, then lift pancake, roll it loosely and put onto warm plate. Cover with foil. Repeat this process with remaining oil and batter until you have cooked all the dosas.

Unroll pancakes, then fill with potato, ginger and coriander filling, fold over to enclose filling and enjoy.

Speedy Potatoes

If you have just 10 minutes to make a meal and want to use potatoes, just cut and cook them as follows. Potatoes cut into 1cm/½in-thick slices will cook in moments in a covered frying pan in a mix of melted butter and oil, maybe with some sliced mushrooms and a sliced onion. The same slices, even if cut a bit thicker, will steam in a few minutes, ready to be lightly tossed with chopped fresh herbs. Or for a complete meal, put slices on a baking paper-lined baking tray (not overlapping them) and add fillets of a not-too-thick fish (such as King George whiting or flathead), or tenderloins of skinless chicken, both brushed with butter or spread with a spice paste and scattered with herbs, then bake for 10 minutes in a 180°C/Gas 4 oven.

Moong Dal with Potato and Green Vegetables

SERVES 6–8 This is a very fancy dal. Served with a bowl of rice, it could be a complete meal. Alternatively, it would be a very delicious accompaniment to a meat or fish curry or alongside the Spiced Chicken and Rice with Mint on page 403. Like all dals it thickens on standing, so either make it and serve it straight away or reheat it gently in a bowl over a pan of hot water or in the microwave. Moong dal (or *mung dal*) is a small, husked all-yellow variety of pulse, actually a skinned split mung bean that in its unskinned form is green. Lentils are often known collectively as dals in many Indian books, but it is true that the dal recipes include split peas and some beans, as here. They are all readily obtainable from Indian food stores. The addition of green peppers is not traditional, but when I went to the garden to gather green leaves for this dish I did not have enough and there were plenty of crisp green peppers on the bushes. You can leave them out and make up the weight with extra green leaves if preferred.

EXTRA EQUIPMENT
speed peeler (see page 47)

200g/7oz moong dal (see page 704)
150g/5oz green leaves (spinach, rainbow chard, small silverbeet or beetroot leaves)
1 litre/1¾ pints water
80ml/3fl oz vegetable oil
1 onion, finely chopped
1 × 2cm/¾in-long piece ginger, finely chopped
100g/3½oz green peppers (optional), seeded, peeled (see page 487) and sliced

1 teaspoon cumin seeds
250g/9oz waxy potatoes, diced and placed in a bowl of cold water
½ teaspoon ground turmeric
1 fresh green chilli, seeded and thinly sliced
1 teaspoon salt
250g/9oz tinned chopped tomatoes, with juice

Soak dal in cold water for 15 minutes. Meanwhile, wash green leaves and cook them, covered, over medium heat in a small saucepan in water clinging to leaves. Once leaves collapse, tip into a colander and press to remove excess water, then coarsely chop and set aside.

Drain dal and transfer to a large heavy-based saucepan with the water. Bring to simmering point over high heat, then reduce heat to medium. Skim surface with a ladle and simmer gently for 20 minutes, stirring with a wooden spoon from time to time.

Heat oil in a large heavy-based frying pan over medium heat. Cook onion, ginger, green pepper (if using) and cumin seeds for 4–5 minutes, stirring. Add drained potato, turmeric, chilli, salt and tomato. Stir to mix well, then reduce heat to low and cook for 10 minutes.

Transfer onion mixture to saucepan of cooked dal. Mix and continue to cook over low heat, stirring frequently for 15 minutes or until potato is quite soft. Increase heat to evaporate excess liquid if necessary. Stir in reserved green leaves. Mix together and taste for salt, then season if desired and serve.

PUMPKINS

Cucurbitaceae family (includes cucumber, melons and zucchini) Annual

Soil type
Moist, well-drained soil enriched with organic matter.

Soil preparation
Plant after a legume crop or dig in well-rotted manure or organic matter a few weeks prior to planting.

Climate
Suitable for warmer areas; sensitive to frosts and cold.

Position
Prefer full sun and warmth.

How to grow
In April, sow seed in small pots in a heated propagator in a heated greenhouse or on an indoor windowsill, the seed needs 20°C to germinate. Grow on at 13–18°C and gradually harden-off (see page 692) young plants. Plant out once there is no danger of frost (usually mid May–

early June). Allow 1m between plants. Water the young plants in until they are growing away. Keep the ground weed-free until the vine is established.

Water requirements
If the weather is dry, water once the fruits start to swell, but don't water the vine stem or leaves.

When to fertilise
To improve growth, add liquid fertiliser (see page 691) when the first flower appears. Too much fertiliser improves vine growth at the expense of fruit development.

Harvest period
20 weeks after planting out.

Pests and organic control
Plants can get a virus that causes the foliage to develop a characteristic yellow mottling, there is no cure so pull up and destroy plants (do not compost). Slugs and mice can nibble the fruit skins and mould can then take hold.

Companion planting
Corn, marigolds, sunflowers to encourage bees; and nasturtiums and calendula as bait plants for aphids.

Special information
Keep the soil moist and free from weeds by mulching.

Quantities to plant for a family of four
4–6 vines.

Pumpkin (*Cucurbita maxima*)

Growing and Harvesting Pumpkins are such beautiful fruits. Some of the most dramatic pumpkins or winter squashes are not necessarily the best to eat but they are wonderful to grow because of their gorgeous shapes and colours. Happily, there are many cultivars, including several heirlooms, that are both beautiful and delicious. There are now cultivars available, such as 'Becky', that take up less space. As always, I recommend you check seed catalogues.

Pumpkin plants can grow to startling sizes. Unless there is unlimited space, train the vines over a high mound or a trellis, or up a strong fence. Growing on a mound is beneficial as it will ensure good drainage. The vines will need to be gently secured to the support when they are about 1 metre long. It always surprises me that the weight of a maturing pumpkin does not tear the vine from the fence. It is just as surprising that the heavy fruit does not drop from the vine!

During the hottest part of the day, the leaves will look wilted; this is not necessarily due to lack of water if the soil has been kept moist. Like us, pumpkins will wilt after a lot of sun and, like us, they revive once the day-time temperature drops. Place straw under developing fruit to reduce fruit rot, or allow the fruit to romp over randomly placed logs or preloved bits and pieces.

When harvesting pumpkins, ensure that you pick or cut them with at least 5 centimetres of stem still attached, otherwise insects can invade through the top and rot can set in. This is especially important if you are hoping to store the pumpkins for a few weeks. If this is the case, they must be fully mature and will need to be cured. Curing involves leaving the fruit in the sun in order to dry the skin for a week or so. In times gone by our grandparents would have kept stored pumpkins in a dry airy shed, or even on a bench outside the shed, and they would have expected them to last for months. A centrally heated house is not suitable for storing pumpkins, nor should they be stored in a damp cellar.

Pumpkins sometimes fail to set fruit. Pumpkins that fall off the vine during early development indicate poor pollination. To counter this, plant bee-attracting flowers in the garden, such as sunflowers, borage and lavender, and be prepared to hand-pollinate. Early in the morning, hand-pollinate the female flowers (the smaller flower with a round swelling behind it) by transferring pollen from the male flower (the one on the long stalk) using a paintbrush, or break off the male flower, bend back its petals and press it against a female flower. For best results, choose a female flower that is only partly opened. The Cucurbitaceae family provides a dramatic way to introduce concepts of fertilisation and reproduction to children. All members of the Cucurbitaceae family are incestuous if conditions permit. If seed-saving, plant your pumpkins well away from other family members (cucumber, melon and zucchini) to avoid cross-pollination.

Pinching out the growth tips will improve branching and encourage increased fruiting. Some pumpkins can be picked before they attain full size and this can assist the vine to produce more fruit. Vines that are overloaded will shed developing fruit.

Try to leave fruits on the plants for as long as possible so they can ripen fully. Frost will kill the plants and can damage fruits so harvest fruits beforehand.

Container Planting One pumpkin plant will grow well in a large container such as a half-wine barrel, as long as you dig plenty of organic matter into the soil before planting. The vine will spill over the sides and over anything in its path, so it is advantageous to place the barrel near a trellis, so you can lift and secure the growing vine. It is not unusual for a single pumpkin to produce more than 6 metres of vine.

Preparing and Sharing Whole pumpkins, with their different shapes, sizes and colours, can provide a beautiful autumn display on your harvest table or kitchen bench for at least several weeks. On many country farms, harvested pumpkins are stored for months in a cold, dry environment such as a garage or garden shed. If the area where you are keeping them is heated, the pumpkins will not last as long and may start to develop soft patches. It might be better to keep the display in the garden, but out of the rain.

Many pumpkins have edible skin (one of the best is butternut) and, after roasting, the skin becomes quite thin and has a deliciously nutty flavour. Pumpkin skin cooked in water is horrible, so if the pumpkin chunks are to be boiled or steamed they must be peeled first.

Pumpkins are very versatile, and can be eaten in sweet as well as savoury dishes. Pumpkins can be deep-fried as chips, roasted, sautéed, steamed, mashed, made into a gratin, used to make gnocchi and, of course, the 'soup of the day' on many menus is almost always pumpkin! In the United States, a sweet pie made from spiced puréed pumpkin is a mandatory offering for the Thanksgiving table (see page 514).

My favourite filled pasta is the classic specialty of Modena, *tortellini di zucca*. What makes this especially exciting is the combination of dry mashed pumpkin with parmesan and crushed almond-flavoured amaretti biscuits. These little tortellini are usually served with nut-brown butter and crisp sage – a flavour and texture combination that is as near to perfection as I have experienced. Roasted diced pumpkin can be mixed with chopped sautéed onion, toasted pine nuts and hot chunky pasta such as rigatoni, then drizzled with extra-virgin olive oil and seasoned with sea salt, freshly ground black pepper and grated nutmeg for a quick and satisfying meal.

Pumpkin flowers are as edible as those from zucchini plants and can be deep-fried dipped in batter just as for zucchini flowers (see page 678). The male flowers, which grow from central stems (as opposed to the female, which become the pumpkins in time), can be harvested after the vine has set sufficient fruit. The cleaned seeds from cut pumpkin can be roasted (see page 515) – another activity that will intrigue any children in the household.

I am grateful to a fine Italian cook for telling me that the growing tips, pinched off to stop the vine from growing (so its energy is diverted to the fruit), are a seasonal delicacy that can be dipped in batter and fried, just as one does with pumpkin or zucchini flowers. They are known as *cime di zucca* in Italian. The tips can also be included in a stir-fry or steamed with other quick-cooking green vegetables such as peas of all sorts.

I encourage you to consider growing spaghetti squash one season. Its spaghetti strand-like flesh definitely gives it 'wow' factor. To cook this squash, first pierce the ends with a skewer so the heat can reach the centre, then simmer in a saucepan of lightly salted water for about 25 minutes until the skin feels tender. Cut the spaghetti squash in half either widthways or lengthways, remove the seeds and then twirl the strands of flesh onto a hot serving plate. The strands can be mixed with homemade Pesto (see page 119) or a herb-flavoured butter such as the Parsley Butter on page 457.

Especially for Kids Pumpkins are difficult to cut safely. Children will need to be shown how to do this. An adult helper should make the very first cut to split open the pumpkin, then stay right alongside the young cook. The flat side of a chunk needs to be turned down on the chopping board and the peel removed in sections with a sharp, heavy knife.

Many children dislike pumpkin. I suspect this is because they have only experienced the soft, squashy texture of some varieties, often poorly drained, dished up as an orange lump on the side of their plate. This is a great shame as pumpkin can be so much more interesting than this. Ask children what they like or dislike about pumpkin and see if there are new words to be added to the kitchen vocabulary. Encourage children to think about the texture of food. Adjectives such as crusty, crunchy, chewy and slippery are all words to describe texture. Are they relevant in describing pumpkin? Will they also dislike pumpkin gnocchi or pumpkin scones? Or pumpkin chips or pumpkin pie? Try making some Pumpkin-filled Pasta (see opposite) and see if they find this marvellous dish appealing.

Young cooks and gardeners will love to roast pumpkin seeds (see page 515). The best seeds for this are not too big.

Pumpkin and Pumpkin Seed Tart

SERVES 6 Almost any cooked vegetable can be used to make this sort of open tart. The vegetable must be cooked first and drained well so as not to spoil the texture of the filling or crispness of the pastry. Another time, you could try carrot, silver beet or Jerusalem artichokes, cut into chunks, chopped or puréed. The chunks of brightly coloured pumpkin make this a very cheerful-looking tart. Pepitas, the inner pumpkin seed kernels, can be bought and used instead of the roasted pumpkin seeds. It is quite rich if made with cream and yet not sufficiently luscious if made with milk. I compromise and make it with half thickened cream and half milk, and always use the best free-range eggs.

2 tablespoons extra-virgin olive oil
1 onion, halved and sliced into half-moons
400g/14oz peeled and seeded pumpkin, cut into 1cm/½in cubes
1 teaspoon sea salt
2 tablespoons Roasted Pumpkin Seeds (see page 515) or pepitas (see page 705)
3 free-range eggs
2 free-range egg yolks
250ml/9fl oz milk

250ml/9fl oz thickened cream
50g/2oz grated parmesan
freshly grated nutmeg
freshly ground black pepper

BASIC SHORTCRUST PASTRY
240g/8½oz plain flour, plus extra for dusting
a pinch salt
180g/6⅓oz butter, chopped
60ml/2fl oz ice-cold water

EXTRA EQUIPMENT
food processor
20cm/8in tart tin with removable base
pastry weights

To make the shortcrust pastry, sift flour and salt into a food processor, then add butter. Pulse briefly to combine butter and flour until mixture looks like breadcrumbs. With motor running, add ice-cold water and process until mixture forms a rough ball. Lightly dust a workbench, then tip dough out and knead briefly. Wrap in plastic film and chill in the refrigerator for 20 minutes.

Remove pastry from refrigerator and dust workbench lightly with flour, then roll pastry to fit a 20cm/8in tart tin with removable base. Line tin with pastry, trimming edge with a small sharp knife. Cover with foil and place pastry weights (or dried chick peas) on foil. Chill in the refrigerator for 30 minutes.

Preheat oven to 200°C/Gas 6.

Blind-bake pastry for 20 minutes. Remove from oven, leave tart shell to cool for a few minutes, then remove pastry weights and foil. Reduce oven temperature to 170°C/Gas 3.

Heat olive oil in a large non-stick frying pan that has a lid over medium heat, then sauté onion for 5–8 minutes or until limp and starting to colour. Add pumpkin and salt and stir. Cover pan, reduce heat to low and cook for 10 minutes. Remove lid and test that pumpkin is tender, then increase heat to high and stir until pumpkin and onion have started to catch at the edges; the tart will taste better if there are a few caramelised bits. Tip pumpkin mixture into a mixing bowl and add roasted pumpkin seeds.

In another bowl, lightly whisk eggs and yolks together. Whisk in milk and cream just enough to mix. Tip in pumpkin and onion mixture and stir, then stir in two-thirds of the parmesan and the nutmeg. Taste and adjust seasoning with salt and pepper.

Put blind-baked tart shell on a baking tray and place it on the oven shelf. Carefully pour in filling, moving pumpkin around if necessary with a spoon or fork to ensure an even distribution. Sprinkle top with remaining parmesan.

Bake tart for 20–25 minutes or until just set. Remove tart tin on baking tray to a cake cooling rack and leave to cool a little before cutting. This tart is best served warm rather than hot.

Pumpkin-filled Pasta

SERVES 4 Steam 500g/1lb dry-fleshed pumpkin (butternut or kent), dry the chunks in a 150°C/Gas 2 oven for 15 minutes, then mash and mix with 20g/¾oz crushed amaretti biscuits, 20g/¾oz fresh breadcrumbs and a generous handful of grated parmesan. Season with freshly ground black pepper, a little sea salt and a grating of fresh nutmeg. Use to fill fresh pasta sheets cut into ravioli shapes and cook in batches in a large saucepan of boiling salted water for 6 minutes, then remove with a slotted spoon, or fill and roll squares of cooked thin pasta into cannelloni. Brush the filled pasta with butter and bake, covered, until heated through.

Pumpkin, Coconut and Seafood Soup

SERVES 4 This is a very speedily made soup. By separately poaching or steaming a generous piece of chunky fish or pan-searing some fat scallops (or both), this soup can become a one-dish dinner. The soup contains shrimp paste, also known as blachan, and fish sauce. Both ingredients are available in most large supermarkets and in all Asian grocery stores. The strength of flavour varies, depending on the brand. Add the amount suggested and then add more if you want greater pungency.

400g/14oz peeled and seeded
    pumpkin, cut into 1cm/½in-
    thick slices
1 tablespoon vegetable oil
1 onion, finely chopped
4 cloves garlic, finely chopped
1 fresh long green or red chilli,
    seeded and chopped
2 teaspoons shrimp paste
    (see page 706)
750ml/27fl oz water

2 teaspoons fish sauce
200ml/7fl oz coconut milk
8 scallops and/or 1 × 400g/14oz
    thick fillet of white fish, such as
    barramundi, hapuka or blue eye
    trevalla, cut into bite-sized pieces
1 × 2cm/¾in-long piece ginger, very
    finely chopped or grated
¼ small handful roughly chopped
    coriander

EXTRA EQUIPMENT
wok
bamboo steamer
   with lid
enamelled cast-iron
   or other heavy-
   based casserole
blender or food
   processor

Half-fill a wok with water, place bamboo steamer in position, and when water boils, drop in pumpkin pieces in a single layer and steam, covered, for 10 minutes, then check. If tender, transfer to a plate, otherwise steam until tender.

Heat oil in an enamelled cast-iron casserole over medium heat and sauté onion, garlic and chilli for 8–10 minutes or until onion is well softened. Stir in shrimp paste and then add pumpkin, water and fish sauce. Bring to a simmer over high heat and simmer for 3 minutes.

Transfer soup in batches to a blender (or food processor) and cover blender lid with a thick dry tea towel; hot liquids can force up the lid, spraying hot liquid that can burn. Carefully blend until smooth. Tip each batch into a bowl. Continue until all soup is smoothly blended. Rinse out saucepan and return soup to the pan. Add coconut milk. Bring to a simmer over medium heat and taste for salt and pungency, then adjust with more salt or fish sauce if desired. Set aside.

Sear scallops in a non-stick frying pan over high heat for 1 minute on each side. If using fish, half-fill wok with water, place bamboo steamer in position, and when water boils, place fish in a single layer and steam, covered, for 5–8 minutes, then check. It should be cooked through (if not, continue cooking until it is).

Reheat soup and stir in ginger and coriander. Transfer scallops and/or fish to hot soup. Ladle into warmed soup bowls and serve at once.

Pumpkin Hotcakes

MAKES ABOUT 16 These delicious little hotcakes will convert many pumpkin haters to pumpkin lovers. They have irresistible crisp edges and tender middles, and are a sunny golden colour. They are marvellous with maple syrup or can be served with breakfast eggs in any form, with grilled tomatoes and with crisp bacon. Or try them just by themselves topped with a small dollop of sour cream and a generous sprinkling of chopped chives. Leftovers can be gently reheated the next day in a non-stick frying pan with a brush of extra-virgin olive oil.

300g/10½oz peeled and seeded
    pumpkin, cut into 1cm/½in-
    thick slices
125ml/4½fl oz buttermilk
30g/1oz butter, melted

1 free-range egg
115g/4oz plain flour
½ teaspoon bicarbonate of soda
¼ teaspoon salt
vegetable oil, for pan-frying

EXTRA EQUIPMENT
wok
bamboo steamer
    with lid
food processor

Half-fill a wok with water, place bamboo steamer in position, and when water boils, drop in pumpkin in a single layer and steam, covered, for 10 minutes, then check. If tender, transfer to a plate until needed, otherwise steam until tender. Process pumpkin in a food processor to form a smooth purée. Transfer to a measuring cup; you should have about 250ml/9fl oz purée.

Tip purée into a mixing bowl. Stir in buttermilk and butter. Whisk in egg. Sift flour, bicarbonate of soda and salt into another bowl. Gradually whisk flour mixture into pumpkin mixture.

Heat a film of vegetable oil in a large non-stick frying pan over medium heat. Working in batches, cook tablespoonfuls of pumpkin batter for 3 minutes; little bubbles will form on the tops. Flip to cook other sides. Add a little more oil to the pan if necessary. Serve the hotcakes at once.

New England Pumpkin Pie

SERVES 6–8 Blind-bake a 20cm/8in pastry shell (see page 510). Make the pumpkin purée in the recipe above, then put it into a bowl. You will need approximately 250–375ml/9–13fl oz pumpkin purée to fill a tart shell of this size. Put pumpkin purée into a bowl. For each 250ml/9fl oz pumpkin purée add 40g/1½oz melted butter, 75g/2½oz white sugar, 80ml/3fl oz maple syrup, 1 teaspoon ground cinnamon and ½ teaspoon grated nutmeg. In a separate bowl, whisk 2 free-range egg yolks with 80ml/3fl oz milk and 2 tablespoons cream, then mix with pumpkin mixture. Using hand-held electric beaters, whisk egg whites to form soft peaks and fold in. Pour filling into prepared pastry shell and bake for about 35 minutes. Serve warm with a bowl of cream whipped with a little maple syrup.

Roasted Pumpkin Seeds

MAKE AS MANY AS YOU LIKE Roasted pumpkin seeds, also called pepitas, are addictive. Children will love to make this and may never yearn for a potato crisp again after trying them! The most delicious roasted seeds are from varieties where each seed is quite small, such as a jap (also known as kent) pumpkin. If you start with big pumpkin seeds, the outer casing remains a bit too hard for pleasant munching. The inner kernels will still be delicious, but they are very fiddly to extract. I have suggested two different spice mixtures for the final sprinkling.

EXTRA EQUIPMENT
large metal spoon
mortar and pestle

a chunk pumpkin (with small seeds
   for preference)
extra-virgin olive oil

MIDDLE EASTERN SPICED SALT
2 teaspoons coriander seeds
½ teaspoon cumin seeds
1 teaspoon sea salt

SPANISH SPICED SALT
1 teaspoon sweet paprika
1½ teaspoons sea salt

Using a large metal spoon, gouge out pulp and seeds from pumpkin. Tease seeds away from stringy pulp and drop seeds into a small saucepan; discarded pulp goes into the compost bucket. (The pulp and seeds can be saved over a few days as long as it is kept covered and refrigerated. But as with everything from the garden, freshest is best.)

Preheat oven to 180°C/Gas 4.

Cover the seeds generously with cold water and bring to the simmer, then simmer over low heat for 10 minutes. Drain seeds in a sieve and transfer to a dry tea towel. Rub them dry; they will be quite clean.

Put a little olive oil in a bowl and turn seeds in the oil. Spread seeds on a baking tray and bake for 15–20 minutes.

To make the Middle Eastern spiced salt, dry-roast coriander and cumin seeds separately in a small frying pan over medium heat until fragrant. Tip seeds into a mortar, then add salt and grind to a fine powder with the pestle.

To make the Spanish spiced salt, mix paprika and sea salt in a small bowl.

Remove the baking tray from oven and tip roasted seeds into a bowl. Spoon over some of your selected spice mix. Shake to mix and then cool. These seeds are very delicious warm but are also good cold. Although they can be stored for a day or so I think it is more fun to prepare and serve them as quickly as possible. Any excess spiced salt mixture can be stored in an airtight container and used for other dishes.

Sweet-and-sour Pumpkin with Mint

SERVES 4 Use a dry-fleshed pumpkin such as a green-and-yellow-splashed jap or kent for this dish to make sure the slices don't break up when sautéing. The texture is best if eaten within a few hours of cooking. If intended as part of an antipasti platter, don't refrigerate it. If it is to be used to top a pizza (see below), then the finished pumpkin can be stored, covered, in the refrigerator for one to two days. This recipe is based on one in the excellent book *Verdura: Vegetables Italian Style* by Viana La Place, a treasure-house of marvellous vegetable dishes.

2 tablespoons extra-virgin olive oil
2 cloves garlic, unpeeled
  and bruised
250g/9oz peeled and seeded
  pumpkin, cut into
  5mm/¼in-thick slices

1 tablespoon caster sugar
2 tablespoons red-wine vinegar
sea salt and freshly ground
  black pepper
12 mint leaves, torn
  or roughly chopped

Heat olive oil in a large non-stick frying pan over low heat, drop in garlic cloves and sauté for 5 minutes or until golden. Discard garlic. Carefully arrange pumpkin slices in a single layer in the pan. Increase heat to low–medium and cook for 2–3 minutes. Turn pumpkin carefully and cook for a further 2–3 minutes on the other side; the slices should be well coloured and cooked through when inserted with a skewer. Lift pumpkin from pan and place in a single layer on a plate.

Discard any oil in the pan, then place over high heat. Tip in sugar and vinegar, then swirl to dissolve sugar and slightly reduce vinegar. Spoon vinegar syrup over pumpkin slices and season with salt and pepper. Scatter with mint.

Leave at room temperature for at least 1 hour before eating.

Sweet-and-sour Pumpkin and Sage Pizza

SERVES 4 Make a simple pizza dough by combining 200g/7oz plain flour and 1 teaspoon salt with 2 teaspoons instant dry yeast in the bowl of an electric mixer. Mix 1 tablespoon olive oil with 125ml/4½fl oz warm water and beat into dry ingredients until smooth and elastic. Cover dough with a dry cloth and leave for about 1½ hours or until doubled in size. Knock back dough, shape into a ball and allow to rise again. After about 30 minutes, roll on a floured workbench to form a thin 26cm/10in round and transfer to a floured pizza tray. Top with sweet-and-sour pumpkin slices (see above), then dot with 2–3 tablespoons goat's cheese or fresh mozzarella (see page 704). Scatter over fresh sage leaves and drizzle with extra-virgin olive oil before baking in a 220°C/Gas 7 oven for 15 minutes or until crisp at the edges and the cheese is bubbling.

RADISHES

Brassicaceae family (includes broccoli, cabbage, cauliflower, cresses and turnips)
Annual

Soil type
Well-drained, light soil.

Soil preparation
As long as the soil is well drained and rich in organic matter, no additional preparation is required.

Climate
Suitable for all climates.

Position
Sunny or partially shaded.

How to grow
Summer radish are small and grow quickly, they need to be sown little and often as if they get too big they are woody. Winter radish is a larger root, usually sown once and harvested in the autumn. Sow summer radish from March to August. Sow direct into weed-free ground at 5mm deep, sow thinly and leave 15cm between rows.

Thin seedlings out to 3cm. Keep plants well watered and the ground well weeded. Sow winter radish from July, 1mm deep, in rows 25cm apart. Thin seedlings to 15cm. Harvest in October.

Water requirements
Water frequently to encourage rapid growth and prevent woodiness.

Successive planting
Leave about 2–3 weeks between each planting, throughout the growing season.

When to fertilise
While plants are at the seedling stage, use a liquid fertiliser (see page 691) weekly.

Harvest period
4–6 weeks after planting summer radish; 12 weeks for winter radish.

Pests and organic control
Summer radish rarely suffer pest problems apart from flea beetle, this peppers the leaves with small holes. Use a crop

cover of fleece or fine netting to keep them off the leaves. Winter radish is prone to cabbage root fly, again a crop cover of fine netting will prevent the flies getting access. Winter radish is prone to clubroot, a serious soil disease where the plant wilts and the roots are swollen and disorted, pull up and destroy affected plants (do not compost). Crop rotation is important for both types of radish.

Companion planting
Peas, nasturtiums, lettuce, carrots, kohlrabi, onions, cucumbers and spinach. Don't plant near tomatoes, grapes, cabbages or cauliflowers.

Quantities to plant for a family of four
20 plants every 2 weeks, throughout the growing season.

Growing and Harvesting Because radishes are such speedy growers, their seeds are often mixed with beetroot or carrot seeds to act as row-markers for the slower growing vegetables. They are pulled long before the carrots or beetroot need the space. Radishes use little space, so planting them among other crops that can provide shade and have the same water requirements will ensure a good crop. And don't think you have to plant them in rows – why not a spiral or a circle? One of the Kitchen Garden Program schools planted radishes so that the plants spelt out a welcome message to visitors. My radishes grow near my main supply of salad leaves, which provide filtered shade. As I pull one row, I start another in a different part of the garden bed.

Summer radishes are round or long and narrow; red, white or pink-and-white striped. Best in spring and early summer, radishes should feel solid and firm and be crisp and crunchy. Pull them before they are too big, when they can become very spicy and also 'cottony'. If you have overlooked some plants and they have flowered, leave them where they are, as they are said to attract beneficial insects to the garden.

There are many types of radish, including the large group of Winter radishes, of which white daikon is the most familiar. These are much slower growing, taking months to mature, and are not commonly grown in home gardens. However, their constant presence in Asian markets indicates that they are grown in quantity by market gardeners specialising in Asian vegetables. Other names for white daikon are Japanese radish, *lo baak* and *lo bok*.

Container Planting Radishes grow very successfully in containers. They are ideal for growing in a pot or tub with other salad plants or root vegetables as mentioned above, or with potatoes. The radishes will be ready for harvesting before the other plants or, in the case of potatoes, before you need to start earthing up the potato plants with mulch or extra soil.

Preparing and Sharing As a Francophile I admit to a preference for the pink-and-white 'French Breakfast' cultivar (see opposite) that I have long enjoyed served in the French manner with a tiny dab of unsalted butter and flakes of sea salt, or as the Italians do, with a drop of extra-virgin olive oil and sea salt. But truthfully, their flavour is indistinguishable from that of any round red summer radish. To make this French treat, a deep cross is cut in the non-stalk end of a radish. The radishes are put into water for about one hour, by which stage they will have opened up. A tiny piece of softened unsalted butter is forced into the opening and the radishes can be assembled on a plate with a small saucer of sea salt. Yum!

This combination of radish, butter and sea salt can be enjoyed as a sandwich. It offers the same appeal and crunch of a cucumber sandwich, another of my favourites. Thinly slice the radishes with a plastic vegetable slicer (see page 46) or very carefully with a knife. Thickly butter some wholegrain bread and cover with a pattern of overlapping radish slices. Sprinkle on a very little salt and either top with a second slice of buttered bread, or cut the open sandwich into triangles or squares to offer as a savoury or serve alongside freshly shucked oysters.

The crisp crunch of quickly grown radishes is a delightful addition to any salad, or to accompany any picnic meats or terrines. Radishes grown speedily are never too peppery or hot.

Most radish lovers don't eat the leaves, but I do. Radish tops can be included in small quantities in a salad to add punch and a peppery bite. They can also be quickly stir-fried or added to a soup such as the Spring Kitchen Garden Soup on page 473. Don't use any yellow, wilted or very large and coarse leaves.

Japanese cooks sometimes push a whole red chilli into the flesh of a large white daikon. They then grate this section with a box grater, resulting in fiery red-and-white gratings that are used as a relish or dip alongside seafood or sushi rolls. Fun to do but be careful with quantities! Thin slices of daikon can be 'sandwiched' with slices of sashimi-grade raw or smoked fish, or pesto (see page 119) or other herb-based (or vegetable) spreads for a surprising snack.

Especially for Kids Radishes are especially popular as a crop to grow with young children as they reward the young gardener's efforts with quick results. They germinate within three to five days and have a brief growing season of twenty to thirty days.

Even though you may not choose to grow the Asian white daikon at home it can be interesting to buy one to display alongside garden-grown radishes – a bit like David and Goliath. Flavour and texture can be compared and commented upon.

There are inexpensive daikon graters available from Asian kitchenware shops that enable you to pare fine strings of daikon (or carrot) by turning the handle. Children will *love* to do this and the grated vegetables can be used in rice-paper rolls, dipping sauces and salads.

'French Breakfast' radishes

Radish, Orange and Fennel Salad

SERVES 4 AS A SIDE DISH This is a super-crunchy salad, perfect to serve alongside plainly grilled fish. The slicing blade of most food processors does an excellent job of slicing radishes safely, although some cooks might prefer to use a plastic vegetable slicer (see page 47). They should never be used by a young cook without the closest supervision.

EXTRA EQUIPMENT
food processor with
  slicing attachment
  or plastic
  vegetable slicer
  (see page 47)
salad spinner

a handful of ice cubes
1 small bulb fennel, trimmed
  of any damaged outer leaves
  and halved lengthways
12 radishes, washed, dried
  and trimmed

2 oranges
2 handfuls rocket leaves, trimmed,
  washed and dried
sea salt and freshly ground black pepper
1 tablespoon extra-virgin olive oil
1 teaspoon red-wine vinegar

Put ice cubes in a bowl with a small amount of water. Slice fennel bulb halves in a food processor with the slicing attachment. Drop fennel slices into iced water for 3–4 minutes only. Lift crisped fennel from iced water, spin dry in a salad spinner, then wrap in a paper towel-lined tea towel and store in the refrigerator until needed.

Slice radishes in the food processor with the slicing attachment, then transfer to a mixing bowl.

Carve the skin from the oranges with a small serrated knife or paring knife, removing all white pith. Holding peeled orange over radish bowl, proceed to separate segments of flesh from membrane by slipping the knife down one side of a single segment and then down the other side of the segment to release it. Allow each piece of orange to fall into the mixing bowl. When all segments are removed, squeeze orange 'skeletons' so that juice falls into bowl.

Add rocket and fennel to bowl with radish and orange and mix, then season to taste with salt and pepper. Drizzle over olive oil and vinegar, then pile onto plates and serve.

Radish with Raw Tuna

SERVES 4 AS A STARTER This combination was inspired by a meal I enjoyed at the Melbourne restaurant Attica created by chef Ben Shewry. My version is far less intricate but still has the wonderful textural contrast of soft and melting (the tuna) with crunchy (the radish), as well as interesting and appropriate accompaniments. Either drizzle the sauce over the tuna just before serving or divide it between tiny Asian sauce bowls for dipping the tuna in with chopsticks.

a handful coriander sprigs

a few ice cubes

12 radishes, washed, dried and
   trimmed

1 × 200g/7oz piece sashimi-grade
   tuna

½ teaspoon sesame seeds (optional)

8 small slices pickled ginger (see
   page 705)

SAUCE

2 tablespoons peanut oil

½ onion, thinly sliced into
   half-moons

2 tablespoons rice vinegar

2 tablespoons light soy sauce

1 tablespoon mirin (see page 704)

1 tablespoon white sugar

EXTRA EQUIPMENT

fine-meshed sieve

salad spinner

food processor
   with grating
   attachment or
   a box grater

To make the sauce, heat peanut oil in a small frying pan and cook onion over lowest heat very gently for 10 minutes or until onion is crisp and a deep golden brown. Drain onion in a fine-meshed sieve over a bowl. Set onion aside until you wish to serve and reserve onion oil. Add reserved onion oil, vinegar, soy, mirin and sugar to a small saucepan and bring to the boil over high heat, stirring to ensure sugar has dissolved. Tip into a small container and chill. The sauce will keep for up to 1 week in the refrigerator.

Drop coriander sprigs into a bowl with a little cold water and ice cubes. Leave for 3–4 minutes, then gently dry in a salad spinner, wrap in a paper towel-lined tea towel, then store in the refrigerator until needed.

Grate radish coarsely in a food processor with a grating attachment (or use a box grater) and refrigerate (don't grate unless you are going to serve in the next hour as otherwise the radish will start to ooze juices and become rather limp).

With a clean, very sharp knife, cut tuna into 1cm/½in-thick strips.

On each of 4 chilled plates or shallow bowls, place a pile of grated radish. Place tuna strips on top of radish, then spoon over some of the sauce, if desired. Scatter over sesame seeds, if using, crisped onion and coriander sprigs, and place a little pickled ginger on the side of each plate or bowl. Serve at once with a bowl of the sauce to the side for dipping.

RASPBERRIES

Rosaceae family (includes apples, pears, quinces and strawberries)
Deciduous perennial, can live for up to 10 years

Soil type
Well-drained, fertile soil enriched with organic matter. Better on a neutral or slightly acid soil.

Soil preparation
Prepare beds a few weeks ahead by digging in well-rotted organic matter such as garden compost. Summer-fruiting raspberries will need a row of post and wire supports put in to tie the cane to.

Climate
Suitable for all areas.

Position
Prefers sun and an open but sheltered site.

How to grow
Buy bare-rooted canes in the dormant season (October–February). Plant summer-fruiting ones along a row of wires, leave 1.8–2m between rows. Autumn-fruiting ones do not usually need support, leave 1–1.5m between rows. Water in plants, tie the canes to the wires with soft ties. Cover with netting or grow in a fruit cage to stop fruit getting eaten.

Water requirements
Water in dry spells to keep soil moist but not waterlogged.

When to fertilise
Raspberries are heavy feeders so sprinkle an organic general purpose feed on the soil surface in spring and water in.

Harvest period
The summer-fruiting varieties crop from end June to July, the autumn fruiting ones sometimes start end July and go on until October or the first frosts.

Pests and organic control
Birds are the main pests as they take the fruit, netting the crop or growing fruit in a walk in netted fruit cage is an essential precaution. Raspberries are a long-lived crop but they can suffer from various diseases such as viruses (spread by aphids), cane blight and cane spot – all are serious and there is no cure apart from to dig up and start again on new ground. Yellowing leaves are usually because the soil is too alkaline, apply sulphur chips in spring.

Special information
An annual mulch in spring will keep weeds down and help to conserve moisture. Prune each year (see overleaf).

Quantities to plant for a family of four
At least 3 canes of each type.

Raspberry (*Rubus idaeus*)

Growing and Harvesting   Sadly I have never had enough space at home to grow raspberries, but in several of the Kitchen Garden Program schools, the raspberry patch has proved to be a very popular place for students to forage.

Raspberries are truly one of the most glorious fruits. Such soft texture, such perfumed flesh and what an exquisite colour! I have a nameless and very thorny rose bush that blooms in my front garden and it has petals that are the exact colour of bruised raspberries that have faded to the colour of a piece of old silk. Passers-by have been known to knock at the door and ask its name. Perhaps because of my infatuation with the colour of a ripe raspberry I am not that excited by the lesser-known golden and black cultivars. They do not spill their glorious juice in the same way.

Raspberries that fruit only in summer and those that fruit in both summer and autumn are known as floricanes. Cultivars that only fruit in autumn are known as primocanes. If you are growing a mix of cultivars, keep them separate, as their pruning needs can be quite different. Raspberries at the top of the branch ripen first, and the fattest, sweetest berries are those that hide deep in the bushes where you are sure to get the most scratches!

Raspberries need to be pruned each year, and how you do so depends on when they fruit. Summer-fruiting cultivars: In winter, remove all the canes that fruited during summer; they will look dead. The canes that are left behind will have grown during the summer and will not have fruited. Of these you should remove any weak or small canes then tie up the remainder 45cm apart onto the wire supports. Autumn-fruiting cultivars: All canes should be removed absolutely flush to the ground in winter (February). All raspberries can throw up suckers some way from the plant. Dig these out or the raspberries will take over the plot.

Container Planting   Raspberries are not suitable for container planting.

Preparing and Sharing   All the same ideas apply for raspberries as **STRAWBERRIES**. Raspberries are very delicate and must be handled as little as possible and if necessary, only stored very briefly in a single layer on a paper-towel-lined plate. One mouldy raspberry will easily taint the rest. Should you ever find yourself with a glut, raspberries freeze perfectly.

Especially for Kids   If you are often away during the Summer holiday period, it may be worth selecting a raspberry variety that will crop in autumn, so you are there to enjoy its bounty.

Raspberry Muffins

MAKES 12 This simple recipe is a great way of using up any raspberries that make it into the kitchen rather than being eaten straight from the canes. When raspberries aren't available, it is equally delicious when made with mashed banana or cooked apple instead.

EXTRA EQUIPMENT
12 paper cupcake cases (optional)
1 × 12-hole muffin tin

20g/¾oz butter, melted (optional)
220g/8oz self-raising flour
110g/3¾oz caster sugar
180ml/6fl oz buttermilk

1 free-range egg
180ml/6fl oz vegetable oil
100g/3½oz raspberries

Preheat oven to 180°C/Gas 4.

If using paper cupcake cases, drop into holes of muffin tin. Otherwise, grease holes with melted butter.

Sift flour into a large bowl, add sugar and mix. Put buttermilk, egg and oil in another bowl and whisk to mix well, then stir in raspberries. Make a well in flour mixture, then pour in egg mixture. Stir lightly until just mixed but do not over-mix or the muffins will become tough.

Divide mixture among holes, filling each one just over two-thirds full. Bake muffins for 20–25 minutes or until firm and golden brown. Cool muffins for a few minutes in the tin, then turn out onto a cake cooling rack to cool further.

Honey Wafers with Bruised Raspberries

SERVES 6 This very fancy dessert is really child's play to assemble – the wafers take a minute to make and just a few minutes to cook, not to mention they are crunchy and delicious! You could also crush other berries into the cream or use stoned and diced ripe peaches instead.

EXTRA EQUIPMENT
food processor
9cm/3½in biscuit cutter
flexible spatula
hand-held electric beaters

150g/5oz butter, softened
240g/8½oz caster sugar
125ml/4½fl oz honey
120g/4oz plain flour, sifted
1 teaspoon ground ginger

2 free-range egg whites
500ml/18fl oz thickened cream
500g/1lb raspberries
grated zest of 1 lime
icing sugar, to serve

Preheat oven to 180°C/Gas 4.

Cream butter and sugar in a food processor. With motor running, add honey, flour, ginger and egg whites and blend until a smooth, spreadable paste forms.

>>>

Line 2 baking trays with baking paper, then use a 9cm/3½in biscuit cutter to trace 18 rounds well apart. Spread batter on the rounds, using the back of a spoon to smooth. Bake for 7–8 minutes or until golden brown. Cool wafers on trays for 1 minute, then use a flexible spatula to transfer to a cake cooling rack and leave to cool completely.

Meanwhile, whip cream with hand-held electric beaters to form soft peaks. Add half of the raspberries, then whip to form firm peaks; the berries will be crushed and turn the cream pink. Fold in lime zest.

Place a tiny dob of cream on each of 6 serving plates to hold wafers in place, then put a wafer on top of each dob of cream. Add a generous spoonful of cream and some of the remaining raspberries, then top with another wafer and repeat with more cream and raspberries, finishing the layering with a final wafer on top of each one. Dust with icing sugar and serve at once.

Berry Crumbles

SERVES 4 There is something very special about the deep crimson juice from raspberries. This crumble is one of my favourite dishes. Try it with blackberries and mulberries too. It deserves being served with the very best cream.

50g/2oz unsalted butter
400g/14oz raspberries (or
  mulberries or blackberries or
  a mixture)
75g/2½oz caster sugar
double or clotted cream, to serve

CRUMBLE TOPPING
60g/2oz soft brown sugar
1 teaspoon baking powder
1 teaspoon ground ginger
60g/2oz unsalted butter, chopped
100g/3½oz plain flour

EXTRA EQUIPMENT
4 × 125ml/4½fl oz-
  capacity individual
  gratin dishes

Preheat oven to 200°C/Gas 6.

To make the crumble topping, mix sugar, baking powder and ginger in a bowl. In another bowl, crumble butter into flour with your fingertips to make pea-sized pieces, then toss flour mixture with sugar mixture. Set aside.

Use some of the butter to grease four 125ml/4½fl oz-capacity gratin dishes. Divide berries among dishes. Press them down lightly with the back of a spoon. Scatter over sugar. Spoon over crumble topping; it should be no more than 1cm/½in deep (any extra crumble topping can be put into a suitable container, labelled and frozen, ready for a crumble some other day). Divide remaining butter into small pieces and dot over tops of crumbles. Set dishes on a baking tray with a lip to catch any overflowing juices.

Bake crumbles for 15 minutes or until topping is golden and berry juices are bubbling through. Leave crumbles to cool for several minutes before serving with spoonfuls of double or clotted cream.

RHUBARB

**Polygonaceae family
(includes sorrel)
Herbaceous perennial**

Soil type
Adaptable to most soils, but prefers moist, well-drained soil enriched with organic matter.

Soil preparation
Prepare with plenty of organic matter and well-rotted manure.

Climate
Suitable for all climates.

Position
Prefers full sun, but will tolerate partial shade.

How to grow
Buy crowns that can be planted during winter. Dig a hole 25cm wide and 30cm deep, making sure there is enough room for the roots to spread, and cover the crown with soil. Maintain a space of 1m between plants. Ensure the crown is just below the surface.

Water requirements
Water regularly.

When to fertilise
Use a liquid fertiliser (see page 691) every 4 weeks.

Harvest period
Don't harvest more than 50 per cent of the plant while it is young; this will allow the plant to develop a strong crown. Start harvesting in March but stop by July. Rhubarb can be blanched (see overleaf).

Pests and organic control
Few, although the crown can rot and the stems fail to grow. There is no cure. Destroy affected plants.

Companion planting
Rhubarb can be planted among border plants but as a perennial it is best kept out of crop rotation beds.

Special information
Keep the soil moist and free from weeds by mulching. Plants can be divided into new crowns and replanted during winter. Remove flowering stems as they appear and enjoy their beauty in a vase. The stems are edible but the leaves are too poisonous to eat.

**Quantities to plant
for a family of four**
2 plants.

Rhubarb (*Rheum rhabarbarum*)

Growing and Harvesting Rhubarb is a handsome plant in the garden, where it can be planted randomly, offering shade to smaller and more delicate plants nearby. It grows from crowns planted just under the surface of very well-prepared soil. The crowns accumulate nutrients through the winter. When the weather is favourable in spring, the leaves and a major harvest of stalks will shoot in a new plant or re-shoot in well-established plants.

After a cold winter, rhubarb is the first crop from the kitchen garden that can be eaten as a dessert. Uncovered stems are ready for harvesting around March but there are a two techniques that can bring stems on earlier in the year and make them even more tender and pink. The easiest is to blanch (see page 687) the stems by depriving them of light. Cover established clumps in December-January with a clean plastic dustbin or a terracotta forcing pot. A few weeks later, long stems with yellow leaves will appear. Harvest these until March, then uncover the plant and let it regain its natural growth. The second technique known as forcing, involves lifting the rhubarb from the ground and bringing it into a warm, dark place. Dig up an established crown in November and leave it on the ground for two weeks until the temperature has dropped below 10°C. Pack the roots into boxes or pots of moist potting compost and store somewhere dark and cool but frost-free. The sticks should be ready to pull five weeks later. Discard the crown after harvesting.

Remind young gardeners to harvest stalks of rhubarb with a twisting action rather than by pulling at the stalks. Unless the plant is very well established, pulling a stalk risks dislodging the whole plant, whereas a twist of a stalk and a slight tug will leave the plant unscathed and able to continue growing without too much of a shock. For the first harvest of a young plant it may be better to cut the stalks with a knife. To ensure that growth continues, don't harvest more than half of the stems. Spring stalks will be more tender than those harvested in summer, and stalks harvested in a drought year will also be less succulent.

There seems to be confusion as to what causes rhubarb leaves to be poisonous. Oxalic acid is usually cited as the culprit. Scientist Harold McGee in *On Food and Cooking: The Science and Lore of the Kitchen* claims that the edible stalks also contain significant quantities of this acid and that the leaf toxin is unknown. *The New Oxford Book of Food Plants* declares that the problem is a combination of a high concentration of oxalic acid and anthraquinone (an organic compound that is the basis for many natural plant pigments). Whatever it is, children need to be told not to eat the rhubarb leaves. The leaves can quite happily be added to the compost heap, however.

Although rhubarb is a perennial plant, you should divide old crowns after several years. Some gardeners insist on removing the flowering heads of rhubarb, believing they weaken the plants. Others leave them or pick them because they are highly decorative, and these gardeners claim there is no difference in the strength of their plants afterwards.

Container Planting A single rhubarb plant will do quite well in a large pot as long as its basic needs are catered for. Plant it in good soil with plenty of organic matter dug in, keep it moist at all times, and fertilise every four weeks.

Preparing and Sharing Once again, here's a reminder that the leaves of the rhubarb plant are poisonous. Cut them away and consign to the compost. Depending on personal taste, rhubarb stalks can be sliced into 3 centimetre lengths and strewn with sugar (raw or brown for preference), left overnight at room temperature for the juices to run and then baked, covered, in a 160°C/Gas 3 oven without any extra liquid. Alternatively, rhubarb can be sliced and cooked with sugar and a few spoonfuls of water quite quickly on the stovetop over medium heat and using a simmer mat to prevent sticking. Be careful as this method needs stirring – you need to watch it, as it can stick. The first method produces pieces of rhubarb, the second a rough purée. When you have a supply of your own home-grown rhubarb, why not try it both ways and see which you prefer? Pieces are prettier for breakfast, but a purée is better if intending to make ice cream. Either way works well when combined with cooked apple chunks in a crumble. Remember too – always cook rhubarb in stainless-steel pans.

The addition of a rose-scented geranium leaf to the pan adds an intriguing perfume to rhubarb. Cooled rhubarb purée can be mixed with whipped cream to make a fool or stirred into a vanilla custard and churned in an ice cream machine to make a delicious ice cream.

Rhubarb combines very well with other fruit. In summer, combine it with strawberries or raspberries; in autumn with apples and figs; and in winter with oranges and dried fruits.

Especially for Kids When I was a child I was never told that rhubarb was good for me, so I grew up loving it. There is a lesson here about not presenting food to children as 'good for you' or 'not good for you'. Children's tastebuds are as individual as any other part of their personality and it is a great shame when parents insist on saying things like, 'Darling, you won't like this.' How do they know what 'Darling' will or will not like? Palates change and develop. As long as there is no negative connotation attached to a food, a child is much more likely to try it again sometime.

However, the tartness of rhubarb can be a shock to some children. When you combine it with other fruit, sugar, butter and nuts in a pie or tart such as the Rhubarb and Strawberry Freeform Tart on page 536 it usually proves to be a winner. If you grow angelica in your garden, a leaf or two cooked with rhubarb will lessen its acidity.

Because of the poisonous nature of the leaves, some of the participating schools in the Kitchen Garden Program prefer not to grow rhubarb in their kitchen gardens, and you may choose not to at home for the same reason. While I respect this decision, I believe that once children are over a certain age, they are well able to understand and be suitably alarmed at the idea of becoming seriously ill and will not wish to eat the leaves of this plant. My own rather laissez-faire approach to this is that in most instances children will not persist with eating anything that tastes nasty or bitter. I can't think of any plant in a kitchen garden that would do much damage if a little was eaten by mistake, including an experimental nibble on a rhubarb leaf – or a snail or mouthful of dirt, for that matter. However, of course adults need to supervise a child in the garden.

Rhubarb and Strawberry Freeform Tart

SERVES 6 I once supervised and helped to cook this tart for 150 people in a woolshed in country Victoria, where it was served with the most sensational farm cream. Raspberries could be substituted for the strawberries, as could slices of juicy plum. Whatever is selected as the second fruit, it must take no more than ten minutes to cook. The amaretti and crushed almond mixture that is scattered over the pastry and through the fruit was inspired by a mention of the combination in Alice Waters' book *Chez Panisse Fruit*. If you don't want to include almonds, substitute ground-up gingernut biscuits for the Italian amaretti biscuits and the crushed almonds. Amaretti biscuits include sweet and bitter almonds and are flavoured with the oil from almond kernels or almond essence.

plain flour, for dusting
1 quantity Basic Shortcrust Pastry
 (see page 510)
750g/1lb 10½oz rhubarb stalks, washed
 and trimmed, leaves discarded
125ml/4½fl oz hot water
110g/3¾oz caster sugar
juice of 1 orange
6–8 strawberries, hulled and halved
double cream, to serve

**ALMOND AND AMARETTI
 MIXTURE**
2 tablespoons plain flour
2 tablespoons white sugar
50g/2oz raw almonds,
 coarsely crushed
2 tablespoons crushed amaretti
 biscuits (about 6–8)

EXTRA EQUIPMENT
mortar and pestle

On a workbench dusted with plain flour, roll pastry until 5mm/¼in thick to form a 26cm/10in round. Transfer to a baking paper-lined baking tray and chill.

If rhubarb stalks are more than 2cm/¾in wide, slit in half lengthways (my home-grown rhubarb stalks were quite thin, so this wasn't necessary) and then cut widthways into 3cm/1½in-long pieces.

Simmer water, sugar and orange juice in a small stainless-steel saucepan over low heat, stirring until sugar dissolves. Drop rhubarb into syrup, turn to mix, then cover and cook for 3 minutes only. Drain rhubarb in a sieve resting over a bowl, reserving syrup. Transfer rhubarb to another bowl and leave to cool.

To make the almond and amaretti mixture, mix flour, sugar, crushed almonds and crushed biscuits.

Preheat oven to 200°C/Gas 6.

Mix 40g/1½oz almond/amaretti mixture into cooled rhubarb. Scatter another 3–4 tablespoons of this mixture over the chilled pastry round, leaving a 4cm/1½in border. Pile rhubarb over almond/amaretti mixture, then even it out and 'trap' it by folding pastry edges up and over fruit, crimping and pleating as you go. Bake for 30 minutes.

Meanwhile, tip reserved poaching syrup into a small frying pan and reduce over high heat for 1–2 minutes until syrupy. Set aside. Remove tart from oven, >>>

press rhubarb down with an egg lifter and place halved strawberries on top. Brush some syrup over pastry edges and dab a little over the fruit. Bake for a further 10 minutes.

Slide baking tray onto a cake cooling rack. Cool tart for a few minutes and then brush with more syrup, then leave to cool further. Don't attempt to slide tart onto a serving platter until it has cooled down. Serve slices of cooled tart with spoonfuls of double cream.

Rhubarb and Ricotta Turnovers

MAKES 8 Now that it is possible to buy outstanding ready-made and rolled all-butter puff pastry, these turnovers are a very fast and delicious dessert option. It is also a way of using up any extra Almond and Amaretti Mixture you may have left if you made the Rhubarb and Strawberry Freeform Tart on page 536.

150g/5oz rhubarb stalks, washed and trimmed, leaves discarded
150g/5oz fresh ricotta
2 tablespoons currants
75g/2½oz caster sugar, plus 1 teaspoon extra
1 tablespoon white sugar
1 teaspoon ground cinnamon

1 tablespoon plain flour
1 tablespoon ground almonds (optional)
1 tablespoon coarsely crushed gingernuts or amaretti biscuits
1 free-range egg
a pinch salt
2 × sheets ready-made all-butter puff pastry, cut into quarters
double cream or ice cream, to serve

Slit rhubarb stalks in half lengthways and then cut widthways into 5mm/¼in-thick slices. Transfer to a bowl with ricotta, currants, sugars, cinnamon, flour, almonds and biscuits, and mix with a fork.

Mix egg with salt and set aside. Put 1 heaped tablespoonful of rhubarb mixture on each pastry square. Fold over to form turnovers. Press edges to seal. Brush pastry with egg mixture, scatter with extra caster sugar and place on a baking paper-lined baking tray. Cut a tiny slit in top of each turnover for steam to escape during baking. Chill in refrigerator for at least 15 minutes.

Preheat oven to 200°C/Gas 6.

Bake turnovers for 10 minutes, then reduce temperature to 180°C/Gas 4 and bake for a further 15 minutes or until turnovers are a rich golden brown. Transfer turnovers to a cake cooling rack. The contents are boiling hot so delay serving for 5 minutes or so. Serve with double cream or ice cream.

ROCKET

Brassicaceae family (includes broccoli, cabbage, cauliflower, cresses, radishes and turnips) Annual

Soil type
Well-drained, fertile soil enriched with organic matter.

Soil preparation
Plant after a legume crop, if possible.

Climate
Suitable for all climates.

Position
Prefers full sun in spring and partial shade in summer.

How to grow
Directly sow from March–September or raise seeds in modular trays. Plant at a depth of 2cm and about 15cm apart. If sown in trays, plant out seedlings when 10cm tall.

Water requirements
Keep soil moist to encourage rapid growth.

Successive planting
Regular rocket: 3–4 plants every 4 weeks, throughout the growing season. When the new seedlings can be picked, compost older plants, which will have become too spicy for enjoyment.
Perennial rocket: Not required. Cut off yellow flowers and long stems to keep it producing tender leaves.

When to fertilise
Use a liquid fertiliser (see page 691) every 4 weeks to improve growth.

Harvest period
Pick young leaves as required, 5 weeks from planting.

Pests and organic control
Use crushed eggshells around the base of the young plants to deter snails and slugs.

Companion planting
Other salad plants and herbs.

Special information
Plants will go to seed if they lack water or if exposed to too much hot sun. Keep the soil moist and free from weeds by mulching.

Quantities to plant for a family of four
Regular rocket: 3–4 plants every 4 weeks throughout the growing season.
Perennial rocket: 3–4 plants planted at the same time will be sufficient if kept trimmed of flowers.

Wild perennial rocket (*Diplotaxis tenuifolia*)

Growing and Harvesting This delightful salad plant (*Eruca sativa*) is also known as roquette, arugula, rucola and Italian cress. It has white flowers. Another variety with slimmer leaves that are more grey-green than bright green is described as wild rocket (*Diplotaxis tenuifolia*), although it is not at all wild. I suspect the 'wild' part refers to the plant's tendency to run wild all over the garden if allowed to do so! It is sold in nurseries as perennial rocket and has yellow flowers.

I found a note in a holiday diary that records my first experience of wild rocket. My host had an extensive walled vegetable garden and part of the excitement of the holiday was stepping into the garden and deciding what to cook for dinner.

The wild rocket is a delightful surprise. It has all the virtues (more of them, actually) and none of the disadvantages of the commercially sold variety. Its slender leaflets are a soft grey-green and are easily stripped from each central stem. It is soft to touch, tender in the mouth and yet hardy. The same winds that have scorched and burnt the basil have left this rocket unscathed. The commercial varieties always need time-consuming sorting for insect damage and yellow leaves, and one must discard the giant leaves that are unacceptably tough and too hot. This rocket smells marvellous as one brushes it – memories of Italy are evoked at once – it is peppery and invigorating and equally good mixed into a salad or strewn over soft white goat's cheese or added to a ham sandwich. Last evening I picked and sliced zucchini with their blossoms still open and added handfuls of wild rocket to our risotto.

Both types have become very popular in recent years as a garnish and a salad vegetable, and I now have them growing in my own garden. Rocket grows very easily, although it is worth remembering that rocket does not like fierce sun and that hot weather makes hot leaves. Young, tender leaves are irresistible as a slightly peppery, mustardy salad green with a bit of a punch, but as it matures the plant rapidly becomes unbearably spicy and off-putting – and not just to young palates! Picked in its prime, it is wonderful added to a salad of mixed greens or to top a just-cooked pizza.

Patches of rocket in the garden can be treated as seedling crops and small quantities can be constantly pulled or picked for the salad bowl. Alternatively, a patch of mixed salad seeds or seedlings including rocket can be treated as a mesclun or a cut-and-come-again crop. Plant them close and pick the small seedlings as needed when they are about 10 centimetres high.

Once rocket has grown out of control, the clumps can be cut back ruthlessly by two-thirds of their height, after which they will send out tender new shoots. If the plant has already flowered, pull the clumps. By then you should have another crop coming along anyway, if you have planted continuously over the growing season.

Container Planting Rocket is an ideal crop to grow in a container, either on its own, with several other lettuces, or closely planted as described above so you can pick individual leaves and continually re-sow the seed.

Preparing and Sharing Freshly harvested rocket wilts quickly and is not stored very successfully for more than a few hours. If I had to pick rocket in advance (why I wonder – a storm threatening perhaps?) I would pick and store it, unwashed, in one of the green vegetable storage bags you buy at the supermarket.

However rocket is to be used, remember to wash and dry the leaves very well using a salad spinner and, most importantly, pinch off excess stems before adding the leaves to the salad bowl. Those long spindly stems can catch in the throat and cause someone to choke.

Rocket is best regarded as a seasoning leaf for salads, rather than the principal ingredient, especially if the eaters are young. It is at its best tossed with delicate and mild salad greens such as butter lettuce, oak leaf or hearts of cos.

Some salad combinations that have delighted me are: rocket with ripe figs or beetroot; rocket with sharp and salty things such as goat's cheese and capers; and rocket with Caramelised Onion (see page 461). Rocket is also great scattered over a potato or mushroom pizza before serving.

Rocket can be substituted for watercress to make a delicious potato and rocket soup (see page 265). In this case you could use a fair proportion of the larger leaves, as their final punch will be softened by the potato. Try serving this with grilled slices of sourdough bread rubbed with garlic and spread with fresh ricotta mixed with chopped rocket leaves. Apart from this, while not all cooks agree, I don't find cooked rocket very appetising. An exception might be cooked pasta tossed in a hot bowl with a simple sauce that includes some well trimmed and only briefly wilted rocket, such as the recipe for Linguine with Ricotta and Rocket on page 545.

Especially for Kids Because rocket quickly flowers and becomes coarse if not picked early, there is a tendency to pick too much of it and then try and use quantities of overgrown leaves with lots of stalk. Please remember that it is absolutely counter-productive to offer bitingly hot leaves to young children and then expect them to be enthusiastic about salads.

Encourage your young gardeners to pick the largest and toughest leaves and give them to the chickens, if you have them, as they will love them.

Linguine with Ricotta and Rocket

SERVES 4 This is a very delicate and gently flavoured pasta dish. The rocket should just have been harvested and, perhaps even more importantly, the ricotta must be absolutely fresh! As ricotta is a fresh cheese without any salt or other preservative, it has to be eaten within two days of making to be truly delicious. This dish is successful made with homemade pasta or with bought dried pasta. Homemade linguine will cook in two to three minutes, making this a super-speedy treat (see Fresh Pasta on page 474). Dried pasta will probably take eight to ten minutes to be al dente.

EXTRA EQUIPMENT
salad spinner

salt
400g/14oz dried or fresh
    linguine or fettuccine
50g/2oz butter
250g/9oz fresh ricotta, crumbled

2 small handfuls loosely packed rocket
    leaves, washed and dried
sea salt and freshly ground
    black pepper
35g/1¼oz grated parmesan

Preheat oven to 100°C/Gas ¼ and put an ovenproof bowl inside to warm.

Bring a pasta pot or large heavy-based saucepan of well-salted water to the boil over high heat. If using dried pasta, drop into water and wait 8 minutes before beginning to make the sauce. If using homemade pasta, drop into water just as you add rocket leaves to frying pan.

Melt butter in a large non-stick frying pan over medium heat. When foaming, drop in ricotta. Stir gently but don't try to break up the lumps; bite-sized snowy lumps of ricotta will look much more attractive in the finished dish than white crumbs. Drop in rocket leaves and stir to coat with buttery juices. Cover with a lid for 45 seconds–1 minute. The leaves should just be wilted, not collapsed. Remove from heat and season very well with salt and pepper.

Drain pasta in a colander over a sink and give it a good shake, then tip it into the warmed bowl. Tip over sauce, add parmesan, toss to mix and serve at once.

Rocket, Chestnut and Bacon Salad

SERVES 4 This combination was inspired by the work of Skye Gyngell, a good friend and a fine chef. I did not have all the ingredients called for in Skye's recipe so I had to adapt the idea. I love to eat the crisped pieces of lemon zest, but remove them if you like before serving. I use convenient frozen, peeled chestnuts, which need to be thawed before using. In early autumn this would be even more delicious made with fresh chestnuts. Peeling chestnuts is an especially tedious task in the kitchen, but interesting to do at least once. It is a good job to share. If everyone peels half-a-dozen, the task will be completed quickly.

30 cooked and peeled fresh
   chestnuts or frozen chestnuts,
   thawed for 2 hours
100ml/3½fl oz extra-virgin olive oil
20 sage leaves
zest of 1 small lemon, removed in
   thin strips

2 slices streaky bacon, rind
   removed and thinly sliced
4 small handfuls loosely packed
   rocket leaves, trimmed,
   washed and dried
sea salt and freshly ground
   black pepper

EXTRA EQUIPMENT
salad spinner

If using fresh chestnuts, cut a slit on the outer skins and simmer the nuts in a saucepan of water over low heat for 15 minutes. Remove one chestnut at a time, then peel – it is easier to remove the outer and inner skin when the chestnut is hot.

Heat olive oil in a large non-stick frying pan over low heat and drop in sage leaves and lemon zest, then gently heat on lowest possible heat for 5 minutes. Drop in thawed or freshly cooked and peeled chestnuts and infuse with sage-infused oil for another 5 minutes. Remove pan from heat until needed.

Heat 1 tablespoon of the sage oil in a small non-stick frying pan over medium heat and sauté bacon until it starts to sizzle. Tip bacon and its oil into large frying pan with sage leaves, lemon zest and chestnuts and place over medium heat. Toss and stir for about 5 minutes or until bacon is crisp and chestnuts have taken on a little colour. Remove from heat and cool for 1–2 minutes.

Drop rocket leaves into a large mixing bowl. Tip over bacon/chestnut mixture. Add sea salt and pepper to taste and toss to mix well. Serve at once.

Making Rocket Salads

Remember the guidelines:
- either regular or wild rocket can be used in any salad recipe calling for rocket – while regular rocket adds more bulk, the flavour of both types is identical. If using wild rocket, you may want to add bulk by including other soft leafy greens or watercress.
- only use freshly picked young leaves (home-picked rocket wilts quickly and doesn't store successfully for more than a few hours)
- pick over the leaves, trim, wash, dry in a salad spinner and refrigerate wrapped in a dry cloth until needed
- no long straggly stems for family or guests to choke on
- mix with other mild leaves if your leaves are very peppery
- add the dressing at the very last minute – bedraggled, collapsed leaves look horrible and are not nice to eat

Here are a some other successful salad combinations:
- Combine rocket with thinly sliced fennel (crisped in iced water as described on page 523), slices of firm pear, shavings of either ricotta salata (see page 705) or parmesan, then drizzle with extra-virgin olive oil and lemon juice or wine vinegar and season with sea salt and freshly ground black pepper.
- Make an autumn salad of rocket, green grapes, sliced green or red pepper and the last greenish tomatoes of the season. Dress with extra-virgin olive oil and lemon juice or red- or white-wine vinegar and season with sea salt and freshly ground black pepper.
- Toss rocket with sliced avocado in a sharper than usual dressing of extra-virgin olive oil, sherry vinegar, sea salt and freshly ground black pepper to provide a contrast to the creaminess of the avocado.

Rocket Pesto

MAKES 250ML/9FL OZ I am a bit of a purist when it comes to classic combinations, but if you substitute regular rocket leaves (be sure to remove the straggly stems) for the basil in the recipe for Pesto on page 119, you will have a quick pasta sauce or sandwich spread.

ROSEMARY

**Lamiaceae family
(includes basil, mint and sage)
Evergreen woody perennial**

Soil type
Well drained.

Soil preparation
As long as the soil is well drained
and rich in organic matter,
no additional preparation
is required.

Climate
Suitable for most climates.
It will tolerate frost and drought,
but not waterlogged soil or
damp shade.

Position
Prefers full sun and sheltered
spot.

How to grow
Buy a young potted plant in
late spring and plant in a sunny
spot. Take a woody cutting
about 15–20cm long and place
just over one-third of the length
in a gritty potting mix. Once
the roots have taken you can
plant the cutting in a permanent
position in the garden. All
herbs are great planted among
vegetables – they attract
beneficial insects.

Water requirements
Don't over-water.

When to fertilise
Rosemary is tolerant of poor soil,
so avoid using fresh manure.
Use a liquid fertiliser (see page
691) or worm tea (see page 695)
a couple of times a year to
assist growth.

Harvest period
Can be harvested at any time.

Pests and organic control
A new pest is rosemary beetle.
Pick off any small metallic green
or purple beetles you find

Companion planting
Cabbages, beans, carrots
and sage benefit from being
near rosemary as rosemary
attracts beneficial insects. It
deters cabbage moth, bean
beetles and carrot fly.

Special information
Keep the soil free from weeds
by mulching. Prune back
once flowering has finished
to maintain shape and
encourage growth.

**Quantities to plant
for a family of four**
1–2 plants.

Rosemary (*Rosmarinus officinalis*)

Growing and Harvesting Rosemary is a beautiful hedging and edging plant and deserves a place in every garden. It accommodates different growing conditions, as long as it gets lots of sun and is not planted in boggy ground. After all, rosemary grows wild on stony hillsides in the Mediterranean without any care from anyone. I have a low hedge of rosemary backing onto terracotta paving, against which the deep green of the leaves and the brilliant-blue flowers look so lovely. The effect is even more marvellous after rain, when the terracotta glows a pinky-red and the green leaves are shiny with raindrops. I have scattered my father's ashes around these rosemary bushes – after all, rosemary is for remembrance, as Shakespeare tells us.

There are several types of rosemary and all of them are aromatic. Some of the trailing specimens can tumble over walls, softening harsh edges, or can be used as an effective and aromatic groundcover that suppresses weeds. All rosemary plants have beautiful flowers and attract bees to the garden. Most varieties bloom for months, from spring through summer and into autumn. Rosemary needs hard pruning to retain its shape and to encourage bushiness. Any woody stalks are valuable as grilling skewers. Dry and store the prunings or add them to a mix for making potpourri or a scented pillow (see page 381 or 565).

Container Planting As with all herbs, rosemary will be very happy in a pot. It can have a container to itself or maybe share the space with parsley or a thyme bush. See **HERBS**.

Preparing and Sharing Another diary note from a wonderful holiday in Italy:

> Of all the herbs it is rosemary that evokes Italy most powerfully and last year we tucked rosemary sprigs into roasts of pork and under small birds grilling over the open fire; chopped them into dishes of gnocchi; warmed them in oil for our lunch-time bread and chopped the leaves into the *soffritto* that was the basis of our wonderful slow-cooked dishes. At roadside vans and market squares throughout the countryside around Lazio, Tuscany and Umbria one is offered portions of *porchetta* – a whole pig stuffed with startling amounts of garlic, fennel and rosemary and then roasted.

Rosemary is a powerful herb that is generally best used on its own although it has an affinity with thyme, fennel and savory, all of which also grow wild on Mediterranean hillsides. It overpowers delicate herbs like chervil or tarragon. Its pungent aroma fills the kitchen when I open the oven door on a rosemary-scented roast lamb (see page 554) or pan of roasted vegetables (see page 553); the rosemary needles roast to a crisp and can be enjoyed. Rosemary also pairs well with fish, bread, cheese, garlic, chicken, pork and rabbit, as well as dried beans in soups and purées.

I learnt from an Italian friend to marinate a thin beefsteak in a little olive oil, crushed juniper and quite a lot of stripped rosemary for 1 hour at room temperature. The herbs stick to the meat as it grills over a very hot flame or coals and you can brush them away or not before eating. I quite like the flavour of the brittle, charred rosemary needles. Another Italian specialty is slowly braising a shoulder of lamb or kid on a bed of par-cooked dried borlotti or cannellini beans, with lots of rosemary and garlic, barely covering them with stock or broth. Baste the beans and meat during cooking; the meat should come away from the bone.

Roughly chopped rosemary is excellent mixed with extra-virgin olive oil to brush over or drizzle onto pizzas and savoury tarts. Always finely chop the stripped needles if they are to be included in a dish such as a bread dough or casserole, as the needles can be tough and the stems will not soften in such dishes. Save the stalks to make skewers to spear oiled and seasoned lamb's kidneys or cubes of calf's liver for the barbecue, or to press very finely minced spiced beef or lamb into a fat cigar around and grill on a hot grill-plate, turning once.

Especially for Kids Encourage children to bruise fresh rosemary and inhale deeply. Note how spicy it smells – smell is such an important part of stimulating appetite. After roasting potatoes with garlic and rosemary ask, 'Does rosemary smell the same after it is cooked?'

Rosemary, Barley and Beer Scones

MAKES 8 These scones are fast to mix and to bake, if you have leftover cooked barley on hand. Try them alongside a vegetable soup. If you prefer, substitute cooked white or brown rice for the barley.

EXTRA EQUIPMENT
pastry scraper

300g/10½oz plain flour, plus extra
  for dusting
2 teaspoons cream of tartar
1 teaspoon bicarbonate of soda
1 teaspoon salt
1 tablespoon finely chopped
  rosemary leaves
30g/1oz butter, softened
60g/2oz feta, crumbled

1 tablespoon grated parmesan
110g/3¾oz cooked barley (see page
  228) or white or brown rice
125ml/4½fl oz beer
125ml/4½fl oz buttermilk, plus extra,
  for brushing
1 tablespoon fine semolina,
  for dusting
butter or soft cream cheese, to serve

Preheat oven to 180°C/Gas 4.

Sift flour, cream of tartar, bicarbonate of soda and salt into a large mixing bowl. Stir in rosemary. Quickly rub in softened butter. Mix in cheeses. Stir in the cooked barley, or rice if using.

Combine beer and buttermilk. Make a well in flour/barley mixture and tip in liquid, then quickly mix to form a soft dough. Sprinkle a workbench with extra flour and press the dough into a round loaf about 6cm/2½in high.

Using a pastry scraper, cut loaf in half, then in quarters, and then in eighths. Place the 8 wedges well apart on a baking paper-lined baking tray. Brush top of each wedge with extra buttermilk and scatter with semolina. Bake for 20–25 minutes or until wedges are golden brown on top and sound hollow when tapped. Cool on a cake cooling rack for a few minutes. Eat with butter or cream cheese.

Roasted Vegetables with Rosemary

SERVES 4 This is one of my standbys. The version given here usually accompanies a roast of beef or lamb when the family visits. I roast a rib of beef or a leg of lamb directly on the oven rack with these vegetables sitting in a roasting pan on the rack underneath (see page 554). The vegetables benefit from the delicious drippings. When I'm cooking just for myself, I frequently prepare a smaller quantity and put the roasting pan straight into a cold oven when I get home, even before taking off my jacket. (Famous food writer and excellent cook Marcella Hazan impressed and amused me many years ago by dumping chopped onion in a pan with oil, shrugging her shoulders most expressively and saying, 'It will get hot sooner or later!') I then turn the oven on and proceed to read the paper or my emails, listen to some music, open a bottle of wine and just relax, knowing that my dinner is cooking itself and that in forty-five minutes or so it will be ready. Sometimes I open the oven door after thirty minutes and add some halved tomatoes or lightly oiled mushrooms to the pan. This is just one possible combination of vegetables. Depending on what I have harvested (or bought) I might use whole small onions (see opposite) rather than wedges of large onions or chunks of celeriac, sweet potato or Jerusalem artichokes instead.

4 waxy or all-purpose potatoes (desirees or nicolas are my favourites), washed, dried and halved (or 8–10 small potatoes)

2 onions, cut into wedges

400g/14oz peeled and seeded pumpkin, cut into 4 chunks

4 chunky carrots, peeled and halved if large

4 parsnips, peeled and halved if large

8 cloves garlic, unpeeled and pierced with a fine skewer

60ml/2fl oz extra-virgin olive oil

sea salt and freshly ground black pepper

2 tablespoons rosemary leaves

Preheat oven to 200°C/Gas 6. (Although it doesn't really matter if oven has reached temperature or not; the vegetables just may take an extra 10 minutes to cook if the oven is still heating up when you are ready to put the pan in.)

Place vegetables and garlic in a large mixing bowl. Pour over olive oil, then season with salt and pepper. Mix through rosemary.

Tip vegetable mixture into a roasting pan and move around so the vegetables fit compactly in a single layer without too much extra space. Roast for 45–60 minutes or until vegetables are golden and tender, shaking the pan once during this time, and serve.

Roast Lamb with Rosemary and Garlic

SERVES 4–6 When I made this to be photographed I also roasted halved potatoes directly on the oven rack alongside the lamb for one hour. Cooked this way, they develop a crackling exterior that I find irresistible (see opposite).

1 × 1.5kg/3lb leg lamb
sea salt and freshly ground black pepper
extra-virgin olive oil, for drizzling
2 cloves garlic, cut into slivers
2 rosemary sprigs, cut into 4 pieces each

1 quantity prepared vegetables (see Roasted Vegetables with Rosemary on page 553)
150ml/5fl oz white wine, for gravy (optional)

Preheat oven to 200°C/Gas 6.

Season lamb with salt and pepper and rub with olive oil, then stud with garlic and rosemary and put into a roasting pan. Roast lamb for 15 minutes. Remove lamb from roasting pan and place it directly onto the oven shelf, then tip prepared vegetables into the pan and return it to the oven shelf underneath. Cook for 55 minutes for deliciously rose-pink lamb and golden roasted vegetables – the juices from the meat will drip onto the vegetables as they cook.

To make a quick gravy from the pan juices, transfer lamb and vegetables to a serving plate, then pour away any fat in the pan. Place roasting pan over high heat, then deglaze with a little wine, scraping up any caught bits and leaving the sauce to bubble and reduce slightly. Strain, then serve gravy with roast lamb and vegetables.

Rosemary, Garlic and Tomato Sauce

Many Italian cafes offer the ever-popular side dish of potatoes tossed in olive oil and roasted with garlic cloves and rosemary until golden and crusty. Another way of using this classic combination of flavourings is to slowly cook thinly sliced garlic in a saucepan over low heat with rosemary sprigs and a generous quantity of your best extra-virgin olive oil. Once the lovely, pine needle-like aroma of the rosemary appears, tip in a bowl of peeled, seeded and chopped tomatoes. Season with sea salt and freshly ground black pepper and stir. Increase the heat to high and cook for another 5 minutes and you'll have a marvellous sauce for a piece of grilled tuna or a pork chop, or to stir through pasta or freshly picked and cooked broad beans.

SAGE

**Lamiaceae family
(includes basil, mint,
rosemary and thyme)
Woody perennial**

Soil type
Well-drained, loose soil.
Sage is tolerant of poor soil.
Dislikes boggy soil.

Soil preparation
Providing soil is well drained and
rich in organic matter, no special
preparation is required.

Climate
Suitable for most climates, can
tolerate frost and drought but
not waterlogged soil in winter
and damp shade.

Position
Prefers full sun, open site.

How to grow
Buy small potted plants in spring
and plant them in a sunny spot
or in a container with gritty
potting mix. Sage is short-lived
so it is worth taking cuttings.
Take 10cm stem tip cuttings in
early summer, remove lower
leaves and insert cuttings
into pots of gritty cutting mix.
Keep pots on a windowsill
indoors overwinter, plant out
following spring.

Water requirements
Water in new plants until they
are growing away, thereafter no
watering required unless sage is
in a container.

When to fertilise
Little feed needed but container
plants can have liquid feed
(see page 691) or worm tea
(see page 695) a couple of
times a year.

Harvest period
Pick the leaves as needed during
the growing season, dry some in
summer for use in winter when
the foliage is poor quality.

Pests and organic control
A new pest is the rosemary
beetle, a small metallic green
and purple beetle. Pick off and
destroy any you find.

Companion planting
When planted with rosemary,
cabbage and carrots, sage
deters cabbage white butterfly
and carrot fly. Don't plant near
cucumber, onion or wormwood.

Special information
Stems may die off overwinter
and eventually plants become
woody and unattractive, so it is
worth pruning them when they
are young (see overleaf).

Quantities to plant
for a family of four
2–3 plants.

Left to right: Variegated sage (*Salvia officinalis* 'Icterina'); purple sage (*Salvia officinalis* 'Purpurascens')

Growing and Harvesting My favourite herb book, *The Herb Garden Displayed* by Gilian Painter and Elaine Power, tells me that there are about 700 sage (*Salvia*) species in the world, but most of us grow one of just three or four types for culinary use. Other sage species, usually called salvias, are often grown in the garden for their attractive flowers and to attract beneficial insects, even though their leaves have no culinary potential. Sages will remain compact and attractive if pruned regularly; neglected old specimens are best replaced. Cut back plants to 15–20 centimetres about ground in March, feed with an organic balanced fertiliser if the soil is poor.

Culinary sage is a most attractive shrub, with its silvery-grey, purple-silver or variegated leaves, all with pretty flowers. It forms a shapely bush, much-loved by bees when in flower. Plant it in clumps among other flowers and herbs. Many gardeners plant sage alongside brassicas, believing that sage repels the cabbage white butterfly.

Pineapple sage (*Salvia elegans*) is a delightful plant that gives off the aroma of a ripe pineapple when brushed or stroked, and has attractive edible scarlet flowers. Pineapple sage is tender so is best grown in a small pot, bring undercover into a heated greenhouse or indoor windowsill in autumn.

Container Planting Like all herbs, sage is ideal for growing in a pot or container. Maybe combine it with a trailing rosemary plant, or alternatively plant a purple-leafed sage and a variegated sage together with the standard variety for a most attractive effect. See **HERBS**.

Preparing and Sharing The Italians make the best use of sage. Sage leaves crisped in melted butter and/or olive oil are absolutely stunning and make the perfect sauce for gnocchi, rice and pasta-based dishes, summer vegetables cooked in a little olive oil or a sautéed piece of veal or liver. Crisped sage leaves are also fantastic stirred into mashed pumpkin or added to a warm white bean or chestnut salad, such as the Rocket, Chestnut and Bacon Salad on page 546.

An anchovy fillet, or half a fillet (halved along the length of the fillet), can be sandwiched between large sage leaves, dipped into a crisp batter (see page 560) and fried for a fiddly but delicious appetiser before a special meal. Tuck small sage sprigs between scrubbed unpeeled small potatoes, drizzle with extra-virgin olive oil and season with salt and pepper, then roast at 180°C/Gas 4 for about 1 hour or until crisp.

As I never use chemical sprays in my garden I don't need to wash my freshly picked sage. However, I do closely inspect the leaves, particularly the under-sides, to check there are no insects present before using them.

Especially for Kids For something completely different, try adding a little chopped pineapple sage to a fruit salad, a perennial childhood favourite, or float it in a fruit punch.

Onion and Sage Risotto

SERVES 6 This is a variation on the recipe I gave for Lemon Risotto in *The Cook's Companion*. It is important to cook the onions until they have passed the softened stage to become a deep-golden (almost) brown.

1.5 litres/2¾ pints chicken stock
200ml/7fl oz dry white wine
120g/4oz unsalted butter
2 tablespoons extra-virgin olive oil
3 large onions, thinly sliced
400g/14oz Arborio rice (see page 703)
sea salt and freshly ground

black pepper
grated zest and juice of
  1 lemon
2 tablespoons chopped
  flat-leaf parsley
90g/3oz parmesan, grated
12 large sage leaves, torn into
  small pieces

Heat stock and wine in a saucepan. Melt 60g/2oz of the butter in a deep heavy-based frying pan over low heat, then add olive oil and onion and cook for 15 minutes or until a deep golden brown, stirring from time to time. Add rice, stirring to mix and coat with buttery juices. Increase heat to medium, then add 250ml/9fl oz hot stock mixture. Simmer, stirring constantly and adding 250ml/9fl oz stock mixture at a time as the liquid is absorbed, making sure the rice is always just covered (the liquid required can vary, so always taste before adding the last 250ml/9fl oz stock). The rice should have just the faintest bite left in it. Adjust seasoning. Stir in lemon zest and juice, parsley and parmesan, then cover and leave to stand for 3 minutes. Divide risotto among warm bowls.

Heat remaining butter and sage leaves in a clean frying pan over medium heat. Cook for 1–2 minutes until butter has just started to darken, then quickly spoon sage butter over each bowl of risotto and serve at once.

Parmesan-crumbed Veal Chops with Sage

Recently I cooked large veal chops for a dinner at home with friends. A couple of hours beforehand, I dipped the chops in beaten egg, then in a mixture of breadcrumbs and grated parmesan and sealed them on both sides in a hot frying pan with olive oil. I arranged them on a baking tray and topped each one with a bouquet of raw sage, ready for a speedy roast in the oven at 200°C/Gas 6 when my friends had arrived. In 15 minutes the chops cooked through and the sage crisped most beautifully.

Fritto Misto with Sage Leaf Fritters, Fish, Zucchini and Prawns

SERVES 4 These fritters are absolutely delicious. Almost everyone loves deep-fried food (but not indulging in it too often has to be the message). It's important to be mindful of offering a balance with what you offer for the rest of the meal. The batter recipe uses one egg and as it is difficult to make less than this quantity, unless you are providing sage leaf fritters for a large party, it is probably best of all to plan for a fritto misto as an entire meal. When preparing the sage leaves, retain a bit of stalk to help lift them in and out of the batter (see opposite). I suggest accompanying fritto misto with something fresh or crunchy, such as a tomato salad, a fennel salad such as Luke Palmer's Peach Salad with Fennel, Rocket and Almonds on page 612, or a leafy green salad. After such an indulgent main course, fresh fruit would be the best way to finish the meal.

5 anchovy fillets, halved
   lengthways
20 large sage leaves
vegetable oil, for deep-frying
4 raw prawns, heads and tails
   removed and de-veined
4 fillets bone-free white fish,
   such as pollock or
   halibut
2–4 small zucchini, cut lengthways
   into 2–3 slices
4 zucchini flowers (optional)

½ small handful other small pieces
   of vegetable (such as broccoli
   or cauliflower florets)
sea salt
lemon wedges, to serve

BEER BATTER
150g/5oz plain flour
125ml/4½fl oz milk
125ml/4½fl oz beer
1 free-range egg (at room
   temperature), separated

EXTRA EQUIPMENT
hand-held electric
   beaters
wok
long-handled
   brass skimmer or
   a slotted spoon

To make the batter, put flour into a medium-sized mixing bowl. In another bowl, put milk, beer and egg yolk and whisk to mix. Make a well in flour, tip in egg yolk mixture and whisk until smooth. Just before you are going to start frying, whisk egg white with hand-held electric beaters to form stiff peaks and fold into batter.

Preheat oven to 100°C/Gas ¼ and put a baking tray inside to keep warm.

Sandwich an anchovy piece between 2 sage leaves and press together lightly. Repeat with remaining anchovies and leaves. Pour vegetable oil into a wok or deep-sided frying pan to a depth of 4cm/1½in in the centre and heat over high heat until hot. Test oil with a drop of batter; it should sizzle and turn golden almost immediately. Dip fritters into batter, drain off excess and carefully place into hot oil; don't crowd the pan. Turn fritters to brown other side. Lift fritters out with a skimmer or slotted spoon, allowing excess oil to drain into the pan. Place on a baking tray thickly lined with paper towel, then keep warm in oven. Working in batches, dip seafood and vegetables into batter and fry until golden and crisp, then transfer to oven. Lightly season with salt and serve with lemon wedges.

SCENTED GERANIUMS

Geraniaceae family
Tender perennial

Soil type
Well-drained soil or a free-draining potting mix if growing plants in containers.

Soil preparation
Little soil preparation is required, grit can be forked into soils to improve drainage. An alternative is to sink potted plants into the ground while still in their containers, this makes it easier to lift to overwinter at season's end.

Climate
All scented geraniums are tender in the UK, so use them as summer bedding or container plants. Overwinter stock plants underglass or indoors on a windowsill.

Position
Prefers full sun.

How to grow
All scented geraniums can be propagated by taking cuttings in summer. Take cuttings 10cm long, strip the lower leaves, insert into pots of gritty cutting mix. Water pots and put them uncovered somewhere light but out of direct sunlight, cuttings should root in 2–3 weeks. Overwinter in a cool greenhouse. In spring start watering as plant comes into growth, tidy up foliage and repot if needed. In autumn, bring in stock plants before first frosts.

Water requirements
Very little water is required as the plants are drought-tolerant.

When to fertilise
Very little feed is required, use a liquid fertiliser (see page 691) or worm tea (see page 695) 6 weeks after potting on if plants are failing to thrive.

Harvest period
Pick leaves in the growing season.

Pests and organic control
Whitefly and red spider mite can be a problem underglass. Use a soap spray (see page 700) or try a biological control (see page 698). Scented geraniums can suffer from blackleg virus and grey mould if conditions are too wet and cold, keep compost on the dry side and keep greenhouses well ventilated.

Quantities to plant for a family of four
1–2 plants.

Scented geranium (*Pelargonium* sp.)

Growing and Harvesting These lovely plants are indigenous to South Africa. There are a great number of different species that vary considerably in height, hardiness and delicacy of perfume. Most have exquisite flowers with little scent – the aroma is all in the leaves. My favourites are first and foremost rose-scented (I specify *Pelargonium capitatum*, as there are other rose-scented geraniums that are less subtle), then nutmeg-, lemon- and peppermint-scented varieties. Others include coconut-, lime- and apple-scented ones.

Plants are sometimes divided into low-growing, medium-growing and large sprawling varieties. The ones that tumble and sprawl are lovely for softening a rough garden edge, and they also attract bees to the garden.

Cuttings of scented geraniums are frequently passed from gardener to gardener as they strike readily. They do like sunshine, although to prove the exception I have a sprawling peppermint-scented geranium that is happily filling a very dark corner of my garden.

Container Planting Scented geraniums are perfect specimens for growing in pots and are commonly grown in window boxes, along with their non-aromatic cousins. They flower very freely throughout summer.

Preparing and Sharing It only takes one or two geranium leaves to transfer their scent to cream, sugar or syrup, so don't use too many, then strain out the leaves before serving the dish. I have made geranium-scented custards, panna cotte, coeurs à la crème to serve with berries, small sponge cakes and sorbets, and cooked rhubarb flavoured with rose-scented geranium. Try adding a single leaf to the hot water and caster sugar when making the Orange or Mandarin Jellies on page 372. The leaf is strained out of the syrup before it is added to the juice.

Especially for Kids Crushing one of the leaves can be part of a 'sniff and tell' identifying game for children in the garden. They will enjoy identifying the different scented geraniums growing in their garden and will want to add sprigs to a posy to decorate the table.

Raspberry and Rose-scented Geranium Sorbet

MAKES ABOUT 1 LITRE/1¾ PINTS The mouth-filling flavour of ripe raspberries still dominates this delicious sorbet, but the rose-scented geranium adds a haunting after-note that is appealing and not at all cloying.

EXTRA EQUIPMENT
food processor
coarse-meshed
  stainless-steel
  sieve
ice cream machine

500g/1lb fresh or frozen
  raspberries
250g/9oz caster sugar

4 rose-scented geranium leaves
250ml/9fl oz hot water
juice of ½ a lemon, to taste

Purée raspberries in a food processor, then press through a coarse-meshed stainless-steel sieve into a bowl to extract all the seeds. You should have about 300ml/½ pint purée.

Bring sugar, geranium leaves and water to simmering point in a saucepan over low heat, stirring from time to time until sugar has dissolved. Simmer for a further 10 minutes. Leave syrup to cool with geranium leaves still in it. When syrup is cool, remove and compost leaves, then stir in raspberry purée. Add lemon juice to taste.

Churn mixture in an ice cream machine following manufacturer's instructions. Alternatively, freeze mixture in a shallow tray, then after 30 minutes scrape setting edges towards centre and return tray to the freezer. Do the same again twice at 15-minute intervals and you will have a raspberry and rose-geranium scented granita instead.

Rose Potpourri

This recipe comes from Gilian Painter and Elaine Power's book *The Herb Garden Displayed*. For a geranium-scented potpourri, mix 6 small handfuls rose petals, 2 small handfuls rose-scented geranium leaves, 1 small handful lavender flowers, 1 tablespoon each ground allspice, cinnamon and cloves, and 2 tablespoons orris root (available from pharmacies) with 12 drops rose oil or rose-scented geranium oil. Store in an airtight glass jar or use to fill sachets or pillows.

Rhubarb Purée

MAKES 250ML/9FL OZ This speedily made purée is very versatile. It can be enjoyed just as it is with thick yoghurt or be folded into an Egg Custard (see page 296) and churned to make an interesting ice cream. Alternatively, combine it with berries or cooked apple and a crumble mixture such as the one on page 76 to become a baked crumble. When the purée is folded into an equal quantity of whipped cream it becomes a rhubarb fool.

350g/12oz rhubarb stalks, washed and trimmed, leaves discarded
2–3 tablespoons white, raw or soft brown sugar

80ml/3fl oz cold water
1 rose-scented geranium leaf
½ teaspoon rosewater (optional)

EXTRA EQUIPMENT
food processor
(optional)

Slit each rhubarb stalk in half lengthways, then cut widthways into 3 cm-long pieces. Place rhubarb, sugar, water and geranium leaf in a stainless-steel saucepan. Bring to simmering point over medium heat, stirring. Cover and cook for 6–8 minutes. Check after 6 minutes as rhubarb will start to stick once it has collapsed and cooked as there will be so little liquid. Transfer rhubarb to a bowl and remove geranium leaf, then add rosewater, if using. Leave to cool and use as desired. Purée keeps well covered in the refrigerator for up to 1 week.

If you want a silky smooth purée, transfer rhubarb to a food processor and process until smooth.

Scented Geranium Ice Cream

A very simple way to add a note of mystery to a basic ice cream is to add several washed scented geranium leaves to 375ml/13fl oz warmed milk and 125ml/4½fl oz cream to infuse to use when making the custard base – keep the mixture warm until you think the flavour is strong enough. Pour the strained milk mixture onto 5 egg yolks whisked with 110g/3¾oz caster sugar, then cook the custard until it is thick enough to coat the back of a wooden spoon. Chill and churn in an ice cream machine according to the manufacturer's instructions. The resulting geranium-scented ice cream is an excellent partner for fresh berries.

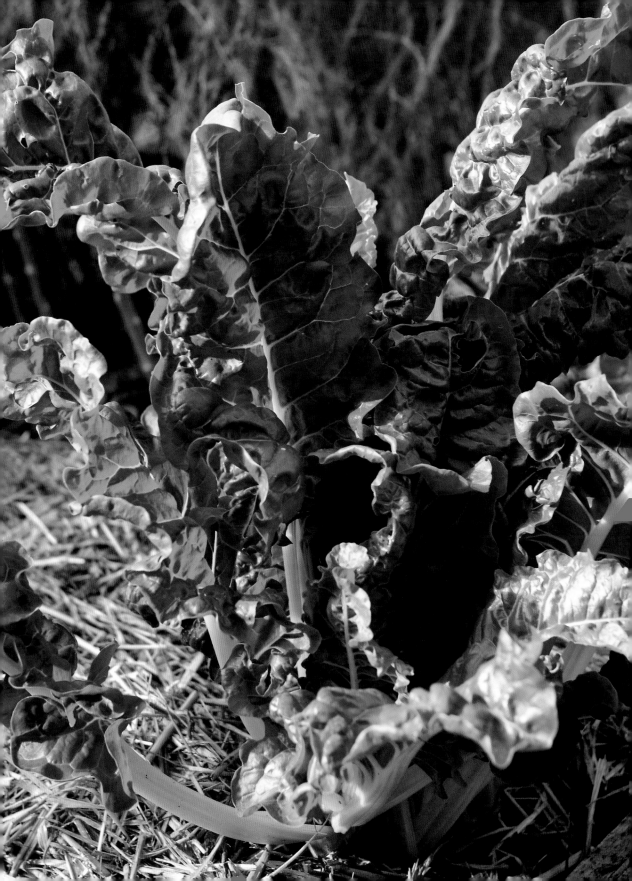

SILVER BEET

Chenopodiaceae family (includes beetroot and spinach)
Biennial

Soil type
Well drained and rich in organic matter.

Soil preparation
Not required.

Climate
Suitable for all climates.

Position
Prefers full sun or partial shade.

How to grow
Directly sow or raise seeds in modular trays in April-June. Plant seeds at a depth of 1cm in clumps of 2–3, with 30cm between the clumps for direct-sowing. Soaking seeds overnight will improve germination, which should occur within 10–14 days. Thin the seedlings when they are 3cm tall, leaving the strongest. When seedlings reach 10cm, transplant from tray to permanent position.

Water requirements
Keep soil moist in dry spells.

Successive planting
Leave about 3 weeks between each planting, throughout the growing season.

When to fertilise
Use a liquid fertiliser (see page 691) or worm tea (see page 695) every 4 weeks.

Harvest period
Silver beet (Swiss chard) has a long cropping period. Leaves can be harvested as soon as the plants are large enough, usually 8–10 weeks after planting.

Pests and organic control
Use crushed egg shells around the base of plants to deter snails and slugs. Caterpillars may eat the mature leaves. Rotate crops every year.

Companion planting
Corn, onions, beetroot, lavender, broccoli, garlic and kohlrabi. Avoid growing with climbing beans.

Special information
To increase leaf production, remove the flower stems as they appear. Keep the soil moist and free from weeds by mulching.

Quantities to plant for a family of four
1 plant every 3 weeks until you have 4 in the ground.

Silver beet (*Beta vulgaris* subsp. *cicla*)

Growing and Harvesting Silver beet (Swiss chard) is one of the most successful crops in any kitchen garden. It grows easily and quickly and just goes on and on into a second season, as long as it likes its position and is well watered and mulched for protection from frosts or super-hot days. It can be grown before or after most other vegetables, which makes it even more appealing to the organic gardener concerned with crop rotation to minimise soil-borne diseases. The colourful cultivar known as 'Bright Lights' looks spectacular in the garden, with stems that can be red, orange, yellow, pink or white. It can be planted among flowering shrubs rather than being consigned to just the vegetable patch.

Rainbow chard is a mixture of red-, white- and yellow-stemmed varieties. They are not as broad stemmed as the original Swiss chard but they are very decorative and so very popular for potagers.

When harvesting silver beet, supervise young gardeners and show them how to always pick from the outside of the plant, breaking the stalk with a downwards and sideways action. If they leave a few centre stalks, the plant will produce new leaves quickly.

Container Planting Silver beet will grow readily in a pot or container. 'Rainbow Chard' tends to have more compact growth than the standard variety.

Preparing and Sharing Many cooks throw away the stems or feed them to the chooks. This is a big mistake. The stems are to be as prized as the leaves and a gratin of the stems in a cheesy sauce (see page 577) has been a successful way of introducing them to students of the Kitchen Garden Program. The strings of the stems may need to be removed with a sharp paring knife. This doesn't need to be done for the more delicate 'Rainbow Chard' stems, whose thinner, finer stems cook more quickly.

Wash silver beet leaves very well in at least one change of water (remember to take the rinsing water back to the garden and dribble it around a needy plant). If you are cooking enough for one or two there will be sufficient water still on the leaves when you drop them into the pan. Stir the leaves to ensure they are not sticking to the pan. While they will shrink, silver beet leaves retain their texture far better than the more delicate spinach leaves, so they are well suited to being used in pies, stuffings, frittatas and long-simmered vegetable soups. The leaves make excellent wrappers instead of grapevine leaves for rice stuffings. In Provence, there is a tradition of using the leaves, combined with dried fruit, to make a sweet tart.

If you are cooking for a crowd and have an armful of leaves it is better to drop it into a large pasta pot or saucepan of lightly salted boiling water. Stir until the water returns to the boil, then drain, cool quickly either by running a little cold water over the leaves (which is wasteful of precious water), or plunge into a basin of very cold water that can later be poured onto the garden, or simply spread out on a tray and use quickly. 'Rainbow Chard' retains its colour best of all if sautéed in olive oil rather than being blanched in water. Steaming also works well for both types.

Especially for Kids Children may be interested to know that in some parts of Europe the stems are prized more than the leaves, which are sometimes fed to the rabbits.

One-pot Silverbeet, Potato and Sausage 'Comforter'

SERVES 4 This is such a good dish for a family cooking session as it is quick and easy to prepare and the whole meal is cooked in the one pot. Do buy good-quality all-pork sausages. If you happen to have picked a few carrots or some young turnips from your garden as well, even better – just peel them and cut into chunks or leave whole and add them to the pot to cook when you add the potatoes.

EXTRA EQUIPMENT
enamelled cast-iron or other heavy-based casserole

salt

4 waxy potatoes (about 200g/7oz), cut into 2cm/¾in-thick slices

500g/1lb silverbeet leaves and stems, washed well, leaves and stems separated

60ml/2fl oz extra-virgin olive oil

300g/10½oz pure pork sausages, skins removed and meat crumbled into bite-sized pieces

2 cloves garlic, finely chopped

2 tablespoons tomato paste

125ml/4½fl oz hot water

¼ teaspoon chilli flakes

Bring a pasta pot or heavy-based saucepan of lightly salted water to the boil over high heat. Drop in potato and simmer for 10 minutes or until tender. Scoop out potato and set aside. Bring pan of water back to simmering point.

Bundle silverbeet leaves together and cut into 2cm/¾in-wide ribbons. Slice really thick stems lengthways into 1cm/½in-wide strips and then into 1cm/½in pieces. Drop stems into the pan of simmering water for 2 minutes. Add leaves and cook for a further 2 minutes. Drain in a colander. Run cold water over to stop silver beet from cooking further or plunge into a basin of ice-cold water and drain again, then press with a saucepan lid or the back of a saucer and tip cooked leaves and stems onto a spread-out dry tea towel. Roll tea towel and twist the ends in opposite directions to extract as much liquid as possible.

Heat 2 tablespoons of the olive oil in an enamelled cast-iron or other heavy-based flameproof casserole over medium heat. Sauté sausage pieces and potato for 8 minutes or until well sealed. Add garlic and stir for 30 seconds, then add silverbeet leaves and stems.

Mix tomato paste with the hot water and add to casserole with chilli flakes. Stir to mix, cover with a lid and reduce heat to low, then cook for 5 minutes. (If it looks too sloppy at this stage, increase heat, remove lid and cook briskly until it looks suitably saucy.) Check for seasoning, adding salt if necessary, and drizzle with remaining olive oil, then serve at once.

Crustless Silverbeet, Pine Nut and Olive 'Tart'

SERVES 6 This tart can be cut into wedges and served for a light lunch, perhaps with a juicy tomato salad to the side. It might be baked in a rectangular tin and then cut into squares or fingers to be offered as part of a mixed antipasto. On another occasion, it can be baked in a pastry crust (see the Basic Shortcrust Pastry recipe on page 510). If you like, chopped sun-dried tomatoes could be used instead of, or as well as, the olives.

300g/10½oz silverbeet leaves and
   stems, washed well, leaves and stems
   separated
2 tablespoons extra-virgin olive oil
1 tablespoon pine nuts
4 spring onions, trimmed and finely
   chopped
2 cloves garlic, finely chopped
12 black olives, pitted and
   coarsely chopped (optional)

20g/¾oz fresh breadcrumbs
sea salt and freshly ground
   black pepper
2 free-range eggs
95g/3⅓oz Greek-style yoghurt
   (see page 706)
20g/¾oz butter, melted, plus
   20g/¾oz extra butter, softened
2 tablespoons grated parmesan

EXTRA EQUIPMENT
food processor
1 × 20cm/8in
   non-stick flan tin
   with removable
   base or ceramic
   or terracotta
   pie plate

Preheat oven to 180°C/Gas 4.

Bundle silverbeet leaves together and cut into 2cm/¾in-wide ribbons. Using a paring knife, pull any strings from silverbeet stems. Slice really thick stems lengthways into 1cm/½in-wide strips and then into 1cm/½in pieces. Drop stems into a pan of simmering water for 2 minutes. Add leaves and cook for a further 2 minutes. Drain in a colander. Run cold water over to stop silver beet from cooking further or plunge into a basin of ice-cold water and drain again, then press with a saucepan lid or the back of a saucer and tip cooked leaves and stems onto a spread-out dry tea towel. Roll tea towel and twist the two ends in opposite directions to extract as much liquid as possible. Pulse silver beet in a food processor for a few seconds to chop. Tip it into a bowl.

Heat 2 teaspoons of the olive oil in a large non-stick frying pan over medium heat and sauté pine nuts until golden. Tip pine nuts onto a paper towel-lined plate. Add remaining oil to pan and sauté spring onion and garlic for 30 seconds or until garlic smells fragrant. Add silverbeet and mix well, then sauté for 1 minute. Tip silverbeet mixture back into bowl, then stir in olives, pine nuts and 2 tablespoons of the breadcrumbs. Season to taste with salt and pepper and leave to cool.

Lightly whisk eggs and stir in yoghurt, then tip into cooled silverbeet mixture. Thoroughly grease a 20cm/8in non-stick flan tin or pie dish with melted butter, then coat base and sides with remaining breadcrumbs. Tip in silverbeet mixture and scatter over parmesan. Dot with softened butter. Bake for 25 minutes or until firm. Serve warm or cold.

Silverbeet and Cheese Filo Triangles

MAKES 15 The proper Greek name for these delicious savoury pies is *spanakotiropitakia*. Every non-Greek speaker stumbles on this word, so I have taken the easy option and anglicised the recipe title.

8 silverbeet leaves and stems, washed well, leaves and stems separated
2 spring onions, trimmed and thinly sliced
10 mint leaves, chopped
6 stalks flat-leaf parsley, chopped
60g/2oz butter, chopped
1 tablespoon extra-virgin olive oil
1 small onion, chopped

1 free-range egg
100g/3½oz feta
100g/3½oz fresh ricotta
50g/2oz parmesan or pecorino, grated
freshly grated nutmeg, to taste
sea salt and freshly ground black pepper
5 sheets filo pastry

Cut silverbeet stems lengthways into 2–3 strips, then thinly slice. Roll silverbeet leaves, then shred. Put stems and leaves into a mixing bowl, then add spring onion, mint and parsley.

Melt butter in a small saucepan and set aside.

Heat oil in a small frying pan over high heat and sauté onion for 2–3 minutes or until well softened. Add silverbeet mixture, stir to mix well and cook for 5 minutes or until all liquid evaporates. Tip into a colander and press with the back of spoon to extract as much liquid as possible. Leave to drain for 5–6 minutes.

Preheat oven to 180°C/Gas 4.

Break egg into a large bowl and mix with a fork. Crumble in feta and ricotta, then add parmesan or pecorino and silverbeet mixture. Season with nutmeg, salt and pepper.

Unwrap filo and select 5 sheets. Return remaining pastry to container and place in refrigerator. Place 1 filo sheet on a workbench with its shortest side facing you and cover remaining filo sheets with a foil-lined damp tea towel. Use a sharp knife to cut filo lengthways into 3 even long strips. Brush with melted butter. Place 1 heaped teaspoonful of silverbeet mixture in the top right-hand corner of the first strip. Fold pastry over filling to form a triangle shape, then keep folding over to enclose filling and form a neat triangle. Repeat with remaining pastry and filling to form 15 triangles. Brush surface of each triangle with melted butter.

Place triangles on 2 baking paper-lined baking trays and bake for 20 minutes or until golden brown. Serve warm or at room temperature.

Silverbeet Stem 'Chips'

SERVES 4 This is a delicious and surprising way of using a part of the silver beet that is often discarded. It is a wonderful accompaniment to a grilled piece of fish. You could serve the fish on a bed of the softly cooked silverbeet leaves with these chips alongside. A squeeze of lemon juice is all that is needed.

EXTRA EQUIPMENT
wok (optional)
long-handled brass
    skimmer or slotted
    spoon

salt
1 lemon, halved
250g/9oz silverbeet stems (10–12 depending on size), well washed (reserve leaves for another use)

2 teaspoons thyme leaves
50g/2oz plain flour
80ml/3fl oz extra-virgin olive oil
sea salt

Bring a large pan of lightly salted water to the boil over high heat. Squeeze in juice of half a lemon. Using a paring knife, pull away any strings from silverbeet stems, slice lengthways into 1cm/½in-wide strips and then into 5–6cm/2–2½in lengths. Drop into simmering water, cook for 10 minutes, then drain. Run cold water over stems to stop them cooking further or plunge into a basin of ice-cold water and drain again. Pat dry with a tea towel. Mix thyme leaves and plain flour in a bowl. Tip in dried silverbeet stems. Toss to mix well.

Preheat oven to 100°C/Gas ¼ and put a paper towel-lined ovenproof plate inside to keep warm.

Pour olive oil into a medium-sized non-stick frying pan or a wok to a depth of 1.5cm/½in in the centre, then heat over high heat. Drop stems into hot oil in batches; be careful as the pieces may spit initially. Don't crowd the pan. As stems become a light golden brown, scoop from oil with a brass skimmer or slotted spoon and transfer to warm plate in oven. Continue until all stems are fried and drain on a paper towel-lined plate. Serve with a sprinkling of sea salt and with the remaining lemon half cut into wedges.

Silverbeet and Ricotta Filling for Pasta

SERVES 6 I have given the recipe for a ricotta-based fresh pasta filling using spinach in detail under **SPINACH** (see Spinach and Ricotta Pasta 'Roly-poly' on page 595); however, it is just as delicious made with silverbeet instead. To make the same quantity, substitute 300g/10½oz silverbeet leaves and stems for the 500g/1lb spinach leaves called for. The resulting filling will yield enough to fill at least 60 pieces of ravioli or tortellini, which is enough to serve 6. For this quantity of filling you will need 300g/10½oz fresh pasta (see Fresh Pasta on page 474), a little more than is needed for the 'Roly-poly'.

Silverbeet Stem Gratin

SERVES 4 This is another way of using silverbeet stems. Be careful not to over-season this dish as both the anchovies and the olives are already salty.

EXTRA EQUIPMENT
1 × 1 litre/1¾ pint-capacity shallow gratin dish

salt
½ lemon
450g/15½oz silverbeet stems (about 20 depending on size), well washed (reserve leaves for another use)
125ml/4½fl oz pouring cream
4 anchovy fillets, finely chopped
10 black olives, pitted and finely chopped

2 tablespoons chopped flat-leaf parsley
25g/1oz fresh breadcrumbs
freshly ground black pepper
20g/¾oz butter, melted
2 tablespoons grated parmesan
1 tablespoon extra-virgin olive oil

Preheat oven to 190°C/Gas 5.

Bring a large saucepan of lightly salted water to the boil over high heat. Squeeze in juice of half a lemon. Using a paring knife, pull away any strings from silverbeet stems, slice lengthways into 1 cm-wide strips and then cut into 5–6cm/2–2¼in lengths. Drop into simmering water and cook for 10 minutes. Drain in a colander. Run cold water over stems to stop them cooking further or plunge into a basin of ice-cold water and drain again. Pat dry with a tea towel and transfer to a bowl.

Mix cream, anchovy, olives and parsley with half the breadcrumbs. Tip in drained stems and mix through. Season to taste with pepper.

Brush a 1 litre/1¾ pint-capacity gratin dish with melted butter. Tip in silverbeet mixture and smooth top. Scatter with remaining crumbs mixed with grated parmesan and drizzle with olive oil.

Bake for 15 minutes or until golden and bubbling at the edges, then serve.

Sautéed Silver Beet with Garlic

SERVES 1 There are few speedier preparations than this. Collect 6 or so silverbeet leaves from the garden. Wash and roughly shred both leaves and stems and put into a frying pan with 1 teaspoon olive oil and 1 sliced clove garlic. Cover and cook over medium heat for maybe 3 minutes. Lift off the lid, increase heat if there is any visible liquid left to reduce, and then serve with a fillet of fish or a speedily cooked minute steak. This is one of my standby mid-week meals. A variation is to cook the leaves in butter and to add a generous quantity of either grated parmesan or ricotta salata (see page 705) before serving.

SORREL

**Polygonaceae family
(includes rhubarb)
Herbaceous perennial**

Soil type
Light soil, enriched with
organic matter.

Soil preparation
Plant after a legume crop or
dig in compost or well-rotted
manure a few weeks prior
to planting.

Climate
Suitable for all climates.

Position
Prefers full sun to partial shade.

How to grow
Directly sow seeds at a depth
of 1.5cm in moist soil, then
thin seedlings to 30cm apart
after 4 weeks. Plants can be
divided during autumn or early
spring. Dig up a plant and divide
it into several pieces, ensuring
each piece has a stem and root
system. Replant the pieces
30m apart.

Water requirements
Water frequently. Don't allow
the soil to become dry.

When to fertilise
Use a liquid fertiliser (see page
691) every 4 weeks to improve
growth.

Harvest period
After 8 weeks, harvest the
leaves as required.

Pests and organic control
Snails, slugs and caterpillars will
attack the leaves. Use crushed
egg shells around the base of
the young plants to deter
snails and slugs.

Companion planting
Grows well with onions, lettuce
and spinach.

Special information
If you are not growing the plant
for seed, cut the flower stalks as
they appear.

**Quantities to plant
for a family of four**
1 plant, or more if your family
loves sorrel, which shrinks very
dramatically when cooked.

Sorrel (*Rumex* sp.)

Growing and Harvesting There are two types of sorrel you might come across, both are hardy perennials that can be lifted, divided and replanted but it is often preferable to sow afresh each year for the youngest leaves. True sorrel (*Rumex acetosa*) is a spreading plant with broad, lance-shaped leaves, it is a British native but do not pick it from the wild as it is easy to raise from seed. Buckler leaf sorrel or French sorrel (*R. scutatus*) has a neater habit and has squatter shield-like leaves, when young it can be used as salad leaf.

Sorrel is easy to grow and an attractive plant in the garden. In no time at all you can plant out a row of sorrel plants that will be ready for picking in less than two months. Snails also love sorrel, so always have a good hunt among the leaves whenever you are in the garden. Pick leaves from the outside of the plant, and cut out the long stems that shoot from the centre to prevent the plant going to seed.

Container Planting Sorrel will grow readily in a pot or container. Ensure that the soil is kept moist at all times and cut the flower stems as they appear to keep the plant productive.

Preparing and Sharing Wash sorrel well and inspect it carefully for any hidden tiny snails. The central stalk needs to be removed by bending the leaf lengthways and ripping out the stem – it's a bit like pulling up a zip.

Raw sorrel leaves are very acidic (due to the presence of oxalic acid). While I don't care for them at all in a mixed leaf salad, other cooks are happy to mix in a few sorrel leaves with more tender salad greens.

Once cooked, sorrel has a sharp but pleasant lemon flavour. Like spinach and silver beet (Swiss chard), sorrel is best cooked in a stainless-steel (non-reactive) pan – it can be combined with either of these to extend it and lessen its acidity. It collapses dramatically and four cups of firmly packed and stemmed sorrel leaves will reduce to half a cup of very intensely flavoured greyish-green purée (see opposite) that is good combined with cream and/or eggs, or served with oily fish such as salmon or rainbow trout. A sorrel purée can also be combined with mashed potato or creamed rice and both options are perfect to serve with oily fish or simply roasted quail.

Especially for Kids Sorrel soup has been surprisingly popular with Kitchen Garden Program students. It is worth trying at home as a way of introducing sorrel to young palates. It is a good idea to start the soup with a finely chopped onion and a few diced potatoes sweated in butter before adding the carefully washed and trimmed sorrel leaves to the pan.

Why not surprise the family (or the class) by making a green risotto with young nettle tops and sorrel leaves?

After rain, a snail hunt among the sorrel plants will almost certainly yield a very tasty lunch for chickens, if you keep them.

Sorrel Purée

SERVES 4 (MAKES 125ML/4½FL OZ) It takes a heap of sorrel to make a substantial amount of purée. Its flavour is very concentrated, so a little bit of this goes a long way. A spoonful of purée gives a lovely sharpness to an omelette. I have enjoyed sorrel purée served alongside pan-fried veal chops or stuffed inside a whole baked ocean trout or under a scallop grilled on its own half-shell. If serving a small spoonful of this purée under grilled scallops, the Anchovy Sauce on page 450 would be a delicious final touch drizzled over each scallop.

EXTRA EQUIPMENT
food processor

200g/7oz sorrel leaves (about 50–60 leaves, to yield 100g/3½oz after picking from stems), well washed

1 teaspoon Dijon mustard
2 tablespoons pouring cream
2 free-range egg yolks

Fold each sorrel leaf along its stem-line with rough side uppermost, then pull stem up and along leaf (a bit like pulling up a zipper). The stem end and central stem will come away leaving you with two pieces of leaf. Put all stems in compost bucket. Plunge trimmed sorrel leaves into a basin of cold water and give them a good swish.

Drop sorrel into a small stainless-steel saucepan with just the water clinging to leaves. Cover and cook over low heat, stirring once, for 2–3 minutes or until it has just collapsed into a greyish-green mass. Tip sorrel into a sieve and press it gently to extract as much liquid as possible.

Immediately process sorrel, mustard and cream in a food processor for a few seconds to form a smooth purée. Add egg yolks and process again.

Scrape purée into a small saucepan and cook over low heat, stirring constantly for 1 minute or until purée has thickened slightly. Remove from heat and serve warm or cold.

Salmon with Sorrel Sauce Remembered

SERVES 6 The inventiveness of French chefs Jean and Pierre Troisgros in creating their iconic dish of salmon with sorrel sauce at the three-Michelin-starred Restaurant Troisgros was revolutionary in the late seventies. The combination of flavours and textures was perfect – oily rich fish with a cream sauce built on a reduction of herby vermouth and the sharp acidity of sorrel. Not only was the sorrel roughly torn and served only just collapsed (instead of the classic purée) but the salmon itself was flattened into a thin escalope and seared for just a moment in the all-new Teflon pans so that it was still practically raw in the centre. I spent a week in the kitchens of the Restaurant Troisgros in the early eighties and watched with fascination as this dish was cooked over and over again – perfect each time. Cream sauces are rarely seen nowadays but they can still charm if served in small portions as part of a well-balanced meal. Prepare the fish before starting the sauce, as the sauce will take maybe 15 minutes to complete and the fish will take about 4 minutes to cook. Otherwise, you can prepare the sauce several hours in advance, then refrigerate it closely covered with plastic film. When needed, return the sauce to simmering point over medium heat, add the torn sorrel and stir to reheat thoroughly, then proceed with the recipe.

1 small handful sorrel leaves
6 × 150g/5oz Atlantic salmon or ocean
   trout fillets, skin removed and
   pin-boned (ask your fishmonger
   to do this)
olive oil, for cooking
sea salt and freshly ground
   black pepper
600ml/1 pint pouring cream

3 French shallots, finely chopped
125ml/4½fl oz dry white wine
60ml/2fl oz dry vermouth
500ml/18fl oz Homemade Fish
   Stock (see opposite)
a large sprig thyme
juice of ½ lemon, strained
10g/⅓oz butter

EXTRA EQUIPMENT
meat mallet

Fold each sorrel leaf along its stem-line with rough side uppermost, then pull stem up and along leaf (a bit like pulling up a zipper). The stem end and central stem will come away leaving you with two pieces of leaf. Wash leaves well.

Place a salmon fillet inside a clean plastic bag and, with the flat side of a meat mallet, gently flatten fattest part of the fillet to make it an even thickness. Remove from plastic bag, brush with olive oil, season with salt and pepper and refrigerate, covered with plastic film. Repeat with remaining fillets.

Reduce cream in a large non-stick frying pan over medium heat for 5 minutes, stirring until you have 400ml/14fl oz. Strain into a bowl and set aside.

Simmer shallot, wine, vermouth, stock and thyme in a stainless-steel saucepan over medium heat for 8–10 minutes or until you have 100ml/3½fl oz liquid. Strain into a bowl, pressing hard on solids.

Preheat oven to 100°C/Gas ¼ and put in a baking tray and 6 plates to warm.

Rinse and dry saucepan. Add strained reduced fish stock and bring to simmering point over medium heat, then whisk in reduced cream. Add lemon juice and season to taste with salt and pepper. Drop in torn sorrel leaves and stir thoroughly, then swirl in butter to add extra richness. Keep warm.

Heat 2 large non-stick frying pans over high heat until very hot. Place 2 salmon fillets in each pan with less attractive side down. Cook for 30 seconds, then turn and cook for a further 30 seconds (if you don't enjoy rare salmon, cook for a little longer). Transfer to baking tray in oven and cook remaining salmon.

Spoon a portion of sauce onto each plate, spreading it with the back of a spoon. Place a salmon fillet in centre of each plate and add a few sea salt flakes, then serve at once.

Homemade Fish Stock

The success of the Salmon with Sorrel Sauce Remembered on page 581 lies in using good-quality fish stock, which is available in good food stores and some supermarkets. It is also easy to make by simmering a chopped, washed white fish head such as snapper with an onion, a stick of celery and a generous bouquet garni (see page 635) and approximately 2 litres/3½ pints water (or enough to just cover the other ingredients) for about 20 minutes only and then straining it, without pressing down on the solids, as this will cloud the stock.

Sorrel, Sausage and Green Leaf Picnic Loaf

SERVES 8–10 This is a very simple and quite rustic preparation. The sorrel contributes an olive-green hue to the loaf, which is a bit unnerving, but delicious nonetheless. In no way should the cook expect a matured, complex blend of flavours such as you would achieve in a carefully made classic terrine – but then this recipe doesn't take the many hours of marinating, mixing, baking, sealing and maturing that such a terrine requires. With crusty bread rolls, freshly picked ripe tomatoes and this savoury loaf, you have the makings of an instant picnic. The egg white can be frozen for another use, or used to make a few meringues to take on the picnic also!

EXTRA EQUIPMENT
potato ricer
1 × 1 litre/1¾ pint-
    capacity terrine
    mould
food processor
large metal spoon

2 large potatoes, cut into chunks
80g/3oz (20–25) sorrel leaves
1 tablespoon extra-virgin olive oil
20g/¾oz butter
salt
150g/5oz leafy greens (spinach,
    silverbeet leaves, beetroot leaves,
    outside lettuce leaves), well washed
    and cut into 2cm/¾in-wide strips

2 cloves garlic,
    finely chopped
100g/3½oz bacon
450g/15½oz pure pork
    sausages, skins removed
    and meat crumbled
freshly ground black pepper
1 free-range egg yolk
2 bay leaves

Cook potato in a saucepan of simmering water for 10 minutes or until quite tender. Press through a potato ricer, cover with plastic film and set aside until needed.

Fold each sorrel leaf along its stem-line with rough side uppermost, then pull stem up and along leaf (a bit like pulling up a zipper). The stem end and central stem will come away leaving you with two pieces of leaf. Put all stems in compost bucket. Wash leaves well.

>>>

Preheat oven to 200°C/Gas 6. Use a little of the olive oil to oil a 1 litre/1¾ pint-capacity terrine mould.

Melt butter in a large non-stick frying pan and drop in sorrel leaves. Stir with a wooden spoon until the leaves have collapsed into a purée. Tip into a sieve resting over a bowl and press with a spoon to extract as much liquid as possible. Discard liquid and add sorrel to potato.

Bring a large saucepan of lightly salted water to the boil over high heat. Drop in greens and cook for 2 minutes. Drain greens in a colander. Run cold water over greens or plunge into a bowl of ice-cold water and drain again to stop them cooking further, then press with a saucepan lid or the back of a saucer and tip cooked leaves and stems onto a spread-out dry tea towel. Roll tea towel, then twist the ends in opposite directions to extract as much liquid as possible. Roughly chop greens.

Heat remaining olive oil in a frying pan over high heat, then add garlic and stir for 30 seconds. Tip in chopped greens and sauté, stirring to evaporate any remaining liquid. Tip into bowl with potato and sorrel.

Coarsely mince bacon in a food processor. Place crumbled sausage meat and bacon in a bowl and grind on some pepper, then add egg yolk. Add potato/sorrel/greens mixture and mix everything together very well with wet hands.

Pack mixture into the oiled terrine mould, then smooth top with the back of a large metal spoon. Place bay leaves on top, then cover with a sheet of foil. Bake for 40 minutes or until juices run clear when centre of terrine is pierced with a skewer and top of terrine feels firm. Remove foil, then bake for another 15 minutes. Cool terrine completely before turning out and refrigerating. The loaf is best eaten the next day, or it could be stored for a day or two (cooked green leaves lose their charm after 1–2 days in the refrigerator).

Sorrel, Sausage and Green Leaf Sausage Rolls

MAKES 18 The Sorrel, Sausage and Green Leaf Picnic Loaf mixture in the above recipe makes an absolutely delicious filling for sausage rolls. Cut 2 all-butter puff pastry sheets into 3 strips each. Divide the sausage/sorrel mixture into 6, then spoon 1 portion along the centre of each pastry strip. Brush pastry edges with lightly beaten egg, then fold over to enclose filling, pinching edges tightly together. Brush pastry with the beaten egg, then cut into 3cm/1½in-wide sausage rolls. Transfer rolls to a baking paper-lined baking tray, then chill in the refrigerator for 20 minutes. Bake at 200°C/Gas 6 for 30 minutes or until golden. Serve at once or cool completely before storing in an airtight container in the refrigerator for 1–2 days. Reheat at 200°C/Gas 6 for 5 minutes.

SPINACH

**Chenopodiaceae family
(includes beetroot and
silver beet)
Annual**

Soil type
Moist, well drained and fertile.

Soil preparation
Dig in organic matter or
well-rotted manure a few
weeks prior to planting.

Climate
Grows in most areas.

Position
Prefers full sun, but will
tolerate partial shade.

How to grow
Directly sow the seeds at
a depth of 1cm, and 30cm
apart if sowing in rows. Sow
from March-May. Some varieties
are suitable for autumn sowing.
Seedlings will emerge within
2–3 weeks. Germination will
improve if you soak the seeds
in water overnight.

Water requirements
Keep the soil moist but avoid
getting the foliage wet.

Successive planting
Leave about 3 weeks between
each planting, throughout the
growing season.

When to fertilise
Use a liquid fertiliser (see
page 691) or worm tea
(see page 695) every 4 weeks
to improve growth.

Harvest period
Spinach has a long cropping
period and the leaves can
be harvested as soon as the
plants are large enough.
This will usually be 6–7 weeks
after planting.

Pests and organic control
Use crushed egg shells around
the base of the young plants to
deter snails and slugs. Downy
mildew can spoil crops in cold,
wet summers. Look for disease-
resistant varieties.

Companion planting
Celery, onions, eggplant,
cabbages, peas
and strawberries.

Special information
Prone to bolting so sow little and
often and cut when young.

**Quantities to plant
for a family of four**
4 plants every 3 weeks
throughout the growing season.

Spinach (*Spinacea oleracea*)

Growing and Harvesting Spinach is the most aristocratic of the leafy green vegetables and holds a special place in the repertoire of French, Italian, Chinese, Indian and Middle Eastern cooks. True spinach is an annual so quickly runs to seed but there are other alternatives such as leaf beet or perpetual spinach and chards, these are biennials so less likely to bolt the first year.

Spinach can be harvested as individual leaves. Pick the outside leaves while they are young and tender. To encourage further growth, don't pick them all in one go. If the leaves of an entire plant are cut, leaving 10–15 centimetres of stem, the plant will sprout again.

Blocks of spinach plantings scattered among suggested companion plants (see page 587) is a good way to deter leaf-eating pests and offer wind protection. This year I have grown my spinach near some roses, where it received filtered sunshine and did quite well. I mulched the plants thickly with straw, which kept the leaves clean.

As spinach shrinks ten-fold when cooked, it is worth growing *lots* of it. Those plants not picked small for salads will continue to grow and produce much larger (but just as succulent, if stronger tasting) leaves.

Container Planting Spinach will grow in a container or pot. The pot will need to be positioned so that the young plants are protected from wind. Keep the pot moist and mulch well.

Preparing and Sharing Spinach needs very careful washing and is usually cooked just with the water from washing clinging to it unless you are cooking a huge quantity. If a snail has taken a bite from the leaf it is still edible as long as the leaf has been washed well. If you intend to make a smooth purée, each leaf must have the central stem removed. Fold the leaf lengthways and then rip out the stem – it's a bit like pulling up a zip. Like sorrel, spinach needs to be cooked in a roomy stainless-steel (non-reactive) saucepan.

Don't wash spinach unless you intend to cook it immediately. When stored damp it quickly becomes an evil-smelling slime. On the other hand, spinach keeps well if cooked, squeezed to remove excess moisture and kept covered in the refrigerator for a day or two. It is then ready to be sautéed or chopped to make a filling for a pie or pasta; for mixing with other ingredients to make vegetable 'burgers'; or added to Italian-style meatballs (*polpette*). Balls of bright-green cooked and drained spinach are a commonplace convenience food in good Italian delicatessens – in Italy, anyhow.

Pick the youngest leaves for a salad as the larger they become the more pronounced the flavour of oxalic acid, which has a puckering effect on the mouth and can leave an unpleasant aftertaste that will discourage young gourmets. It is more interesting to combine some tiny spinach leaves with young rocket and other salad leaves, then dress with a vinaigrette such as the one on page 389. I recommend including an ingredient that has a bit of richness to offset the oxalic acid, such as: snipped crisp bacon; toasted breadcrumbs tossed with sunflower or pumpkin seeds (see page 515); moist boiled eggs (cooked for 7 minutes so the whites are firm but the yolks are still a little soft); small garlic-rubbed baked croûtons (see page 313); or crisp-fried onion rings. Make sure you remove any long spinach stems to prevent choking.

A spinach purée is an elegant accompaniment to an escalope of veal or a fillet steak. Drain the cooked leaves quickly and squeeze dry in a very thick clean tea towel. Immediately transfer to a food processor with a generous quantity of butter and process until you have a velvety green purée. Season with salt, pepper and freshly grated nutmeg. This purée can be reheated in a microwave or steamer for a minute or so when required. It takes a lot of spinach to make a small quantity of this butter-rich purée, so serve it in small portions.

A small amount of spinach will make either a pasta stuffing when combined with ricotta, parmesan and seasoning (see page 595) or a pie or tart filling, when mixed with roasted vegetables. Indian cooks mix spinach with potatoes and spices, or stir spinach and spices into yoghurt as a side dish for a curry (see page 590). Finally, cooked spinach does love butter!

Especially for Kids Before the school vacation or the family holiday, if there is a super-sized crop of spinach, cut and cook as described opposite, squeeze very dry and freeze it in suitably sized containers to use later on.

I have delighted quite a few children by making spinach-leaf fritters. Three or four of the larger leaves are laid one on top of the other. The bundle is dipped into batter (see page 560 or 678), fried in very clean hot oil, drained very, very well and served drizzled with honey.

Yoghurt with Spinach

SERVES 6 AS AN ACCOMPANIMENT Although this recipe is intended as a side dish to serve with a curry, I have also enjoyed it with grilled lamb chops, especially if they have been rubbed with a few spices before cooking. Some cooks might like to double the spice quantities listed in this recipe and use half to cook the spinach and rub the remainder into double-cut lamb chops or racks of lamb. Yoghurt side dishes like this are also very popular with Middle Eastern meals.

250g/9oz spinach (to yield 150g/5oz leaves after stemming)
1 teaspoon cumin seeds
1 tablespoon vegetable oil
1 teaspoon brown mustard seeds
⅛ teaspoon chilli powder
280g/10oz Greek-style yoghurt (see page 706)
sea salt, to taste
paprika, for sprinkling

EXTRA EQUIPMENT
mortar and pestle

Fold each spinach leaf along its stem-line with the rough side uppermost, then pull the stem up and along the leaf (a bit like pulling up a zipper). The stem end and the central stem will come away leaving you with two pieces of leaf. Wash leaves well.

Put washed spinach leaves into a medium-sized stainless-steel saucepan with water clinging to them. Cover and cook over medium heat, stirring once, for 4 minutes or until spinach is collapsed and well softened. Tip spinach into a sieve, then press on it with a metal spoon to remove as much liquid as possible. Roughly chop, then set aside to cool.

Dry-roast cumin seeds in a small frying pan over medium heat for 30 seconds or until fragrant. Grind with a mortar and pestle briefly to form a coarse powder. Heat vegetable oil in the frying pan over medium heat, then add mustard seeds. As soon as they start to pop (a few seconds), add ground cumin and chilli powder, then stir and quickly remove from heat. Scrape spices and oil into a mixing bowl. Leave to cool.

Mix yogurt, spinach and spice mixture together, then add salt to taste. Dust with a little paprika before serving.

Spinach Burghul

SERVES 4 AS AN ACCOMPANIMENT Burghul or cracked wheat (sometimes labelled 'bulgur') deserves to be better known. It is wheat that has been boiled and baked before being cracked so it only needs reconstituting with liquid to make it edible, making it extremely quick to prepare. Its nutty flavour is very appealing. Burghul comes in two textures, fine or coarse. I prefer the coarse one for this dish. This recipe is from Julie Le Clerc, a friend from New Zealand. It can accompany many dishes, from hamburgers to grilled fish or a juicy stew.

EXTRA EQUIPMENT
blender or food
processor

265g/9oz coarse burghul (see
   page 703)
375ml/13fl oz chicken stock
2 cloves garlic,
   finely chopped

150g/5oz spinach leaves or young
   silverbeet leaves, excess stalks
   removed and washed well
sea salt and freshly ground
   black pepper

Place burghul in a bowl. Put stock and garlic into a medium-sized saucepan and bring slowly to the boil over low heat. Drop in spinach and stir with a wooden spoon for 30 seconds. As soon as spinach has wilted, tip spinach/stock mixture into a blender (or food processor). Cover blender lid with a dry tea towel, as hot liquids can force up the lid of a blender, spraying hot liquid that can burn. Carefully blend until a smooth green-flecked liquid forms. Immediately pour liquid over burghul and stir briefly. Cover bowl with plastic film and leave to steam for 10 minutes or until burghul has softened.

Remove plastic film, fluff up burghul with a fork, season to taste with salt and pepper and serve at once. If burghul has become too cool, transfer to a microwave-safe container and reheat, covered, in a microwave for 1 minute.

Spinach 'Breadballs' (*Polpette*)

MAKES 10 Follow the method I've given for Parsley and Parmesan 'Bread Balls' on page 456, substituting 100g/3½oz cooked chopped spinach (about 200g/7oz raw) for the parsley, then proceed with the recipe.

Tony Tan's Beef and Spinach Curry

SERVES 6 This recipe was put together by my friend Tony Tan after we visited the Slow Food Farmers' Market at the Abbotsford Convent in Melbourne and I had bought huge bunches of lovely spinach. I had friends coming for dinner and decided that the menu had to include this vegetable. The curry was quick to make and murmured away in the oven for several hours, requiring no attention and filling the house with lovely aromas. Serve with the Moong Dal on page 505 and the Yoghurt with Spinach on page 590, or, for a grander spread, serve with the Chickpea and Tomato Curry on page 656 and a bowl of Mint and Tamarind Chutney on page 409 (see opposite). Or simply serve with basmati rice or flatbread.

50g/2oz tamarind pulp (see page 706)
60ml/2fl oz boiling water
2 onions, roughly chopped
1 × 6cm/2½in-long piece ginger, roughly chopped
4 cloves garlic, roughly chopped
80ml/3fl oz peanut oil
1 cinnamon stick
6 whole cloves
6 cardamom pods, lightly bruised
1½ tablespoons ground coriander

2 teaspoons ground cumin
1½ teaspoons chilli powder
1.5kg/3lb beef oyster blade, cut into 3cm/1½in pieces
1 × 400g/14oz tin chopped tomatoes
1 tablespoon tomato paste
500ml/18fl oz water
1 teaspoon salt
250g/9oz spinach (to yield 150g/5oz leaves after stemming), washed
basmati rice or flatbread, to serve

EXTRA EQUIPMENT
food processor
1 × 4 litre/ 7 pint-capacity enamelled cast-iron or other heavy-based casserole with tight-fitting lid

Make tamarind water using tamarind and the boiling water, following instructions on page 409, and set aside. Process onion, ginger and garlic in a food processor to form a paste.

Preheat oven to 150°C/Gas 2.

Heat peanut oil in a 4 litre/7 pint-capacity enamelled cast-iron casserole over medium heat and fry onion paste, cinnamon stick, cloves and cardamom pods for 5 minutes, stirring frequently to prevent sticking. Stir in coriander, cumin, chilli and tamarind water and cook for 2–3 minutes. Add meat and stir, turning to coat with spice mixture. Tip in tomato, tomato paste, water and salt. Stir again. Cover and bring to simmering point over medium heat, then transfer to oven and cook for 3 hours. At the end of this time the meat will be tender. Leave to stand, and skim off and discard any excess oil that has risen to the surface.

Meanwhile, fold each spinach leaf along stem-line with rough side uppermost, then pull stem up and along the leaf (a bit like pulling up a zipper). The stem end and central stem will come away leaving two pieces of leaf. Wash leaves well.

Ten minutes before serving, place curry over low heat to reheat, then drop in spinach leaves, season to taste with salt and serve with basmati rice or flatbread.

Spinach and Ricotta Pasta 'Roly-poly'

SERVES 4–6 This is a good party dish as, although it seems to involve many stages, the final baking is very simple and it can be served with a lot less anxiety than is the case when cooking and dividing up pasta for a crowd. The recipe could be doubled if you want to make enough 'roly-poly' for eight to ten friends. It seems that all children love making pasta. They also seem to enjoy handling and washing spinach, and mixing the filling is deliciously squishy, so the 'roly-poly' can be a fun family activity. Here the spinach is cooked in a saucepan of water rather than just with the washing water clinging to the leaves, because it is a much larger quantity than in other recipes. As mentioned under **SILVER BEET** (see page 575), the 'roly-poly' can be made using silver beet instead of spinach, and the filling can be used to stuff small pasta shapes such as tortellini or ravioli. If using silver beet, reduce the weight to 300 grams and follow the instructions for trimming, cooking and draining on page 570.

EXTRA EQUIPMENT
food processor
hand-cranked pasta
  machine
long-handled
  brass skimmer
  (optional)
30cm × 22cm/12in
  × 9in baking dish

500g/1lb spinach leaves (to yield
  250g/9oz after stemming)
salt
2 tablespoons extra-virgin olive oil
1 onion, finely chopped
100g/3½oz sliced pancetta, 6 slices
  reserved, the rest finely chopped
3 cloves garlic, finely chopped
500g/1lb fresh ricotta
150g/5oz blue cheese of choice,

crumbled
100g/3½oz parmesan, grated
½ teaspoon freshly grated nutmeg
sea salt and freshly ground
  black pepper
300g/10½oz Fresh Pasta (see
  page 474)
20g/¾oz butter, for greasing
200ml/7fl oz pouring cream
8–10 sage leaves

Fold each spinach leaf along its stem line, with rough side uppermost, then pull stem up and along leaf (a bit like pulling up a zip). The stem end and central stem will come away leaving you with two pieces of leaf. Wash leaves well.

Bring a large saucepan of lightly salted water to the boil over high heat and drop in spinach. Cover and cook over medium heat, stirring once, for 4 minutes or until spinach has collapsed. Drain in a colander. Run cold water over spinach or plunge it into a basin of ice-cold water to stop it from cooking further, then drain again and press with a saucepan lid or the back of a saucer. Tip cooked spinach onto a spread-out dry tea towel. Roll cloth and twist the ends in opposite directions to extract as much liquid as possible. Drop spinach into a food processor and pulse-chop for a few seconds.

Heat oil in a large non-stick frying pan over medium heat. Sauté onion and pancetta for 8–10 minutes, stirring until onion is well softened and pancetta started to colour. Add garlic and sauté for 30 seconds, then stir in spinach. Stir well and cook for 1–2 minutes to evaporate moisture. Tip onto a tray, spread out and leave to cool.

>>>

In a bowl, combine ricotta, blue cheese and two-thirds of the parmesan. Add nutmeg and season with some salt and pepper. (This next part is for the kids!) Roll up your sleeves and with clean hands mix spinach mixture with cheese mixture. Really squeeze and press to mix very well together. Taste and adjust seasoning with salt and pepper.

Roll pasta sheets using pasta machine, moving through each setting until the second last notch, then cut into 5 even pieces about 20cm/8in long. (Pasta sheets will expand when cooked.)

Bring a pasta pot or large heavy-based saucepan of well salted water to the boil over high heat. Have a large bowl of cold water and 2 dry tea towels spread out on a workbench alongside the stove. Drop 3 pasta sheets into simmering water and cook for 3 minutes. Carefully lift out each cooked sheet with a brass skimmer or the handle of a wooden spoon and drop into cold water. Lift each sheet from cold water and spread out on a dry tea towel; don't overlap the sheets as they will stick and tear. Repeat with remaining pasta sheets.

Preheat the oven to 180°C/Gas 4. Butter a 30cm × 22cm/12in × 9in baking dish and set aside.

Lay 2 sheets of pasta side by side in buttered dish and overlapping down centre of dish by 2–3cm/1in; pasta sheets will come up sides of baking dish. Cover the 'seam' by laying 1 pasta sheet down the centre of the baking dish. Put half of the filling down the centre and flatten it into a squared-off 'log' of filling. Cover filling with another pasta sheet. Spread remaining filling over pasta sheet. Fold overhanging pasta sheets over second layer of filling. Now finish and neaten the pasta roll by placing an extra sheet of pasta over the top and tucking it down the sides of the roll. If the 'roly-poly' fits a little too snugly in the baking dish, then it is fine to curve it a little to make it fit.

Brush top and sides of pasta with cream. Drape over reserved pancetta. Place sage leaves down length of 'roly-poly'. Scatter with remaining parmesan and drizzle remaining cream over and around 'roly-poly'.

Cover baking dish with foil and bake for 20 minutes. Remove foil and bake for a further 10 minutes. Leave 'roly-poly' to cool and settle for a few minutes before slicing and serving.

SPRING ONIONS AND FRENCH SHALLOTS

**Alliaceae family
(includes garlic and leeks)
Biennial**

Soil type
Any well-drained, fertile soil.

Soil preparation
Dig in organic compost or well-rotted manure a few weeks prior to planting.

Climate
Suitable for all climates.

Position
Prefer full sun. Shallots will tolerate partial shade.

How to grow
Spring onions and shallots:
Sow from March–July, directly into ground, at a depth of 1cm, pressing firmly into soil. When 12cm tall, thin to 10cm apart with 15cm between rows. *Shallots:* Plant sets so they are just covered with soil. Allow 10–20cm between bulbs in rows 30cm apart.

Water requirements
Keep soil moist.

Successive planting
Leave 4 weeks between each planting, throughout the growing season.

Harvest period
Spring onions: 8–12 weeks to mature. Harvest as slender stalks or leave to develop a small bulb. *Shallots:* Up to 4 months; pull bulbs at 3–4 months when leaves begin to die.

Pests and organic control
Growing in well-spaced rows for good ventilation reduces diseases such as mildew. White rot is a serious fungal disease that remains in the soil for many years. There is no cure. Pull up and destroy affected plants, and do not compost).

Companion planting
Spring onions: Tomatoes, broccoli and carrots confuse onion fly. Chamomile is said to improve flavour. Don't plant near peas, beans, sage, corn, cabbages or potatoes. *Shallots:* Brassicas, beetroot, carrots, mint and chamomile. Plant near radishes to break up soil. Don't plant near peas and beans.

Special information
Shallots: Warm weather promotes bulb growth. Cool weather promotes top growth. Keep soil moist, cool and weed-free by mulching. Don't cover maturing shallot bulbs with soil.

**Quantities to plant
for a family of four**
Spring onions: 12 every 4–6 weeks. *Shallots:* 20 bulbs.

Clockwise from bottom left: Golden shallots (Aggregatum group); pink-skinned shallots (Aggregatum group); spring onions (*Allium fistulosum*)

Growing and harvesting The onion family comes in all shapes and sizes, and in white, cream, green, brown and red. There are onions for all seasons of the year and numerous specialty cultivars as well as heirloom cultivars. Large onions intended for extended storage have a long growing time and, more importantly, need to be spread out and dried for several weeks. They can't be harvested until the tops have turned brown and collapsed. All of this means that storage onions are greedy for space and will occupy that area for a long time. Many home gardeners, like me, will prefer to buy their large onions and concentrate their growing efforts on the faster and neater growing habits of spring onions and shallots. All growing onions have grass-like leaves that need to be kept weed-free so they aren't overshadowed. Onions are thought to help deter the cabbage white butterfly, so plant them near brassicas. If onions are planted near carrots they are thought to deter aphids and other carrot pests.

Spring onions True spring onions form slender white stalks rather than bulbs. There are also bulbing onions that can be pulled early like spring onions but if left will form a small bulb that is pulled when the tops are still green. These are usually called salad onions. Both varieties are often referred to as 'green onions', which confuses things a great deal, especially as the bulbs of some salad onions are red!

Shallots Shallots grow in a cluster of small bulbs held together at the base, rather like bulbs of garlic. The cluster is covered with a skin which in most cases is a reddish-brown. However, there are varieties known as either pink or grey shallots that have a dull-pinkish skin. They are more tedious to peel, as the skins are thicker and the bulbs inside tend to be smaller. Pink-skinned or greyish/purplish-fleshed shallots are much milder than golden shallots, which taste closer to a regular onion. These golden shallots are larger, have an orange-brown skin and are much more widely available. Shallots are milder in flavour than storage onions. Harvested shallots should be dried for a few days in the open air, then stored in an airy spot and used within a few weeks, although you can enjoy shallots as soon as they are harvested, while they are still juicy and damp.

Container Planting Spring onions and shallots are ideal for growing in a pot. They can grow around the edge of a small potted tree, such as a bay, or can be part of a mixed aromatic pot including chives and coriander. As with all containers, ensure that the pot is kept moist and free of weeds by mulching.

Preparing and Sharing Onions are the workhorse of the kitchen. We rarely commence any savoury cooking without some member of the onion family being involved. Onion, carrot and celery chopped with thyme or oregano and a bay leaf is the start of countless preparations – think stocks, soups, casseroles and braises. Salad onions are very delicious and very mild. I think they are at their most succulent when the bulb is around 4–5 centimetres in diameter. They can be grilled on a barbecue, roasted with root vegetables, or used in the same way as a fully dried storage onion – that is, chopped and used with carrot and celery as a base for soups, casseroles and braises.

Spring onions Spring onions are often used raw in salads, especially Asian combinations. They are indispensable in stir-fries, and they can be cut into sections, then braised and simmered with other vegetable combinations. They can also be quickly blanched (see page 703), dried, oiled, grilled and served as an accompaniment to meatballs or burgers. And they are fun to cut into 'brushes' for serving with pancakes if the menu includes grilled duck.

To prepare chopped spring onions, pull off any damaged leaves and trim the root ends. Cut off one-third of the darkest leaves and discard (onion family members are not a favourite ingredient in the compost heap – apparently the worms don't like them). Gather the spring onions in a bundle in one hand and slice as finely as you can with a knife in the other. (Some recipes may instruct you to cut the spring onions into larger pieces, and that is fine too.)

Shallots The flavour of shallots is generally less aggressive than that of onions and their flesh is denser and less watery; however, they are fiddly to peel. If you are braising or sautéing shallots, start them off, unpeeled, in a stainless-steel pan covered with cold water, then bring them slowly to the boil over medium heat and drain – they will be much easier to peel. The bulbs can then be separated and cooked slowly in a frying pan over low heat in some olive oil for about an hour until soft, dark-gold and melting. Prepared like this, they add a wonderful sweetness and subtlety to the pan juices left after sautéing a small steak, a slice of calf liver or a piece of tuna. They are also an inspired topping for fried eggplant, a base for a rare roast beef sandwich and a fine last-minute addition to a stew.

This method can't be used if the shallots are needed raw. Very finely chopped raw shallot is included in many savoury sauces and vinaigrettes such as the Sauce Ravigote on page 235.

Cut-up shallot develops 'off' flavours quickly so either cover it with red or white-wine vinegar if it is being used in a dressing, or with olive oil if you are not cooking it straight away. If it is to be lightly cooked or used raw I often tame its bite by covering the chopped shallot with a little red-wine vinegar for an hour. The drained shallot still has its crunch and might be scattered over a grilled steak or young green beans. The classic French preparation, *sauce mignonette*, which consists of finely chopped shallots, freshly ground black pepper and red-wine vinegar, is the traditional accompaniment for freshly shucked oysters in France.

Especially for Kids All children, and many adults, complain loudly when cutting onions as the compounds released make their eyes water. Practise to see whether any of these popular preventative measures work!
- wear goggles, spectacles or sunglasses
- breathe through your mouth, not your nose
- hold a mouthful of water while cutting
- chop with a slice of bread in your mouth
- wear a peg on your nose (sounds painful)
- chop under water (sounds impossibly dangerous)

Hokkien Noodles with Spring Onion and Ginger Sauce and Takeaway Roast Duck

SERVES 4 Most large cities have at least one centre for Asian food shopping, where there is sure to be a roast meat shop with rows of shiny brown ducks and glistening chickens hanging on hooks in the window. It is not unusual to buy half a duck or chicken, or even a quarter. You will be asked if you want it chopped or not. Unless you are handy with a cleaver it will be far simpler to allow the expert to chop the bird for you. The chopped duck or chicken can be reheated in a microwave or included in a curry, but a far better idea is to stir-fry it with noodles or vegetables, or both.

1 tablespoon salt	**SPRING ONION AND GINGER SAUCE**	EXTRA EQUIPMENT
500g/1lb fresh thick Hokkien-	2 spring onions, trimmed and chopped	wok
style noodles	2 cloves garlic, finely chopped	wok sang
2 tablespoons peanut oil	1 tablespoon finely chopped ginger	(see page 47)
½ Chinese roasted duck,	2 tablespoons peanut oil	
chopped	2 tablespoons light soy sauce	
	1 tablespoon mirin (see page 704)	
	1 teaspoon sesame oil	

Preheat oven to 100°C/Gas ¼ and put a large ovenproof plate inside to warm.

To make the spring onion and ginger sauce, mix spring onion, garlic and ginger in a small heatproof bowl. Heat oil to smoking point in a small frying pan over high heat (a Chinese friend tells me that he tests that the oil is really hot by standing the end of a bamboo chopstick in it. If the oil around the chopstick hisses instantly, it is hot!). Carefully pour the very hot oil over spring onion mixture. Stir and add soy, mirin and sesame oil and set aside.

Meanwhile, bring a large pasta pot or heavy-based saucepan of salted water to simmering point over high heat. Drop in noodles and separate with a chopstick or wooden spoon handle. Cook for 3 minutes, then drain noodles in a colander and give them a good shake.

Heat a wok over high heat, then add peanut oil, drop in duck pieces and toss with a wok sang to heat through quickly. Toss in noodles and mix with duck, then add sauce. Scoop onto the hot serving plate, then serve at once.

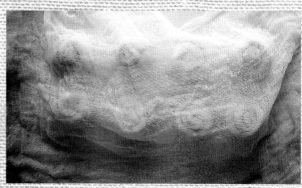

Spring Onion Cakes

MAKES 8 Children love to make these as lots of rolling and squashing with fingers is involved. I first tasted these at a street stall in one of the last remaining traditional *hutong* neighbourhoods in Beijing, where life seemed to go on as it had for generations, just metres away from the encroaching skyscrapers. They were sold as a breakfast snack but they would also be good alongside stir-fried vegetables or served with a dipping sauce of soy sauce with sliced chilli alongside (see opposite).

EXTRA EQUIPMENT
muslin
rolling pin
wok (optional)

125g/4½oz plain flour, plus extra
    for dusting
½ teaspoon salt
20g/¾oz lard
100ml/3½fl oz water
1 teaspoon sesame oil, plus extra
    for brushing
peanut oil, for shallow-frying

SPRING ONION FILLING
1 teaspoon salted black beans
    (see page 705)
1 × 1cm/½in-long piece ginger
3 spring onions, trimmed and
    finely chopped

Sift flour and salt into a mixing bowl. Melt lard in the water in a small saucepan over medium heat, then tip into flour. Mix with a wooden spoon until flour is incorporated. As soon as you can touch dough (it will be hot!), knead it for 1 minute or until smooth, then return it to the bowl and cover with a damp muslin cloth or tea towel. Leave for 30 minutes.

To make the spring onion filling, put black beans into a small bowl and crush with the back of a teaspoon. Finely chop black beans on a chopping board with ginger. Return to bowl and stir in spring onion, then set aside.

Take the ball of dough and roll it into a fat sausage shape, then cut the roll into 8 equal pieces. Shape each piece into a small ball and dust with extra flour. Roll each ball into a thin 12cm/5in round with a rolling pin. Repeat with the remaining balls. Brush each round very lightly with sesame oil.

Scatter filling over dough rounds, dividing it evenly. Using your fingers, roll each circle up like a fat cigar to enclose filling. Slightly flatten each 'cigar' and then roll it into a snail shape. Pinch ends firmly. Lay rolled 'snails' on a baking tray and cover with a slightly damp tea towel. Leave for 30 minutes.

Lightly dust 'snails' with flour. Flatten each one gently with your hand and roll out to a thin 10cm/4in round with a rolling pin. Leave for 30 minutes.

Preheat oven to 100°C/Gas ¼ and put a paper towel-lined ovenproof plate inside to warm. Pour oil into a medium-sized non-stick frying pan or wok to a depth of 1cm/½in in the centre and heat over high heat. Add sesame oil. When hot, put in as many pancakes as will fit in a single layer. They should bubble and blister after about 1 minute. Turn to cook other side, then drain on paper-towel lined plate in oven. Serve warm.

Beancurd Salad (*Hiya-Yakko*)

SERVES 4 Many years ago I worked with a chef whose mother was Japanese. Steven often made this little pick-me-up when we felt a bit stressed. The combination of silken tofu, spring onion, ginger and light soy sauce is inspired. Its success depends on using the freshest silken tofu, and assembling and eating it at once. If there is to be any delay, serve the chilled tofu in individual bowls and offer tiny condiment bowls of the seasoning ingredients separately.

1 × 250g/9oz packet silken tofu, drained
135g/4½oz crushed ice
1 sheet nori (see page 705)
15g/½oz finely chopped ginger

2–3 spring onions, trimmed and thinly sliced
½ fresh small red chilli (optional), seeded and thinly sliced
2 tablespoons light soy sauce

Rinse tofu in a colander, then cut into 2cm/¾in cubes. Put cubes into a mixing bowl and add crushed ice. Chill in refrigerator. Meanwhile, carefully pass nori sheet across a gas flame for a few seconds to toast, holding it with tongs. Tear or cut into bite-sized pieces. Set aside. Drain tofu and place in a mixing bowl. Mix ginger, spring onion and chilli, if using, and scatter generously over tofu cubes. Mix gently and divide among rice bowls, then top each bowl with nori. Drizzle a little soy over and serve at once.

Slow-cooked Shallots

MAKES 250ML/9FL OZ I like to use these slow-cooked shallots to garnish meat dishes or add them to braised vegetables. They will keep for up to one week in the refrigerator, stored in an airtight container.

1 tablespoon duck or pork fat or olive oil
20 French shallots, bulbs separated and peeled

a few sprigs thyme
1 fresh bay leaf
250ml/9fl oz dry red wine

EXTRA EQUIPMENT
sauté pan with lid
simmer mat
(optional)

Heat fat in a sauté pan with a tight-fitting lid that fits shallots in a single layer. Add shallots, turn to coat with fat, then add herbs. Sauté shallots for 5 minutes, shaking pan. Add wine, reduce heat to low and cover. Cook for 35 minutes or until shallots are tender. If using at once, increase heat and shake pan until shallots are glazed. If not, cool and refrigerate in cooking liquid. To reheat, transfer shallots and liquid to a saucepan and cover tightly. Gently warm on a simmer mat over low heat. Increase heat, uncover and shake pan until shallots are glazed.

Preparing Beancurd Salad

STONE FRUIT

Rosaceae (includes apples, pears, quinces, raspberries and strawberries)
Deciduous trees

Soil type
Light, well-drained, fertile soil.

Soil preparation
Dig nitrogen-rich fertiliser and well-rotted manure into the hole a few weeks before planting.

Climate
Best in areas with hot summers and chilling period over winter but not very cold.

Position
Prefers sun, warmth and shelter. Avoid winds and frost pockets.

How to grow
Purchase a tree, either container-grown, root-balled in hessian or bare-rooted. Prepare the planting hole (see overleaf) and put up supports if growing against a wall or fence. Water in well and keep ground beneath weed-free. Protect emerging buds and blossom from late frosts with several layers of fleece. Pruning requirements will vary but those growing against walls or fences will need training and tying in, plus fruitlets will need to be thinned out.

Water requirements
Regular, even watering during dry spells for the first two years after planting. Once established, an annual mulch will help retain soil moisture so regular watering is only needed in dry spells or for trees in containers.

When to fertilise
An annual mulch of well-rotted manure in spring plus chicken manure pellets will help. Or use an organic fruit fertiliser. Trees in pots may need extra feed during the growing season.

Harvest period
Mid-late summer depending on the fruit.

Pests and organic control
Birds peck at fruit as well as spoiling the produce diseases can enter causing fruit to rot. Smaller trees can be netted, otherwise put bird scarers in or near larger trees. Peach leaf curl is a serious fungal disease of peaches and nectarines, an easy way to prevent it infecting wall-trained forms is to cover the plant with clear polythene from January-mid May (allow ends free for pollinating insects). Silverleaf is a fungal disease of all stone fruits that enters through wounds and cuts, spores are most active in autumn and winter so by doing any pruning in summer the chances of disease are reduced.

Companion planting
Borage and lavender attracts bees to assist pollination.

Special information
Ensure the tree you buy is self-fertile, such as apricot, or there are compatible trees nearby. Check the eventual size of the tree is suitable for the site.

Peach (*Prunus persica*)

Growing and Harvesting Stone fruit trees are seeing a revival in popularity in the UK. It is still a challenge for the home gardener to get them cropping consistently every year here but milder climate and new varieties, rootstocks (see page 693) and growing techniques make it more likely and also mean the these fruits can be grown in smaller spaces than previously. Apricots are perhaps the best stone fruit to illustrate this. The traditional variety 'Moorpark', grown on a conventional rootstock would form a tree around 3 x 4.5 metres, a long growing season was required for fruit so it was prone to late frosts and crops were ready towards the end of August. New varieties such as 'Flavorcot' (or others ending in 'cot') flower later (thus avoiding late frosts and lack of insects) yet crop sooner (July to August), modern rootstocks can now produce a tree at a more manageable size around 2.4 x 3 metres and it starts cropping earlier in its life.

Another successful technique to help ensure fruiting in borderline climates is to grow plants trained into a fan against a south-facing wall or fence. This not only provide extra warmth but makes it easier to care for fruits, even in cold areas peaches, nectarines and plums can grown if you can find the right microclimate.

Before taking delivery of the trees, prepare the hole. It should be wide enough to spread the roots well, but no more than 30 centimetres deep. Include nitrogen-rich fertiliser and well-rotted manure. Drive a stake into the hole before planting the tree. Soak the root ball for an hour in a bucket of water before planting or, if in a container, soak the bottom of the plant while still in its container. Loosen the tree roots if they are at all twisted when removed from the pot. Slightly mound the soil in the centre of the hole and settle the tree over this mound, spreading the roots carefully and shaking the tree very gently into the hole to settle it well. Backfill the hole with soil to cover the roots, pressing it firmly. Finish filling the hole, shaping the surface into a slight saucer shape to maximise water penetration. The graft (the bump on the lower trunk) must always be above the soil line. Trim branches so they are no wider than the spread of the roots. Drip irrigation is worth considering in dry areas if you are planning to grow a lot of fruit.

Pruning is important for all stone fruit trees, especially peaches. However, pruning these trees properly can be complex and you should seek expert advice. Most fruit is produced on shoots made the previous year (particularly in the case of peaches and nectarines). Apricots bear fruit both on the previous year's growth and on spurs (see page 695). If a stone fruit tree is left unpruned, the branches will continue to grow and produce fruit further and further away from the main stem. It is also necessary to cut back fruiting shoots to encourage new growth.

Many stone fruit trees have their major crop in summer, which will influence your choice of what to plant if you are often away from home at that time. If you have children, it will be pretty disappointing for them to watch over a tree all year and then to miss out on the fruit altogether because they are holidaying away from home during the harvest period. Plums are the latest to fruit, from late summer and into autumn.

Be sure to cut fruit cleanly from your trees (a long-handled cutting tool is ideal for this), rather than simply twisting it off, as this prevents damage to the branches.

Container Planting Dwarf or miniature stone fruit trees are ideal specimens for large pots or tubs of at least 60 centimetres. More varieties are becoming available all the time. They should be re-potted every two to three years.

Preparing and Sharing You need freestone fruit if you want perfectly shaped peach or nectarine halves for whatever you are making. Poached stone fruit halves make lovely individual fruit tarts. When poaching apricots, always remove the stones first, then crack a few of them on a chopping board with the flat side of a large knife, extract the white kernel and add it to the pan – they add a faint scent of bitter almond to the fruit and syrup. Reduce a little of the poaching syrup by boiling it rapidly, then dab it on the fruit to make a shiny glaze. Poached stone fruit also provides the perfect acid counterfoil to a creamy rice pudding such as the one on page 657. Sometimes a few pieces of stonefruit may collapse in the poaching process. Don't worry – I suggest you purée it with some of the syrup and spoon this lightly thickened sauce over your perfectly poached fruit for a very simple dessert. Another good way to use poached stone fruit is to cut 1.5 centimetre-thick slices from a panettone or brioche. Lay the slices on a baking tray and sprinkle generously with caster sugar. Bake in a 200°C/Gas 6 oven until the sugar has melted and started to caramelise. Now settle the well-drained poached fruit on top and brush with melted jam or fruit jelly. Return to the hot oven for a further 5 minutes, then leave to cool a little before taking the first bite.

Pêches cardinale is a rather fancy but achievable classic way with peaches. It requires poached freestone peaches, ripe strawberries and fresh almonds; that is, almonds fully formed but still tightly encased in their suede-like green coats – all of which is possible to attain during the summer months. Arrange poached peach halves at the bottom of a shallow serving dish. Purée strawberries with a little icing sugar and spoon over the peach halves. Extract the almonds from their shells and slice them carefully lengthways, then scatter them over the strawberry sauce. And of course we must not forget Peach Melba. Arrange a layer of vanilla ice cream (or several scoops) in a shallow serving dish, top with poached freestone peach halves, and generously spoon on a sweetened and strained raspberry purée before serving.

Some of the simplest fruit desserts are those where ripe fruit, such as peaches, is dunked or drizzled with dessert wine or red wine.

Especially for Kids If you are away from home over summer, older children may be interested in helping net the trees before you leave. They will be fascinated by the ghostly, billowing shapes of the netted trees, and share in the satisfaction of knowing that any birds wanting to raid the fruit have been outwitted.

One of the challenges is to teach children how to recognise ripe fruit and to wait for it to ripen naturally. Small green balls on a tree at graspable height present a serious temptation – they can be seen as ammunition to throw and kick. As the tree grows taller and the fruit is less accessible to small hands, the chances of such a premature harvest will hopefully lessen.

Luke Palmer's Peach Salad with Fennel, Rocket and Almonds

SERVES 4 What could be more relaxing than sitting with a good friend in a beautiful garden, shaded by an umbrella, watching bees buzzing among the luxuriant, aromatic border of summer savory, and enjoying delicious fresh food featuring produce being grown in the same garden? That is what's on offer at Fork to Fork Café at Heronswood, the home of Digger's Club in Dromana on Victoria's Mornington Peninsula. Among many lovely tastes I enjoyed that day, this salad was a stand-out. The chef, Luke Palmer, has kindly allowed me to reproduce it here. My salad was made with yellow peaches; however, it would be just as delicious with white peaches or with white or yellow nectarines. Luke likes to serve this salad with cured, smoked or grilled local fish.

40g/1½oz raw almonds
3 ripe yellow freestone peaches
2 tablespoons extra-virgin olive oil
a handful ice cubes
2 small bulbs fennel, halved
   lengthways with fronds reserved

juice of 1 orange
4 small handfuls young rocket
   leaves, washed and dried
½ small red onion, very thinly sliced
sea salt and freshly ground black
   pepper

EXTRA EQUIPMENT
salad spinner
food processor with
   slicing attachment
   or plastic
   vegetable slicer
   (see page 46)

Put almonds into a bowl. Place peaches in another bowl. Pour boiling water over nuts and peaches. Leave peaches for 1–2 minutes, then gently drain in a colander resting over a bowl. Peel and place on a plate. Drain nuts, then peel and discard skins.

Heat 1 tablespoon of the olive oil in a small non-stick frying pan over medium heat. Fry almonds, stirring constantly with a wooden spoon, for 3–4 minutes until golden brown. Tip onto a paper towel-lined plate.

Place ice cubes in a bowl with water. Thinly slice fennel halves using a food processor with a slicer attachment or a plastic vegetable slicer. Drop fennel into iced water for 2 minutes. While fennel crisps, tip orange juice into a mixing bowl. Pat fennel slices dry with a clean tea towel and add to orange juice.

Lightly score peaches around their natural curve with a paring knife. Twist peach halves away from stones. Place each half cut-side down on a chopping board and slice widthways. Either keep as slices or cut each slice into thin sticks. Toss peach slices with rocket and onion in a salad bowl. Lift fennel from orange juice and squeeze it gently. Add to salad bowl. Drizzle with remaining olive oil and season with salt and pepper to taste.

Divide salad among 4 plates and scatter fried almonds and reserved feathery fennel fronds over each one, then serve at once.

Baked Peaches Stuffed with Amaretti Biscuits

SERVES 8 This well-known Italian dessert is delicious made with any ripe stone fruit. You will need to use freestone rather than clingstone stone fruit (see page 610) as they need to be neatly halved and the stones slipped out. The bigger the fruit selected, the more stuffing it will hold. If you don't wish to use nuts, substitute another hard crunchy biscuit for the amaretti crumbs (chocolate ripple or ginger snaps would be good) and leave out the extra nuts. If you love nuts, like me, think of different ones for different fruits – pistachios for peaches, pecans for plums, almonds for apricots and so on.

butter, for greasing
8 large freestone peaches,
   halved and stoned
juice of 2 oranges
double cream or yoghurt,
   to serve

AMARETTI BISCUIT STUFFING
60g/2oz amaretti biscuits
35g/1¼oz shelled pistachios
90g/3oz unsalted butter, softened
2 tablespoons caster sugar
1 free-range egg, lightly beaten

EXTRA EQUIPMENT
22cm × 28cm/9in ×
   11in gratin dish
parisienne spoon
   (see page 46)
rolling pin
food processor

Preheat oven to 200°C/Gas 6. Grease a 22cm × 28cm/9in × 11in gratin dish.

Using the large end of a parisienne spoon, scoop a hollow in the cavity of each peach half. Set scooped fruit pulp aside in a bowl until needed.

To make the amaretti biscuit stuffing, tip amaretti into a clean tea towel and crush coarsely with a rolling pin. Tip crumbs into another bowl. Pulse pistachios in a food processor until chopped and add to amaretti crumbs. Without washing processor, cream butter and sugar together. Add scooped fruit pulp and blend until smooth. Mix in egg. Scrape this cream into amaretti/pistachio mixture and mix.

Divide stuffing among halved fruit. Place peach halves in gratin dish, close together and filled-side up. Pour orange juice over and around stuffed peaches. Bake for 25 minutes. Serve with double cream or yoghurt.

Basic Poaching Syrup for Stone Fruit

MAKES ENOUGH FOR 4–6 PIECES OF FRUIT Poaching fruit needs to be covered by the simmering liquid for the cooking duration. Before starting to prepare any fruit, place it in the saucepan you plan to use to check that it fits comfortably without being too crowded. You also don't want to choose a pan that is so wide that you will need to make huge quantities of syrup. Several varieties of fruit can be poached one after the other in the same syrup. The final syrup will gain in complexity of flavour and probably colour if this is done.

Make sure that you wash the fruit before poaching. Peaches can be peeled after poaching, while apricots and nectarines probably won't be. Plums often lose their skins during poaching.

You could also add the juice of a lemon to the syrup to cut through any excessive sweetness, and serve the fruit lightly chilled. Don't ignore the fact that carefully poached fruit can be delicious with cream, yoghurt or ice cream.

EXTRA EQUIPMENT
slotted spoon

4–6 pieces stone fruit, washed

BASIC POACHING SYRUP
330g/11½oz white sugar
750ml/27fl oz hot water (up to 250ml/
    9fl oz can be replaced by orange juice
    or red or white wine)

FLAVOURING
a vanilla bean, lemon verbena
    or scented geranium leaf,
    citrus peel, cardamom
    pods, a cinnamon stick
    or star anise

To make the basic poaching syrup, put sugar, hot water and your choice of flavouring into a heavy-based saucepan and heat over medium heat to dissolve sugar, stirring. Once all sugar has dissolved, simmer syrup for 3–4 minutes then carefully slip in fruit.

Cut a piece of baking paper to just fit inside the pan and press it down onto surface of syrup; this will inhibit evaporation and also help keep fruit submerged. You may need to weight the paper with a saucer to keep fruit under syrup. Poach fruit until just tender; test with a very fine skewer. This will take 3–6 minutes depending on variety, size and ripeness of stone fruit used.

Lift fruit from poaching syrup with a slotted spoon and drain on a baking tray. Leave syrup to cool. If you have used peaches, once they are cooled the skins can be lifted away and, depending on the variety, they will have a beautiful pink blush. If the poached fruit is not needed immediately, store it in the refrigerator covered with the cooled syrup.

Easy Plum Cake

SERVES 6–8 This is a loose interpretation of the plum *kuchen* enjoyed by my friend Anna during a six-month stay in Frankfurt. It could be made with other stone fruit, although they will not produce the same dramatic effect as plums, which leave deep-purple juice oozing into the cake. This is a cake to make and eat on the same day. The texture is not as irresistible if the cake has been refrigerated, and the quantity of oozing fruit makes it very vulnerable to spoilage if left at room temperature for more than a day. If your serving plate is ovenproof you can loosely cover the cake with foil and reheat it at 180°C/Gas 4 for about 10 minutes to serve as a warm dessert. Individual portions can also be reheated in this way.

90g/3oz butter, softened, plus extra
   for greasing
150g/5oz plain flour
1 teaspoon cream of tartar
½ teaspoon bicarbonate of soda
a pinch salt
1 free-range egg
2–3 tablespoons buttermilk or milk
65g/2¼oz caster sugar
6–8 large ripe plums (preferably purple-
   fleshed, such as a blood plum), halved,
   stoned and cut into 2–3 pieces

2 teaspoons pure icing
   sugar (optional)
double cream, to serve

STREUSEL MIXTURE
30g/1oz soft brown sugar
½ teaspoon baking powder
½ teaspoon ground
   cinnamon
50g/2oz plain flour
30g/1oz unsalted butter,
   chopped

EXTRA EQUIPMENT
18cm/7in square
   cake tin or
   20cm/8in
   springform
   cake tin
food processor

Preheat oven to 180°C/Gas 4. Grease an 18cm/7in-square cake tin and line base with baking paper, leaving some overhanging to help ease cake out (it can't be inverted onto a cooling rack). Or grease a 20cm/8in springform cake tin.

To make the streusel mixture, mix sugar, baking powder, cinnamon and flour in a bowl. Rub in butter so mixture is a bit crumbly and lumpy. Set aside.

Sift flour, cream of tartar, bicarbonate of soda and salt into a bowl. Whisk egg with 2 tablespoons of the buttermilk or milk. Cream butter and sugar until pale and thick in a food processor. Tip in flour mixture and pulse to mix quickly. Add egg/buttermilk mixture and process just until you have a smooth batter; it should be a dropping consistency. If it is quite stiff, mix in remaining buttermilk (this will depend on size of egg used).

Scrape batter into prepared tin and smooth the top. Press plum into batter in rows or circles. Scatter over streusel mixture. Bake for 35–40 minutes or until a skewer inserted in the edges comes out clean (it will still test soft in the middle where plum juice has oozed into cake batter). Cool cake in tin on a cake cooling rack until just warm. Lift cake out using overhanging baking paper to assist, then transfer to a plate. Carefully lift base of cake with a wide spatula and ease paper out. Dust cake with icing sugar, if desired, and serve with double cream.

STRAWBERRIES

Rosaceae family (includes apples, pears, quinces, raspberries and stone fruit) Herbaceous perennial, producing for 2–3 years

Soil type
Well-drained fertile soil, rich in organic matter.

Soil preparation
Add lots of organic matter 4 weeks before planting.

Climate
Suitable for all climates.

Position
Prefer full sun.

How to grow
Purchase guaranteed virus-free plants from a nursery. Plant in spring or late summer-early autumn. Plant in a staggered fashion, 30–45cm apart. Be sure crowns (tops of the roots) are at soil level to avoid rot. It is more productive to establish 3 strawberry beds if space allows.

Water requirements
Water well after planting. Avoid overhead watering to reduce fungal disease. Water frequently.

When to fertilise
Use a liquid fertiliser (see page 691) or worm tea (see page 695) every 2 weeks.

Harvest period
July-October is harvesting time; cover plants with a bird net or you will be left with no fruit. Ripen on the plant.

Pests and organic control
Prone to many diseases and pests. Use crushed egg shells around base of young plants to deter snails and slugs. Grey mould (botrytis) can spread quickly. It is worse in wet summers or where fruit is splashed with water. Well-spaced plants and careful watering will help prevent it.

Companion planting
Lettuce, spinach, borage, chamomile, chives, sunflowers and garlic. Avoid growing with cabbages.

Special information
Remove early runners as they appear and re-plant to increase fruit production. Keep soil moist and free from weeds by mulching; this will also keep fruit clean. To reduce chance of viral diseases, avoid planting where a previous crop of other berries or tomatoes (Solanaceae family) have grown. They are sensitive to frost, so mulch well.

Quantities to plant for a family of four
10–20 plants to begin with, replanting runners as they appear.

Strawberry (*Fragaria* sp.)

Growing and Harvesting Strawberries are one of the most popular fruits of all. Gardeners in most parts of the country have the option of growing summer, ever-bearing (or perpetual-fruiting), woodland or alpine strawberries. Summer strawberries have the most intense flavour and are propagated by runners. As stressed on page 619, it is imperative to start with virus-free runners. Many insects are attracted to strawberries. Organic gardeners rely on companion planting to assist in controlling and/or distracting pests in the garden. In this case, grow plants that will attract beneficial insects that in turn will attack the aphids or spider mites that can infest the strawberry crop. Sunflowers are one of these; not only are they spectacular to look at but will eventually yield seeds for roasting. I have recently discovered that inserting a few bamboo skewers in the soil among the growing strawberry plants discourages birds from coming too close.

Some gardeners choose to grow their strawberries out of the reach of many chewing pests such as slugs and snails. While hanging baskets are one attractive option (they will need to be kept well watered), why not construct a 'strawberry table' instead? This is an open-air frame with a base (a conveniently slatted bench could be used instead) that can support a bag of premium potting mix on top. Slits are made at least 20 centimetres apart, directly into the bag of potting mix, and a strawberry plant is planted into each one. Fertilise fortnightly with a liquid compost or seaweed fertiliser.

Ever-bearing strawberries are smaller plants and fruit for a longer period. Alpine and woodland strawberries are tiny. Some cultivars have intensely flavoured fruit; others have tiny tasteless berries. Select varieties for taste rather than other attributes listed in nursery catalogues. Alpine and woodland strawberries do not produce runners and require little special attention, and can form an attractive groundcover in the garden. (However, even the tasteless ones are useful as a weed-suppressing groundcover, and are easy to pull out if you decide to plant something more productive.)

If you have enough space, consider establishing three strawberry beds. These beds should be rotated and not replanted with strawberries for up to five years. In the first year, bed one will be highly productive and produce runners. After fruiting, these runners should be removed and planted into bed two. Bed three can be planted with runners from bed one or two the following year. After three years the plants in bed one will have finished and the plants should be composted.

Container Planting Ever-bearing strawberries, being smaller plants than summer strawberries, are ideally suited to growing in containers and, even better, in hanging baskets, as long as they are kept moist. Alpine or woodland strawberries are also good for growing in hanging baskets, from which they will tumble most attractively.

Preparing and Sharing If you do need to wash strawberries don't remove the green calyx before placing them in a colander otherwise they will absorb water and their flavour will be diluted. Dunk the colander into a bowl of cold water and move the berries around gently with your hand. Lift the colander from the bowl, allow the water to drain away and then tip the berries onto a thick, dry tea towel to drain. Tip the water onto a thirsty plant.

Strawberries are usually eaten fresh, either whole and just enjoyed as they are with cream, yoghurt or mascarpone, or crushed and used to make a fool (a sweetened fruit purée folded into firmly whipped cream), or served as a cold puréed sauce. Sliced strawberries are often sandwiched in between sponge cakes, or can be stirred into slightly softened ice cream that is then returned to the freezer. Thickly sliced strawberries sautéed in a knob of melted butter in a frying pan with a little sugar and a squeeze of lemon make a delicious sauce for pancakes (see page 622) or ice cream.

Especially for Kids The strawberry patch is sure to be one of the most popular areas in your kitchen garden, perfect for snacking in the garden. The challenge for the adult gardener is to allow some of the crop to become fully ripe before picking as the ripening berries seem to be irresistible to children. However, both young gardeners and birds alike will attack strawberries at the first sign of colour. To protect at least part of the crop from eager children and hungry birds, I recommend covering perhaps two-thirds with fine netting.

It might help to conduct a taste test with some carefully selected purchased ripe strawberries (maybe from an organic stall or a farmers' market) against the sour half-ripe ones picked too early. A picking patch is a fine idea but it troubles me that so many of these delicious fruits are eaten unripe.

As I've mentioned opposite, it is useful to grow giant sunflowers alongside your strawberry patch as a distraction for insects that can damage your crop. Children are always fascinated by sunflowers and, once the big nodding heads have finished flowering and are thoroughly dried, they are very adept at digging out the seeds from the flowers' centre, each one striped like a black-and-white bumblebee, to reveal the tiny, succulent inner seed or kernel inside. The inner seeds are saved and taken to the kitchen to be added to all manner of bread doughs and salads.

Fluffy Buttermilk Pancakes with Strawberries and Blueberries

MAKES ABOUT 12 These pancakes, originally included in *The Cook's Companion*, are the sort often served with maple syrup, whipped butter or honey. I like to include plenty of berries in the batter, then warm extra berries in a pan with butter and maple syrup to spoon over as a delicious sauce.

3–4 free-range eggs (at room
   temperature), separated
60g/2oz butter, melted, plus extra
   for cooking
500ml/18fl oz buttermilk
300g/10½oz plain flour
1 teaspoon salt
1 teaspoon bicarbonate of soda
400g/14oz strawberries, hulled
   and sliced

300g/10½oz blueberries
maple syrup (optional), to serve

BERRY SAUCE
20g/¾oz butter
1 tablespoon maple syrup
140g/5oz mixed strawberries and
   blueberries

EXTRA EQUIPMENT
large metal spoon
electric mixer
small ladle

Preheat oven to 100°C/Gas ¼ and put a baking dish inside to warm.

Put egg yolks into a large mixing bowl. Add melted butter and buttermilk to yolks and whisk well. Sift flour, salt and bicarbonate of soda over egg yolk mixture and fold in with a large metal spoon. Stir in berries. The batter should be of a thick, dropping consistency.

When ready to cook, whisk egg whites in clean bowl of the electric mixer to form soft peaks, then fold into the batter.

Lightly grease a non-stick frying pan with extra butter. Working in batches, ladle in 60ml/2fl oz batter per pancake. Cook pancakes until bubbles form on the uncooked side. Flip and cook on the other side, adding a little extra butter if pan seems too dry. Transfer to warm baking dish until all pancakes are cooked.

To make the berry sauce, heat butter and maple syrup in a small saucepan over medium heat, then add berries. Cover and cook for 3–4 minutes or until the syrupy juices bubble but the berries still retain some shape.

Spoon berry sauce over pancakes and serve at once with a jug of maple syrup if desired.

Strawberries on a Crisp Almond Filo Base

SERVES 6–8 Whenever you use filo pastry you need to keep the unused sheets covered or they dry out quickly and are too brittle to use. I use a lightly dampened tea towel lined with foil to spread over the stack of filo pastry sheets with the foil-side touching the pastry. Quickly return pastry not used for the recipe to its plastic envelope and put it back into the refrigerator (a packet of filo contains such a lot of pastry that it is a good idea to plan to make some Silverbeet and Cheese Filo Triangles, see page 574, with the leftovers). Other fruit could be substituted for the strawberries – I have made this with ripe nectarines and, of course, with any other berries I've bought from my local farmers' market at the time. Prepared in this manner the pastry becomes very crisp and delicious with its almond-filled layers.

EXTRA EQUIPMENT
food processor
2 heavy baking
 trays (about
 28cm × 26cm/
 11in × 10in)

3 sheets filo pastry
30g/1oz butter, melted
1 tablespoon caster sugar
375ml/13fl oz pouring or thickened
 cream
500g/1lb strawberries, hulled
 and halved if large

ALMOND FRANGIPANE CREAM
40g/1½oz unsalted butter,
 softened
40g/1½oz caster sugar
40g/1½oz ground almonds
1 free-range egg yolk

Preheat oven to 200°C/Gas 6.

To make the almond frangipane cream, process butter and sugar in a food processor until creamy. Add ground almonds, then process to mix and add egg yolk. Scrape frangipane cream into a small bowl.

Line a heavy-based baking tray with a sheet of baking paper. Cover the 3 filo sheets with a foil-lined damp tea towel. Place 1 filo sheet on the baking tray so that half its length hangs over and away from you. Brush half of the sheet with melted butter, then sprinkle with 1 teaspoon of the caster sugar. Fold unbuttered half over buttered half.

Spread top layer with half of the almond frangipane cream. Lay a second filo sheet over almond frangipane cream, also allowing half the sheet to hang over the tray away from you. Butter half of this sheet, sprinkle with another teaspoon caster sugar, fold the unbuttered pastry over the buttered half and cover it with the rest of the almond cream. Cover with the third sheet of pastry. Butter half of it, sprinkle with another teaspoon caster sugar and fold unbuttered side over buttered side. Butter this side and sprinkle with remaining caster sugar.

Lay a piece of foil over the pastry stack and weight it with a second heavy baking tray. Place in oven for 5 minutes. Remove top baking tray and foil, and bake pastry for another 5–7 minutes or until a rich golden brown. Cool completely.

Whip cream to firm peaks. Cut pastry stack into 6 or 8 pieces using a serrated knife. Spoon over whipped cream and top with strawberries, then serve.

TARRAGON

Asteraceae family (includes globe artichokes, Jerusalem artichokes and lettuce)
Herbaceous perennial

Soil type
Well-drained soil.

Soil preparation
Providing soil is well-drained and rich in organic matter, no special preparation is required.

Climate
Suitable for all climates.

Position
Prefers full sun, warmth and shade.

How to grow
Buy a young potted plant in spring or early summer.

Water requirements
Frequent watering is required in dry spells.

When to fertilise
Tolerant of poor soil; use a liquid fertiliser (see page 691) or worm tea (see page 695) to assist new growth.

Harvest period
Through spring to autumn, pick leaves as required.

Pests and organic control
Few problems or pests, but it can be lost over winter.

Companion planting
Everything in the garden loves tarragon.

Special information
French tarragon seeds are not available to buy because it is infertile and therefore bears no seeds. Obtain a cutting from a friend if you can, or a herb nursery. Keep the soil free from weeds by mulching.

Quantities to plant for a family of four
1–2 plants.

Growing and Harvesting You must ensure that you are growing French tarragon, or *Artemisia dracunculus* (its aniseed flavour is quite pronounced when you nibble a narrow leaf, and it leaves a distinctive numbing sensation on the tongue) rather than Russian tarragon, or *Artemisia dracunculoides* (a coarser leaf that tastes of nothing much). Encourage young gardeners to bruise a tarragon leaf and inhale deeply to note the delicate aniseed aroma. Interestingly, the leaves have no aroma until bruised or chopped. This is one of the reasons why mistakes happen when buying a tarragon plant. You must eat or crush a leaf to be sure it is French tarragon.

True French tarragon is delicate, delicious and can be difficult to grow, but once it likes its position it will spread to form an aromatic mat. If tarragon does not grow well it probably needs to be moved, especially if it has wet feet. It dies down in winter but can be successfully divided and replanted once the new shoots appear.

Now and then gardeners grow Mexican marigold or tarragon (*Tagetes lucida*), which has a most pronounced aniseed flavour. The plant is a tender perennial, grown as an annual, with small, pretty yellow flowers. In Mexico it is used as an infusion for herbal teas. Its flavour is much coarser than that of French tarragon and is not, in my opinion, an appropriate substitute. It is far better, I think, to grow true tarragon.

Container Planting Like all herbs, tarragon is ideal for growing in a pot. It is relatively shallow-rooted and therefore well suited to a window box or shallow trough. It can also be grown together with its classic *fines herbes* partners: chives, parsley and chervil. Situate the container to provide partial shade during the hottest part of the day. See **HERBS**.

Preparing and Sharing Tarragon needs to be combined with delicate partners. It would be entirely overpowered by rosemary, for example, but it is an essential ingredient in the classic French mixture *fines herbes,* together with chervil, chives and flat-leaf parsley. While tarragon is good with fish or eggs, or added to a creamy sauce, it is at its absolute best when paired with a good (that is organic, free-range) chicken, either roasted (see page 630) or poached (see opposite).

When I use tarragon in a sauce or as a stuffing, I find that it is a good idea to add some of the freshly chopped leaves to the dish just before serving, to heighten the flavour.

If you have a robust crop in early summer, stuff several tarragon branches into a sterilised bottle and top with a good-quality red- or white-wine vinegar. Leave for at least a month. This tarragon vinegar is superb as a basis for salad dressings and makes the perfect base for a classic *sauce béarnaise*, where eggs are whisked to an emulsion with butter. *Sauce béarnaise* is often served with a thick steak – a delicious dish for a special occasion that never goes out of style.

Especially for Kids As with all herbs, children like to pick tarragon and rub it to smell. In a school situation I would recommend a class discussion about enjoying 'everything in its proper season', which leads to thinking about the wisdom of using a poor substitute (such as a purchased dried herb) instead of the real thing.

Tarragon Butter

MAKES 60G/2OZ The delicate aniseed flavour of true French tarragon cannot be mistaken; it is such a lovely herb. If I am feeling French I will rub a free-range chicken with this tarragon butter and work quite a bit of it under the skin (see page 630). As spring or summer is when tarragon is at its best, I may just be able to pick green peas or the first green beans from my garden to serve as well. A little tarragon butter shaken into just-cooked peas or small carrots is also delightful. The instructions here are to form the butter into a roll and to store any leftovers in the freezer. Make sure the tarragon butter is well wrapped, and use it within a few weeks or it risks tasting 'fridgey'. And make sure you use very fresh butter.

EXTRA EQUIPMENT
food processor

60g/2oz softened unsalted
  butter, chopped
1 clove garlic, finely chopped

sea salt and freshly ground black pepper
few drops lemon juice
¼ small handful chopped French tarragon

Process all ingredients in a food processor until thoroughly combined. Tarragon butter can be used immediately but for longer storage or to store excess, scrape onto a sheet of baking paper. Fold paper over and roll to form a sausage shape. Twist ends of paper to firm up and enclose butter mixture. Wrap in a doubled sheet of foil and place in the refrigerator. Slice as needed. Label and freeze what is not needed within 2 days, then use within a few weeks. A slice can be fairly readily cut from the frozen roll if you use a knife dipped in boiling water.

Poached Chicken with Tarragon Mayonnaise

SERVES 4 While poached chicken is never as popular as a roasted bird, this lovely dish deserves pride of place at a summer lunch table. Arrange 2 free-range chicken breasts, still on the bone, on a bed of sliced onion, some flat-leaf parsley stalks, several sprigs of tarragon, and a thick slice of lemon in an enamelled cast-iron pan or similar. Barely cover with water. Place a sheet of baking paper right down over the chicken, then cover and bring very slowly to simmering point over low heat and simmer for 20 minutes. Turn off heat and leave chicken to cool in the liquid. Transfer chicken to a plate, discard bones, cover tightly and refrigerate. Reserve stock for another dish. To make a well-seasoned mayonnaise, follow the method on page 229, using 2 free-range egg yolks, the juice of 1 lemon and 250ml/9fl oz oil. Stir in 2 tablespoons finely chopped French tarragon and 80ml/3fl oz softly whipped cream. Remove skin from poached chicken, cut into thick slices and serve with the tarragon mayonnaise.

Tarragon Roast Chicken for Holly and Lisa

SERVES 4 My daughters love roast chicken and this recipe is very often the first choice when we get together around the table. It was first published twenty years ago in one of my earliest books, *Stephanie's Feasts and Stories,* and has appeared with slight variations in other places. A special treat in summer would be to serve this with freshly picked green beans. You could also roast a selection of seasonal vegetables, or French shallots or small onions in the pan at the same time (see opposite). It is always a milestone when a young person cooks his or her first roast chicken. And it is so easy. Just be sure to buy a free-range bird. It may be easier for a first-time chicken cook to use portions of free-range chicken instead of a whole bird. In which case, the total cooking time, with one turn halfway through, would be more like 45 minutes.

1 × 1.6kg/3½lb free-range chicken
sea salt and freshly ground
 black pepper
3 good-sized sprigs French tarragon
1 thick slice lemon

1 clove garlic, unpeeled and bruised
60g/2oz butter, chopped
1 tablespoon extra-virgin olive oil
250ml/9fl oz dry white wine
1 tablespoon pouring cream

EXTRA EQUIPMENT
kitchen string
 (optional)

Place unwrapped chicken breast-side up and uncovered on a plate in the refrigerator to allow skin to dry out for at least 1 hour.

Preheat oven to 220°C/Gas 7.

Wipe chicken inside and out with paper towel. Remove giblets and neck, if present, and reserve them for making stock for another dish. Season chicken inside and out with salt and pepper. Place tarragon, lemon and garlic in cavity. Rub 30g/1oz of the soft butter all over breast and legs and put rest inside cavity. Truss chicken with kitchen string if you wish (I usually don't).

Brush a roasting pan with olive oil and place chicken in it on its side. Roast for 20 minutes. Carefully turn chicken to the other side, trying not to tear skin, and roast for a further 20 minutes. Reduce heat to 180°C/Gas 4 and turn the chicken breast-side up. Baste with pan juices and roast for a further 20 minutes. Remove roasting pan from oven and tip bird so that juices, herbs, lemon and garlic inside cavity fall into pan. Place chicken on a warmed ovenproof dish and keep warm while you make a simple sauce. Tip away fat and place pan over high heat. Press garlic, lemon and tarragon with a wooden spoon and cook for 1 minute, stirring and scraping with the wooden spoon. Stir in wine. When bubbling strongly, stir in cream. Strain sauce into a warm jug.

Joint the chicken to make self-service easier. Remove legs and wings, and cut the breast meat into chunks (I use strong kitchen scissors to do this). Pour over sauce, or offer it separately, and take the platter proudly to the table.

THYME

**Lamiaceae family
(includes basil, mint and sage)
Perennial**

Soil type
Well-drained, low-nutrient soils.

Soil preparation
Providing soil is well drained, no special preparation is required. Otherwise, fork in some grit or grow in a pot.

Climate
Suitable for all climates.

Position
Prefers full sun.

How to grow
Buy young plants in spring. Thyme is propagated by root division (see page 693) or cuttings (see page 689). Avoid doing this on hot days. Cuttings work best in autumn.

Water requirements
Keep soil moist during dry spells.

When to fertilise
Thyme responds well to liquid fertiliser (see page 691) or worm tea (see page 695) at the beginning of spring.

Harvest period
Cut as required 3 months after planting. If you wish to dry thyme for winter use, harvest just as the plant is coming into flower.

Pests and organic control
Few problems or pests, but root rot and mildew can occur.

Companion planting
Thyme protects cabbages and is a popular bee plant.

Special information
To keep leaves clean from mud, grow in a pot and mulch with fine chippings or grit.

**Quantities to plant
for a family of four**
1–2 plants.

Thyme (*Thymus*)

Growing and Harvesting All thymes like well-drained soil with plenty of sun, if you have had the good fortune to see thyme growing on stony hillsides in the South of France or in Greece you will know that common thyme at least can tolerate almost complete neglect! It will do much better, however, when grown in wetter, cold climates if it is grown in containers of gritty potting mix.

There are many species of thyme and throughout the summer months most are covered in pretty flowers that attract bees to the garden. Some are more prostrate in habit than others. Common thyme (*Thymus vulgaris*) is an essential plant for any kitchen garden. Lemon thyme (*Thymus × citriodorus*) is another attractive type, sometimes seen with variegated leaves.

Both common and lemon thyme become a little ragged in the winter months but can still be harvested and used. If your garden has plenty of thyme plants, leave one or two for winter cooking and cut the others back after flowering. The roots can be divided and replanted. If you have enough for your own use, pot up these divisions and give them to friends as gifts.

Container Planting As with all herbs, thyme will do well in a pot or container. It could be grown around a small bay tree in a pot, or with other Mediterranean herbs such as rosemary and oregano. You could fill any spaces left in the pot with another member of the Lamiaceae family such as basil or sage or another herb. Don't plant with mint, as it will smother the thyme after a short period. Thyme is best picked just before it flowers if the stems are to be dried. See **HERBS**.

Preparing and Sharing I rarely use common thyme as a final garnishing herb on its own. Instead, I invariably cut a few sprigs to add to most casserole dishes and soup pots and find it easiest to strip the leaves from the stalks first to avoid having to fish out stringy stalks later on. It is a key ingredient in every Bouquet Garni (see opposite). I have included a recipe for savoury biscuits flavoured with thyme that are perfect topped with a dob of soft cheese and a halved cherry tomato (see page 637).

Greek cooks use thyme (or oregano) with lemon juice and olive oil as their preferred garnish for cooked seasonal vegetables to be eaten at room temperature and for grilled fish or as a marinade on lamb to be grilled.

Don't be nervous about using lots of thyme. Cut a large handful of sprigs (at least fifteen) and rub them over an oiled and seasoned rack of lamb. Leave the lamb at room temperature in a baking dish sitting atop a thick bed of thyme sprigs for 30 minutes before roasting it in the oven at 200°C/Gas 6. Lemon thyme is best added to dishes after cooking as something of its aroma is lost when cooked. Both types of thyme go well with soft, fresh cheeses.

Especially for Kids An unusual use for lemon thyme is as a flavouring in a buttery biscuit (see page 638). See if children can guess what the unusual flavour is.

Green Tomatoes and Red Onions with Thyme and Wine Vinegar

SERVES 2 This unusual baked vegetable combo is excellent served alongside something grilled – sausages or lamb chops especially. Or it could be served with a fluffy omelette as a breakfast dish. The ingredients can easily be doubled if you are cooking for four. The last of the season's tomatoes may have a blush of pink on them or they may be quite green. Either will do for this dish, but the acidity of green tomatoes works especially well. The skins of green tomatoes don't slip off easily by dunking in boiling water, so if you prefer the skin to be removed, peel the tomatoes with a speed peeler, as I have done here.

EXTRA EQUIPMENT
speed peeler
(see page 47)

2 green tomatoes (200g/7oz)
1 tablespoon extra-virgin olive oil
20g/¾oz butter
1 large red onion, cut into
  1cm/½in-thick slices
2 cloves garlic, finely chopped

1 fresh bay leaf
2 teaspoons thyme leaves
2 tablespoons red-wine vinegar
  or verjuice (see page 706)
sea salt and freshly ground
  black pepper

Preheat oven to 180°C/Gas 4.

Peel tomatoes with a speed peeler. Using a serrated knife, cut tomatoes widthways into 5mm/¼in-thick slices.

Heat oil and butter in a small ovenproof frying pan over medium heat until foaming. Add onion and cook, turning once or twice, for 8 minutes or until it is a lovely golden brown. Scatter over garlic and mix through. Immediately add tomato, bay leaf and thyme. Mix through, turning so everything is buttery.

Carefully tip in vinegar or verjuice (which will hiss and sputter). Shake pan to spread juices, then transfer to the oven for 10 minutes. Remove pan and turn onion and tomato, then baste with pan juices. Return to the oven for a further 5 minutes. Season with salt and pepper before serving.

Bouquet Garni

Thyme is included in every bouquet garni, along with a bay leaf, some flat-leaf parsley stalks, sometimes a piece of orange peel, and sometimes a piece of celery, all tied with a piece of kitchen string for easy retrieval from the stew or braise you are cooking.

Savoury Thyme Biscuits

MAKES 35 Although these biscuits may look like a well-known commercial product, they taste far superior.

EXTRA EQUIPMENT
food processor
6cm/2½in fluted
biscuit cutter

175g/6oz plain flour, plus extra
   for dusting
a pinch salt
150ml/5fl oz double cream

2 teaspoons thyme leaves
10g/⅓oz butter, softened
1 free-range egg yolk
sea salt, for sprinkling

Preheat oven to 200°C/Gas 6.

Place flour, salt, cream, thyme and butter in a food processor and pulse to form a dough. As soon as dough starts to form a ball, remove dough and knead quickly. Wrap in plastic film and chill in the refrigerator for 15 minutes.

On a lightly floured workbench, roll dough out thinly and cut into rounds with a 6cm/2½in fluted biscuit cutter. Transfer dough rounds to a baking paper-lined baking tray or trays and prick each one with a fork. Whisk egg yolk lightly, then brush very lightly over dough. Crush a few sea salt flakes onto each piece of dough.

Bake dough rounds for 10–12 minutes or until golden and crisp. Cool completely on a cake cooling rack, then store in an airtight container.

Labna with Thyme and Toasted Sesame Seeds

Children love making this 'cheese' from yoghurt. I have showed my young friends how to squash the balls onto toasted Turkish bread, and then to sprinkle them with stripped thyme leaves and some toasted sesame seeds. Take 600ml/1 pint plain Greek-style yoghurt (see page 706) and mix it with 1 teaspoon salt. Spoon into a damp doubled sheet of muslin lining a strainer which is resting over a large bowl. Tie muslin into a firm shape and leave yoghurt to drain in the refrigerator for a day. Discard whey that collects in the large bowl. Rinse and dry the bowl and then tip in drained yoghurt. Scatter over plenty of stripped thyme leaves and season with sea salt and freshly ground black pepper. To serve as a dip, scoop into a bowl. Spread onto hot toast and add a sprinkling of toasted sesame seeds. Or for a more traditional way of serving, roll the drained yoghurt into small balls and place in a plastic storage container. Drizzle balls with extra-virgin olive oil and seal the container. Leave overnight. Flavour with your favourite fresh herb combination before serving.

Buttery Lemon Thyme and Vanilla Boomerangs

MAKES 30 The flavour of these popular shortbread biscuits is given a bit of intrigue by the inclusion of a generous quantity of chopped lemon thyme. Once rolled in icing sugar and allowed to cool completely, the biscuits can be stored in an airtight container for more than a week.

150g/5oz plain flour
30g/1oz caster sugar
100g/3½oz ground almonds
1 teaspoon lemon thyme leaves

125g/4½oz cold butter, chopped into
  4–5 pieces
½ vanilla bean, broken into small pieces
110g/3¾oz pure icing sugar

EXTRA EQUIPMENT
food processor

Put flour, sugar, ground almonds and lemon thyme into a food processor and process for a few seconds. With motor running, feed butter quickly through processor tube. Stop machine as soon as mixture forms a dough.

Tip dough onto a sheet of foil. Divide dough into two 4cm/1½in-diameter logs. Wrap each one in foil and chill in the refrigerator for 30 minutes.

Preheat oven to 180°C/Gas 4.

Cut logs into 1cm/½in-wide slices. Roll each piece between palms of your hands to form a 5–6cm/2–2½in-long boomerang-shaped crescent. Place crescents on a baking paper-lined baking tray. Chill crescents in the refrigerator for 10 minutes.

Bake crescents for 15 minutes or until light golden brown. Cool for a few minutes before handling as they are very fragile at this point.

Meanwhile, process vanilla bean with icing sugar in washed and dried food processor until vanilla bean is pulverised. Tip vanilla sugar onto a baking tray and gently roll the cooled biscuits in the sugar.

Store completely cold biscuits in an airtight container. They firm up after 24 hours in their container and are not nearly as fragile.

TOMATOES

Solanaceae family (includes eggplant, peppers and potatoes)
Annual

Soil type
Moist but well-drained and fertile soil or use potting mix.

Soil preparation
Work plenty of well-rotted manure or organic matter into the soil several weeks before planting.

Climate
Suitable for warm, mild areas as a patio container crop, or grow undercover in other areas.

Position
Requires a sunny, sheltered site.

How to grow
Sow seeds in late Feb-early March to grow tomato plants undercover or wait until March before sowing if you are growing them outdoors. Sow in small pots, either on an indoor windowsill or in a propagator in a heated greenhouse. A germination temperature of 18– 20°C needed but as seedlings develop grow on at a minimum of 15°C. Alternatively buy small plants from a garden centre.

Water requirements
Plants in the ground will need watering when conditions are dry. Container grown plants will need daily attention to keep the compost moist but do not over water young plants.

Successive planting
Just 1 sowing or planting is done.

When to fertilise
When the first flowers start to form, feed once or twice a week with liquid fertiliser (see page 691), worm tea (see page 695) or an organic tomato feed.

Harvest period
4–5 months from sowing, harvest July to the first frosts (October).

Pests and organic control
Whitefly are a problem underglass, use a biological control (see page 698). Fruits can suffer from grey mould (botrytis) and blossom end rot, prevent by removing infected fruits and foliage and by regular by careful watering. Blight is an increasingly serious fungal problem outdoors in wet summers, Bordeaux mixture can help if applied early enough.

Companion planting
Basil, onion, garlic, carrots, parsley, marigolds and nasturtiums. Aromatic herbs deter whitefly. Planting mustard, beetroot, silver beet (Swiss chard) and brassicas before and after tomatoes will rid soil of pests and diseases. Don't plant with fennel, potatoes or stone fruit.

Special information
Don't plant where members of the Solanaceae family have grown in the last 2 years. Stake tall plants to protect from wind.

Quantities to plant for a family of four
3 plants every 4 weeks, throughout growing season.

Yellow cherry tomato variety (*Lycopersicon lycopersicum*)

Growing and Harvesting All home gardeners will want to grow tomatoes of one sort or another. Nothing tastes as good as a ripe home-grown tomato. There is a wide range to choose from, including the reintroduction of many Heritage tomatoes – older cultivars that were in danger of disappearing. Heritage tomatoes were selected for flavour, disease resistance and a long harvesting period.

Gardeners can select from a range of heritage tomatoes, including salad tomatoes, paste tomatoes (ideal for drying or stuffing, as they have fewer seeds), beefsteak tomatoes and cherry tomatoes. One favourite of mine is the late-ripening heritage beefsteak cultivar 'Brandywine'. Each fruit is large, heavy and a deep rose-pink with a silk-like sheen. The flesh is dense and full of rich flavour. It is the perfect tomato to have with the freshest mozzarella, torn basil and the very best fruity olive oil.

When you have found a favourite tomato cultivar, slice one thinly and arrange the slices, spacing them well apart, on some paper towel resting on a tray. Write the name of the tomato and the date on the paper, then leave the tray in a dry, draught-proof place. When the tomato slices and seeds are thoroughly dry, cut the paper into seedling pot-sized squares and store away from dust (I slip mine into envelopes). When it comes time to plant next year's tomatoes, fill seedling pots with seed-raising mix, place one of your paper squares into each pot, sprinkle on some more seed-raising mixture and water well, then wait for the seeds to germinate. Of course, this is only possible if your favourite tomato produces viable seeds (which means it is not a hybrid).

Bushy type varieties in containers can produce small crops in most areas of the country if given a sunny spot and regular water and feed. For tomatoes on a larger scale, and to grow some of the more unusual types, it is worth investing in a polytunnel or a greenhouse with a soil border. Tall upright (cordon) types will need a single stake or string support, easily attached to the roof of the greenhouse or polytunnel. Cordons are vigorous and high yielding, they need their sideshoots pinched out each week and the main stem stopping once 5–6 trusses have formed. A halfway house between growing tomatoes in container such as a hanging basket and a large greenhouse or polytunnel is to purchase a tomato house which is small enough to house a couple of plants in growing bags. There are also integrated containers with supports, irrigation and feed specially designed for growing tomatoes on patios. You may need to return container-grown plants with green fruit to greenhouse towards the end of the season if the first frosts are likely to come before all the fruit has ripened.

Non-staking varieties are short, bushy and have an in-built growth meter. They usually have a shorter, earlier harvest. They will benefit from straw mulch so that the fruit is not in contact with the soil. Pests are much more likely to attack low-growing fruit on bush tomatoes than staked ones.

Whichever variety you grow, don't over-water as this dilutes their flavour, and pick the tomatoes when they are well coloured. Cut fruit, rather than pulling, to avoid stem damage. Tomatoes will continue to ripen after harvesting, and their colour will deepen for a few days. Once the days start to shorten and there is a distinct chill in the air, trusses of partly coloured tomatoes can be hung in a dry place, where they will continue to ripen. At some point you must decide that there will be no more ripening; you can then use the remaining green fruit for making pickles or for frying.

Container Planting Dwarf and miniature tomatoes can be grown in pots or tubs. They will tumble most attractively. Do try to keep the pot elevated, on bricks or something similar, so that the dangling fruit does not touch the ground. Medium-sized tomatoes will do well in a pot or container but will need to be staked and tied with soft ties as the plant grows. Attempting to shore up a collapsing tomato bush once it is well grown will almost certainly mean broken branches and fewer fruit.

Preparing and Sharing Tomatoes are all about summer and warm weather. It is so rewarding to grow your own. During the colder months when your own plants have died, don't be tempted to buy tomatoes out of season. If a dish requires some tomato in winter or early spring, it is better to buy good quality tinned tomatoes or, better still, open a jar or bottle of your own preserved tomatoes from the prior season.

My garden diary from last summer reminds me of a bumper harvest that year:

The cherry tomato bushes are still festooned with scarlet balls, so many I cannot consume them all. I have found that if I put a single layer in a pan over moderate heat with some extra-virgin olive oil, a sliced clove of garlic and a few leaves of torn basil, and cover the pan, in ten minutes the skins pop and I have a delicious sweet pasta sauce with lots of red-gold juices.

There are so many speedy and delicious preparations that start with a ripe tomato. Tomatoes plus garlic, salt, good bread and olive oil can become either bruschetta; the well-known Tuscan soup *pappa al pomodoro;* a bread salad such as *panzanella*; or the Catalan version of bruschetta, *pa amb tomàquet.* I cannot resist quoting another diary entry from a wonderful holiday in Barcelona, also briefly mentioned on page 311:

Every table was served a round loaf of bread with a hollow in the middle like a large bagel. In the hole was balanced two fresh tomatoes and a fat clove of garlic. This was to create one's own *pa amb tomàquet.* It went like this. Cut a piece of bread from the circle, slice it open. Douse it with olive oil from the decanter on the table, then rub with the cut garlic clove. Now cut the tomato crosswise and then rub vigorously until there is nothing left of the tomato but the skin. The bread is now damp and a lovely blush-pink.

My friend Australian cook Maggie Beer owns a well-used classic preserving pan and thermometer; each year she invites friends over and together they bottle their excess tomatoes into glass preserving jars. Maggie says she has had no trouble finding preserving jars in her local charity shop. Both new rings and lids are essential.

Other ways of dealing with a glut of ripe tomatoes is to make a tomato sauce (see pages 646, 648, 649 and 651), chutney or relish. Simple cooked tomato purées can be frozen in airtight containers. To freeze excess raw tomatoes, pick and wash them, then place them in plastic freezer bags and freeze just as they are for up to three months. To use, run a frozen tomato under the tap or pour boiling water over for 30 seconds to remove the skin, then use as you wish.

There are many dishes that require peeled tomatoes, such as stews and casseroles where scraps of tomato skin would be unpleasant in the sauce, or when diced raw tomato is needed (these are also the only occasions when I'd take the trouble to remove the seeds as well). While young cooks can cut a cross on the base of a tomato and peel away the softened skins, an adult should be on hand to pour the boiling water over the fruit, and to lift each tomato into a bowl of cold water after a minute.

Tomatoes can be dried in a slow oven for long-keeping. To do this, halve them lengthways, then place them cut-side up on a cake cooling rack over a baking tray in a 120°C/Gas ½ oven. Brush generously with extra-virgin olive oil, season with sea salt and freshly ground black pepper and scatter with torn basil, then roast for four to five hours. Cool on the rack and store in the refrigerator for up to two weeks in single layers separated by baking paper.

Tomatoes can also be dried in the sun. It will only be successful in areas with high summer and autumn temperatures and low humidity. Even so, the tomatoes will need to be brought in at night to protect them from condensation. It can take up to a week to dry tomatoes and one unexpected rainfall will ruin the lot. Meaty egg-shaped roma tomatoes are best for drying as they contain less moisture than other varieties.

It could be an interesting project to construct a simple drying rack. You will need a stainless-steel (or plastic mesh) screen supported on bricks or cement blocks to raise the screen and the tomatoes well above the ground. (Don't use aluminium or galvanised mesh or copper. These metals can oxidise and leave harmful residues on the fruit.) Place the drying rack on concrete or asphalt, well away from cars or foot traffic and over a sheet of aluminium. The sun's reflection on the metal increases the temperature and hastens the drying process.

Cut tomatoes in half, squeeze to remove most of the seeds and sprinkle the cut surface with sea salt. The drying tomatoes will need to be covered with a layer of muslin to keep away curious birds or insects. Peg the muslin to the underneath screen securely. Once well dried, the tomato halves will have a leathery texture and they can then be stored in an airtight container layered with rosemary, basil or thyme and covered with extra-virgin olive oil. Be sure that you have pressed the tomatoes down well to remove any little air pockets. Alternatively, pack the dried tomatoes into freezer bags and freeze.

An easier but less interesting way to dry tomatoes is to purchase a home dehydrator and follow the manufacturer's instructions.

Don't refrigerate tomatoes as this destroys their acid level and much of their flavour with it. The best place to store tomatoes is indoors, not in direct sunlight or on the windowsill as many of us were told by our mothers, but in less direct natural light at room temperature.

At the end of summer or in early autumn when our tomato bushes are laden (we hope), most of us think of using them in sauces, salads and sandwiches. My preferred simple suggestions are on pages 646–657. Any extra tomato sauce, made in whichever way you prefer, can be frozen in ice cube trays; the frozen tomato iceblocks can be stored in an airtight container. Use within a month. There is no need to thaw the tomato iceblock if it is to be dropped into a curry or stew. Next to homemade stock, homemade tomato sauce would be my favourite item in the freezer.

Especially for Kids Children will enjoy poring over seed catalogues to select unusual heritage cultivars with marvellous names such as 'Black Krim', 'Brandywine', 'Tigerella', 'Green Zebra' and 'Lemon Drop'. They are usually surprised and intrigued by the idea of green, yellow and striped tomatoes and will enjoy making markers to identify each type.

Children will also be interested to know that tomatoes are actually a fruit. In China two years ago I was invited to three special banquets and each meal ended with a gorgeous fruit platter. Yellow, pink and deep-red oval tomatoes, each the size of a large olive, were tucked in alongside the watermelon and strawberries.

Encourage children to bruise a tomato leaf and inhale deeply, then note the spicy aroma. The sense of smell is very important in awakening appetite.

Every visit to the tomato patch should include a grub hunt. Hand-pick caterpillars from young plants and feed them to the chooks or destroy them.

Remember to plant a pick-me patch of cherry tomatoes in your garden for impromptu grazing. Once your crop is being harvested, why not set out a tasting table and try the different varieties. Which one has the best flavour? Is one juicier than the other? Which one has the most tender skin to bite through?

Spanish and Mexican cooks often roast and then peel their tomatoes (and also chillies) to intensify their flavour, making them slightly smoky, before using in sauces and salsas. This is an interesting thing to do at home or in a school kitchen garden class. It is easily done on a barbecue grill-plate or a heavy-based frying pan in lieu of the traditional flat-plate (*comal*) used in Mexico.

To Peel Tomatoes

First, remove the cores from tomatoes and make a cross on the other end. Put tomatoes in a bowl, then cover with boiling water and leave for a minute. Drain the tomatoes in a colander and return to the bowl, then cover with cold water. Peel away skins and transfer peeled tomatoes to a clean bowl. (If using green-skinned tomatoes you will have to peel them with a speed peeler (see page 47) as the skins stick tight and can't be dislodged by the boiling water method.) Halve each tomato widthways and gently squeeze out the seeds, if desired. Either keep the seeds for planting next year (see page 642) or discard them with any peel to the compost heap.

Oven-baked Tomato Sauce

MAKES 500ML/18FL OZ This is an out-of-sight, out-of-mind sauce that is ideal for when you have other things to do and can't stand by a stove to watch a sauce bubbling. Cook it for at least 2 hours or even up to 3 or 4, if you want a drier, more concentrated sauce. You can add the sauce to any stew or casserole. It's also a good sauce for meatballs (see page 649). The recipe can be doubled or tripled.

500g/1lb ripe tomatoes, cored
  and roughly chopped
1 carrot, thinly sliced
1 onion, finely chopped
2 cloves garlic, finely chopped
80ml/3fl oz extra-virgin olive oil

80ml/3fl oz red wine or
  red-wine vinegar
8 basil leaves, torn
sea salt and freshly ground
  black pepper

EXTRA EQUIPMENT
1 × 1.5–2 litre/2¾–
  3½ pint-capacity
  enamelled cast-
  iron casserole with
  tight-fitting lid or
  roasting pan
food mill with
  medium disc

Preheat oven to 150°C/Gas 2.

Mix all ingredients (except salt and pepper) in a 1.5–2 litre/2¾–3½ pint-capacity cast-iron casserole or roasting pan. Cover and bake for at least 2 hours or for up to 4 hours, depending on how reduced you want the sauce to be.

Set up a food mill fitted with a medium disc resting comfortably over a mixing bowl. Carefully pour tomato mixture into food mill. Turn handle to press out all the good stuff, leaving tomato skins and seeds behind. A good bit of energy is required to do this. Get help if your arms are tired; there should only be shreds of skin left in the mill. Lift food mill away from bowl and scrape any mixture on bottom of disc into bowl. Season to taste with salt and pepper. Store covered in the refrigerator for up to 1 week, or in an airtight container in the freezer for up to 1 month.

Stuffed Tomatoes

Cut the lids from tops of ripe tomatoes, scoop out seeds, then place tomatoes upside-down to drain. Meanwhile, assemble the stuffing. This varies depending on what I have on hand – I might have a little leftover rice to mix with plenty of chopped herbs and some grated parmesan. Otherwise, I might mix sautéed onion and garlic with fresh breadcrumbs, a chopped anchovy fillet or two, plenty of chopped parsley and oregano or basil, sea salt, freshly ground black pepper and a free-range egg to bind. Spoon the stuffing loosely into the drained tomatoes and transfer them to a well-oiled gratin dish. Dribble with more olive oil, then bake at 200°C/Gas 6 for 30 minutes or until tomatoes are wrinkled and filling is golden. Serve warm or at room temperature.

Buttery Tomato Sauce

MAKES 375ML/13FL OZ This is a very delicate sauce that is marvellous served with simply cooked fish or shellfish. It is also good with fried eggs or fluffy omelettes. The instructions are to purée the mixture, which results in a smooth sunset-coloured sauce. It can also be used without being puréed; at this stage, the tomatoes will have almost melted into the buttery juices and the colour will be a red-gold mix. A splendid variation is to use tomatoes that are green with just a blush of colour and to scatter in a handful of blanched slivered almonds and some flat-leaf parsley, oregano or basil before tossing the sauce with cooked dried pasta such as spaghettini.

750g/1lb 10½oz ripe tomatoes, cored, peeled and seeded
100g/3½oz unsalted butter, chopped
2 cloves garlic, thinly sliced
sea salt and freshly ground black pepper

2 tablespoons torn basil
1 tablespoon pouring cream or 20g/¾oz extra butter (optional)

EXTRA EQUIPMENT
blender or food processor (optional)

Remove the core from tomatoes. Make a slit in the bottom of each tomato, then place in a bowl and pour boiling water over. Wait for 1 minute, then drain and run cold water over tomatoes. Peel and halve tomatoes, then gently squeeze out seeds (put seeds into compost or save for next season). Roughly chop tomatoes.

Melt butter in a large non-stick frying pan over medium heat. Add garlic and cook for 1 minute, then add tomato. Cook, stirring frequently, over low heat for 15–20 minutes or until tomato has collapsed completely. Add salt and pepper to taste.

If you wish to make a smooth sauce, transfer tomato mixture to a blender (or food processor) and blend until smooth. Cover blender lid and the flask with a dry tea towel; hot liquids can force up the lid of a blender spraying hot liquid that can burn.

Scatter sauce with basil and serve as it is or stir in either 1 tablespoon cream or extra butter just before serving.

Fast Basic Tomato Sauce

MAKES 375ML/13FL OZ This is the simplest tomato sauce of all. Although it is fast to make, you must watch it to prevent it from sticking. It can be varied – a chopped chilli can be included at the beginning of cooking, as can a roasted and peeled red pepper (see page 488). It can be reduced over high heat to make a more concentrated sauce, or puréed to make it baby-food smooth.

EXTRA EQUIPMENT
food mill with
medium disc

80ml/3fl oz extra-virgin
  olive oil
1 onion, finely chopped
1 fresh bay leaf
500g/1lb ripe tomatoes,
  cored and roughly chopped

2 cloves garlic, finely chopped
8 sprigs basil, oregano or mint
sea salt and freshly ground pepper
  (or a shake of chilli flakes)
extra freshly torn herbs (optional), to serve

Heat oil in a large non-stick frying pan over medium heat, add onion and bay leaf, then cover and cook for 5 minutes or until onion is well softened but hardly coloured. Uncover and add tomato, garlic and herbs. Cook over medium heat, stirring frequently for 10 minutes or until tomato has collapsed. Add salt and pepper or chilli flakes to taste.

Set up a food mill fitted with a medium disc resting comfortably over a mixing bowl. Carefully pour tomato mixture into food mill. Turn handle to press out all the good stuff, leaving tomato skins and seeds behind. Lift food mill away from bowl and scrape any mixture on bottom of disc into bowl. Season with salt and pepper. Scatter with extra herbs, if using, just before sauce is served.

Very Basic Meatballs

SERVES 4 Cook 1 finely chopped onion and 2 cloves finely chopped garlic in a frying pan in 2 teaspoons olive oil over medium heat for 8 minutes or until well softened. Leave to cool. Using your hands, mix cooled onion mixture with 400g/14oz minced veal, lamb or beef, 1 tablespoon chopped oregano, basil or flat-leaf parsley, 1 free-range egg, 2 tablespoons fresh breadcrumbs and a little sea salt and freshly ground black pepper. Pinch off a spoonful of the mixture and fry over low heat in the frying pan, then taste and adjust salt or pepper. Divide mixture into meatballs. Add another 2 teaspoons olive oil to the pan and fry meatballs over medium heat until well browned on all sides. Reduce heat to low and cook for 5 minutes or until cooked through. Add the Fast Basic Tomato Sauce (see above) and heat through, then serve with cooked pasta, if desired.

Spicy and Speedy Cherry Tomato Sauce for Pasta

SERVES 2 This cheerful little sauce can be made in less time than most dried pasta takes to cook. The cherry tomatoes burst their skins quickly and that is the moment to spoon the sauce onto freshly drained pasta. The recipe can easily be doubled to serve four but it is important that the pan chosen allows the tomatoes to sit in a single well-packed layer rather than layering tomatoes on top of each other. A drizzle of Chilli-infused Oil (see page 486) is a good final flourish for this dish.

200g/7oz spaghetti or casarecce, small maccaroni or other short pasta
salt
80ml/3fl oz extra-virgin olive oil
6 spring onions, trimmed and cut into 3cm/1½in lengths

2 cloves garlic, finely chopped
1 fresh green chilli, seeded and thinly sliced
10 sprigs basil or mint, roughly chopped
300g/10½oz cherry tomatoes
freshly torn herbs, to serve

Cook pasta in a saucepan of boiling salted water, following manufacturer's instructions, until al dente. Drain.

Meanwhile, heat olive oil in a medium-sized non-stick frying pan over medium heat, then add spring onion, garlic, chilli and herbs. Stir for 1 minute or so until spring onion is brilliantly green and somewhat softened. Add cherry tomatoes, reduce heat to low, then cover and cook for 5 minutes or until skins burst and juices start to flow. Remove from heat, then add salt to taste and freshly torn herbs.

Spoon sauce over pasta and serve at once.

Tomato and Goat's Curd Tart

SERVES 6 This tart recipe assumes you have made your own pesto (see page 119). If not, then finely chop some basil and garlic and make it into a paste with a small quantity of extra-virgin olive oil and use that instead. I used striped Tigerella tomatoes when I made this (see opposite). All-butter puff pastry is sold frozen and it is best thawed overnight in the refrigerator or at room temperature in a cool place for about one hour.

1 × 25cm/10in-square sheet ready-
   made all-butter puff pastry,
   thawed
1 free-range egg yolk
400g/14oz (8) tomatoes, cut
   widthways into 1cm/½in-
   thick slices

1 tablespoon Pesto (see page 119)
sea salt and freshly ground
   black pepper
2 teaspoons extra-virgin olive oil
50g/2oz goat's curd
6 basil leaves

Place pastry on a baking paper-lined baking tray. With a very sharp knife, score a border 2cm/¾in in from pastry edge on all sides. Lightly whisk egg yolk with a fork and then brush it over pastry, taking care not to drip egg over edges (this prevents pastry layers from rising). Prick all over pastry base with a fork and chill in the refrigerator for 1 hour.

Meanwhile, using a teaspoon, flick out most tomato seeds (either keep for planting next year by spreading out on paper towel and leaving to dry before labelling and storing in a dry place, or discard them to the compost heap). Cover a tray with a doubled layer of paper towel, and then lay tomato slices on top. Cover them with more paper towel and leave to drain while pastry chills.

Preheat oven to 200°C/Gas 6.

Bake pastry sheet for 10 minutes, then lower temperature to 170°C/Gas 3 and continue cooking for a further 15 minutes. Remove from oven. Press middle of pastry lightly with a dry tea towel if it has risen.

Dot pastry with pesto, spreading it lightly with the back of a teaspoon. Lay tomato slices over, slightly overlapping. Season with a little salt and pepper, then drizzle with olive oil. Return tart to the oven for a further 15 minutes.

Cool tart slightly on a cake cooling rack. Transfer to a chopping board and use a serrated knife to cut into 6 rectangles. Top each portion with a dollop of goat's curd and a basil leaf, then season again, if desired, and serve.

Friselle

SERVES 4 While holidaying in southern Puglia I was served a delicious lunch 'sandwich' called a *friselle*. It was very close to the well-known and much-loved bread salad of Tuscany, *panzanella*, but in Lecce the tomato salad was served piled onto a hard-baked rusk that had been soaked in water and vinegar. At every table locals were munching on these friselle. Several toppings were offered. My version is a compromise as the authentic bread rusks are time-consuming and complicated to make. I was happy with using thickly sliced two-day-old sourdough, dipped in water and vinegar, with my favourite *panzanella* mix piled on top instead. I left the crusts on the bread to give the salad a better foundation. It's not elegant to eat, and a knife and fork are necessary. On another occasion you could tear the bread into chunks and toss it with the filling so you have a *panzanella* salad. To do this, remove the bread crusts, then tear the bread into bite-sized pieces and toss through the salad ingredients. If you need crunch, another option is to use Turkish bread and to cut it into cubes, brush the cubes with olive oil and bake in a preheated 180°C/Gas 4 oven until lightly golden and then toss these crunchy croûtons through the salad.

4 × 2cm/¾in-thick slices
  2-day-old sourdough
250g/9oz ripe firm tomatoes
  (oxheart or beefsteak tomatoes
  are ideal for this), cut into
  2cm/¾in pieces
1 small cucumber, quartered
  lengthways and cut into
  1cm/½in-wide pieces
1 pale inner stalk celery,
  very thinly sliced
¼ red onion, very thinly sliced

½ clove garlic, finely chopped
sea salt and freshly ground
  black pepper
20 basil leaves, torn into
  small pieces
2 tablespoons extra-virgin olive oil

SOAKING BATH
60ml/2fl oz water
2 tablespoons red-wine vinegar
a pinch sea salt

To make the soaking bath, combine all ingredients in a shallow bowl. Dip each bread slice into bath for 1 minute or until it is quite wet but crust still has shape. Set aside on a plate until needed.

Place tomato, cucumber and celery in a bowl. Separate onion slices and add to bowl. Mix through garlic, salt, pepper, basil and olive oil. Leave to stand for at least 30 minutes before piling salad onto damp bread, then serve.

Pilaf of Rice, Tomato and Basil

SERVES 4 This recipe comes from one of my favourite cookbooks, *Lulu's Provençal Table: The Exuberant Food and Wine from the Domaine Tempier Vineyard* by the late Richard Olney. I have adjusted the quantities only and agree with the author that it is the perfect accompaniment for grilled or roasted lamb. With a generous strewing of grated parmesan I think it can stand alone as a lunch dish. This method is for the classic pilaf. On another occasion, such as during winter when tomatoes and basil are scarce but silver beet grows plentifully, you could use chopped spring onion and a selection of strongly flavoured herbs (such as thyme or oregano) in place of the onion, together with sliced silverbeet stems, at the beginning of the cooking process. Instead of the tomato flourish, substitute shredded silverbeet leaves and sorrel leaves cooked with garlic and butter in the same way.

EXTRA EQUIPMENT
1 × 2.5 litre/4½ pint enamelled cast-iron or other heavy-based casserole with lid simmer mat (see page 45)

300g/10½oz (3–4) ripe tomatoes
2 tablespoons extra-virgin olive oil
½ onion, finely diced
200g/7oz long-grain rice
1 teaspoon sea salt
500ml/18fl oz boiling water

2 cloves garlic, finely chopped
12 basil leaves, torn into
  small pieces
freshly ground black pepper
20g/¾oz cold unsalted butter,
  cut into 3–4 pieces

Cut a cross in the bottom of each tomato, then place in a bowl and pour boiling water over. Wait for 1 minute, then drain and run cold water over tomatoes. Peel and halve tomatoes, then gently squeeze out seeds (put seeds into a compost bucket). Coarsely chop tomatoes and put them on a doubled sheet of paper towel resting on a plate.

Heat 1 tablespoon of the olive oil in a 2.5 litre/4½ pint-capacity cast-iron casserole over medium heat. Sauté onion for 5 minutes, stirring until it is well softened but has not started to colour. Add rice and salt and stir well to coat grains with oil and onion. Stir for about 1 minute.

Pour the boiling water onto rice. Give a good stir, and then settle casserole on a simmer mat over low heat and cover tightly. Cook for 20 minutes.

After 15 minutes' cooking time has elapsed, scoop tomato from paper into a small bowl. Heat remaining olive oil in a small frying pan over medium heat and quickly sauté garlic for about 30 seconds. Before garlic starts to colour, add tomato and basil. Grind on some black pepper. Toss for 1 minute, then add cold butter and shake pan until butter melts.

Remove lid from casserole and tip in tomato mixture. Work it through rice with a fork; the rice should turn a lovely rosy pink. Taste for seasoning; it should be well seasoned. Serve without delay, either straight from the casserole or spooned into a hot dish.

Chickpea and Tomato Curry

SERVES 4 This could be a meal by itself, served with a fresh chutney such as the Green Chutney on page 250 and some yoghurt and flatbread or it could be served alongside a meat-based curry as part of an Indian-style meal. You could cheat and use a tin of chick peas instead of soaking and cooking them yourself. You will then need to moisten the curry with chicken or vegetable stock or water in place of the reserved chickpea cooking liquid.

160g/5½oz chick peas, soaked overnight in cold water (to yield 360g/12½oz)
2 onions, 1 finely chopped and 1 roughly chopped
2 cloves garlic, roughly chopped
1 × 2cm/¾in-long piece ginger, roughly chopped
2 tomatoes
60ml/2fl oz vegetable oil
1 cinnamon stick
½ teaspoon chilli flakes or chilli paste (or to taste)
juice of 1 lemon

SPICE PASTE
½ teaspoon cumin seeds
1 teaspoon black peppercorns
4 cloves
4 cardamom pods, lightly crushed and seeds removed
½ teaspoon ground turmeric
½ teaspoon garam masala

EXTRA EQUIPMENT
food processor
mortar and pestle
1 × 2 litre/3½ pint-capacity enamelled cast-iron or other heavy-based casserole with a tight-fitting lid

Drain chick peas, rinse with fresh water, then place in a heavy-based saucepan and cover with cold water. Bring to the boil over high heat, then reduce heat to low and cook until tender; this can take anywhere from 45–90 minutes, depending on how fresh your chick peas are. When tender, turn off the heat and leave to cool. Drain cold chick peas, reserving cooking liquid.

Put the finely chopped onion into a bowl. Purée the roughly chopped onion, garlic and ginger in a food processor, then set aside; don't wash the processor.

Cut a cross in the bottom of each tomato, then place in a bowl and pour boiling water over. Wait for 1 minute, then drain and run cold water over tomatoes. Peel and halve tomatoes, then gently squeeze out seeds and purée in food processor. Set aside.

To make the spice paste, crush cumin seeds, black peppercorns, cloves and cardamom seeds with a mortar and pestle. Stir in turmeric and garam marsala.

Heat oil in a heavy-based casserole over medium heat. Add finely chopped onion and sauté for at least 10 minutes, stirring until it is a deep gold. Add puréed onion mixture and cook for a further 5 minutes, stirring. Add spice mixture, cinnamon stick and chilli flakes. Stir and cook for 5 minutes. Stir in tomato.

Add chick peas and just enough cooking liquid to barely cover. Stir well, cover and cook gently over low heat for 25 minutes. Taste for salt and spiciness and season if desired, then stir in lemon juice and serve.

Candied Tomato Rice Pudding with Pistachios

SERVES 4 This creamy pudding is quite rich so the quantities I've given make enough to offer satisfying small portions. The rice will still retain a bit of texture. I've garnished the pudding with candied tomato, a recipe given to me by Bruno Loubet, an excellent French chef when he was working in Queensland. These lovely, surprising morsels are perfect with creamy rice desserts. The pudding should be served within a few hours of making it. It should not be chilled. If tomatoes are not in season, it is also delicious made with four finely chopped dried apricots which have been soaked overnight in two tablespoons water. Stir them into the pudding when you add the sugar.

EXTRA EQUIPMENT
mortar and pestle

4 cardamom pods, lightly crushed
  and seeds removed
200g/7oz short-grain rice
600ml/1 pint milk
125ml/4½fl oz water
1 tablespoon caster sugar or to taste
250ml/9fl oz thickened cream, lightly
  whipped
2 tablespoons roughly
  chopped pistachios

BRUNO'S CANDIED TOMATO
4 large tomatoes, ripe but firm
300g/10½oz caster sugar
200ml/7fl oz hot water
1 vanilla bean, split lengthways
rind of ½ orange, removed in
  wide strips

To make the candied tomato, preheat oven to 100°C/Gas ¼. Cut a cross in the bottom of each tomato, then place in a bowl and pour boiling water over. Wait for 1 minute, then drain and run cold water over tomatoes. Peel and quarter tomatoes, then gently extract as many seeds as possible, using a teaspoon. The aim is to end up with shapely curved pieces of tomato, sometimes referred to as tomato 'petals'. Place tomato on a baking paper-lined baking tray and bake for 45 minutes or until they are dry and firm.

Meanwhile, put sugar, hot water, vanilla bean and orange rind into a heavy-based pan. Bring to the boil over low heat, stirring continuously until sugar dissolves. Slip in dried tomato and simmer very gently over low heat for 10–15 minutes. Cool tomato completely in syrup, then transfer both to an airtight container and seal. Candied tomato can be stored in the refrigerator for up to 1 week.

Crush cardamom seeds to a fine powder with a mortar and pestle. Combine rice, milk, water and ground cardamom in a medium-sized saucepan. Stir and bring to the boil over lowest heat. Cook for up to 30 minutes, stirring from time to time, until rice has absorbed all milk and is soft with just the faintest 'bite' left in each grain. Stir in sugar well and taste, then add more sugar if desired. Leave to cool to room temperature.

Stir a little of the cream into rice to loosen it and then fold in remainder. Scatter pudding with pistachios, then arrange candied tomato on top and serve.

TURNIPS AND SWEDE TURNIPS

Brassicaceae family (includes broccoli, cabbage, cauliflower, cresses and radishes)
Biennial grown as an annual

Soil type
A loose soil, moist but well-drained and slightly alkaline.

Soil preparation
Does not need organic matter but should follow a crop that was manured the previous year, if not they will need some balanced fertiliser. Lime can be added to increase pH. Rake and level soil ready for sowing seed direct.

Climate
Can be grown in any climate but especially suited to cooler, wetter climates.

Position
Full sun or partial shade in summer.

How to grow
Summer turnips: In March-April directly sow seeds into the ground at a depth of 1cm in rows 15cm apart. Thin seedlings to 15cm apart. *Swede*: Sow in May-June, 2cm deep in rows 35–40cm apart. Thin seedlings to 23cm. Use modular trays if ground space still occupied, this saves time on thinning too. *Winter turnips*: Sow in July-August in rows 30cm apart, thin to 15cm.

Water requirements
Summer turnips need to grow fast with no check to their growth, soil should be evenly moist so water in dry spells. Swede and winter turnip do not need regular watering unless conditions are very dry.

When to fertilise
Rake in a balanced organic fertiliser before sowing outdoors.

Successive planting
3 Summer turnips sown at 3-week intervals from March-July. Just a single sowing of swede and winter turnip.

Harvest period
Pull summer turnips when they are golf ball to tennis ball size, usually May-September. Lift all swede and winter turnip in September-October and store, or harvest a few and leave the remainder for winter harvesting.

Pests and organic control
Cabbage root fly, flea beetle and other pests can damage plants, use a fine mesh crop cover when insects are active. Swede can suffer from powdery mildew or clubroot, there are varieties such as 'Marian' that have some resistance to both diseases. Liming can combat clubroot.

Companion planting
Peas, Brussels sprouts, nasturtiums, lettuce, corn and cucumber for turnips and peas, onion and lettuce for swede. Don't plant with potatoes.

Special information
Even watering is essential to stop roots splitting.

Quantities to plant for a family of four
Summer turnips: 4 plants every three weeks. *Swede or winter turnips*: 4 plants in total.

Turnip (*Brassica rapa*)

Growing and Harvesting Turnips and swede are closely related. They are actually not root vegetables, as the 'root' is not a root at all but, in fact, the swollen base of the stem. It is a mystery to me why turnips and swedes are not more widely appreciated. Could it be that many adults' first experience of turnip and swede was as pale greyish or yellowish watery blobs? So sad, I think, as the sweetness of turnip in particular is absolutely delicious and a buttered purée of well-drained swedes is a very comforting thing alongside a rich beef stew.

Summer turnips in particular should be grown fast or they can become woody. They are particularly delicious if grown close together and pulled early when golf-ball sized. Large turnips can not only be woody but also very watery and strong-flavoured. Young turnip tops can be cooked and eaten if in good condition. Flying insect pests can be prevented from attacking plants by fine mesh crop covers.

The *cime di rapa* (meaning 'turnip tops') often mentioned in Italian recipe books is a different leafy green from the turnip tops referred to here. *Cime di rapa* has many different names in Italian and in English (*broccoli di rapa*, rapini, for example) and is delicious but quite bitter. If grown quickly, the bitterness is much reduced. It would not be my first choice for a school kitchen garden, and may not appeal to children at home either.

Swede is usually in the ground longer than turnips and can withstand heavier frosts, so they are a good choice for growing in the colder parts of the country. Swede is very popular in Scandinavia and Scotland, both known for their chilly weather. Another name for swede turnips is rutabaga, which is apparently a corruption of the Swedish for 'red bags', referring to the bulbous shape of the usual swede. Swede is usually harvested much larger than turnips. A large swede is milder tasting than an equally large turnip and its flesh is drier.

Container Planting Summer turnips and swede can be grown in a tub or pot. They will occupy the space for several months and there will be just the one crop to harvest, but productivity from that pot could be increased by planting lettuce, carrots or radishes, which will be harvested before the others are ready.

Preparing and Sharing Turnips and swede should be picked and used when they are hard and solid-feeling, not soft or spongy. Most of them need peeling, although turnips pulled when they are marble-sized just need a good scrub as peeling them would leave very little to cook. Both turnips and, even more so, swede, are absolutely delicious if cooked with care. Both vegetables are especially good when prepared with butter and homemade broth.

French cooks celebrate the arrival of the first young turnips as a sign that spring has arrived. They would probably braise the turnips tucked around a chicken, duck or some other piece of meat. Turnips absorb the flavours of roasting juices and become translucent. For my own take on this marvellous combination, see the Grilled Duck with Scorched Turnips and Figs recipe on page 667. Turnips are also delicious caramelised in a pan with a tiny bit of sugar and a little stock, becoming sticky and shiny as the stock reduces (see page 662).

If the turnip tops are in good condition then keep the leaves, wash them well and steam or sauté them. They are excellent blanched, then chopped and sautéed in olive oil with garlic and tossed with pasta. Alternatively, they can be stirred into a wok-braised dish or a coconut milk-based curry or shredded and added to Asian soups.

Swede is fantastic mashed with butter and pepper. Known as 'bashed neeps' in Scotland, this dish is often served with haggis. I once made tiny forcemeat balls with oatmeal, turnip tops and duck liver, rolled them in caul fat and baked them alongside a grilled pigeon, which I then served with a rich swede purée. The little forcemeat balls were excellent, but in no way resembled the flavour of a good haggis.

Especially for Kids Summer turnips picked at golf-ball size are very appealing to children. Maybe you have also grown round carrots to the same size? And maybe the vegetable patch has some small salad onions too. Learning how to cook this sort of vegetable combination, using just one pan and minimal liquid, so that all the vegetables become tender at the same time, is a wonderfully useful skill and can be applied to many other vegetables. It also saves on the washing up.

Get children to help you make a jar of Middle Eastern pickled turnip (see below). The turnips turn purple due to the addition of a few chunks of beetroot. This is not a long-keeping pickle, so plan to serve the pickles soon with other Middle Eastern nibbles such as falafel, hummus and some flatbread. Or make spicy lamb meatballs (such as the kofta on page 249) and serve them with flatbread, yoghurt and a little bowl of lipstick-pink pickled turnip as a way of appealing to young eyes as well as palates.

Glazed Turnips

SERVES 4 This is a master recipe, and works equally well for either small golf-ball sized turnips or larger ones. If the turnips you have pulled from the garden are more cricket-ball size, it is a good idea to blanch them first as outlined below. This can become a dish in its own right if you include some small round carrots and small salad onions. In this case, the sugar is optional. When all the vegetables are tender, drop in a couple of handfuls of the first spring peas and toss the pan gently to coat everything with a veil of the shiny sauce.

400g/14oz turnips, peeled
  (to yield 325g/11½oz)
salt
40g/1½oz butter
2 teaspoons caster sugar

250ml/9fl oz chicken or vegetable
  stock or water
1 fresh bay leaf (optional)
sea salt and freshly ground
  black pepper

EXTRA EQUIPMENT
sauté pan or
  medium-sized
  non-reactive wide-
  based saucepan
  with lid

Blanch peeled turnips in a saucepan of lightly salted simmering water for 5 minutes if large or not in the first flush of youth. Drain and cut large ones into 2cm/¾in pieces or halve medium-sized turnips. Keep tiny ones whole.

Heat butter and sugar in a sauté pan or wide-based saucepan over medium heat until sugar has dissolved. Tip in turnips and shake to coat with syrupy liquid. Add stock and bay leaf, if using, then cover and simmer for 12 minutes. Test turnips with a skewer. If tender, remove lid, increase heat to high and shake pan so liquid evaporates, coating turnips with the golden sauce. If turnips are not cooked and stock seems to evaporate too quickly, add a little water, cover again and test after another 2 minutes. Season with salt and pepper to taste, then serve.

Roasted Swede Wedges with Rosemary

Peel and cut swedes into fat wedges, then roll in extra-virgin olive oil. Bake at 225°C/Gas 7 with several rosemary sprigs for about 1 hour or until tender and golden, turning after 30 minutes.

Turnip Bliss Bombs

SERVES 4 These delicious morsels are best cooked with golf-ball sized turnips and are ideal to make when you have harvested a large quantity of such small turnips. Larger turnips cut into 3 centimetre/1½ inch pieces can be used as long as they have been blanched for five minutes to lessen any very strong flavours or bitterness. Traditionally the turnips would be cooked in duck fat rather than olive oil – the choice is yours. Duck fat is available in larger supermarkets in jars or tins and lasts indefinitely if kept covered in the refrigerator (providing you always use a clean spoon to scoop fat from the jar). I eat these as an antipasto item. They are also stunning served with any grilled lamb dish – in fact, with almost anything.

400g/14oz turnips, peeled (to yield about 325g/11½oz)
salt
2 tablespoons duck fat or extra-virgin olive oil

2 tablespoons fresh breadcrumbs
2 tablespoons chopped flat-leaf parsley
sea salt and freshly ground black pepper

EXTRA EQUIPMENT
medium-sized sauté pan or non-reactive wide-based saucepan with lid

Blanch peeled turnips in a saucepan of lightly salted simmering water for 5 minutes if large or not in the first flush of youth. Drain and cut large ones into 3cm/1½ inch pieces.

Melt fat or heat oil in a medium-sized sauté pan or wide-based saucepan and add turnips; they must fit snugly in a single layer. Cover with lid and cook over low–medium heat for about 12 minutes, shaking pan every few minutes. Remove lid; all turnips should be a deep golden brown all over. If not, increase heat to medium–high, then cook uncovered, stirring turnips constantly so they colour evenly.

Once all turnips are a deep golden brown, add breadcrumbs and parsley. Increase heat a little and stir with a wooden spoon for about 1 minute or just until breadcrumbs become crisp. Tip into a serving dish and season with sea salt and pepper, then serve at once or cool and serve at room temperature.

Turnip Gratin

SERVES 4 Everyone loves a creamy vegetable gratin. For the cook the appeal is that it bakes in the oven without requiring any extra attention and can then be brought directly to the table, minimising the number of items needing to be coordinated at dinner time. Five or ten extra minutes in the oven will never hurt a gratin and they hold their heat for some time. I have given quantities for an all-turnip gratin – a real treat for turnip lovers. If you want a creamier result, substitute sliced potatoes for one-third of the turnips; the potatoes contain more starch than turnips. This is an ideal dish to make if the turnips you have picked are large. Given the cream content it is good menu planning to serve the gratin with a grilled lamb rack or a grilled lean steak. When I recently cooked this dish I had a small quantity of delicious pan juices left from roasting some pork. I substituted it for some of the cream, and this stock/cream version was also wonderful. If made in advance, the gratin can be successfully reheated in a 150°C/Gas 2 oven for about twenty minutes, covered with foil.

EXTRA EQUIPMENT
food processor with
  slicing attachment
  (optional)
24cm × 20cm/
  9½ × 8in gratin
  dish

750g/1lb 10½oz turnips, peeled
  (to yield 600g/1lb 5oz)
salt
300ml/½ pint pouring cream (or
  substitute 100ml/3½fl oz with
  good homemade stock)
1 clove garlic, thinly sliced

1 teaspoon thyme leaves
½ teaspoon red or white-wine
  vinegar
1 teaspoon butter, for greasing
sea salt and freshly ground
  black pepper

Preheat oven to 180°C/Gas 4.

Blanch peeled turnips in a large saucepan of lightly salted simmering water for 5 minutes. Drain in a colander and pat dry.

Put cream, garlic, thyme and vinegar into a small saucepan and simmer over medium heat for 3 minutes. Stir in stock, if using. Set aside.

Thinly slice turnips in a food processor using the slicing attachment or with a sharp knife. If turnips are too large for feeder tube, halve or even quarter them. The slices should be around 3mm/⅒in thick.

Butter a 24cm × 20cm/9½in × 8in gratin dish. Layer turnip slices in the dish, seasoning each layer with salt and pepper as you go. Try and make each layer as flat as possible, hiding any scrappy slices under the best ones for the top layer. When all turnip is used, pour over cream mixture and press down gently on surface with an egg lifter to push turnip evenly under cream.

Bake for 45–50 minutes until turnip is completely tender and creamy and top is golden. Leave to rest for at least 5 (or up to 15) minutes before serving.

Grilled Duck with Scorched Turnips and Figs

SERVES 2 This is a bit fiddlier to prepare than many of the recipes in this book but it is speedy to cook and so delicious that I am sure many will want to give it a go. It would be a perfect dish for a special dinner for two. Duck and turnips is the very best combination, closely followed by duck with figs, and here they are all together! A green salad would be the nicest accompaniment to this dish.

EXTRA EQUIPMENT
ridged char-grill pan

2 × 200g/7oz duck breast fillets, skin on
sea salt and freshly ground black pepper
3 sprigs thyme, leaves stripped
2 teaspoons extra-virgin olive oil
100g/3½oz Glazed Turnips (see page 662), cut into 5mm/¼in-thick slices

2 ripe figs, halved
2 tablespoons chicken stock
1 teaspoon red-wine vinegar
2 tablespoons vino cotto (see page 706, optional)
finely grated zest of ½ orange

Preheat oven to 100°C/Gas ¼. Put in 1 large plate and 2 dinner plates to warm.

Score skin of duck breasts on the diagonal with a sharp paring knife to create a diamond pattern; don't cut through to meat, just skin and fat under skin. Season duck on both sides, rub in thyme leaves and drizzle over 1 teaspoon of the olive oil. Refrigerate, uncovered, for at least 1 hour so duck skin dries out. When ready to cook, bring to room temperature.

Fold a 25cm/10in sheet of foil in half widthways and cut to form 2 12.5cm/5in squares. Brush with remaining olive oil. Divide glazed turnips between oiled foil sheets, pushing slices close together but not overlapping, to form a 'circle', then set aside. Put fig halves on a warm plate in the oven.

Heat a ridged char-grill pan over high heat until very hot, then place duck breasts skin-side down in the pan. Cook for 6 minutes. Carefully pour away accumulated fat, turn duck breasts and cook for 3 minutes on other side. Transfer duck breasts, skin-side down, to plate in oven with figs and leave to rest for 10 minutes.

Heat a large non-stick frying pan over high heat. Lift 1 square of turnip-covered foil and place it turnip-side down in the pan. Wait for 30 seconds and then peel away and discard the foil. After 1 minute, turn turnip over with an egg lifter (still in its circle, if possible). It should be well scorched at the edges. Cook for another 1 minute, then slide scorched turnip onto the centre of one of the dinner plates in oven, keeping turnip slices in their circles if possible. Repeat with second square of foil. Quickly deglaze the pan with stock, red-wine vinegar and vino cotto, if using. Tip pan juices over duck on the resting plate. Leave for a good 5–10 minutes before serving.

To serve, using your sharpest knife, thinly slice duck breasts on the diagonal. Place 2 fig halves in centre of each turnip circle. Arrange duck slices around figs. Drizzle with pan juices, then season with salt and pepper and scatter over orange zest. Serve at once.

ZUCCHINI AND ZUCCHINI FLOWERS

**Cucurbitaceae family
(includes cucumber,
melons and pumpkin)
Annual**

Soil type
Moist, well-drained soil, enriched
with organic matter.

Soil preparation
Plant after a legume crop or
dig in well-rotted manure
or compost prior to planting.

Climate
Suitable for all climates; sensitive
to frosts and cold.

Position
Prefers full sun.

How to grow
In May sow seed in small pots,
seeds germinate at a minimum
of 18°C. Young plants grow
quickly but are very sensitive to
frost, harden-off (see page 692)
gradually and plant out once
there is no more danger of frost
(usually late May-beginning of
June). If plants outgrow their
pots and outside conditions

are not suitable then, pot on
into bigger pots. Mound up the
soil and plant in centre, space
plants 60–90cm apart in each
direction depending on vigour of
the variety. Water young plants
carefully, avoiding the foliage
until they start to grow away or
plants can rot.

Water requirements
Water frequently. Don't water vine
stem or leaves. Under-watering
may make vines drop fruit.

When to fertilise
Use liquid fertiliser (see page
691) after first fruit has set.
Too much fertiliser will improve
vine growth at expense of fruit
development.

Harvest period
8 weeks after planting, when
10–15cm long. This promotes
new growth.

Pests and organic control
Aphids can spread mosaic virus
so be on the look out for them,
nasturtium can act as a bait plant
but you may need to spray with

an appropriate insecticide. Once
a plant has the virus, there is no
cure so destroy the plant (do
not compost). Powdery mildew
can be a serious problem if it
strikes young plants, you may
need to treat with plant and fish
oil blend, but it often occurs
towards the end of the season
with little effect on cropping.

Companion planting
Chamomile, comfrey, marigolds,
borage and sunflowers to
encourage bees; nasturtiums
and calendula as a bait plant
for aphids. Don't plant
near potatoes.

Special information
If seed-saving keep away from
other family members (such as
pumpkin, melons and cucumber)
to avoid cross-pollination.

**Quantities to plant
for a family of four**
2–3 plants.

Growing and Harvesting Also known as courgettes, there are many varieties of zucchini. Two of my favourites are the pale-green, slightly bulging varieties known variously as white zucchini or Lebanese zucchini. I also like a striped, slightly ridged-skin variety known as zucchini romanesco.

A delicious zucchini of whatever shape or colour will have shiny skin, almost squeak when stroked and should feel solid and unyielding. Harvest them frequently and harvest them small, as keeping the bushes picked regularly is the best way to keep them producing. One plant can produce up to 40 fruit a season. The optimum size is 8–15 centimetres long. You will sadly have to accept that the inevitable really giant runaways are really tasteless and, apart from grating and using to make a slice or cake or stuffing a few, they have no future in the kitchen. They do offer a useful source of seeds for the following year, though. As one family will need only a small number of seeds, dry the rest, bag and label them and give them as gifts. If the seeds are from a special variety, draw a picture of it on the bag.

Zucchini need good ventilation, so avoid growing them near bushy and tall plants. During the hottest part of the day the leaves will look wilted; this is not necessarily due to lack of water if the soil has been kept moist. Powdery mildew is a fungus that frequently attacks zucchini and other Cucurbitaceae family members such as cucumbers, melons and pumpkin. At first white patches appear on the leaves; these can then spread to cover entire leaves, which eventually become twisted and shrivelled. It may be necessary to spray the plants with an organically approved fungicide. Remove any affected leaves promptly, as the spores that spread this fungal infection are dispersed by the wind.

Zucchini sometimes fail to set fruit due to poor pollination. It might be that it is too cold for bees or there might not be enough bee-attracting plants nearby. Hand-pollination will solve the problem. Early in the morning, hand-pollinate the female flowers by transferring pollen from the male flower using a paint brush, or break off the male flower, bend back its petals and press it against a female flower. For best results, choose a female flower that is only partially opened. The female flower is smaller and you can see a tiny swelling behind it, as opposed to the thin stalk of the male flower. The flower opens boldly at first, waiting to be pollinated by bees, then collapses as the fruit swells. By the time you pick a zucchini, the flower has withered or fallen off.

The male flower is larger and stays open longer. Once the bees have collected its pollen and deposited it in the female flowers there is no further use for the male, so it is the preferred flower for stuffing and deep-frying. No sensible Italian farmer or home gardener would sacrifice the potential of growing zucchini in order to stuff the smaller flower! There are usually plenty of male flowers on each bush. You can pick a male flower from a plant, leaving a few as pollinators, and allow the female flowers to continue growing the zucchini. If you have an excess of fruit, you can also stuff female flowers.

Some gardeners are unaware that the flowers are a delicacy that should be picked quickly while fully open in the morning, as they close after a few hours. Place them very carefully in a plastic bag or takeaway container with a lid and refrigerate; this way the flowers will be usable for a few hours more. An Italian friend advises me that if the flowers are to be fried without stuffing (also delicious), they can be picked even earlier in the morning, before they have opened. They are not nearly so fragile then.

Container Planting Zucchini can be successfully grown in a large container. I have planted mine this year in a half wine barrel. I planted four seeds just in case, but they all germinated and I have removed two of the seedlings. That said, zucchini crop very heavily and need space to romp so make sure your container is large enough.

Preparing and Sharing The simplest way with freshly picked zucchini is to put them, whole or sliced, into a pan where they fit without too much extra space, then add a tiny amount of water, a slice of butter or a drizzle of extra-virgin olive oil and then cover the pan tightly and cook over medium heat. They will be ready in less than 5 minutes. Remove the lid, increase the heat and bubble to evaporate almost all the liquid, then season with sea salt and freshly ground black pepper and eat. Delicious!

Chunks of zucchini cooked slowly in a covered pan with extra-virgin olive oil, chopped garlic, sea salt and freshly ground black pepper until very soft make a complete change from the more usual lightly cooked zucchini. Once soft, crush with a fork, add lemon juice and flat-leaf parsley and serve warm. If you have also boiled some small new potatoes, gently combine the two for another delicious vegetable dish. Don't forget, zucchini also make delicious chips and fritters.

Another favourite way of mine is to grate them coarsely, squeeze briefly in a clean tea towel and toss for 2–3 minutes in butter. Season and add some chopped flat-leaf parsley and/ or French tarragon. Now and then, make a zucchini slice (see page 672) from the gratings of a large runaway zucchini, or use them in a cake. Or make an interesting zucchini mash by combining cooked and well-drained chunks of giant zucchini with cooked potato, butter, parsley and parmesan.

Zucchini are also lovely raw. Slice them thinly on an angle, either carefully with a sharp knife, or more easily using a plastic vegetable slicer (see page 46). These are extremely sharp and should never be used by a child without the closest supervision. To make one of my favourite summer salads, dress thinly sliced zucchini with extra-virgin olive oil, lemon juice and freshly chopped flat-leaf parsley or French tarragon – I sometimes add some freshly picked rocket leaves.

If you make the slices a little thicker and brush each one with olive oil and blister them quickly under a hot griller, they make a lovely addition to a bowl of pasta tossed with grated parmesan and lemon juice. Season judiciously (the parmesan will already add salt) and add herbs of your choice, as so many are wonderful with zucchini. I would always include flat-leaf parsley, probably with one other herb – maybe mint, French tarragon or oregano. You could also serve the slices just as they are either as a salad or to accompany a pan-fried escalope of veal.

At the end of zucchini season the last little shoots of the plant, including any embryonic undeveloped fruit, can be picked when about 6–8 centimetres long and then sautéed or dipped in tempura batter. These are known as *cime di zucchini* and are considered a delicacy (see page 678). Another Italian friend showed me how to strip the prickly outer covering on young zucchini stems, just as you might string a celery stalk or a cardoon. These young stalks can also be cooked and eaten in the same way as *cime di zucchini*.

Before stuffing or frying zucchini flowers, always check that there is not an insect nestled deep inside. I see no reason to remove the stamens or the calyx – they are both perfectly edible. Fill the flowers with a very simple ricotta stuffing, twirl them in a light batter and fry them (see page 679). Damaged blossoms can be chopped and sautéed, then added to frittatas, pasta, risotto, omelettes and so on.

Especially for Kids Zucchini grow so fast that they will be endlessly fascinating for home gardeners. Harvesting the crop is nearly as exciting as collecting the eggs from chickens.

Children are always intrigued to discover that they can eat some flowers and that the plants have male and female flowers. The first time they are offered a platter of fried zucchini flowers (see pages 679 and 681) they are truly amazed. This is indeed magic.

Both at home and in school kitchen gardens it is inevitable that the bulk of the harvest will be during the long summer holiday period. The marvellous volunteers who visit the gardens over the summer should pick the zucchini and take them home as a bonus.

Anna-Maria's Zucchini Slice

MAKES 12–16 PIECES First published in *Stephanie's Australia*, here again with a few minor adjustments, the original recipe was a gift from Anna-Maria Bruno. This dish freezes well. Individual pieces can be reheated for a few minutes in a preheated 200°C/Gas 6 oven.

60ml/2fl oz olive oil	2 large eggs, lightly beaten	**EXTRA EQUIPMENT**
500g/1lb zucchini, coarsely grated	sea salt and freshly ground black pepper	1 × 25cm/10in-square cake tin or
1 large onion, finely chopped	150g/5oz streaky bacon, finely chopped (optional)	30cm × 20cm/
170g/6oz parmesan, grated	3 large ripe tomatoes, thickly sliced	12in × 8in
150g/5oz self-raising flour		rectagular tin

Preheat oven to 200°C/Gas 6. Brush a 25cm/10in-square cake tin or 30cm × 20cm/12in × 8in rectangular tin with a little of the oil and line base with baking paper. Combine remaining ingredients, except tomato and remaining oil. Pour into prepared tin and smooth out top. Cover with tomato slices and dribble over oil. Bake for 30 minutes or until firm. Cut into 12–16 pieces. Serve warm or cold.

Zucchini Parmigiana

SERVES 4 This variation on the popular veal dish makes an excellent lunch. I am indebted to Antonio Carluccio for suggesting the use of a pungent washed-rind cheese in between the layers of zucchini. His suggestion was taleggio, a marvellous Italian washed-rind cheese. This recipe, like some of those that follow, requires zucchini slices to be fried. If making this with children, it would be a good moment to teach young cooks how to add food to hot oil. Always carefully place the food in the oil, never drop it, as it will be certain to splash and possibly lead to burns. I recommend always adding slices to the oil away from you so any splash is not in your face.

EXTRA EQUIPMENT
1 × 2 litre/3½pint-
capacity baking
dish

2 tablespoons plain flour
sea salt and freshly ground black pepper
2 free-range eggs
500g/1lb zucchini, trimmed and cut
  lengthways into 5mm/¼in-thick slices
60ml/2fl oz extra-virgin olive oil

250ml/9fl oz Fast Basic Tomato
  Sauce (see page 649)
80g/3oz washed-rind cheese
  (such as taleggio)
50g/2oz parmesan, grated

Preheat oven to 200°C/Gas 6.

Put flour onto a plate and season it lightly with salt and pepper. Break eggs into a wide bowl and whisk lightly. Dip zucchini slices into flour, coating well and tapping off excess.

Heat 1½ tablespoons of the oil in a non-stick frying pan over high heat. Working in batches, quickly dip floured slices into whisked egg, allowing any excess to drip back into the bowl, then carefully place away from you in hot oil to fry. Reduce heat to medium, turn after 1 minute or when the slices are golden brown, then cook until other side is golden brown. Transfer to a paper towel-lined plate. Add remaining oil and reheat until hot, then continue with remaining zucchini, flour and egg until all slices are fried and drained.

Brush a 2 litre/3½ pint-capacity baking dish with a little of the frying oil. Spoon one-third of the tomato sauce over the bottom of the dish. Closely cover with half of the zucchini slices. Cover with another one-third of the tomato sauce, then dot with half of the washed-rind cheese and sprinkle with half of the parmesan. Place remaining zucchini on top of cheese. Cover with remaining tomato sauce and cheeses.

Bake for 25 minutes until bubbling and golden. Leave to settle for 10 minutes before cutting to serve.

Stuffed Zucchini with Zucchini Flowers

SERVES 4 AS A SIDE DISH This stuffing is sufficient to fill two large zucchini or one 'runaway' zucchini. In both cases, the stuffed zucchini are cut into thick slices to serve together with other dishes as part of an antipasti platter. The stuffing includes excess male flowers. If there are none available, the stuffing will still hold together and taste good without them.

2 × 14cm/5½in zucchini or
   1 × 20–22cm/8–9in zucchini
1 tablespoon extra-virgin olive oil,
   plus 1 teaspoon extra for drizzling
½ onion, finely chopped
6 male zucchini flowers (see page
   670), chopped (optional)
1 free-range egg
2 sprigs thyme, leaves stripped

1 tablespoon chopped flat-leaf
   parsley
1 clove garlic, finely chopped
2 tablespoons fresh breadcrumbs,
   plus extra for scattering
25g/1oz parmesan, grated
sea salt and freshly ground
   black pepper

EXTRA EQUIPMENT
wok
bamboo steamer
   with lid
baking dish long
   enough to hold
   the stuffed
   zucchini in 1 layer

Preheat oven to 180°C/Gas 4.

Half-fill a wok with water and place a bamboo steamer over water, then bring to the boil over high heat. Once water is boiling, drop whole zucchini into steamer, then cover and steam for 5 minutes (for 2 smaller ones) or 10 minutes (for 1 larger one). Put bamboo steamer with zucchini on a chopping board and leave to cool. Dry zucchini.

Meanwhile, heat olive oil in a small frying pan over medium heat, then sauté onion for 8–10 minutes or until very soft and golden. Tip into a large bowl.

Cut zucchini in half lengthways. With a sharp teaspoon, gouge a channel in the flesh so that all seeds and some flesh are removed, then chop removed flesh and add to bowl with onion. Brush a baking dish with a little extra olive oil and place zucchini halves inside, then set aside.

Add chopped flowers (if using), egg, thyme, parsley, garlic, breadcrumbs and parmesan to onion/zucchini mixture and mix together. Taste and adjust the seasoning with salt and pepper. Fill hollowed-out zucchini with stuffing. Scatter over extra breadcrumbs and drizzle with a little more olive oil.

Bake for 20 minutes. Leave to cool a little before cutting into thick slices and serving.

Zucchini and Marjoram Gratin

SERVES 4 AS A SIDE DISH This is an excellent dish for young cooks to master – simple to prepare and cook, it looks splendid. When it is taken out from the oven it is certain to elicit compliments from the rest of the family.

EXTRA EQUIPMENT
1 × 1.5 litre/2¾pint-capacity baking dish

60ml/2fl oz olive oil
1 small onion, finely chopped
3 zucchini (about 400g/14oz), cut into 5mm/¼in-thick slices
50g/2oz long-grain rice
25g/1oz fresh breadcrumbs
250ml/9fl oz milk

2 teaspoons chopped marjoram
1 free-range egg, lightly beaten
50g/2oz parmesan, grated
sea salt and freshly ground black pepper
2 tablespoons pouring cream

Preheat oven to 180°C/Gas 4.

Lightly brush a 1.5 litre/2¾ pint-capacity baking dish with a little olive oil.

Heat 1 tablespoon of the oil in a non-stick frying pan over low heat, then add onion and sauté for 8 minutes or until very soft and just starting to colour. Transfer onion to a plate. Add a little more of the oil to the pan, then, working in batches so as not to crowd the pan, sauté zucchini for 4 minutes or until lightly coloured. Transfer to plate with onion.

Put rice in a small saucepan and cover with boiling water, then simmer for 5 minutes and drain well.

Put breadcrumbs in a bowl and cover with milk. Stir in rice, marjoram, egg and two-thirds of the parmesan. Leave for 10 minutes or until bread swells. Stir in zucchini and onion, then taste and season with salt and pepper. Transfer mixture to baking dish, drizzle with cream and scatter over remaining parmesan.

Bake gratin for 30 minutes or until it is golden and feels firm in the centre. Serve hot or warm.

Male zucchini flower (bottom); and female zucchini flower

Warm Sauté of Zucchini, Pine Nuts and Currants

SERVES 4 The combination of pine nuts and currants is frequently encountered in Sicilian-inspired dishes. A similar combination, with the addition of oil-moistened fresh breadcrumbs, can be used as a stuffing for sardine fillets (see below). This dish is speedy to prepare and cook, and is at its best immediately after cooking, when the pine nuts are warm and the zucchini slices are still a little crisp.

2 tablespoons currants
2 tablespoons red-wine vinegar
2 tablespoons extra-virgin olive oil
40g/1½oz pine nuts
400g/14oz zucchini, cut lengthways
   into 5mm/¼in-thick slices

1 clove garlic, finely chopped
2 teaspoons lemon juice
12 mint leaves, finely shredded
sea salt and freshly ground
   black pepper
sprig mint (optional), to serve

Preheat oven to 100°C/Gas ¼ and put in an ovenproof serving dish to keep warm.

Soak currants in vinegar for 10 minutes, then drain and set aside.

Heat 2 teaspoons of the oil in a frying pan over medium heat and fry pine nuts for 2 minutes or until golden, then tip onto a paper towel-lined plate and set aside.

Heat remaining oil in a large non-stick frying pan over high heat and add zucchini slices in a single layer (remember to carefully place them in the hot oil, not drop them). Don't shake the pan. The aim is for each slice to colour evenly and quickly. Turn slices carefully and cook until well coloured but still crisp, then transfer to the warm serving dish in oven. Wipe out pan with paper towel and place over high heat.

Add garlic to pan and cook for a few seconds, then add currant/vinegar mixture; the vinegar will hiss, splutter and reduce almost instantly. Add pine nuts to the pan, shaking to mix with currant mixture, then spoon over zucchini. Add a few drops of lemon juice and mint, then season with salt and pepper and top with a mint sprig, if using. Serve at once.

Stuffed Sardines

Scatter sardine fillets with the pine nut and currant mixture above, then scatter with olive oil-moistened fresh breadcrumbs. Roll up stuffed sardine fillets and pack tightly into an oiled baking dish. Drizzle with a small amount of Fast Basic Tomato Sauce (see page 649) and bake at 180°C/Gas 4 for 15 minutes. Serve warm.

Cime di Zucchini

MAKES 2 CUPS Rose Gray from the wonderful River Café in London showed me how to nip off the very last tender shoots and the embryonic zucchini left on the plants at the end of the season. An Italian friend told me that the appearance of handfuls of these tiny treasures in the local markets in Umbria marks the very end of the crop. They are considered a seasonal treat so please don't pull up your plants in early autumn without gathering this very special harvest. (The tender shoots can also be gathered from pumpkin plants, to halt further growth as well as at the end of their season, then cooked in this manner.)

The tiny shoots and fruit can be served on garlic-rubbed grilled bread as a bruschetta or tossed through homemade pasta (see page 474). If you decide to cook the shoots in a bamboo steamer, put them on a plate or shallow bowl before placing them inside the steamer as the flavour of bamboo that comes from cooking directly in the basket is inappropriate to these little morsels.

2 small handfuls *cime di zucchini* (you will
   have a mixture of growing tips, stems,
   tiny leaves and tiny undeveloped fruit)
1 tablespoon extra-virgin olive oil

1 clove garlic, finely chopped
sea salt and freshly ground
   black pepper

EXTRA EQUIPMENT
pasta pot or large
   saucepan with
   steamer insert and
   lid or wok with
   bamboo steamer
   plus lid

Bring water to the boil in a pasta pot or large saucepan with a steamer insert in place (or place a bamboo steamer over a wok of simmering water). Drop in *cime di zucchini*, cover and steam for 6 minutes.

Meanwhile, heat olive oil in a small non-stick frying pan over medium heat and briefly sauté garlic until fragrant, then remove from heat. Tip steamed shoots into frying pan, carefully stir with a wooden spoon to coat with garlic and oil, season with salt and pepper and serve at once.

Eggwhite Batter for Deep-fried Zucchini Flowers or Zucchini Chips

MAKES ENOUGH TO COAT 12 ZUCCHINI FLOWERS This batter is crisp and has a lighter texture than the Beer Batter on page 560 although it could be used instead. It will give a more transparent coating and you will be able to glimpse the gold of the flowers more readily. When there are no zucchini flowers to fry, battered sticks or slices of zucchini make absolutely wonderful chips that I have never seen any child reject. Sift 250g/9oz cups plain flour and 1 teaspoon salt into a bowl and make a well. Mix 125ml/4½fl oz olive oil and 375ml/13fl oz warm water and tip into well. Whisk until batter is smooth. Leave at room temperature for at least 1 hour. Beat 2 free-range egg whites in an electric mixer until soft peaks form and then fold into batter. Use batter immediately.

Deep-fried Zucchini Flowers with Three-Cheese Stuffing

MAKES 12 Remember that it is the male flower that is stuffed. This flower is larger, there are more of them and, most importantly, you are not robbing the bush of developing fruit. In Italy it is more likely that you will be offered a plate of fried flowers that have been dipped in batter and fried without any stuffing. They tend to be crisper than stuffed flowers as the moisture in many filling mixtures can make the petals quite damp. Stuffed flowers can't sit around; fill them, dip them in batter, then fry and eat them. Other possible stuffing ingredients include chopped buffalo mozzarella; leftover risotto; ricotta mashed with anchovies and herbs or cooked spinach; or finely chopped cooked meat with fresh breadcrumbs and herbs.

EXTRA EQUIPMENT
wok (optional)

120g/4oz fresh ricotta
25g/1oz parmesan, grated
50g/2oz goat's curd or other
  soft goat's cheese
1 free-range egg
2 tablespoons chopped
  flat-leaf parsley

sea salt and freshly ground black pepper
12 male zucchini flowers, stamens
  removed (optional)
vegetable or olive oil, for deep-frying
1 × Beer Batter (see page 560) or
  Eggwhite Batter (see opposite)

Put ricotta in a sieve resting over a bowl and drain for 15 minutes. Transfer to a mixing bowl and add parmesan, goat's curd, egg and parsley, then season with salt and pepper to taste.

Preheat oven to 100°C/Gas ¼ and put a baking tray lined thickly with paper towel inside to warm.

Put a spoonful of ricotta stuffing mixture into each zucchini flower and gently fold petals around filling. Twirl petal ends to seal.

Pour oil into a large non-stick frying pan or a wok to a depth of 1.5cm/½in in the centre, then heat over high heat. To test whether it is hot enough, add a drop of batter; it should sizzle and turn golden almost immediately. Working in batches, dip stuffed flowers into batter, letting excess drain back into bowl. Fry until golden brown. Don't crowd the pan. Turn to brown on other side. Lift out with tongs and allow excess oil to drain back into pan. Place on baking tray in oven to keep warm until all zucchini flowers are fried. Lightly season with salt and pepper and serve at once.

Zucchini Flowers with Mortadella and Bread Stuffing

MAKES 12 This alternative stuffing for zucchini flowers includes delicately flavoured and smoothly textured mortadella. It can also be used to stuff 'runaway' zucchini which are to be baked (see page 674).

EXTRA EQUIPMENT
food processor
wok (optional)

25g/1oz fresh breadcrumbs
1 tablespoon water
100g/3½oz mortadella,
  roughly chopped
1 clove garlic, finely chopped
2 tablespoons chopped
  flat-leaf parsley
25g/1oz parmesan, grated

1 tablespoon extra-virgin olive oil
sea salt and freshly ground black pepper
12 male zucchini flowers, stamens
  removed (optional)
vegetable or olive oil, for deep-frying
1 quantity Beer Batter (see page 560)
  or Eggwhite Batter (see page 678)

Put breadcrumbs and water into a mixing bowl and leave for 10 minutes. Process mortadella in a food processor until finely chopped. Scrape into bowl with breadcrumbs and add garlic, parsley, parmesan and olive oil. Taste and adjust the seasoning with salt and pepper.

Preheat oven to 100°C/Gas ¼ and put a baking tray lined thickly with paper towel inside to keep warm.

Put a spoonful of breadcrumb stuffing mixture into each zucchini flower and gently fold petals around filling. Twirl petal ends to seal.

Pour oil into a large non-stick frying pan or a wok to a depth of 1.5cm/½in in the centre, then heat over high heat. To test whether it is hot enough, add a drop of batter; it should sizzle and turn golden almost immediately. Working in batches, dip stuffed flowers into batter, letting excess drain back into bowl. Fry until golden brown. Don't crowd the pan. Turn fritters to brown on other side. Lift out with tongs and allow excess oil to drain back into pan. Place on baking tray in oven to keep warm until all zucchini flowers are fried. Serve at once.

Fettuccine with Zucchini, Lemon, Ricotta and Fried Almonds

SERVES 4 This is a light and summery combination of flavours that goes particularly well with delicate homemade pasta.

80g/3oz unsalted butter
40g/1½oz slivered or flaked almonds
salt
400g/14oz dried fettuccine or
300g/10½oz Fresh Pasta (see page 474), cut into fettuccine
1 tablespoon extra-virgin olive oil
4 × 10cm/4in-long zucchini, quartered lengthways, then cut into 1cm/½in-wide slices

2 cloves garlic, thinly sliced
250ml/9fl oz chicken stock
juice and finely grated zest of 1 lemon
125g/4½oz fresh ricotta, crumbled
sea salt and freshly ground black pepper
2 tablespoons chopped flat-leaf parsley

Preheat oven to 100°C/Gas ¼ and put an ovenproof serving bowl inside to warm.

Melt 40g/1½oz of the butter in a large non-stick frying pan over medium heat, then fry almonds until golden brown. Drain in a sieve to remove excess butter and reserve almonds until needed; discard butter. Wipe out pan with a paper towel.

Bring a pasta pot or large heavy-based saucepan of well salted water to the boil over high heat. If using dried pasta, drop into water now and cook following manufacturer's instructions until al dente, then drain and give it a good shake.

Put remaining butter, olive oil, zucchini, garlic, stock, lemon juice and half of the lemon zest into the pan and gently cook, covered, over low heat, for 10 minutes or until zucchini is tender. Set aside until needed.

If using fresh fettuccine, drop into pan of boiling water now and cook for 2–3 minutes or until al dente, then drain and give it a good shake.

Place zucchini mixture over high heat and return to simmering point, then add ricotta chunks and season with salt and pepper. Stir gently, trying not to break up ricotta (bite-sized snowy lumps of ricotta will look much more attractive in the finished dish than a mass of white crumbs).

Tip well drained pasta into warmed serving bowl. Tip over sauce and mix through gently, adding parsley and remaining lemon zest. Scatter with reserved almonds and serve at once.

GARDENING GLOSSARY

Blanching In gardening, this means to exclude air and light by covering the growing vegetable in order to keep the edible part pale. This is done to celery, cauliflowers, endive, leeks, rhubarb and white asparagus.

Bolting The term 'to bolt' describes a plant that is putting its energy into flowering and getting ready to reproduce. This can happen when the weather is very hot, when a plant is stressed with insufficient water, or when a plant has been sown in its incorrect season. Leafy plants that have bolted, such as lettuces, develop a bitter taste. Some plants that have bolted or gone to seed can be left to scatter their seed over the garden and new plants will eventually appear.

Cloches These are simple plastic tunnels that protect young seedlings from late frosts or cold weather and allow them to be planted out a little earlier than would otherwise be possible. In the same way, simple protection can be given to individual plants by covering them with plastic bottles that have had their bases cut away. The cut-off edge is pushed down into the soil. The extra benefit of this method is that it protects the young seedling from snails and slugs.

Alternatively, inexpensive clear polythene such as that sold in hardware stores for use as drop sheets can be cut to size and secured over bamboo hoops, sticks or other supports in the garden to work as a simple hothouse. The plastic can be pulled back while the plant absorbs the sun and secured again with stakes or tent pegs in the evening.

Coir pots The most practical plant-starter pots are made from organic materials such as coir (coconut fibres). When ready the little pots may be planted into the ground together with the seedlings they contain, thus avoiding any transplanting shock (see **Container planting**).

Grapefruit (*Citrus paradise*)

Comfrey tea Collect comfrey leaves (the amount is up to you), place them in a bucket, cover with water and leave for about four weeks. The mixture will become very smelly. Strain and dilute 2 litres tea with 1 litre water and spray. Comfrey tea is a wonderful fertiliser and plant tonic.

Companion planting The term 'companion planting' covers several practices. It can refer to planting one species close to another as a protection against or distraction for pests; planting one species near another in order to lend shelter or support for a less robust plant; or planting a species near another in order to improve the yield or flavour of the first plant. The benefits may be due to the two plants liking similar conditions, not competing with each other on a nutritional level, and possibly providing some extra chemical to each other to improve yield and flavour. (Some plants do, however, exude chemicals through their roots that are detrimental to others.) Sometimes one is also advised to plant a fast-growing plant with a slower-growing plant, as the speedy crop will be harvested before the other is ready.

I have spoken with many gardeners and consulted a wide range of gardening references, and there is much contradiction regarding which plants offer distraction for pests or protection from pests. My advice is to listen to the experiences of as many organic gardeners as possible, experiment widely and observe your results.

Container planting Garden supply stores and online retailers sell a range of containers made from terracotta, plastic, wood or corrugated iron (see page 16). Found objects such as enamelled bath tubs, wheelbarrows and watering cans can also be used.

Include a proportion of well-rotted manure or garden compost mixed with certified organic potting mix when using large pots. In areas where water supply is an ongoing challenge, add some water gel or wetting crystals to the mix. If your pot has nurtured an annual crop it is a good idea to replace the entire contents at the end of the harvest. (See also **Window boxes.**) Perennial potted plants such as small fruit trees should be repotted into a pot one size larger every two years (when the roots fill the pot, but before they get too crowded or 'pot bound') with fresh mix filling the gap. As drainage is limited in all pots, and the roots cannot draw sufficient nutrients from the soil, regular fertilising is essential.

Crop rotation This is the practice of growing a sequence of plants from different families in the same soil through different seasons or years. Crop rotation is partly about soil nutrients, but mostly it is a preventative measure against the build-up of pests and disease in the soil. I find crop rotation quite difficult to manage in my small home vegetable garden, where it is completely impossible to create four separate beds (the ideal for effective crop rotation). Some of my plants have to be tucked into less-than-ideal spaces. It can also be mind-bogglingly complicated. Here is an example:

Year 1: In well-composted soil plant 'heavy feeders' (such as cabbages, cauliflowers, leeks, corn).
Year 2: Plant a legume crop (such as beans, peas) to replace nitrogen in the soil.
Year 3: Plant 'light feeders' (such as carrots, beetroots, radishes, turnips).
Year 4: Start the cycle again.

More and more home gardeners are prepared to say that replenishing soil with plenty of well-rotted manure and/or compost will permit the same crop to be planted successfully in the same position for two seasons. If space is not a problem in your garden, do rotate crops as suggested above.

Crowns This term applies to asparagus, rhubarb and strawberries. Crowns are the nutrient storage vessels by which plants manage to survive cold winters underground and then shoot up when the soil temperature is correct. They can live like this for many years.

Cultivars It is botanically correct to refer to specific plants as either cultivars or varieties of a family. In common usage, however, we tend to refer just to 'varieties'.

In simple terms 'cultivar' stands for cultivated variety. Plants can have naturally occurring variations within the same species, for example different coloured flowers, or adaptations to local climate. These are sometimes referred to as a distinct variety of a species. A cultivar is where a plant has been deliberately selected or bred for one or a combination of attributes, and those attributes are stable and able to be reproduced through appropriate means of propagation. Heritage plants can also be cultivars.

Cuttings, how to take To take a woody cutting, snip a section 5–10 cm long, cutting just below a leaf junction, and place just over half of the length in good soil or potting mix, after gently removing the leaves from the lower half of the cutting. Keep moist. A clear plastic bag or bottle with a hole in the top can help keep the air moist. Once the roots have taken, you can plant it in a permanent position in the garden.

Direct sowing of seeds This involves sowing seeds directly into their final position in a garden bed or container, essential for many plants and acceptable for many others.

Some seeds are incredibly fine, however, and it is difficult to plant just one seed at a time. Mixing fine seed with clean sand is often recommended as an aid. If more than the ideal one or two seedlings appear in close proximity, once they have developed 'true leaves' (the second pair of leaves to emerge), thin the group to one healthy plant.

Espalier This term is used to describe a way of training plants, usually fruit trees, so that they grow flat against a wall or training wires. Plants trained in this way take up less space while still permitting light to penetrate the branches. Often, though, the crop is reduced.

Families The classification of plants is complex and mostly beyond the scope of this book. But new gardeners can readily grasp the idea of plant families. The family of each plant covered in this book is given in the gardening notes for growing the plant. In the kitchen garden context, knowing which plants are in the same family helps gardeners understand their similar needs. In crop rotation it is recommended not to plant species from the same family in the same area more than once every three years (see **Crop rotation**).

Fertilisers Many soils need improving with fertiliser before they will grow healthy fruit and vegetables. All plants need various levels of nitrogen, phosphorous and potassium to thrive.

These nutrients can be provided by organic fertilisers, including fish, blood and bone, compost, mulch or green manure crops. It is impossible to exaggerate the importance of ensuring that your plant receives the nutrients it needs. (See also **Liquid fertiliser**.)

Garden compost This is the ultimate soil improver, and can be made from a mixture of recycled vegetable scraps and garden gleanings such as lawn clippings, prunings, well-rotted raked leaves, straw and torn paper. It is not used until it has decomposed (see **Organic matter**). If you need to supplement your own garden compost by purchasing it, ensure you buy bagged organic soil improvers such as those approved by the Soil Association. By digging in garden compost the soil becomes more porous, allowing air and water to reach growing roots more easily. Garden compost also releases much goodness from the organic matter as it decomposes. It is a must for any garden!

Greenhouse A walk-in building (typically 1.8 by 2.4m) with glass walls and roof designed for growing plants under controlled conditions. Greenhouses with electricity fitted can be heated so they are frost free and have accessories such as heating mats and propagators for seed raising.

Gloves All gardeners should develop the habit of wearing gardening gloves outside, not just because they might be handling powerful fertilisers (such as manure, blood, fish and bone, or lime), but because there are also sharp sticks, thorns and stakes in many gardens.

Green manure This refers to annual plant crops, usually nitrogen-rich legumes such as peas and beans, that are known to improve the soil. If grown as a green manure crop rather than for the kitchen, the plants are dug into the soil before they flower, when they have maximum nitrogen. By chopping up these growing plants and digging them into the soil, drainage is also improved. They break down very rapidly and the bed can be planted just a few weeks afterwards. A green manure crop is often planted in a bed deliberately left empty after growing plants that are 'heavy feeders' (see **Crop rotation**).

Hand-pollination This refers to pollinating the female flower manually with the pollen from the male flower of certain plants. See entries for Cucumber, Melon, Pumpkin and Zucchini. Early in the morning, hand-pollinate female flowers (the smaller flower with a swelling) by transferring pollen from the male flower (the one on the long stalk) using a paintbrush; or break off the male flower, bend back its petals and press it against a female flower.

Heritage plants These are traditional cultivars of food plants that were bred for their flavour, disease resistance, adaptation to various local conditions and for their long harvesting period. These older cultivars were in danger of disappearing as many commercial growers turned to hybrids bred to accommodate the needs of supermarkets. Seed Savers exchanges around the world have pioneered the reintroduction of heritage fruits and vegetables. In the UK, Garden Organic run the Heritage Seed Library (**www.gardenorganic.org.uk**). The seed from many heritage fruits and vegetables can be saved and replanted the following season, and the plant will still grow true to type.

Hybrid plants/seeds Modern hybrids are plants often bred with the ability to be harvested by machine, to withstand the transporting process over long distances, and to be refrigerated. If you save the seed from generation to generation with a hybrid, they won't necessarily produce plants the same as the parent as the seed is often sterile.

Kitchen gardens The French term '*potager*' means 'kitchen garden'. It refers to a garden attached to a house that grows a mixture of both annual and perennial fruits, vegetables and culinary herbs. It exists to service a household with food.

Liquid fertiliser Cheaper than buying a commercial product is to make your own liquid fertiliser, using manure, garden compost or seaweed. If using seaweed, wash it well first to rid it of excess salt. You will need a large plastic bin with a lid. Place a large armful of the chosen material (approximately one-third of your bin's capacity) into a hessian sack. Suspend the sack by a rope tied to a stick placed across the top of the bin. Fill with water, cover with the lid to protect it from rain and leave until the water turns brown – this should take about 10–14 days. Dilute to the colour of weak tea before using, and apply only when the ground is damp following rain or irrigation. Liquid fertiliser made with garden compost is commonly referred to as 'compost tea'.

Manure Fresh manure will burn plants if it is not well rotted. If possible, find out where it has come from in case it contains harmful residues from herbicides which could damage your crops. There is confusion regarding the term 'organic' as it has several meanings. All manure, garden compost, straw and so on, are organic in that they are carbon-based; that is, they once lived. Often bagged products will claim to be 'organic' but are not necessarily produced without artificial chemicals on uncontaminated sites according to strict guidelines. The Soil Association (**www.soilassociation.org**) runs a certification scheme with a well-known logo which is used on food, it is available to gardening suppliers but few take it up because of the lengthy and costly certification. The other alternatives are to look carefully at the packaging or contact the supplier direct..

No-dig gardens/raised beds Whole books are devoted to the theory and construction of no-dig gardens, which were first pioneered in the 1970s by Esther Deans. Her little book *No-dig Gardening & Leaves of Life* is a delight and very inspirational. A no-dig garden is one that is built on top of existing soil or other surfaces and not made by digging the soil to form a bed. It can be built anywhere: on top of a lawn, on top of unworkable clay soil, even on concrete. It is constructed from layers of organic material that settle and break down rapidly, providing a nutrient-rich soil ready for planting. (See **What is a No-dig Garden?** on page 20.)

Open-pollinated seed This term refers to the free and open exchange of pollen between plants that occurs naturally by wind and bees, as opposed to the deliberate manipulation of pollen involved in producing hybrids. All heirloom varieties can be open-pollinated (see **Heritage plants**). Open-pollinated seeds are those that you can save from year to year as long as seed-saving procedures to prevent cross-pollination are followed, such as providing distance between plants known to cross-pollinate (see **Seed-saving**).

Organic gardening At home and at school where families and children are often eating produce straight from the garden, there are commonsense reasons to avoid gardening methods that use harmful chemicals. Organic gardening doesn't just mean no chemicals. In order to have a healthy organic garden you literally have to start from the ground up with resilient soils and plants. Organic gardening means not using treated pine, tyres or old corrugated iron in the food production area as edging or as supports in order to avoid arsenic, chromium or other undesirable chemicals leaching into the garden soil. Western Red cedar is a good alternative, although not as generally available. It may need to be ordered in advance.

Organic matter In this book, the term 'organic matter' usually refers to a mixture of soil, compost and well-rotted animal manure. See **Manure** for the difference between 'organic' and 'certified organic'.

pH A measure of alkalinity or acidity of a soil on a scale 1-14 where pH7 is neutral, above pH7 is alkaline and below is acid. It is worth measuring the pH of the soil every couple of years using a simple kit. Members of the cabbage family prefer a slightly alkaline soil, lime can be added to raise the pH. It is harder to lower the pH of a soil, many fruits such as blueberries prefer acid conditions, so these are often grown in containers of lime-free peat-based compost.

Permaculture A practice highly respected in organic gardening circles, permaculture is concerned with gardening for sustainability. The term was coined in the 1970s by Bill Mollison and David Holmgren. It links the concepts 'permanent', 'agriculture' and 'culture', and proposes that it is not possible for any culture to survive for long without sustainable practices being followed, and that this applies to agriculture as well as other social systems.

Planting out This refers to transferring young plants from a seedling tray or small pot into the open ground or garden proper. It is advisable to sow seeds in trays or pots rather than to sow them directly into the garden for many reasons. Seedlings in pots or trays can be better protected from wind and hot sun until they are strong enough to cope. Similarly, seedlings in pots or trays can be better defended from birds, ants and other chomping insects. If using a heated propagator, the germination rate improves. The seedlings should usually be 'hardened off' for a few days, which means removing any covers from the trays, before being planted out into the garden bed.

Propagation containers These are simply seedling trays. A cardboard egg carton works well if you poke a hole in the bottom of each hollow. Alternatively, try a plastic ice-cream container; again, make sure you have punched a series of holes in the bottom (a heated metal sharpening steel or metal skewer does a good job). Fill the container with moist seed-raising mix; add seeds, then cover them with another layer of seed-raising mix. Once the seedlings have developed six leaves, they are ready for planting out (see **Planting out**).

Rooster Pelleted Manure This is a commercially available, certified organic fertiliser consisting of pelleted chicken poo. It is used in the compost 'lasagne' recipe (on page 12).

Root division Some plants, such as tarragon, thyme and oregano, are propagated by dividing their roots and replanting as several smaller plants. For propagation by division, dig up a plant and divide it into several pieces with a clean, sharp knife. Be sure each piece has a stem and root system, and replant the pieces.

Root stock A plant used to provide the root system for a grafted plant. Many fruit trees are grafted and by choosing a particular rootstock the vigour of the tree can be controlled.

Seaweed Using seaweed in its natural state as a mulch is controversial, and it is in fact illegal to harvest seaweed on some beaches. While seaweed is a good supplier of nitrogen, potash and trace elements, others decry it because of its high sodium content. However, making a seaweed 'tea' (see **Comfrey tea**) results in a good all-purpose fertiliser. There are also many proprietary brands of concentrated liquid seaweed fertiliser available at every garden supplier.

Seed-raising bed A well raked patch of ground outside where seeds of vegetables are first sown in short rows and grown on until they are ready to be transplanted to their final positions. A seed bed is useful for crops that need space to mature, many members of the cabbage family and leeks are often started off in seed-raising beds.

Seed-saving This is the practice of allowing healthy plants to go to seed and collecting the seed for use the following season. To collect seeds, pull the plant out of the ground before the seeds start to fall and hang it upside-down in a dry, well-ventilated space. (Some gardeners prefer to enclose the dry heads or pods in paper bags tied with string before harvesting the plant.) Ensure the plant is completely dry before picking off the seeds. Place newspaper or white paper on the ground to catch any seeds that may fall.

There are other seed collection methods, depending on the type of plant. These include opening the pods, shaking the plant in a large sieve or rubbing the flowers with both hands to release seeds. These methods are best done over a white or light-coloured sheet, so that the seeds are visible. Collecting seed from tomatoes is a bit more complicated (see page 642).

Store the collected seeds in an airtight container (old film canisters are great, as are small jars), label them and store them in a cool, dry place (this means indoors, not in a non-insulated garden shed) away from the light. Use any stored seeds in the next planting season.

Self-sufficiency We might aspire to grow all the fruit and vegetables our families require, and in this book the suggested amounts to plant per fruit, vegetable or herb are based on this aspiration, for the average needs of a family of four. However, many readers will not have the necessary space to grow such quantities. Instead, you should grow what you can manage and be delighted and proud to have produced some proportion of your family's food.

Slug and snail pellets Growing Success Advanced Slug Killer are the least toxic slug pellets currently available and approved for organic farming. It is a bait containing ferric phosphate which can be used around children, pets and wildlife as it only targets slugs. It also remains effective after both rain and watering and does not contain metaldehyde or methiocarb found in conventional pellets.

Soil Home gardeners start work with whatever soil their garden happens to have. There are three main textures or types of soil, ranging from light or sandy to loam to heavy clay. Soil is made up of four components: mineral particles, air, water and biological elements (living organisms and decaying organic matter such as worms, roots, fungi and bacteria).

All types of soil will benefit from and be improved by the digging in of organic matter, which improves drainage, nutrient availability and water-holding capacity (see **Organic matter**). New gardeners may have to purchase manure and soil improvers until they have established their own garden compost supply. A good all-purpose ratio for soil feeding is one part chicken manure, two parts certified organic compost and three parts cow manure. All manures used must be well-rotted, as fresh manure can burn plants (see **Manure**).

All vegetables prefer well-drained soil. Some will tolerate soggy or dry conditions better than others. Almost all vegetables prefer soil with plenty of organic matter worked into it.

If you are a new gardener, the challenge is to get to know the soil in your garden: to recognise those areas that get maximum sun and maximum wind as well as the areas that tend to hold moisture and so on. You can group plants that need extra feeding and give them extra care. Similarly, you can position less fussy plants in the driest or poorest areas in the garden. Lastly, you can plant legumes to improve the soil for future crops as they return essential nitrogen to the soil.

Gardeners whose only available space for a vegetable garden is taken up by lawn or paving should consider constructing a raised no-dig garden (see **No-dig gardens/raised beds**).

Soil temperature It's important to plant out seeds or seedlings in soil that is the right temperature for the individual plant. A succession of sunny days can inspire an inexperienced gardener to plant out seeds or seedlings too early. Most spring sown crops should not be sown until the soil temperature is at least 5°C. You can buy a soil thermometer at any garden supply store.

Soil toxicity Soil can be tested for toxicity. If you have reason to believe that your soil is contaminated, contact the Contaminated Land Officer at your local authority. Constructing a no-dig garden will not help if the soil is contaminated. You will need to lay down a physical barrier such as Geo fabric, which is non-permeable, before constructing the garden bed on top (see **No-dig gardens/raised beds**).

Spurs These are short permanent side stubs that grow from the shoots or growing branches on fruit trees. Some trees (such as apricots) produce fruit on both the shoots and the spurs; some (such as peaches) on shoots only; and some (such as cherries) bear fruit mainly on these short spurs. This is another reason to consult expert advice before carrying out any pruning on your fruit trees.

Transplanting seedlings If your seedlings have been grown in an organic plant-starter pot, the pot and all its contents can be planted directly into the ground (see **Coir or pots**). If not, the seedlings have to be 'pricked out'. Begin by choosing the hardiest, strongest-looking seedling. Seedlings are delicate, so be careful not to harm the root system. Handle the seedling very gently by a leaf so as not to damage the fragile stem. A dibbler or wooden plant-marker stick (or even an icypole stick or a pencil) can be used to create a hole at the right depth in the soil into which the seedling will be transplanted. If the transplanted seedling has a long stem, replant the seedling a little deeper. Keep the soil around the newly transplanted seedling moist, and only remove the number of seedlings from their pot or tray that you can plant in 15 minutes.

Window boxes Apartment dwellers are often encouraged to grow a few herbs in a window box. It's a lovely idea but remember that the amount of soil available to plants in window boxes either planted directly or in small pots is limited. If the window box is in full sun the plants will inevitably be stressed. They may also have to cope with reflected heat from glass and poor air flow, as well as limited root run. The best idea, if you have a little more space, is to have 'back-up' pots of your favourites positioned in the backyard, and every few weeks rotate the pots in the window box with those grown out of doors. This is not possible, of course, with plants grown directly in a window box.

Worms and worm tea Worms are a gardener's friend. Not only do they aerate the soil by tunnelling through it and leaving 'castings', which are a valuable fertiliser, but worms work tirelessly in the compost heap, helping to break it down. They are then transferred to the soil with the compost and continue to improve the soil.

Special composting worms (as opposed to earthworms) can be farmed in a worm farm (see page 13). Their draining liquid ('worm juice' or 'worm wee') is diluted to a ratio of 1 cup worm juice to 9 litres water to make worm tea, which can be used as a fertiliser throughout the garden.

PEST AND WEED CONTROL

As more gardeners become aware of the dangers posed by chemical sprays, there is an increasing demand for effective organic prevention and control measures. Many businesses and organisations offer products and guidance: the leading organic gardening charity in the UK is Garden Organic (www.gardenorganic.org.uk), there is a lot of information on their website for the public but if you become a member you also get a magazine The Organic Way.

There are now many specialist suppliers of organic or environmentally-friendly products for controlling pests such as the Organic Gardening Catalogue (www.organiccatalogue.com) but also local garden centres have increased their range of such products due to the restricted number of chemical controls now available to amateur gardeners in the UK.

Gardeners can also utilise beneficial creatures to help control pests, these are available as biological controls and have been prepared to make them easy for the home gardener to use, either in an enclosed environment such as a greenhouse or watered on to outside soil or potting mixes. Choose a mail order supplier that provides plenty of advice as the temperature and time the control is used is often critical. Try: www.harrodhorticultural.com; www.just-green.co.uk; www.defenders.co.uk; www.greengardener.co.uk).

Exclusion (or barrier methods) are the most effective organic preventative measure of all. Fine mesh crop covers that allow light, air and water through to growing crops but prevent flying insects to eat and lay eggs on crops are a major innovation for gardeners. Drape the covers over hoops and secure the edges of the netting so it does not fly open. Ripening fruit is well worth netting to prevent the birds eating it, you can either temporarily net each bush or wall-trained specimen or erect a permanent walk-in fruit cage and grow the fruit inside. Winter crops are often attacked by pigeons so it is worth netting these overwinter.

It is illegal in the UK to use any chemical pesticide unless it has been cleared and approved for that use for amateur gardeners, this extends to home-made remedies. So do not be tempted

Onion, red variety (*Allium cepa*)

to use commercial pesticides in a domestic situation or to make up your own brews. Fertilisers and feeds are not covered by the regulations, so many organic treatments claim to be general plant tonics rather than make specific claims to kill certain pests and diseases. Whatever you use, always make sure you read and follow the instructions – many products cannot be used on edible crops near to harvesting, for example.

Barrier method Pests are prevented from reaching the plant by a barrier such as fine netting on cabbages, copper tape on plant pots or grease bands on apple tree trunks.

Beer Shallow containers or citrus skins (see below) filled with beer and left in the garden are excellent traps for slugs and snails..

Biological control The use of a natural predator to control a pest. You need to know what pest you have then buy a suitable biological control to tackle it. The range of controls is growing all the time, some are microscopic nematode worms that release a bacteria into the host such as slugs. Others are parasitic wasps or tiny flies that lay eggs on young aphids. The biological control can be killed by sprays and traps, so remove yellow sticky traps in the greenhouse before introducing whitefly or aphid predators. Stop using pyrethrum 4 days before introducing predators.Insecticidal soap can be used up to 1 day before.

Cabbage collars Cabbage root fly lays its eggs in the soil near the stem of vulnerable plants. By placing a 12cm diameter mat or collar around the base of the plant egg laying is prevented. Collars can be purchased or made out of carpet underlay or similar material.

Citrus skins Halved orange, lemon or grapefruit skins left upturned in the garden will trap snails and slugs. They will still need to be killed or fed to the chickens.

Comfrey tea see page 688.

Copper Snails and slugs get a slight electric shock when they attempt to cross a band of copper, so they usually do not cross over. Copper tape can be fitted around the rims of containers or raised beds to protect the plants within. Solid copper rings that are popped over individual plants can be used in borders.

Crop covers There are various types of material that can protect plants ranging from clear polythene and horticultural fleeces that raise the temperatures underneath for early sowings to fine mesh covers that protect plants from flying pests. Both types of cover can be draped over metal hoops, it is usual to replace fleece after the last frost date with fine mesh cover which can then stay on until the autumn.

Egg shells Crushed egg shells scattered around new seedlings will discourage snails and slugs, neither of which enjoy sliding over rough, sharp surfaces.

Grease bands Sticky bands wrapped and secured around fruit tree trunks to prevent the wingless female winter moths crawling up the trunk to lay her eggs in the tree branches.

Horticultural oils Pests can be controlled by spraying plants with products containing natural vegetable oils such as rapeseed oil. The oil blocks the small insects breathing holes and they suffocate while the larger, beneficial insects such as bees and ladybirds are left un-harmed but keep oils away from ponds. Edible crops can be picked and eaten on the same day they are sprayed.

Hose Pieces of old hose left in the garden will be seen as attractive gathering places for earwigs, which can then be disposed of.

Ladybirds I have read that a single ladybird can eat 400 aphids in a week. They also eat many other damaging insects. Plant a diverse garden with flowering companion plants to attract beneficial predators of all kinds. Leave habitat such as logs and chunks of wood.

Nettle spray Soak 300 g nettles in 3 litres water for 3 weeks and dilute to spray in the garden. Use as a general fertiliser as nettles are rich in nitrogen and iron. This spray may also help with powdery mildew, aphids and bean fly.

Pheromone traps Pheromones are chemicals secreted by an animal, especially an insect, that enables the creature to communicate with others of the same species. There are many different pheromones. In the garden pheromone traps are used most often to minimise the damage to fruit trees caused by codling moth. These traps are a specific kind of sticky trap. A sticky trap is bated with a synthetic version of the chemical secreted by a female moth to attract the male. The traps are hung in the branches of the tree. The male is caught in the trap rather than mating with a female which would result in more eggs and more damage to the tree.

Potassium bicarbonate A spray to fight powdery mildew and downy mildew on a range of plants including fruit, courgettes and cucumbers. Dilute one teaspoon per litre of water and spray weekly.

Pyrethrum A plant-based contact insecticide that breaks down quickly and fully. While it is effective against things that chew leaves including caterpillars and smaller beetles, it will kill bees and beneficial insects too, so it has to be used carefully. Don't spray in temperatures above 32degreeC. Use in the early morning or evening to avoid killing bees.

Soap spray A fatty acid spray giving effective control of aphids, red spider mite, whitefly and other pests. For general use on fruit vegetables and flowers.

Sticky traps Useful for trapping small, flying, leaf-eating insects. The disadvantage is that they can also trap the 'good' insects. You can buy yellow plastic sheets covered with a non-drying glue which traps insects such as whitefly, thrips and gnats in greenhouses. The traps can indicate when to introduce a biological control.

Wasp traps To deter wasps from crops such as plums, hang traps nearby. Either purchase glass traps that hold jam and water but are shaped so it is difficult for the wasp to fly out once it enters. The home-made alternative is a jam jar filled with a bit of jam ans water with a paper cover with a hole in the middle.

Water Many insects can be dislodged with a jet spray of water from a hose gun. Remember to hose the underside of the leaves as well as the tops.

A tussie mussie – a bunch of flowers that contains herbs

COOKING GLOSSARY

Acidulated water Water to which an acid ingredient has been added (usually lemon juice but it might be wine vinegar) to delay the natural darkening of some ingredients when they are peeled or cut and exposed to the air (for example, celeriac, artichokes, apples or pears).

Arborio rice This is the best-known variety of rice sold specifically to make Italian risotto. It is a medium-grain rice with a soft texture and a chalky centre. During the cooking of the risotto some of the starch from the rice is released and creates the desired creaminess. Other varieties of risotto rice, which are often recommended, are Carnaroli and Vialone Nano.

Blanching There are two quite different meanings of 'to blanch'. In the kitchen 'to blanch' means to dunk something briefly in boiling water in order to loosen an outer skin (such as with broad beans or tomatoes), to fast-cook tender green leaves (as with baby spinach) or to extract bitterness (such as with garlic). In the garden it means to exclude air to keep a vegetable pale.

Burghul Sometimes called bulgur or cracked wheat. It is wheat that has been roasted and the kernels coarsely milled ('cracked'). It comes in two textures: coarse and fine. Burghul only requires a short soaking period in water before being ready to eat. Commonly recognised as the grain in tabbouleh.

Cartouche A piece of baking paper cut or torn to fit the inside diameter of a saucepan or pot so that it settles directly over the food to prevent evaporation, often of braising juices or a poaching syrup.

Garden-picked tomatoes are always sweeter

Clarified butter Butter heated until the milk solids fall to the bottom of the pan and the clear butter oil can be spooned off (see page 258). Clarified butter is less likely to burn when heated than regular butter, yet it still retains the true taste of butter.

Cornichons Very small pickling cucumbers that are salted and then pickled in wine vinegar. Best with terrines and cold meats.

Cream The fat component of milk. There are many cream products on the market. They vary mainly in the amount of butterfat they contain: from 25 per cent for low-fat or 'light', to 50 per cent for a super-thick cream for dolloping. In between are products sold as pure cream or pouring cream; double cream; whipping cream (which has been thickened with a small quantity of gelatine), and crème fraîche (which has had a lactic acid culture added to it).

Fresh and firm mozzarella This cheese comes in various sizes and as fresh or matured. The standard-sized balls of fresh, white mozzarella are a little larger than a golf ball. Smaller sizes are sold as 'bocconcini' and even smaller, 'milk cherries'. The small size of milk cherries makes them ideal for handing around on little skewers because they require no further cutting. Once mozzarella has been hung to dry and all the whey has drained from it, the balls become firm and are golden-yellow in colour and become the firm mozzarella used for grating on pizzas and gratins.

Gelatine An odourless, tasteless thickening agent produced from the connective tissue of animals, usually cows. There are two types of gelatine: powdered and leaf. I prefer to use leaf gelatine, which dissolves quickly and without lumps. It needs soaking in cold water for a few minutes to make it pliable and dissolve well before being added to a small quantity of hot liquid. If you buy gold-strength leaf gelatine, 1 leaf is the equivalent of a rounded half teaspoon of powdered gelatine (which is 2g/.07oz).

Ghee A standard ingredient in Indian cooking. It is butter that has been clarified and then cooked further until it develops a nutty flavour and a deep-golden colour (see **Clarified butter**).

Harissa A fiery condiment that is a blend of chillies and other spices that is served alongside or added to many Moroccan and North African dishes. Sometimes it is served as a blob on a flat plate ringed with olive oil. One tears off a piece of bread and drags it through the harissa and the oil.

Mirin This is Japanese rice wine that is used for cooking only. It is often combined with equal quantities of soy sauce, when it is known as teriyaki sauce, and is then used as a dipping sauce or as a glaze. It is sweeter than Chinese shao hsing wine.

Moong dal or mung dal 'Dal' usually refers to lentils, but this is actually a skinned, split mung bean. In its unskinned form it is green; once skinned it is yellow. Many pulses look quite different once skinned and it is easy to be confused. Dal with rice provides an inexpensive and balanced meal for many Indian families.

Nori A seaweed or sea vegetable best known as a wrapping for sushi. It is farmed in Japan and sold in flat, dried sheets. If soaked in boiling water for 10-15 minutes it becomes soft and can be added to soups or mixed with other vegetables. It can be toasted over a flame and added to salads.

Orange flower water Flavours sweet dishes and pastries in India, the Middle East and in the Eastern Mediterranean. It is made by distilling the flowers of Seville orange trees. It is very intense and rarely should one use more than a few drops.

Palm sugar A sweetener with a distinctive flavour derived from the concentrated sap of several different palm trees. It is used in Thai and other South-East Asian cuisines.

Pandan leaf or pandanus leaf As popular in South-East Asia as vanilla is to Western cooks, pandan leaves are used to flavour both sweet and savoury dishes. A whole narrow leaf may be used to wrap food to be grilled or a strip from a leaf is often cooked with rice. The leaf is discarded before the dish is eaten.

Pearl barley This is barley that has had the external husk or bran removed. While still taking some time to cook it is speedier than 'pot barley', which has not been 'pearled'.

Pepitas These are a commercial product made from the inner kernels of a pumpkin that has very large seeds. They are olive-green in colour. The inner kernels of the seeds of most pumpkins I have grown or seen in other gardens are much smaller. You could substitute some of your own small roasted pumpkin seeds (see recipe on page 515).

Pickled ginger This is ginger that has been thinly sliced and pickled in sweetened vinegar. Used as a condiment in Japanese cooking, it becomes pale pink and is always served with raw fish.

Preserved lemons Traditionally used in Moroccan and Middle Eastern cooking, jars of these can be bought in many larger supermarkets and speciality food shops. However, they are very easy to make (see recipe on page 371).

Red rice vinegar A mild vinegar with a hint of sweetness, which is frequently used in Chinese dipping sauces.

Ricotta salata This is a firm yet creamy, pressed and lightly salted ricotta that has a lovely sharp, lemony flavour. Available from Italian-owned delicatessens.

Salted black beans These soy beans have been preserved in salt and are available in all Asian food stores. They are often crushed and soaked in water or rice wine before using.

Shao hsing wine Chinese rice wine that is a little sweet and very aromatic. Available at all Asian food stores, it adds a distinctive flavour to Chinese sauces. The nearest substitute is dry sherry. Mirin, or Japanese rice wine, is frequently substituted but it is sweeter.

Shrimp paste A very powerful paste made from fermented prawns. It has a pungent smell but adds a magical subtlety to many Asian dishes. It has many local names, among them *trasi*, *blachan* and *kapi*.

Spanish smoky paprika All paprikas are made from various varieties of peppers. The colour of paprika depends on the variety with which it was made. Smoky paprikas are made by smoking the peppers before they are dried and ground to a powder. Spanish smoky paprikas are sold as either *dulce* (sweet), *agridulce* (semi-sweet) or *picante* (hot).

Sterilised jars Jars and their lids should be washed thoroughly in hot, soapy water, rinsed well and dried in a low oven for at least 10 minutes. Alternatively run the empty glasses and lids in the dishwasher (without other dirty dishes) and fill as soon as they come hot and dry from the machine.

Tamarind pulp Obtained from the pods of a large shade tree grown throughout Asia, the pulp inside the pod is both sweet and sour, and is used to add its special character to curries, relishes and other dishes. Pulp can be bought seed-free or with seeds from Asian food stores and many supermarkets. The pulp is soaked to achieve a liquid that is added to dishes (see page 409).

Verjuice Made from the juice of unripe grapes, verjuice is used as a delicate acidulant. It is often used in sauces and dressings, especially for poultry, pork and seafood.

Vino cotto (or 'vincotto' – literally 'cooked wine'). A relative newcomer to food shelves, this has been used in Italy for a long time. This magic ingredient is both sweet and sour. It is made by reducing cooked grape must (the residue after pressing) until thick and syrupy. Vino cotto can be used in marinades, sauces, to baste meat before grilling or to brush onto grilled vegetables.

Yoghurt Milk that has been soured by the addition of various live cultures. It varies as to butterfat content and as to how much whey is left in the final product. Greek-style yoghurt has approximately 10 per cent butterfat and has less whey than other styles, whereas other plain yoghurts have less butterfat and more whey. There is also low-fat yoghurt and flavoured, sweetened yoghurt. When cooking, seek out unflavoured, unsweetened yoghurt.

Clockwise from top left: A selection of frying pans;
tea towels; ceramic moulds; and bamboo steamers

BIBLIOGRAPHY

Adey Family, *Fresh from the Garden*, Simon & Schuster, Sydney, 1995

Alexander, Stephanie, *The Cook's Companion*, 2nd edn, Lantern, Melbourne, 2004

—— *Kitchen Garden Cooking with Kids*, Lantern, Melbourne, 2006

Alexander, Stephanie & Beer, Maggie, *Stephanie Alexander & Maggie Beer's Tuscan Cookbook*, Lantern, Melbourne, 2009

Beer, Maggie, *Maggie's Harvest*, Lantern, Melbourne, 2007

Bertrand, Bernard, *Les secrets de l'Ortie*, 3rd edn, Éditions de Terran, Aspet, 1997

Blazey, Clive & Varkulevicius, Jane, *The Australian Fruit & Vegetable Garden*, Digger's Club, Dromana, 2006

Bown, Deni, *Herbal*, Pavilion, London, 2001

Bradley, Fern Marshall, *Find-it-Fast: Answers for Your Vegetable Garden*, Rodale, New York, 2007

Brennan, Georgeanne & Ethel, *The Children's Kitchen Garden*, Ten Speed Press, Berkeley, 1997

Brennan, Georgeanne, *Potager*, Ebury Press, London, 1992

Brown, Lynda, *The Cook's Garden*, Random Century Group, London, 1990

Burke, Don, *The Lazy Gardener*, New Holland, Sydney, 2008

Byrne, Josh, *The Green Gardener*, Viking, Melbourne, 2006

Cameron, Susie, Crook, Caroline & Webster, Caroline, *Small Fry: Outdoors*, ABC Books, Sydney, 2008

Caplin, Adam, *New Kitchen Garden*, Ryland, Peters & Small, London, 2003

Carluccio, Antonio, *Antonio Carluccio's Vegetables*, Hodder Headline, London, 2000

Carluccio, Antonio & Priscilla, *Carluccio's Complete Italian Food*, Quadrille Publishing, London, 1997

Cherikoff, Vic & Isaacs, Jennifer, *The Bush Food Handbook*, Ti Tree Press, Sydney, 1989

Creasy, Rosalind, *The Edible Mexican Garden*, The Edible Garden series, Periplus Editions, Hong Kong, 2000

David, Elizabeth, *French Provincial Cooking*, Penguin Books, London, 1964

Davidson, Alan (ed.), *The Oxford Companion to Food*, Oxford University Press, Oxford, 1999

Deans, Esther, *No-dig Gardening & Leaves of Life*, HarperCollins, Sydney, 2001

Demaio, Pietro, *Preserving the Italian Way*, Burwood East, Vic: Memoirs Foundation, Melbourne, 2006

De Pieri, Stefano, *Modern Italian Food*, Hardie Grant, Melbourne, 2004

Esbensen, Mogens Bay, *Thai Cuisine*, Nelson, Melbourne, 1986

Feridun, Bruno, *Jardiner avec les enfants*, Éditions Ouest-France, 2005

Glowinski, Louis, *The Complete Book of Fruit Growing in Australia*, Lothian, Melbourne, 1991

Grigson, Jane, *Jane Grigson's Vegetable Book*, Atheneum, New York, 1979

—— *The Observer Guide to British Cookery*, Michael Joseph, London, 1984

Grover, Harry, *The Vegetable Gardener's Diary for Australia and New Zealand*, Hyland House, Melbourne, 1994

Hazan, Marcella, *Marcella Cucina*, Macmillan, London, 1997

Hemphill, John & Rosemary, *John & Rosemary Hemphill's What Herb is That?*, Lansdowne, Sydney, 1995

Holt, Geraldine, *The Gourmet Garden*, Pavilion, London, 1990

—— *Recipes from a French Herb Garden*, Conran Octopus, London, 1989

Hutton, Wendy, *Singapore Food*, Times Books International, Singapore, 1989

Jaine, Tom, *Cooking in the Country*, Chatto & Windus, London, 1986

Jaffrey, Madhur, *Climbing the Mango Trees*, Ebury Press, London, 2005

—— *Eastern Vegetarian Cooking*, Arrow Books, London, 1990

—— *A Taste of India*, Pavilion, London, 1985

Jenkins, Nancy Harmon, *Flavors of Puglia*, Broadway Books, New York, 1997

Johns, Leslie & Stevenson, Violet, *Fruit for the Home and Garden*, Angus & Robertson, Sydney, 1979

Katzen, Molly, *Molly Katzen's Sunlight Café*, Hyperion, New York, 2002

Kwong, Kylie, *Heart and Soul*, Lantern, Melbourne, 2006

—— *My China*, Lantern, Melbourne, 2007

—— *Simple Chinese Cooking*, Lantern, Melbourne, 2006

Kyritsis, Janni, *Wild Weed Pie*, Lantern, Melbourne, 2006

La Place, Viana, *Verdura*, Macmillan, London, 1994

Larkcom, Joy, *The Organic Salad Garden*, Frances Lincoln, London, 2001

—— *Oriental Vegetables*, John Murray, London, 1991

Little, Brenda, *Companion Planting in Australia*, 4th edn, New Holland, Sydney, 2000

Lloyd, Christopher, *Gardener Cook*, Francis Lincoln, London, 1997

Low, Tim, *Wild Food Plants of Australia*, Angus & Robertson, Sydney, 1988

McGee, Harold, *On Food and Cooking*, Scribner, New York, 1984

Madison, Deborah, *The Savory Way*, Bantam Books, New York, 1990

Malouf, Greg & Lucy, *Arabesque*, Hardie Grant, Melbourne, 2002

Marshall, Tim, *Composting*, ABC Books, Sydney, 2008

Matthews, Julian, *The Kitchen Garden*, Fairfax Books, Sydney, 2007

Murray, David, *Successful Organic Gardening*, 2nd edn, Kangaroo Press, Sydney, 2006

Norman, Jill, *Herb & Spice*, Dorling Kindersley, London, 2002

Norrington, Leonie, *Tropical Food Gardens*, Bloomings, Melbourne, 2008

Nuttall, Carolyn & Millington, Janet, *Outdoor Classrooms*, PI Productions, Palmwoods, Queensland, 2008

O'Brien, Charmaine, *Recipes from an Urban Village*, The Hope Project, New Delhi, 2003

Olney, Richard, *Lulu's Provençal Table*, HarperCollins, New York, 1994

—— (ed.), *Grains, Pasta & Pulses*, The Good Cook series, Time-Life, New York, 1980

Owen, Sri, *The Rice Book*, Doubleday, London, 1993

Painter, Gilian & Power, Elaine, *The Herb Garden Displayed*, Hodder & Stoughton, Auckland, 1978

Palazuelos, Susanna, *Mexico the Beautiful Cookbook*, Collins, San Francisco, 1991

Panjabi, Camellia, *50 Great Curries of India*, Kyle Cathie, London, 1994

Robins, Juleigh, *Wild Lime*, Allen & Unwin, Sydney, 1996

Roseman, Pam, *Vegetables in the Home Garden*, rev. edn, Viking O'Neil in association with the Dept of Agriculture and Agmedia, Melbourne, 1993

Sartori, Loretta, *Patisserie*, Tertiary Press, Melbourne, 2004

Scaravelli, Paola & Cohen, Jon, *Cooking from an Italian Garden*, Henry Holt & Co, New York, 1984

Schneider, Elizabeth, *Vegetables: From Amaranth to Zucchini*, William Morrow, New York, 2001

Solomon, Charmaine, *Encyclopedia of Asian Food*, Hamlyn, Melbourne, 1997

Stanton, Rosemary, *Vegetables*, Allen & Unwin, Sydney, 2000

Taruschio, Ann & Franco, *Bruschetta: Crostoni and Crostini*, Pavilion, London, 1995

Vaughan, J G & Geissler, C A, *The New Oxford Book of Food Plants*, Oxford University Press, Oxford, 1997

Wallace-Crabbe, Chris, *Selected Poems*, 1st edn, Carcanet Press, Manchester, 1999

Waters, Alice, *The Art of Simple Food*, Clarkson Potter, New York, 2007

—— *Chez Panisse Fruit*, William Morrow, New York, 2002

Woodward, Penny, *Pest-repellent Plants*, Hyland House, Melbourne, 1997

ACKNOWLEDGEMENTS

The initial impetus to write this book came from my seven – going on eight – years working with the Stephanie Alexander Kitchen Garden Foundation (SAKGF). I would like to thank my friend, former colleague and founding board member Anna Dollard, for her initial enthusiasm for this project, which, rather in the manner of *The Cook's Companion*, was first conceived of as a small pamphlet!

My colleague Jacqui Lanarus, Senior Project Officer at the SAKGF, wrote the plant profiles that are to be found at the beginning of each entry. Her brief was to compress all that she knew about each plant into one small page. I think she has done an outstanding job. Jacqui also contributed many of the organic pest control recipes. Thank you Jacqui (and thanks also for lending your children, and your neighbour's children, as talent). Neither gardening nor cooking is an exact science and both Jacqui and I realise that there may be those who would do things differently. Do it differently by all means, but 'just do it!'.

There are many people to thank who have assisted in the planning and production of this book. Many of them are part of the team at Penguin and its special imprint Lantern.

I want to thank my friend and publisher Julie Gibbs, who once again gave me free rein to expand on an original idea that just seemed to grow and grow – just as she did for *The Cook's Companion*.

I have thoroughly enjoyed working closely with Senior Editor Kathleen Gandy, and together we have explored an extraordinary range of topics, always conscious of accuracy and accessibility, with a good splash of humour. Managing Editor Ingrid Ohlsson has provided further support and I gratefully acknowledge the additional editorial assistance given by Saskia Adams, Rachel Carter, Jocelyn Hungerford, Jane Morrow and Bethan Waterhouse. Thank you also to Caroline Pizzey for her painstaking proofreading. Thank you to horticulturalist Renee Wierzbicki, who kindly read the plant profiles and made helpful suggestions. And thank you so much to John Canty for his lively design for the book, with help from Claire Wilson. I love it.

Thank you to my photographers: Mark Chew, for the delicious food shots; and Simon Griffiths, for the sexy vegetables and garden shots. And a special thank you to food stylist Caroline Velik, for her unfailingly cheerful and reassuring manner, as well as to kitchen assistant Fiona Rigg. My cupboards have never been so organised!

Thank you to my personal assistant Carly Skinner, who worked hard in the background to keep my life running smoothly and sustained us all with coffee and kind words through long days of shooting.

Thank you to Scullerymade for lending us some of their wonderful equipment for the photo shoots.

I am grateful to the Ian Potter Foundation Children's Garden in Melbourne, in particular to Katie O'Brien, for allowing us to shoot there.

Special thanks also to the Royal Botanic Gardens in Melbourne for allowing us to shoot in their wonderful grounds.

A special thank you to all the children who allowed me into their gardens and kitchens: Zak Aldenhoven, Audrey McAllister, Angus Norman, Molly and Lily Phillips, Tim Pope, Maisy and Ezra Ronchi-Banay, Grace Russell, Nina Underwood; Guy, Sabrina and Charlotte Velik; and Anna, Zara and Richard Wotherspoon.

Many years ago I visited the Galleria Palatina in the Pitti Palace in Florence and first saw the breathtakingly beautiful still-life paintings of (female!) Florentine artist Giovanna Garzoni. Painted in the first half of the seventeenth century, these paintings are for me the measure by which all other representations of fruit and vegetables are considered. They are unforgettable. The figs burst from their skins, a snail crawls away from a cracked-open pomegranate, a dish of medlars nestles against almonds. The four lovely still-life photographs that have been composed for this book, one for each season of the year, are inspired by the work of Garzoni.

There are many recipes and ideas in these pages gleaned from the work of friends, colleagues and some food writers whom I know only through their work. They have been acknowledged in the text and permission has been sought from published works. I would like to thank each one of you (in alphabetical order): the Adey family, Maggie Beer, Anna-Maria Bruno, Antonio Carluccio, Diana Clarke, Louis Glowinski, Skye Gyngell, Kathy Howard, Madhur Jaffrey, Tom Jaine, Mollie Katzen, Kylie Kwong, Janni Kyritsis, Viana La Place, Julie LeClerc, Bruno Loubet, Debra Maffescioni, Greg Malouf, Sean Moran, Richard Olney, Luke Palmer, Kat Phillips, Damien Pignolet, Loretta Sartori, Ben Shewry, Patrizia Simone, Annie Smithers, Tony Tan, Melita Vlassopoulos and Chris Wallace-Crabbe.

Finally, thank you to all the kitchen specialists and garden specialists and all of the children presently engaged in a Stephanie Alexander Kitchen Garden primary school for all that they have shown me and taught me and for being a constant source of inspiration and delight.

INDEX

COOKING INDEX

Recipe for Spiced Cauliflower Masala (p 215) from *Singapore Food: A Treasury of More Than 200 Time-tested Recipes*
by Wendy Hutton, 2008, Marshall Cavendish Cuisine, an imprint of Marshall Cavendish International (Asia) Pte Ltd.
Recipe for Lemon Pickle (p 369) from *Cooking in the Country* by Tom Jaine,
Published by Chatto & Windus. Reprinted by permission of Random House Group Ltd.
Parsley and Parmesan 'Bread Balls' (p 456) adapted from the recipe Meatless Meatballs from *Flavors of Puglia* by Nancy Harmon Jenkins,
published by Broadway, copyright 1997, and new edition published by Congedo Editore, Galatina, Italy, 2006.
Christopher Lloyd quote (p 129) from *Gardener Cook* by Christopher Lloyd. Copyright © Frances Lincoln 1997.
Harold McGee broad bean quote (p 169) reprinted with permission of Scribner, a Division of Simon & Schuster, Inc.
from *On Food and Cooking* by Harold McGee. Copyright © 1984 by Harold McGee.
Greg Malouf's Lemon and Date Chutney (p 368) from *Arabesque* by Greg & Lucy Malouf, 2002, reprinted with permission of Hardie Grant.

First published in the UK in 2010 by
Quadrille Publishing Limited
Alhambra House
27-31 Charing Cross Road
London WC2H 0LS
www.quadrille.co.uk

First published in 2009 by
Penguin Group (Australia)
250 Camberwell Road
Camberwell
Victoria 3124
Australia
www.penguin.com.au

1 3 5 7 9 10 8 6 4 2

Text copyright © Stephanie Alexander and Jacqui Lanarus 2009
Recipes copyright © Stephanie Alexander 2009
Kitchen photography © Mark Chew
Garden photography © Simon Griffiths
Illustrations © John Canty

Design and illustration by John Canty © Penguin Group (Australia)
Photography by Mark Chew and Simon Griffiths
except photographs pp 330 and 462 by Fresh Food Images; pp 206, 298 by Getty Images; p 562 by Marina Oliphant

Diagram on page 22 by Ed Merritt, based on original drawing by Megan Carter, no-dig-vegetablegarden.com
Typeset in 11.25/14 Adobe Garamond by Post Pre-Press Group, Carina Heights, Queensland
Colour reproduction by Splitting Image Pty Ltd, Clayton, Victoria

British Library Cataloguing-in-Publication Data:
A catalogue record for this book is available from the British Library

978 1 84400 878 0

Printed and bound in China